POLITICAL
PSYCHOLOGY

POLITICAL PSYCHOLOGY

Classic and Contemporary Readings

EDITED BY

NEIL J. KRESSEL

PARAGON HOUSE PUBLISHERS
New York

To Dorit

First edition, 1993

Published in the United States by

Paragon House
90 Fifth Avenue
New York, N.Y. 10011

Library of Congress Cataloging-in-Publication Data

Political psychology : classic and contemporary readings / edited by
Neil J. Kressel.—1st ed.
p.   cm.
Includes bibliographical references.
ISBN 1-55778-452-3
1. Political psychology.   I. Kressel, Neil Jeffrey.
JA74.5.P635   1993
320'.01'9—dc20
92-28018
CIP

Manufactured in the United States of America

CONTENTS

PREFACE

Political psychology applies theory and research methods from psychology to the comprehension and improvement of political processes. This interdisciplinary endeavor has developed steadily during the past few decades and, as a result, political psychology in the 1990s looks very different than it did in the 1960s.

- The cognitive "revolution" has reached every subfield of political analysis.
- Classical Freudian approaches to politics have diminished in popularity, but psychoanalytic historiography has grown more sophisticated.
- Political psychologists are less apt to trace the drive for political power to psychopathological roots and more likely to see participation in politics as a manifestation of healthy personalities.
- Feminists, nuclear freeze advocates, and other political activists have become increasingly involved in the generation of research in political psychology.
- Various biological approaches to the analysis of political behavior have been introduced.

Political psychologists also have enriched our understanding of how policy elites make decisions, how the mass media influence the public, and how genocidal massacres can occur. Currently, we show much greater methodological expertise than several decades ago in our measurement of political opinions. In these areas and others, political psychology shows the growth spurts of adolescence and promises exciting developments in the years to come.

Political Psychology provides a representative sampling of important and influential works by psychologists, political scientists, psychiatrists, sociologists, and others. About a third of the selections are journal articles or chapters from anthologies reprinted in their entirety; the remainder are excerpts from books.

Two-thirds of the selections in this volume were written during the past decade; many just appeared during the past few years and stand in the forefront of knowledge in the field. While several of the remaining works can be designated classics, all have acquired a time-honored respectability.

The primary audience for this anthology is students in advanced undergraduate and including Political Behavior, Psychology of Politics, Psychological Perspectives on Politics, Personality and Politics, and Behavioral Approaches to Politics.

Professors who teach these courses often lament the scarcity of suitable texts in political psychology. Many believe, as I do, that no textbook can substitute for exposure to original works, especially in a field as methodologically and theoretically diverse as the psychology of politics. *Political Psychology* can serve as a stand-alone text for political psychology courses, or may be used together with additional books.

Professors also may find the reader useful for other psychology and political science courses, including Psychology of Social Issues, Political Communication, Public Opinion, Psychohistory, and Social Psychology. Moreover, scholars in political science and psychology should find *Political Psychology* convenient as a source book and reference.

In a young, rapidly growing intellectual venture, such as political psychology, it is difficult to reach agreement concerning selection of works for inclusion in an anthology. No book can cover all areas adequately and, regrettably, important pieces must be omitted because of space limitations. My goals in choosing readings were:

1) To ensure broad coverage of the field, focusing on the topics I consider the most important, exciting, and popular.
2) To select well-written articles, suitable for students with backgrounds in either psychology or political science.
3) To expose readers to a wide range of methodological and theoretical approaches, without catching them in webs of jargon or statistical analysis.
4) To maintain a balance among time-honored classics, solid articles written several years ago, and the latest research.
5) To keep the reader affordable.

To accomplish these goals, I generally chose case studies, theoretical essays, and literature reviews over original empirical contributions; most can be understood without any quantitative background. Nonetheless, I did include a few studies that assume an understanding of elementary statistical concepts. Of course, an instructor may omit these selections if he or she feels that students lack sufficient quantitative expertise.

Political Psychology includes twenty-seven selections by thirty-two scholars. By including these readings in this volume, I have indicated my judgment that the authors have something important to say, and that they say it well. I do not agree with all the arguments expressed in these works; indeed, an effort has been made to include a wide spectrum of positions, many of which conflict. My views emerge in two of my own articles (3, 26), reprinted in the reader.

In the chapter introductions, I highlight basic issues, raise key questions, and place readings in the context of other work in political psychology. In addition, I briefly compare and contrast approaches taken by the authors.

Political Psychology is organized into six main chapters. The first, "Political Psychology as a Discipline," includes selections by (1) Heinz Eulau, (2) David O. Sears, and (3) myself. These readings provide an overview of political psychology, discussing its history, objectives, and basic findings; in addition, the selections provide some insight into the sociopolitical context of research in the field.

The second chapter, "Politics and Human Nature," includes selections by (4) Sigmund Freud, (5) B. F. Skinner, (6) Hadley Cantril, (7) Herbert A. Simon, and (8) Karl Marx. These readings consider political implications of several influential theories of human nature: psychoanalysis, behaviorism, humanism-existentialism, information-processing, and Marxism.

In the third chapter, "Personality and Political Leadership," we examine the personal and motivational sources of political leadership. Five readings develop perspectives based on different aspects of the psychology of personality. Readings are by (9) Lloyd S. Etheredge, (10) James David Barber, (11) David G. Winter, (12) Paul M. Sniderman, and (13) Geoffrey Cocks.

Chapter Four takes a close look at a defining attribute of the twentieth century—genocide. This chapter focuses on the social and political psychology of destructive obedience, sanctioned mass murder, and dictatorial control. It includes readings by (14) John P. Sabini and Maury Silver, (15) Robert Jay Lifton, (16) Herbert C. Kelman and V. Lee Hamilton, and (17) John King Fairbank.

From consideration of human capabilities under extreme conditions in dictatorships, we move to examination of political attitudes and actions under more typical conditions. More specifically, Chapter Five focuses on the relationship among public opinion, the mass media, and political behavior in a democratic system. Four readings are included. The first two selections—by (18) W. Russell Neuman, and (19) Herbert McClosky and John Zaller—offer current perspectives on public attitudes and American government. The next reading, a classic by (20) Sidney Verba and Norman H. Nie, analyzes modes of public participation in the American political system. Finally, a selection by (21) Shanto Iyengar, Mark D. Peters, and Donald R. Kinder highlights the role of the mass media in politics and opinion formation.

The last chapter applies political psychology to international conflict, focusing on foreign policy formation, elite decision-making, misperception, and the role of the mass media and public opinion. This chapter includes six selections by (22) Philip E. Tetlock, (23) Stanley Hoffmann, (24) Irving L. Janis, (25) Janice Gross Stein, (26) myself, and (27) Bernard C. Cohen.

The editor of any anthology owes a tremendous debt to the contributors. However, my own intellectual debt to the authors of these readings goes well beyond this. Whether I agree with their analyses or not, their own quest for excellence has been personally inspiring. I hope that *Political Psychology: Classic and Contemporary Readings* will bring their writings to the attention of the next generation of students, and that they will continue to stoke intellectual fires and provoke curiosity about the fascinating interface between psychology and politics.

Finally, I would like to thank my agent, Susan Ann Protter, and my editors at Paragon House for their encouragement and support.

ACKNOWLEDGMENTS

Selection 1, from *The Behavioral Persuasion in Politics* by Heinz Eulau. New York: Random House, 1963. Reprinted by permission of the author.

Selection 2, David O. Sears, "Political Psychology," reproduced with permission, from the *Annual Review of Psychology*, Vol. 38, © 1987 by Annual Reviews, Inc.

Selection 3, Neil J. Kressel, "The Politics of Knowledge Production in Social Psychology," from "Systemic Barriers to Progress in Academic Social Psychology," *Journal of Social Psychology*, Vol. 130, Issue No. 1, pp. 5–28, February, 1990. Reprinted with permission of the Helen Dwight Reid Foundation. Published by Heldref Publications, 4000 Albemarle St., N.W., Washington, D.C. 20016. Copyright © 1990.

Selection 4, from *Civilization and Its Discontents* by Sigmund Freud. Translated and edited by James Strachey, by permission of W. W. Norton & Company, Inc. Copyright © 1961 by James Strachey. Copyright renewed 1989.

Selection 5, "The Design of a Culture," from *Beyond Freedom and Dignity* by B. F. Skinner. Copyright © 1971 by B. F. Skinner. Reprinted by permission of Alfred A. Knopf, Inc.

Selection 6, Hadley Cantril, "The Human Design," reprinted from the *Journal of Individual Psychology*, Volume 20 (1964) by permission of the University of Texas Press.

Selection 7, Herbert A. Simon, "A Cognitive Approach to Human Nature in Politics," from "Human Nature in Politics," *American Political Science Review*, Vol. 79, 1985, pp. 293–304. Reprinted by permission of the author and the American Political Science Association.

Selection 8, Karl Marx, "Political Consciousness and the Means of Production," from *Marx's Concept of Man* by Erich Fromm. Copyright © 1961, 1966, Erich Fromm. Reprinted by permission of The Continuum Publishing Company.

Selection 9, "The Hardball Practitioner," from Lloyd S. Etheredge, *Can Governments Learn?: American Foreign Policy and Central American Revolutions*, pp. 148–157. New York: Pergamon Press, 1985. Copyright © 1985, Pergamon Press, Inc.

Selection 10, from James David Barber, *The Presidential Character: Predicting Performance in the White House* (third edition, 1985). Reprinted by permission of the author.

Selection 11, from David G. Winter, "Leader Appeal, Leader Performance, and the

Motive Profiles of Leaders and Followers," *Journal of Personality and Social Psychology*, Vol. 52, No. 1, pp. 196–202, 1987. Copyright © 1987 by the American Psychological Association. Reprinted by permission.

Selection 12, from Paul M. Sniderman, *Personality and Democratic Politics*, pp. 305–323. Berkeley, CA: University of California Press, 1975. Copyright © 1975, The Regents of the University of California.

Selection 13, from Geoffrey Cocks, "Contributions of Psychohistory to Understanding Politics," pp. 139–151. In M. G. Hermann (ed.), *Political Psychology: Contemporary Problems and Issues*. San Francisco, CA: Jossey-Bass, 1986. Reproduced with permission of publisher.

Selection 14, from John P. Sabini and Maury Silver, "Destroying the Innocent with a Clear Conscience: A Sociopsychology of the Holocaust," from J. E. Dimsdale, ed., *Survivors, Victims, and Perpetrators*. New York: Hemisphere, 1980. Reprinted by permission.

Selection 15, from *The Nazi Doctors: Medical Killing and the Psychology of Genocide*, by Robert Jay Lifton. Copyright © 1986 by Robert Jay Lifton. Reprinted by permission of Basic Books, Inc., Publishers, New York.

Selection 16, "Sanctioned Massacres," from Herbert C. Kelman and V. Lee Hamilton, *Crimes of Obedience: Toward a Social Psychology of Authority and Responsibility*, pp. 12–20. New Haven, CT: Yale University Press, 1990. Reprinted by permission.

Selection 17, John King Fairbank, "Thought Reform in China." From *The United States and China* by John King Fairbank. Cambridge, MA: Harvard University Press. Copyright © 1948, 1958, 1971, 1972, 1979 by the President and Fellows of Harvard College, © 1976 by John King Fairbank. Reprinted by permission of the publishers.

Selection 18, from *The Paradox of Mass Politics* by W. Russell Neuman. Cambridge, MA: Harvard University Press. Copyright © 1986 by the President and Fellows of Harvard College. Reprinted by permission of the publishers.

Selection 19, from *The American Ethos: Public Attitudes Toward Capitalism and Democracy* by Herbert McClosky and John Zaller. Cambridge, MA: Harvard University Press. Copyright © 1984 by the Twentieth Century Fund, Inc. Reprinted by permission of the publishers.

Selection 20, from Sidney Verba and Norman H. Nie, *Participation in America*. New York: Harper & Row, 1972. Reprinted by permission of Sidney Verba.

Selection 21, from Shanto Iyengar, Mark D. Peters, and Donald R. Kinder, "Experimental Demonstrations of the 'Not-So-Minimal' Consequences of Television News Programs," *American Political Science Review*, Vol. 76, 1982, pp. 848–858. Reprinted by permission of the authors and the American Political Science Association.

Selection 22, from Philip E. Tetlock, "Psychological Advice on Foreign Policy: What Do We Have to Contribute?," *American Psychologist*, Vol. 41, pp. 555–567, 1986. Copyright © 1986 by the American Psychological Association. Reprinted by permission.

Selection 23, from Stanley Hoffmann, "On the Political Psychology of Peace and War: A

Critique and an Agenda," *Political Psychology*, Vol. 7, pp. 1–21, 1986. Reprinted by permission of Plenum Publishing Corporation.

Selection 24, Irving L. Janis, "Groupthink," from *Yale Alumni Magazine*, Vol. 36, 1973. Reprinted by permission.

Selection 25, from Janice Gross Stein, "Building Politics into Psychology: The Misperception of Threat," *Political Psychology*, Vol. 9, 245–271, 1988. Reprinted by permission of Plenum Publishing Corporation.

Selection 26, from Neil J. Kressel, "Biased Judgments of Media Bias: A Case Study of the Arab-Israeli Dispute," *Political Psychology*, Vol. 8, No. 2, pp. 211–227, 1987. Reprinted by permission of Plenum Publishing Corporation.

Selection 27, from Bernard C. Cohen, *The Public's Impact on Foreign Policy*. Boston: Little, Brown and Company, 1973. Reprinted by permission of the author.

CHAPTER ONE

POLITICAL PSYCHOLOGY AS
A DISCIPLINE

Politics needs psychology. As Heinz Eulau argues, it is difficult, if not impossible, to say anything meaningful about the governance of human beings without speaking of human acts, goals, drives, feelings, beliefs, commitments, and values. Psychological assumptions pervade the works of contemporary political scholars, even those who do not consider themselves political psychologists or adherents to "the behavioral persuasion."

One sees this dependence on principles of behavior, personality, perception, motivation, cognition, and interpersonal interaction throughout political science. Frequently, however, the psychological principles remain between the lines, unstated and sometimes unacknowledged. Consider, for example, how several authors use psychological concepts in a recent (Winter 1991) issue of *Foreign Affairs*:

1) Historian Richard Pipes claimed that Perestroika, by exposing the fraudulence of the communist system, led the Soviet population to "nervous exhaustion" and "national malaise." His prognosis was that "no tampering with institutions or procedures can overcome" these problems (p. 72).
2) German political scientist Karl Kaiser traced the rapidity of Germany's unification, in part, to a constellation of truly exceptional personalities at the heads of major world powers in 1989–90 (p. 179).
3) Syndicated columnist Charles Krauthammer argued that American political leaders dressed the American unilateral military action in the Persian Gulf in a shroud of pseudo-multilateralism. He saw a danger in the possibility that these leaders might come to believe their own pretense (p. 26).

1

These three examples all rely on assumptions about the connection between psychological principles and politics. Pipes hypothesizes about a mass psychological disorder, Kaiser alludes to the impact of leaders' personal traits on political negotiation, and Krauthammer suggests potential problems in cognitive processing and perception. The three *Foreign Affairs* articles are typical of analysis in international politics; implicit psychological assumptions work their way into other subfields of political science as well.

The political psychology approach differs from more traditional political interpretation by *focusing on psychological principles, clarifying them and making them more explicit.* Moreover, political psychologists generally subject their psychological assumptions to critical analysis and, sometimes, empirical investigation. As a discipline, political psychology seeks to apply the highest caliber of psychological thinking to the comprehension and solution of political problems. Political psychology at its best does not invoke reductionistic explanations that see political phenomena as wholly understandable in psychological terms; instead, scholars seek to determine the proper level of analysis for various issues and the appropriate role for psychology in political explanation (Greenstein, 1987; Telhami, 1990).

Jeanne Knutson, a well-known advocate of political psychology, suggested that the objective of the discipline should not be merely to understand political behavior as it is, but also to discover what, under more favorable psychic conditions, it might become. According to Knutson, political psychology should encourage psychological growth in order to bring about a more stable and creative open society (Knutson, 1973). Others have continued to develop her humanistic approach to political psychology (Greening, 1984). Political psychologists with many different political and theoretical orientations have been characterized by a drive toward prescription and political relevance as well as empirical description.

The eminent political psychologist James David Barber has suggested that "the relevance of psychology to politics escalates daily, because situations once primarily presented by nature are now primarily presented by humans" (Barber, 1990, p. 173). Yet Barber does not assume that political psychology must necessarily realize its promise. He warns against a dark alternative:

> the development of yet another sub-sub-specialty of academic technicism, invented by scholars to protect themselves from the challenge of argument. Fleeing from the field to the closet, such technicists form their mini-clubs and share their jargonized whispering. That kind of intellectual fragmentation sadly produces thousands upon thousands of printed pages no scholar across the street will bother to read. Nor will any grappling politician, however much he needs knowledge to guide action. (p. 173)

By gathering together some of the best thinking in the discipline, I hope to show in this volume that political psychology has made a good start toward "applying the best of psychology to the generation of political peace and freedom and justice" (Barber, p. 173).

The blending of psychological and political analysis has been the hallmark of many works of scholarship since the early twentieth century. Graham Wallas, Harold Lasswell, Walter Lippmann, Erich Fromm, Erik Erikson, Theodor Adorno, Kenneth Keniston, David McClelland, M. Brewster Smith, Robert Lane, Robert Jay Lifton, Herbert C. Kelman, and many others wrote important works of political psychology in the five decades between 1920 and 1970.

However, the origins of political psychology as a formal, self-conscious discipline can be traced to the late 1970s. The formation of the International Society of Political Psychology and the introduction of the journal *Political Psychology* are key historical markers.

The three articles included in this chapter—by Eulau (1), Sears (2), and Kressel (3)—deal with the intellectual foundation, history, and current status of the discipline. Their main purpose is to familiarize readers with the academic organization of political psychology. The first two articles raise many central questions to which we will return in subsequent chapters; they establish the intellectual justification for political psychology and introduce its main content areas. The third article discusses the sociopolitical context of social psychology, a field closely related to political psychology and from which most research in political psychology originated. Knowledge production does not take place in a vacuum, and important perspectives on research can emerge from an analysis of the social, historical, intellectual, and political surroundings in which books and articles are written.

The first selection in the chapter is titled, "The Root Is Man," and drawn from political scientist Heinz Eulau's influential book, *The Behavioral Persuasion in Politics* (1963). Although this book predates the establishment of political psychology as a self-conscious discipline, it does highlight the approach to politics that focuses on political *behavior*, rather than ideas, institutions, and processes. Eulau defines political science as the "study of why man finds it necessary or desirable to build government, of how he adapts government to his changing needs or demands, of how and why he decides on public policies." Politics "is concerned with the conditions and consequences of human action." Some contemporary political psychologists might judge Eulau's language sexist, but many would endorse his definition of political science.

In the excerpt included in this reader, Eulau calls for greater use of empirical methodology. He claims that political science

> must build from the bottom up by asking simple questions that can, in principle, be answered; it cannot be built from the top down by asking questions that, one has reason to suspect, cannot be answered at all, at least not by the methods of science.

Eulau criticizes "traditional" approaches to political inquiry for assuming that *theory* is the same as *knowledge*. Moreover, he suggests that the "behavioral persuasion" in political science is, in reality, a continuation by different means of the intellectual quest that began with the ancient political theorists. Eulau also raises the important issue of how to distinguish between trivial and "simple but important" political issues.

By pointing the way to a *scientific* study of politics, Eulau contributed to the ground-work from which a more mature political psychology sprouted in the late 1970s. On the other hand, some political psychologists—for example, those of a psychoanalytic bent—would question the requirement of systematic empirical inquiry. See, for example, the selection in this book on psychohistory by Cocks (13).

The second selection, social psychologist David O. Sears' review article from *Annual Review of Psychology*, provides a masterful overview of the current state of political psychology. Since the 1960s, Sears has been a major contributor to political psychology as well as to other areas of social psychology. His selection in the reader discusses the historical origins of research on many subfields of political psychology including: 1) personality and politics, 2) public opinion and voting behavior, 3) political socialization, 4) political participation, 5) mass media effects, 6) international conflict, and 7) political murder. The breadth of his coverage, I hope, will leave the reader thirsting for more background and depth. The topics he raises receive attention throughout *Political Psychology: Classic and Contemporary Readings*.

Sears' article surveys trends in research. He summarizes major approaches, reviewing the evidence and noting the strengths and weaknesses of each. Perhaps more importantly, Sears conveys his enthusiasm for political psychology. He writes that "one of the charms of the field is its relative looseness, which provides for more original and imaginative flights of fancy than are usually permitted in more staid and methodologically proper basic disciplines." It is not certain that Heinz Eulau would regard this as a positive feature, though, and Sears, himself, cautions that "this leads to the unavoidable hazard of mixing sound analyses in with the naive and poorly informed." Sears also calls attention to the important tension between political psychology as an intellectually tough-minded discipline and ever-present tendencies toward political reformism.

The third selection, my own article, discusses several barriers to progress in social psychology. This field is sometimes considered a parent of political psychology and, in any case, is the discipline from which much political psychology research originated. Yet social psychology fails to meet its potential as a source of theory and research for political and other areas of application.

My article discusses three broad categories of nonintellectual influence on research production: 1) social movements and political ideologies, 2) student selection and socialization processes, and 3) systemic survival demands. The article can be viewed as a study in the politics of psychology as well as a discussion of pitfalls likely to be encountered by political psychologists.

In a recent article, political scientist Robert Jervis considered similar impediments to the development of political psychology. He claimed that:

• Disciplinary incentives within both political science and psychology did not support work in political psychology.
• Scholars in the parent disciplines had inadequate contact with each other, and were often unaware of the latest work in the other parent discipline.

- Decision makers seldom saw political psychology as a source of knowledge relevant to problems in public policy.
- Too much psychological theory was based on laboratory experiments with possibly low external validity.
- A "dovish," left-of-center political cast characterized many analyses and conclusions in political psychology. (Jervis, 1989)

Jervis concluded, sensibly, that these disciplinary issues should not preoccupy us, but that "we ignore them at our peril because they are vital to the health of our field and are not entirely divorced from the validity of the approaches we use" (p. 482).

REFERENCES

Barber, J. D. (1990). "The Promise of Political Psychology." *Political Psychology*, *11*(1), 173–183.

Eulau, H. (1963). *The Behavioral Persuasion in Politics*. New York: Random House.

Greening, T. (ed.). (1984). *American Politics and Humanistic Psychology*. New York: Saybrook.

Greenstein, F. I. (1987). *Personality and Politics: Problems of Evidence, Inference, and Conceptualization* (new ed.). Princeton, NJ: Princeton University Press.

Jervis, R. (1989). "Political Psychology: Some Challenges and Opportunities." *Political Psychology*, *10*(3), 481–494.

Knutson, J. N. (ed.). (1973). *Handbook of Political Psychology*. San Francisco, CA: Jossey-Bass.

Telhami, S. (1990). *Power and Leadership in International Bargaining: The Path to the Camp David Accords*. New York: Columbia University Press.

1

The Root Is Man

HEINZ EULAU

The root is man. I don't think it is possible to say anything meaningful about the governance of man without talking about the political behavior of man—his acts, goals, drives, feelings, beliefs, commitments, and values. Man has built nations and empires, created customs and institutions, invented symbols and constitutions, made wars, revolutions, and peace. Politics is the study of why man finds it necessary or desirable to build government, of how he adapts government to his changing needs or demands, of how and why he decides on public policies. Politics is concerned with the conditions and consequences of human action.

A study of politics which leaves man out of its equations is a rather barren politics. Yet such is the propensity of man that he can consider his own creations without measuring them by himself. Political science has studied political ideas, values, customs, symbols, institutions, processes, and policies without reference to their creators for a long time, but the cost has been high. I do not want to belabor this point. I mention it only because the simple question I want to ask—Why do people behave politically as they do?— seems to have explosive consequences for the study of politics.

Just what *is* political behavior? I have been asked the question many times, by students as well as by colleagues, in and out of political science. Is it a field of study, a method, or an approach? If it is a field, it must have content and boundaries. If it is a method, it must have rules. If it is an approach, it must have direction. I cannot say that it is one or the other. It is none of them alone, and it is not all of them together. This leaves the questioner confused, perhaps irritated, even hostile. It is not considered a virtue to tolerate ambiguity. I would certainly not argue that ambiguity is preferable to clarity, though it may be preferable to false or easy answers.

The difficulty begins with definitions. If taken seriously, definitions commit and constrain. They orient their user and reveal his orientation. They are embedded in his concepts and his theorizing, are a source of sense, but also of nonsense. So it is with "political behavior." For some years now, I have asked my students to define politics. Politics, they tell me, has something to do with government, power, policy, influence, decision making, conflict, or even "authoritative allocation of values." I cannot but marvel at such ingenuity. But when I ask just what people *do* when they *act* in ways to which these concepts presumably refer, there is a perplexing silence.

I wonder why this is so. Evidently, we are the victims of our own sophistication. However, this is not the case when I ask what people do when they practice religion. The students will tell me that a man is religious when he prays, attends mass, sings hymns, listens to sermons, immerses himself in baptismal water, senses the presence of divine guidance, abides by the Ten Commandments, or believes in immortality. And there is no trouble with economics: man produces, buys, sells, exchanges, invests, speculates, consumes, and so on. Not so with politics. When I suggest that what makes man's behavior political is that he rules and obeys, persuades and compromises, promises and bargains, coerces and represents, fights and fears, my students are baffled.

Certainly these verbs do not define politics. But they do refer to those of man's acts that are at the core of what we study when we talk about politics. And there are many more. If human behavior is the root of politics, they are more useful in studying political things than nouns like authority, power, conflict, allocation, or government. It seems to me that behavior comes first: ruling before government, obeying before authority, voting before decision, demanding before value, fearing before sanction, coercing before power, persuading before influence, fighting before conflict, believing before ideology.

But such is the enterprise, whether we call it politics, political study, or political science, that we must define first and then sense, rather than sense first and then define. As we define politics, so we behave politically, for our definitions of politics are themselves evidence of political behavior. They determine, at least in part, what we observe and how we explain it. It would be silly to deny that man in politics, being a defining animal, has various definitions of politics. I am merely pleading that in seeking, clarifying, or refining our definitions of politics, we turn to what men do as they behave politically and why they do it. Definitions unrelated to the behavior of man, in politics as in any other area of human activity, have no content.

The behavioral persuasion in politics is concerned with what man does politically and the meanings he attaches to his behavior. Politics asks about ancient traditions and grandiose designs, about complex systems and intricate processes, about fearful atrocities and superb achievements. But as an eminent physicist once remarked, it is a subject "more difficult than physics." The physical scientist seems to have one great advantage over the political scientist: whatever meanings he may give his objects of study, they do not talk back to him. Atoms, neutrons, or electrons do not care how they are defined; political actors do mind. This is precisely why a political science that ignores man is necessarily a very incomplete science of politics.

However, the fact that men give meanings to their behavior need not be a handicap. On the contrary, what men say about themselves and others represents an infinitely rich source of information about behavior. And the meanings that people give to politics are appropriate data for scientific analysis because people behave in terms of these meanings. These meanings do not provide the scientific observer with the kind of definitions he needs in order to proceed with his investigation. He must develop his own. But, whatever definition of politics the political scientist adopts, it cannot be altogether arbitrary. It must itself be "meaningful" in terms of the meanings that men give to their political behavior. In the language of science, definitions must be operational. No matter how concrete or abstract conceptually, they must be relevant empirically. The meanings that political actors, consciously or unconsciously, attribute to their own behavior are of interest to the political scientist because they provide a partial explanation of the motives for that behavior.

Defining political behavior is a delicate problem, partly because people in politics define and interpret what they do differently, and partly because political scientists are by no means agreed on what they mean when they say that they are studying political behavior. One way to avoid the dilemma is to ignore it, offer a definition as succinctly as possible, and go on from there. The researcher must do this. He cannot get entangled in problems of definition if he hopes to come up with a piece of research. The only criterion is that his definition suit his research objectives, and this is probably all that can be reasonably expected. The problem of definition must ultimately be solved by empirical research.

A rigorous approach to definitions alone will not spur progress in the study of politics. In fact it might well stifle in infancy a new approach which requires not definitional rigor so much as new categories and concepts with which to explore new terrain. In returning to the behavior of man as the root of politics, the behavioral persuasion has opened up new possibilities in the study of politics. If this has created more problems than it has solved, including those of definition, it is more of a challenge than a defeat.

The return to the behavior of man as the root of politics is a new beginning. For in dealing with the conditions and consequences of man's political conduct, the behavioral persuasion represents an attempt, by modern modes of analysis, to fulfill the quest for political knowledge begun by the classical political theorists. The behavioral persuasion in politics, as I understand it, is a return to the bases of man's political experience in which the great theorists of the past found nurture and sustenance. What makes the so-called classic theories great are their sometimes explicit, sometimes implicit assumptions about human nature in politics. The theoretical constructions of the polity found in the classics are "peopled systems," model communities based on some notion of how men behave politically as they do and why, in addition to frequently being prescriptions for how men ought to behave in the polity and what the polity should look like. Of course, the psychology, sociology, and even anthropology involved in these images is, from the contemporary perspective, primitive, underdeveloped, and often mistaken. I certainly do not advise a reading of the classics for the purpose of learning about political behavior, not even of the empirical Machiavelli. But this is not the point. The point is that classical political theory, as the modern behavioral persuasion in politics, has at its base the conduct of man, even if, counter to the behavioral persuasion, it is predominantly prescriptive rather than descriptive.

It may seem startling that the behavioral persuasion is a continuation of the classical tradition of political inquiry. On the face of things, the discontinuities between the ancient and the modern approaches seem more significant than the continuities. Modern modes of thought, criteria of validation, and methods of investigation are so radically different that the link between classical political theory and the behavioral persuasion would seem to be rather tenuous. A good deal depends on what one means by continuity. If one means continued textual exegesis of the classics as if they were sacred writings, the behavioral persuasion does, in fact, make a radical break with political theory. But if by continuity one means, as I think one should, the application of modes of thought and techniques of inquiry appropriate to one's own time to the political problems of the time, then the behavioral persuasion is a direct and genuine descendant of the classical tradition. The classical theorists, from Plato to Mill and beyond, in building their models of the polity, sought to bring to political inquiry the best conceptual and technical tools at their disposal. The modern political scientists who adapt the new theories, methods, and techniques of behavioral science to political analysis are in the tradition of the classical political theorists.

Concern with the political behavior of man has posed the following questions: Does it encourage dealing in trivia while the "really important" problems of politics are neglected? Does it not lead to cultivating areas of research where access to data is easy, regardless of the "significance" of the political problem? What does political behavior research contribute to the solution of the great issues of politics? These questions are not so much unwarranted as they are misdirected. It is perfectly true that much behavioral research on politics is concerned with simple questions. But a simple question is not necessarily a simple matter. The line between asking simple but important questions and asking trivial ones is often very narrow. Moreover, there is much confusion as to just what "significance" means. If it is *only* defined in terms of the so-called great issues, then politics as science is likely to become the handmaiden of policy, for better or for worse. . . . But whatever other relevance the great-issues criterion may have, it does not necessarily help to define significance from the point of view of political behavior research.

A question may be simple, then, without being trivial. From the standpoint of empirical research, it is trivial only if it does not yield answers that "significantly" add to knowledge. In fact, many answers given to questions, simple or complex, from the point of view of policy, do not add to knowledge. By knowledge I mean, of course, a set of verified statements about reality. If the statements hang together and do not contradict each other, we have knowledge. This is as true of politics as of any other area of human endeavor.

Now, the interesting thing about this chain of reasoning is that it is based on hindsight, although when we call a question trivial, we speak as if we had foresight. This is so because knowledge is transmitted. A trivial question is one we assume has been answered already, or, if it has not been answered, that it can be answered easily enough. A trivial question, it is implied, is one that every fool can answer. We simply predict, from hindsight, that a trivial question will not significantly contribute to new knowledge.

However this approach to knowledge does not lead anywhere. Knowledge is the process of knowing, always undergoing change. If this is so, we cannot call a question trivial, for we cannot *know* whether it is trivial or not until it has been asked and answered. Triviality is not a matter of the kind of *questions* we ask, but of the *answers* we get. Only after a question has been answered can we say that it has been trivial. Without an answer, one can call a question trivial only if one assumes that everything worthy of being known is known already. It is sometimes advantageous to assume that we don't know what we think we know. In other words, it may sometimes be advisable to ask old questions as if they were fresh.

It is the function of science to understand and interpret the world, not to change it. A science of politics which deserves its name must build from the bottom up by asking simple questions that can, in principle, be answered; it cannot be built from the top down by asking questions that, one has reason to suspect, cannot be answered at all, at least not by the methods of science. An empirical discipline is built by the slow, modest, and piecemeal cumulation of relevant theories and data. The great issues of politics, such as the conditions and consequences of freedom, justice, or authority, are admittedly significant topics, but they are topics compounded with a strong dose of metaphysical discourse. I don't think that they are beyond the reach of behavioral investigation, but before they can be tackled, the groundwork must be laid.

There is little glory to be had in the patient analysis of mass political behavior (and elite behavior is, indeed, much more glamorous as a topic of inquiry). But the hundreds of studies of electoral behavior, some good, some not, accumulated in the last sixty years, allow us to make some statements about democracy that are true with a reasonably high degree of probability, certainly higher than if these studies had not been made. This is all one can hope for in the present stage of political inquiry, an early stage in spite of the great thinkers who have influenced our notions of significance. But we cannot decide whether an Aristotle's concerns should be our concerns by appealing to Aristotle. We can decide this only by questioning our own experiences in the world of politics in which we live. If our experiences lead us back to the great issues, all to the good; if they do not, little is lost.

In returning to man as the root of politics, the behavioral persuasion reveals itself as a "radical" orientation in the study of politics. But its practitioners are neither wide-eyed prophets nor blind apostles. They are self-consciously sensitive to the difficulties involved in the behavioral study of politics. The way ahead is never clear or straight. One may not always know the destination, and even if in sight, one may never reach it. But it makes an exciting journey, if not always a rewarding one.

What the behavioral persuasion challenges in the traditional study of politics, if it challenges anything, is the comfortable assumption that theory is the same thing as knowledge. But theory is only a tool. If it is a tool, like all tools it tends periodically to wear out and need replacement. The behavioral persuasion in politics is both theoretical and empirical in direction. Its radicalism stems from the conviction that a proposition may be worn out when, on being tested, it can be disproved.

2

Political Psychology

DAVID O. SEARS

Political psychology has become a self-conscious, if small, academic specialty in its own right. The International Society of Political Psychology is a professional organization with over 500 members and its own journal, *Political Psychology*. There are a few textbooks (Stone 1974, Freedman and Freedman 1975, Elms 1976, Segall 1976, Barner-Barry and Rosenwein 1985) though none has yet received wide acceptance. Two editions of *Handbook of Political Psychology* have been published (Knutson 1973a, Hermann 1986).

Nevertheless, political psychology is primarily an interdisciplinary field. It has mainly attracted psychologists (social, personality, and clinical), political scientists (in politics and international relations), historians, and psychiatrists, with a smattering of sociologists, anthropologists, lawyers, and educators. The dominant outlets for work in political psychology have thus far been the disciplinary journals and associations (especially the Society for the Psychological Study of Social Issues); there are extensive handbook chapters in the disciplinary handbooks of social psychology and political science. And while two political science departments have explicitly offered doctoral specializations in political psychology (Yale and SUNY-Stony Brook), by and large, political psychologists have been trained in regular disciplinary specialties, with Yale, Michigan, UC Berkeley, and UCLA being particularly active in this regard.

In general, political psychology has very much been stimulated by the urgent political problems of the day, especially those with actually or potentially devastating human consequences, whether maniacs in high office, the rise of totalitarianism, anti-Semitism, the radical right, the Cold War, Arab-Israeli conflict, the specter of nuclear war, or the transitional problems in postcolonial nations. Whether or not these concerns result in basic research (and many of them do), the field of political psychology tends to reflect the headlines; it also reflects the continuing influence of a few basic theoretical traditions—most notably psychoanalytic and Lewinian field theories.

PERSONALITY AND POLITICS

Perhaps the first major work in the field was *Human Nature in Politics* by Graham Wallas (1921). Consistent with the prevailing views of the day, this work was characterized by a strong Darwinian emphasis on instinct, natural selection, and thus irrationality; mob rule and irrational elite decision making were staples of political life (Stone and Smith 1983).

The dominant influence over political psychology in the next three decades, however, was psychoanalytic theory. The psychobiographical tradition began with Freud's study of Leonardo da Vinci. The psychoanalytic macrolevel analysis of society was introduced by Freud in his two monographs, *The Future of an Illusion* and *Civilization and Its Discontents*. Given the fundamental data base of psychoanalytic research, its main legacy became the psychobiographical analysis of specific individuals in politics.

To many, a "psychological" approach to politics has simply meant looking at the effects of personality in politics. While this is obviously too narrow, the topic has always been an important one. For useful reviews of this literature, see Greenstein (1975), Elms (1976), and Hermann (1977).

The Role of Personality

A focus on personality raises a number of conceptual and methodological questions. The larger context is the situation versus disposition question that preoccupies both personality and attribution theorists. When applied to politics, this turns into the "man versus the times" question of leadership. Simonton (1985), for example, raises it explicitly in the case of vice-presidential succession to the presidency, and concludes that success results more from situational than personal factors.

Most psychologists presumably would define personality in terms of generalized predispositions to behave in a particular way, regardless of time, situation, role, etc. The focus on such personality predispositions drew great strength in the first half of the century from the psychoanalytic and psychometric traditions. More recently it has come under attack with the complaint that empirical research does not reveal the tight consistency of behavior with personality in varying situations as had been claimed by personality theorists. As a result, political psychologists have more recently looked at a wider variety of personal predispositions, including attitudes, motives, decision style, modes of interpersonal interaction, stress responses, and expertise (Greenstein 1975).

Despite this broadening of focus, it remains important to assess the impact of personality per se. Only a limited set of assessment techniques are available, each with its own well-known assets and liabilities: questionnaires and interviews, observation, archival content analyses, biographical data, and experiments or simulations (Hermann 1977, Tetlock 1983a). Most of these techniques have even more severe liabilities in the study of political leaders than in the study of ordinary people because of the greater self-presentational pressures on persons in public life. Efforts to trace personality to earlier life confront the problem of lack of evidence; one cannot identify political leaders until it is too late to observe formative experiences directly, which has led to some unfortunate examples of excess speculation. Moreover, the person of interest is often dead, which adds even greater limitations.

Another quasi-methodological question is how personality explanations differ from others that emphasize demographic variables, situations, or roles, etc. Greenstein (1975) has made an extraordinarily careful and discerning analysis, which can be commended even to those with no particular interest in politics per se.

Substantive Questions

A major substantive interest has been in political recruitment: Who becomes a political leader? In his well-known formula, Lasswell (1930) asserted that in politics, private conflicts become displaced onto public objects and then are rationalized in terms of the public interest. People are recruited to political life for neurotic personal reasons, by this account. He later (1948) argued that a compensatory need for power was a particularly strong motive. Lane (1959) later argued the contrary, that to be a successful democratic politician one needed to have a healthy, well-balanced personality. Such disagreement concerning the mental health of those recruited to politics recurs throughout the personality-and-politics literature.

A second major area of interest is the impact of personality upon the behavior of political elites. Lasswell's early work provided numerous examples of the deleterious effects of neurotic patterns. Rogow's (1963) biography of Forrestal, the first U.S. Secretary of Defense, argued that his suicide was brought on by progressive paranoia, a possibly dangerous quality for someone in that high position. The Georges' (1956) excellent biography of Woodrow Wilson depicts his identification with, along with his repressed hostility toward, his stern and demanding father. When Wilson became frustrated, this conflict could be expressed by rage and rigidity. The Georges suggest that this aspect of Wilson's personality was partly responsible for his failure to have the United States join the League of Nations. Mazlish's (1972) biography of Richard Nixon described Nixon's need to risk failure to prove himself and his need to create crises in order to cope with his fear of death, along with such potentially hazardous characteristics as suspiciousness, social isolation, difficulty in decision making, and a need for an emotional enemy. Some more recent examples of this approach include Rintala's (1984) analysis of the childhood origins of Churchill's need for power, and the continuing conflict over whether Woodrow Wilson's root problems were physical or mental [see also Post (1983) and others in the same issue].

Various multidimensional typologies of political actors have been proposed to capture major differences in political orientation. Lasswell (1930) suggested agitators, administrators, and theorists; Barber (1965) proposed four types of state legislators; Stewart (1977) discussed several types of Soviet politicians, and so on. Barber's (1985) typology of American presidents is perhaps the best known. In his scheme, the most dangerous are the "active negatives," such as Woodrow Wilson, Herbert Hoover, Lyndon Johnson, and Richard Nixon. This type is characterized by unusual self-concern, perfectionism, an all-or-nothing quality in self-perception, denial of self-gratification, and great concern with controlling aggression. When threatened, the active-negative type has a tendency to rigidify. One consequence is that he may focus anger on a personal enemy; another is to cling tightly to a failing policy, to stand and fight, and even to order others to die for him.

Certain specific needs or motives have been thought to have special driving force for political leaders. Power has been especially salient (Lasswell 1930, Rintala 1984, Rothman 1984). The projective testing tradition had promoted the use of fantasy to measure personality, and was applied to power motivation in politics (e.g., Winter 1973). Maslow's (1954) hierarchy of needs has had some influence in political psychology, especially in Davies's (1963) and Knutson's (1973b) suggestions that political activism is likely only when more basic needs have been satisfied. Following in that line, Inglehart (1981) has suggested that postwar affluence has generated postmaterialist values and political values, since basic subsistence needs have been satisfied. Rothman (1984), on the other hand, has suggested that the leftist activists of the 1960s have strong narcissistic needs today.

In studying the role of personality in mass political behavior, two approaches have been most common. The first has correlated self-report questionnaire or interview measures of various personality traits with political attitudes. The most obvious examples are the role of authoritarianism and dogmatism in intolerance (Adorno, et al 1950, Sanford 1973, Sullivan, et al 1982), machiavellianism (Christie and Geis 1970), or the cluster including paranoia, hostility, rigidity, etc., behind conservatism and isolationism (McClosky 1958, 1967). Two more positive dimensions are self-esteem (see Sniderman 1975) and a sense of personal control (Renshon 1974). The life history or idiographic approach is a second alternative that looks at individuals in greater detail to understand their idiosyncratic functioning (Smith, et al 1956, Lane 1962).

PUBLIC OPINION AND VOTING

A second major influence was the development of survey research, especially its application to public opinion and voting behavior. Sociologists introduced it with their community studies in the 1940s. Lazarsfeld, et al (1948) at first emphasized the origins of the vote in large social groupings (class, religion, etc.) and then shifted to an emphasis upon direct interpersonal influence (Berelson, et al 1954). However, the desire for more representative samples, and the development of increased technological capability, resulted (beginning in 1952) in a long series of voting studies that have been conducted in even-numbered years by the Survey Research Center at the University of Michigan, and are now called the American National Election Studies. These studies led to an individual decision-making analysis best developed in *The American Voter* (Campbell, et al 1960). The relevant chapters include those by Lipset, et al (1954), Sears (1969), Converse (1975), Kinder and Sears (1985).

Party Identification

In this pivotal book Campbell, et al used simple Lewinian field theory to argue that voters, largely nonideological and minimally informed, used their underlying, stable party identifications, which had been developed early in their lives, to organize partisan attitudes toward the various major elements of an election campaign. *The American Voter* has been challenged from a number of perspectives in the years since it was published. Much of the criticism has contended that the key factors are political and economic realities rather than longstanding psychological dispositions. The underlying issue has usually been one that is at the heart of the political psychological approach: Is *homo politicus* informed, consistent, sensible, and rational, operating from a set of stable preferences and values, and responsive to external reality—or is he/she uninformed, inconsistent, irrational, operating from anachronistic preferences and prejudices that are out of touch with current reality?

Not surprisingly, specialists in political psychology and political economy often arrive at opposing answers to this question. For useful contrasts, see Converse (1975) and proponents of a "symbolic politics" approach (Edelman 1971, Sears and Citrin 1985), on the one hand, who emphasize the power of early learning, myths, and symbols, and Fiorina (1981), Nie, et al (1979), and Mann and Wolfinger (1980), on the other hand, who emphasize consistency, rationality, and responsiveness to current economic and political realities (whether in voters' personal economic situations, the actual competence of incumbents, their service to their constituents, etc.).

At an empirical level, the role of party identification has been a focal point. The authors of *The American Voter* contended that voters are ill-informed and thus vote on the basis of party because it is a simplifying cue, especially in Congressional elections. Its critics instead emphasize the role of constituency service (Mann and Wolfinger 1980) and hence incumbency. Others suggest that voters both vote on the basis of reasonable judgments of the incumbent's performance in office and actually adjust their party identification accordingly (Kinder and Kiewiet 1979, Fiorina 1981), and that policy preferences affect the vote and even party identification (Markus 1979) when the parties and candidates differ unmistakably in policy positions.

At the macro level, this challenge focuses on the dynamics of voting that result from an apparent decline in the strength and power of party identification: "party dealignment" is indicated in the declining intensity of party commitments and increased defection and split-ticket voting (Wattenberg 1984).

Economic Realities

A central area of contention is the role of current economic realities. Kramer (1971) argued that macroeconomic conditions play a major role in determining the outcome of elections. Kinder and Kiewiet (1979) observed that the voters' "sociotropic" judgments of the incumbent's management of the economy were the deciding factor rather than more egocentric, self-interested judgments about their own financial situations.

This explanation of macro political changes generated some contention, but not much modification, of the basic psychological point that material self-interest plays a relatively minor role in the individual's vote. That was the judgment also of a series of studies showing minimal effects of self-interest on such policy preferences as busing (Kinder and Sears 1981, Sears and Allen 1984), national health insurance (Sears, et al 1980), or tax and spending policies (Sears and Citrin 1985). Even unemployment has surprisingly few direct political effects on the individual (Schlozman and Verba 1979). Predispositions such as party identification and racial intolerance seem to play a much stronger role. Strong self-interest effects do seem to occur when the positive stakes are high and clear or when the threat is high and ambiguous, and the political remedy is clear and certain (Sears and Allen 1984, Sears and Citrin 1985), but these prove to be rather rare circumstances in the political world of the ordinary citizen.

Consistency and Ideology

Another question that has drawn much attention is the degree of consistency and ideological thinking in public opinion. At first this discussion centered on whether or not the public mirrored the standard abstract ideological categories used by political elites to organize political life cognitively (Campbell, et al 1960, Converse 1964). This quickly raised issues of consistency, since Converse (1964) suggested that the low level of "constraint" in the average individual's belief system (i.e., functional interdependence among elements as indexed by correlations across attitudes on issues) indicated a low level of ideological thinking in the mass public.

A number of key areas of public opinion also have been marked by logical inconsistencies that coexist with some reasonable degree of affective consistency. For example, inconsistencies have frequently been noted between tolerance in the abstract and intolerance in concrete situations, both in terms of such civil liberties issues as freedom of speech and in terms of racial integration (Sullivan, et al 1982, Sears and Allen 1984). The general resistance to higher taxes and a desire in the abstract for smaller government, on the one hand, also is widely believed to be inconsistent with broad-based support for maintaining specific government social programs, on the other hand (Sears and Citrin, 1985).

This view of the public as inconsistent and illogical has been extensively challenged. Much of the argument again concerns whether or not citizens are responding in a rational way to political realities. On the reality-oriented side, it is argued that the public will think ideologically only when political elites offer genuinely different ideological alternatives, as they did in the mid-1960s and early 1970s (Nie, et al 1979); that freedom of speech for national enemies such as Communists is denied only when they are perceived as being dangerous, as in the early 1950s (Stouffer 1955, Sullivan, et al 1982); that the white public supports integration, but not busing, which is perceived to be ineffective; and that it supports radical tax cuts but not cuts in essential government services because of high levels of waste in government, the many "frills" in these services, or a willingness to pay user fees.

This conflict has stimulated much methodological controversy. One question is whether consistency is more properly reflected in uniform patterning of attitudes across individuals or in idiosyncratic patterns within the individual (Lane 1962, 1973). Over the years, changes in item wording in time-series surveys may have given rise to artifactual increases in consistency (Sullivan, et al 1978). Changes in the groups thought to pose danger to the nation may have given rise to illusory increases in tolerance, as tolerance items were not revised to focus on the newest enemies (Sullivan, et al 1982). And social desirability pressures may have given rise to deceptively high levels of racial tolerance in the abstract (McConahay, et al 1981, Jackman and Muha 1984).

One new approach centers on "political cognition," which applies innovations in social cognition to politics. In particular, political schemas and various cognitive representations of political candidates are emphasized [see the various articles in Lau and Sears (1986); also Lane's contrast of market and political cognition (1983); Hamill, et al (1985) on schemata]. A major challenge here is to explain the relatively high level of affect and emotionality associated with politics while using cognitive theories that normally ignore affect.

Racial Conflict

Though social and political groups were emphasized by the early voting studies, they tended not to be given such close attention in later work. Recently they have staged a comeback. Part of the reason is a renewed interest in racial conflict in politics. Three general problem areas seem to have sparked the most recent interest.

A major new theoretical approach has grown out of various cognitive theories. Kluegel and Smith (1986) have developed attributional models of the theories people have about racial differences. And a wide variety of interesting insights have emerged from Tajfel's (1981) theorizing and experiments on the effects of social categorization on in-group biases [see Stephan (1985) and Worchel and Austin (1986) for a comprehensive treatment of the range of these cognitive approaches].

Racial attitudes have liberalized markedly over time (McConahay 1982, Schuman, et al 1985), leading to the question of what form politically potent racial attitudes now take.

Racial attitudes clearly play an important role in determining racial policy preferences and evaluations of black political candidates (see Kinder and Sears 1981, Sears and Allen 1984). Some argue that the key content of racial attitudes is "symbolic racism," a blend of antiblack affect and traditional values (Kinder and Sears 1981, McConahay 1982). Others disagree (Bobo 1983) and see group conflict or racial threat at work. Realistic racial threats generally have a much weaker effect than does symbolic racism, but the role of group conflict is still not clear (Vanneman and Pettigrew 1972, Sears and Allen 1984). Social desirability biases may also threaten measurement validity of old-fashioned racism (McConahay, et al 1981, Jackman and Muha 1984).

A second important applied area concerns the effects of interracial contact, and desegregation, upon the reduction of prejudice. There is much experimental evidence that such contact does reduce prejudice under the right conditions, which include cooperative task interdependence, mutual competence, successful task performance, etc. (Aronson, et al 1978, Cook 1984). Unfortunately, these conditions are infrequently found when desegregation is implemented (Stephan 1985).

Gender

The women's movement and the many postwar changes in women's roles in society have prompted renewed attention to women's roles in politics. The conventional wisdom in the early days of political behavior research was that women had lower levels of political involvement than men, which was reflected in lower interest, opinionation, sense of efficacy, and turnout, presumably because of a female sex role that made women dependent on men, uninterested in power, and distasteful of conflict (Lane 1959, Campbell, et al 1960, Sears 1969, Shapiro and Mahajan 1986). Presumably, few gender differences in attitudes existed except in matters of morality, such as sex and prohibition.

Today, registration and turnout now seem to be quite similar for men and women (Wolfinger and Rosenstone 1980, Poole and Zeigler 1985), and women are nearly as opinionated as men (Shapiro and Mahajan 1986). There is the well-heralded evidence of a "gender gap" in attitudes, especially in women's greater opposition to Ronald Reagan, which, since 1980, accompanies gender differences in party identification (Frankovic 1982).

An interesting line of research has begun to look for the effects of changes in women's social roles upon their group consciousness, and thus upon their political attitudes (Klein 1984). Women today are much more likely to be working, highly educated, unmarried, and free of caretaking for small children. This new reality clearly has the potential for increasing sensitivity to discrimination against women and, in turn, converting those perceptions into potent partisan instruments, whether through a sense of self-interest, group consciousness, or through conversion to feminist ideology by the women's movement.

The evidence is mixed. Young, single women are clearly the most liberal (Frankovic 1982). But women's private lives have rather little spillover into their political lives

(Sapiro 1983), and the findings generally do not follow a simple self-interest pattern. Evidence that women voters place extra weight on women's issues is mixed (Klein 1984, Mansbridge 1985). Women's sense of group consciousness, though increasing, remains relatively weak, and so is not believed to be strong enough to explain women's political attitudes (Gurin 1985). Rather, the best evidence is that the "gender gap" is better explained by women's longstanding greater aversion to force (Smith 1984) than by gender differences on such gender issues as ERA or affirmative action for women, which in any case are very small (Frankovic 1982, Mansbridge 1985). In that sense, despite clear polarization of the two parties in the 1980s on women's issues, the "gender gap" does not seem to depend very strongly on self- or group-interest.

Another possibility is that differential sex role socialization promotes greater concern about compassion, violence, and risk to people, because women are taught to be more responsible for others (Gilligan 1982). While this is consistent with gender differences in policy preferences, no such direct links have yet been demonstrated, and indeed women showing the greatest departure from men's political attitudes generally were reared in the least traditionally feminine manner.

POLITICAL PARTICIPATION

The form and level of participation in political life represent another important category of dependent variables. Economic, sociological, and political explanations always must be given their due, and have much to recommend them. Still, psychological explanations have a clear role. Much of the relevant literature has been reviewed elsewhere by Lane (1959), Nie and Verba (1975), Milbrath and Goel (1977), and Kinder and Sears (1985).

Political participation differs widely in its form—from such mainstream behavior as voting, the main activity of ordinary citizens, to engaging in protest or revolutionary behavior, or serving as an official in a legitimate government. Voting turnout has been analyzed principally by social psychologists, in terms of citizenship attitudes (especially "citizen duty," the norm of an obligation to vote, and "political efficacy," the sense that one's vote counts), attitudes about the election itself (whether or not the contenders differ very much), interpersonal pressures (such as being contacted by a party worker, interviewed in a survey, or driven to vote by a neighbor), and the political context (e.g., how easy it is to register) (see Kinder and Sears 1985).

Early analyses of participation in mass movements were inspired by Freud's analysis of group psychology, perhaps most notably Fromm's *Escape from Freedom* (1941). More sociological treatments focused particularly on the rootlessness or alienation produced by migration and the disintegration of primary group ties (Kornhauser 1959), the consequences of working class life (Lipset 1981), or the costs associated with an open, mobile society (Bettelheim and Janowitz 1964).

Protest and revolutionary activity have been analyzed recently in more sociopsychological terms. Such attitudes as political disaffection, relative deprivation (especially fraternal, rather than egoistic, deprivation), and realistic grievances all play a part (see Vanneman and Pettigrew 1972, Lipset and Raab 1978, Seeman 1984). In recent years, analyses of black, feminist, student, and antiwar protest in the United States have emphasized the role of political socialization, or resocialization, particularly of social and political values, and have in turn traced outbreaks of protest to prior changes in social and economic conditions. Black protest is partly linked to rising expectations stemming from the widespread migration by blacks from the rural South to Northern and Western metropolises (Sears and McConahay 1973); feminism is associated with a rising sense of discrimination against women among the better-educated, working women of recent decades who are less burdened by child care or economic dependency on a male (Klein 1984); and youth or student protest has been linked to the early family learning of liberal values in an affluent society (Flacks 1967, Inglehart 1981).

Personality explanations have been employed to some degree. Contrary to the early views of Lasswell (1930), most data on the mass public tend to show that political participation is associated with such indicators of a healthy personality as high self-esteem, a strong sense of personal efficacy, and satisfaction of basic physical, safety, and social needs (Lane 1959, Knutson 1973b, Renshon 1974, Sniderman 1975). In contrast, case studies of political leaders frequently turn up pervasive feelings of insecurity, low self-esteem, early deprivation, and ungratified social and personal needs (see Chapter Three of Burns 1978; see also Lasswell 1948, Wolfenstein 1967, Mazlish 1972, Glad 1973, Elms 1976, Barber 1985). These findings have supported Lasswell's view that political participation compensates for personal disabilities in at least these cases.

Psychobiographical studies of political leaders are, of course, vulnerable to criticism in terms of the availability of data and the intrusion of the biographers' own motives (Glad 1973, Falk 1985). But these contradictory findings are also likely to be due to the much more detailed examination of the inner lives of the elite, especially their particular conflicts and anxieties. Surely according to standardized personality tests, or other relatively superficial instruments, such individuals as Nixon, Lenin, Wilson, Lincoln, and Eleanor Roosevelt would, relative to humanity at large, appear to be strikingly strong, confident, effective human beings. It would seem more pertinent to ask how particular disabilities interact with specific political tasks or roles rather than attempt to gauge the overall level of mental health among the politically active.

POLITICAL SOCIALIZATION

The psychoanalytic emphasis on personality development, and research on such predispositions as party identification, racial prejudice, and disaffection, led to an early interest in preadult political socialization. So did studies that attempted to account for variability in the strength of democratic traditions across countries (Almond and Verba

1963; for other reviews see Sears 1975, Dawson, et al 1977, Renshon 1977, Kinder and Sears 1985).

Diffuse System Support

One major focus has been on preadult socialization that results in "proper" citizenship attitudes, loyalty to the regime, law-abiding behavior, and compliance with the political rules of the game. According to Easton and Dennis (1969), the major theorists in this area, these are key elements in the development of "diffuse system support," the tendency to support the regime in general, which in turn is a regime's ability to maintain order and authority, an orderly succession of political leadership, the legitimacy of authority, a willingness to fight external enemies, and other such contributors to its persistence. Easton and Dennis (1969), in developing this theory, distinguished diffuse system support from "specific support," or support for the current incumbents and their policies. A regime could persist over many years with the former, even in the absence of the latter.

Their early evidence persuaded them that preadult socialization was crucial in determining diffuse support. They and others observed that young children tend to have extraordinarily positive views of the President and to be aware of very little else in the political arena (Greenstein 1965, Hess and Torney 1967). They theorized that children idealize the President as a result of transferring affect from their fathers and/or such proximal quasi-political figures as the local policeman. As the child matured, he/she began to recognize other more impersonal political objects such as the Congress and practice of voting, to which that positive affect was generalized, thus producing support of the diffuse system.

But later research challenged both the psychological basis of this early idealization and its impact on later regime support. Adelson (1971), Tapp and Kohlberg (1971), and other cognitive developmentalists documented the fact that such positive affects toward authority represented a predictable but usually transitory developmental stage in late childhood and early adolescence, which might therefore have little lasting impact in adulthood. Second, much research indicated that such early idealization was quite specific to the place, samples, and era; such idealized views were not so characteristic in other nations or minority groups, or toward later presidents, and there was no noticeable cost in terms of regime persistence. Hence social learning explanations, rather than psychoanalytic, seemed most appropriate. Third, the distinction between diffuse support and specific support proved extremely difficult to make empirically; evaluations of the most general procedures and institutions seem to be strongly influenced by evaluations of specific current incumbents and their practices (for a review on these points, see Sears 1975). Finally, indices of systemic support, such as they were, proved to have relatively little stability across the life span (Jennings and Niemi 1981) or little impact on such indicators of regime support as support for energy conservation in the 1974 energy crisis (Sears, et al 1978) or participation in ghetto riots (Sears and McConahay 1973).

Thus the outcome is unfortunately somewhat murky, the problems perhaps methodological and perhaps substantive.

Partisanship

The second major issue concerns the persisting divisions within any polity—those based on party, ideology, class, ethnicity, race, religion, and region. Early empirical research demonstrated that such divisions were the most powerful factors in voting behavior (Lazarsfeld, et al 1948, Campbell, et al 1960). Attitudes toward them seemed to be acquired early in life, within the family (Hyman 1959, Campbell, et al 1960), pointing again to the political socialization process.

This view contained several propositions that lent themselves to more detailed testing. One is the assertion of persistence of such predispositions across a life span. This has been investigated with several research paradigms: the individual's retrospections, longitudinal studies, cohort analyses, and tests of the effects of environmental changes. Each has its strengths and weaknesses (see Kinder and Sears 1985). Persistence clearly varies considerably by attitude object and life stage; it is quite high for party identification and racial attitudes, is quite low for system attitudes (Jennings and Niemi 1981, Jennings and Markus 1984), and it is lower in early adulthood than in later life (Glenn 1980, Sears 1983). Political events such as wars, racial conflict, or poor performance by one's party when it is in power can disrupt it, especially early in adulthood (Markus 1979, Fiorina 1981), as can major changes in social environment, again especially in early adulthood (Brown 1986). And of course times change; party identification has not been socialized as strongly in early life in recent years as in earlier times (Wattenberg 1984). Overall, the emphasis among researchers has probably shifted away from childhood and early adolescence toward early adulthood as a possibly formative period with lasting effects (see Jennings and Niemi 1981, Jennings and Markus 1984). There is a greater appreciation for how people adjust their preferences (even if only modestly) later in life to accommodate changed realities.

The effects of events occurring in formative life stages are of considerable interest. The long-term consequences of affluence, and consequent value changes (Abramson and Inglehart 1986), or of the introduction of new democratic institutions (Barnes, et al 1985), tend to follow a generational model. Some research has been done on the effects of war experiences in childhood or of military service (Jennings and Markus 1977) or the possibly traumatic effects upon children of the assassination of a president (Wolfenstein and Kliman 1965). Considerable work has been done on socialization experiences during the adult years, especially on occupation and workplace, status and social mobility, and other environmental events (Sigel and Hoskin 1977, Elden 1981).

Parents were thought to be the central socializing agents, a view based largely on individual retrospections and consistent with the psychoanalytic and learning views of the postwar era. Later research (Jennings and Niemi 1981), based on more thorough measurement of both parents' and children's attitudes, cast doubt on this assumption (though see Dalton 1980). Limits on the parents' role are due especially to lack of political communication in the family (Tedin 1974). There also was much interest in the role of schools as socializing agents, but with some disappointing results (Torney-Purta 1984). Newcomb and colleagues' (1967) study of attending Bennington College as a politically socializing experience is very well known, but it likely is an exceptional case. Recent research has reviewed the role of the military and specially prepared curricula that deal with issues such as value clarification and peace (Jennings and Markus 1977). The role of the media in children's political socialization, always an interesting topic, continues to be somewhat uncertain (see Chaffee 1977).

THE MASS MEDIA

Social scientists' views of the mass media have undergone some cycling since the widespread use of the electronic media, but recurrent themes can be recognized in each era. The invention of the radio coincident with its creative use in the 1930s by demagogues such as Hitler, Goebbels, Huey Long, and Father Coughlin gave rise to the belief that the mass public was a vast, captive, and gullible audience, easy prey for these demagogues' "tricks of the trade" (Institute for Propaganda Analysis, 1939). Inferences of massive effects rested on no particular empirical data other than some loose estimates of audience size and informal content analyses.

A second era followed the introduction of mass survey techniques. Early voting studies found campaign propaganda and the mass media not to be especially influential (Lazarsfeld, et al 1948). Early media research led to a general view that might be described as the "minimal effects model"; mass communications normally reinforced prior attitudes, rather than producing converts, except under some special circumstances (Hovland 1959, Klapper 1960).

Most of this research was conducted prior to the sophisticated political uses of television that began to appear in the 1960s. Hence a third era of studies portrayed television as particularly powerful, and with socially dangerous effects.

Concerns about television's ill effects took several forms. One focused on the President's ability to gain prime-time coverage for essentially uncontested defenses of Administration policy (Minow, et al 1973). Network news was criticized for attacking mainstream institutions and thus producing "videomalaise" (Robinson 1976), or for taking a stance of "belligerent neutrality" that produced confusion and partisan dealignment (Schultz 1986). Television commentators were criticized for being biased toward the left, or for emphasizing "hoopla" and failing to educate voters about the issues (Patterson and McClure 1976). Subtle nonverbal techniques were used by media consultants to artificially enhance candidates' popularity.

As in the 1930s, these observations of persuasive power were often based on little more than loose estimates of audience size. Audience exposure estimates often were based on the large number of television sets in use and on evidence about the amount of time they were turned on (see Minow, et al 1973). Disregarded were more discouraging data about widespread inattention, poor learning, and even the substantial fraction of time that television sets are turned on but with no humans watching or even in the same room (Neuman 1976, Comstock, et al 1978, Sears and Chaffee 1979).

Persuasive Effects

The current era thus is marked by the search for the effects of television viewing. Graber (1984a), Comstock, et al (1978), and Kraus and Davis (1976) have provided useful overviews. Nevertheless, much of this literature indicates, in my judgment, that partisan communications still have "minimal effects." The clearest examples are perhaps presidential debates (Sears and Chaffee 1979), but other political and entertainment programs seem to follow suit (Kinder and Sears 1985). Hence some researchers have looked for persuasive effects under conditions that are considered to be exceptions by the minimal effects model, e.g., conventions, primary elections, nonpartisan elections, etc. (Kraus and Davis 1976), though even then the effects have often not been very powerful. Perhaps the most creative explorers for persuasive effects have been the Langs (1983, 1984), who have investigated the effects of conventions, debates, early announcements of voting returns, and, most extensively, the Watergate episode.

Insofar as money spent on media in a political campaign indexes media effort, its association with the vote might indirectly reflect a persuasive effect. More money spent in a political campaign does not, on the average, produce more votes. So increasingly, analyses have tried to define the conditions under which it does affect voting, e.g., with several obscure candidates for open seats, or in districts with weak party organizations (Grush, et al 1978, Wattenberg 1982). The "belligerent neutrality" hypothesis is particularly interesting because it predicts that the most media-attentive will become the most confused, least partisan, most volatile and unstable elements of the electorate. Schultz (1986) provides surprisingly strong evidence for this effect from the 1980 campaign. This is quite a shift from past views of the effects of information flow (Klapper 1960, Sears 1969). Finally, if verbal communications normally do not have major effects, it has been thought that subtle nonverbal cues might. Various facial displays influence emotional and attitudinal responses to televised news coverage of political leaders (though usually in interaction with prior attitudes; see Lanzetta, et al 1985).

Agenda-Setting

Some feel the media's main role may be in "agenda-setting": media coverage can place a particular issue or problem foremost on the public's agenda, where it can become the central determinant of the public's evaluations of incumbent performance and/or voting behavior. This phenomenon has now been investigated with experiments (Iyengar and Kinder 1985), surveys (McCombs and Shaw 1972), and time-series analyses of aggregate data (MacKuen 1981). The research raises interesting questions, especially about the magnitude and duration of coverage required to produce an effect, the role of steady coverage versus vivid single cases, and impact on political judgments. An especially important case is the massive attention, and thus boost in popularity, given to early front-runners during the American presidential primary season (Patterson 1980).

The central implication of the agenda-setting approach is that the media can make certain political symbols salient, and in that way determine which predispositions form the basis of voter choice. Edelman (1971) argues that this is a prime technique by which elites control public opinion. For some, a symbolic politics approach focuses particularly on the learning of appropriate feelings about regime symbols (Baas 1984, Feldman 1985), and for others, the learning of values of any kind (Sears and Citrin 1985).

Brief mention, at least, should also be given to more cognitive approaches to media effects. The role of schemata as filters of media messages has begun to be explored in considerable depth (Graber 1984b, Lau and Sears 1986). And, finally, others have conceded that most of the public is not likely to be massively politically persuaded by the media because they use the media for entertainment, not as sources of information; this has generated considerable work under the "uses and gratifications" rubric (Garramone 1985).

INTERNATIONAL CONFLICT

A third major influence on political psychology has been international conflict; initially the Cold War and later international tensions in and around the Mideast. A comprehensive psychological approach to international conflict would require consideration of mutual perceptions of contending parties, attitudes toward each other (such as nationalism and outgroup antagonisms), economics, social roles, organizational behavior and group dynamics within decision making groups, and bargaining and negotiation (e.g., Stagner 1967). Most recent work has taken up these factors in a more piecemeal fashion.

Images and Misperception

A convenient starting point is the images that contending adversaries hold about themselves and each other. Whether focusing on nations, political leaders, or populaces, these images can be held by elites or the public. This point is sufficiently central that about half of the major handbook in this area was devoted to the nature and determinants of international images (see Kelman 1965).

The first priority has been to identify patterns of misperception. Finlay, et al (1967) described the delights of perceiving another country as an enemy. White (1970) described a number of other common misperceptions, such as "the diabolical enemy," "the moral self," and "the virile self." He described a mutual pattern of distortion as "the mirror image," in which each side believes it has peaceful intentions, is afraid of the other side because the latter is perceived as aggressive and threatening (at least the rulers are, if not the common people), and endorses its own militarism as self-defense. He has carefully applied these general biases to the cases of Soviet-American relations and the Vietnam conflict (White 1965, 1970). Tetlock (1983b) has contrasted the "spiral" and "deterrence" images of Soviet-American relations, and Herrmann (1985) has dealt with "communist expansionism," "real politik expansionism," and "real politik defensive." These authors, in addition, make heroic efforts to evaluate the accuracy of these images.

These misperceptions need to be described in basic cognitive terms. Most analyses have particularly emphasized black-and-white, oversimplified thinking and egocentric perceptions that satisfy self-serving motives. Jervis (1976) has rooted elites' misperceptions in international relations most clearly and coherently in psychological theory. He particularly emphasizes overestimations of the unity and planfulness of behavior, wishful thinking, egocentricity, and dissonance-reducing defense of prior commitments.

A third line of analysis has focused on the more distal psychological determinants of international images. These have rounded up the usual suspects. The several chapters on this point in the Kelman (1965) handbook emphasize cultural socialization, education and propaganda, political events, cross-national contact, and such personal predispositions as values and personality (personal security, aggressiveness, etc.). When applied to concrete cases, these result in excessive loyalty to one's own nation and conformity to its norms, overly enthusiastic adherence to social roles (e.g., in the military), unconsciously expressed motives such as hostility, and the oversimplification and intolerance of ambiguity that personal insecurity is presumed to produce (White 1970). Etheredge (1978) has particularly emphasized the role of male machismo, or the "male narcissism syndrome," in producing leaders that like to "play hardball" or threaten force; they excessively perceive international relations in competitive, coercive, combative, and adversarial terms. In common with the current drift of psychology toward the cognitive, Jervis (1976, 1986) emphasizes the tendency to minimize cognitive effort through theory-driven inference from belief systems (or schemas).

Public Opinion

In dealing with international relations, it is even more important than usual to distinguish leaders' perceptions from those of the mass public. Public opinion proves particularly responsive to bold international acts by national leaders, demonstrated most dramatically by Mueller (1973) in the support given American presidents when they attacked the enemy in the Vietnam and Korean wars. There is a similar "rally round the flag" effect when some disaster occurs (such as the Bay of Pigs or Tet invasions, or the Russian shooting down of the American U-2 plane), which is evidenced in a strong tendency to support presidents in foreign policy (Sears 1969). Mueller goes further and identifies the well-educated and the young as the "followers" who follow most.

Numerous efforts have been made to uncover simple dimensions of public opinion on foreign policy, e.g., interventionism/isolationism, or hawk/dove. They generally find more complex patterns, even toward such apparently well-known issues as the Vietnam

War (see Modigliani 1972) or nuclear war (Fiske, et al 1983). Part of the problem is that political candidates often do not take distinctive positions, thus preventing simple links to voting preferences.

Elite Decision Making

Political psychologists, like many other social scientists, have tried to develop comprehensive theories of elite decision making. Janis and Mann's (1977) conflict theory of decision making centers upon emotion-laden decisional conflicts, the various patterns of coping behavior that are common in such conflicts, the antecedents of such coping patterns, and their various consequences for decisional rationality. The authors attempt to develop a unique but comprehensive theory of decision making, and they draw examples (or evidence) from a wide variety of arenas. At the other extreme is George's (1980) eclectic theory of presidential decision making; George explains specifically presidential behavior with theories drawn from wherever required: e.g., information processing, belief systems, small group behavior, and organizational behavior. Etheredge (1985) makes a similar attempt in the case of American foreign policy toward Central America.

Political psychologists have developed some insights that seem unique to the psychological approach. One point is that decisional conflicts are inherently emotional and thus stressful (Janis and Mann 1977). Stress can have a number of negative effects, e.g., it can reduce the complexity of information processing (Tetlock 1983a), and it can lead to defensive avoidance and wishful thinking. Various techniques, primarily relying on vigilance, are offered by Janis and Mann for coping constructively with stress.

Some personality characteristics may be particularly relevant to and dangerous in foreign policy decision-making. The "male narcissism" or machismo syndrome described by Etheredge (1978) is an example. Even that humble individual difference variable, birth order, may have considerable consequence. Stewart (1977) believes that first-borns and only children tend to lead us into crisis, war, and civil conflict. The "Machiavellian" personality (Christie and Geis 1970), who demonstrates a lack of interpersonal affect, ideological commitment, and concern with conventional morality, may be highly appropriate for foreign minister positions (such as those held with great effect by Bismarck and Kissinger), but may be utterly unsuited for head of state (Elms 1976).

Cognitive consistency theories generate numerous examples of decision-makers' biases in favor of decisions consistent with their predispositions and images; e.g., in their treatment of their enemies (Finlay, et al 1967). An especially important notion is that of a leader's "operational code" (Leites 1951, George 1969), his beliefs about the nature of politics, political conflict, historical developments, and strategy and tactics. Leites suggests that the beliefs of Bolshevik leaders were quite different from those of contemporary American leaders; they were willing to engage in high-risk activities as long as subsequent events could be controlled, so that the sequence could be aborted in the event of failure (for other analyses of operational codes of heads of state and U.S. statesmen, see Johnson 1977).

Recent information processing theories in psychology offer similar insights. Most of these fall under the rubric of social cognition (Fischer and Johnson 1986, Lau and Sears 1986). One central tenet is that information processing tends to be "theory-driven" rather than "data-driven." Some of the most interesting implications involve elite decision-makers' "learning from history" (Jervis 1976); too often those lessons are learned too early and hence prove to be anachronistic when applied, or are overly responsive to firsthand or especially vivid experiences, or are too responsive to successes—even accidental successes.

Most foreign policy decisions arise from extensive small group deliberation, so it is perhaps not surprising that one of the most influential efforts by a political psychologist involves "groupthink"—factors inherent in highly cohesive small groups that can produce terrible foreign policy fiascoes (Janis 1982). High group cohesiveness produces pressures toward conformity, and thus suppression of dissent and of one's own doubts, as well as illusions of unanimity and invulnerability. Janis persuasively argues for the critical role of groupthink in generating such American fiascoes as the Bay of Pigs, Pearl Harbor, Watergate, and Vietnam (for critiques, see Longley and Pruitt 1980, Tetlock 1983a).

Interactive Processes

A final area of application focuses on relations between adversaries or those in conflict. A considerable sociopsychological literature deals with the issues of interdependence, influence, bargaining, negotiation, escalation, and conflict resolution. Space limitations prevent detailed discussion. Some of the most influential work is by Deutsch (e.g., 1973), who uses extrapolations from simulation and experimental games. The "deterrence" and "spiral" models are central (Jervis 1976). An early innovation was the gradual unilateral initiatives (Osgood 1962), which Etzioni (1967) believed were employed by President Kennedy in unilaterally stopping atmospheric nuclear testing. For a useful recent collection in this area, see White (1985); also see Tetlock (1983a, pp. 69–71). Those working in this field also have a proclivity for action, so numerous workshops and training programs in negotiation, mediation, and conflict management are offered (Kelman and Cohen 1986). The best early overview of this distinctively psychological perspective is by Kelman (1965, Chapters 9–15).

DEATH AND HORROR

All historical eras must confront the horrible acts committed in the quest for political power. Our era is no exception. We live under the nuclear cloud as well, arguably a new element (though the plagues, pestilences, and wars of the past may hardly have seemed less devastating and all-encompassing). Economists are obviously uncomfortable with the irrational, and political scientists with the disorderly and impractical. Many psychologists, on the other hand, seek out the extremes—the irrational, the deep, the mysterious, the sense of horror and despair—and even, from another perspective, the astonishing ability of the human being to weather, adapt to, and even ultimately find some small pleasures in many intrinsically quite unpleasant situations.

Americans' responses to the assassination of President Kennedy were examined in great detail (Greenberg and Parker 1965, Wolfenstein and Kliman 1965), in terms of their emotionality, grieving, and overidealization of the dead president; particular attention was given to the impact on children. Reactions to the Nazi Holocaust have become a matter of great interest—for example, the apparent passivity of so many Jews (e.g., Zuckerman 1984). The mass suicide of residents of Jonestown raises questions both about individual charisma (of Jones himself) and collective action, perhaps in terms of collective regression (Ulman and Abse 1983). Terrorism has provoked much analysis of the personalities and motives of terrorists themselves, of course, but also of its effects on the population it attempts to influence. So far, it seems indeed to inspire fear and anxiety (among Israelis), but a hardening of attitude against the terrorists' causes (see Friedland and Merari 1985).

The nuclear stalemate has inspired considerable research as well. The relative lack of public concern, despite some realistic estimates of nuclear effects, has been a source of puzzlement (Fiske, et al 1983). Adolescents' perceptions, and efforts at public education and media presentations, have been assessed (Goodman, et al 1983, Zweigenhaft 1985). All these matters heighten the salience of death of oneself or others, but the political consequences of this variable have generally not been considered explicitly (though see Peterson 1985).

CONCLUSIONS

Political psychology as an emerging self-conscious specialty has now attracted a fairly stable cadre of workers. Like most interdisciplinary ventures, it is difficult to do well because it requires a sophisticated understanding of two (or more) quite different disciplines. To date understanding of the second discipline has mostly been self-taught. One of the charms of the field is its relative looseness, which provides for more original and imaginative flights of fancy than are usually permitted in the more staid and methodologically proper basic disciplines. Concomitantly, this leads to the unavoidable hazard of mixing sound analyses in with the naive and poorly informed.

As an identifiable specialty, political psychology has drawn together a variety of intellectual strands previously located solely in the traditional social science disciplines. It has done so partly because it does offer a unique perspective on politics, one emphasizing such familiar psychological concerns as emotion and stress, mechanisms of information processing, interpersonal relationships, and the irrational, among others.

The coalescence of these strands seems to me particularly valuable at this time because of the surging popularity within the discipline of political science of political economy, which offers a strikingly different account of human behavior.

One of the necessary consequences of this focus upon individuals and their irrationalities is a strong normative undercurrent that usually leads to a caring, understanding, good-hearted empathy for them. The political reformist impulse that follows close behind can produce a soft-headed science. The tension between this impulse and scientific tough-mindedness is but one of the several that promise to keep political psychology lively and provocative in the years to come.

REFERENCES

Abramson, P., Inglehart, R. 1986. Generational replacement and value change in six West European societies, *Am. J. Polit. Sci.* 30:1-25

Adelson, J. 1971. The political imagination of the young adolescent. In *12 to 16: Early Adolescence*, ed. J. Kagan, R. Coles. New York: Norton

Adorno, T. W., Frenkel-Brunswik, E., Levinson, D. J., Sanford, R. N. 1950. *The Authoritarian Personality*, New York: Harper & Row

Almond, G. A., Verba, S. 1963. *The Civic Culture.* Princeton: Princeton Univ. Press

Aronson, E., Stephan, C. W., Sikes, J., Blaney, N., Snapp, M. 1978. *The Jigsaw Classroom.* Beverly Hills, CA: Sage

Baas, L. 1984. The primary sources of meaning of a secondary symbol: The case of the Constitution and Mrs. Murphy. *Polit. Psychol.* 5:687–705

Barber, J. D. 1965. *The Lawmakers.* New Haven: Yale Univ. Press

―――. 1985. *The Presidential Character: Predicting Performance in the White House.* Englewood Cliffs, NJ: Prentice-Hall. 3rd ed.

Barner-Barry, C., Rosenwein, R. 1985. *Psychological Perspectives on Politics.* Englewood Cliffs, NJ: Prentice-Hall

Barnes, S. H., McDonough, P., Pina, A. L. 1985. The development of partisanship in new democracies: The case of Spain. *Am. J. Polit. Sci.* 29:695–720

Berelson, B. R., Lazarsfeld, P. F., McPhee, W. N. 1954. *Voting: A Study of Opinion Formation in a Presidential Campaign.* Chicago: Univ. Chicago Press

Bettelheim, B., Janowitz, M. 1964. *Social Change and Prejudice.* New York: Free Press

Bobo, L. 1983. Whites' opposition to busing: Symbolic racism or realistic group conflict? *J. Per. Soc. Psychol.* 45:1196–1210

Brown, T. A. 1986. *Migration and Politics in America.* Chapel Hill: Univ. North Carolina Press

Burns, J. M. 1978. *Leadership.* New York: Harper & Row

Campbell, A., Converse, P. E., Miller, W. E., Stokes, D. E. 1960. *The American Voter.* New York: Wiley

Chaffee, S. H. 1977. Mass communication in political socialization. See Renshon 1977, pp. 223–58

Christie, R., Geis, F. L. 1970. *Studies in Machiavellianism.* New York: Academic

Comstock, G., Chaffee, S., Katzman, N., McCombs, M., Roberts, D. 1978. *Television and Human Behavior.* New York: Columbia Univ. Press

Converse, P. E. 1964. The nature of belief systems in mass publics. In *Ideology and Discontent,* ed. D. E. Apter, pp. 206–61. New York: Free Press

———. 1975. Public opinion and voting behavior. In *Handbook of Political Science,* ed. F. I. Greenstein, N. W. Polsby, 4:75–170. Reading, MA: Addison-Wesley

Cook, S. W. 1984. Cooperative interaction in multiethnic contexts. In *Groups in Contact: The Psychology of Desegregation,* ed. N. Miller, M. Brewer, pp. 156–86. New York: Academic

Dalton, R. J. 1980. Reassessing parental socialization: Indicator unreliability versus generational transfer. *Am. Polit. Sci. Rev.* 74:421–31

Davies, J. C. 1963. *Human Nature in Politics: The Dynamics of Political Behavior.* New York: Wiley

Dawson, R. E., Prewitt, K., Dawson, K. S. 1977. *Political Socialization.* Boston: Little, Brown. 2nd ed.

Deutsch, M. 1973. *The Resolution of Conflict.* New Haven: Yale Univ. Press

Easton, D., Dennis, J. 1969. *Children in the Political System: Origins of Political Legitimacy.* New York: McGraw-Hill

Edelman, M. 1971. *Politics as Symbolic Action: Mass Arousal and Quiescence.* Chicago: Markham

Elden, J. M. 1981. Political efficacy at work: The connection between more autonomous forms of workplace organization and a more participatory politics. *Am. Polit. Sci. Rev.* 75:43–58

Elms, A. C. 1976. *Personality in Politics.* New York: Harcourt, Brace Jovanovich

Etheredge, L. S. 1978. *A World of Men: The Private Sources of American Foreign Policy.* Cambridge, MA: MIT Press

———. 1985. *Can Governments Learn?: American Foreign Policy and Central American Revolutions.* New York: Pergamon

Etzioni, A. 1967. The Kennedy experiment *West. Polit. Q.* 20:361–80

Falk, A. 1985. Aspects of political psychobiography. *Polit. Psychol.* 6:605–19

Feldman, D. L. 1985. Ideology and the manipulation of symbols: Leadership perceptions of science, education, and art in the People's Republic of China, 1961-1974. *Polit. Psychol.* 6:441–60

Finlay, D. J., Holsti, O. R., Fagen, R. R. 1967. *Enemies in Politics.* Chicago: Rand-McNally

Fiorina, M. P. 1981. *Retrospective Voting in American National Elections.* New Haven: Yale Univ. Press

Fischer, G. W., Johnson, E. J. 1986. Behavioral decision theory and political decision making. See Lau & Sears 1986, pp. 55–65

Fiske, S. T., Fischhoff, B., Milburn, M. A., eds. 1983. Images of nuclear war. *J. Soc. Issues* 39(I):41–65

Flacks, R. 1967. The liberated generation: An exploration of the roots of student protest. *J. Soc. Issues* 23:53–75

Frankovic, K. A. 1982. Sex and politics—new alignments, old issues. *PS* 15:439–48

Freedman, A. E., Freedman, P. E. 1975. *The Psychology of Political Control.* New York: St. Martin's Press

Friedland, N., Merari, A. 1985. The psychological impact of terrorism: A double-edged sword. *Polit. Psychol.* 6:591–604

Fromm, E. 1941. *Escape from Freedom*. New York: Holt

Garramone, G. M. 1985. Motivation and political information processing: Extending the gratifications approach. See Kraus & Perloff 1985. pp. 201–19

George, A. L. 1969. The "operational code": A neglected approach to the study of political leaders and decision making. *Int. Stud. Q.* 13:190–222

———. 1980. *Presidential Decision-making in Foreign Policy: The Effective Use of Information and Advice*. Boulder, CO: Westview

George, A. L., George, J. L. 1956. *Woodrow Wilson and Colonel House: A Personality Study*. New York: Day

Gilligan, C. 1982. *In a Different Voice*. Cambridge, MA: Harvard Univ. Press

Glad, B. 1973. Contributions of psychobiography. See Knutson 1973a, pp. 296–321

Glenn, N. D. 1980. Values, attitudes, and beliefs. In *Constancy and Change in Human Development*, ed. O. G. Brim Jr., J. Kagan, pp. 596–640. Cambridge, MA: Harvard Univ. Press

Goodman, L. A., Mack, J. E., Beardslee, W. R., Snow, R. M. 1983. The threat of nuclear war and the nuclear arms race: Adolescent experience and perceptions. *Polit. Psychol.* 4:501–30

Graber, D. A. 1984a. *Mass Media and American Politics*. Washington, DC: Congressional Quarterly. 2nd ed.

———. 1984b. *Processing the News: How People Tame the Information Tide*. New York: Longman

Greenberg, B. S., Parker, E. B. 1965. Summary: Social research on the assassination. In *The Kennedy Assassination and the American Public*, ed. B. S. Greenberg, E. B. Parker, pp. 361–82. Stanford, CA: Stanford Univ. Press

Greenstein, F. I. 1965. *Children and Politics*. New Haven: Yale Univ. Press

———. 1975. Personality and politics. In *Handbook of Political Science*, ed. F. I. Greenstein, N. W. Polsby, 2:1–92. Reading, MA: Addison-Wesley. 2nd ed.

Grush, J. E., McKeough, K. L., Ahlering, R. C. 1978. Extrapolating laboratory exposure research to actual political elections. *J. Pers. Soc. Psychol.* 36:257–70

Gurin, P. 1985. Women's gender consciousness. *Public Opin. Q.* 49:142–63

Hamill, R. C., Lodge, M., Blake, F. 1985. The breadth, depth, and utility of class, partisan, and ideological schemata. *Am. J. Polit. Sci.* 29:850–70

Hermann, M. G., ed. 1986. *Political Psychology: Contemporary Problems and Issues*. San Francisco: Jossey-Bass

———. ed. 1977. *A Psychological Examination of Political Leaders*. New York: Free Press

Herrmann, R. K. 1985. American perceptions of Soviet foreign policy: Reconsidering three competing perspectives. *Polit. Psychol.* 6:375–411

Hess, R. D., Torney, J. V. 1967. *The Development of Political Attitudes in Children*. Chicago: Aldine

Hovland, C. I. 1959. Reconciling conflicting results derived from experimental and survey studies of attitude change. *Am. Psychol.* 14:8–17

Hyman, H. 1959. *Political Socialization*. Glencoe, IL: Free Press

Inglehart, R. 1981. Post-materialism in an environment of insecurity. *Am. Polit. Sci. Rev.* 75:880–900

Institute for Propaganda Analysis. 1939. *The Fine Art of Propaganda: A Study of Father Coughlin's Speeches*. New York: Harcourt & Brace

Iyengar, S., Kinder, D. R. 1985. Psychological accounts of agenda-setting. See Kraus & Perloff 1985, pp. 117–40

Jackman, M. R., Muha, M. J. 1984. Education and inter-group attitudes: Moral enlightenment, superficial democratic commitment, or ideological refinement. *Am. Sociol. Rev.* 49:751–69

Janis, I. L. 1982. *Victims of Groupthink.* Boston: Houghton Mifflin. 2nd ed.

Janis, I. L., Mann, L. 1977. *Decision Making.* New York: Free Press

Jennings, M. K., Markus, G. B. 1977. The effect of military service on political attitudes: A panel study. *Am. Polit. Sci. Rev.* 71:131–47

_____. 1984. Partisan orientations over the long haul: Results from the three-wave political socialization panel study. *Am. Polit. Sci. Rev.* 78:1000–18

Jennings, M. K., Niemi, R. G. 1981. *Generations and Politics.* Princeton: Princeton Univ. Press

Jervis, R. 1976. *Perception and Misperception in International Politics.* Princeton: Princeton Univ. Press

_____. 1986. Cognition and political behavior. See Lau & Sears 1986, pp. 319–36

Johnson, L. K. 1977. Operational codes and the prediction of leadership behavior: Senator Frank Church at midcareer. In *A Psychological Examination of Political Leaders,* ed. M. G. Hermann, pp. 80–119. New York: Free Press

Kelman, H. C. 1965. *International Behavior: A Social-Psychological Analysis.* New York: Holt, Rinehart & Winston

Kelman, H. C., Cohen, S. P. 1986. Resolution of international conflict: An interactional approach. In *Psychology of Intergroup Relations.* ed. S. Worchel, W. G. Austin. Chicago: Nelson-Hall. 2nd ed.

Kinder, D. R., Kiewiet, D. R. 1979. Economic discontent and political behavior: The role of personal grievances and collective economic judgments in congressional voting. *Am. J. Polit. Sci.* 23:495–527

Kinder, D. R., Sears, D. O. 1981. Prejudice and politics: Symbolic racism versus racial threats to the good life. *J. Pers. Soc. Psychol.* 40:414–31

_____. 1985. Public opinion and political action. In *Handbook of Social Psychology,* ed. G. Lindzey, E. Aronson, 2:659–741. New York: Random House. 3rd ed.

Klapper, J. T. 1960. *The Effects of Mass Communications.* Glencoe, IL: Free Press

Klein, E. 1984. *Gender Politics: From Consciousness to Mass Politics.* Cambridge, MA: Harvard Univ. Press

Kluegel, J. R., Smith, E. R. 1986. *Beliefs about Inequality.* New York: Aldine

Knutson, J. N., ed. 1973a. *Handbook of Political Psychology.* San Francisco: Jossey-Bass

_____. 1973b. *The Human Basis of the Polity: A Psychological Study of Political Man.* Chicago: Aldine

Kornhauser, W. 1959. *The Politics of Mass Society.* Glencoe, IL: Free Press

Kramer, G. H. 1971. Short-term fluctuations in U.S. voting behavior, 1896–1964. *Am. Polit. Sci. Rev.* 65:131–43

Kraus, S., Davis, D. 1976. *The Effects of Mass Communication on Political Behavior.* University Park, PA: Penn. State Univ. Press

Kraus. S. A., Perloff, R. M., eds. 1985. *Mass Media and Political Thought: An Information-Processing Approach.* Beverly Hills, CA: Sage

Lane, R. E. 1959. *Political Life: Why People Get Involved in Politics.* Glencoe, IL: Free Press

_____. 1962. *Political Ideology: Why the American Common Man Believes What He Does.* New York: Free Press

_____. 1973. Patterns of political belief. See Knutson 1973a, pp. 83–116

————. 1983. Political observers and market participants: The effect on cognition. *Polit. Psychol.* 4:455–82

Lang, G. E., Lang, K. 1983. *The Battle for Public Opinion: The President, the Press, and the Polls During Watergate.* New York: Columbia Univ. Press

————. 1984. *Politics and Television Re-viewed.* Beverly Hills, CA: Sage

Lanzetta, J. T., Sullivan, D. G., Masters, R. D., McHugo, G. J. 1985. Emotional and cognitive responses to televised images of political leaders. See Kraus & Perloff 1985, pp. 85–116

Lasswell, H. D. 1930. *Psychopathology and Politics.* New York: Viking

————. 1948. *Power and Personality.* New York: Norton

Lau, R. R., Sears, D. O., eds. 1986. *Political Cognition: The 19th Annual Carnegie Symposium on Cognition.* Hillsdale, NJ: Erlbaum

Lazarsfeld, P. F., Berelson, B., Gaudet, H. 1948. *The People's Choice.* New York: Columbia Univ. Press. 2nd ed.

Leites, N. 1951. *The Operational Code of the Politburo.* New York: McGraw-Hill

Lipset, S. M. 1981. *Political Man: The Social Bases of Politics.* Baltimore, MD: Johns Hopkins Univ. Press (expanded ed.)

Lipset, S. M., Lazarsfeld, P. F., Barton, A. H., Linz, J. 1954. The psychology of voting: An analysis of political behavior. In *Handbook of Social Psychology,* ed. G. Lindzey, 2:1124–75. Reading, MA: Addison-Wesley

Lipset, S. M., Raab. E. 1978. *The Politics of Unreason.* Chicago: Univ. Chicago Press. 2nd ed.

Longley, J., Pruitt, D. 1980. Groupthink: A critique of Janis's theory. In *Review of Personality and Social Psychology,* Vol. 1, ed. L. Wheeler, Beverly Hills, CA: Sage

MacKuen, M. B. 1981. Social communication and the mass policy agenda. In *More than News: Media Power in Public Affairs,* ed. M. B. MacKuen, S. L. Coombs, pp. 19–144. Beverly Hills, CA: Sage

Mann, T. E., Wolfinger, R. E. 1980. Candidates and parties in congressional elections. *Am. Polit. Sci. Rev.* 74:617–32

Mansbridge, J. J. 1985. Myth and reality: The ERA and the gender gap in the 1980 election. *Public Opin. Q.* 49:164–78

Markus, G. B. 1979. The political environment and the dynamics of public attitudes: A panel study. *Am. J. Polit. Sci.* 23:338–59

Maslow, A. H. 1954. *Motivation and Personality.* New York: Harper

Mazlish, B. 1972. *In Search of Nixon: A Psychohistorical Inquiry.* New York: Basic Books

McClosky, H. 1958. Conservatism and personality. *Am. Polit. Sci. Rev.* 52:27–45

————. 1967. Personality and attitude correlates of foreign policy orientations. In *Domestic Sources of Foreign Policy,* ed. J. Rosenau, pp. 51–109. New York: Free Press

McCombs, M. E., Shaw, D. L. 1972. The agenda-setting function of the media. *Public Opin. Q.* 36:176–87

McConahay, J. B. 1982. Self-interest versus racial attitudes as correlates of anti-busing attitudes in Louisville: Is it the buses or the blacks? *J. Polit.* 44:692–720

McConahay, J. B., Hardee, B. B., Batts, V. 1981. Has racism declined in America? *J. Confl. Resolut.* 25:563–79

Milbrath, L. W., Goel, M. L. 1977. *Political Participation.* Chicago: Rand McNally

Minow, N. N., Martin, J. B., Mitchell, L. M. 1973. *Presidential Television.* New York: Basic Books

Modigliani, A. 1972. Hawks and doves, isolationism and political distrust: An analysis of public opinion on military policy. *Am. Polit. Sci. Rev.* 66:960–78

Mueller, J. E. 1973. *War, Presidents, and Public Opinion.* New York: Wiley

Neuman, W. R. 1976. Patterns of recall among television news viewers. *Public Opin. Q.* 40:115–23

Newcomb. T. M., Koenig, K. E., Flacks, R., Warwick, D. P. 1967. *Persistence and Change: Bennington College and its Students After 25 Years.* New York: Wiley

Nie, N. H., Verba, S. 1975. Political participation. See Greenstein & Polsby 1975, 4:1–74

Nie, N. H., Verba, S., Petrocik, J. R. 1979. *The Changing American Voter.* Cambridge, MA: Harvard Univ. Press. (enlarged ed.)

Osgood, C. 1962. *An Alternative to War or Surrender.* Urbana, IL: Univ. Illinois Press

Patterson, T. E. 1980. *The Mass Media Election: How Americans Choose Their President.* New York: Praeger

Patterson, T. E., McClure, R. D., 1976. *The Unseeing Eye.* New York: Putnam's

Peterson, S. A. 1985. Death experience and politics: A research note. *Polit. Psychol.* 6:19–27

Poole, K. T., Zeigler, L. H. 1985. *Women, Public Opinion and Politics: The Changing Political Attitudes of American Women.* New York: Longman

Post, J. M. 1983. Woodrow Wilson reexamined: The mind-body controversy redux and other disputations. *Polit. Psychol.* 4:289–306

Renshon, S. A. 1974. *Psychological Needs and Political Behavior: A Theory of Personality and Political Efficacy.* New York: Free Press.

———. ed. 1977. *Handbook of Political Socialization: Theory and Research.* New York: Free Press

Rintala, M. 1984. The love of power and the power of love: Churchill's childhood. *Polit. Psychol.* 5:375–90

Robinson, M. J. 1976. Public affairs television and the growth of political malaise: The case of "the selling of the Pentagon." *Am. Polit. Sci. Rev.* 70:409–32

Rogow, A. A. 1963. *James Forrestal: A Study of Personality, Politics, and Policy.* New York: Macmillan

Rothman, S. 1984. Ideology, authoritarianism and mental health. *Polit. Psychol.* 5:341–63

Sanford, N. 1973. Authoritarian personality in contemporary perspective. See Knutson 1973a, pp. 139–70

Sapiro, V. 1983. *The Political Integration of Women.* Urbana, IL: Univ. Illinois Press

Schlozman, K. L., Verba, S. 1979. *Injury to Insult: Unemployment, Class, and Political Response.* Cambridge, MA: Harvard Univ. Press

Schultz, C. K. 1986. *The belligerent neutrality of the news: Creating an environment of informed confusion.* Unpublished doctoral dissertation. Univ. Calif., Los Angeles

Schuman, H., Steeh, C., Bobo, L. 1985. *Racial Attitudes in America: Trends and Interpretation.* Cambridge, MA: Harvard Univ. Press

Sears, D. O. 1969. Political behavior. In *Handbook of Social Psychology,* ed. G. Lindzey, E. Aronson, 5:315–458. Reading, MA: Addison-Wesley. 2nd ed.

———. 1975. Political socialization. See Greenstein & Polsby 1975, 2:96–136

———. 1983. The persistence of early political predispositions: The roles of attitude object and life stage. In *Review of Personality and Social Psychology,* ed. L. Wheeler, P. Shaver, 4:79–116. Beverly Hills, CA: Sage

Sears, D. O., Allen, H. M. Jr. 1984. The trajectory of local desegregation controversies and whites' opposition to busing. In *Groups in Contact: The Psychology of Desegregation,* ed. N. Miller, M. B. Brewer, pp. 123–51. New York: Academic

Sears, D. O., Chaffee, S. H. 1979. Uses and effects of the 1976 debates: An overview of empirical studies. In *The Great Debates, 1976: Ford vs. Carter,* pp. 223–61. Bloomington: Indiana Univ. Press

Sears, D. O., Citrin, J. 1985. *Tax Revolt: Something for Nothing in California.* Cambridge, MA: Harvard Univ. Press (enlarged ed.)

Sears, D. O., Lau, R. R., Tyler, T. R., Allen, H. M. Jr. 1980. Self-interest vs. symbolic politics in policy attitudes and presidential voting. *Am. Polit. Sci. Rev.* 74:670–84

Sears, D. O., McConahay, J. B. 1973. *The Politics of Violence: The New Urban Blacks and the Watts Riot.* Boston: Houghton Mifflin

Sears, D. O., Tyler, T. R., Citrin, J., Kinder, D. R. 1978. Political system support and public response to the 1974 energy crisis. *Am. J. Polit. Sci.* 22:56–82

Seeman, M. 1984. A legacy of protest: The "Events of May" in retrospect. *Polit. Psychol.* 5:437–64

Segall, M. H. 1976. *Human Behavior and Public Policy: A Political Psychology.* New York: Pergamon

Shapiro, R. Y., Mahajan, H. 1986. Gender differences in policy preferences: A summary of trends from the 1960s to the 1980s. *Public Opin. Q.* 50:42–61

Sigel, R. S., Hoskin, M. B. 1977. Perspectives on adult political socialization—areas of research. See Renshon 1977, pp. 259–93

Simonton, D. K. 1985. The vice-presidential succession effect: Individual or situational basis? *Polit. Behav.* 7:79–99

Smith, M. B., Bruner, J. S., White, R. W. 1956. *Opinions and Personality.* New York: Wiley

Smith, T. W. 1984. The polls: Gender and attitudes toward violence. *Public Opin. Q.* 48:384–96

Sniderman, P. M. 1975. *Personality and Democratic Politics.* Berkeley: Univ. Calif. Press

Stagner, R. 1967. *Psychological Aspects of International Conflict.* Belmont, CA: Brooks/Cole

Stephan, W. G. 1985. Intergroup relations. In *Handbook of Social Psychology,* ed. G. Lindzey, E. Aronson, 2:599–658. New York: Random House. 3rd ed.

Stewart, L. H. 1977. Birth order and political leadership. See Hermann 1977, pp. 205–36

Stone, W. F. 1974. *The Psychology of Politics.* New York: Free Press

Stone, W. F., Smith, D. C. 1983. Human nature in politics: Graham Wallas and the Fabians. *Polit. Psychol.* 4:693–712

Stouffer, S. A. 1955. *Communism, Conformity, and Civil Liberties.* New York: Doubleday

Sullivan, J. L., Piereson, J. E., Marcus, G. E. 1978. Ideological constraint in the mass public: A methodological critique and some new findings. *Am. J. Polit. Sci.* 22:233–49

——. 1982. *Political Tolerance and American Democracy.* Chicago: Univ. Chicago Press

Tajfel, H. 1981. *Human Groups and Social Categories.* New York: Cambridge Univ. Press

Tapp, J. L., Kohlberg, L. 1971. Developing senses of law and legal justice. *J. Soc. Issues* 27:65–92

Tedin, K. L. 1974. The influence of parents on the political attitudes of adolescents. *Am. Polit. Sci. Rev.* 68:1579–92

Tetlock, P. E. 1983a. Policymakers' images of international conflict. *J. Soc. Issues* 39:67–86

——. 1983b. Psychological research on foreign policy: A methodological overview. In *Review of Personality and Social Psychology,* ed. L. Wheeler, P. Shaver, 4:45–78. Beverly Hills, CA: Sage

Torney-Purta, J. 1984. Political socialization and policy: The United States in a cross-national context. In *Child Development and Social Policy*. Vol. 1, ed. H. W. Stevenson, A. E. Siegel, Chicago: Univ. Chicago Press

Ulman, R. B., Abse, D. W. 1983. The group psychology of mass madness: Jonestown. *Polit. Psychol.* 4:637–61

Vanneman, R. D., Pettigrew, T. F. 1972. Race and relative deprivation in the urban United States. *Race* 13:461–86

Wallas, G. 1921. *Human Nature in Politics*. New York: Knopf. Originally published 1908

Wattenberg, M. P. 1982. From parties to candidates: Examining the role of the media. *Public Opin. Q.* 46:216–27

——. 1984. *The Decline of American Political Parties, 1952-1980*. Cambridge, MA: Harvard Univ. Press

White, R. K. 1965. Images in the context of international conflict: Soviet perceptions of the U.S. and the U.S.S.R. In *International Behavior: A Social-Psychological Analysis*, ed. H. C. Kelman, pp. 236–76. New York: Holt, Rinehart & Winston

——. 1970. *Nobody Wanted War: Misperception in Vietnam and Other Wars*. Garden City, NY: Doubleday

——. ed. 1985. *Psychology and the Prevention of Nuclear War: A Book of Readings*. New York: New York Univ. Press

Winter, D. G. 1973. *The Power Motive*. New York: Free Press

Wolfenstein, E. V. 1967. *The Revolutionary Personality*. Princeton: Princeton Univ. Press

Wolfenstein, M., Kliman, G., eds. 1965. *Children and the Death of a President*. Garden City, NY: Doubleday

Wolfinger, R. E., Rosenstone, S. J. 1980. *Who Votes?* New Haven: Yale Univ. Press

Worchel, S., Austin, W. G., eds. 1986. *Psychology of Intergroup Relations*. Chicago: Nelson-Hall. 2nd ed.

Zuckerman, A. S. 1984. The limits of political behavior: Individual calculations and survival during the Holocaust. *Polit. Psychol.* 5:37–52

Zweigenhaft, R. L. 1985. Providing information and shaping attitudes about nuclear dangers: Implications for public education. *Polit. Psychol.* 6:461–80

3

The Politics of Knowledge Production in Social Psychology

NEIL J. KRESSEL

Many social psychologists admit to general dissatisfaction with the style, focus, originality, and caliber of much research within the discipline. In one survey, Lewicki (1982)
found that only 16% of social psychologists believe the criteria typically employed for
selection of research topics are appropriate and only 15% regard as acceptable the
discipline's mechanisms for evaluating research. Similarly, fewer than one social psychologist in five thought that the contents of the 1977 volume of the generally top-
ranked *Journal of Personality and Social Psychology* constituted a gain for the field
(Diamond and Morton, 1978). It is not unreasonable to suspect that similar sentiments
would be expressed concerning more recent volumes of that journal and others in social
psychology.

For the past two decades, and consistent with these survey findings, social psychology
journals have been inundated with articles criticizing the field for a wide range of
theoretical and methodological shortcomings (Argyris, 1975; Boutilier, Roed, and
Svendsen, 1980; Buss, 1975; Elms, 1975; Gergen, 1973, 1976, 1978; House, 1977;
Koch, 1976, 1981; McGuire, 1967, 1973; Moscovici, 1972; Ring, 1967; Rosnow, 1981;
Sherif, 1970, 1977; Smith, 1973a, 1973b, 1976, 1980; Wachtel, 1980). Nonetheless,
few harbingers of significant metamorphosis emerged during the 1970s (Fried, Gumpper, and Allen, 1973; Gergen, 1978; Helmreich, 1975; Higbee and Wells, 1972; Sherif,
1977). Notwithstanding a slight trend toward more "applied" research (Leary, Jenkins,

39

and Shepperd, 1984; Mark and Bryant, 1984; Stricker, 1982), mainstream social psychology in the 1980s does not appear to have been substantially influenced by the deluge of intradisciplinary criticism either (Carlson, 1984; Jones, 1986; Sears, 1986).

One source of failed reform is intellectually based theoretical, methodological, and epistemological disagreement with analyses made in the critical literature. However, it is the thesis of this article that a comprehensive understanding of the crisis in contemporary social psychology requires us to look beyond intellectual matters. McGuire's (1973) suggestion that more time was the necessary ingredient has proven false, unless, of course, still more time is needed. Much of social psychologists' reported discontent with the field stems from problems that are not generally disputed on intellectual grounds. Moreover, a complex array of nonintellectual forces conspire to maintain the status quo. Thus, even when proposed reforms are disputed intellectually, the outcome of these disputes is often preordained by nonintellectual forces that bear upon the conduct of research.

It is surprising that most critical analyses of social psychology have been based upon the assumption—curious for social psychologists—that scientists engage primarily in rational choice designed to ensure maximum intellectual payoff for the discipline when they select topics, methods, styles, and theoretical orientations for research. Even if one accepts a rational choice paradigm, it must be acknowledged that published criticisms have ignored the full range of rewards and punishments that influence the research act.

Although no comprehensive analysis of the nonintellectual underpinnings of the crisis in social psychology has appeared, a few commentators have questioned the assumption that critiques directed solely toward upper-level cognitive processes will lead to significant change. Buss (1975) has called for a "sociology of psychological knowledge." He has reviewed some sociology-of-knowledge research and explored how this outlook might be fruitfully applied to several subfields of psychology, including social psychology. House (1977) concurs when he writes that ". . . the particular substantive and methodological nature of each face [of social psychology] largely reflects the intellectual *and* [italics added] institutional contexts in which each developed rather than purely intellectual and scientific imperatives" (p. 162). Gergen (1978) hints at the utility of an organizational or social psychological approach to the crisis in social psychology when he laments that "in spite of emerging doubts, the experimental tradition has continued unabated. . . . And doubting graduate students may have paused fitfully before pushing on with an experimental thesis that would ensure passage to a secure professional niche" (p. 508). Wachtel (1980) also alludes to the importance of considering organizational and sociological constraints on the production of psychological research. Similarly, Stinchcombe (1975) and Petras and Curtis (1972) have suggested the need for a reflexive sociology, that is, a sociology of sociology.

Although these analyses have pointed to the desirability of developing a comprehensive approach to knowledge production in social psychology, no one has systematically defined the components of such an approach. This is particularly unfortunate because, as psychologists know, the prospects for change are enhanced by a thoroughly reasoned understanding of the forces involved in maintaining the status quo.

SOURCES OF DISCONTENT

A prima facie analysis of the crisis literature might lead one to conclude that intellectual disagreement constitutes a sufficient explanation of current dissatisfaction with the discipline. After all, for more than 15 years, social psychology has been ridden with intellectual controversies: science versus history (Gergen, 1973, 1976; Schlenker, 1974, 1976; Smith, 1976), applied versus basic research (Kenrick, 1986), the value of significance testing (Meehl, 1978), the importance of a unified psychological science (Koch, 1976; Smith, 1980). Nonetheless, it should be pointed out that it is often easiest to perpetuate controversy around broad epistemological and symbolic issues. Even the most ardent opponents of experimentation concede its appropriateness under certain conditions (Gergen, 1978; Mitroff and Bonoma, 1978), and the strongest supporters of experimental methodology admit to frequent limitations in generalizability of experimental results (Kenrick, 1986). Moreover, there is sometimes considerably greater agreement about what constitutes a particular instance of high-quality research. According to Diamond and Morton (1978), journal editors generally do not cite critical tests between competing theories as examples of excellence—for a discussion of this matter from a philosophy-of-science perspective, see Lakatos (1970) and Meehl (1978). Journal editors are most likely to cite experiments that are, in Smith's (1980) terms, "sensitization to social phenomena." Many defenders of experimentation in the general case would nonetheless agree with Gergen's (1978) position that the method is overused in contemporary social psychology research.

Commentators on social psychology have highlighted at least four categories of criticism about which there can be little epistemological, methodological, or theoretical debate (Gergen, 1978; Sears, 1986; Sherif, 1970; Smith, 1980). They suggest that present-day social psychology is (a) fad-ridden and noncumulative, (b) trivial, (c) artificial, and (d) parochial. Disagreement concerning these areas cannot center upon their desirability but only upon the extent to which they are perceived as characteristic of the contemporary discipline.

Fad-ridden and noncumulative character of research. Perhaps most frequently, social psychologists have complained that research does not cumulate in the sense of successive advances being built upon prior ones (Allport, 1960; Smith, 1980). Meehl (1978) observed that old theories "suffer the fate that General MacArthur ascribed to old generals [sic]—they never die, they just slowly fade away." He continues:

> There is a period of enthusiasm about a new theory, a period of attempted application to several fact domains, a period of disillusionment as the negative data come in, a growing

bafflement about inexplicable empirical results, multiple resorts to ad hoc excuses, and then people just sort of lose interest in the thing and pursue other endeavors. (p. 807)

Ring (1967) called social psychology a field of many "frontiersmen but few settlers." Sherif (1970) labeled it a "jungle of activity shooting in all directions." Dunnette (1966) pointed to the recycling of old research under new, more glamorous names as an especially disturbing manifestation of the lack of cumulation.

Triviality of research. Several critics have suggested that social psychologists study trivial issues at the expense of more important social problems. They point out that the value and relevance of social psychology research is often determined against prior research alone without any external reality testing (Pencil, 1976). A direct manifestation of the perceived triviality of much research has been the flood of calls for a better developed applied social psychology in which basic research informs applied work (Argyris, 1975; Deutsch, 1975; Rossi, Wright, and Wright, 1978; Triandis, 1978). Although, according to several commentators (Leary, Jenkins, and Shepperd, 1984; Mark and Bryant, 1984), high-caliber applied social psychology has been occurring more frequently than in the past, and several applied texts have appeared, applied research seems to be retaining its lower status within the discipline (Carlson, 1984; Gergen, 1973; Kenrick, 1986). Nogami's (1982) call for an "applicable" as opposed to "applied" social psychology may be interpreted as one more manifestation of continuing dissatisfaction with the perceived low utility of research findings.

Moreover, as Koocher's (1977) analysis of Middlemist, Knowles, and Matter's (1976) lavatory investigation suggests, field research is not necessarily a cure for the triviality ailment. Several critics have suggested that the triviality of many findings may derive in part from the methodological orientations of the discipline. Variables of interest are frequently operationalized inadequately. Meehl (1978) explains:

It is as if we were interested in the effect of sunlight on the mating behavior of birds, but not being able to get directly at either of these two things, we settle for correlating a proxy variable like field-mice density (because birds like to destroy the field mice) with, say, incidence of human skin cancer (since you can get that by spending too much time in the sun!). (p. 823)

Dunnette (1966) is more explicit about the process.

The investigator shrewdly fails to state the question he is trying to answer, gathers data to provide answers to simpler questions, and then behaves as if his research has been relevant to other unstated but more important and interesting problems. (p. 348)

In addition, triviality may develop out of social psychologists' tendency to overemphasize independent (theoretical) variables at the expense of dependent (social issues) variables (Pencil, 1976). Often, research proceeds from the selection of an interesting independent variable to the search for areas where such a variable might be relevant. Finally, the emphasis on significance testing (Meehl, 1978) and the relative lack of concern for effect sizes may contribute to the triviality of many findings. Dunnette (1966) refers to this issue as the "A difference doesn't need to make a difference if it's a real difference" game.

Artificiality of research. Many different lines of criticism have suggested that social psychology research is plagued by artificiality and a lack of generalizability. Rosenthal's (1966) discussion of experimenter bias casts doubts on the validity of much empirical research. Laboratory experimentation, according to many critics (Gergen, 1978), is applied to problems for which it is unsuitable. Social psychologists—even when they are not conducting experimental research—pay insufficient attention to social context (Armistead, 1974; Boutilier, Roed, and Svendsen, 1980; Carlson, 1984; Lynn and Oldenquist, 1984). College students are relied upon for far too large a percentage of social psychology's subject pool, and volunteer participants constitute an unusual breed of nonrandom sample (Rosenthal and Rosnow, 1969). Sears (1986) has suggested that many aspects of the emerging social psychology concept of human nature may be artifacts of the field's overuse of college student samples.

Parochialism and methodological rigidity of research. Critics have scored the field for its reliance upon positivistic epistemology (Israel and Tajfel, 1972), its "masochistic love affair with the physical sciences" (Smith, 1980), and the verbal pseudo-rigor of its journals.

Smith (1973a, 1973b, 1976) has criticized social psychologists for failing to engage in collaborative research with scholars and scientists from other disciplines. Social psychology is not a field that can afford the luxury of disciplinary isolation; its subject matter, correctly conceived, will often carry it into the domain of other social scientists. Deutsch, Platt, and Senghaas (1971) found that nearly half of all major advances in social science from 1900 to 1929 and nearly two thirds of those from 1930 to 1970 derived from interdisciplinary work. When social psychologists attempt to address interdisciplinary questions without adequate background or assistance in the neighboring fields, the result is often unsatisfactory. According to many critics, social psychologists display a lamentable lack of familiarity with relevant research from outside the field (Smith, 1973a, 1973b). This intellectual isolation has characterized social psychology's relationship with many areas of learning: sociology (Boutilier, Roed, and Svendsen, 1980; Wilson and Schafer, 1978), philosophy (Feigl, 1959), intellectual history (Allport, 1969), social history (Gergen 1973; Smith, 1980), political history (Kressel, 1981, 1984), and others. House (1977) has argued that most social psychology research proceeds even on the basis of an insufficient awareness of studies in other domains of social psychology.

Critics have also discussed American social psychologists' lack of awareness of

research done abroad and despaired about the inaccessibility of foreign-language publications to English speakers (Smith, 1978; Lewicki, 1982). An extension of this problem
concerns the limitation of social psychology research to issues that emerge in the
English-speaking world, because it is there where most psychologists are able to apply
their research skills. As it happens, however, many of the most interesting and important
social phenomena of the present day, for example, genocide, modernization, authoritarianism, occur primarily outside the English-speaking world.

The call for methodological diversity sometimes entails acceptance of nonstatistical
approaches to aspects of social behavior that cannot easily be subjected to rigorous
quantitative analysis (Gergen, 1978; Wachtel, 1980). On the other hand, critics have
charged that overly simplistic statistical methods are frequently relied upon. Broader use
of multivariate statistical methods might facilitate construction of theoretical models
that better represent the multidimensional causal patterns that typify social behavior
(Cohen and Cohen, 1975; McGuire, 1973).

It is argued in the following section that many of the problems highlighted above can
be best understood in the context of an analysis of nonintellectual factors bearing upon
research. For a comprehensive overview of social psychology's self-criticism, see reviews by Boutilier, Roed, and Svendsen (1980) and Elms (1975).

A SYSTEMATIC APPROACH TO THE RESEARCH ACT

It is useful to distinguish three categories of nonintellectual influence on knowledge
production in social psychology: (a) broad extradisciplinary forces such as Zeitgeist,
social movements, and prevalent political ideologies of professors; (b) student selection
and socialization processes; and (c) survival demands of the academic system. For a
given act of research, any, all, or none of these forces may affect the research product.
We may also postulate, without too much blushing, a strong motive to discover the truth,
a motive that often counteracts many of the nonintellectual influences on the research
act. In any case, it should be understood that the present approach is not offered as a
substitute for the intellectual level of analysis. As many sociologists of knowledge and
philosophers of science have argued (Berger and Luckmann, 1967; Popper, 1962), the
social and psychological sources of an idea cannot determine its validity. Popper
counseled avoidance of explanations based upon the sociology of knowledge in order to
control the temptation to explain away opponents without dealing with the scientific and
intellectual validity of their claims. The present interpretation adopts the position that an
examination of nonintellectual influences on research should be considered as an adjunct
level of analysis, subordinate to definitive intellectual arguments, but, nonetheless,
meaningful. Considered as part of a composite model, the systemic influences upon
knowledge production constitute a useful but sometimes ignored explanation for the
persistence of the crisis in social psychology.

Before we proceed, we ought to consider another caveat concerning the present approach. Social psychologists are not the only academics who respond to systemic forces of a nonintellectual nature. Indeed, the growing body of research in the sociology of science is concerned primarily with the natural sciences (Barber and Hirsch, 1962; Merton, 1973). In addition, despite the systemic pressures identified in this analysis, social psychologists have been responsible for many widely acknowledged advances in social science since the turn of the century (Deutsch et al., 1971). It is most accurate to construe this analysis as a specific instance of a form of analysis that could, no doubt, be applied to a wide range of academic institutions.

Broad Extradisciplinary Forces

The broad orientation and predilections of American social psychology derive to some extent from the sociohistorical context in which studies are conceived and conducted. Zeitgeist, Volksgeist, class identity, and prevalent Weltanschauungen all may have an impact upon a discipline's shape (Merton, 1973). Such influences, however, are extremely difficult to identify and document without the benefit of historical hindsight. A systematic investigation of the relationship between sociohistorical forces and knowledge production in academic social psychology would be a worthy but monumental endeavor. The present essay attempts merely to suggest in skeletal form some key instances of this sort of nonintellectual influence.

One of the most far-reaching examples of a Zeitgeist effect concerns the tremendous respect accorded to the physical sciences in Western (especially American) society during the past few centuries. The attempt to model social science upon the physical sciences has had unquestionably positive consequences for social psychology. Concepts of quantification and operationalization have resulted in major advances for the discipline. As Moscovici (1972) and others have argued, however, another impact of the overwhelming success of physics has been to encourage a "fetishism of the trappings of science." In other words, "physics-envy" has led to an unthinking scientism.

Although there is no compelling reason to accept uncritically the belief that advances in social psychology will follow patterns similar to advances in physical science (Gergen, 1973), alternative nonpositivistic epistemologies have never achieved much acceptance among American social psychologists. However, as Edelman (1978) has argued, contemporary psychological notions of valid scientific methodology rest largely on a Newtonian worldview, and developments in modern quantum mechanics and relativity theory may, in fact, support research frequently characterized as less rigorous by "scientific" psychologists.

In any event, the scientistic orientation of mainstream social psychology may be related to the failure of the discipline to confer high status upon research that does not fit neatly into quantitative (especially experimental) designs. It also may explain the prevalence of dry, passive prose in the discipline. Social psychology envies the certainty and control possible in the hard sciences, yet clearly, the field cannot attain hard science status. Identity problems ensue, which are resolved in part by concentration upon phenomena and environments in which control is greatest. Problems in social psychology outside the laboratory highlight the discipline's ambiguous character and, consequently, are deemphasized. As Smith (1976) has argued, whether you consider social psychology a science or not is essentially irrelevant, but when the desire for a scientific appearance weakens judgment, the discipline is in trouble. Clinical psychologists might advise that the identity problems be faced squarely.

Sometimes, unthinking acceptance of scientific methodology obscures the centrality of conceptual, normative, and political judgments in evaluating social psychological phenomena; Kressel (1987a) provides a case study of the misleading role played by quantitative, scientific studies in investigations of media coverage and public attitudes toward the Arab-Israeli conflict.

Other aspects of Zeitgeist and Volksgeist may have had an influence upon the development of contemporary social psychology. Examples include the following:

1. Kagan (1980) showed the impact of a strong Western belief in (and longing for) scientific conceptions of human psychosocial development in the academic psychological literature.
2. Many social psychological studies of antisemitism were conducted during the three decades following Hitler's ascent to power; the growing influence of Freudian psychology in America during this same period may explain, in part, the strong psychoanalytic coloration of a large portion of research on fascism and antisemitism (Kressel, 1981).
3. Western, modernized attitude structures and belief in the efficacy of technological solutions to social problems (Clark, 1982) undoubtedly contribute to the popularity of research on the diffusion of innovations (Rogers, 1983) and, in particular, to the conceptualization of the technological laggard as an undesirable type.
4. The incompatibility of Marxist and dialectical approaches with American political values may contribute to the relative unpopularity of these orientations in American social psychology (Jay, 1973).

Of course, the fact that a body of research is consistent with the Zeitgeist or Volksgeist does not invalidate it.

The predominant political ideology of social psychologists also may have substantial impact upon knowledge production. Bem (1970) cited evidence documenting the overwhelmingly liberal political predispositions of most social psychologists. These political sympathies undoubtedly color topic selection and knowledge transmission in the discipline; they may also influence interpretation of research results. Formal statements by the American Psychological Association and, especially, the Society for the Psychological Study of Social Issues, contribute to the institutionalization of a left-of-center and left-center political agenda. This tendency may discourage and downplay research from other perspectives, including those from the extreme left and the right and some from the political center. A comparison of the values of American social psychologists and the American public might be revealing in this regard.

Contemporary social movements in the outside world also tend to influence knowledge production by academic social psychologists. Blumer (1971) has shown that social movements often have predictable lives of their own, influencing research trends by calling for a plethora of research on a given topic—often with preordained conclusions. Research on child rearing (Adelson, 1981), date rape, child abuse, pornography (Wilson, 1971), televised violence (Wilson, 1971), sexual terrorism, education about nuclear war (Adelson and Finn, 1985), efficacy of social programs (Boone and Kressel, 1988), public attitudes toward international conflict (Kressel, 1987a), and many other topics may fall into this category.

Student Selection and Socialization

Selection. Social psychology's image among undergraduate students and their professors influences the type of people who enter the field. Justifiably or not, the image of social psychology among many undergraduates and professors from other disciplines is often one of atheoretical "number crunching" on trivial topics. Wachtel (1980) has argued that psychology's emphasis on empirical work discourages students with theoretical skills or inclinations from becoming academic psychologists. This emphasis could be one source of Deutsch and Krauss's (1965) lamentation about the state of social psychological theory. Students whose skills and interests concern computers and statistics are much more likely to feel comfortable in the contemporary environment of academic social psychology. In addition, social psychology's failure to establish and promote itself as a remunerative, applied profession may influence the type of students attracted to the field; ambitious, high-caliber students who wish to have an impact upon the social, political, or business worlds may be selecting other career paths perceived—rightly or wrongly— as more relevant (Kressel, 1987b). Also, the common admissions requirement of an undergraduate psychology major may discourage students with relatively mature inter-disciplinary orientations from entering the field.

Finally, student self-selection also tends to perpetuate social psychology's left-of-center political bias. As a result, politically conservative students and to a lesser extent politically moderate and radical students with interests in social psychology may perceive that they will not be well received by their colleagues; they may opt for other fields and careers, leaving social psychology to suffer the weaknesses associated with academic in-breeding.

Socialization. Gergen (1978), Jones (1986), McGuire (1973), and others have identified a change in students' orientations to research that occurs during the years of graduate education. McGuire wrote:

The young student typically enters graduate study wanting . . . to engage in a direct confrontation with reality. All too often, it is our graduate programs which distract him with shadows. Either by falling into subjectivism and twice-removed scholarly studies of what other subjectivists have said; or, if he falls under the influence of scientific psychologists, he becomes preoccupied with twice-removed sanitized data in the form of computer printouts. (p. 453)

During the Ph.D. program and the early postdoctoral years, the discipline confers career honors and rewards primarily upon those who conform to certain professional norms. Those craving recognition and success, and few talented graduate students do not, find themselves under powerful pressure to play the game ("Do you want your union card or not?"), a pressure that probably has increased through two decades of academic job scarcity.

Sociologist Stinchcombe's (1975) "structural analysis of sociology"—a tongue-in-cheek application of Levi-Strauss's work—provides insight into socialization processes in contemporary social psychology as well. Stinchcombe writes:

Clearly the discipline of sociology (especially within a country) is a system of exchange, in which students correspond to women as being people of low status and power who must be "placed" in other departments, job offers correspond to material goods which are exchanged partly to show mutual respect, partly to improve each others' material positions, and scientific papers are symbols exchanged . . . Raw creativity in a wide variety of fields does not produce a social object which can "fill a slot" in the normatively defined needs of other departments . . . (pp. 57–58)

Stinchcombe identifies a central myth of sociology that seems equally descriptive of social psychology:

That for all the internal distinctions, we are engaged in a common intellectual enterprise whose collective purpose is different from that of anthropology, political science, economics or history. There is an attempt to create the sense of a distinctive competence . . . (p. 59)

Stinchcombe uses Levi-Strauss's distinction between the "raw" and the "cooked" to explain the difference between students who have bright, creative, but undeveloped ideas and students whose ideas are suitably prepared for digestion by the discipline. Pretenure publications are seen to exist primarily to prove one's worth according to the norms of the group. Insofar as a large number of papers in social psychology are written prior to the granting of tenure, this does not bode well for the field's overall creative productivity. Stinchcombe's analysis, if applicable, would help explain the lack of interdisciplinary work in social psychology, the lack of awareness of foreign research, the existence of fads, and the ritualistic style of much research.

It is necessary, however, to consider several other aspects of the process by which students are moved from a raw to a cooked state. Graduate students assimilate disciplinary norms and rules, some of which can have negative implications for the production of quality research. For example, an astute graduate student might perceive the following:

1. Young social psychologists should stick to one subfield, or they will be labeled dilettantes.
2. Disciplinary criticism is an "old man's game" to be engaged in only by those who have paid their dues.
3. A good theory is one that stimulates a lot of research; Dunnette (1966) suggests that this position is a bit like claiming that an accidental fire is a good thing because it keeps so many firemen busy.
4. A good experimenter is one who can demonstrate an effect, no matter how small, even if that effect exists nowhere in the world besides in the experimental situation.
5. Pure research has higher status than applied research; the *Journal of Personality and Social Psychology* is the best journal.
6. The way to get a good job is to do dissertation research on a hot topic, e.g., cognitive social psychology.
7. The formal recommendation to avoid college students as subjects for research is not to be taken seriously.
8. High-level statistical manipulations can be an acceptable and even preferable substitute for careful data collection and creative research designs (cf. Lipsey, 1978).
9. Little of enduring value about human social behavior was written prior to Triplett's first experiment in the late 19th century, and novelists, poets, psychoanalysts, and philosophers say few things about human social interaction worthy of the attention of trained social psychologists.

In addition to these norms, rules, and precepts, the socialization process operates through the specification of certain skills as important and others as unnecessary. For example, foreign language requirements have been dropped in many graduate departments and, although the option still exists, the academic reward system discourages the requisite investment of time. As a result, cross-cultural research is made much less likely. Similarly, there are few encouragements for obtaining background in domains for the application of social psychology such as business, government, health, law, or clinical psychology. A few courses in these areas will generally be tolerated, but, again, the reward structure argues against the investment of time outside of mainstream social psychology.

Survival Demands of the Academic System

Merton (1973) has argued convincingly that in order to understand the productivity of scientists, we must focus upon the reward structure of science. The search for truth is one motivation for scientific activity, but scientists generally wish to maintain or improve their job status, job security, and income. Certain survival rules must be followed to retain professional identity and fulfill these objectives.[1]

Graduate students generally resolve the tension between reality and their own ideal-ized expectations of the discipline by pursuing studies in those areas defined as critically important by the powers-that-be within the field. As a result, manageable officially sanctioned topics are studied and other areas, often more central to the students' original interests, are neglected. After all, most successful role models are engaged in research topically and methodologically sanctioned by the discipline. Moreover, graduate stu-dents have little time for nonessential intellectual development, given the time demands of rigid mainstream training activities. Once they have developed competence in these areas, for example, experimental design, multivariate quantitative methods, content areas of experimental social psychology, they are probably at least 28 years old. They have been students, often impoverished, for nearly a decade; they may have families to support. In short, the time is ripe for some modicum of worldly success, and the system's clear message is that professional success requires mainstream publications, not further learning or maverick explorations. Originally, students may have accepted the argument that graduate school was not the place for intellectual revolution. Now, having finished their doctoral training, they no longer possess the energy or inclination to acquire the skills or background once deemed necessary. Perhaps, they reason, after tenure, the time will be right; perhaps, after promotion.

Initial hiring, tenure, promotion, recognition, salary, merit awards, and even self-esteem can depend upon the number of articles one has published in prestigious, refereed journals. In theory, articles should be of high quality, but rumor has it that articles are not always read, let alone thoughtfully evaluated, by those people who possess power over one's future. Even when quality is assessed, it is often measured on the basis of the journal's reputation; recent measures of departmental quality have been based solely upon counts of publications in American Psychological Association journals (Cox and Catt, 1977; Crandall, 1978; Howard, Cole, and Maxwell, 1987; Rubin, 1978; Simon, 1968). The "quality" journals in social psychology are precisely those that endorse the mainstream orientation of the field; they are not known for their openness to inter-disciplinary, applied, or innovative research. Social psychologists who publish in less prestigious publications or even in equally prestigious outlets from related disciplines do so at their own risk.

If a social psychologist wishes to thrive in an academic context, he or she will tend to do the following:

1. Avoid originality and imagination because such qualities decrease the likelihood of publication in prestigious mainstream outlets (Farrell, Markley, and Matulef, 1967).
2. Strive for a dry, passive, and turgid writing style in order to fulfill the demands of the field's appetite for the trappings of science.
3. Publish tentative results as soon as they can be written up, following an ethic of "Publish first, ask questions later."
4. Avoid investing time and research resources into experimental setups unless it is

reasonably sure from the outset that the results will be significant (Farrell, Markley, and Matulef, 1967).

5. Ignore treatments of similar matters in other disciplines because the new "language" takes too long to learn and too long to explain to other social psychologists.
6. Select topics for research that fit neatly into experimental designs or, failing this, other sophisticated quantitative designs.
7. Select quickie topics suitable for treatment in journal article format, as opposed to books, because publications must be produced rapidly.
8. Select college students for subjects because they are easier to recruit, cheaper, more cooperative, and more respectful of college professors. The same resources often are required to test 60 college sophomores as to test 30 randomly sampled adults; the former sample, of course, is more likely to yield statistically significant, publishable results. Moreover, findings based upon this population may be more likely to support currently fashionable orientations in social psychology (Sears, 1986).

It is worth stating that despite this somewhat dreary litany of disciplinary bad habits, some graduate students do manage to produce excellent works. The forces discussed here simply tend to make such accomplishments significantly more difficult.

Mythic modes of response to survival demands. Edelman (1979), Gergen (1978), Simon (1968), and others have identified feelings of disappointment, disillusionment, and despair that frequently befall students during the course of their graduate education in social psychology. For many, a realization of the conflict between survival within the system and intellectual fulfillment may contribute to these negative feelings. Successful students typically fulfill the systemic demands placed upon them even though they do not agree with these demands. After a while, they may engage in sanctioned activities simply to prove that the field was right all along and that they have not sold out. Festinger's (1957) cognitive dissonance theory may also be relevant, to the extent that social psychologists may modify their belief systems to match their behavioral patterns. According to Berger and Luckmann (1967),

All human activity is subject to habitualization. Any action that is repeated frequently becomes cast into a pattern, which can then be reproduced with an economy of effort. (p. 53)

To ward off further negative feelings and to assume an integrated identity, graduate students tend to abandon their own reality testing of the importance and credibility of research, substituting the field's definition of scientific worthiness. Janis's (1972) examination of the groupthink phenomenon demonstrates how stress can lead to the reduction or abandonment of reality testing. Put more bluntly, the social psychologist's worldview incorporates various elements of a make-believe universe à la Peters (1980). It is a fairly safe strategy, because only infrequently will journal reviewers ask how well a piece of research describes the real world or contributes to the solution of an important dilemma; more often, reviews focus on statistical questions such as whether the factor analytic method is Wherry-Wherry, Rao's Canonical, or Alpha Factoring.

Berger and Luckmann's (1967) complex discussion of the origins of symbolic universes is relevant here. Symbolic universes are socially constructed systems for organizing knowledge that do not, at a gut level, correspond to everyday reality. The function of a symbolic universe is to put everything in its right place. In addition, symbolic universes help to integrate discrepant meanings actualized within everyday life in society. In other words, part of the motivation to construct a symbolic universe stems from the complexity of the social world; a "reduction of ambiguity" motive is operating. The world is reduced to a comprehensible format. Furthermore, the professional identity of the social psychologist is reinforced by collective faith in the symbolic universe. A comprehensive discussion of academic social psychology as a symbolic universe might explore the conceptual machinery for universe maintenance, the social organization for universe maintenance, and the interaction between the individual's intellectual processes and the official recognition of reality. An example of the latter issue is the process by which trivial research topics are legitimized through the addition of a "more research is required" clause and connection to a "larger research project" that fails to materialize. Also, a tendency to avoid real-world applications of research might be explained in part as an unwillingness to enter environments likely to highlight the perceived inadequacies of the mythic universe.

Leisure class and recreational implications of research. Social psychologists may derive differing amounts of enjoyment from activities associated with various topical areas and research methodologies. The recreational implications of social psychological research probably increase in importance as the perceived likelihood of significant, real-world contributions declines. Dunnette (1966) explains some trends in psychology as the outcome of "games psychologists play." He discusses a game called "The Fun We Have":

> . . . the underlying theme of the game . . . is the compulsion to forget what we are really doing—because of the fun we may be enjoying with our apparatus, our computers, our models, or the simple act of testing statistical null hypotheses. (p. 345)

For social psychologists, the personal pleasure of being a laboratory scientist may influence the selection and evaluation of research activities.

Veblen's *The Theory of the Leisure Class* (1899/1979) may help explain the preference of many social psychologists for research that is low in practical significance. According to Veblen, the ability to remain free of activities that are even indirectly industrial or productive is a key marker of social status, often more respected than even the ability to engage in conspicuous consumption. Thus, although academics have lower incomes than many other people in society, they generally are considered to possess high status.

Within academia, philosophy and other branches of the humanities were traditionally granted very high status precisely because they were far removed from worldly productivity. Although psychology was not yet a well-established discipline in 1899 when Veblen's book was first published, it is fair to say that the field as a whole lies towards the productive end of the academic spectrum. Nonetheless, the relative low status afforded to applied work within the discipline may stem in part from the leisure class motive. Even within the domain of applied social psychology research, the topics with the highest status appear to be those least likely to have implications for economic productivity or personal income (Kressel, 1987b).

Another related matter concerns perceived status hierarchies within academia; however chauvinistically and misguidedly, some social psychologists may perceive psychology as a profession more highly esteemed than sociology in the eyes of other scholars and the general public. Consequently, a reluctance to focus upon social context and other topics perceived as "sociological" may derive from their desire to teach within psychology departments and retain identities as psychologists.

CONCLUSION

Although the present analysis can account for the frequent failure of intellectual appeals to result in substantial disciplinary change, it does not rule out the possibility that such appeals might influence individual social psychologists. Differences in responsiveness might depend upon career aspirations, personal definitions of success, and ego ideals. Wealth, marital status, age, intellectual background, and personal dispositions may also be relevant predictors. The ability and desire to tolerate pariah status may be particularly important.

According to Levinson (1976), an organizational consultant's best leverage comes from the pain felt by those people with the power to bring about change. An attempt to resolve the disciplinary crisis might therefore focus upon the pain felt by social psychologists themselves. If the above analysis is correct, however, many social psychologists may feel very little pain because they have adopted symbolic universes and other mythic modes of response; nonetheless, there probably remains some residual frustration and disillusionment growing out of the field's collective inability to make much difference in the world.

Some general benefit may derive from the mere identification of the nonintellectual underpinnings of social psychology's crisis. As sociologists of knowledge have maintained, an understanding of the social forces involved in buttressing various outlooks may tend to weaken those forces. This approach, socioanalysis, is in many ways analogous to the talking cure of psychoanalysis. Presumably, guilt and hope are two emotions that will tend to increase the likelihood of successful socioanalysis. On the other hand, the structural forces supporting the status quo are strong and the power of socioanalysis is weak. If intellectual appeals are to achieve substantial success, they must be reinforced by structural changes.

A comprehensive program for disciplinary change lies beyond the scope of this essay. It seems, however, that such an intervention might incorporate the following suggestions:

1. Change the reward system in social psychology.
   - Change journal acceptance policies and select editors who will assign greater importance to external validity, social relevance, potential for practical application, and connection to prior literature. For every article, one reader should come from another academic discipline and one from an applied setting.
2. Modify criteria for appointment, promotion, and tenure to provide more encouragement and reward for work that deviates from mainstream social psychological scholarship (Deutsch, 1975).
   - Until mainstream journals change, give more consideration to work published outside of traditional high-status channels.
   - At research universities, limit the number of works submitted for hiring, tenure, and promotion evaluation to an applicant's three best works (cf. Wachtel, 1980).
3. In making decisions concerning research grants, pay more attention to potential applicability and social relevance of research findings.
4. Initiate new categories for American Psychological Association awards to young scholars: best nonempirical work, most innovative methodology, best research conducted in a non-English-speaking culture, best application of social psychology to economics, medicine, history, political science, education, and so forth.
5. Change the way graduate students are selected.
   - Actively seek some students who majored in fields other than psychology.
   - Select some students whose main strengths are verbal as opposed to quantitative.
   - Attempt to avoid political bias in introductory courses and texts in social psychology, stressing that one need not have left-of-center political views in order to be a social psychologist.
6. Change graduate education.
   - Require proficiency in a foreign language.
   - Permit some students to substitute skills in an additional foreign language for advanced statistics.
   - Require students to develop expertise in at least one area of application, for example, health, politics, psychotherapy, education.
   - Increase status and support for nonempirical doctoral dissertations.
   - Arrange internships in various applied settings (Deutsch, 1975) such as hospitals, government agencies, and market research firms.
   - Place greater emphasis upon hypothesis generation, perhaps following McGuire's (1973) suggestions.
   - Teach a wider range of techniques in research methodology classes, deemphasize experimentation, and allow students to select areas in which they will develop expertise.

- Support development of applied specialties in social psychology such as social–clinical, public affairs (Elms, 1972), and marketing–persuasion specialties.
- Encourage and reward participation in interdisciplinary institutes focused on the solution of social problems.
- Encourage students to obtain joint degrees in other fields, for example, business administration, law, public affairs, public health.
- Support development and licensure of a profession of social psychology that permits practitioners to earn a living and retain their identity as social psychologists (Kressel, 1987b).

Despite the length of this list, many potentially constructive interventions have been omitted. It should be noted, too, that several key extradisciplinary forces are not readily subject to manipulation. Also, for a percentage of the powers-that-be, the present reward structure is satisfactory, the survival demands acceptable, and the symbolic universe firmly entrenched. Thus, the prognosis for broad disciplinary change is not good and, for the foreseeable future, the best research in social psychology may emanate from the periphery of the discipline. Some of the suggestions have already been adopted by various institutions, but what is required is an overall disciplinary effort.

Until this occurs, individual social psychologists who wish to escape the confining symbolic universe of contemporary mainstream social psychology will, no doubt, follow one of these paths:

1. Leave academia to assume positions in business, government, health care, or psychotherapy—often abandoning the identity of social psychologist in the process or struggling hopelessly to retain that identity in relatively inhospitable environments.
2. Set up independent practices as professional social psychologists, carving out new territory but frequently encountering licensure laws and other boundaries established by competing professions.
3. Adopt dual personalities that permit them to conduct mainstream research for professional advancement within academia and nonmainstream research for intellectual fulfillment and personal reward.
4. Select careers in less competitive colleges on the academic periphery that permit and reward research activities further from the mainstream of social psychology.

NOTE

1. It should be noted that survival demands operate within many different career areas; for example, Peters (1980) offers superb insight into the operation of survival demands in the Washington political culture.

REFERENCES

Adelson, J. (1981, May). Letty in Pogrebinland. *Commentary*, 82–86.

Adelson, J., and Finn, C. E. (1985, April). Terrorizing children. *Commentary*, 29–36.

Allport, G. W. (1960). The open system in personality theory. *Journal of Abnormal and Social Psychology, 61*, 301–310.

––––––. (1969). The historical background of modern social psychology. In G. Lindzey (Ed.), *Handbook of social psychology* (Vol. 1, pp. 1–80). Cambridge, MA: Addison-Wesley.

Argyris, C. (1975). Dangers in applying results from experimental social psychology. *American Psychologist, 30*, 469–485.

Armistead, N. (Ed.) (1974). *Reconstructing social psychology*. Baltimore: Penguin.

Barber, B., and Hirsch, W. (Eds.). (1962). *The sociology of science*. New York: Free Press.

Bem, D. J. (1970). *Beliefs, attitudes and human affairs*. Belmont, CA: Brooks/Cole.

Berger, P. L. and Luckmann, T. (1967). *The social construction of reality: A treatise in the sociology of knowledge*. New York: Anchor.

Blumer, H. (1971). Social problems as collective behavior. *Social Problems, 18*, 298–306.

Boone, S. L., and Kressel, N. J. (1988). *Speaking of families*. Wayne, NJ: William Paterson College, Family Studies Institute.

Boutilier, R. G., Roed, J. C., and Svendsen, A. C. (1980). Crises in the two social psychologies: A critical comparison. *Social Psychology Quarterly, 43*, 5–17.

Buss, A. R. (1975). The emerging field of the sociology of psychological knowledge. *American Psychologist, 30*, 988–1002.

Carlson, R. (1984). What's social about social psychology? Where's the person in personality research? *Journal of Personality and Social Psychology, 47*, 1304–1309.

Clark, R. (1982). *Power and policy in the third world*. New York: Wiley.

Cohen, J., and Cohen, P. (1975). *Applied multiple regression/correlation analysis for the behavioral sciences*. Hillsdale, NJ: Wiley.

Cox, W. M., and Catt, V. (1977). Productivity ratings of graduate programs in psychology based on publication in journals of the American Psychological Association. *American Psychologist, 32*, 793–813.

Crandall, R. (1978). The relationship between quantity and quality of publications. *Personality and Social Psychology Bulletin, 4*, 379–380.

Deutsch, K., Platt, J., and Senghaas, D. (1971). Conditions favoring major advances in social science. *Science, 171*, 450–459.

Deutsch, M. (1975). Graduate training of the problem-oriented social psychologist. In M. Deutsch and H. Hornstein, (Eds.), *Applying social psychology* (pp. 261–278). Hillsdale, NJ: Erlbaum.

Deutsch, M., and Krauss, R. M. (1965). *Theories in social psychology*. New York: Basic Books.

Diamond, S. S., and Morton, D. R. (1978). Empirical landmarks in social psychology. *Personality and Social Psychology Bulletin, 4*, 217–221.

Dunnette, M. D. (1966). Fads, fashions, and folderol in psychology. *American Psychologist, 21*, 343–352.

Edelman, P. D. (1978). *Physics and psychology: From the Newtonian to the modern worldview*. Unpublished bachelor's thesis, Massachusetts Institute of Technology, Cambridge, MA.

_____. (1979). *Hospital patients and graduate students: Analogous roles?* Unpublished manuscript, Harvard University, Cambridge, MA.

Elms, A. C. (1972). *Social psychology and social relevance.* Boston: Little, Brown.

_____. (1975). The crisis of confidence in social psychology. *American Psychologist, 30,* 967–976.

Farrell, G. P., Markley, O. W., and Matulef, N. J. (Eds.). (1967). *Special bulletin of the National Committee on Graduate Education in Psychology.* Washington, DC.

Feigl, H. (1959). Philosophical embarrassments of psychology. *American Psychologist, 14,* 115–128.

Festinger, L. (1957). *A theory of cognitive dissonance.* Evanston, IL: Row, Peterson.

Fried, S., Gumpper, D., and Allen, J. (1973). Ten years of social psychology: Is there a growing commitment to field research? *American Psychologist, 28,* 155–156.

Gergen, K. J. (1973). Social psychology as history. *Journal of Personality and Social Psychology, 26,* 309–320.

_____. (1976). Social psychology, science, and history. *Personality and Social Psychology Bulletin, 2,* 373–383.

_____. (1978). Experimentation in social psychology: A reappraisal. *European Journal of Social Psychology, 8,* 507–527.

Helmreich, R. (1975). Applied social psychology: The unfulfilled promise. *Personality and Social Psychology Bulletin, 1,* 548–560.

Higbee, K. L., and Wells, M. G. (1972). Some research trends in social psychology during the sixties. *American Psychologist, 27,* 963–966.

House, J. S. (1977). The three faces of social psychology. *Sociometry, 40,* 161–177.

Howard, G. S., Cole, D. A., and Maxwell, S. E. (1987). Research productivity in psychology based upon publication in the journals of the American Psychological Association. *American Psychologist, 42,* 975–986.

Israel, J., and Tajfel, H. (Eds.). (1972). *The context of social psychology: A critical assessment.* New York: Academic Press.

Janis, I. L. (1972). *Victims of groupthink.* Boston: Houghton Mifflin.

Jay, M. (1973). *The dialectical imagination.* Boston: Little, Brown.

Jones, P. A. (1986). Social psychological research and clinical practice: An academic paradox. *Professional Psychology, 17,* 535–540.

Kagan, J. (1980). Perspectives on continuity. In J. Kagan and O. G. Brim (Eds.), *Constancy and change in human development* (pp. 26–74). Cambridge, MA: Harvard University Press.

Kenrick, D. T. (1986). How strong is the case against contemporary social and personality psychology? A response to Carlson. *Journal of Personality and Social Psychology, 50,* 839–844.

Koch, S. (1976). Language communities, search cells and the psychological studies. In J. K. Cole and W. J. Arnold (Eds.), *Nebraska Symposium on Motivation 1975* (Vol. 23, pp. 477–559). Lincoln: University of Nebraska Press.

_____. (1981). The nature and limits of psychological knowledge: Lessons of a century qua "science." *American Psychologist, 36,* 257–269.

Koocher, G. P. (1977). Bathroom behavior and human dignity. *Journal of Personality and Social Psychology, 35,* 120–121.

Kressel, N.J. (1981). Hating the Jews: A new view from social psychology. *Judaism, 30,* 269–275.

————. (1984). The Holocaust as history. *Midstream, 30*(4), 57–59.

————. (1987a). Biased judgments of media bias: A case study of the Arab–Israeli dispute. *Political Psychology, 8*, 211–227.

————. (1987b). The development of social psychology as a profession. *The Journal of Training and Practice in Professional Psychology, 1*, 43–48.

Lakatos, I. (1970). Falsification and the methodology of scientific research programs. In I. Lakatos and A. Musgrave (Eds.), *Criticism and the growth of knowledge* (pp. 91–196). Cambridge, England: Cambridge University Press.

Leary, M. R., Jenkins, T. B., and Shepperd, J. A. (1984). The growth of interest in clinically relevant research in social psychology 1965–1983. *Journal of Social and Clinical Psychology, 2*, 333–338.

Levinson, H. (1976). *Psychological man.* Cambridge, MA: The Levinson Institute.

Lewicki, P. (1982). Social psychology as viewed by its practitioners: A survey of SESP members' opinions. *Personality and Social Psychology Bulletin, 8*, 409–416.

Lipsey, M. W. (1978). Occupational socialization and midcareer orthodoxy among academic psychologists. *Personality and Social Psychology Bulletin, 4*, 169–172.

Lynn, W. M., and Oldenquist, A. (1984). American social psychologists. *Academic Psychology Bulletin, 6*, 43–48.

Mark, M. M., and Bryant, F. B. (1984). Potential pitfalls of a more applied social psychology. *Basic and Applied Social Psychology, 5*, 231–253.

McGuire, W. J. (1967). Some impending reorientations in social psychology. *Journal of Experimental Social Psychology, 3*, 124–139.

————. (1973). The yin and yang of progress in social psychology: Seven koan. *Journal of Personality and Social Psychology, 26*, 446–456.

Meehl, P. E. (1978). Theoretical risks and tabular asterisks: Sir Karl, Sir Ronald, and the slow progress of soft psychology. *Journal of Consulting and Clinical Psychology, 46*, 806–834.

Merton, R. K. (1973). *The sociology of science.* Chicago: University of Chicago Press.

Middlemist, D. R., Knowles, E. S., and Matter, C. F. (1976). Personal space invasions in the lavatory. *Journal of Personality and Social Psychology, 33*, 541–546.

Mitroff, I., and Bonoma, T. V. (1978). Psychological assumptions, experimentation, and real world problems. *Evaluation Quarterly, 2*, 235–260.

Moscovici, S. (1972). Society and theory in social psychology. In J. Israel and H. Tajfel (Eds.), *The context of social psychology* (pp. 17–68). New York: Academic Press.

Nogami, G. Y. (1982). Good–fast–cheap; pick any two: Dilemmas about the value of applicable research. *Journal of Applied Social Psychology, 12*, 343–348.

Pencil, M. (1976). Salt passage research: The state of the art. *Journal of Communication, 26*, 31–36.

Peters, C. (1980). How Washington really works. Reading, MA: Addison-Wesley.

Petras, J. W., and Curtis, J. E. (1972). Note on "Bibliography on the Sociology of Sociology." *Journal of the History of the Behavioral Sciences, 8*, 405–406.

Popper, K. R. (1962). *The open society and its enemies: Hegel and Marx* (Vol. 2). Princeton, NJ: Princeton University Press.

Ring, K. (1967). Experimental social psychology: Some questions about some frivolous values. *Journal of Experimental Social Psychology, 3*, 124–139.

Rogers, E. M. (1983). *Diffusion of innovations* (3rd ed.). New York: The Free Press.

Rosenthal, R. (1966). *Experimenter bias in behavioral research.* New York: Appleton-Century-Crofts.

Rosenthal, R., and Rosnow, R. L. (Eds.). (1969). *Artifact in behavioral research.* New York: Academic Press.

Rosnow, R. L. (1981). *Paradigms in transition: The methodology of social inquiry.* New York: Oxford.

Rossi, P., Wright, J., and Wright, S. (1978). The theory and practice of applied social research. *Evaluation Quarterly, 2,* 171–191.

Rubin, Z. (1978). On measuring productivity by the length of one's vita. *Personality and Social Psychology Bulletin, 4,* 197–198.

Schlenker, B. R. (1974). Social psychology and science. *Journal of Personality and Social Psychology, 29,* 1–15.

———. (1976). Social psychology and science: Another look. *Personality and Social Psychology Bulletin, 2,* 384–390.

Sears, D. O. (1986). College sophomores in the laboratory: Influences of a narrow data base on social psychology's view of human nature. *Journal of Personality and Social Psychology, 51,* 515–530.

Sherif, M. (1970). On the relevance of social psychology. *American Psychologist, 25,* 144–156.

———. (1977). Crisis in social psychology. *Personality and Social Psychology Bulletin, 3,* 368–382.

Simon, W. B. (1968). What every young psychologist should know. *Journal of Social Issues, 24,* 115–126.

Smith, M. B. (1973a). Criticisms of a social science. *Science, 180,* 610–612.

———. (1973b). Is psychology relevant to new priorities? *American Psychologist, 28,* 463–471.

———. (1976). Social psychology, science and history: So what? *Personality and Social Psychology Bulletin, 2,* 437–443.

———. (1980). Attitudes, values and selfhood. In H. E. Howe, Jr. and M. M. Page (Eds.). *Nebraska Symposium on Motivation 1979* (pp. 305–350). Lincoln: University of Nebraska Press.

Smith, R. J. (1978). The future of an illusion: American social psychology. *Personality and Social Psychology Bulletin, 4,* 173–176.

Stinchcombe, A. L. (1975). A structural analysis of sociology. *The American Sociologist, 10,* 57–64.

Stricker, L. J. (1982). Social psychology of everyday life. *Contemporary Psychology, 27,* 200–201.

Triandis, H. (1978). Basic research in the context of applied research in personality and social psychology. *Personality and Social Psychology Bulletin, 4,* 383–387.

Veblen, T. (1979). *The theory of the leisure class.* New York: Penguin. (Original work published 1899)

Wachtel, P. (1980). Investigation and its discontents: Some constraints on progress in psychological research. *American Psychologist, 35,* 399–408.

Wilson, D. W., and Schafer, R. B. (1978). Is social psychology interdisciplinary? *Personality and Social Psychology Bulletin, 4,* 548–552.

Wilson, J. Q. (1971). Violence, pornography, and social science. *The Public Interest, 22,* 45–61.

CHAPTER TWO

POLITICS AND HUMAN NATURE

According to Hadley Cantril (1964), a humanistic social psychologist, "Every social and political system can be regarded as an experiment in the broad perspective of time. . . . The human design will in the long run force any experiment to accommodate it."

Throughout history, political theorists have attempted to articulate the connection between government and the human essence, sometimes seeking merely to describe and sometimes hoping to provide prescriptions for change. During the past century, the development of modern psychology has spawned increasingly sophisticated efforts to ground political science in a sound understanding of human nature.

For better or worse, however, no straightforward and consensual psychological science has arisen to meet the needs of political scholars. Instead, modern psychologists, sociologists, and biologists forge competing images of human nature and a convergence of outlooks appears unlikely in the foreseeable future (Mischel, 1986; Sahakian, 1982). Thus, political psychologists often confront the same array of issues that face other students of human behavior and mental processes. And the way one answers these fundamental psychological questions has important implications for how one views government. For example,

- Do environmental forces play a more significant role than innate tendencies in determining political behavior?
- How much, if any, of political behavior is the result of unconscious motivation?
- How much of an individual's political thinking and activity follows a consistent pattern throughout the life-span?
- Does the evolutionary past of our species continue to influence political life?

- To what extent can human nature be modified or molded?
- Do existential needs such as "the search for meaning" or the related "need for self-actualization" have an impact on political behavior?

Scholars and scientists have applied many methodologies to answer these questions and others about our political existence. To some extent, substantive conflicts may reflect more fundamental disagreements concerning rules of evidence. Even when people share perspectives on human nature, there is much room for debate about implications for the design and amelioration of political systems; for example, psychoanalytic theory has been employed by Marxists, e.g., the Frankfurt School, as well as political conservatives, e.g., Philip Rieff (Jay, 1972; Muller, 1991).

This chapter includes five readings on human nature and politics by Freud (4), Skinner (5), Cantril (6), Simon (7), and Marx (8). The first four selections discuss influential psychological theories of human nature—psychoanalytic, behaviorist, humanistic, and cognitive. The next selection searches beyond contemporary psychology for clues about human nature. Marx sees human consciousness as a consequence of one's relation to the means of production.

No one of the views presented in this chapter has found anywhere near universal acceptance among contemporary psychologists or political scientists. It is fair to say that each continues to exert influence on scholars and researchers in political psychology. Beyond this, assessments of the relative influence of the approaches become difficult, often conveying more about the biases of the assessor than anything else. Freudian, Skinnerian, and Marxist viewpoints are less common in psychology and political science than they once were. Humanistic psychology continues to have a small but loyal following. Cognitive orientations are currently popular. Although a variety of biological approaches are gaining support, they are still relatively new. (Schubert, 1983; Wiegele, 1979.)

What will be the case in twenty or thirty years, one cannot say. We can, however, be certain that the questions addressed by the thinkers in this chapter will continue to occupy political psychologists.

Sigmund Freud's long-term place in intellectual history is as secure as anyone's. For many political psychologists, the founder of psychoanalysis was at his best in *Civilization and Its Discontents*, the 1930 book from which this chapter's brief selection has been excerpted (Freud, 1961). Even for scholars who reject Freud's therapy and the more esoteric aspects of his developmental and personality theories, *Civilization and Its Discontents* remains a thought-provoking classic. Freud maintains that a terrible tension exists between human nature and the necessarily harsh demands of civilized society. One consequence of this tension is that utopian schemes must fail. Humans have exchanged a portion of their happiness for security so some discontent will characterize all political systems. In passing, Freud offers a brief but insightful analysis of the incompatibility between communist theory and human nature.

The next selection, The Design of a Culture, a passage from B. F. Skinner's (1971)

Beyond Freedom and Dignity, draws out the social and philosophical implications of behaviorist psychology. Skinner's views have been dubbed pessimistic because he rejects the notion of free will and consequently believes that humans cannot meaningfully feel pride concerning their achievements. However, Skinner claims that he offers an optimistic vision of human potential based on social and political experimentation. By planning, focusing on behavior and manipulating environmental contingencies, Skinner believes humans can greatly improve their condition. Although most contemporary psychologists place less emphasis on operant conditioning than they did several decades ago, many of Skinner's ideas continue to exert a powerful influence on academic psychology. Political psychologists have seldom considered themselves Skinnerians but, as this chapter's selection shows, his ideas are relevant to the central concerns of the discipline.

In The Human Design, Hadley Cantril (1964) sets forth an approach to human nature that flows mostly from humanistic and existential psychology. Although he does not articulate in this article the intellectual origins of his observations, he sketches a portrait of humans as creatures of hope, continuously seeking to "enlarge the range and enrich the quality of their satisfactions." People desire security but, at the same time, seek a value system to which they can feel committed and for which they might even risk their lives. Cantril considers the generalizations he discusses empirically valid, although he does not provide the "hard" evidence that some scientifically-minded political scientists would require. Maslow, Frankl, and other humanistic-existential psychologists would agree with many of Cantril's generalizations. His attempt to outline their political implications remains one of the best statements of the humanistic approach to political psychology.

Herbert A. Simon's view of human nature arises out of theory and empirical research in cognitive psychology and artificial intelligence. In this 1985 article, he compares two notions of rationality employed by social scientists. The first, "global, substantive rationality," prevails among economists and is also widely employed by political scientists. This type of rationality ignores the characteristics of the choosing organism, considering only constraints from the external situation. The second type of rationality, "procedural rationality," is determined by considering the limitations in the chooser's knowledge and computing power. Simon favors the latter definition of rationality and believes that its use would facilitate the advance of political science. Simon's argument for grounding political science in procedural rationality translates into advocacy for a cognitive psychological approach to political behavior. This cognitive orientation shows up in many aspects of political psychology but Simon is one of the first to relate a cognitive theory of human nature to the study of government.

The excerpt from Karl Marx's *The German Ideology* is the oldest selection in this reader, dating back to the mid-nineteenth century, but it still offers a relevant perspective. Marx's brief selection can be read as a critique of psychological notions of human nature. For Marx, consciousness derives from one's relationship to the social system and the means of production. Consciousness is "from the very beginning a social product, and remains so as long as men exist at all." Thus, attempts to understand politics through a psychological focus on individuals would be regarded by Marxist theory as beside the point. Improvement of human psychological and political conditions requires modification of prevailing social and economic structures. This critique remains powerful, even for many who reject Marxism as an ideology.

Perhaps psychologists William Gamson and Andre Modigliani offer the best vantage point from which we may explore the relationship between human nature and politics. They suggest that:

> It is misleading to ask which of . . . [the] competing images is more or less true. The question, rather, is which is more or less useful and for what purposes. Some images of man may seem particularly helpful in highlighting an issue that is left obscure by others; these others, in turn, may have their own uses. (Gamson and Modigliani, 1974, p. 1.)

On the other hand, we might be wise to guard against the easy tendency—call it pragmatic or atheoretical—to pick and choose among great ideas, without regard for the consistency or compatibility of their tenets. The pasting together of bits of classic works does not necessarily result in an integrated, meaningful theory of human nature.

REFERENCES

Cantril, H. (1964). The human design. *Journal of Individual Psychology, 20,* 129–136.
Freud, S. (1961). *Civilization and Its Discontents.* Translated by James Strachey. New York: W. W. Norton.
Gamson, W. A., and Modigliani, A. (1974). *Conceptions of Social Life.* Boston: Little, Brown.
Jay, M. (1972). *The Dialectical Imagination.* Boston: Little, Brown.
Mischel, W. (1986). *Introduction to Personality: A New Look.* Philadelphia: Holt, Rinehart and Winston.
Muller, J. Z. (1991, 2). A neglected conservative thinker. *Commentary,* pp. 49–52.
Sahakian, W. S. (1982). *History and Systems of Social Psychology.* New York: Hemisphere.
Schubert, G. (1983). Evolutionary politics. *Western Political Quarterly, 36,* 175–193.
Simon, H. A. (1985). Human nature in politics. *American Political Science Review, 79,* 293–304.
Skinner, B. F. (1971). *Beyond Freedom and Dignity.* New York: Alfred Knopf.
Wiegele, T. C. (1979). *Biopolitics: Search for a More Human Political Science.* Boulder, CO: Westview Press.

4

Civilization and Its Discontents

SIGMUND FREUD

The existence of this inclination to aggression, which we can detect in ourselves and justly assume to be present in others, is the factor which disturbs our relations with our neighbour and which forces civilization into such a high expenditure [of energy]. In consequence of this primary mutual hostility of human beings, civilized society is perpetually threatened with disintegration. The interest of work in common would not hold it together; instinctual passions are stronger than reasonable interests. Civilization has to use its utmost efforts in order to set limits to man's aggressive instincts and to hold the manifestations of them in check by psychical reaction-formations. Hence, therefore, the use of methods intended to incite people into identifications and aim-inhibited relationships of love, hence the restriction upon sexual life, and hence too the ideal's commandment to love one's neighbour as oneself—a commandment which is really justified by the fact that nothing else runs so strongly counter to the original nature of man. In spite of every effort, these endeavours of civilization have not so far achieved very much. It hopes to prevent the crudest excesses of brutal violence by itself assuming the right to use violence against criminals, but the law is not able to lay hold of the more cautious and refined manifestations of human aggressiveness. The time comes when each one of us has to give up as illusions the expectations which, in his youth, he pinned upon his fellow-men, and when he may learn how much difficulty and pain has been added to his life by their ill-will. At the same time, it would be unfair to reproach civilization with trying to eliminate strife and competition from human activity. These things are undoubtedly indispensable. But opposition is not necessarily enmity; it is merely misused and made an *occasion* for enmity.

The communists believe that they have found the path to deliverance from our evils. According to them, man is wholly good and is well-disposed to his neighbour; but the institution of private property has corrupted his nature. The ownership of private wealth gives the individual power, and with it the temptation to ill-treat his neighbour; while the man who is excluded from possession is bound to rebel in hostility against his oppressor. If private property were abolished, all wealth held in common, and everyone allowed to share in the enjoyment of it, ill-will and hostility would disappear among men. Since everyone's needs would be satisfied, no one would have any reason to regard another as his enemy; all would willingly undertake the work that was necessary. I have no concern with any economic criticisms of the communist system; I cannot enquire into whether the abolition of private property is expedient or advantageous.[1] But I am able to recognize that the psychological premises on which the system is based are an untenable illusion. In abolishing private property we deprive the human love of aggression of one of its instruments, certainly a strong one, though certainly not the strongest; but we have in no way altered the differences in power and influence which are misused by aggressiveness, nor have we altered anything in its nature. Aggressiveness was not created by property. It reigned almost without limit in primitive times, when property was still very scanty, and it already shows itself in the nursery almost before property has given up its primal, anal form; it forms the basis of every relation of affection and love among people (with the single exception, perhaps, of the mother's relation to her male child[2]). If we do away with personal rights over material wealth, there still remains prerogative in the field of sexual relationships, which is bound to become the source of the strongest dislike and the most violent hostility among men who in other respects are on an equal footing. If we were to remove this factor, too, by allowing complete freedom of sexual life and thus abolishing the family, the germ-cell of civilization, we cannot, it is true, easily foresee what new paths the development of civilization could take; but one thing we can expect, and that is that this indestructible feature of human nature will follow it there.

It is clearly not easy for men to give up the satisfaction of this inclination to aggression. They do not feel comfortable without it. The advantage which a comparatively small cultural group offers of allowing this instinct an outlet in the form of hostility against intruders is not to be despised. It is always possible to bind together a considerable number of people in love, so long as there are other people left over to receive the manifestations of their aggressiveness. I once discussed the phenomenon that it is precisely communities with adjoining territories, and related to each other in other ways as well, who are engaged in constant feuds and in ridiculing each other—like the Spaniards and Portuguese, for instance, the North Germans and South Germans, the English and Scotch, and so on.[3] I gave this phenomenon the name of 'the narcissism of minor differences', a name which does not do much to explain it. We can now see that it is a convenient and relatively harmless satisfaction of the inclination to aggression, by means of which cohesion between the members of the community is made easier. In this respect the Jewish people, scattered everywhere, have rendered most useful services to the civilizations of the countries that have been their hosts; but unfortunately all the massacres of the Jews in the Middle Ages did not suffice to make that period more peaceful and secure for their Christian fellows. When once the Apostle Paul had posited universal love between men as the foundation of his Christian community, extreme intolerance on the part of Christendom towards those who remained outside it became the inevitable consequence. To the Romans, who had not founded their communal life as a State upon love, religious intolerance was something foreign, although with them religion was a concern of the State and the State was permeated by religion. Neither was it an unaccountable chance that the dream of a Germanic world-dominion called for anti-semitism as its complement; and it is intelligible that the attempt to establish a new, communist civilization in Russia should find its psychological support in the persecution of the bourgeois. One only wonders, with concern, what the Soviets will do after they have wiped out their bourgeois.

If civilization imposes such great sacrifices not only on man's sexuality but on his aggressivity, we can understand better why it is hard for him to be happy in that civilization. In fact, primitive man was better off in knowing no restrictions of instinct. To counterbalance this, his prospects of enjoying this happiness for any length of time were very slender. Civilized man has exchanged a portion of his possibilities of happiness for a portion of security. We must not forget, however, that in the primal family only the head of it enjoyed this instinctual freedom; the rest lived in slavish suppression. In that primal period of civilization, the contrast between a minority who enjoyed the advantages of civilization and a majority who were robbed of those advantages was, therefore, carried to extremes. As regards the primitive peoples who exist to-day, careful researches have shown that their instinctual life is by no means to be envied for its freedom. It is subject to restrictions of a different kind but perhaps of greater severity than those attaching to modern civilized man.

When we justly find fault with the present state of our civilization for so inadequately fulfilling our demands for a plan of life that shall make us happy, and for allowing the existence of so much suffering which could probably be avoided—when, with unsparing criticism, we try to uncover the roots of its imperfection, we are undoubtedly exercising a proper right and are not showing ourselves enemies of civilization. We may expect gradually to carry through such alterations in our civilization as will better satisfy our needs and will escape our criticisms. But perhaps we may also familiarize ourselves with the idea that there are difficulties attaching to the nature of civilization which will not yield to any attempt at reform.

NOTES

1. Anyone who has tasted the miseries of poverty in his own youth and has experienced the indifference and arrogance of the well-to-do, should be safe from the suspicion of having no

understanding or good will towards endeavours to fight against the inequality of wealth among men and all that it leads to. To be sure, if an attempt is made to base this fight upon an abstract demand, in the name of justice, for equality for all men, there is a very obvious objection to be made—that nature, by endowing individuals with extremely unequal physical attributes and mental capacities, has introduced injustices against which there is no remedy.

2. [Cf. a footnote to Chapter VI of *Group Psychology* (1921*c*), *Standard Ed.*, **18**, 101*n*. A rather longer discussion of the point occurs near the end of Lecture XXXIII of the *New Introductory Lectures* (1933*a*).]

3. [See Chapter VI of *Group Psychology* (1921*c*), *Standard Ed.*, **18**, 101, and 'The Taboo of Virginity' (1918*a*), ibid., **11**, 199.]

5

The Design of a Culture

B. F. SKINNER

When a culture induces some of its members to work for its survival, what are they to do? They will need to foresee some of the difficulties the culture will encounter. These usually lie far in the future, and details are not always clear. Apocalyptic visions have had a long history, but only recently has much attention been paid to the prediction of the future. There is nothing to be done about completely unpredictable difficulties, but we may foresee some trouble by extrapolating current trends. It may be enough simply to observe a steady increase in the number of people on the earth, in the size and location of nuclear stockpiles, or in the pollution of the environment and the depletion of natural resources; we may then change practices to induce people to have fewer children, spend less on nuclear weapons, stop polluting the environment, and consume resources at a lower rate, respectively.

We do not need to predict the future to see some of the ways in which the strength of a culture depends upon the behavior of its members. A culture that maintains civil order and defends itself against attack frees its members from certain kinds of threats and presumably provides more time and energy for other things (particularly if order and security are not maintained by force). A culture needs various goods for its survival, and its strength must depend in part on the economic contingencies which maintain enterprising and productive labor, on the availability of the tools of production, and on the development and conservation of resources. A culture is presumably stronger if it induces its members to maintain a safe and healthful environment, to provide medical care, and to maintain a population density appropriate to its resources and space. A culture must be transmitted from generation to generation, and its strength will presumably depend on what and how much its new members learn, either through informal instructional contingencies or in educational institutions. A culture needs the support of its members, and it must provide for the pursuit and achievement of happiness if it is to prevent disaffection or defection. A culture must be reasonably stable, but it must also change, and it will presumably be strongest if it can avoid excessive respect for tradition and fear of novelty on the one hand and excessively rapid change on the other. Lastly, a culture will have a special measure of survival value if it encourages its members to examine its practices and to experiment with new ones.

A culture is very much like the experimental space used in the analysis of behavior. Both are sets of contingencies of reinforcement. A child is born into a culture as an organism is placed in an experimental space. Designing a culture is like designing an experiment; contingencies are arranged and effects noted. In an experiment we are interested in what happens, in designing a culture with whether it will work. This is the difference between science and technology.

A collection of cultural designs is to be found in the utopian literature. Writers have described their versions of the good life and suggested ways of achieving them. Plato, in *The Republic*, chose a political solution; Saint Augustine, in *The City of God*, a religious one. Thomas More and Francis Bacon, both lawyers, turned to law and order, and the Rousseauean utopists of the eighteenth century, to a supposed natural goodness in man. The nineteenth century looked for economic solutions, and the twentieth century saw the rise of what may be called behavioral utopias in which a full range of social contingencies began to be discussed (often satirically).

Utopian writers have been at pains to simplify their assignment. A utopian community is usually composed of a relatively small number of people living together in one place and in stable contact with each other. They can practice an informal ethical control and minimize the role of organized agencies. They can learn from each other rather than from the specialists called teachers. They can be kept from behaving badly toward each other through censure rather than the specialized punishments of a legal system. They can produce and exchange goods without specifying values in terms of money. They can help those who have become ill, infirm, disturbed, or aged with a minimum of institutional care. Troublesome contacts with other cultures are avoided through geographical isolation (utopias tend to be located on islands or surrounded by high mountains), and the transition to a new culture is facilitated by some formalized break with the past, such as a ritual of rebirth (utopias are often set in the distant future so that the necessary evolution of the culture seems plausible). A utopia is a total social environment, and all its parts work together. The home does not conflict with the school or the street, religion does not conflict with government, and so on.

Perhaps the most important feature of the utopian design, however, is that the survival of a community can be made important to its members. The small size, the isolation, the internal coherence—all these give a community an identity which makes its success or failure conspicuous. The fundamental question in all utopias is "Would it really work?"

The literature is worth considering just because it emphasizes experimentation. A traditional culture has been examined and found wanting, and a new version has been set up to be tested and redesigned as circumstances dictate.

The simplification in utopian writing, which is nothing more than the simplification characteristic of science, is seldom feasible in the world at large, and there are many other reasons why it is difficult to put an explicit design into effect. A large fluid population cannot be brought under informal social or ethical control because social reinforcers like praise and blame are not exchangeable for the personal reinforcers on which they are based. Why should anyone be affected by the praise or blame of someone he will never see again? Ethical control may survive in small groups, but the control of the population as a whole must be delegated to specialists—to police, priests, owners, teachers, therapists, and so on, with their specialized reinforcers and their codified contingencies. These are probably already in conflict with each other and will almost certainly be in conflict with any new set of contingencies. Where it is not too difficult to change informal instruction, for example, it is nearly impossible to change an educational establishment. It is fairly easy to change marriage, divorce, and child-bearing practices as the significance for the culture changes but nearly impossible to change the religious principles which dictate such practices. It is easy to change the extent to which various kinds of behavior are accepted as right but difficult to change the laws of a government. The reinforcing values of goods are more flexible than the values set by economic agencies. The word of authority is more unyielding than the facts of which it speaks.

It is not surprising that, so far as the real world is concerned, the word utopian means unworkable. History seems to offer support; various utopian designs have been proposed for nearly twenty-five hundred years, and most attempts to set them up have been ignominious failures. But historical evidence is always against the probability of anything new; that is what is meant by history. Scientific discoveries and inventions are improbable; that is what is meant by discovery and invention. And if planned economies, benevolent dictatorships, perfectionistic societies, and other utopian ventures have failed, we must remember that unplanned, undictated, and unperfected cultures have failed too. A failure is not always a mistake; it may simply be the best one can do under the circumstances. The real mistake is to stop trying. Perhaps we cannot now design a successful culture as a whole, but we can design better practices in a piecemeal fashion. The behavioral processes in the world at large are the same as those in a utopian community, and practices have the same effects for the same reasons.

The same advantages are also to be found in emphasizing contingencies of reinforcement in lieu of states of mind or feelings. It is no doubt a serious problem, for example, that students no longer respond in traditional ways to educational environments; they drop out of school, possibly for long periods of time, they take only courses which they enjoy or which seem to have relevance to their problems, they destroy school property and attack teachers and officials. But we shall not solve this problem by "cultivating on the part of our public a respect it does not now have for scholarship as such and for the practicing scholar and teacher." (The cultivation of respect is a metaphor in the horticultural tradition.) What is wrong is the educational environment. We need to design contingencies under which students acquire behavior useful to them and their culture— contingencies that do not have troublesome by-products and that generate the behavior said to "show respect for learning." It is not difficult to see what is wrong in most educational environments, and much has already been done to design materials which make learning as easy as possible and to construct contingencies, in the classroom and elsewhere, which give students powerful reasons for getting an education.

A serious problem also arises when young people refuse to serve in the armed forces and desert or defect to other countries, but we shall not make an appreciable change by "inspiring greater loyalty or patriotism." What must be changed are the contingencies which induce young people to behave in given ways toward their governments. Governmental sanctions remain almost entirely punitive, and the unfortunate by-products are sufficiently indicated by the extent of domestic disorder and international conflict. It is a serious problem that we remain almost continuously at war with other nations, but we shall not get far by attacking "the tensions which lead to war," or by appeasing warlike spirits, or by changing the minds of men (in which, UNESCO tells us, wars begin). What must be changed are the circumstances under which men and nations make war.

We may also be disturbed by the fact that many young people work as little as possible, or that workers are not very productive and often absent, or that products are often of poor quality, but we shall not get far by inspiring a "sense of craftsmanship or pride in one's work," or a "sense of the dignity of labor," or, where crafts and skills are a part of the caste mores, by changing "the deep emotional resistance of the caste superego," as one writer has put it. Something is wrong with the contingencies which induce men to work industriously and carefully. (Other kinds of economic contingencies are wrong too.)

Walter Lippmann has said that "the supreme question before mankind" is how men can save themselves from the catastrophe which threatens them, but to answer it we must do more than discover how men can "make themselves willing and able to save themselves." We must look to the contingencies that induce people to act to increase the chances that their cultures will survive. We have the physical, biological, and behavioral technologies needed "to save ourselves"; the problem is how to get people to use them. It may be that "utopia has only to be willed," but what does that mean? What are the principal specifications of a culture that will survive because it induces its members to work for its survival?

The application of a science of behavior to the design of a culture is an ambitious proposal, often thought to be utopian in the pejorative sense, and some reasons for skepticism deserve comment. It is often asserted, for example, that there are fundamental differences between the real world and the laboratory in which behavior is analyzed.

Where the laboratory setting is contrived, the real world is natural; where the setting is simple, the world is complex; where processes observed in the laboratory reveal order, behavior elsewhere is characteristically confused. These are real differences, but they may not remain so as a science of behavior advances, and they are often not to be taken seriously even now.

The difference between contrived and natural conditions is not a serious one. It may be natural for a pigeon to flick leaves about and find bits of food beneath some of them, in the sense that the contingencies are standard parts of the environment in which the pigeon evolved. The contingencies under which a pigeon pecks an illuminated disk on a wall and food then appears in a dispenser below the disk are clearly unnatural. But although the programming equipment in the laboratory is contrived and the arrangement of leaves and seeds natural, the schedules according to which behavior is reinforced can be made identical. The natural schedule is the "variable-ratio" schedule of the laboratory, and we have no reason to doubt that behavior is affected by it in the same way under both conditions. When the effects of the schedule are studied with programming equipment we begin to understand the behavior observed in nature, and as more and more complex contingencies of reinforcement have come to be investigated in the laboratory, more and more light has been thrown on the natural contingencies.

And so with simplification. Every experimental science simplifies the conditions under which it works, particularly in the early stages of an investigation. An analysis of behavior naturally begins with simple organisms behaving in simple ways in simple settings. When a reasonable degree of orderliness appears, the arrangements can be made more complex. We move forward only as rapidly as our successes permit, and progress often does not seem rapid enough. Behavior is a discouraging field because we are in such close contact with it. Early physicists, chemists, and biologists enjoyed a kind of natural protection against the complexity of their fields; they were untouched by vast ranges of relevant facts. They could select a few things for study and dismiss the rest of nature either as irrelevant or as obviously out of reach. If Gilbert or Faraday or Maxwell had had even a quick glimpse of what is now known about electricity, they would have had much more trouble in finding starting points and in formulating principles which did not seem "oversimplified." Fortunately for them, much of what is now known in their fields came to be known as the result of research and its technological uses, and it did not need to be considered until formulations were well advanced. The behavioral scientist has had no such luck. He is all too aware of his own behavior as part of his subject matter. Subtle perceptions, tricks of memory, the vagaries of dreams, the apparently intuitive solutions of problems—these and many other things about human behavior insistently demand attention. It is much more difficult to find a starting point and to arrive at formulations which do not seem too simple.

The interpretation of the complex world of human affairs in terms of an experimental analysis is no doubt often oversimplified. Claims have been exaggerated and limitations neglected. But the really great oversimplification is the traditional appeal to states of mind, feelings, and other aspects of the autonomous man which a behavioral analysis is replacing. The ease with which mentalistic explanations can be invented on the spot is perhaps the best gauge of how little attention we should pay to them. And the same may be said for traditional practices. The technology which has emerged from an experimental analysis should be evaluated only in comparison with what is done in other ways. What, after all, have we to show for nonscientific or prescientific good judgment, or common sense, or the insights gained through personal experience? It is science or nothing, and the only solution to simplification is to learn how to deal with complexities.

A science of behavior is not yet ready to solve all our problems, but it is a science in progress, and its ultimate adequacy cannot now be judged. When critics assert that it cannot account for this or that aspect of human behavior, they usually imply that it will never be able to do so, but the analysis continues to develop and is in fact much further advanced than its critics usually realize.

The important thing is not so much to know how to solve a problem as to know how to look for a solution. The scientists who approached President Roosevelt with a proposal to build a bomb so powerful that it could end the Second World War within a few days could not say that they knew how to build it. All they could say was that they knew how to go about finding out. The behavioral problems to be solved in the world today are no doubt more complex than the practical use of nuclear fission, and the basic science by no means as far advanced, but we know where to start looking for solutions.

A proposal to design a culture with the help of a scientific analysis often leads to Cassandran prophecies of disaster. The culture will not work as planned, and unforeseen consequences may be catastrophic. Proof is seldom offered, possibly because history seems to be on the side of failure: many plans have gone wrong, and possibly just because they were planned. The threat in a designed culture, said Mr. Krutch, is that the unplanned "may never erupt again." But it is hard to justify the trust which is placed in accident. It is true that accidents have been responsible for almost everything men have achieved to date, and they will no doubt continue to contribute to human accomplishments, but there is no virtue in an accident as such. The unplanned also goes wrong. The idiosyncrasies of a jealous ruler who regards any disturbance as an offense against him may have an accidental survival value if law and order are maintained, but the military strategies of a paranoid leader are of the same provenance and may have an entirely different effect. The industry which arises in the unrestrained pursuit of happiness may have an accidental survival value when war matériel is suddenly needed, but it may also exhaust natural resources and pollute the environment.

If a planned culture necessarily meant uniformity or regimentation, it might indeed work against further evolution. If men were very much alike, they would be less likely to hit upon or design new practices, and a culture which made people as much alike as possible might slip into a standard pattern from which there would be no escape. That would be bad design, but if we are looking for variety, we should not fall back upon accident. Many accidental cultures have been marked by uniformity and regimentation. The exigencies of administration in governmental, religious, and economic systems breed uniformity, because it simplifies the problem of control. Traditional educational establishments specify what the student is to learn at what age and administer tests to make sure that the specifications are met. The codes of governments and religions are usually quite explicit and allow little room for diversity or change. The only hope is *planned* diversification, in which the importance of variety is recognized. The breeding of plants and animals moves toward uniformity when uniformity is important (as in simplifying agriculture or animal husbandry), but it also requires planned diversity.

Planning does not prevent useful accidents. For many thousands of years people used fibers (such as cotton, wool, or silk) from sources which were accidental in the sense that they were the products of contingencies of survival not closely related to the contingencies which made them useful to men. Synthetic fibers, on the other hand, are explicitly designed; their usefulness is taken into account. But the production of synthetic fibers does not make the evolution of a new kind of cotton, wool, or silk any the less likely. Accidents still occur, and indeed, are furthered by those investigating new possibilities. It might be said that science maximizes accidents. The physicist does not confine himself to the temperatures which occur accidentally in the world at large, he produces a continuous series of temperatures over a very wide range. The behavioral scientist does not confine himself to the schedules of reinforcement which happen to occur in nature, he constructs a great variety of schedules, some of which might never arise by accident. There is no virtue in the accidental nature of an accident. A culture evolves as new practices appear and undergo selection, and we cannot wait for them to turn up by chance.

6

The Human Design

HADLEY CANTRIL

The human being seems at last to be entering the main body of psychology with a vengeance. For years he has all too often been shorn of his most characteristic attributes, until he has been scarcely recognizable. Variables such as appetites, wants, values, and temperament have been neglected because they are not easily manipulated in the laboratory and can so disturb otherwise neat experimentation. As Henry A. Murray pointed out nearly two decades ago (1948, p. 466), "The main body of psychology started its career by putting the wrong foot forward, and it has been out of step with the march of science much of the time. Instead of beginning with studies of the whole person adjusting to a natural environment, it began with studies of a segment of a person responding to a physical stimulus in an unnatural laboratory environment." One consequence of this false start has been a proliferation of model building which often takes on the aspect of playing games. Another consequence has been an overemphasis by some investigators on a single variable which proves at best tentative and partial after the fad for it has run its course.

It is therefore no wonder that so many students of psychology have found it an insufferably dull subject and that many social scientists and inquiring laymen feel that most of the psychology they read provides them unconvincing, unrewarding concepts from which to choose as they try to give plausible accounts of the behavior of men and women in real-life situations. They sense that somewhere along the line too much of human experience has been left out of account.

It is appropriate, then, for those of us concerned with human experience and behavior in all its subtle ramifications to spell out what seems to us to ring true and what appear to be the demands that the genetically built-in design of the human being imposes on any

75

society, political culture, or enduring social relationship. It is all too easy to neglect the basic functional uniformities which take diverse forms and to leave the accounting or explanation at that level. Differences are often dramatic and simpler to detect than the similarities they may obscure. Here I shall try to orchestrate into some systematic unity the diversities of mankind found in different societies and contexts.

The aspects of "human nature" differentiated here are those which seem to me to be pointed to by the data of psychology and by the observations sensitive observers have made of the way people live their lives in a variety of circumstances. I shall try to use a level of accounting appropriate both to an understanding of people and to an understanding of social and political systems. In doing this, some of the absurdities may be avoided that result when a single man-made abstraction, usually devised to account for some single aspect of behavior, is the sole theme song. As the different characteristics of the human design are reviewed here, it must be recognized and emphasized that they all overlap, intertwine, and are interdependent. One must differentiate artificially in order to focus and describe.

Man Requires the Satisfaction of His Survival Needs. Any listing of the characteristics of any living organism must begin here. Neurophysiologists have located and described in a most general way two built-in appetitive systems found in higher animals: one system propelling them to seek satisfying and pleasurable experiences, and the other protecting them from threatening or unpleasant experiences (Cantril and Livingston, 1963). These two systems together can be thought of as the basic forces contained within all human beings, which not only keep them and the species alive as their simple survival needs for food, shelter, and sex are gratified but also are involved in the desire for life itself.

These appetitive systems, of course, become enormously developed, refined, and conditioned—especially in humans—as new ways are learned to achieve satisfactions and avoid dangers and discomforts. It has often been noted that unless the survival needs are satisfied, a person devotes himself almost exclusively to a continued attempt to fulfill them, a preoccupation which preempts his energies and repels any concern for other activities. Most people in the world today are still concerned with living a type of life that constitutes well-being on a relatively simple level with what amenities their cultures can provide.

Man Wants Security in Both Its Physical and Its Psychological Meaning to Protect Gains Already Made and to Assure a Beachhead from Which Further Advances May Be Staged. Man wants some surety that one action can lead to another, some definite foothold which provides an orientation and integration through time. People invariably become embittered if they nurse a dream for what they regard as a long time with no signs of it becoming a reality.

In this connection, it should be recalled that the story of evolution seems to tell us that members of every species stake out some territory for themselves within which they can provide for their needs and carry on their living; the size of this territory is dependent on what is required for the survival of the species, and is increased if this will contribute to such survival. In the present era, the territories human beings stake out for themselves are largely bounded by the nation-state, a territorial unit rapidly replacing narrower geographical and psychological identifications. Yet it is doing so just at the time when it is becoming more and more apparent that the concept of nation itself limits and threatens man's development in an age of increasing interdependence and highly developed weaponry.

Man Craves Sufficient Order and Certainty in His Life to Enable Him to Judge with Fair Accuracy What Will or Will Not Occur if He Does or Does Not Act in Certain Ways. People want sufficient form and pattern in life to be sure that certain satisfactions already enjoyed will be repeatable and will provide a secure springboard for takeoffs in new directions.

The conflict of old loyalties with emerging new loyalties in the case of developing people is bound to create uncertainties, doubts, and hesitations. If people become frustrated and anxious enough, they will do almost anything in a desperate attempt to put some order into apparent chaos or rally around new symbols and abstractions that enable them to identify with a new order that promises to alleviate the uncertainties experienced in the here and now.

In stressing process and change, the desire of people to preserve the *status quo* when it has proved satisfying and rewarding and to protect existing forms against alteration must never be overlooked. This craving for certainty would include the satisfactions that come from the sense of stability provided by our habitual behavior—including much of our social and political behavior.

Human Beings Continuously Seek to Enlarge the Range and Enrich the Quality of Their Satisfactions. Man is engaged in a ceaseless quest to extend the range and improve the quality of his satisfactions through the exercise of his creative and inventive capacities. This is, of course, a basic reason why order of any kind is constantly being upset. Whitehead expressed the point eloquently and repeatedly, for example, in his statements that "the essence of life is to be found in the frustrations of established order" (1938, p. 119) and that "the art of progress is to preserve order amid change, and to preserve change amid order" (1929, p. 515).

The distinguished British philosopher John Macmurray has used the phrase "the self as agent" as the title of his book analyzing the role of action in man's constant search for value satisfactions (1957). In a companion volume, he has noted that ". . . human behavior cannot be understood, but only caricatured, if it is represented as an adaptation to environment" (1961, p. 46). The search for an enlargement of satisfactions in the transactions of living can also be phrased as the *desire for development in a direction*, the desire to do something which will bring a sense of accomplishment as we experience the consequences of successfully carrying out some intention and which will thus give us an occasional feeling that our lives are continuous creations in which we can take an active part. During a conversation in Beirut, a wise man once remarked to me that "people are hungry for new and good experiences."

It seems worthwhile to differentiate this search for value satisfactions into two varieties: (1) value satisfactions that are essentially new, different, more efficient, more reliable, more pleasurable, or more status-producing results of activity along familiar and tried dimensions and (2) value satisfactions that are new in the sense of being emergent, a new quality a person discovers or creates himself for the first time. The latter is exemplified in the child who tries out and relishes new experiences as his own developmental pattern unfolds. The former variety, like the growth on the limb of a tree, builds people out and extends their range, while the latter, like the new growth at the top of the tree, lets them attain new heights and see new vistas. The satisfactions sought by a newly developing people are at first most likely to be of the former type.

The particular value satisfactions man acquires are the result of learning. Some of the values learned will serve as the operative ideals of a people; others will be chiefly instrumental. People in rich countries have learned to want and to expect many aspects of a good life that less favored people have not yet learned are possibilities. From this point of view, one might say that the competition between social and political systems is a competition in teaching people what to want and what is potentially available to them, and then in proving to them in their own private experience that these wants are best attainable under the system described.

Human Beings Are Creatures of Hope and Are Not Genetically Designed to Resign Themselves. This characteristic of man stems from the characteristic just described: that man is always likely to be dissatisfied and never fully "adapts" to his environment.

Man seems continually to hope that the world he encounters will correspond more and more to his vision of it as he acts within it to carry out his purposes, while the vision itself continuously unfolds in an irreversible direction. The whole process is a never-ending one. It is characteristic of man in their ongoing experience to ask himself, "Where do I go from here?" Only in his more reflective moods does a person ask, "Where did I come from?" or "How did I get this way?" Most of the time, most people who are "plugged into" the changing world around them are future-oriented in their concerns.

Human Beings Have the Capacity to Make Choices and the Desire to Exercise This Capacity. Any mechanical model of man constructed by a psychologist or by anyone else is bound to leave out the crucially important characteristic of man as an "appetitive-perceptive agency." Perceptions are learned and utilized by people to provide prognoses or bets of a variety of kinds to weigh alternative courses of action to achieve purposes. Consciously or without conscious awareness, people are trying to perceive the probable relation between their potential acts and the consequences of these acts to the intentions that constitute their goals.

The human nervous system, including the brain, has the capacity to police its input, to determine what is and what is not significant for it, and to pay attention to and to reinforce or otherwise modify its behavior as it transacts in the occasions of living (Cantril and Livingston, 1963). In this sense, the human being is a participant in, and producer of, his own value satisfactions: People perceive only what is relevant to their purposes and make their choices accordingly.

Human Beings Require Freedom to Exercise the Choices They Are Capable of Making. This characteristic of man related to freedom is deliberately worded as it is, rather than as a blanket statement that "human beings require freedom," since the freedom people want is so relative to their desires and the stage of development they have attained. Human beings, incidentally, apparently require more freedom than other species of animals because of their much greater capacity to move about and to engage in a much wider variety of behavior.

It seems true that maximum freedom is a necessary condition if a highly developed individual is to obtain maximum value satisfaction. It is equally true, as many people have pointed out, that too much freedom too soon can be an unbearable burden and a source of bondage if people, like children, are insufficiently developed to know what to do with it. For freedom clearly involves a learning of responsibility and an ability to take advantage of it wisely.

The concept of freedom is essentially a psychological and not a political concept. It describes an individual's opportunity to make his own choices and to act in accord with them. Psychologically, freedom refers to the freedom to experience more of what is potentially available, the freedom to move about and ahead, to be and to become. Freedom is thus less and less determined and more of a reality as man evolves and develops; it emerges and flowers as people learn what it can mean to them in terms of resolving some frustrations under which they are living.

The authoritarian leadership sometimes required to bring about man's awakening and to start him on the road to his definition of progress appears to go against the grain of the human design once man is transformed into a self-conscious citizen who has the desire to exercise the capacity latent within him. The definition of freedom in the Soviet dictionary, *Ushakov*, as "the recognition of necessity" is valid only during those periods in the lives of individuals or the history of a people when they are willing to let others define what is necessary and to submerge their own individuality.

Human Beings Want to Experience Their Own Identity and Integrity (More Popularly Referred to as the "Need for Personal Dignity"). Every human being craves a sense of his own self-constancy, an assurance of the repeatability of experience in which he is a determining participant. He obtains this from the transactions he has with other individuals.

People develop significances they share with others in their membership and reference groups. If the satisfaction derived from and the significance of participation with others cease to confirm assumptions or to enrich values, then a person's sense of self-constancy becomes shaken or insecure, and his loyalties become formalized and empty or are given up altogether. He becomes alienated or seeks new significances, new loyalties that are more operationally real.

People Want to Experience a Sense of Their Own Worthwhileness. This differentiation is made from the desire for personal identity and integrity to bring out the important relationship between this search for identity and the behavior and attitudes of others toward us. A human being wants to know he is valued by others and that others will somehow show through their behavior that his own behavior and its consequences make some sort of difference to them in ways that give him a sense of satisfaction. When this occurs, not only is a person's sense of identity confirmed, but he also experiences a sense of personal worth and self-respect. The process of extending the sense of self both in space and in time appears also to involve the desire that one's "presence" not be limited merely to the here and now of existence, but extend into larger dimensions. These human cravings seem to be at the root of man's social relationships.

People acquire, maintain, and enrich their sense of worthwhileness only if they at least vaguely recognize the sources of what personal identity they have: their family, their friends and neighbors, their associates or fellow workers, their group ties, or their nation. The social, religious, intellectual, regional, or national loyalties formed play the important role of making it possible for individuals to extend themselves backward into the past and forward into the future and to identify themselves with others who live at more or less remote distances from them. This means the compounding of shared experiences into a bundle that can be conceptualized, felt, or somehow referred to in the here and now of daily living, thus making a person feel a functional part of a more enduring alliance. Man accomplishes such feats of self-extension largely through his capacity to create symbols, images, and myths which provide focal points for identification and self-expansion. After reviewing the lessons from history, Muller noted as one of the "forgotten simplicities" the fact that "men have always been willing to sacrifice themselves for some larger cause, fighting and dying for their family, tribe, or community, with or without hope of eternal reward" (1954, p. 392).

Human Beings Seek Some Value or System of Beliefs to Which They Can Commit Themselves. In the midst of the probabilities and uncertainties that surround them, people want some anchoring points, some certainties, some faith that will serve either as a beacon light to guide them or as a balm to assuage them during the inevitable frustrations and anxieties that living engenders.

People who have long been frustrated and who have searched for means to alleviate their situations are, of course, particularly susceptible to a commitment to a new system of beliefs or an ideology that they feel holds promise of effective action.

Beliefs are confirmed insofar as action based on them brings satisfying consequences, and they are denied with growing skepticism if disastrous results consistently occur because they are followed.

Commitment to a value or belief system becomes more difficult among well-informed and sophisticated people who self-consciously try to reconcile what they believe with what they know and what they know with what they believe. In such circumstances, beliefs become more secular and less important as personal identifications.

Human Beings Want a Sense of Surety and Confidence that the Society of Which They Are a Part Holds out a Fair Degree of Hope that Their Aspirations Will be Fulfilled. If people cannot experience the effectiveness of social mechanisms to accomplish some of the potential goals they aspire to, then obviously their frustrations and anxieties mount, and they search for new means to accomplish aims. On the other hand, they make any sacrifice required to protect a society which they feel is fulfilling their needs but which appears seriously threatened.

It cannot be stressed too strongly that any people will become apathetic toward, or anxious about, ultimate goals they would like to achieve through social organizations if they continually sense a lack of reliability in the means provided to accomplish these goals. Obviously, any society that is to be viable must satisfy basic survival needs, must provide security, must ensure the repeatability of value satisfactions already attained, and must provide for new and emerging satisfactions. The effective society is one that enables individuals to develop personal loyalties and aspirations which overlap with, and are congenial to, social values and loyalties and that at the same time takes full account of the wide range of individual differences that exist.

Such a social organization must, too, become the repository of values, must provide symbols for people's aspirations, and must comprise and contain customs, institutions, laws, economic arrangements, and political forms which enable individuals in various ways to give concrete reference to their values in their day-to-day behavior. If the gap between what society actually provides in terms of effective mechanisms for living and what it purports to provide becomes too great, the vacuum created will sooner or later engender the frustrations that urge people on to seek new social patterns and symbols. Whitehead wrote (1927, p. 88):

> The major advances in civilization are processes which all but wreck the societies in which they occur—like unto an arrow in the hand of a child. The art of free society consists first in the maintenance of the symbolic code; and secondly in fearlessness of revision, to secure that the code serves those purposes which satisfy an enlightened reason. Those societies which cannot combine reverence to their symbols with freedom of revision, must ultimately decay either from anarchy, or from the slow atrophy of a life stifled by useless shadows.

Every social and political system can be regarded as an experiment in the broad perspective of time. Whatever the experiment, the human design will in the long run force any experiment to accommodate to it. This has been the case throughout human history. Few would deny that the varied patterns of experiments going on today hold out more promise of satisfying the human condition for a greater number of people than ever before.

REFERENCES

Cantril, H., and Livingston, W. K. The concept of transaction in psychology and neurology. *Journal of Individual Psychology,* 1963, **19**, 3–16.

Macmurray, J. *The self as agent.* New York: Harper & Row, 1957.

_____. *Persons in relation.* London: Faber, 1961.

Muller, H. J. *The uses of the past.* New York: Mentor Books, 1954.

Murray, H. A., et al. *The assessment of men.* New York: Holt, Rinehart and Winston, 1948.

Whitehead, A. N. *Symbolism: Its meaning and effect.* New York: Macmillan, 1927.

_____. *Process and reality.* New York: Macmillan, 1929.

_____. *Modes of thought.* New York: Macmillan, 1938.

7

A Cognitive Approach to Human Nature in Politics

HERBERT A. SIMON

This article is concerned with the nature of human reason and the implications of contemporary cognitive psychology for political science research that employs the concept of rational behavior. I shall begin with a bit of history, written from a rather personal viewpoint, to provide a setting for the discussion.

The older and/or more scholarly among you will recognize the essay's title as having been plagiarized from Graham Wallas, whose seminal book, *Human Nature in Politics*, appeared in 1908. When I began graduate study, in the middle 1930s, that book, along with Walter Lippmann's *Public Opinion*, was still wholly fresh, and both stood out as harbingers of the "behavioral revolution" that was then just getting under way at the University of Chicago.

Not that we graduate students thought of ourselves as participants in a scientific revolution. The realities of the political process had long since replaced the formal legal structure of political institutions as the main subject for study in political science—at least at the University of Chicago. Merriam's studies of power, Gosnell's quantitative methods, Lasswell's psychoanalytic probes seemed to us merely (paraphrasing Clausewitz) "the continuation of political realism by other means."[1]

I was little prepared, therefore, for the violence of the polemic pro and con "behavioralism" that echoed over the land in the first two decades after World War II. Nowadays, my periodic soundings in the *American Political Science Review* reassure me that this civil strife in the profession is largely over, and that the behavioral revolution is now seen as continuity rather than discontinuity in the development of political science. I am not sure it would even qualify, in today's revisionist view, as one of Thomas Kuhn's major paradigm shifts. Perhaps what we were doing was not revolutionary science at all, but just everyday normal science.

This is probably the right moment, while I am alluding to behavioralism, to record a *culpa mea* for my part in popularizing that awkward and somewhat misleading term. It appeared, of course, in the title of *Administrative Behavior* (Simon, 1947/1976a), and also in the title of my chief epistle to the economists, "A Behavioral Model of Rational Choice," published in the *Quarterly Journal of Economics* in 1955. However, I doubt that I was the main culprit. That honor belongs to the Ford Foundation, which at that same time introduced and diligently popularized the phrase "behavioral sciences."

Whatever its origins, the term was picked up with enthusiasm—as an epithet—by the opponents of behavioralism, who frequently employed it as though it were synonymous with the Behaviorism then rampant in the discipline of psychology. In fact, there was never any substantive connection between the two labels, and much of what went on in political science, sociology, economics, and anthropology under the heading of behavioralism would have been anathematized by the psychological Behaviorists if they had been aware of it—which they mainly weren't.

However, my aim here is not to reminisce about old battles. We should rejoice that political scientists are devoting all their efforts to advancing the science, and we should do nothing to encourage a renewal of the Methodenstreit. Instead, I shall offer a commentary on the role of the rationality principle in recent political science research.

I emphasize that this is a commentary and not a new piece of substantive research. The basic values for political science to which I and my contemporaries were and are committed include sound empirical data as the foundation for theory and for normative recommendations; new sources of data including polls, structured interviews, and systematic samples; the use of statistics, mathematics, and computer simulation where appropriate as tools for data analysis and theory construction; and the analysis of phenomena in terms of basic categories like power, decision making, rationality, and systems.

The research on which I shall comment exemplifies those values: it is empirically based, employing many different kinds of data-gathering methods, often uses mathematical and other formal techniques, and is sophisticated in its use of theory. My commentary will not touch on any of those aspects of the work except the last, and in particular its employment of ideas derived from the theory of human rationality.

The commentary will take us through three main topics. First, I shall have to say something about the two main forms of theories of human rationality that prevail in social science today—the one of them having its center in cognitive psychology, the other in economics. Next, I shall consider the implications, for the balance in political science between rationalism (or a priorism) and empiricism, of adopting one or the other of these two paradigms of rationality. In particular, I will argue that there is a natural alliance between empiricism and the psychological version of rationality, on the one hand, and an alliance between rationalism and the economic version of rationality, on the other. Finally, I will comment on the balance between reason and passion—"radical" irrationality—in political affairs.

THE FORMS OF RATIONALITY

The term "rational" denotes behavior that is appropriate to specified goals in the context of a given situation.[2] If the characteristics of the choosing organism are ignored, and we consider only those constraints that arise from the external situation, then we may speak of substantive or objective rationality, that is, behavior that can be adjudged objectively to be optimally adapted to the situation.

On the other hand, if we take into account the limitations of knowledge and computing power of the choosing organism, then we may find it incapable of making objectively optimal choices. If, however, it uses methods of choice that are as effective as its decision-making and problem-solving means permit, we may speak of procedural or bounded rationality, that is, behavior that is adaptive within the constraints imposed *both* by the external situation and by the capacities of the decision maker.

The terms "procedural" and "substantive" were, of course, borrowed from constitutional law, in analogy with the concepts of procedural and substantive due process, the former judging fairness by the procedure used to reach a result, the latter by the substance of the result itself. In the same way, we can judge a person to be rational who uses a reasonable process for choosing; or, alternatively, we can judge a person to be rational who arrives at a reasonable choice.

There is a fundamental difference between substantive and procedural rationality. To deduce the substantively, or objectively, rational choice in a given situation, we need to know only the choosing organism's goals and the objective characteristics of the situation. We need to know absolutely nothing else about the organism, nor would such additional knowledge be of any use to us, for it could not affect the objectively rational behavior in any way.

To deduce the procedurally or boundedly rational choice in a situation, we must know the choosing organism's goals, the information and conceptualization it has of the situation, and its abilities to draw inferences from the information it possesses. We need know nothing about the objective situation in which the organism finds itself, except insofar as that situation influences the subjective representation.

If we review the history of political science over the past 40 years, I believe we will see that it was mainly the procedural view of rationality that was embraced by behavioralism, but that during the past two decades this view has received growing competition from the substantive view. Anthony Downs's *Economic Theory of Democracy*, published in 1957, may be used to date the first nudgings of this new camel into the tent.

I should now like to develop a little further the fundamental characteristics and theoretical structures of the two views of rationality, and then consider the implications of employing them, separately or jointly, in the study of political behavior.

Procedural Rationality and Cognitive Psychology

A central theme for Graham Wallas in *Human Nature in Politics* was the interplay of the rational and nonrational components of human behavior in politics. That, of course, was also a central theme for Harold Lasswell in *Psychopathology and Politics* (1934) and *World Politics and Personal Insecurity* (1935). But while Lasswell's psychological apparatus comes largely from Freud, Wallas acknowledges as his principal mentor William James. Although Lasswell was concerned with borderline and not-so-borderline pathology, Wallas was interested in the ubiquitous workings of instinct, ignorance, and emotion in normal behavior. Wallas, like his mentor William James, is the more closely attuned to the contemporary orientation in psychology.

What is that orientation? I expressed skepticism, earlier, that political science has experienced, since World War II, any change that deserves being called a revolution. I have no such doubts about the field of psychology. Cognitive psychology, in the past 30 years, has undergone a radical restructuring, from a severe Behaviorism (no relation, I remind you, to behavioralism) to a framework that views thinking as information processing.

In psychology, Behaviorism carefully avoided speaking about what went on inside the head—it preferred to stick to the observable facts of stimuli and responses. It preferred rats to humans as subjects in its experiments, presumably because rats could not be induced to give unacceptable introspective accounts of their mental experiences. Even the term "cognitive" was eschewed, as implying an illicit mentalism.

Today, all of these barriers are down. The term "cognition" is uttered openly and proudly to refer to the human thought processes and to distinguish them from the processes of sensation and emotion. Most experiments use human subjects, and many instruct the subjects to speak aloud as they perform the experimental tasks, the tape-recorded protocols from such sessions being now regarded as wholly objective and analyzable data.[3] Theories, in modern cognitive psychology, are expected to provide detailed descriptions of the information processes that go on in the human head when it is performing problem solving and other tasks in the laboratory.[4]

Within this new paradigm, cognitive psychology has made great strides toward understanding how an information processing system like the human brain solves problems, makes decisions, remembers, and learns. That understanding has advanced so far that psychology is no longer limited to dealing with "toy" tasks—puzzles and nonsense syllables—in the laboratory, but can give rather impressive accounts of adult performance in professional-level tasks: making medical diagnoses, solving physics and mathematics problems at high school and college level, learning new mathematics and chemistry, and even making new scientific discoveries, to mention just a few examples.

As examples of explicit applications of the new theories to political science, I can mention the models of public budget-making behavior constructed by Crecine (1969) and Gerwin (1969) and their students, and Carbonell's (1979) ingenious "Goldwater machine," which predicts the response of an appropriately specified political figure to a situation or set of events. Later, I will cite a number of other accounts of procedural rationality at work in the political process, but in most of these the appeal to cognitive theory and research is only implicit.

The human capabilities for rational behavior that are described by contemporary cognitive psychology are very congenial to the paradigm of bounded rationality as that is described in *Administrative Behavior*. The models of problem solving describe a person who is limited in computational capacity, and who searches very selectively through large realms of possibilities in order to discover what alternatives of action are available, and what the consequences of each of these alternatives are. The search is incomplete, often inadequate, based on uncertain information and partial ignorance, and usually terminated with the discovery of satisfactory, not optimal, courses of action.

To understand the behavior of this kind of problem solver, who is provided in advance with a knowledge of neither alternatives nor consequences—and who may even discover what his or her goals are in the course of the problem-solving process—it is necessary to specify what the problem solver wants, knows, and can compute. Within the framework of these conditionalities, the mere assumption of rationality provides little basis for the prediction of behavior. To be of much use, that assumption must be supplemented by considerable empirical knowledge about the decision maker.

Substantive Rationality and Economics

Just as procedural, bounded rationality is most extensively developed in modern cognitive psychology, so substantive, objective rationality finds its principal base in neoclassical economics and statistical decision theory.[5] The two conceptions of rationality are radically different. The foundation for the theory of objective rationality is the assumption that every actor possesses a utility function that induces a consistent ordering among all alternative choices that the actor faces, and, indeed, that he or she always chooses the alternative with the highest utility.

If the choice situation involves uncertainties, the theory further assumes that the actor will choose the alternative for which the expected utility is the highest. By expected utility of an alternative is meant the average of the utilities of the different possible outcomes, each weighted by the probability that the outcome will ensue if the alternative in question is chosen.

The theory of objective rationality assumes nothing about the actor's goals. The utility function can take any form that defines a consistent ordering of preferences. Nor does the theory postulate anything about the way in which the actor makes probability estimates of uncertain events; in fact one version of the theory, the so-called subjective expected utility, or SEU, theory, explicitly denies that these probabilities are to be identified with objective probabilities of the events, determined by some outside observer. In this one respect, the label "objective" for this version of the theory must be qualified.

In principle (i.e., in a wholly idealized laboratory setting), it should be possible to obtain independent evidence about the nature and shape of any particular person's utility function, as well as evidence of the probabilities that person assigns to events. In practice, this is completely infeasible. In fact, when such experiments have been run, it has generally been found that human subjects do not possess consistent utility functions or probability assignments.[6]

In application, therefore, auxiliary assumptions about utility and expectations must usually be supplied before the theory of objective rationality can be applied to real situations. In economic applications, for example, it is customary to identify the utility function of a firm with its profit, and to assume that actors generally are trying to maximize economic well-being—perhaps some weighted average of income and leisure. In applications to political science, it may be assumed that the goal is to maximize power, or to maximize economic well-being as a function of the policies pursued by the government. (I will have more to say later about the assumptions that are made regarding political "utility" in applying the principle of rationality to problems in political science.)

In the same way, in applying the theory of objective rationality to real-world behavior, either uncertainty must be ignored, or auxiliary postulates must be provided to define the expectation-forming process. In contemporary economics, for example, the very lively "rational expectations" school, whose leaders include such figures as Robert Lucas and Thomas Sargent, assumes that each economic actor has a more or less accurate model of the economic system, and expects that system to proceed toward its equilibrium in the near future. Of course, there is much doubt whether this particular assumption about the formation of expectations bears any close resemblance to the reality, and a majority of neoclassical economists have different, and simpler, beliefs about how economic actors cope with uncertainty.

When neoclassical economics in its purest form addresses itself exclusively to questions of the existence, stability, and Pareto optimality of equilibrium, it can generally get along without introducing auxiliary assumptions about the utility function or the nature of the expectation-forming processes. In fact, it usually finesses the latter by ignoring uncertainty. The price that is paid is that the conclusions reached by this kind of analysis are extremely general and abstract: roughly, that under conditions of perfect competition, the economic system has a stable equilibrium, and that this equilibrium is, indeed, Pareto optimal (not everyone can simultaneously be made better off than the equilibrium).

When economists want to draw conclusions about nonequilibrium phenomena, matters get stickier. The theory of business cycles provides an important illustration of the difficulties.[7] The economic theory of Keynes and that of neoclassical economists like Friedman or Lucas are only inches, not miles, apart. Most of Keynes's general theory can be (and has been) interpreted as an exercise in quite orthodox neoclassical reasoning— except at one or two critical points, the most important being the supply of labor. At these points economic actors depart from objective rationality and suffer from persistent illusions or confusions. The assumption in Keynes's theory that produces a business cycle and the possibility of long-continuing unemployment is that labor mistakes its money wage for its real (purchasing power) wage. It is not human rationality, but the limits on that rationality and its breakdown, that accounts for Keynes's important predictions.

But the same thing can be said of the other, non-Keynesian, theories of the business cycle. (I must except Milton Friedman (1968), who essentially denies that there is such a phenomenon as real unemployment.) For example, Lucas (1981), among the most orthodox of neoclassical economists, attributes the business cycle to a different limit on human rationality. In his theory, it is not labor but businessmen who behave irrationally. When general price changes occur (e.g., inflation), they mistake these changes for *relative* changes affecting only prices in their own industry. It is this departure from objective rationality that produces the cycle in Lucas's model.

I have developed this example at some length because it is perhaps the most dramatic illustration of a widespread phenomenon that is not well understood outside the profession of economics, and perhaps not even within the profession: A large part of the "action" of economic models—the strong conclusions they support—does not derive from the assumptions of objective rationality at all, but depends on auxiliary assumptions that are introduced to provide limits to that rationality, assumptions about the process of decision.

This being the case, one would suppose that a great deal of attention would be devoted to the empirical validity or plausibility of the auxiliary assumptions—in the examples just cited, the assumptions that labor or business, as the case may be, suffers from a money illusion. However, this is not the way the practices and traditions of economics have developed. Instead, there is a tradition that is often referred to, within economics itself, as "casual empiricism." Assumptions about the shape of the utility function or the limits on the rationality of economic actors are commonly made in an armchair, on the basis of feelings of "plausibility" or "reasonableness," and without systematic support from empirical evidence. The assumptions are never tested directly, but only in the context of the models in which they are embedded. The goodness of fit of a model, usually to aggregate data, is regarded as the best justification for the assumptions embedded in that model, whatever their source.[8]

Bounded Rationality Is Not Irrationality

Skepticism about substituting a priori postulates about rationality for factual knowledge of human behavior should not be mistaken for a claim that people are generally "irrational." On the contrary, I think there is plenty of evidence that people are generally quite rational; that is to say, they usually have reasons for what they do. Even in madness, there is almost always method, as Freud was at great pains to point out. And putting madness aside for a moment, almost all human behavior consists of sequences of goal-oriented actions.

When, in spite of the evidence for this goal-oriented character of human behavior, we call some of that behavior "irrational," we may mean any one of several things. We may deem behavior irrational because, although it serves some particular impulse, it is inconsistent with other goals that seem to us more important. We may deem it irrational because the actor is proceeding on incorrect facts or ignoring whole areas of relevant fact. We may deem it irrational because the actor has not drawn the correct conclusions from the facts. We may deem it irrational because the actor has failed to consider important alternative courses of action. If the action involves the future, as most action does, we may deem it irrational because we don't think the actor uses the best methods for forming expectations or for adapting to uncertainty. All of these forms of "irrationality" play important roles in the lives of every one of us, but I think it is misleading to call them "irrationality." They are better viewed as forms of bounded rationality.

To understand and predict human behavior, we have to deal with the realities of human rationality, that is, with bounded rationality. There is nothing obvious about these boundaries; there is no way to predict, a priori, just where they lie.

THE RATIONALITY PRINCIPLE IN POLITICS

After this long excursion into the views of human rationality that are commonly held in psychology and economics, let me come back now to the subject of political science. What kind of rationality does *Homo politicus* exhibit? Is he or she a creature of objective, substantive rationality; or instead, one of subjective, procedural rationality? But I am afraid that I have already tipped my hand and made it quite clear that I believe the latter to be the case.

If that is true, the rationality principle, as it is incorporated in theories of substantive rationality, will provide us with only limited help in understanding political phenomena. Before we apply the methods of economic reasoning to political behavior, we must characterize the political situation, not as it appears "objectively" to the analyst, but as it appears subjectively to the actors. We can only select the appropriate model of adaptation after we undertake the requisite empirical study to determine this subjective representation both of goals and of the situation or draw upon research in cognitive psychology to tell us about the nature of that representation. A few examples drawn from the political science literature will show what is involved.

An Example: Duverger's Law

Recently, William Riker (1982) provided us with an instructive account of a descriptive generalization that usually goes by the name of Duverger's Law. In its roughest form, the law asserts that plurality election rules bring about and maintain two-party, rather than multi-party, competition. In an informative way, Riker takes us through the history of the empirical research that has been done to test, to confirm, refute, or amend, this law. He also shows that political scientists have not been content simply to assert the law, or to test it empirically; they have also sought to "explain" it. He says:

From the first enunciation by Droop, the law has been implicitly embedded in a rational choice theory about the behavior of politicians and voters. This theory has been rendered more and more explicit, especially in the last two decades, so that recent empirical work consciously invokes the rational choice model. (1982, p. 766)

The so-called rational choice argument for Duverger's Law goes something like this. If a number of candidates are running for office under a plurality election rule, and if candidates A and B are well ahead of the pack so that it is unreasonable to suppose that any other candidate will win, then it is rational to limit your vote to your preference between A and B. The argument has to be elaborated somewhat to account for two-party configurations that are stable over time, but I think that I have conveyed the general idea.

What assumptions does this argument make about you, the voter. First, it assumes that you have a preference ranking among candidates and wish to vote so as to secure the election of a candidate who is as high as possible on your ranking. Second, it assumes that you believe that one vote may decide the election (otherwise it is indifferent, in terms of the stated goal to whom the vote goes). Third, it assumes that you have an assessment of the relative prospects of the candidates, and a considerable confidence in that assessment (e.g., you do *not* believe that one more vote could bring success to any but one of the two candidates judged to have the most support). Fourth, it assumes that you do not attach a large value to providing public evidence that your most preferred candidate has extensive, even if not pluralistic, public support.

Since I have not tried to construct a formal axiomization of this choice, perhaps there are other assumptions that must be made, in addition to those listed above. For the purposes of the present argument, however, my inventory of assumptions will suffice. What the assumptions show is that only a small part of the work of explaining Duverger's Law is being done by the rationality principle. Most of the work is being done by propositions that characterize the utility function of the voter and his or her beliefs, expectations, and calculations—that is to say, the limits of rationality. These propositions are subject to empirical test.

Perhaps the key assumption here is the postulate of "sophisticated voting," that a rational voter believes "his vote should be expended as part of a selection process, not as an expression of preference" (Downs, 1957, p. 48). But this postulate is wholly independent of the usual definition of objective rationality. There is no irrationality in a utility function that regards a vote as an expression of preference rather than an attempt to influence the selection. In fact, it is realistic to believe that one can express a preference (i.e., change the numerical result of the vote, if only by a unit), but seldom realistic to believe that one can affect the outcome of an election. Moreover, a voter might correctly (or incorrectly, but certainly not irrationally) believe that expression of preference for a party could increase the chances of that party's succeeding in subsequent elections.

There are many more changes we can ring on the possible beliefs of voters without impugning their (subjective) rationality. With these alternative sets of beliefs are associated different voting behaviors. It is not at all hard to build a rational model of the voter who stays home from the polls and does not vote at all. Hence, we get very little understanding or explanation of voting behavior simply from invoking the principle of utility maximization. That principle does not exempt us from the arduous task of testing all the auxiliary empirical assumptions about voters' values, beliefs, and expectations. And, as Riker shows us, when we subject an auxiliary assumption like the postulate of sophisticated voting to empirical test, we discover that the actual pattern of human response can be very complex indeed. We are then constructing and testing theories of bounded rationality, not theories of substantive rationality.

Additional Examples

It should not be thought that Duverger's Law is an isolated case and that rational choice theories derived from the assumption of utility maximization and unalloyed with auxiliary assumptions about preferences and beliefs have much more predictive and explanatory power in most other cases. Recent issues of the *American Political Science Review* provide a rich mine of examples that support our analysis of the respective roles of reason and fact. One can stumble upon such examples by opening the pages almost at random, and it appears to make little difference whether the author is a behavioralist or an economic rationalist by persuasion. (Or if there is a difference, it is that the behavioralist makes fewer explicit claims for rationality as the source of his or her conclusions than does the rational choice theorist.)

My next example is a study by Hibbs (1982) of "Economic Outcomes and Political Support for British Governments among Occupational Classes." Hibbs demonstrates that various indicators of the health of the British economy are related to voting preferences. Score one for the objective rationality principle. Presumably voters vote for the party that they think will enhance their economic well-being. But how do we get from that general proposition to a prediction of their vote? We can make the leap only if we can discover how voters *judge* which party will do the better job of managing the economy. There are many ways in which that judgment could be made, none of them, probably, having high objective validity.

Hence, the interesting and significant finding of Hibbs's study is not that people employ a rationality principle. The interesting finding, which does not follow from such a principle, is that "voters evaluate the cumulative performance of the governing party relative to the prior performance of the current opposition," weighting current performance more heavily than past performance (p. 259).

Now I don't know if Hibbs's model will hold up under further analysis or will apply equally well to other times and places. However valid or invalid the model, its powerful motor is not a theory of objectively rational choice but a very specific empirical assumption, based on notions of bounded rationality, about how voters form their beliefs regarding the connections between the economy and government. If Hibbs's model is correct, voters do this not by solving a maximization problem but by setting an aspiration level (the opposition's past performance) against which to measure the performance of the incumbents. This is what modern cognitive theory would lead us to expect, but not what would be predicted by a theory of utility maximization.

A third example has to do with the application of rationality principles to a game resembling the prisoners' dilemma, but allowing the players the additional alternative of exiting from the situation (Orbell, Schwartz-Shea, and Simmons, 1984). In their abstract, the authors, using the usual distinction between defectors and cooperators in the prisoners' dilemma, sum up the matter very well:

> We derive the prediction that the exit option will drain the community or group more of cooperators than of defectors.
>
> But experimental data do not support this prediction; cooperators do not leave more frequently than defectors. . . . [We] present data supporting the hypothesis that cooperators often stay when their personal interest is with exiting because of the same ethical or group-regarding impulse that (presumably) led them to cooperate in the first place.

In this experiment, again, the principle of objective rationality contributes little to predicting or explaining the findings. Everything rests, instead, on the assumptions that are made about the utility functions of two classes of players, those who are prepared to cooperate with the other players and those who are prepared to betray them. What is more, to explain the behavior of the cooperators, a strong component of altruism must be introduced into their utility functions.[9]

Other research within a game-theoretical framework shares many of the characteristics of this study. The predicted outcome depends sensitively upon assumptions not derivable from the principle of objective rationality, about participants' beliefs and values. For example, in a study involving the conditions under which subjects would contribute to the provision of public goods, the authors summarize their findings thus (van de Kragt, Orbell, and Dawes, 1983, p. 112):

> We present hypotheses about why designating a minimal contributing set works. . . . The essential property of the minimal contributing set . . . is *criticalness*: the contributions of the members of the minimal contributing set are each critical to obtaining the public good the members desire, and they know it. It is reasonable (albeit not a dominant strategy) to contribute because reasonable behavior can be expected from other minimal contributing set members who are in the same situation.

What is called reasonable behavior here is clearly the behavior we might expect of a creature of bounded rationality. And its reasonableness depends on expectations about the behavior of others.

Perhaps the major contribution of game theory to political science has been to demonstrate how rare and unusual the situations are where a game has a stable equilibrium solution consistent with the principle of objectively rational choice. Under these circumstances, the task of determining how people actually do behave in situations having game-like characteristics must be turned over to empirical research: research that seeks to determine what values people actually act on, and how they form their expectations and beliefs.

My final example concerns considerations of economic advantage in voting decisions. Weatherford (1983) points out that the concept of economic voting is ambiguous. It may mean voting in response to perceptions of one's own economic well-being, or voting in response to perceptions of the health of the economy. But this distinction is itself ambiguous, for it may refer to differences in utility functions or to differences in the voter's model of reality.

You, the voter, may want to vote for the candidate who will do best for you (for example, support the "right" kinds of tax laws, impose or remove the "right" kinds of regulations), or for the candidate who will best foster the vigor of the whole economy, even if it costs you, personally, a loss of income or of a job. Put in these terms, the difference lies in the structure of your utility function.

But we can look at the matter in a different way. How do you judge the state of the economy or your well-being? You can use the immediate evidence of your personal situation—your employment or unemployment, your salary, your taxes. Or you can look at published economic indexes. And, because the question before you is not the current state of the economy, but how it is likely to be affected if one candidate or another is elected, there are still other kinds of evidence that may influence you. You may consider the candidates' past voting records or the economic predispositions of the parties to which they belong.

Differences in the kinds of evidence you respond to may have nothing to do with your utility function. Instead, they may reflect the model you have of the world, the beliefs you have formed about the meanings and predictive value of different kinds of available information, and what information has come to your attention.

All of these examples teach us the same lesson: the actors in the political drama do appear to behave in a rational manner—they have reasons for what they do, and a clever researcher can usually obtain data that give good clues as to what those reasons are. But this is very different from claiming that we can predict the behavior of these rational actors by application of the objective rationality principle to the situations in which they find themselves. Such prediction is impossible, both because, even within the framework of the SEU theory of substantive rationality, behavior depends on the structure of the actors' utility functions, and because it depends on their representation of the world in which they live, what they attend to in that world, and what beliefs they have about its nature.

The obvious corollary is that rationalism can carry us only a little way in political analysis, even in the analysis of the behavior of boundedly rational people. The rest of the path requires continuing, painstaking empirical investigation within the framework of modern cognitive theories of human behavior.

Rationalism and Empiricism

I should not like my comments to be interpreted as a complaint that political science worships at the altar of rational choice theory. On the contrary, I think we political scientists have generally been behaving quite well in this respect. If I take the pages of the *American Political Science Review* as representing the attitudes and methods of our discipline, then I observe that there is a healthy respect for sophisticated empirical research. Assumptions of rationality are used to provide a framework for analyzing behavior, but they are generally used tentatively, and with a sensitivity to the assumptions of value, expectation, and belief that have to be added to the models before they can yield predictions of behavior.

Authors who use rational choice models are not always conscious of the extent to which their conclusions are independent of the assumptions of those models, but depend, instead, mainly upon auxiliary assumptions. Nor is advantage taken as often as it could be of the knowledge of cognitive mechanisms to be found in the psychological literature. But these defects, if defects they be, are easily remedied.

It is also a good omen for the future of our science that empirical work means both the study of social aggregates, whose behavior is recorded in public statistics, and the study of the individual actors at the microscopic and face-to-face level of the interview and the poll. The graduate training we provide our students gives them opportunities to acquire skill in both kinds of empirical methodology, and others (e.g., historical inquiry) as well. In this respect, we are better off than our brethren in economics, who are seldom trained in the skills of observing economic phenomena at first hand.

We sometimes, perhaps, experience a mild malaise in that our research does not seem to be taking us in the direction of a few sweeping generalizations that encompass the whole of political behavior. A hope of finding our "three laws of motion" was probably a major part of the appeal of rational choice theory in its purer forms. But a more careful look at the natural sciences would show us that they, too, get only a little mileage from their general laws. Those laws have to be fleshed out by a myriad of facts, all of which must be harvested by laborious empirical research. Perhaps our aspirations for lawfulness should be modeled upon the complexities of molecular biology—surely a successful science, but hardly a neat one—rather than upon the simplicities of classical mechanics.

RADICAL IRRATIONALITY

Thus far, I have dealt with the picture of procedural rationality that emerges from modern cognitive psychology and the relation between that picture and the economist's notion of substantive rationality. My main conclusion is that the key premises in any theory that purports to explain the real phenomena of politics are the empirical assumptions about goals and, even more important, about the ways in which people characterize the choice situations that face them. These goals and characterizations do not rest on immutable first principles, but are functions of time and place that can only be ascertained by empirical inquiry. In this sense, political science is necessarily a historical science, in the same way and for the same reason that astronomy is. What will happen next is not independent of where the system is right now. And a description of where it is right now must include a description of the subjective view of the situation that informs the choices of the actors.

But you may feel that I have not gone far enough in my skepticism about reason in political behavior. Surely even the concept of bounded rationality does not capture the whole role of passion and unreason in human affairs. Don't we need to listen to Lasswell and Freud as well as to Wallas and James?

Assuredly we do. From the earliest times it has been seen that human behavior is not always the result of deliberate calculation, even of a boundedly rational kind. Sometimes it must be attributed to passion, to the capture of the decision process by powerful impulses that do not permit the mediation of thought. The criminal law takes explicit account of passion in assigning different penalties to deliberate and impulsive acts.

In psychoanalytic theory, passion takes mainly the form of unconscious drives, largely unknown to the actor, that provide the "real" wellsprings of action. This approach, whether it be correct or false, has always been troublesome for empirical research, because it makes suspect human testimony about motives.[10] If we don't know why we act, if our motives are unconscious, then we can't report them, no matter how much we wish to cooperate with the researcher.

Let me take a more conservative approach, which accords well with what we know about the mechanisms that link emotions to reason (Simon, 1978, chapter 1.3). People are endowed with very large long-term memories, but with very narrow capacities for simultaneous attention to different pieces of information. At any given moment, only a little information, drawn from the senses and from long-term memory, can be held in the focus of attention. This information is not static; it is continuously being processed and transformed, with one item being replaced by another as new aspects of a stimulus are sensed, new inferences drawn, or new bits of information retrieved from long-term memory. Nevertheless, of all the things we know, or can see or hear around us, only a tiny fraction influences our behavior over any short interval of time.

If a particular strong drive takes control of our attention, determining not only our goals of the moment but also selecting out the sensory and memory facts that we will consider, then behavior can be determined by that drive or passion as long as its control persists. But passionate behavior in this extreme form is exceptional and not common in human behavior. The control process is usually more complex.

Even in the case of a person like Hitler, whose behavior might be interpreted by some clinicians as a pure instance of an all-consuming hatred or self-hatred, a large cognitive element intrudes into the behavior. Hitler was not just angry; he directed his hatred toward a particular group of people, Jews, and he made decisions that were arguably rational on the premise that the Jewish people were to be extirpated to satisfy that hatred.

For some purposes of political analysis, it may be enough to postulate the overtly expressed values and goals without seeking their deeper roots in the unconscious, or at least without trying to explain how they arrived there.

The methodological lesson I would draw is that we need to understand passion and to provide for it in our political models, but we need particularly to provide in those models for the limited span of attention that governs *what* considerations, out of a whole host of possible ones, will actually influence the deliberations that precede action. In particular, we need to understand the conditions that predispose human beings to impulsive action that disregards much of the potentially relevant reality. I would like to comment on three aspects of this question: the nature of the attention mechanism, the role of uncertainty, and the process whereby novel ways of viewing situations are evoked or generated.

Attention

The human eye and ear are highly parallel devices, capable of extracting many pieces of information simultaneously from the environment and decoding them into their significant features. Before this information can be used by the deliberative mind, however, it must proceed through the bottleneck of attention—a serial, not parallel, process whose information capacity is exceedingly small. Psychologists usually call this bottleneck short-term memory, and measurements show reliably that it can hold only about six chunks (that is to say, six familiar items) of information.

The details of short-term memory and the bottleneck of attention are not important for our purposes. What is important is that only one or a very few things can be attended to simultaneously. The limits can be broadened a bit, but only modestly, by "time-sharing"—switching attention periodically. The narrowness of the span of attention accounts for a great deal of human unreason that considers only one facet of a multi-faceted matter before a decision is reached.

For example, it has been hypothesized that the art of campaign oratory is much more an art of directing attention (to the issues on which the candidate believes himself or herself to have the broadest support) than an art of persuading people to change their minds on issues.[11] Similarly, shifts in expressed voting intentions during the course of an election campaign have been explained as caused by evocation of beliefs and attitudes already latent in voters' minds (e.g., party loyalties) (Lazarsfeld et al., 1948, chapter 9). Another example, highly characteristic of the political process, was the shift of attention from environmental problems to problems of energy supply that took place immediately after the Oil Shock, and that greatly altered public priorities for a number of years.

The unreason associated with attention focusing has no necessary connection with passion—cold reasoning can be as narrow and one-sided as hot reasoning. But the existence of these narrow limits on the span of human attention is a principal reason why we must distinguish between the "real" situation and the situation as perceived by the political actors when we try to apply the rationality principle to make predictions of behavior. People are, at best, rational in terms of what they are aware of, and they can be aware of only tiny, disjointed facets of reality.

Uncertainty

Lack of reliable knowledge and information is a major factor in almost all real-life decision making. In our soberer moments, we realize how little we know and can predict about the decision-making premises and processes of the rulers of the USSR. Yet the content of a rational foreign policy is highly sensitive to our hypotheses about these matters. The effects of the policies of the President upon the well-being of the American economy are only slightly less uncertain. At least there is often little consensus in the economics profession about these effects.

Wherever such uncertainties are present, an enhanced opportunity is provided for unconscious, or only partly conscious, drives and wishes to influence deliberation. Where the facts are clear (to the actors as well as to us), we have some chance, by application of the principles of reason, to calculate what the choice will be. Where evidence is weak and conflicting, a rationality principle has little independent predictive power.

Evocation

Finally, to understand political choices, we need to understand where the frame of reference for the actors' thinking comes from—how it is evoked. An important component of the frame of reference is the set of alternatives that are given consideration in the choice process. We need to understand not only how people reason about alternatives, but where the alternatives come from in the first place. The process whereby alternatives are generated has been somewhat ignored as an object of research.

But not wholly ignored! Turning again to my favorite source of information on the state of the profession, I find in a recent issue of the *American Political Science Review* another imaginative paper by William Riker, in fact his 1983 Presidential Address to the Association, on precisely this issue. (I could wish that he had not invented the word "heresthetics" to conceal the heresies he is propagating.) Riker traces the history of proposals in the Constitutional Convention for electing the President, with particular concern for the generation of new alternatives, and for the shifts in attention and emphasis on issues that accompanied their introduction.

Riker speaks of these matters in terms of "artistry within the rational choice context." I think that the generation of alternatives is much more than that: that it is an integral component of any veridical account of human decision making, or of human bounded rationality generally. The theory of the generation of alternatives deserves, and requires, a treatment that is just as definitive and thorough as the treatment we give to the theory of choice among prespecified alternatives.

But is such a treatment possible? Are we not treading upon the sacred precincts of creativity? Indeed we are; but I think the precincts are no longer sacrosanct. The same cognitive psychology that has been elaborating the theory of human bounded rationality has made considerable progress toward constructing models of the processes of discovery and creativity that can account for these processes in terms quite akin to those it uses to account for ordinary problem solving. Again, I cannot tell that story here but must limit myself to pointers to the literature (Bradshaw, Langley, and Simon, 1983; Lenat, 1983).

CONCLUSION

In this essay I have tried to provide an overview—a very general one—of our current knowledge of human nature in politics. I first undertook to compare the two principal theories of human rationality that have found application in political research: the procedural bounded rationality theory that has its origins in contemporary cognitive psychology, and the substantive global rationality theory that has been nurtured chiefly in economics. Then, by means of a series of examples, I examined the relative roles played by rationality principles and by the auxiliary assumptions that accompany them, respectively, in predicting and explaining human behavior in political contexts. Finally, I commented on the more extreme deviations from the objective rationality model that exhibit themselves in political affairs, and showed how they could be explained, in considerable measure, in terms of the mechanisms of attention and the severe limits that the architecture of the mind places on the span of human attention.

My overview, if it is even partly valid, carries a number of implications for research in political science. First, it dissipates the illusion, if anyone holds it, that an application of principles of rationality can discharge us, to any considerable degree, from the need to carry on painstaking empirical research at both macro and micro levels. It is far easier (for the political scientist and for the political actor) to calculate the rational response to a fully specified situation than it is to arrive at a reasonable specification of the situation. And there is no way, without empirical study, to predict which of innumerable reasonable specifications the actors will adopt.

Second, my overview suggests that the study of the mechanisms of attention directing, situation defining, and evoking are among the most promising targets of political research. In particular, the question of where political ideas come from is not only highly deserving of study, but also within the competence of our contemporary research techniques. I join Bill Riker in commending it to you as one of the truly exciting and significant areas of investigation in our field.

Nothing is more fundamental in setting our research agenda and informing our research methods than our view of the nature of the human beings whose behavior we are studying. It makes a difference, a very large difference, to our research strategy whether we are studying the nearly omniscient *Homo economicus* of rational choice theory or the boundedly rational *Homo psychologicus* of cognitive psychology. It makes a difference to research, but it also makes a difference for the proper design of political institutions. James Madison[12] was well aware of that, and in the pages of the *Federalist Papers* he opted for this view of the human condition (*Federalist*, No. 55):

> As there is a degree of depravity in mankind which requires a certain degree of circumspection and distrust, so there are other qualities in human nature which justify a certain portion of esteem and confidence.

—a balanced and realistic view, we may concede, of bounded human rationality and its accompanying frailties of motive and reason.

NOTES

1. See David Eastman's perceptive account of this history in his article on political science in the *International Encyclopedia of the Social Sciences* (1968).
2. For a more extensive discussion of the concepts of substantive and procedural rationality, see Simon (1976b), reprinted as chapter 8.3 in Simon (1982).
3. See Ericsson and Simon (1984).
4. See, for example, Newell and Simon (1972), Simon (1979), and Anderson (1983).
5. A classical treatment is Savage (1954).
6. For a number of examples and references to the literature, see Kahneman, Slovic, and Tversky (1982).
7. This account is based on Simon (1984).
8. Friedman's well-known methodological essay transforms these methodological practices into a strongly defended doctrine. Friedman argues that direct tests of the behavioral assumptions underlying an economic model are superfluous at best, and positively misleading at the worst.
9. For a discussion of the problems of reconciling altruism with rationality in systems subject to evolutionary selection, see Simon (1983, chapter 2).
10. For a review of some reasons why we should suspect testimony about motives, see Nisbett and Wilson (1977). The authors of that study draw conclusions that are rather too broad for their evidence, but their main point about reports of motivation is well taken. See also Ericsson and Simon (1984).
11. For a classic statement of this hypothesis, see Lazarsfeld, Berelson, and Gaudet (1948, chapter 8).
12. Or was it Hamilton? Mosteller and Wallace (1964) attribute No. 55 of *The Federalist* to Madison, but it is the least certain of their attributions of the numbers whose authorship has been disputed. Since the sentiment quoted here is certainly consistent with the beliefs of both authors, we need not be too concerned with the uncertainty of authorship.

REFERENCES

Anderson, J. *The architecture of cognition.* Cambridge, Mass.: Harvard University Press, 1983.

Bradshaw, G. F., Langley, P. W., and Simon, H. A. Studying scientific discovery by computer simulation. *Science*, 1983, *222* (Dec. 2), 971–975.

Carbonell, J. G. *Subjective understanding: Computer models of belief systems.* New Haven, Conn.: Yale University Dept. of Computer Science, 1979.

Crecine, J. P. *Governmental problem solving: A computer simulation of municipal budgeting.* Chicago: Rand McNally, 1969.

Downs, A. *An economic theory of democracy.* New York: Harper & Row, 1957.

Eastman, D. Political science. In D. L. Sills (Ed.). *International encyclopedia of the social sciences* (vol. 12). New York: Macmillan, 1968, pp. 282–298.

Ericsson, K., and Simon, H. A. *Protocol analysis: Verbal reports as data.* Cambridge, Mass.: MIT Press, 1984.

Friedman, M. The methodology of positive economics. In *Essays in positive economics.* Chicago: University of Chicago Press, 1953.

_____. The role of monetary policy. *American Economic Review*, 1968, *58*, 1–17.

Gerwin, B. *Budgeting public funds: The decision process in an urban school district.* Madison: University of Wisconsin Press, 1969.

Hibbs, D. A., Jr. Economic outcomes and political support for British governments among occupational classes: A dynamic analysis. *American Political Science Review*, 1982, *76*, 259–279.

Kahneman, D., Slovic, P., and Tversky, A. (Eds.). *Judgment under uncertainty: Heuristics and biases.* New York: Cambridge University Press, 1982.

Keynes, J. M. *The general theory of employment, interest and money.* London: Macmillan, 1936.

van de Kragt, A. J. C., Orbell, J. M., and Dawes, R. M. The minimal contributing set as a solution to public goods problems. *American Political Science Review*, 1983, *77*, 112–122.

Lasswell, H. *Psychopathology and politics.* Chicago: University of Chicago Press, 1934.

_____. *World politics and personal insecurity.* New York: McGraw-Hill, 1935.

Lazarsfeld, P. S., Berelson, B., and Gaudet, H. *The people's choice* (2nd ed.). New York: Columbia University Press, 1948.

Lenat, D. B. EURISKO. A program that learns new heuristics and domain concepts. *Artificial Intelligence*, 1983, *21*, 61–98.

Lippmann, W. *Public opinion.* New York: Macmillan (1922/1944).

Lucas, R. E., Jr. *Studies in business cycle theory.* Cambridge, Mass.: MIT Press, 1981.

Lucas, R. E., Jr., and Sargent, T. J. (Eds.). *Rational expectation and economic practice.* Minneapolis: University of Minnesota Press, 1981.

Mosteller, F., and Wallace, D. W. *Influence and disputed authorship: The Federalist.* Reading, Mass.: Addison-Wesley, 1964.

Newell, A., and Simon, H. A. *Human problem solving.* Englewood Cliffs, N.J.: Prentice Hall, 1972.

Nisbett, R. E., and Wilson, T. D. Telling more than we know: Verbal reports on mental processes. *Psychological Review*, 1977, *84*, 231–259.

Orbell, J. M., Schwartz-Shea, P., and Simmons, R. T. Do cooperators exit more readily than defectors? *American Political Science Review*, 1984, *78*, 147–162.

Riker, W. H. The heresthetics of constitution-making. The presidency in 1787, with comments on determinism and rational choice. *American Political Science Review*, 1984, *78*, 1–16.

———. The two-party system and Duverger's Law: An essay on the history of political science. *American Political Science Review*, 1982, *76*, 753–766.

Savage, L. J. *The foundation of statistics*. New York: Wiley, 1954.

Simon, H. A. *Administrative behavior*. New York: Free Press, 1947/1976. (a)

———. A behavioral model of rational choice. *Quarterly Journal of Economics*, 1955, *69*, 99–118. Reprinted in H. A. Simon. *Models of bounded rationality* (vol. 2, chap. 7.2). Cambridge, Mass.: MIT Press, 1982.

———. From substantive to procedural rationality. In S. J. Latsis (Ed.). *Method and appraisal in economics*. Cambridge: Cambridge University Press, 1976, pp. 129–148. (b)

———. *Models of bounded rationality*. Cambridge, Mass.: MIT Press, 1982.

———. *Models of thought*. New Haven, Conn.: Yale University Press, 1979.

———. Motivational and emotional controls of cognition. In *Models of thought*. New Haven, Conn.: Yale University Press, 1978, chap. 1.3.

———. On the behavioral and rational foundation of economic dynamics. *Journal of Economic Behavior and Organization*, 1984, *5*, 35–55.

———. *Reason in human affairs*. Stanford, Calif.: Stanford University Press, 1983.

Wallas, G. *Human nature in politics* (4th ed.). Gloucester, Mass.: Smith, 1908/1944.

Weatherford, M. S. Economic voting and the "symbolic politics" argument: A reinterpretation and synthesis. *American Political Science Review*, 1983, *77*, 158–174.

8

Political Consciousness and the Means of Production

KARL MARX

The fact is . . . that definite individuals who are productively active in a definite way enter into . . . definite social and political relations. Empirical observation must in each separate instance bring out empirically, and without any mystification and speculation, the connection of the social and political structure with production. The social structure and the State are continually evolving out of the life-process of definite individuals, but individuals, not as they may appear in their own or other people's imagination, but as they really are; i.e., as they are effective, produce materially, and are active under definite material limits, presuppositions and conditions independent of their will.

The production of ideas, of conceptions, of consciousness, is at first directly interwoven with the material activity and the material intercourse of men, the language of real life. Conceiving, thinking, the mental intercourse of men, appear at this stage as the direct efflux of their material behavior. The same applies to mental production as expressed in the language of the politics, laws, morality, religion, metaphysics of a people. Men are the producers of their conceptions, ideas, etc.—real, active men, as they are conditioned by a definite development of their productive forces and of the intercourse corresponding to these, up to its furthest forms. Consciousness can never be anything else than conscious existence, and the existence of men is their actual life-process. If in all ideology men and their circumstances appear upside down as in a *camera obscura*, this phenomenon arises just as much from their historical life-process as the inversion of objects on the retina does from their physical life-process.

In direct contrast to German philosophy which descends from heaven to earth, here

103

we ascend from earth to heaven. That is to say, we do not set out from what men say, imagine, conceive, nor from men as narrated, thought of, imagined, conceived, in order to arrive at men in the flesh. We set out from real, active men, and on the basis of their real life-process we demonstrate the development of the ideological reflexes and echoes of this life-process. The phantoms formed in the human brain are also, necessarily, sublimates of their material life-process, which is empirically verifiable and bound to material premises. Morality, religion, metaphysics, all the rest of ideology and their corresponding forms of consciousness, thus no longer retain the semblance of independence. They have no history, no development; but men, developing their material production and their material intercourse, alter, along with this their real existence, their thinking and the products of their thinking. Life is not determined by consciousness, but consciousness by life. In the first method of approach the starting-point is consciousness taken as the living individual; in the second it is the real living individuals themselves, as they are in actual life, and consciousness is considered solely as *their* consciousness.

This method of approach is not devoid of premises. It starts out from the real premises and does not abandon them for a moment. Its premises are men, not in any fantastic isolation or abstract definition, but in their actual, empirically perceptible process of development under definite conditions. As soon as this active life-process is described, history ceases to be a collection of dead facts as it is with the empiricists (themselves still abstract), or an imagined activity of imagined subjects, as with the idealists.

Where speculation ends—in real life—there real, positive science begins: the representation of the practical activity, of the practical process of development of men. Empty talk about consciousness ceases, and real knowledge has to take its place. When reality is depicted, philosophy as an independent branch of activity loses its medium of existence. At the best its place can only be taken by a summing-up of the most general results, abstractions which arise from the observation of the historical development of men. Viewed apart from real history, these abstractions have in themselves no value whatsoever. They can only serve to facilitate the arrangement of historical material, to indicate the sequence of its separate strata. But they by no means afford a recipe or schema, as does philosophy, for neatly trimming the epochs of history. On the contrary, our difficulties begin only when we set about the observation and the arrangement—the real depiction—of our historical material, whether of a past epoch or of the present. The removal of these difficulties is governed by premises which it is quite impossible to state here, but which only the study of the actual life-process and the activity of the individuals of each epoch will make evident. We shall select here some of these abstractions, which we use to refute the ideologists, and shall illustrate them by historical examples.

The ideas of the ruling class are in every epoch the ruling ideas: i.e., the class, which is the ruling material force of society, is at the same time its ruling intellectual force. The class which has the means of material production at its disposal, has control at the same time over the means of mental production, so that thereby, generally speaking, the ideas of those who lack the means of mental production are subject to it. The ruling ideas are nothing more than the ideal expression of the dominant material relationships, the dominant material relationships grasped as ideas; hence of the relationships which make the one class the ruling one, therefore the ideas of its dominance. The individuals composing the ruling class possess among other things consciousness, and therefore think. In so far, therefore, as they rule as a class and determine the extent and compass of an epoch, it is self-evident that they do this in their whole range, hence among other things rule also as thinkers, as producers of ideas, and regulate the production and distribution of the ideas of their age: thus their ideas are the ruling ideas of the epoch. For instance, in an age and in a country where royal power, aristocracy and bourgeoisie are contending for mastery and where, therefore, mastery is shared, the doctrine of the separation of powers proves to be the dominant idea and is expressed as an "eternal law." The division of labor, which we saw above as one of the chief forces of history up till now, manifests itself in the ruling class as the division of mental and material labor, so that inside this class one part appears as the thinkers of the class (its active, conceptive ideologists, who make the perfecting of the illusion of the class about itself their chief source of livelihood), while the others' attitude to these ideas and illusions is more passive and receptive, because they are in reality the active members of this class and have less time to make up illusions and ideas about themselves. Within this class this cleavage can even develop into a certain opposition and hostility between the two parts, which, however, in the case of a practical collision, in which the class itself is endangered, automatically comes to nothing, in which case there also vanishes the semblance that the ruling ideas were not the ideas of the ruling class and had a power distinct from the power of this class. The existence of revolutionary ideas in a particular period presupposes the existence of a revolutionary class; about the premises for the latter sufficient has already been said above.

If now in considering the course of history we detach the ideas of the ruling class from the ruling class itself and attribute to them an independent existence, if we confine ourselves to saying that these or those ideas were dominant, without bothering ourselves about the conditions of production and the producers of these ideas, if we then ignore the individuals and world conditions which are the source of the ideas, we can say, for instance, that during the time that the aristocracy was dominant, the concepts honor, loyalty, etc., were dominant, during the dominance of the bourgeoisie the concepts freedom, equality, etc. The ruling class itself on the whole imagines this to be so. This conception of history, which is common to all historians, particularly since the eighteenth century, will necessarily come up against the phenomenon that increasingly abstract ideas hold sway, i.e., ideas which increasingly take on the form of universality. For each new class which puts itself in the place of one ruling before it, is compelled, merely in order to carry through its aim, to represent its interest as the common interest of all the members of society, put in an ideal form; it will give its ideas the form of universality, and represent them as the only rational, universally valid ones. The class making a revolution appears from the very start, merely because it is opposed to a *class*, not as a class but as the representative of the whole of society; it appears as the whole mass of society confronting the one ruling class. It can do this because, to start with, its interest really is more connected with the common interest of all other non-ruling classes, because under the pressure of conditions its interest has not yet been able to develop as the particular interest of a particular class. Its victory, therefore, benefits also many individuals of the other classes which are not winning a dominant position, but only in so far as it now puts these individuals in a position to raise themselves into the ruling class. When the French bourgeoisie overthrew the power of the aristocracy, it thereby made it possible for many proletarians to raise themselves above the proletariat, but only in so far as they become bourgeois. Every new class, therefore, achieves its hegemony only on a broader basis than that of the class ruling previously, in return for which the opposition of the non-ruling class against the new ruling class later develops all the more sharply and profoundly. Both these things determine the fact that the struggle to be waged against this new ruling class, in its turn, aims at a more decided and radical negation of the previous conditions of society than could all previous classes which sought to rule.

This whole semblance, that the rule of a certain class is only the rule of certain ideas, comes to a natural end, of course, as soon as society ceases at last to be organized in the form of class-rule, that is to say as soon as it is no longer necessary to represent a particular interest as general or "the general interest" as ruling.

Once the ruling ideas have been separated from the ruling individuals and, above all, from the relationships which result from a given stage of the mode of production, and in this way the conclusion has been reached that history is always under the sway of ideas, it is very easy to abstract from these various ideas "the idea," "die Idee," etc., as the dominant force in history, and thus to understand all these separate ideas and concepts as "forms of self-determination" on the part of *the* concept developing in history. It follows then naturally, too, that all the relationships of men can be derived from the concept of man, man as conceived, the essence of man, *man*. This has been done by the speculative philosophers. Hegel himself confesses at the end of *The Philosophy of History* that he "has considered the progress of *the concept* only" and has represented in history "the true theodicy." Now one can go back again to the "producers of the concept," to the theoreticians, ideologists and philosophers, and one comes then to the conclusion that the philosophers, the thinkers as such, have at all times been dominant in history: a conclusion, as we see, already expressed by Hegel. The whole trick of proving the hegemony of the spirit in history (hierarchy, Stirner calls it) is thus confined to the following three tricks.

1. One must separate the ideas of those ruling for empirical reasons, under empirical conditions and as empirical individuals, from these actual rulers, and thus recognize the rule of ideas or illusions in history.

2. One must bring an order into this rule of ideas, prove a mystical connection among the successive ruling ideas, which is managed by understanding them as "acts of self-determination on the part of the concept" (this is possible because by virtue of their empirical basis these ideas are really connected with one another and because, conceived as *mere* ideas, they become self-distinctions, distinctions made by thought).

3. To remove the mystical appearance of this "self-determining concept" it is changed into a person—"self-consciousness"—or, to appear thoroughly materialistic, into a series of persons, who represent the "concept" in history, into the "thinkers," the "philosophers," the ideologists, who again are understood as the manufacturers of history, as "the council of guardians," as the rulers. Thus the whole body of materialistic elements has been removed from history and now full rein can be given to the speculative steed.

While in ordinary life every shopkeeper is very well able to distinguish between what somebody professes to be and what really is, our historians have not yet won even this trivial insight. They take every epoch at its word and believe that everything it says and imagines about itself is true.

This historical method which reigned in Germany (and especially the reason why), must be understood from its connection with the illusion of ideologists in general, e.g., the illusions of the jurists, politicians (of the practical statesmen among them, too), from the dogmatic dreamings and distortions of these fellows; this illusion is explained perfectly easily from their practical position in life, their job, and the division of labor.

CHAPTER THREE

PERSONALITY AND POLITICAL LEADERSHIP

In this chapter, we explore the link between personality and politics, focusing on politically influential leaders. Our approach shares Fred Greenstein's (1987) assumption that,

> as one's perspective on political activity becomes closer and more detailed, the political actors begin to loom as full-blown individuals who are influenced in politically relevant ways by the various strengths and weaknesses to which the human species is subject. (p. 1)

Political participants, therefore, must be viewed "as more than role-players, creatures of situation, members of cultures, and possessors of social characteristics, such as occupation, class, sex, and age" (p. 1). Although it has been argued that the importance of personality variables is illusory and that they play only a minor part in comparison to objective, rational interests, the selections in this chapter proceed from an alternative orientation. They seek the keys to leaders' political behavior in the psychology of personality.[1]

The traits and styles of kings, presidents, prime ministers, generals, rebel leaders, and dictators provide the past with its color and texture. Exploits of the famous and infamous endow political history with magnificent plots, rescuing it from the tedium of social, political, and economic analysis. Nonetheless, exciting stories do not provide sufficient justification for the serious study of personality and politics.

In many eras, the personality characteristics of a few powerful people seem to shape the epoch. Consider, for example, the likely course of modern Western history if George Washington, Napoleon Bonaparte, Karl Marx, Prince Metternich, Abraham Lincoln, Otto von Bismarck, Woodrow Wilson, Josef Stalin, Adolf Hitler, and Franklin Delano

Roosevelt had never lived. Even small changes in the political activities of any one of these men might have shifted the course of world history. In each case, strong arguments can be made that the source of the leader's political actions and strength lay within his character.

Political psychologists devote much effort to identifying the psychological origins of the behavior of political leaders. Comprehensive political history requires political biography, and political biography calls for the interpretation of personality.

Nonetheless, the marriage of these areas of inquiry often breeds errors of reductionism. Despite the literary appeal of a focus on colorful individuals, we must consider the possibility that personalities merely tint rather than shape diagrams of the past. In addition, we should be careful not to reduce the behaviors of leaders operating in complex political environments to fodder for simplistic psychological theories.

Greenstein (1987) has theorized that the individual actions of leaders are most likely to influence political events under three conditions: (1) if the political environment "admits of restructuring," (2) if the leader is strategically placed within that environment, and (3) if the leader possesses the personal and cognitive skills necessary to manipulate the environment. Greenstein further speculates about the conditions under which the personal characteristics of leaders are most likely to affect their actions. Personality is apt to have the greatest impact when (among other conditions):

- The political situation is ambiguous;
- The political leader lacks "socially standardized mental sets" that might lead to the structuring of perceptions and the resolution of ambiguities;
- The leader does not face social sanctions for all alternative courses of action;
- The leader does not make his/her decision in a group context;
- The leader does not have an intense need to take cues from others;
- The leader possesses a strong affective involvement in politics;
- The political act in question is either spontaneous, a matter of style, or demands a great deal of effort.

Greenstein's model is complex, but plausible; he carves out a well-defined and important place for personality psychology in the study of political leadership. Other theorists have defined a smaller role for personality in the explanation of politics (Telhami, 1990), laying greater emphasis on the rational interests of political actors.

While mainstream political scientists fail to pay appropriate attention to personality (Holsti, 1989; Jervis, 1989), researchers of political personality have sometimes committed the opposite error—assuming personality is always relevant. A reasonable middle course would be to attend carefully to Greenstein and other theorists who attempt to specify the conditions under which personality affects political outcomes.

This chapter includes some of the more careful and insightful analyses. To better comprehend their contributions, we will briefly review the origin of psychological attempts to understand political leadership.

Throughout the history of political theory, philosophers have speculated about the traits of good and bad leaders. Machiavelli stands out as timeless, psychologically rich, and ethically provocative. In *The Prince*, he argues that the successful leader must engage in rational, hard-nosed, and unsentimental behavior. In Machiavelli's day—and even more so in our own—people had to struggle to obtain and keep power. We are left with the question of what type of person seeks political power and succeeds in acquiring it.

Harold Lasswell's (1930, 1948) early attempts to answer this question led to several extremely influential works in political psychology. Lasswell's (1948) main thesis was that the power-seeker pursues power to compensate against deprivation. "Power is expected to overcome low estimates of the self" (p. 39). Lasswell's framework was heavily psychoanalytic and, thus, emphasized the decisive importance of deprivation in early years as well as the unconscious nature of self-evaluation. But he realized that not all psychologically deprived people with low self-esteem become power-seeking politicians. This response is most likely when high self-estimates co-exist along with the low. In addition,

the reaction occurs when opportunities exist both for the displacement of ungratified cravings from the primary circle to public targets and for the rationalization of these displacements in the public interest; and, finally, when skills are acquired appropriate to the effective operation of the power-balancing process. (p. 53)

Lasswell's *homo politicus*, in his pure form, leaves us with a pessimistic theory of leadership; the power-seeker will sacrifice "anyone and everyone at convenience for his power, and does not conceive of power as a means of advancing the value position of family, neighborhood, nation, or any other group" (p. 56). He wants power for himself alone.

According to Lasswell, this pure type seldom emerges to fill positions of power. (A poignant exception was the "mad King Ludwig" of Bavaria who liked a little bit of human blood in his hunting bag.) Less intense variations on the same psychological theme abound in political history and provide cause for some concern.

Alexander George (1968), reflecting on his earlier (1956) biography of Woodrow Wilson, assessed the match between Wilson's case and Lasswell's theory. George concluded that the theory, in some respects, fit Wilson's behavior (and that of psychologically similar leaders) but that several caveats were in order. George concludes that,

If we may generalize provisionally from this one case, the demand or need for power in compensation-seeking personalities does not operate uniformly in the individual's political motivation under all conditions . . . *homo politicus* is likely to be a multi-valued personality; his striving for power as compensation may be reinforced by, or conflict with strong personal needs for other values that he may pursue in the political arena. (p. 89)

Although Lasswell is widely acknowledged as the most important early student of the psychology of political leadership, few contemporary scholars accept his compensation hypothesis in its original form. The power-seeking type has not been discredited, but many other political types have been identified (Greenstein, 1987; Lane, 1953; Stone & Schaffner, 1988). Moreover, most current approaches tend to focus less on pathological origins of political involvement and more on normal, even "healthy," roots of political ambition.

This chapter includes five influential approaches to the study of personality and political leadership: Etheredge (9), Barber (10), Winter (11), Sniderman (12), and Cocks (13).

Lloyd Etheredge's description of the practitioner of hardball politics resembles Lasswell's power-seeking personality. Etheredge's type is more limited in scope, however. It draws on Heinz Kohut's (1971) neo-Freudian discussion of narcissism (Etheredge, 1979). The hardball player is a cynically calculating, tremendously ambitious self-promoter; nonetheless, he or she, often, vies for power under an idealistic veneer. Hardball players instinctively understand Machiavelli's lessons and they display many tendencies of Christie and Geis' (1970) "machiavellian personality." Nonetheless, as Etheredge argues, they possess a complex psychoanalytic substructure.

James David Barber's typology of American presidents (10) has been very influential in political science, although it has also produced many critics. Barber's earlier work on the personalities of state legislators identified four types based upon two variables: activity in the legislature and attitude toward legislative membership. Barber suggested that superior performances most often came from Lawmakers, i.e., legislators high in activity and positively inclined toward their membership in the legislature (Barber, 1965). His similar typological model of presidential character first appeared in the late 1960s. It is important to note that Barber's theory is not merely a theory of presidential personality but also one that incorporates the power situation, the climate of expectations, the presidential style, and the president's worldview. He focuses on character, but he acknowledges the importance of other variables too. In the final chapter of the 1985 edition of *The Presidential Character*, Barber provides a spirited and detailed response to his critics; interested readers should consult that work.

In the next reading, David Winter also attempts to understand the personality of United States presidents. However, he applies a different psychological model to the task: David McClelland's theory of human motivation. McClelland's approach focuses on three central needs—for power, affiliation, and achievement. People differ in how much of each need they possess and, through scoring of unconscious content in a variety of materials created by the subject, McClelland identifies needs profiles. McClelland has used this approach to select appropriate personnel for jobs in government and industry; he has also been able to explain some trends in economic development by focusing on need for achievement in populations. Winter uses McClelland's approach to obtain need profiles for American presidents. He then uses this information to predict the appeal and performance of the presidents. Finally, Winter discusses his work in the context of other studies (Simonton, 1981) that downplay personality traits and motivation in the study of presidential performance.

The selection from Paul Sniderman's *Personality and Democratic Politics* develops a perspective that applies to the personalities of leaders and followers alike. For him, low self-esteem correlates with a wide array of attitudes that indicate suspicion of—or hostility toward—democracy. Those who participate in democratic politics, however, generally display signs of high self-esteem. Sniderman also offers an important perspective on the mechanism by which personality may influence political beliefs. While many prior studies had emphasized the relationship between personality and motivation, Sniderman concentrates on how personality characteristics can affect social learning. In light of this, he also hypothesizes that self-esteem can have radically different impacts on political beliefs, depending on the political situation in which the persona finds himself.

Geoffrey Cocks represents in this volume the psychohistorical tradition. He believes that careful analysis of psychoanalytic theorizing about historical figures can enhance our understanding of political leadership in the past.

Cocks's essay delineates the history of the psychohistorical approach and discusses the conditions under which psychoanalysis can be applied to the study of the past. (The second half of Cocks's essay, discussing psychobiographies of Hitler, is not included.) Even among those who accept the validity of psychoanalytic tenets and their applicability to historical analysis, there is widespread agreement that past psychobiographies often missed the mark. For example, Freud's own psychological study of Leonardo is now cited mainly as an example of how careless psychohistorians can commit egregious errors of interpretation (Elms, 1988). Geoffrey Cocks's thoughtful guidelines merit careful consideration by those who believe that psychohistory can make important contributions to historiography and political psychology.

NOTE

1. Although readings in this chapter pay particular attention to influential political leaders, personality psychology has been applied fruitfully to the explanation of mass political attitudes and behavior (Stone and Schaffner, 1988; Altemeyer, 1981; Inkeles, 1983). Research has considered variables such as authoritarianism, dogmatism, machiavellianism, locus of control, self-esteem, and others.

REFERENCES

Altemeyer, B. (1981). *Right-Wing Authoritarianism*. Winnepeg, Canada: University of Manitoba Press.

Barber, J. D. (1965). *The Lawmakers*. New Haven, CT: Yale University Press.

———. (1985). *Presidential Character* (Third ed.). Englewood Cliffs, NJ: Prentice-Hall.

Christie, R., & Geis, F. L. (1970). *Studies in Machiavellianism*. New York: Academic Press.

Elms, A. C. (1988). Freud as Leonardo: Why the first psychobiography went wrong. *Journal of Personality*, *56*(1), 19–40.

Etheredge, L. (1979). Hardball politics: A model. *Political Psychology*, *1*, 3–26.

George, A. L. (1968). Power as a compensatory value for political leaders. *Journal of Social Issues*, *24*, 29–49.

George, A. L., & George, J. L. (1956). *Woodrow Wilson and Colonel House*. New York: John Day.

Greenstein, F. I. (1987). *Personality and Politics: Problems of Evidence Inference and Conceptualization* (New ed.). Princeton, NJ: Princeton University Press.

Holsti, O. (1989). The political psychology of international politics: More than a luxury. *Political Psychology*, *10*(3), 495–500.

Inkeles, A. (1983). Exploring Individual Modernity. New York: Columbia University Press.

Jervis, R. (1989). Political psychology: some challenges and opportunities. *Political Psychology*, *10*(3), 481–494.

Kohut, H. (1971). *The Analysis of the Self.* New York: International Universities Press.

Lane, R. E. (1953). Political character and political analysis. *Psychiatry*, *16*, 387–398.

Lasswell, H. D. (1930). *Psychopathology and Politics*. Chicago: University of Chicago Press.

_____. (1948). *Power and Personality*. New York: W.W. Norton.

Simonton, D. K. (1981). Presidential greatness and performance: Can we predict leadership in the White House? *Journal of Personality*, *49*, 306–323.

Stone, W. F., & Schaffner, P. E. (1988). *The Psychology of Politics* (Second ed.). New York: Springer-Verlag.

Telhami, S. (1990). *Power and Leadership in International Bargaining: The Path to the Camp David Accords*. New York: Columbia University Press.

9

The Hardball Practitioner

LLOYD S. ETHEREDGE

The defining feature of a practitioner of hardball politics is the simultaneous existence of two different and unintegrated experiences of the self. Each is linked with a companion imagination system of larger-than-life drama that arrays other people and nations— regardless of physical reality—in this drama above or below the relevant sense of the self (viewpoint) of the knower.

In the foreground of the mind is a "lower," depleted, insecure self. Here is a sense of low self-esteem and of self-doubt, a strong propensity to feel inadequate and ashamed, continuing worry about social acceptability, discomfort with intimacy, fear of genuineness, candor, and self-revelation, insecurity and apprehension about (vaguely defined) impending disaster. But above and in the background there exists a wholly different, relatively split-off sector of the mind, a "grandiose self."[1] This sector includes fantasies and drives for grandiose accomplishment, total recognition and admiration, complete dominance of events of the world, and a complete self-confidence. It is a highly charged sector, and much of the individual's life is organized by it as an effort to establish himself subjectively in the ongoing social and political drama so that he will achieve recognition as its director, superior to the other participants.[2]

Moving from this basic description of two selves (and associated dramas) of a hardball-politics decision maker (HP), let me now elaborate the outline, jointly aligning personality tendencies and characteristics of hardball politics in a discussion of eight themes: ambition for the self; deficiencies of love and superficial interpersonal relations; twinship images of hardball opponents; weak ethics and disconnected moral restraint; defective humor; aggressiveness, tactical manipulativeness, and vanity; moderately dreamlike and emotionally organized mental processes; and hyperactivity.

Ambition

One could view the job of a politician or president solely as a tedious, stressful, overly demanding, ethically compromising, uncertain job, a psychodrama role forcing the individual to act out public fantasies and anxieties and be the target of everyone's complaints. But to the HP, in his internal psychodrama, it is inconceivable that anyone would want anything else, or any other associations, as the fulfillment of a life.[3] Looking upward, the HP manifests what is known as "idealizing transference" to the institutions (and especially to the major symbols and highest offices of those institutions) of which he is a part. This aspect of the internal topography of upward ambition reflects faith there is something above worth being ambitious for. The "higher" the office, the more it is idealized as a location of prestige, honor, recognition, and power, the more desirable it seems. The HP feels an almost religious awe of these offices, his upward distance to personal salvation is a political distance.[4]

It is important to be clear that what the HP wants primarily is to realize the experience of directorship atop the unfolding social and political drama of his times. He seeks a position of power less to use power to accomplish certain specific goals than for the personal gratification of being engagé and a top dog. Although he may genuinely dedicate himself to certain ideals of grandiose accomplishment, these typically are stylistic and symbolic, and seldom involve thoughtful and well-elaborated programs.[5] The major story is that, above all, he wants to succeed; he imagines a better society to follow (he is vague about details) once his own will occupies the idealized "over-mind" location of high office.

This "upward" ambition has the character of a single-minded obsession, fusing a desire for personal integration (and salvation) within a political quest. (In the American political scene, to be in the White House or as close to it—even to the Oval Office—as possible.) It organizes an entire life in its service.[6] But it is a quest whose consummation is always in the distance and there is little genuine pleasure in the striving.[7] The tragic fact is that in his ambitious "upward" quest for personal salvation and fulfillment, the HP is not a satisfied man; he is caught up in the push and pull of an ambition that gives him little rest or deep satisfaction. Simpler pleasures pass him by; he is a man made for more important things.

The upward striving of the HP involves also what is known as "mirror transference."[8] That is, he relates implicitly to most other people (i.e., of lower status) with the expectation and need that they confirm his grandiose strivings, give him public recognition that shows him as he wishes himself to appear. He seeks an echo of applause, love, and unbounded admiration and respect coming back.[9] And he is certain such response is out there, albeit latent and mobilizable, that "in their hearts," in their "hearts and minds," the people, the silent majority, know he is right and eventually will respond.[10]

It is difficult to say whether the HP seeks love, or unbounded admiration, or status, or unlimited power or success; these connotations become joined in high political office. He is on a public ego trip; in fact, he wants all simultaneously. The "public" is not important to him in a genuine sense; he perceives them not as autonomous fellow human beings of equal status and respect with whom he works collaboratively in a specialized role, but as a supporting cast of subordinate parts in his own drama. He will aspire to be a "public servant" only if this status means he will be in a higher status role "looked up to" by the public. Favorable publicity and recognition are, of course, important to the HP "rationally," in order to be elected, but his vanity requires these for more than their strategic value.

Thus, the ambition of the HP involves two kinds of biased drama simultaneously. He subjectively experiences both an idealized goal above himself and—below—a potentially attentive and supportive mass public. In both cases there is probable overdramatization and distortion: the harsher reality is that the majority of a congressman's constituents do not bother to remember his name, and in a pluralistic society, and world, universal acclaim is a chimera, perhaps even for an American president. It is likely that the HP's hopes and fantasies, this selective absence of reality testing in his epistemology, are useful to society since they help to sustain his lifelong quest and the dutiful and energetic performance of his roles.

One particular feature of ambition in the HP is worth additional comment: He vastly overestimates the probability of achieving fulfillment of his long-range grandiose project.[11] He has an almost religious confidence in his own eventual success. Such inner certainty that he will be recognized by future events as the conquering hero is an invaluable aid to perseverance in the skirmishes and setbacks inevitable in the political arena. The HP (as we shall see in detail later) bases his long-range plans substantially on the strength of these internal fantasies and not upon rational assessments derived from external evidence. He will leave his mark upon history, and he is not deterred by ambiguities and low probabilities of success. Success *must* be accomplished.

Deficiencies of Love

The interpersonal relations of the HP are superficial; he has little genuine love and affection for others.[12] He does not become involved (even in marriage) to an extent that would divert him from pursuing his own ambitious self-interest, and he does not let sentimentality or genuine emotion get the better of him. There often is a facade of cordiality and considerable skill at ingratiation, glad-handing, and interpersonal relations—a kind of "Hiya fella, how are you?" (to person A), "Hiya fella, how are you?" (to person B), "Hiya fella, how are you?" (to person C). The essential that is absent is qualitative, true caring for another unique person's welfare, relating to other people as ends rather than as means. The HP operates with cool, even cold, detachment.

There is, however, one area of interpersonal relations—technically, narcissistic object choice—where this inner distance does not apply: In ordinary English, it is the area of loyalty. With people who support or potentially support his grandiose striving, the HP develops intense emotional involvement.[13] But such relations are vampiresque (he does not form strong bonds of mutual respect and love with autonomous individuals) and he denies such people (including, e.g., wives and staff) independent lives, molding them to live for him and expecting them to serve his ambitions. Fundamental disagreement is perceived as disloyalty, and disloyalty engenders a powerful and violent rejection by the HP.[14]

Such a style of interpersonal relations can be quite functional in hardball politics. The HP has "permanent interests but no permanent allies" (in the phrase sometimes used in a *realpolitik* prescription for American foreign policy). He does not let his ambition become encumbered by love or loyalty or personal friendships. He can shift coalitions instrumentally without regret, continuing in the pursuit of his own success and reparative vindication.

Mirror Images of Opponents

The image of opponents evidences what is technically a "twinship transference": the HP experiences other people as essentially like himself, replicas of his own psychodynamics.[15] All participants are expected to be "grown up" (*sic*), to know their self-interest, to look out for "number one" first, and to engage in shrewd, rational calculations in the service of hardball maneuvering for domination, status, and power in the world. He thereby experiences himself to inhabit a fearful, insecure, and dangerous arena, a competitive, Hobbesian world. Other men in the arena are experienced to be as ambitious as he is himself, untrustworthy when egotistical self-interests diverge sharply. He expects others have secret desires to be opportunistic, to outmaneuver and defeat him, dominate and control him, to string him along, trip him up, win away his constituents, expand their spheres of influence, stab him in the back (although this latter is only figurative in American domestic practice these days).[16] And as there is some truth in this—other hardball players *are* like himself—this intuition-based knowledge can stand him in good stead because there *are* people who will try, opportunistically, to outmaneuver him, undermine him, steal his constituency, dominate and control him, string him along, trip him up, or stab him in the back. To ambitious men of this type, then, both foreign and domestic opponents will be expected to press advantages, to be vigilant for weakness, and to take advantage of vulnerabilities if they find an opportunity. Moreover, the presumption of shrewd, self-interested calculation by others eliminates moral qualms: others are imagined to know the risks they are taking in a political arena.

Of course, no politician can afford to be completely treacherous, and there are game rules, norms of accommodation, surface camaraderie, and ethical sensitivities among the powerful.[17] And fortunately not all of American society, politicians, or countries, play hardball, but the hardball politician lives in an uncertain subsystem, a "cold, cruel world" of "dog eat dog."[18] Power politics is partly a collective and uncomfortable *folie à deux*.

Weak Ethics and Disconnected Moral Restraint

The ethics of the HP differ from ordinary morality. He does not have a strong and principled superego.[19] Rather the ideals of his grandiose self (and the fears of social shame and exposure of his insecure, depleted self) join to provide a substitute for ethical restraint. He plays hardball without moral qualms about his typical lack of candor, dissembling, his hypocrisy, or manipulativeness, his using of other people, his wars or invasions for national interest (i.e., to further national power), his covert activities, his "leaks" of information to the press which unfairly damage his opponent's reputation, and so forth.[20] The HP always seeks an edge on what he would achieve by ethical means; while fear of exposure will be a deterrent, his character structure does not inhibit him. And he fears, perhaps with some justification, that in playing hardball "nice guys finish last." "This is not an honorable undertaking conducted by honorable men through honorable means," Secretary of State Henry Kissinger—in the Nixon administration— lectured one of his idealistic subordinates.[21]

But this is not to say the HP lacks a sense of morality. The fantasies embedded in the grandiose self include an almost religious sense of moral justification. The HP feels greater moral virtue to be identical with his higher location in his grandiose dreams. He imagines he will be a high status benefactor to mankind, and achievement and retention of power thus become the sine qua non, his greatest moral guide. He experiences a "higher purpose" served by his day-to-day hardball escapades. In its most rationalized form the HP gives a name to this vaguely specified higher virtue which supersedes normal morality and ethical conduct, "*raison d'ètat*," "*staats-raisen*," "public interest," or "national security."

There are, however, constraints of shame and embarrassment to cope with and, feeling potentially ashamed, the HP does much of his scheming in private and conducts most of his deals in back rooms. He has a penchant for secrecy. And players believe everyone else is calculating and maneuvering backstage. No one is believed to have integrity or to be open, candid, or trustworthy except as a semblance, a strategy. But while the secrecy is sometimes functional, in the hardball power drama it does not arise only from this source. Rather the HP is also afraid to tell the truth about his hardball politics because he presupposes instinctively (and perhaps correctly) that full public knowledge would risk public rejection.[22] What the HP fears most is that such rejection would result in subjective separation from the higher idealized images (i.e., high office) in the larger-than-life drama within which his life is located.

Defective Humor

An additional characteristic of the HP is a defective sense of humor.[23] He lacks a playful, warm detachment about himself and the conduct of human affairs. He takes himself seriously. If he has a sense of humor it favors being unkind about someone else: "Gerald

Ford can't walk and chew gum at the same time," said Lyndon Johnson. The pure form is best captured by Hobbes's theory of humor, that it expressed coolness and dominance, perhaps a touch of malicious superiority, rather than a playful amusement.[24] And the HP does not much care for jokes or funny stories told about himself.

Cold, Condescending Aggression and Vanity

The HP handles many interpersonal and political situations with tactical shrewdness because he retains an aloof inner distance, a lack of major emotional investment in anything save winning. But just as personal disloyalty will stir his wrath, so does a challenger, particularly of lower status (hence unworthy and, comparatively, underestimated) who unsettles the fantasy and threatens the grandiose location and control he is driven to effect. Under such challenge he experiences cold, imperious rage and an aggressive drive for control and reparative revenge, for punishment of those lesser men, upstarts so insolent as to question his natural superiority and benevolent wisdom.[25] Theodore Roosevelt dispatched American troops into Cuba in 1906 and wrote in a private letter, "Just at the moment I am so angry with that infernal little Cuban republic that I would like to wipe its people off the face of the earth."[26]

The fact of emotion-charged vanity increases the sensitivity to "face" and avoidance of embarrassment in the world of power politics. Professional politicians are cautious not to express such ridicule openly (although ambitious aides often will do so in anonymous leaks to the press). The tact of professional diplomats is especially helpful in dealing among such men without arousing complicated emotions of insult and revenge.

The inner nexus of such cold, imperious vanity and anger is the psychology of the grandiose self. One patient in psychoanalysis expressed this typical stance when he was leaving a job and his employers were speculating about a suitable replacement. The thought went through his mind of saying, "How about God?"[27]

But the people who lack an independent power base and are dependent upon the HP, his staff, often get the full force of his vanity and frustrations. He can be a bully and petulant, taking as a personal affront any deviation from perfection and any sign his staff has not absolutely dedicated their lives to him. He gives them little autonomy. Nietzsche's theory appears correct: "One will seldom err if extreme actions are ascribed to vanity, ordinary actions to habit, and mean actions to fear." The HP is especially likely to act from both vanity and fear.[28]

It should be clear, however, that stubbornness, imperial determination, and aggression to effect control of what are seen as lesser men are not always dysfunctional.[29] The capacity to persevere in a course of action despite travails, opposition, and criticism can be a formula for success, whether creating a revolutionary movement or "toughing out" the attacks of critics. HPs have a Darwinian advantage in the competitive quest. And once in office, critics of the direction of policy are more readily ignored: To the HP the *advantage* of being a leader is to be able finally to ignore lower status critics.

Partial Regression: Slightly Drunken, Emotionally Organized Thought

The HP is engaged by power, his mental life preoccupied with it. He cannot get away from it and relax because the concern is part of his personality. He directly, physically, experiences "forces," "threats," and "pressures" moving him to act in various ways. In technical terms, his mental processes are partly regressed and primary process. The HP may have the gift to fashion bold visions or alarums from such material, but he usually lacks the detached executive control to be a first-rate artist; proportion is lacking and often he is only vague, emotionalistic, dull, and vacuous. The HP has a "veil of ambiguity and indirectness"; there is a slight drunkenness to his thought when he thinks or declaims about important issues.[30] His thinking seems to reflect underlying emotional themes and, in perspective, he appears caught up powerfully in a world of his own imagining.

It should be clear that the term "slight drunkenness" is used here in a specialized sense. Power exists in the mind, and the conventional subculture of hardball power is a subculture of mental processes widely shared. The primary process dramatizations of the HP put him in touch with, and allow his intuition to guide him within, this subculture. It is functional; in fact, someone without his sensitivity might be unable to succeed in hardball politics. He would be like Plato's former prisoner in a cave who, returning to the world of shadows and semblances, is unable to perform effectively because his eyes are not attuned to the lack of light.[31]

I do not wish to be misunderstood: The HP can be shrewd, and often effective, in the capture of high office. It is simply that analytically rational intelligence operates in connection with a larger part of his mind that functions as if he were sleepwalking: manipulating vaguely defined, emotionally laden, symbols; adopting dramatic poses; exhorting; attacking; reassuring; defending; declaiming. This is the nature of public rhetoric in hardball politics.[32] What rationalist accounts of such ambiguity and emotionalism (which see such traits as mere stratagems) omit is the deeper cause that men with ambition are psychologically predisposed to be caught in their own imaginations and speak with this slight drunkenness of mind.[33]

There are other important senses in which the HP's mental processes, while common among politicians, are regressed. As discussed above, he lives partially in a world of strong imagination, of empowered abstraction, of viscerally experienced threats, forces, and pressures; as well, his ambition typically involves major psychic investment in his internal dramatization with grandiose fantasies, substantial overestimation of his probability of ultimate success, and his biased perceptions idealize too much (upwards), stereotype too simply (others as like himself), and misconstrue the lower status public as (at least potentially) fully attentive and a responsive cast of supporting characters. In a psychiatric taxonomy his is in part a "borderline" character (Table 1).

Table 1. From Within: The "Hardball Politics" Imagination System

Normality	Borderline (HP)	Psychosis
Integrated subjective self	Structural split into two selves (grandiose/depleted)	Complete fragmentation of subjective self
Mature self-esteem	Grandiosity/shame	Full delusional constitution of grandiose self; cold, paranoid grandiosity/omnipotent persecutor
Mature self-confidence	Imperial, absolute self-confidence/hypochondria, continual worry about well-being, insecurity	Full delusional constitution of grandiose self; cold, paranoid/omnipotent persecutors and malevolent forces
Mature ambition	Compelling drive to merge with ("attain") idealized powerful offices; solipsistic claims for attention; fears of inadequacy	Full delusional constitution of grandiose self; cold, paranoid grandiosity/omnipotent persecutor
Genuine love, warmth with autonomous individuals	Partial withdrawal of object libido; partial narcissistic bonding (loyalty/disloyalty)	Complete withdrawal of object libido; narcissistic bonding
Secondary process (secularized) reality testing and creative use of primary process under ego control	Partially distorting idealizing, twinship and mirror stereotypes; vague awe, primary process "religious" feelings, reified abstractions, and experiences of forces, pressures, power; habitual ambiguity and indirection; marked libidinal intrusions into speech and thought	Massive projection and transference; full deterioration of reality testing; uncontrolled intrusion of primary process, incomprehensible, illogical, fully emotionally expressive speech and thought
Mature, playful humor	Deteriorated humor	Absent
Capacity for enthusiasm	Episodes of hypomanic excitement	Auto-erotic tension state

Hyperactivity

There is a final characteristic of the HP syndrome closely allied to grandiose striving: hyperactivity. When he is engaged in, or associated with, projects he considers heroically important, his being becomes flooded with nervous energy. He walks fast (typically with the grandiose fantasy that his project is essential to preserve the well-being and functioning of the world, that it will come apart or degenerate if he ceases).[34] He over-schedules himself. He works long hours, seldom with time to relax or enjoy recreation. The importance of his own projects may produce so much physiological arousal that he needs to turn to alcohol to calm himself.

CODA

Individuals whose inner worlds are complex, larger-than-life power dramas of enormous grandiosity and apprehensive vulnerability, while they have a basic skeleton in common, are not identical. Some are motivated simply to live out their wish to occupy the role of a high-status benefactor, others have such fantasies infused with genuine ability and socially useful content, a genuine idealism of heroic accomplishment to produce a better world. (But it is, of course, not a world to be produced now by truth, compassion, fairness, the freeing of individuals from warping roles, and the rearrangement of norms. It is a vision predicated on the scenario of grandiose competitive accomplishment, dominance—in the imagination, integration of the self by being above others—and survival of the self against countervailing forces: utopia first requires domination; political control precedes ethics.) The subjective intensity of such a power drama varies in degree and is not a complete description either of all determinants of hardball practice or of other aspects of personality.

COMPASSION AND THE HARDBALL POLITICS PRACTITIONER

This review of hardball politics has drawn upon a psychiatric humanism which diagnoses as pathological, by comparison with its ideals, the behavior I have described. The rationale is that the two "selves" are seen to be parts of a potentially integrated whole; therapy is thought to be a more effective nurturant than the pursuit of worldly ambition to effect such spiritual healing. But this diagnosis—which suggests why psychologists, with a larger perspective, are skeptical of the limited "realism" in international politics—also implies, within a psychiatric mode, compassion for what one sees as the problems of the HP (a compassion which the HP, with his scorn of weakness— including, often, a misinformed view that psychology is only a "soft," liberal viewpoint—seldom would reciprocate).[35] How much sympathy and compassion to accord the hardball player who makes others victims of his irrationalities will have to be left to the reader. But it would be appropriate to recall Ernest Jones's summary of Freud's image of man and to note also that the HP himself is driven by imperatives whose origins are a mystery to him (and especially suffers physically from stress and psychogenic illness when success is problematic or he encounters setbacks), and that his political agendas (an effort at self-therapy—a lifelong quest to integrate his depleted self with the image of a charismatic idealized self) are seldom wholly successful: "The images of the innocent babe or unfolding plant have been replaced," Jones wrote, "by more sympathetic and living ones of creatures pathetically struggling 'with no language but a cry,' to achieve the self-control and inner security that civilized man has so far attempted in vain to attain."[36] Yet the fused quest to effect both inner security and national security simultaneously can be deadly as well as tragically unrealistic.

The prayer for beneficent transformation of the world and the syndrome of its hardball practices is an old one. "From pride, vain-glory, and hypocrisy; from envy, hatred, and malice, and all uncharitableness, good Lord, deliver us" reads the litany of *The Book of Common Prayer*.[37] In his 1837 Phi Beta Kappa address at Harvard, Ralph Waldo Emerson spoke eloquently about the disheartening effects of "business as usual," pointing out that "Young men of the fairest promise, who begin life upon our shores, inflated by the mountain winds, shined upon by all the stars of God, find the earth below not in unison with these, but are hindered from action by the disgust which the principles on which business is managed inspire."[38] An inspired goodwill and "patience" were Emerson's prescriptions to idealistic youth. Yet 124 years later, in 1961, and almost 150 years later in the mid-1980s . . . there was still no effective remedy for this condition.

NOTES

1. This duality is not readily assessed with conventional measures of self-esteem as the HP is ashamed to reveal low self-esteem and in part experiences enormously high self-esteem. For a discussion of several methodological issues and evidence for high manifest self-esteem among the politically active, see P. Sniderman, *Personality and Democratic Politics* (Berkeley, CA: Univ. of California Press, 1975). Psychoanalytic characterizations of this phenomenon are suggested in H. Kohut, *The Analysis of the Self* (New York: International Universities Press, 1971) and his *The Restoration of the Self* (New York: International Universities Press, 1977).

2. Early childhood antecedents appear complex and are not fully documented. They seem to include a mother whose indulgence is self-involved ("narcissistic" in psychoanalytic terminology); that is, the child, rather than being related to as an autonomous person, confirmed and loved for himself, is valued as a being who can fulfill the mother's own aspirations through heroic accomplishment. Thus the child is both empowered while (following Lasswell) he is deprived of power as an autonomous individual. See Kohut, *The Analysis of the Self*; L. Pye, *Mao Tse Tung: The Man in the Leader* (New York: Basic Books, 1976).

3. Ambition drives such men even in the face of extreme objective risk. Commenting on the attractions and the enormous risks of the office of Caesar, M. Grant, *The Twelve Caesars* (New York: Scribner's, 1975), p. 257, observes: "In view of the alarming perils involved, it may seem difficult to understand why anyone could be eager to become ruler of the Roman Empire. Yet signs of reluctance were not greatly in evidence. Even in the third century A.D., when a would-be usurper scarcely needed to be a statistical expert to note that the average reign ended rapidly and violently, candidates for the throne still proliferated on every side."

4. One of the important therapeutic tasks in the integration of the HP is realization that such dramatizations are in his own mind, albeit shared by others in the system to create its reality. This may be especially difficult to achieve among politicians because HPs and others with

similar traits in the news media join in a "collusion of grandiosity" to define and sustain their collective and mutually reinforcing idealized fantasies of "high" public offices as "objective" social reality. See V. Volkan's work, esp. *Primitive Internalized Object Relations: A Clinical Study of Schizophrenic, Borderline, and Narcissistic Patients* (New York: International Universities Press, 1976), p. 269; O. Kernberg, *Borderline Conditions and Pathological Narcissism* (New York: Aronson, 1975), pp. 51–85; J. Gedo and A. Goldberg, *Models of the Mind* (Chicago: Univ. of Chicago Press, 1973) on disillusionment therapy. On efforts mutually to reinforce the prestige of the position they occupy and the institutional ladders they climb, see Mayhew, *Congress*.

5. C. Bowles, *Promises to Keep*, p. 29, for example, laments Kennedy's disinterest in the drafting of the Democratic Party platform on which he ran.

6. In terms of psychological theory, ordinary stimulus-response punishments do not extinguish the HP's long-term behavior, although they may hurt his feelings.

7. The HP, in other words, does not enjoy his work. Contrary to what one might expect in a politician, most British prime ministers have not much enjoyed associating with other people. See H. Berrington, "The Fiery Chariot: British Prime Ministers and the Search for Love" *British Journal of Political Science* 4 (1974): 345–369; Kohut, *The Analysis of the Self*, pp. 120, 144, 199.

8. Kohut, *The Analysis of the Self*, pp. 96–98; 251–253 et passim.

9. There may be a need, too, to receive this comparatively and competitively, by constantly seeking out and winning against challengers and opponents. See also H. Kohut, "Thoughts on Narcissism and Narcissistic Rage" in *The Psychoanalytic Study of the Child* (Chicago: Quadrangle, 1971).

10. There is the anticipated reward (via the mirror transference) of future, perhaps eternal, fame and vindication "in the eyes of history." The reference to "hearts and minds" is to a phrase which is part of this syndrome in the case of America's Vietnam policy. See L. Gelb and R. Betts, *The Irony of Vietnam: The System Worked* (Washington, DC: Brookings Institution, 1979). "Silent majority" refers to a phrase used during the Nixon administration.

11. Kohut, *The Analysis of the Self*, pp. 150–151. However, the observation of political life that "great power is in general gained by running great risks" may be correct. If so, the inherent inability of the HP to believe his personal failure is a realistic possibility may eliminate inhibitions to his upward ambitions that would deter more "normal" men. Hubris may lead to great successes as well as to great tragic disasters. The problem of assessing overconfidence and attitudes toward risk is subtle because, while the HP, in one sector of his mind, worries constantly about failure, in another sector of his mind he is convinced it will never occur. The above quotation is from Herodotus, *The History of Herodotus*. Translated by G. Macaulay. (London: Macmillan & Co., 1904), p. 151. See also the discussion of risk taking by a military HP, Gen. Douglas MacArthur, especially his decision for the Inchon landing and underestimation of the Chinese Communists in the Korean War in J. DeRivera, *The Psychological Dimension of Foreign Policy* (Chicago, IL: Charles E. Merrill, 1968), pp. 175-180. See also Kohut, *The Analysis of the Self*, pp. 150-151.

12. Kohut, *The Analysis of the Self*, pp. 9, 85–88, 97.

13. Ibid., p. 3. To retain power "Daley has intuitively known from the beginning (that) a man must surround himself with servitors, people who are totally loyal and utterly dependent on the man, Daley, for their own well-being." O'Connor, *Court*, p. 11.

14. Ibid., p. 123 et passim.

15. The congressional expert Richard Fenno observes: "One of the dominant impressions of my travels is the terrific sense of uncertainty which animates these Congressmen. They perceive electoral troubles where the most imaginative outside observer could not possibly perceive, conjure up or hallucinate them." Cited in Mayhew, *Congress*, p. 35, note 2.

   During the Watergate cover-up case, President Nixon was often called upon by critics to apologize and ask forgiveness. A hardball practitioner such as Nixon would know (believe) this would not work.

16. Hersh, *The Price of Power* provides a recent discussion of behavior in the national security process in this light. The Nixon administration was more extreme in this regard than the Kennedy years. A general discussion of pervasive, mutual mistrust in the foreign policy process is C. Argyris, *Some Causes of Organizational Ineffectiveness Within the Department of State* (Washington, DC: Department of State. Center for International Systems Research, 1967). See also the sensibility of the self-blocking people portrayed in A. Wildavsky, "The Self-Evaluating Organization" in J. Shafritz and A. Hyde, ed., *Classics of Public Administration* (Oak Park, IL: Moore Publishing Co.), pp. 412–427.

17. See the distinction between normative and pragmatic rules in Bailey, *Stratagems and Spoils*, p. 5. See also S. Huntington, *Political Order in Changing Societies* (New Haven, CT: Yale Univ. Press, 1968) on political development and "arts of association."

18. Unpleasant consequences for a polity and the international political system tend to follow, as James Madison noted in *The Federalist* #10 (J. Cooke, ed., Cleveland and New York: Meridian Books, 1961), p. 59: "an attachment of different leaders ambitiously contending for pre-eminence and power . . . [has], in turn, divided mankind into parties, inflamed them with mutual animosity, and rendered them much more disposed to vex and oppress each other than to cooperate for their common good." Madison did not discuss the breathless dramatizations of the mass media, but his analysis would apply as well.

19. Kohut, *The Analysis of the Self*, p. 232.

20. See Halperin et al., *Bureaucratic Behavior* for an inventory derived partly from personal observation.

21. R. Woodward and C. Bernstein, *The Final Days* (New York: Simon and Schuster, 1976), p. 194. See also Etheredge, *A World of Men*. Dean Acheson made a similar point: Some goings-on in Washington would make the Borgias envious, he thought. He also thought it necessary for a Secretary of State to have "a killer instinct." Another former State Department official thought an ideal preparation for understanding the territoriality, coalitions, in-group secrecy, demands for loyalty, and tough style in national security circles was to have been a member of a juvenile street gang. Acheson is cited in G. Allison, *Essence of Decision: Explaining the Cuban Missile Crisis* (Boston: Little, Brown, 1971), p. 180.

22. Kohut, *The Analysis of the Self*, p. 232.

23. Ibid., pp. 199, 238; H. Kohut, "Forms and Transformations of Narcissism" *Journal of the American Psychoanalytic Association* 14 (1966): 243–272.

24. T. Hobbes. *Leviathan*. C. Macpherson, ed. (Baltimore, MD: Penguin, 1968), p. 126: "Sudden glory is the passion which maketh those grimaces called laughter: and is caused . . . by the apprehension of some deformed thing in another." Hobbes also felt people laughed from delight in self-congratulation. His unpleasant theory is not always true, but perceptive and of local validity if taken as the observation of one of the major observers of politics.

25. H. Kohut, "Thoughts on Narcissistic Rage"; J. Nehemiah, *Foundations of Psychopathology* (New York: Oxford Univ. Press, 1961), pp. 165–166; Etheredge, *A World of Men*, p. 82.

26. Quoted in T. Bailey, *A Diplomatic History of the American People* 10th ed. (Englewood Cliffs, NJ: Prentice-Hall, 1980), p. 500.

27. Quoted in Kohut, *The Analysis of the Self*, p. 149. On competitive "credit-claiming" see Mayhew, *Congress*.

28. F. Nietzsche, *Human, All Too Human: A Book for Free Spirits*. Trans. by P. Cohen. (New York: Russell & Russell, 1964).

29. See O. Fenichel, *The Psychoanalytic Theory of Neurosis* (New York: Norton, 1945), p. 279, on the relation of stubbornness to narcissism.

30. Kohut, *The Analysis of the Self*, pp. 97, 184.

31. Plato, *The Republic*. In E. Hamilton and H. Cairns, ed., *The Collected Dialogues of Plato* (New York: Pantheon, 1961), p. 749.

32. M. Edelman, *The Symbolic Uses of Politics* (Urbana, IL: Univ. of Illinois Press, 1964); D. Graber, *Verbal Behavior and Politics* (Urbana, IL: Univ. of Illinois Press, 1976); and D. Nimmo, *Popular Images of Politics* (Englewood Cliffs, NJ: Prentice-Hall, 1974) discuss these issues.

33. See also R. Robins's introduction to R. Robins, ed., *Psychopathology and Political Leadership* (New Orleans: Tulane Univ. Press, 1977), pp. 1–34 on (potentially visionary) primary process shifts in the discourse of political leaders.

34. The HP is trying to hold himself together in the face of stress. See Kohut, *The Analysis of the Self*, pp. 152–153; also A. Wallace, "Stress and Rapid Personality Changes" *International Record of Medicine* 169 (1956): 761–764. MONGOOSE would qualify as an example.

35. The present analysis suggests how an understanding of psychology may afford a larger perspective, but I do not mean to endorse tender-minded analyses.

36. E. Jones, *Sigmund Freud: Four Centenary Addresses* (New York: Basic Books, 1956), p. 145.

37. Church of England, *The Book of Common Prayer* (London: Oxford Univ. Press, 1960), p. 70.

38. R. Emerson, "The American Scholar" in B. Atkinson, ed., *Selected Writings of Emerson* (New York: Modern Library, 1950), p. 63.

10

The Presidential Character

JAMES DAVID BARBER

When a citizen votes for a Presidential candidate he makes, in effect, a prediction. He chooses from among the contenders the one he thinks (or feels, or guesses) would be the best President. He operates in a situation of immense uncertainty. If he has a long voting history, he can recall time and time again when he guessed wrong. He listens to the commentators, the politicians, and his friends, then adds it all up in some rough way to produce his prediction and his vote. Earlier in the game, his anticipations have been taken into account, either directly in the polls and primaries or indirectly in the minds of politicians who want to nominate someone he will like. But he must choose in the midst of a cloud of confusion, a rain of phony advertising, a storm of sermons, a hail of complex issues, a fog of charisma and boredom, and a thunder of accusation and defense. In the face of this chaos, a great many citizens fall back on the past, vote their old allegiances, and let it go at that. Nevertheless, the citizen's vote says that on balance he expects Mr. X would outshine Mr. Y in the Presidency.

[*The Presidential Character*] . . . is meant to help citizens and those who advise them cut through the confusion and get at some clear criteria for choosing Presidents. To understand what actual Presidents do and what potential Presidents might do, the first need is to see the man whole—not as some abstract embodiment of civic virtue, some scorecard of issue stands, or some reflection of a faction, but as a human being like the rest of us, a person trying to cope with a difficult environment. To that task he brings his own character, his own view of the world, his own political style. None of that is new for him. If we can see the pattern he has set for his political life we can, I contend, estimate much better his pattern as he confronts the stresses and chances of the Presidency.

The Presidency is a peculiar office. The Founding Fathers left it extraordinarily loose

127

in definition, partly because they trusted George Washington to invent a tradition as he went along. It is an institution made a piece at a time by successive men in the White House. Jefferson reached out to Congress to put together the beginnings of political parties; Jackson's dramatic force extended electoral partisanship to its mass base; Lincoln vastly expanded the administrative reach of the office, Wilson and the Roosevelts showed its rhetorical possibilities—in fact every President's mind and demeanor has left its mark on a heritage still in lively development.

But the Presidency is much more than an institution. It is a focus of feelings. In general, popular feelings about politics are low-key, shallow, casual. For example, the vast majority of Americans knows virtually nothing of what Congress is doing and cares less. The Presidency is different. The Presidency is the focus for the most intense and persistent emotions in the American polity. The President is a symbolic leader, the one figure who draws together the people's hopes and fears for the political future. On top of all his routine duties, he has to carry that off—or fail.

Our emotional attachment to Presidents shows up when one dies in office. People were not just disappointed or worried when President Kennedy was killed; people wept at the loss of a man most had never even met. Kennedy was young and charismatic—but history shows that whenever a President dies in office, heroic Lincoln or debased Harding, McKinley or Garfield, the same wave of deep emotion sweeps across the country. On the other hand, the death of an ex-President brings forth no such intense emotional reaction.

The President is the first political figure children are aware of (later they add Congress, the Court, and others, as "helpers" of the President). With some exceptions among children in deprived circumstances, the President is seen as a "benevolent leader," one who nurtures, sustains, and inspires the citizenry. Presidents regularly show up among "most admired" contemporaries and forebears, and the President is the "best known" (in the sense of sheer name recognition) person in the country. At inauguration time, even Presidents elected by close margins are supported by much larger majorities than the election returns show, for people rally round as he actually assumes office. There is a similar reaction when the people see their President threatened by crisis: if he takes action, there is a favorable spurt in the Gallup poll whether he succeeds or fails.

Obviously the President gets more attention in schoolbooks, press, and television than any other politician. He is one of very few who can make news by doing good things. *His* emotional state is a matter of continual public commentary, as is the manner in which his personal and official families conduct themselves. The media bring across the President not as some neutral administrator or corporate executive to be assessed by his production, but as a special being with mysterious dimensions.

We have no king. The sentiments English children—and adults—direct to the Queen have no place to go in our system but to the President. Whatever his talents—Coolidge-type or Roosevelt-type—the President is the only available object for such national-religious-monarchical sentiments as Americans possess.

The President helps people make sense of politics. Congress is a tangle of committees, the bureaucracy is a maze of agencies. The President is one man trying to do a job—a picture much more understandable to the mass of people who find themselves in the same boat. Furthermore, he is the top man. He ought to know what is going on and set it right. So when the economy goes sour, or war drags on, or domestic violence erupts, the President is available to take the blame. Then when things go right, it seems the President must have had a hand in it. Indeed, the flow of political life is marked off by Presidents: the "Eisenhower Era," the "Kennedy Years."

What all this means is that the President's *main* responsibilities reach far beyond administering the Executive Branch or commanding the armed forces. The White House is first and foremost a place of public leadership. That inevitably brings to bear on the President intense moral, sentimental, and quasi-religious pressures which can, if he lets them, distort his own thinking and feeling. If there is such a thing as extraordinary sanity, it is needed nowhere so much as in the White House.

Who the President is at a given time can make a profound difference in the whole thrust and direction of national politics. Since we have only one President at a time, we can never prove this by comparison, but even the most superficial speculation confirms the commonsense view that the man himself weighs heavily among other historical factors. A Wilson re-elected in 1920, a Hoover in 1932, a John F. Kennedy in 1964 would, it seems very likely, have guided the body politic along rather different paths from those their actual successors chose. Or try to imagine a Theodore Roosevelt ensconced behind today's "bully pulpit" of a Presidency, or Lyndon Johnson as President in the age of McKinley. Only someone mesmerized by the lures of historical inevitability can suppose that it would have made little or no difference to government policy had Alf Landon replaced FDR in 1936, had Dewey beaten Truman in 1948, or Adlai Stevenson reigned through the 1950s. Not only would these alternative Presidents have advocated different policies—they would have approached the office from very different psychological angles. It stretches credibility to think that Eugene McCarthy would have run the institution the way Lyndon Johnson did.

The burden of [*The Presidential Character*] . . . is that the crucial differences can be anticipated by an understanding of a potential President's character, his world view, and his style. This kind of prediction is not easy; well-informed observers often have guessed wrong as they watched a man step toward the White House. One thinks of Woodrow Wilson, the scholar who would bring reason to politics; of Herbert Hoover, the Great Engineer who would organize chaos into progress; of Franklin D. Roosevelt, that champion of the balanced budget; of Harry Truman, whom the office would surely overwhelm; of Dwight D. Eisenhower, militant crusader; of John F. Kennedy, who would lead beyond moralisms to achievements; of Lyndon B. Johnson, the Southern conservative; and of Richard M. Nixon, conciliator. Spotting the errors is easy. Predicting with even approximate accuracy is going to require some sharp tools and close attention in their use. But the experiment is worth it because the question is critical and because it lends itself to correction by evidence.

My argument comes in layers.

First, a President's personality is an important shaper of his Presidential behavior on nontrivial matters.

Second, Presidential personality is patterned. His character, world view, and style fit together in a dynamic package understandable in psychological terms.

Third, a President's personality interacts with the power situation he faces and the national "climate of expectations" dominant at the time he serves. The tuning, the resonance—or lack of it—between these external factors and his personality sets in motion the dynamic of his Presidency.

Fourth, the best way to predict a President's character, world view, and style is to see how they were put together in the first place. That happened in his early life, culminating in his first independent political success.

But the core of the argument (which organizes the structure of the book) is that Presidential character—the basic stance a man takes toward his Presidential experience—comes in four varieties. The most important thing to know about a President or candidate is where he fits among these types, defined according to (a) how active he is and (b) whether or not he gives the impression he enjoys his political life.

Let me spell out these concepts briefly before getting down to cases.

PERSONALITY SHAPES PERFORMANCE

I am not about to argue that once you know a President's personality you know everything. But as the cases will demonstrate, the degree and quality of a President's emotional involvement in an issue are powerful influences on how he defines the issue itself, how much attention he pays to it, which facts and persons he sees as relevant to its resolution, and, finally, what principles and purposes he associates with the issue. Every story of Presidential decision-making is really two stories: an outer one in which a rational man calculates and an inner one in which an emotional man feels. The two are forever connected. Any real President is one whole man and his deeds reflect his wholeness.

As for personality, it is a matter of tendencies. It is not that one President "has" some basic characteristics that another President does not "have." That old way of treating a trait as a possession, like a rock in a basket, ignores the universality of aggressiveness, compliancy, detachment, and other human drives. We all have all of them, but in different amounts and in different combinations.

THE PATTERN OF CHARACTER, WORLD VIEW, AND STYLE

The most visible part of the pattern is style. *Style is the President's habitual way of performing his three political roles: rhetoric, personal relations, and homework.* Not to be confused with "stylishness," charisma, or appearance, style is how the President goes about doing what the office requires him to do to speak, directly or through media, to large audiences; to deal face to face with other politicians, individually and in small, relatively private groups; and to read, write, and calculate by himself in order to manage the endless flow of details that stream onto his desk. No President can escape doing at least some of each. But there are marked differences in stylistic emphasis from President to President. The *balance* among the three style elements varies; one President may put most of himself into rhetoric, another may stress close, informal dealing, while still another may devote his energies mainly to study and cogitation. Beyond the balance, we want to see each President's peculiar habits of style, his mode of coping with and adapting to these Presidential demands. For example, I think both Calvin Coolidge and John F. Kennedy were primarily rhetoricians, but they went about it in contrasting ways.

A President's *world view consists of his primary, politically relevant beliefs, particularly his conceptions of social causality, human nature, and the central moral conflicts of the time.* This is how he sees the world and his lasting opinions about what he sees. Style is his way of acting; world view is his way of seeing. Like the rest of us, a President develops over a lifetime certain conceptions of reality—how things work in politics, what people are like, what the main purposes are. These assumptions or conceptions help him make sense of his world, give some semblance of order to the chaos of existence. Perhaps most important: a man's world view affects what he pays attention to, and a great deal of politics is about paying attention. The name of the game for many politicians is not so much "Do this, do that" as it is "Look here!"

"Character" comes from the Greek word for engraving; in one sense it is what life has marked into a man's being. As used here, *character is the way the President orients himself toward life*—not for the moment, but enduringly. Character is the person's stance as he confronts experience. And at the core of character, a man confronts himself. The President's fundamental self-esteem is his prime personal resource; to defend and advance that, he will sacrifice much else he values. Down there in the privacy of his heart, does he find himself superb, or ordinary, or debased, or in some intermediate range? No President has been utterly paralyzed by self-doubt and none has been utterly free of midnight self-mockery. In between, the real Presidents move out on life from positions of relative strength or weakness. Equally important are the criteria by which they judge themselves. A President who rates himself by the standard of achievement, for instance, may be little affected by losses of affection.

Character, world view, and style are abstractions from the reality of the whole individual. In every case they form an integrated pattern: the man develops a combination which makes psychological sense for him, a dynamic arrangement of motives, beliefs, and habits in the service of his need for self-esteem.

THE POWER SITUATION AND "CLIMATE OF EXPECTATIONS"

Presidential character resonates with the political situation the President faces. It adapts him as he tries to adapt it. The support he has from the public and interest groups, the party balance in Congress, the thrust of Supreme Court opinion together set the basic power situation he must deal with. An activist President may run smack into a brick wall of resistance, then pull back and wait for a better moment. On the other hand, a President who sees himself as a quiet caretaker may not try to exploit even the most favorable power situation. So it is the relationship between President and the political configuration that makes the system tick.

Even before public opinion polls, the President's real or supposed popularity was a large factor in his performance. Besides the power mix in Washington, the President has to deal with a national climate of expectations, the predominant needs thrust up to him by the people. There are at least three recurrent themes around which these needs are focused.

People look to the President for *reassurance*, a feeling that things will be all right, that the President will take care of his people. The psychological request is for a surcease of anxiety. Obviously, modern life in America involves considerable doses of fear, tension, anxiety, worry; from time to time, the public mood calls for a rest, a time of peace, a breathing space, a "return to normalcy."

Another theme is the demand for a *sense of progress and action*. The President ought to do something to direct the nation's course—or at least be in there pitching for the people. The President is looked to as a take-charge man, a doer, a turner of the wheels, a producer of progress—even if that means some sacrifice of serenity.

A third type of climate of expectations is the public need for a sense of *legitimacy* from, and in, the Presidency. The President should be a master politician who is above politics. He should have a right to his place and a rightful way of acting in it. The respectability—even religiosity—of the office has to be protected by a man who presents himself as defender of the faith. There is more to this than dignity, more than propriety. The President is expected to personify our betterness in an inspiring way, to express in what he does and is (not just in what he says) a moral idealism which, in much of the public mind, is the very opposite of "politics."

Over time the climate of expectations shifts and changes. Wars, depressions, and other national events contribute to that change, but there also is a rough cycle, from an emphasis on action (which begins to look too "political") to an emphasis on legitimacy (the moral uplift of which creates its own strains) to an emphasis on reassurance and rest (which comes to seem like drift) and back to action again. One need not be astrological about it. The point is that the climate of expectations at any given time is the political air the President has to breathe. Relating to this climate is a large part of his task.

PREDICTING PRESIDENTS

The best way to predict a President's character, world view, and style is to see how he constructed them in the first place. Especially in the early stages, life is experimental; consciously or not, a person tries out various ways of defining and maintaining and raising self-esteem. He looks to his environment for clues as to who he is and how well he is doing. These lessons of life slowly sink in: certain self-images and evaluations, certain ways of looking at the world, certain styles of action get confirmed by his experience and he gradually adopts them as his own. If we can see that process of development, we can understand the product. The features to note are those bearing on Presidential performance.

Experimental development continues all the way to death; we will not blind ourselves to midlife changes, particularly in the full-scale prediction cases. But it is often much easier to see the basic patterns in early life histories. Later on a whole host of distractions—especially the image-making all politicians learn to practice—clouds the picture.

In general, character has its *main* development in childhood, world view in adolescence, style in early adulthood. The stance toward life I call character grows out of the child's experiments in relating to parents, brothers and sisters, and peers at play and in school, as well as to his own body and the objects around it. Slowly the child defines an orientation toward experience; once established, that tends to last despite much subsequent contradiction. By adolescence, the child has been hearing and seeing how people make their worlds meaningful, and now he is moved to relate himself—his own meanings—to those around him. His focus of attention shifts toward the future; he senses that decisions about his fate are coming and he looks into the premises for those decisions. Thoughts about the way the world works and how one might work in it, about what people are like and how one might be like them or not, and about the values people share and how one might share in them too—these are typical concerns for the post-child, pre-adult mind of the adolescent.

These themes come together strongly in early adulthood, when the person moves from contemplation to responsible action and adopts a style. In most biographical accounts this period stands out in stark clarity—the time of emergence, the time the young man found himself. I call it his first independent political success. It was then he moved beyond the detailed guidance of his family; then his self-esteem was dramatically boosted; then he came forth as a person to be reckoned with by other people. The *way* he did that is profoundly important to him. Typically he grasps that style and hangs onto it. Much later, coming into the Presidency, something in him remembers this earlier victory and re-emphasizes the style that made it happen.

Character provides the main thrust and broad direction—but it does not *determine*, in any fixed sense, world view and style. The story of development does not end with the end of childhood. Thereafter, the culture one grows in and the ways that culture is translated by parents and peers shapes the meanings one makes of his character. The going world view gets learned and that learning helps channel character forces. Thus it will not necessarily be true that compulsive characters have reactionary beliefs, or that compliant characters believe in compromise. Similarly for style: historical accidents play a large part in furnishing special opportunities for action and in blocking off alternatives. For example, however much anger a young man may feel, that anger will not be expressed in rhetoric unless and until his life situation provides a platform and an audience. Style thus has a stature and independence of its own. Those who would reduce all explanation to character neglect these highly significant later channelings. For beyond the root is the branch, above the foundation the superstructure, and starts do not prescribe finishes.

FOUR TYPES OF PRESIDENTIAL CHARACTER

The five concepts—character, world view, style, power situation, and climate of expectations—run through the accounts of Presidents in the chapters to follow, which cluster the Presidents since Theodore Roosevelt into four types. This is the fundamental scheme of the study. It offers a way to move past the complexities to the main contrasts and comparisons.

The first baseline in defining Presidential types is *activity-passivity*. How much energy does the man invest in his Presidency? Lyndon Johnson went at his day like a human cyclone, coming to rest long after the sun went down. Calvin Coolidge often slept eleven hours a night and still needed a nap in the middle of the day. In between, the Presidents array themselves on the high or low side of the activity line.

The second baseline is *positive-negative affect* toward one's activity—that is, how he feels about what he does. Relatively speaking, does he seem to experience his political life as happy or sad, enjoyable or discouraging, positive or negative in its main effect. The feeling I am after here is not grim satisfaction in a job well done, not some philosophical conclusion. The idea is this: is he someone who, on the surfaces we can see, gives forth the feeling that he has *fun* in political life? Franklin Roosevelt's Secretary of War Henry L. Stimson wrote that the Roosevelts "not only understood the *use* of power, they knew the *enjoyment* of power, too. . . . Whether a man is burdened by power or enjoys power; whether he is trapped by responsibility or made free by it; whether he is moved by other people and outer forces or moves them—that is the essence of leadership."

The positive-negative baseline, then, is a general symptom of the fit between the man and his experience, a kind of register of *felt* satisfaction.

Why might we expect these two simple dimensions to outline the main character types? Because they stand for two central features of anyone's orientation toward life. In nearly every study of personality, some form of the active-passive contrast is critical; the general tendency to act or be acted upon is evident in such concepts as dominance-submission, extraversion-introversion, aggression-timidity, attack-defense, fight-flight, engagement-withdrawal, approach-avoidance. In everyday life we sense quickly the general energy output of the people we deal with. Similarly we catch on fairly quickly to the affect dimension—whether the person seems to be optimistic or pessimistic, hopeful or skeptical, happy or sad. The two baselines are clear and they are also independent of one another: all of us know people who are very active but seem discouraged, others who are quite passive but seem happy, and so forth. The activity baseline refers to what one does, the affect baseline to how one feels about what he does.

Both are crude clues to character. They are leads into four basic character patterns long familiar in psychological research. In summary form, these are the main configurations:

Active-Positive

There is a congruence, a consistency, between much activity and the enjoyment of it, indicating relatively high self-esteem and relative success in relating to the environment. The man shows an orientation toward productiveness as a value and an ability to use his styles flexibly, adaptively, suiting the dance to the music. He sees himself as developing over time toward relatively well defined personal goals—growing toward his image of himself as he might yet be. There is an emphasis on rational mastery, on using the brain to move the feet. This may get him into trouble; he may fail to take account of the irrational in politics. Not everyone he deals with sees things his way and he may find it hard to understand why.

Active-Negative

The contradiction here is between relatively intense effort and relatively low emotional reward for that effort. The activity has a compulsive quality, as if the man were trying to make up for something or to escape from anxiety into hard work. He seems ambitious, striving upward, power-seeking. His stance toward the environment is aggressive and he has a persistent problem in managing his aggressive feelings. His self-image is vague and discontinuous. Life is a hard struggle to achieve and hold power, hampered by the condemnations of a perfectionistic conscience. Active-negative types pour energy into the political system, but it is an energy distorted from within.

Passive-Positive

This is the receptive, compliant, other-directed character whose life is a search for affection as a reward for being agreeable and cooperative rather than personally assertive. The contradiction is between low self-esteem (on grounds of being unlovable, unattractive) and a superficial optimism. A hopeful attitude helps dispel doubt and elicits encouragement from others. Passive-positive types help soften the harsh edges of politics. But their dependence and the fragility of their hopes and enjoyments make disappointment in politics likely.

Passive-Negative

The factors are consistent—but how are we to account for the man's *political* role-taking? Why is someone who does little in politics and enjoys it less there at all? The answer lies in the passive-negative's character-rooted orientation toward doing dutiful service; this compensates for low self-esteem based on a sense of uselessness. Passive-negative types are in politics because they think they ought to be. They may be well adapted to certain nonpolitical roles, but they lack the experience and flexibility to perform effectively as political leaders. Their tendency is to withdraw, to escape from the conflict and uncertainty of politics by emphasizing vague principles (especially prohibitions) and procedural arrangements. They become guardians of the right and proper way, above the sordid politicking of lesser men.

Active-positive Presidents want most to achieve results. Active-negatives aim to get and keep power. Passive-positives are after love. Passive-negatives emphasize their civic virtue. The relation of activity to enjoyment in a President thus tends to outline a cluster of characteristics, to set apart the adapted from the compulsive, compliant, and withdrawn types.

The first four Presidents of the United States, conveniently, ran through this gamut of character types. (Remember, we are talking about tendencies, broad directions; no individual man exactly fits a category.) George Washington—clearly the most important President in the pantheon—established the fundamental legitimacy of an American government at a time when this was a matter in considerable question. Washington's dignity, judiciousness, his aloof air of reserve and dedication to duty fit the passive-negative or withdrawing type best. Washington did not seek innovation, he sought stability. He longed to retire to Mount Vernon, but fortunately was persuaded to stay on through a second term, in which, by rising above the political conflict between Hamilton and Jefferson and inspiring confidence in his own integrity, he gave the nation time to develop the organized means for peaceful change.

John Adams followed, a dour New England Puritan, much given to work and worry, an impatient and irascible man—an active-negative President, a compulsive type. Adams was far more partisan than Washington; the survival of the system through his Presidency demonstrated that the nation could tolerate, for a time, domination by one of its nascent political parties. As President, an angry Adams brought the United States to the brink of war with France, and presided over the new nation's first experiment in political repression: the Alien and Sedition Acts, forbidding, among other things, unlawful combinations "with intent to oppose any measure or measures of the government of the United States," or "any false, scandalous, and malicious writing or writings against the United States, or the President of the United States, with intent to defame . . . or to bring them or either of them, into contempt or disrepute."

Then came Jefferson. He too had his troubles and failures—in the design of national defense, for example. As for his Presidential character (only one element in success or failure), Jefferson was clearly active-positive. A child of the Enlightenment, he applied his reason to organizing connections with Congress aimed at strengthening the more popular forces. A man of catholic interests and delightful humor, Jefferson combined a clear and open vision of what the country could be with a profound political sense, expressed in his famous phrase, "Every difference of opinion is not a difference of principle."

The fourth President was James Madison, "Little Jemmy," the constitutional philosopher thrown into the White House at a time of great international turmoil. Madison comes closest to the passive-positive, or compliant, type; he suffered from irresolution, tried to compromise his way out, and gave in too readily to the "warhawks" urging combat with Britain. The nation drifted into war, and Madison wound up ineptly commanding his collection of amateur generals in the streets of Washington. General Jackson's victory at New Orleans saved the Madison administration's historical reputation; but he left the Presidency with the United States close to bankruptcy and secession.

These four Presidents—like all Presidents—were persons trying to cope with the roles they had won by using the equipment they had built over a lifetime. The President is not some shapeless organism in a flood of novelties, but a man with a memory in a system with a history. Like all of us, he draws on his past to shape his future. The pathetic hope that the White House will turn a Caligula into a Marcus Aurelius is as naive as the fear that ultimate power inevitably corrupts. The problem is to understand—and to state understandably—what in the personal past foreshadows the Presidential future.

11

Leader Appeal, Leader Performance, and the Motive Profiles of Leaders and Followers: A Study of American Presidents and Elections

DAVID G. WINTER

What is a great leader? What is a popular leader? Are they the same? Are they the result of the same or different factors? Our naive belief in the "great person" theory of leadership, that the person shapes events and the leader creates his or her own greatness, has long been challenged by scholars from diverse disciplines who analyze leadership appeal and performance into broad impersonal forces and social-structural factors. Yet in the real world of politics, the factor of personal appeal or having (in the language of the Harris poll) "an attractive, forceful personality" is of enormous concern to campaign strategists and journalists (even if it is largely treated as error variance by voting analysts; see Nie, Verba, and Petrocik, 1979; Sears, 1969). And in the real world of history, successful leaders such as Abraham Lincoln or Franklin D. Roosevelt display such a blend of wisdom, flexibility, and good tactics that we conclude their greatness must be based, at least in part, on personal characteristics (e.g., see Burns, 1956; Haley, 1969; Vidal, 1984).

Can these phenomena of greatness and appeal among political leaders be analyzed in psychological terms? Several classic theories and a good deal of contemporary social psychological research suggest a variety of models for a leader's appeal and performance. This article presents data on the psychological characteristics of one kind of leader—American presidents—and one series of followers—American society from the 1780s through the 1960s—as an empirical commentary on (not a test of) these theories and issues.

THEORIES AND MODELS OF LEADER APPEAL

Leader Characteristics

Max Weber's concept of charisma (or the "gift of grace") as one base of the legitimacy of authority is obviously related to the leader's personal appeal and performance when structural and traditional factors are held constant. To Weber, the charismatic leader possesses "a certain quality of personality by virtue of which he is set apart from ordinary men and treated as endowed with supernatural, superhuman, or at least specifically exceptional powers or qualities." Followers obey out of duty rather than choice or calculation; as Weber put it, "No prophet has ever regarded his quality [of charisma] as dependent on the attributes of the masses around him." Of course Weber did acknowledge that in the long run the followers' needs and satisfactions are important. "If [the leader] is for long unsuccessful, above all if his leadership fails to benefit his followers, it is likely that his charismatic authority will disappear" (1947, pp. 358–360).

Although Freud analyzed the dynamics of group formation in terms of the followers' identification in their ego ideal or superego with the leader, he emphasized the characteristics of the successful leader in facilitating these identifications. "The leader himself need love no one else, he may be of a masterful nature, absolutely narcissistic, self-confident, and independent" (1921/1955, pp. 123–124).

Thus one psychological model of political leaders' appeal and success focuses on relatively enduring personal characteristics (e.g., narcissism, energy, self-direction) that some leaders simply happen to possess. Although the great-person theory of leadership implicit in this model is now in some disrepute (see Gibb, 1969; Hollander, 1964), many experimental studies do show the modest positive correlations between leadership and self-esteem, self-confidence, and related variables (see Bass, 1981, pp. 74–92) that would be predicted from the Weber-Freud model.

Leader–Situation Match

Nowadays many theorists and most experimentalists would argue that the leader's appeal and success depend on the situation, so that the personality characteristics required for successful, appealing leadership will vary with the situation. Recently Bem and Funder (1978) and Bem and Lord (1979) have expressed this notion more formally in the concept of the degree of match between a person and the *template* (required characteristics) of the situation, and they have gone on to suggest ways of measuring situational demands.

Barber's (1980) recent cyclical model of American elections is an application of the notion of leader–situation template matching or congruence in a political context. According to Barber, American presidential elections follow a regular course: first, a focus on *conflict* of forces; then, a concern for *conscience*: and finally, a need for *conciliation* to bring all parties together again. This leads, in turn, to a renewed conflict orientation. From election to election the requirements for personal appeal and success in office might vary in a corresponding fashion: In a "conflict" year, the candidate who is the best fighter will be appealing and victorious, but when the concern is with conciliation, the candidate who promises to "bring us together" will gain popular appeal. Barber believed that these three issues are derived from the most basic social-political aspects of human nature; that the cyclical dynamic has a force of its own. Thus his theory involves a kind of match between leader and situation, but the situation is conceived in terms of abstract, impersonal forces rather than in terms of particular personal characteristics of the followers.

Leader–Follower Match

In contrast to the impersonal cycle of Barber's theory, Erikson offered a theory of the relation between leaders and their societies that is explicitly focused on the relation between leaders' and followers' characteristics. On the basis of several studies of "inspiring and effective [men] of action" such as Hitler, Luther, and Gandhi (Erikson, 1950, 1958, and 1969, respectively), Erikson concluded that leaders, with their own identities, conflicts, and needs, are "found and chosen by contemporaries possessed of analogous conflicts and corresponding needs" (1964, p. 204). In other words, the success of such leaders depends on a match between their own personal characteristics and the historically conditioned characteristics of their potential followers. Phrased in this way Erikson's theory is supported by the extensive experimental literature relating leadership success to a kind of congruence between leaders' characteristics and followers' characteristics (see Bass, 1981, pp. 31–33). Erikson also mentioned some transsituational abilities of the leader, but they are not formally incorporated into his theory: "An unusual energy of body, a rare concentration of mind, and a total devotion of soul. . . . Intuitive grasp of the actualities of the led . . . [and] ability to introduce himself into that actuality as a new, vital factor (personality, image, style)" (1964, pp. 203, 208).

Taken together, these theories suggest several different kinds of factors that may account for the personal appeal and greatness of political leaders: (a) leader characteristics independent of the situation, (b) leader characteristics that match systematically changing situational demands, and (c) leader characteristics that match characteristics of followers or of the population in general, whatever the determinants of these latter characteristics may be.

The several explanations of leadership are quite parallel to familiar psychological explanations of other behaviors: an initial person or "trait" explanation (e.g., Allport, 1937), later debunked for a time (e.g., Mischel, 1968), and followed by a focus on the interaction of person and situation (e.g., Magnusson & Endler, 1977). The rest of this article will explore the usefulness of these models by analyzing American presidents and presidential elections. Some questions to be asked include: What is the psychological basis of presidential appeal? Does it involve leader characteristics or some kind of leader–situation match? What is the psychological basis of presidential greatness? Are the leaders who appeal the most to the electorate also the greatest or best leaders? In some sense, this last question reaches down to the foundations of democratic political theory. (See Simonton, 1981, for a study of other, nonpsychological determinants of presidential greatness.)

EMPIRICAL STUDIES OF PRESIDENTS AND ELECTIONS

The American presidency is an excellent source of material for studying the appeal and performance of political leaders. Although the size of the population is rather small, the efforts of historians, political scientists, and archivists have accumulated an enormous amount of data. In recent years, many scholars have begun to analyze the presidency with the quantitative and statistical methods familiar to the behavioral sciences (e.g., Maranell, 1970; Murray & Blessing, 1983; Simonton, 1981). Recent advances in the technology for assessing the personalities of key political actors at a distance (cf. Hermann, 1977) and measuring the modal personality of groups of followers over time through coding cultural documents (e.g., McClelland, 1961, 1975, especially Appendix IV) have made it possible to study, in psychological terms, the leadership appeal and performance of American presidents in their society.

For both leaders and followers, this study focuses on three important human social motives: (a) the achievement motive, a concern for excellence, which is associated with moderate risk taking, using feedback, and entrepreneurial success (McClelland, 1961); (b) the affiliation–intimacy motive, a concern for close relations with others, which is associated with interpersonal warmth, self-disclosure, and good overall adaptation to life (McAdams, 1982); and (c) the power motive, a concern for impact and prestige, which is associated with getting formal social power and also profligate impulsive actions such as aggression, drinking, and taking extreme risks (Winter, 1973; Winter & Stewart, 1978).

Motivation focuses on the broad classes of people's goals and goal-directed actions, and so it is a component of personality that is especially important to the relations between leaders and followers. These particular motives are drawn from Murray's comprehensive taxonomy. Although they are not the only human motives, several lines of evidence do suggest that they are major motives involving the most important common human concerns. Power and affiliation, for example, repeatedly emerge as the two fundamental dimensions of social behavior (see Brown, 1965, chapter 2) and interpersonal traits (Conte & Plutchik, 1981; Wiggins, 1980). Achievement reflects the dimension of evaluation that is consistently the most important factor of connotative meaning (Snider & Osgood, 1969). These three motives are closely matched to the three dimensions used by Bales (1970) to describe group functioning (forward–backward, positive–negative, and upward–downward, respectively).

Winter and Stewart (1977) have demonstrated that these three motives are relevant to several important kinds of political action and outcomes. Whereas the motives were originally measured in individuals by content analysis of Thematic Apperception Test (TAT) responses, the new integrated scoring system, developed by Winter (1983) for scoring motive imagery in any kind of verbal material, makes it possible to score presidents at a distance. Thus, both leaders and followers are assessed by means of the same methods and scoring techniques. This makes it possible to describe the characteristics of leaders and situations (or followers) in terms that are both psychologically meaningful and also commensurate with each other. (See Winter, 1973, 1983, for a general description of the psychometric characteristics, including reliability, of the motive measures.)

METHOD

Sources of Data

For each president from Washington through Reagan, the first inaugural address was scored for achievement, affiliation–intimacy, and power motive imagery.[1] (Presidents Tyler, Fillmore, Andrew Johnson, Arthur, and Ford were never elected and inaugurated in their own right and, therefore, are not included.) Although some speeches had been scored in the past by Donley and Winter (1970) and Winter and Stewart (1977), for the present study all speeches were mixed together and newly scored by two trained and reliable scorers (demonstrated category agreement with expert scoring over .85), who discussed and resolved any disagreements that had occurred. Raw scores were expressed in terms of images per 1,000 words and then standardized with an overall mean of 50 and a standard deviation of 10 for each motive. Motive imagery scores for each president, in standardized and raw form, are presented in Table 1.

Motive scores for American society were adapted from the work of McClelland (1975, chapter 9), who collected three kinds of standard cultural documents dating from each decade from the 1790s through the 1960s: popular novels, children's readers, and hymns. A few details of McClelland's procedure should be mentioned at this point. For each kind of document in each decade, selected pages (readers) or 10-line page segments (novels and hymns) were scored for achievement, affiliation, and power motive imagery. The results were expressed in terms of proportion of pages (or 10-line segments) scored for a particular motive. These scores were then standardized across all decades, separately for each motive. Separate scores from each type of document were then averaged (see McClelland, 1975, pp. 330–332, 403–410, for further methodological information). For the present study, these average decade scores were then restandardized, also with an overall mean of 50 and a standard deviation of 10 for each motive. Thus the motive levels of the presidents and of American society at the time of each president's election are measured in comparable ways and expressed in comparable terms.

**Table 1. Motive Imagery Scores of American Presidents'
Inaugural Addresses, 1789–1981**

| President | Date | Motive scores | | | | | |
| | | Standardized | | | Raw | | |
		Ach	Aff	Pow	Ach	Aff	Pow
Washington, George	1789	39	54	41	3.85	3.85	4.62
Adams, John	1797	39	49	42	3.89	3.03	4.76
Jefferson, Thomas	1801	49	51	51	5.65	3.30	6.59
Madison, James	1809	55	51	57	6.84	3.42	7.69
Monroe, James	1817	57	46	51	7.22	2.41	6.62
Adams, John Quincy	1825	48	51	37	5.43	3.40	3.74
Jackson, Andrew	1829	43	47	45	4.48	2.69	5.38
Van Buren, Martin	1837	42	48	40	4.38	2.83	4.38
Harrison, William Henry	1841	32	41	40	2.56	1.52	4.31
Polk, James	1845	33	41	50	2.65	1.43	6.32
Taylor, Zachary	1849	53	53	41	6.39	3.65	4.56
Pierce, Franklin	1853	49	44	50	5.72	2.11	6.33
Buchanan, James	1857	46	47	42	5.05	2.53	4.69
Lincoln, Abraham	1861	36	45	53	3.34	2.23	6.97
Grant, Ulysses	1869	56	47	36	7.02	2.63	3.51
Hayes, Rutherford	1877	51	48	48	6.07	2.83	6.07
Garfield, James	1881	46	35	49	5.09	0.34	6.10
Cleveland, Grover	1885	53	46	63	6.52	2.37	8.89
Harrison, Benjamin	1889	37	45	45	3.49	2.18	5.45
McKinley, William	1897	47	41	46	5.30	1.51	5.55
Roosevelt, Theodore	1905	62	38	38	8.14	1.02	4.07
Taft, William Howard	1909	44	38	58	4.79	0.92	7.93
Wilson, Woodrow	1913	66	49	53	8.83	2.94	7.06
Harding, Warren	1921	48	57	42	5.41	4.51	4.81
Coolidge, Calvin	1925	44	46	45	4.69	2.47	5.43
Hoover, Herbert	1929	68	45	48	9.18	2.16	5.94
Roosevelt, Franklin	1933	53	44	61	6.37	2.12	8.50
Truman, Harry	1949	56	65	78	6.91	5.99	11.98
Eisenhower, Dwight	1953	43	57	49	4.50	4.50	6.14
Kennedy, John	1961	50	85	77	5.90	9.59	11.81
Johnson, Lyndon	1965	55	59	49	6.77	4.74	6.09
Nixon, Richard	1969	66	76	53	8.94	8.00	7.06
Carter, Jimmy	1977	75	59	59	10.60	4.89	8.16
Reagan, Ronald	1981	60	51	63	7.78	3.28	9.01

NOTE: Ach = achievement. Aff = affiliation. Pow = power.

Definitions of Variables

Several characteristics that are important to leader appeal and leader performance in the theories of Freud and Weber, such as energy, impact, prestige, and even narcissism, are closely related to the known action characteristics of the power motive. For example, power-motivated people tend to be energetic, in terms of both self-report and physiological arousal, especially in power-related situations (Steele, 1977). They seek impact on others and are concerned about prestige, while maintaining their own autonomy and self-direction (Winter, 1973; Winter & Stewart, 1978). Their own estimates of their influence, as well as their responses to ingratiation by subordinates, suggest a considerable narcissism (Fodor & Farrow, 1979). Thus power motivation is a leader characteristic of great interest in its own right. Some recent studies of organizations further suggest that the combination of high-power motivation and low affiliation–intimacy motivation—the so-called leadership motive pattern—predicts successful leadership among managers and high morale among followers (McClelland, 1975, chapter 8; McClelland & Boyatzis, 1982; McClelland & Burnham, 1976). In the present case, this motive combination was defined as the difference between standard-scored power motive imagery and standard-scored affiliation–intimacy imagery.[2]

How can Barber's cyclical theory be operationalized with the motive measures? Barber's three issues seem closely related to the three motives: Conflict suggests power, conciliation suggests affiliation, and (more loosely) conscience may involve achievement. A variable reflecting the cycle-appropriate motive was therefore defined as follows: the power motive score for presidents chosen in the conflict elections (1912, 1924, 1948, 1960); the affiliation–intimacy score for presidents taking office in conciliation years (1908, 1920, 1932, 1968); and the achievement score for the winners of conscience elections (1904, 1928, 1952, 1964, 1976).

To determine the extent of congruence between a president and American society at the time of his election, the absolute values of the discrepancies between presidential score and society score for each motive were summed to yield a total discrepancy score. With sign reversed, this was used as a measure of president–society motive congruence.

Dependent variables reflecting presidential appeal and presidential performance were taken from several sources. Presidential appeal was measured by the percentage of popular votes received in their first election to the presidency and by the margin of votes over the second-place candidate. (These two measures intercorrelated +.71, but diverged in years such as 1860, 1912, 1968, and 1980 when there were three or more major candidates.) The four cases where the winning candidate was a former vice president who had taken office on the death of the president (Theodore Roosevelt, Coolidge, Truman, and Lyndon Johnson) were eliminated because these men had not initially gained the presidency in their own right. They had no real first election and first inaugural address to study and score. One other measure of presidential appeal, this time involving not only initial popular appeal but also popular reaction to all 4 years of an administration, is whether the president was reelected. Two separate measures were used to measure reelection; one considered each president as a single case (including the four vice presidents mentioned earlier), and the other treated each attempted reelection as a separate case. Obviously those presidents who died during their first term were not included here.

Next, the total national percentage of votes for the House of Representatives candidates of the president's party was taken as a measure of the appeal of the president's *party* as distinguished from the appeal of the president as a *person*. (Alternatively, this is a measure of the *coattails* effect.) Data for these election variables were taken from the *Historical Statistics of the United States* (Bureau of the Census, 1984).

Generating popular appeal is one kind of political skill, but working successfully with Congress is also important. Although it is difficult to give each president an overall score on his relations with Congress, there are some objective measures that might reflect that relationship, including the number of rejections of court and cabinet appointments (taken from Kane, 1956) and the percentage of vetoes overridden (taken from U.S. Senate Library, 1976). A final aspect of a president's political skill involves his party's election success at the midterm elections 2 years after the inauguration. Normally, the president's party loses seats. In the House of Representatives, the percentage of seats lost varied inversely with the percentage size of the initial majority ($r = -.29$ for 24 midterm elections; percentages rather than raw changes in seats were necessary because of the changing size of the U.S. House of Representatives over time). When the effects of this negative correlation were removed by subtracting the expected loss from the actual loss, the result was an adjusted measure of the performance of the president's party.

Of the many things that can happen in a presidential administration, war and peace are surely among the two most important. In the present study, war entry was defined in terms of the list developed by Richardson (1960), with his definitions used for the years before 1820 and after 1945. (Because of the difficulty of demarcating separate wars and the uncertainty of casualty figures, all Indian conflicts are excluded. Thus in the present context, *war* really means *interstate war*.) Not every crisis necessarily results in war, however. Small (1980), for example, listed 19 crises that could easily have escalated into war but that were in fact settled peacefully. Some examples include the dispute with England about violations of American neutrality (1791), the Oregon boundary dispute (1845), the *Panay* incident (1937), and the Cuban Missile Crisis (1962). These are labeled *war avoidance* in the present study. Another aspect of peacemaking involves the limitation of arms. Starting with the first arms limitation conference at The Hague during McKinley's administration, historical sources were used to identify presidents who concluded treaties with at least one other major power for the limitation or banning of one or more specific weapons systems.

What is presidential greatness? Perhaps it is impossible to define. First, we can never know all the facts about a president's actions and what independent effects these actions had on historical outcomes. Even with these facts, moreover, any ratings of greatness will mostly reflect the values attached by the rater to these outcomes. For example, raters who value military greatness will tend to rate highly presidents who involved the United

States in victorious wars. Second, presidential greatness probably has many separate (and uncorrelated) components. How can these be weighed and synthesized into a single rating?

One approach to measuring presidential greatness is to rely on the judgments of scholars of American history. Although their judgments are undoubtedly affected by their values, historians are presumably in possession of more facts than are most people and are in a better position to make objective evaluations and comparative ratings. Over the past 35 years, historians have often been polled on presidential greatness. In one of the most extensive polls, Maranell (1970) asked 571 historians of the United States to rate the presidents on several dimensions, including general prestige, strength of action, presidential activeness, and accomplishments of the administration. Because these four dimensions were highly intercorrelated, they were standardized and summed to produce a consensus on the relative greatness of the presidents from Washington to Lyndon Johnson. Washington and Lincoln, for example, were the highest rated presidents, whereas Grant and Harding were at the bottom. In a sense, these ratings are only another aspect of presidential appeal, to historians rather than to voters. In fact, though, the correlations between the summed Maranell study ratings and the percentage of vote and margin of victory measures were essentially zero. At the very least, then, rated greatness is different from voter appeal. Another facet of presidential greatness involves making decisions that have historic impact on the country and world, as compiled and judged by Morris (1967). Some examples of "great" presidential decisions include the purchase of Louisiana (by Jefferson), the abolition of central banking (by Jackson), and the attack on business trusts (by Theodore Roosevelt).

RESULTS

Table 2 presents the relations between each of the four major variables assessing presidential motives or president–situation motive match and the dependent variables reflecting presidential appeal, political skill, and presidential performance. Presidential appeal, as measured by success at both election and reelection, is a straightforward function of how congruent the president's motive levels were with those of the American society of the time. The much lower correlation with the total percentage of House of Representatives vote for candidates of the president's party suggests that this motive congruence predicts the specific personal appeal of the president (percentage of votes cast, margin, reelection), rather than the national support for the president's party (or the coattails effect). In general, the summed discrepancy/congruence score gave results more significant than those for the discrepancy scores on any individual motive, suggesting that discrepancies on *each* motive contributed to most overall effects. Algebraically signed discrepancy scores gave no significant results. This suggests that what is important is the *discrepancy* between president and society, rather than whether the president or the society is higher on any particular motive.

Neither presidential power motivation nor power minus affiliation–intimacy, by itself, was related to any aspect of political appeal. The *cyclically appropriate motive* measure, drawn from Barber's theory, actually reversed and was negatively correlated with most of the appeal measures. For political appeal, as reflected in the size of the personal electoral mandate, then, Erikson's theory of leader–follower personality congruence was the theory most strongly supported by the results.

None of the measures of political skill in office was significantly associated with any of the presidential or congruence motive measures. Probably veto overrides and appointment rejections are fragmentary measures that do not adequately reflect presidential political skill and are much affected by particular historical circumstances.

Presidential outcomes showed a very different pattern. Power motivation was strongly related to war entry, as expected on the basis of numerous other findings (e.g., Winter, 1980). It was also related, almost at a significant level, to *avoiding* war in a crisis situation. This suggests that the power motive is a leader characteristic associated with dramatic, crisis-oriented, perhaps confrontational foreign policy, which may end peacefully but which can easily end in war (see Hermann, 1980). Power motivation by itself was also associated with both measures of greatness, more strongly so than power minus affiliation–intimacy or the leadership motive pattern. This latter variable was negatively associated with arms reduction, largely because of the strong positive relation between affiliation–intimacy imagery and arms limitation agreements ($r = .43$). The cycle-appropriate motive measure also showed low, nonsignificant correlations in the same direction as those for the power motive. Congruence between president and society, in contrast, was significantly negatively associated with both measures of greatness as well as war avoidance. It seems those presidents who matched the country's motives at the time were in the end among the least great of the presidents, at least in the judgment of historians.

DISCUSSION

These results suggest two conclusions. First, among American presidents at least, leader appeal is a function of how well the leader's own motives fit the motive imagery profile of the times. Presidential leadership performance, however, is a very different matter. Both rated performance and several of the most significant outcomes were functions more of leader attributes (especially power motivation) than of leader–situation match. Indeed, among American presidents it appears that the greatest presidents were those who were least congruent with the followers of their society.

Some examples will illustrate these two conclusions. Abraham Lincoln is generally considered to be one of the two greatest American presidents. Yet he was one of four major candidates in 1860, elected with only a minority of the total popular vote. His motive profile was highly discrepant with that of American society in the 1860s; in fact, he is among the half dozen most discrepant presidents. Some others with motive profiles

Table 2. Correlations of Variables Assessing Aspects of Presidential Appeal and Performance With Presidential Characteristics and President–Situation Match

Variable	Presidential characteristics		President–situation match	
	Power motive	Power minus affiliation–intimacy	Cycle-appropriate motive	President–society congruence
Electoral appeal				
Vote percentage[a]				
r	-.04	.10	-.38	.60****
n	25	25	9	23
Margin of victory[a]				
r	-.07	.05	-.52	.46**
n	25	25	9	23
Reelected				
r	.06	-.05	-.40	.37
n	25	25	9	25
Reelected, all instances[b]				
r	.27	.16	-.40	.44**
n	30	30	9	30
Percentage vote for party's House candidates				
r	.13	.20	-.11	.21
n	30	30	9	28
Political skills in office				
Court/cabinet rejections				
r	-.19	-.20	-.12	.23
n	24	31	13	23
Percentage vetoes overridden				
r	.01	-.04	.24	-.01
n	27	27	13	26

Adjusted midterm House loss				
r	−.23	.03	−.19	.09
n	24	24	13	23
		Presidential outcomes		
War entry				
r	.52***	.36*	.13	−.05
n	31	31	13	30
War avoidance				
r	.34*	.16	.26	−.39**
n	29	29	11	29
Arms limitation				
r	−.05	−.55**	.44	.03
n	14	14	13	13
Consensus of greatness				
r	.40**	.35	.23	−.46**
n	29	29	11	29
Great decisions cited				
r	.51***	.27	.31	−.37**
n	29	29	11	29

[a] Excluding all vice presidents who assumed office on the death of the president.
[b] Including all attempts at reelection.
* $p < .10$, two-tailed. ** $p < .05$, two-tailed. *** $p < .01$, two-tailed. **** $p < .001$, two-tailed.

highly discrepant from their times include: Washington, Theodore Roosevelt, Truman, and Kennedy—all highly rated by historians. And some congruent presidents include Buchanan, Grant, Harding, and Coolidge—three of whom are considered to be failures if not outright disasters. (To be fair, it must also be noted that Franklin Roosevelt was highly congruent and Nixon highly discrepant.)

These results diverge somewhat from those obtained by Simonton (1981) in his study of presidential greatness (summed ratings along five dimensions, from Maranell) and presidential performance (duration of administration, war years, assassination attempt, and scandal). Simonton found that personality traits, including specifically achievement and power motivation scores, made little predictive contribution to presidential greatness or performance. How can this conclusion be reconciled with the results of the present study? First, there are differences in the motive scores used. Simonton used scores originally reported by Donley and Winter (1970), based on an informal adaptation of the original scoring systems, for the 12 presidents from 1905 to 1969. When the final codified version of the integrated scoring system was developed (Winter, 1983), the first inaugurals of all presidents were mixed together and scored. This resulted in some changed scores for speeches scored earlier, most notably for Theodore Roosevelt and William Howard Taft. The later scorings, shown in Table 1, should be taken as definitive. Thus the present study involved slightly different motive data and used a much larger group of presidents. Second, Simonton used some presidential performance variables that were different from those of the present study and others that were defined differently. For example, Simonton did not measure war avoidance, arms limitation, or great decisions; and the definitions of one overlapping variable—war—seem to be different in the two studies. Finally, Simonton analyzed the effect of motives "within a multivariate framework" (1981, p. 321), which seems to mean hierarchical regression (cf. p. 314), although this is not clear. No doubt different researchers would make different judgments about whether, in predicting performance and greatness, personality variables should be entered before or after variables reflecting other biographical information or administration events. Simonton did not investigate the relation between presidential and societal motives. Overall, then, the differences in the results of these two studies suggest the need for careful definition of variables and explicit theory about the relation of leader motivation to other kinds of variables.

Although the present results are based on a small population of leaders and measures that involve several assumptions, they do suggest some interesting hypotheses about leadership in the real world of politics: (a) Leader *appeal* seems to involve a person–situation (or leader–follower) match of psychological characteristics. (b) Leader *performance* (historically rated greatness and some major outcomes), when it is more than a function of circumstances, may involve more enduring and less situationally defined psychological characteristics of the leader.

Why do these conclusions diverge from much of the experimental social psychological research on leadership? The time-bound constraints of the laboratory often lead researchers to rely on group member sociometric ratings of leadership; that is, leader appeal. Not surprisingly, the results often involve some kind of complex leader–situation interaction. But factors that predict leadership that is sociometrically defined in this way may not necessarily predict long-term effective leader performance and evaluation, which of course is hard to study in the time-foreshortened laboratory microcosm. This divergence of leader appeal and leader performance should underline the importance of studying leadership in the real world, using archival, at-a-distance measures.

The conclusions of the present study are also relevant to the basic philosophical assumptions of democratic political theory. We may vote for the candidate who feels most "comfortable" or congruent to us, who fits our dimly perceived hierarchies of motives and goals. At best, though, such leader appeal has little to do with leader effectiveness. And often enough the "uncomfortable" leader, discrepant in motive from the larger society of the times, turns out to be regarded as the great leader.

NOTES

The research reported in this article was supported by grants from the John and Mary R. Markle Foundation. I am grateful to Joseph M. Healy, Jr., for assistance in the analysis of data.
1. When formal prepared speeches are scored, it is natural to ask whether the results reflect the motives of the president or those of the speech writers. There are, however, several reasons for believing that this is not an important problem. First, any good speech writer knows how to produce words and images that feel appropriate and comfortable to the presidential client. Second, before a speech as important as the first inaugural address, presidents spend a good deal of time reviewing and changing the text, paying special attention to the kinds of images that are coded in the motive-scoring systems. For example, the various drafts of President Kennedy's inaugural address show insertions and deletions of scorable imagery, in Kennedy's own handwriting. Many speeches in the Eisenhower Library archives show the same. Thus, although the words may have originated from many sources, in the end an inaugural address probably says almost exactly what the president wants it to say. The final justification of these scores, of course, is then validity in terms of predicting presidential actions and outcomes, as shown in this article and in other studies using the scores.
2. Subtracting standardized affiliation–intimacy from standardized power motivation follows the practice of these researchers and also yields a single variable combining the two motives that can be simply represented and used in correlations, as in Table 2. It would also be possible to combine the two motive scores by means of multiple regression (in which case an interaction term could also be used). Although such a procedure might be more powerful statistically, it is also more complex and is not the same combination measure used by McClelland and others.

REFERENCES

Allport, G. W. (1937). *Personality: A psychological interpretation.* New York: Holt.
Bales, R. F. (1970). *Personality and interpersonal behavior.* New York: Holt, Rinehart & Winston.

Barber, J. D. (1980). *The pulse of politics: Electing presidents in the media age*. New York: Norton.

Bass, B. M. (1981). *Stogdill's handbook of leadership* (rev. ed.). New York: Free Press.

Bem, D. J., & Funder, D. C. (1978). Predicting more of the people more of the time: Assessing the personality of situations. *Psychological Review, 85*, 485–501.

Bem, D. J., & Lord, C. G. (1979). Template-matching: A proposal for probing the ecological validity of experimental settings in social psychology. *Journal of Personality and Social Psychology, 37*, 833–846.

Brown, R. W. (1965). *Social psychology*. New York: Free Press.

Bureau of the Census. (1984). *Historical statistics of the United States*. Washington, DC: U.S. Government Printing Office.

Burns, J. M. (1956). *Roosevelt: The lion and the fox*. New York: Harcourt, Brace.

Conte, H. R., & Plutchik, R. (1981). A circumplex model for interpersonal personality traits. *Journal of Personality and Social Psychology, 40*, 701–711.

Donley, R. E., & Winter, D. G. (1970). Measuring the motives of public officials at a distance: An exploratory study of American presidents. *Behavioral Science, 15*, 227–236.

Erikson, E. H. (1950). *Childhood and society*. New York: Norton.

———. (1958). *Young man Luther*. New York: Norton.

———. (1964). *Insight and responsibility*. New York: Norton.

———. (1969). *Gandhi's truth*. New York: Norton.

Fodor, E. M., & Farrow, D. L. (1979). The power motive as an influence on use of power. *Journal of Personality and Social Psychology, 37*, 2091–2097.

Freud, S. (1955). Group psychology and the analysis of the ego. In J. Strachey (Ed.), *Standard edition of the complete psychological works of Sigmund Freud* (Vol. 18, pp. 67–143). London: Hogarth. (Original work published 1921).

Gibb, C. A. (1969). Leadership. In G. Lindzey & E. Aronson (Eds.), *Handbook of social psychology* (rev. ed.). Reading, MA: Addison-Wesley.

Haley, J. (1969). *The power tactics of Jesus Christ and other essays*. New York: Grossman.

Hermann, M. G. (ed.). (1977). *A psychological examination of political leaders*. New York: Free Press.

———. (1980). Explaining foreign policy using personal characteristics of political leaders. *International Studies Quarterly. 24*, 7–46.

Hollander, E. P. (1964). *Leaders, groups and influence*. New York: Oxford University Press.

Kane, J. N. (1956). *Facts about the presidents* (3rd ed.). New York: H. W. Wilson.

Magnusson, D., & Endler, N. S. (Eds.). (1977). *Personality at the crossroads: Current issues in interactional psychology*. Hillsdale, NJ: Erlbaum.

Maranell, G. (1970). The evaluation of presidents: An extension of the Schlesinger poll. *Journal of American History, 57*, 104–113.

McAdams, D. P. (1982). Intimacy motivation. In A. J. Stewart (Ed.), *Motivation and society*. San Francisco: Jossey-Bass.

McClelland, D. C. (1961). *The achieving society*. Princeton, NJ: Van Nostrand.

———. (1975). *Power: The inner experience*. New York: Irvington.

McClelland, D. C., & Boyatzis, R. E. (1982). Leadership motive pattern and long-term success in management. *Journal of Applied Psychology, 67*, 737–743.

McClelland, D. C., & Burnham, D. (1976). Power is the great motivator. *Harvard Business Review, 54*, 100–111.

Mischel, W. (1968). *Personality and assessment*. New York: Wiley.

Morris, R. B. (1967). *Great presidential decisions: State papers that changed the course of history* (rev. ed.). Philadelphia: Lippincott.

Murray, R. K., & Blessing, T. H. (1983). The presidential performance study: A progress report. *Journal of American History, 70*, 535–555.

Nie, N. H., Verba, S., & Petrocik, J. R. (1979). *The changing American voter* (enlarged ed.). Cambridge, MA: Harvard University Press.

Richardson, L. (1960). *Statistics of deadly quarrels*. Pittsburgh, PA: Boxwood Press.

Sears, D. O. (1969). Political behavior. In G. Lindzey & E. Aronson (Eds.), *Handbook of social psychology* (Rev. ed., Vol. 5, pp. 315–458). Reading MA: Addison-Wesley.

Simonton, D. (1981). Presidential greatness and performance: Can we predict leadership in the White House? *Journal of Personality, 49*, 306–323.

Small, M. (1980). *Was war necessary? National security and United States entry into war*. Beverly Hills, CA: Sage.

Snider, J. G., & Osgood, C. E. (Eds.). (1969). *Semantic differential technique: A sourcebook*. Chicago: Aldine.

Steele, R. S. (1977). Power motivation, activation, and inspirational speeches. *Journal of Personality, 45*, 53–64.

U.S. Senate Library. (1976). *Presidential vetoes, 1789–1976*. Washington, DC: U.S. Government Printing Office.

Vidal, G. (1984). *Lincoln*. New York: Random House.

Weber, M. (1947). *The theory of social and economic organization*. New York: Free Press.

Wiggins, J. S. (1980). Circumplex models of interpersonal behavior. In L. Wheeler (Ed.), *Review of personality and social psychology* (Vol. 1, pp. 265–294). Beverly Hills, CA: Sage.

Winter, D. G. (1973). *The power motive*. New York: Free Press.

_____. (1980). Measuring the motives of southern Africa political leaders at a distance. *Political Psychology, 2*(2), 75–85.

_____. (1983). *Development of an integrated system for scoring motives in verbal running text*. Unpublished manuscript, Wesleyan University, Middletown, CT.

Winter, D. G., & Stewart, A. J. (1977). Content analysis as a method of studying political leaders. In M. G. Hermann (Ed.), *A psychological examination of political leaders* (pp. 27–61). New York: Free Press.

_____. (1978). Power motivation. In H. London & J. Exner (Eds.), *Dimensions of personality* (pp. 391–447). New York: Wiley.

12

Personality and
Democratic Politics

PAUL M. SNIDERMAN

My concern has been to explore how individual differences in the ways in which people evaluate themselves affect the ways in which they embrace the democratic idea. Up to this point details of measurement and data analysis have been at the center of attention. Now I should like to consider some of the broader implications of the specific findings. For I believe these findings suggest certain marginal notes about larger questions in the study of personality and democratic politics. These notes are appropriately, and I hope usefully, modest. They are conjectures, not conclusions.

POLITICAL EXTREMISM

The evidence seems plain, the conclusion obvious. Low self-esteem encourages a susceptibility to political extremism. Compared to those with high self-esteem, those with low self-esteem show markedly less tolerance, less support for procedural rights, less faith in democracy, and more cynicism about politics. They have a penchant for seeing conspiracies at work, a disenchantment with the established political order, an express desire for large-scale change by whatever means possible, at whatever cost necessary. They set little store by freedom of speech and assembly (unless it is theirs), the importance of diversity in an open society, the principle of equality. In sum, those with low self-esteem give evidence of a pronounced suspicion of—even a certain hostility toward—the democratic idea. Low self-esteem encourages extremist politics, or so it may appear.

Appearances can be deceptive. Low self-esteem works against democratic values; however, it need not work against democratic practice. To the extent that previous analysis of personality and political extremism has concentrated on the factor of motivation and overlooked that of social learning, it has presented a one-sided and possibly misleading picture. If we take account of questions of learning as well as pressures of motives, it becomes evident that the same psychological disposition may encourage extremist sentiments but discourage extremist politics. For example, a person low in self-esteem tends to be less attentive to politics and so less responsive to political cues—whether desirable or undesirable. Compared to the person with high self-esteem, he should be slower to learn of the emergence of a political demagogue, and less able to see the relevance of a demagogue's appeals to his own circumstances. To be sure, once aware of an extremist appeal, he may well be less likely to reject it than are persons with high self-esteem. Nonetheless, he is less likely to be exposed to such appeals, to pay attention to them, or to understand them.

Moreover, low self-esteem increases vulnerability to all the varieties of political extremism. . . . [A] person with low self-esteem is more likely to embrace both extreme right-wing and extreme left-wing values. For example, he is at once likely to believe that the press is in the hands of left-wingers and that the laws of this country are "almost all 'rich man's laws.' " In short, he simultaneously takes his stand with extremist creeds at the very opposite poles of the ideological spectrum, a posture that is likely to prove not only awkward but self-defeating.

In addition, though low self-esteem encourages extremist views, it impedes political involvement. Thus, low self-esteem tends to weaken further the tenuous link between political attitudes and political behavior. More important perhaps, it inhibits the type of participation that is the key to being genuinely effective in a democratic society. When political scientists consider political participation, their attention is usually fixed on such *individual* actions as whether a person is likely to vote or to write a letter of complaint to an official or to contribute money to an election. But what counts most in democratic politics is what a citizen is able and willing to do with others, not what he is inclined to do on his own. As Tocqueville has remarked: "Among democratic countries . . . all the citizens are independent and feeble; they can hardly do anything by themselves, and none of them can oblige his fellow men to lend him their assistance. They all, therefore, become powerless if they do not learn voluntarily to help one another."[1] And the larger the political order becomes, the smaller the chances a citizen can influence the outcome of events by his independent actions. Now more than ever, "the art of association" becomes "the mother of action."[2]

The relationship between low self-esteem and political passivity therefore assumes additional significance. For low self-esteem not only impedes a citizen taking part in politics on his own—for example, by voting. More significantly, it inhibits him from taking part in politics with others. As we have seen, the individual with low self-esteem tends to avoid others, to be ill at ease in their company, to be reluctant to initiate or participate in conversation or social exchange, to be passive and withdrawn particularly in face-to-face contact with others who are unfamiliar to him or who in some way differ from him. Thus the very psychological needs that tend to motivate those with low self-esteem toward extremist politics tend to make it difficult for extremist movements to mobilize them.

Moreover, not only is a person with low self-esteem less likely to become active in politics, he is also less likely to become a leader in politics. His self-doubts stand in the way of attempting to lead a political organization or to organize one. He tends to lack the articulateness, assertiveness, and interpersonal skills necessary to advance himself or his cause politically. And his lack of self-regard encourages an outlook likely to dampen or extinguish altogether his enthusiasm for political action. As he sees the world, few can be trusted and little can be done. Of course, I have painted a particularly dark picture of how the person with low self-esteem views the world, but he does tend to see the world of politics darkly or not at all. And his sense of political futility tends to undermine his chances of taking political action or gaining political power.

In short, the same personality trait which tends to make men strong advocates of extremist values tends to make them weak opponents of democratic institutions.

ELITES AND MASSES

The irrationality of the mass emerged as a major theme in the group psychology of the late nineteenth century and the dynamic psychology of the early twentieth century. The mood then, as Rieff has pointed out, was conservative, pessimistic, and elitist, as psychological forces long hidden from awareness were increasingly uncovered and brought into sight.[3] Freud, Taine, and le Bon, among others, were struck by a new historical force: "the emotion of the masses."[4] Two themes became intertwined. The irrationality of the mass and the consequent fear of the mass, both of which are well illustrated in a letter written by Freud as a medical student in Paris: "The town and the people are uncanny; they seem to be of another species from us. I believe they are possessed of a thousand demons. . . . They are the people of psychical epidemics, of historical mass convulsions."[5] With the emergence of totalitarian politics, the fear of mass movements and mass politics deepened, the more so as classic studies of prejudice and civil liberties highlighted the role of the elite as a repository of democratic values.[6] By contrast, the mass appeared to be to political tinder, readily combustible.

Research on personality and politics has tended to deepen this fear of the mass. Indeed, as my own study has shown, the politically active and influential tend to have significantly higher self-esteem than does the average citizen. And to the extent that high self-esteem is a sign of psychological adjustment,[7] it might be argued that my findings add one further piece of evidence to the now classic theme of the relative irrationality of the mass. For my part, however, I think several findings of this study cast a somewhat different light on this classic problem.

I have considered one aspect of this problem in the discussion of personality and political extremism. But there is another aspect to consider—the relationship between personality and susceptibility to social influence. It is one thing to worry that low self-esteem may lead citizens to hold political values one regards as undesirable. It is quite another to worry that their emotional makeup makes them easy to manipulate politically. For if their psychological makeup renders them readily persuasible, then they may easily be caught up and tossed about by any sudden political storm. From this point of view what matters is not what ordinary citizens may believe but what they can be persuaded to believe.

This fear is far from specious. The experience of the thirties in Europe demonstrated the readiness of large numbers of citizens to embrace totalitarian ideologies. Of course, a variety of forces were at work but, no doubt, personality (and more specifically, authoritarianism) was among them. Authoritarianism as a dimension of personality, it is important to note, refers not to adherence to totalitarian values, but to "a *susceptibility* to anti-democratic propaganda."[8] Such a susceptibility is of special interest to us because of the long-established connection between low self-esteem and conformity. To the extent that low self-esteem leads men to submit to social pressure to conform to one set of political values and to insist that others conform to them too, it places the democratic idea in jeopardy.

The stronger the pressures for conformity, the greater the threat to diversity, to creativity, and ultimately to liberty itself. Increasingly, then, the danger to the democratic idea arises from the power of society and not that of the state to make men's convictions and conduct conform to a common mold, as John Stuart Mill argued in *On Liberty*:

> The circumstances which surround different classes and individuals, and shape their characters, are daily becoming more assimilated . . . Comparatively speaking, they now read the same things, go to the same places, have their hopes and fears directed to the same objects, have the same rights and liberties, and the same means of asserting them . . . And the assimilation is still proceeding. All the political changes of the age promote it, since they all tend to raise the low and to lower the high. Every extension of education promotes it, because education brings people under common influences, and gives them access to the general stock of facts and sentiments. Improvements in the means of communication promote it, by bringing the inhabitants of distant places into personal contact, and keeping up a rapid flow of changes of residence between one place and another. The increase of commerce and manufacture promotes it, by diffusing more widely the advantages of easy circumstances, and opening up all objects of ambition, even the highest, to general competition, whereby the desire of rising becomes no longer the character of a particular class, but of all classes. [And] a more powerful agency than even all these, in bringing about a general similarity among mankind, is the complete establishment, in this and other free countries, of the ascendancy of public opinion in the state.[9]

Men differ in their readiness to yield to established custom and public opinion. Low self-esteem in particular is thought to render a person susceptible to social influence. The person with low self-esteem lacks confidence in himself and in his opinions. As many experimental studies have shown, he is more likely to change his views if placed under social pressure, more ready to comply with social expectations, more likely to yield to social influence. He is more likely to be, in a word, a conformist.

Admittedly, to the extent that low self-esteem impedes social learning, it may lead a person to deviate from the official values of his society rather than conform to them. But the danger to the democratic idea remains; indeed, it may even be increased. For the individual is then unlikely to grasp the principle of democratic restraint and yet still insist on the urgency of conformity. He is all the readier, then, to join attacks on opinions that are unconventional or merely unfamiliar to him. He may be a conformist, without being a conformer.

Low self-esteem, it appears, encourages the desire for conformity and so threatens the principle of liberty. But on further thought the matter becomes more complex. It is plain that high self-esteem encourages the individuality and creativity that Mill so valued; however, it is by no means clear that low self-esteem promotes the societal mediocrity and conformity that Mill so feared.

Low self-esteem may not strongly foster the principles of diversity and creativity, but neither does it directly menace them. Mill and Tocqueville both feared that equality would promote uniformity. But democratic societies have generally proven to be pluralistic societies, comprising exceedingly diverse sentiments and social groups, rather than mass societies in which the largest number are more or less indistinguishable in conviction or vocation. In particular, one feature of American pluralism is the segmentation of society in such a way that only a relatively small fraction of citizens enters directly in the exchange of new ideas. The person with low self-esteem is little or no threat to commerce in this marketplace of ideas, if only because low self-esteem so dulls his awareness of this marketplace's existence or its daily activities.

The individual with low self-esteem may indeed favor conformity and may attempt to oppose ideas or practices which are novel or unfamiliar to him. But he is likely to prove a weak opponent, indeed, not because of the weakness of his desire to oppose diversity, but because of the poverty of his knowledge. Only when new ideas have won wide attention in the society is he likely to become aware of them. But by then those ideas will already have had the opportunity to win at least a foothold, and possibly even strong backing, among those in the society who pay attention to emerging ideas and who introduce and popularize fashions in opinion which the larger society tends—even if erratically—to follow. In short, low self-esteem makes it unlikely a person will frequent the marketplaces for new and creative ideas, and thereby reduces the likelihood that he will impede the liveliness of the commerce in ideas on which both individual genius and social progress depend.

The root problem, of course, is broader than that of conformity, at least as Mill conceived it. What animated Mill was *fear for* genius; what has disturbed later observers more is *fear of* mass politics. The totalitarian movements of the twentieth century have dramatized the risks of mass politics—in particular, by revealing the apparent ease with which mass sentiments can be excited and manipulated. This problem cannot be considered in its entirety here, but the role that psychological characteristics such as low self-esteem are widely believed to play in it should be considered. The classic experimental studies of conformity and persuasibility show that low self-esteem increases the likelihood of yielding to social influence. Yet what many of our arguments to this point suggest is that it is precisely the person low in self-esteem who is the least likely to be susceptible to such influence, at least with respect to politics. The exercise of social influence depends on, among other things, the clarity of the transmission of socially approved standards. A person will tend to bring his behavior into line with such standards, other things being equal, as he becomes aware of (1) his departure from them; (2) the actions he must take to comply with them; and (3), the rewards and punishments contingent on compliance. But one consequence of low self-esteem is that it interferes with the reception of socially approved standards. Compared to the person with high self-esteem, the one with low self-esteem is more likely to deviate from these standards, despite his stronger desire to conform to them, because he is less likely to be aware of what the prevailing standards are; of whether he is actually deviating from them; of what he must do or avoid doing to bring himself into compliance; or of the rewards and punishments he may anticipate if he behaves in one way rather than in another. As we have seen, low self-esteem tends to diminish awareness and comprehension of socially approved standards, all the more effectively, in an area of life such as politics which is ordinarily not of great moment for the average citizen. In short, the person most willing to yield to social influence may often be the least susceptible to it. And both his desire to yield and his failure to do so may spring from the very same personality characteristic, low self-esteem.

However that may be, the contrast between political elites and ordinary citizens has been drawn increasingly sharply. Certainly, men drawn to political life are better informed about politics, more often articulate and aware, more interested in the important issues of the day, more deeply committed to the values of the American political culture and to the programs and philosophy of their party, and frequently better educated than ordinary citizens are.[10] As a consequence, political leaders, more often than the mass public, develop complex systems of ideas that permit them to organize large masses of information in terms of a manageable number of abstract categories and thereby to organize in a relatively consistent manner the variety of opinions they hold on specific subjects.[11] It is understandable, then, if some students of politics go on to draw the inference that political leaders, compared to the mass public, are more rational (in some sense of the term) and further, that personality, or more generally, non-logical "irrational" psychological forces, on the average have little effect on the political elite.

It is understandable, but it may well be wrong, or at least seriously misleading. In the data presented here, self-esteem appears to affect the opinions and values of political leaders as it does those of the general population. Certainly, self-esteem need not always have the same effect on leaders and followers. But we must not lose sight of the forest for the trees. On the whole, personality characteristics such as self-esteem appear to have much the same impact on the beliefs of elites as on those of citizens.

Self-esteem not only has much the same impact on political leaders and followers, it also affects their opinions in much the same way. Students of personality and politics traditionally have concentrated on the connection between personality and motivation. A person's beliefs or behavior have been explained in terms of the rewards experienced or anticipated for adopting a particular point of view or committing a particular act. In this study, I have presented a different view of the connection between personality and belief, a view intended to supplement, not replace, the viewpoint of previous research. Briefly, my aim has been to show that a personality characteristic can affect the acquisition of political opinions by affecting social learning as well as motivation. And as we have seen, this model of political learning applies as well to political leaders as to average citizens.

At a minimum, then, the findings of this study give us good reason to believe that the relevance of personality constructs is not limited to the analysis of mass politics. Personality characteristics such as self-esteem also play an important role in determining what political leaders believe, and very probably, how they behave.

PARTICIPATORY THEORIES OF DEMOCRACY

It has become increasingly fashionable to divide democratic theorists into two camps—one labeled elitist, the other participatory.[12] Up to this point, the contention between the two has turned on the values each supposedly promotes. But which of the two is the more satisfactory must depend in the end on the facts of the matter. All the facts are certainly not in hand, but some of my findings do sound a note of caution against certain claims advanced by participatory theories of democracy.

Before considering the evidence, I think it would be useful to state more clearly the difference between these two conceptions of democratic theory, particularly since the label "elitist" is both invidious and misleading. Both conceptions favor popular participation in politics. They differ not in the value they place in citizen involvement but in the role they assign to it. Citizen participation may be viewed as a political means to *public* ends. In this view, popular involvement promotes the good management of the public business. On this point, both camps of democratic theorists are in agreement, though specific arguments vary from theorist to theorist. Participatory theorists, however, go on to contend that political participation is a political means to a specific *private* end— enhancement of the self. According to Mill, for example, participation in civic affairs improves the character of the citizen. It enlarges his intellectual and moral capacities, promoting a character type hailed by Mill as "active" and by G.D.H. Cole as "nonservile," a character type said by Pateman, a contemporary theorist of democracy, to involve "the belief that one can be self-governing, and confidence in one's ability to participate responsibly and effectively, and to control one's life and environment."[13] Thompson, another contemporary theorist, concurs, contending that participation may be a path to "self-realization."[14]

What distinguishes participatory theories is the view that becoming involved in the political process is likely to work important changes in the basic character of citizens. It is not merely that political participation may increase a person's sense of political efficacy. The claim is broader, if vaguer. Participation is a particularly promising means to affect fundamental changes in the citizen's self-image—to strengthen his sense of confidence and competence, to impress on him his own worth and dignity, in a word, to enhance his self-esteem. This notion that political participation may be a path to self-esteem and self-realization is worth noting, especially at a time when many argue that minorities historically excluded from political life ought to have assurance of office and influence in all major institutions of the society (political, economic, educational and the like), not only to secure representation of their interests, but to redress, at least partly, their damaged self-esteem.

The current emphasis on the self-enhancing function of participation is not without irony. Where contemporary theorists contend that participation enhances, their predecessors warned that power corrupts.[15] Whatever the reasons for this shift in emphasis, it is now widely argued that political participation can engender a sense of efficacy, of self-assurance, and more broadly, of self-esteem.

Does participation in fact pay the psychological dividends that participatory theorists claim it does? The findings of this study bear on this question, though they certainly provide no final answer to it. As we have seen, the politically active have a stronger sense of efficacy, less anxiety, more self-assurance and self-assertiveness, and higher self-esteem than do those who are not active in politics. It is conceivable, then, that participatory theorists may be right in advertising the psychological benefits of participation.

It is conceivable, but in my opinion, unlikely for at least two reasons. First, not all aspects of self-esteem are equally related to participation. As we have seen, the lack of a sense of interpersonal competence is strongly related to taking an active part in politics, but feelings of personal unworthiness or of social inferiority are related only marginally, if at all, to political involvement. Thus participation, even if we were to consider it a cause, rather than a consequence, of self-esteem, could be said to have only a limited power to change self-attitudes. It may change how efficacious a person thinks he is; it is much less likely to change how worthwhile he believes he is. Second, high self-esteem most often appears to be the cause and not the consequence of participation in politics. The question of causal order, of course, is the key to the problem. To sustain the claims of the participatory theorists evidence must be amassed showing that the higher self-esteem of political leaders appeared after and not before they became involved in politics. The evidence available, however, suggests that exactly the opposite is usually the case. Thus there is some suggestive evidence that attitudes toward the self, when they concern basic qualities of the individual's character rather than particular capacities to perform specific tasks, develop early in childhood and are relatively enduring. Moreover, a recent experiment on the consequences of power found that having power did not lead to higher self-esteem.[16] Last, if participation did lead to more favorable self-attitudes, then the more active one is in politics, the higher one's self-esteem should be. But if by participation we mean more than prosaic acts of involvement such as voting—and I take it to be plain that by participation participatory theorists mean taking a genuine and vigorous part in political life—there is no relationship between degree of activity and level of self-esteem. As we have seen, among the sample of political activists, there is no relationship of consequence between self-esteem and how active a person is in politics, or how long he has been active in politics. Nor is there any relationship of consequence between level of self-esteem and position in political life (as indicated by public or party office held). These data do not support the hypothesis that participation in political life tends to promote self-approval. They suggest, instead, that the claims of participatory theorists for such psychological benefits are either exaggerated or erroneous. At a minimum, though the evidence at hand is merely suggestive, it would appear that such claims deserve far more critical scrutiny than they have yet received.

THE GOOD MAN AND THE GOOD CITIZEN

It is no small irony that a classical problem in political philosophy, the relationship between the good man and the good citizen, stimulated the scientific study of personality and politics. It was the pressure to understand the connection between the two in modern society, or more precisely the relationship between the bad man (defined psychologically) and the bad citizen (defined ideologically), that gave rise to the seminal studies of authoritarianism in the 1930s. The rise of fascism in Western Europe fixed the attention of some scholars—not a few of them refugees—on the sources of anti-Semitism. What made some men actually anti-Semitic, and thereby potentially fascistic? Conversely, what made others tolerant and egalitarian in outlook, and thereby well-disposed to the democratic spirit?

Part of the answer seemed to lie in man's psychological makeup. Achieving an understanding of some of the forces leading to totalitarianism of the right or the left entailed developing a psychology of ideology—an analysis of the personal needs, inner conflicts, fantasies, mechanisms of defense and strategies for adaptation that lie beneath antidemocratic creeds. So Aristotle's question, now substantially revised, proved the starting point for the psychological analysis of authoritarianism and thereby the scientific study of personality and politics.

My concern, too, has been with the relationship between personality and commitment to democratic values. My aim, however, has been to learn how such a relationship comes about, not merely to show that it in fact exists. For that reason, my findings both lend support to, and cast doubt upon, hypotheses of previous researchers. More important, the findings of this study help us to better understand the complexity of the connection between personality and political behavior.

Previous researchers have attempted to understand the connection between the two by focusing on the personal motives lying behind political values. Thus, Lasswell and others reasoned that the person low in self-esteem has less commitment to democratic values because he is more hostile, less tolerant, and so forth. And indeed the person with low self-esteem in fact is more hostile, less tolerant, and less committed to democratic values than the one with high self-esteem.

They made the right prediction, then, and for the right reasons, but unfortunately, for only some of the right reasons. As we have seen, the relationship between personality and belief is best thought of as a complex process, comprising a number of separate intervening steps. This process can be viewed in different ways. One alternative is to think of it as involving three *steps*—exposure, comprehension, and the reward value of acceptance. Another alternative is to think of it as involving three *paths*, which account for the causal influence of personality on political belief as mediated by reinforcement contingencies (the reward value of acceptance) and learning contingencies (exposure and comprehension). Both of these conceptions make it plain that a personality characteristic can affect the acquisition of political opinions by affecting social learning as well as motivation. Thus, those with low self-esteem are less likely to acquire democratic values at least as much because of the barriers to social learning raised by low self-esteem as because of the personal motives that accompany it.

Recognizing that the relationship between personality and belief is mediated both by motivation and social learning helps us to understand both why and when the relationship between them will vary. Previous approaches, emphasizing only motivation, tend to suggest a one-to-one correspondence between a personality characteristic such as low self-esteem and a political orientation such as democratic commitment. Thus, Lasswell and others speak of a "democratic character" or the "democratic personality" as if the psychological profile of the democrat (and of the antidemocrat) tend to be always and everywhere alike. Such an approach pays no attention to the interaction of internal and external forces.

Self-esteem, as I have tried to suggest, may well lead to radically different outcomes, depending on the situation. When individual differences in exposure and comprehension are minimized, self-esteem is likely to affect the outcome only insofar as it affects the motivational orientations of individuals. For example, if we were to study a small policy-advisory group whose members were in close contact with each other and were equally able to understand the messages transmitted within the group, we might well expect low self-esteem to reinforce a tendency toward group conformity, or as Irving Janis has labeled it, "groupthink."[17]

However, when individual differences in learning count for a great deal, low self-esteem is likely to lead to deviance, not conformity. Thus, in the circumstances of everyday life, low self-esteem tends to strongly inhibit exposure to and comprehension of the official values of the American political culture. As a result, low self-esteem weakens commitment to democratic values; that is, it leads to deviance, not conformity to institutionalized norms. Thus not only does the same personality characteristic lead to different outcomes, depending on the situation, but paradoxically, the same personality characteristic that motivates a person to conform frequently leads him to deviate.

This argument ought not to be taken as support for the contention of some scholars that personality constructs have little explanatory value because the same individual's behavior is so variable from one situation to another. Personality may well affect behavior, even if the former is constant across different situations. Indeed, a major aim of this study has been to develop an analytic scheme allowing us to suggest when self-esteem should lead to one outcome and when it should lead to another. Admittedly, this scheme is crude; nevertheless, it may be useful in understanding why personality may lead the same person to behave differently in different situations. However that may be, the choice between personality and the situation as determinants of behavior is a false choice. What may well matter most in explaining political belief and behavior is neither the influence of personality nor the impact of the situation *but the interaction between the two*.[18]

A one-to-one correspondence, then, between the good man and the good citizen is unlikely. Whether a citizen embraces democratic politics not only depends on the interaction between personality and the situation, it also hinges on the interaction among personality characteristics themselves. In this regard, the interaction between low self-esteem and psychological inflexibility is especially intriguing. As we have seen, a lack of self-esteem (and particularly, a lack of interpersonal competence) inhibits the tendency to participate in politics. Thus, rigidity raises a barrier to political involvement. Yet, if it is combined with low self-esteem, there is, so to speak, a catalytic reaction: these traits, in combination, potentiate rather than inhibit involvement in democratic politics.

This interaction between low self-esteem and inflexibility suggests something of the complex and as yet poorly understood processes by which personality dimensions become translated into action. Clearly much remains to be learned. But even at this early stage of inquiry, evidence of the interaction of self-esteem and other personality characteristics underlines the need for us to move from trait to profile analysis. Focusing on one personality characteristic is a useful strategy, especially in the early stages of inquiry. Yet it will become increasingly necessary to take account of the interaction among psychological and cognitive attributes, for the same personality trait may lead to very different outcomes, depending on the configuration of psychological characteristics in which it is imbedded.

Last, the interaction of personality and culture deserves mention. A paramount concern of this study has been the connection between personality and democratic citizenship. As we have seen, high self-esteem shows up democratic commitment and practice; low self-esteem undermines them. But the data for this study have been drawn only from the United States. We may expect that high self-esteem buttresses the values of democratic politics in other countries, but this may be so only where the democratic idea has legitimacy. The relationship between personality and political ideology may well differ where authoritarian values are at the center of political culture, for insofar as high self-esteem facilitates social learning, it may promote the learning of all socially approved values, whether democratic or not. And insofar as high self-esteem (and particularly, a sense of interpersonal competence) facilitates political involvement, it may encourage participation in political life, whether democratic or not. Ironically, then, the same personality trait which strengthens democratic commitment here may conceivably weaken it elsewhere.

The good man and the good citizen, Aristotle has argued, are the same—but only in the perfect society. The democratic personality may be the democratic citizen, I would suggest, but possibly only in a democratic society.

NOTES

1. Alexis De Tocqueville, *Democracy in America* (New York: Random House, 1945), vol. 2, p. 125.
2. *Ibid.*, vol. 2, p. 115.
3. Philip Rieff, *Freud: The Mind of the Moralist* (Garden City, New York: Doubleday and Company, Inc., 1961), p. 249ff.
4. *Ibid.*, p. 250ff.
5. *Ibid.*, p. 250.
6. See particularly, Herbert McClosky, "Consensus and Ideology in American Politics," *APSR* 58 (June 1964): 361–382; and Samuel Stouffer, *Communism, Conformity and Civil Liberties* (New York: Doubleday, Inc., 1955). For a recent dissent from this view based on a reanalysis of Stouffer's classic data see Robert W. Jackman, "Political Elites, Mass Publics, and Support for Democratic Principles," *Journal of Politics* 34 (Sept. 1972): 753–773.
7. For a close examination of the extent of which this view is valid see Ruth Wylie, *The Self-Concept* (Lincoln: University of Nebraska Press, 1961).
8. T. W. Adorno et al., *The Authoritarian Personality* (New York: W. W. Norton and Company, Inc., 1950), p. 4. Italics are those of the authors.
9. John Stuart Mill, *Utilitarianism* (New York: Meridian Books, 1962), pp. 203–204.
10. See for example, Philip E. Converse, "The Nature of Belief Systems in Mass Publics," in David Apter, ed., *Ideology and Discontent* (New York: Free Press, 1964).
11. For this distinction see Carole Pateman, *Participation and Democratic Theory* (Cambridge: Cambridge University Press, 1970).
12. The distinction between the two functions of participation has been taken from Carole Pateman's *Participation and Democratic Theory*, p. 28.
13. See Pateman, *Participation and Democratic Theory*, p. 28ff.
14. Dennis F. Thompson, *The Democratic Citizen* (Cambridge: Cambridge University Press, 1970), p. 64ff.

15. For an interesting contemporary experimental test of Acton's Axiom, see David Kipnis, "Does Power Corrupt?" *Journal of Personality and Social Psychology* 24 (Oct. 1972): 26–32.

16. *Ibid*.

17. For a provocative view of conformity forces in policy decision-making, see Irving L. Janis, *Victims of Groupthink* (Boston: Houghton Mifflin Company, 1972).

18. Henry Alker, "Is Personality Situation Specific or Intra-Psychically Consistent?" *Journal of Personality* 40 (March 1972): 1–16.

13

Contributions
of Psychohistory
to Understanding Politics

GEOFFREY COCKS

Modern psychohistory came to professional consciousness in 1957 in a speech in New York to the American Historical Association by its outgoing president, William Langer. Langer (1958), whose brother Walter was a psychoanalyst, declared that if he were a young historian just starting out he would devote his career to the application of psychoanalytic insights to history. Langer then proceeded to sketch an analysis of the irrational dynamics of the human response to the Black Death, which scourged medieval Europe in the fourteenth century. Against the backdrop of the "black death" visited upon twentieth-century Europe by the Nazis, Langer's call to his colleagues to turn to a systematic study of the irrational in history was possessed of undeniable urgency, especially in the realm of political history. No doubt the influence of his brother, who during the war had produced a psychoanalytic study of Hitler for the American Office of Strategic Services, was significant (see Loewenberg, 1983).

This professional appeal, while not falling on deaf ears, nevertheless faced several problems in the way of its acceptance by historians. First, many of Langer's colleagues in their professional conservatism did not like to be told, in effect, that for some time they had been missing the point. Second, Freudian concepts, while not unknown to historians, involved in their application a somewhat daunting degree of intellectual retooling and, even more significantly, the personally threatening prospect of confession upon the couch. Finally, the enthusiastic claim for the utility of psychoanalytic theory in historical inquiry had to overcome the legacy of clumsy attempts at historical psychobiography made by psychoanalysts and other amateur historians during the height of Freudian fashion in the United States during the 1920s. Many of these works were caricatures of history and reinforced the belief of most historians that they had nothing worthwhile to learn from the psychoanalytic school.

On the other hand, Langer's arguments for the historical exploitation of psychoanalytic theory could draw on some advantageous dispositions within the field. First, the twentieth century had witnessed spectacular growth in the social sciences, areas of newly sophisticated human knowledge that offered historians intriguing new perspectives on their material. The Marxist interpretation and some of the work of the *Annales* school in France are only two examples of the many fruitful interactions along the lines of interdisciplinary collaboration. Thus, there was valuable precedent for interdisciplinary work in the field of history. Second, the American cultural and intellectual interest in Freud had remained strong, and historians themselves had not remained unaffected by this interest in the psychoanalytic perspective. Third, and most important, was the fact that historians in their work had of necessity run across and dealt with what in Freudian parlance was called the unconscious. Indeed, the traditional bent within the discipline toward studying leaders and "great men" made the psychoanalytic concern for the total dynamic mental life of the individual a fundamentally appealing one.

During the next several decades, therefore, some noted historians sought to explore and establish the lines of the overlapping boundaries of history and psychoanalysis. Hans Meyerhoff, a philosopher of history, was one of the first colonizers of this new methodological territory. In a paper presented at a Los Angeles symposium in November 1961, he went carefully over the common ground shared by the two disciplines. Meyerhoff (1962, p. 4) concluded that psychoanalysis and history have much in common because "historical method is an integral part of psychoanalytic theory and therapy" and because "psychoanalysis cannot be divorced from a study of society and history." Citing the historiographical work of Wilhelm Dilthey, R. G. Collingwood, Benedetto Croce, and E. H. Carr, Meyerhoff (1962, p. 16) argued that the contemporary historian re-creates the "thought of the past" in order to "discover the inner and hidden 'meaning' behind the overt sequence of events." The historian involves himself emotionally and intellectually in the totality of the individual and collective past, whereby, to paraphrase Pirandello, he fills the limp sack of facts with interpretation. This process leads to "understanding" or "insight" into the special cases with which history, in its concern for the particular, is exclusively filled. Anticipating the criticism of, among others, psychologist Hans Eysenck, Meyerhoff declared that psychoanalysis, like history, is actually empirical in its concern with the individual case study. Science, more strictly defined, strives toward the general and abstract, while history and psychoanalysis in their application eschew this nomothetic quest in favor of idiographic wandering—a characteristic in form and content of the work of psychoanalyst Erik Erikson, whom Meyerhoff cites and who, by his publication in 1958 of *Young Man Luther: A Study in Psychoanalysis and History*, produced the first work of modern psychohistory. Some years later, in 1977, Peter Loewenberg, like Meyerhoff from the University of California at Los Angeles, was to argue that twentieth-century revelations about the nature of human scientific inquiry rendered the smug scientific dismissal of psychoanalysis as science in the broad sense substantially hollow. Indeed, according to Loewenberg, the idiographic rigor demanded by history was an important strengthening of psychoanalysis's own emphasis on the unique and a strong check against any overindulged tendency toward theoretical abstraction.

H. Stuart Hughes, one of the grand masters of European intellectual history, also addressed himself during this period to the question of the use of psychoanalysis in history. In his *History as Art and as Science*, Hughes (1964) devoted a chapter to the historian's search for motive, the "prime quest" for both disciplines, and at the outset wondered why it had taken so long for history and psychoanalysis to find each other. The answer, of course, lay in their history: a mutual misunderstanding stemming from the nineteenth-century traditions surrounding both disciplines, the dry search for facts on the one hand and the mechanistic tradition on the other. Their commonalities appear self-evident now: the stress on plural explanations, the importance of ostensibly trivial detail, the regular confrontation with the irrational in human affairs, the inevitable and indispensable subjective involvement of the investigator in the life of his subjects, and a shared concern for the logical and emotional coherence of an account in place of correspondence to general laws (see Friedländer, 1978).

Writing out of the French psychoanalytic tradition, Alain Besançon also noted the common concerns and methods of psychoanalysts and historians. Besançon (1968, p. 155) emphasized the "echo awakened in [the historian] by the various texts" as a means of understanding a culture or a period through the self-aware study of documents left us by the great and small actors in the human drama of history. Besançon further asserted that the Oedipus complex is crucial for understanding man's social reality, since it is this conflict through which every individual must pass in order to enter the larger society, and, thus, every culture must have historically revealing ways of dealing with it.

The strength of psychohistory as it has evolved is its careful detection of the mix of rational and irrational in political affairs and the intriguing and disturbing combination of inflexibility and flexibility, dysfunction and function, in political leaders as varied as Adolf Hitler and Woodrow Wilson (Greenstein, 1969). Psychohistorical studies, while reminding us of the influence of the past on the present, also provide us with the most complete case studies of the motives and actions of individual policy makers as well as insight into the emotional forces behind specific political movements as a whole.

This chapter will attempt to show how psychohistory, with its concern for the emotional content of human thoughts and actions at particular times and places in history, can illuminate the psychological dimensions of political life. It is from history, with its trove of rich detail of human activity, that political psychology can draw its most complete and instructive examples, confirming, enriching, and correcting models drawn from contemporary observation and theory.

ISSUES IN PSYCHOHISTORY

Psychohistorical Paradigms. Psychiatrist and psychohistorian Robert Jay Lifton (1970) has outlined four paradigms serving the evolution of psychohistory, the first two stemming from Freud's own work. Starting with *Totem and Taboo*, Freud ([1913] 1955) hypothesized what Lifton calls a "prehistorical paradigm" based on the "Oedipal Event." This macrohistorical metaphysic sees all human history as repetition of an original crime (and the attendant guilt) of the sons against the father of the hypothesized "primal horde," in essence leaving nothing important for the historian to do. Freud's other model, closely connected with his role as a pioneer in medical psychology, views individual psychopathology stemming from childhood experiences and fantasies as the key to unlocking the secrets of history. In Lifton's view, both models are insufficient as a basis for genuine psychohistorical inquiry, since they are united in the assumption that history is simply the larger story of the intrapsychic struggles of the individual. Lifton sees partial amelioration of this problem in Erikson's (1958, 1969) studies of Luther and Gandhi as "great men" who, in the coincident realms of ego and society, wrestled with the Freudian instinctual in themselves but in a way that involved and resolved a central historical problem shared by the people and culture of the time. Lifton himself has advanced a fourth paradigm: that of "shared psychohistorical themes." For Lifton the crucial element in understanding human history is an appreciation for collective historical experience that operates not on an instinctual, intrapsychic level but in the cultural realm of the "symbolic" and the "formative." Lifton rejects the causal preoccupations of classical psychoanalysis and emphasizes the interactions over time between personal and cultural predispositions and historical events.

Whatever paradigm is used, however, psychohistory is based firmly, and by and large exclusively, on Freudian psychoanalysis. Although nonpsychoanalytic models have been of some use (Raack, 1970; Crosby and Crosby, 1981), the strength of psychohistory lies in its rigorous, historical concern with the detailed psychological antecedents of individual actions and events. Such a concern has been evinced by psychoanalysis since its inception as a movement in medical psychology directed against a positivist and physicalist psychiatry (Decker, 1977; Cocks, 1985). Psychoanalysis and psychohistory are both idiographic (rather than nomothetic) in nature, wishing to know the motivational details arising from the organism's interaction with the environment in particular cases. The inductive emphasis on evidence, rather than an exclusive deductive reliance on a generalizing theory, was actually an anticipation of a current widespread skepticism about systems in social science. There is a significant contemporary trend, as exemplified by humanistic psychology and "sociology of the everyday," toward a typically historical balance between material and theory. Thus, Barzun (1972) is inaccurate when he claims that psychohistory lies far from history because psychohistory is committed to scientific generalization and jargon. Barzun's further assertion—that historians have gotten along quite well with their intuitive and literary psychological insight—only strengthens Rolle's (1980) counterargument—namely, that the historical profession has been chiefly concerned with rational explanations for events and that the insight into unconscious factors in history displayed by its best practitioners has been enriched by the primarily Freudian twentieth-century advances in the study of the human psyche. (See also Crosby, 1979.)

Psychoanalysis: Artifact or Tool? But whatever its basic orientation, is psychoanalysis in fact a useful mode of inquiry? It has been charged, first of all, that psychoanalysis is outdated, culture bound, and, thus, scientifically worthless. Crews (1980) is one who has turned from an enthusiastic espousal of psychoanalytic theory to vigorous apostatic criticism. Viewing psychoanalysis as an artifact of a dead era, Crews goes on to cite the large amounts of plain bad work done in the various fields of applied psychoanalysis, especially psychohistory. Charging that psychoanalysis is empirically nonsensical, he calls for a more rigorously scientific approach to human behavior. Whatever the failings of psychoanalysis and psychohistory (and there have been many), Crews's gravamina are not so much destroying the psychoanalytic and psychohistorical claim to insight as they are illustrating the tremendously elusive nature of the human mind in historical action. The very controversy among psychoanalysts and psychohistorians over systems, theories, and techniques is a sign not of rigor mortis or decomposition but of further fruitful fermentation in that most difficult realm of thought and inquiry concerned with the human mind and body. Freud's thought is anything but culture bound in its rigorous pursuit of the emotional, the ambiguous, *and the historical* in what people think and do, based as it is on penetrating insights into everyday human behavior. Moreover, the Freudian concepts of the dynamic unconscious, of conflict, and of ambivalence are vital and insightful metaphors for use in the study of human history. No other psychological theory or system has been nearly so useful to the historian.

It will not do, therefore, to maintain that psychoanalysis must be discarded and a fresh start made. Echoing Crews, Stannard (1980) has called for just such a new beginning on a behavioral basis that would dispense with the archaic notion of the unconscious. Stannard declares that psychohistory has failed, but he leaves unanswered the question of what it is at which psychohistory has allegedly failed. Stannard, also an apostate, obviously once expected too much from psychohistory, a common misapprehension that has led in the opposite directions of overenthusiasm and disillusionment.

Psychohistory, properly understood and applied, does not offer a "Freudian" view of history in the sense of an external metaphysical construct that seeks to define the nature and direction of history as a whole. Rather, psychohistory offers a number of means for unlocking an understanding of what Loewenberg (1982) has termed "feeling states." Freud's thought itself was not a monolith. Initially, his concept of the mind was economic and topographical—its functioning the result of energies coursing through the conscious, preconscious, and unconscious. Later, however, he developed a structural model of the mind, conceiving of the agencies of the ego, superego, and id in tension between the inner and outer world (see Yankelovich and Barrett, 1970).

Early Freudian drive, or libido, theory, as Loewenberg (1982) points out, has been

helpful in detailing patterns of behavior beholden to past traumata. Subsequent psychoanalytic models, however, offer more time-specific ways of understanding the dynamics
of human behavior. Instead of concentrating on an essentially static model based on a
pattern of repetition of behavior stemming from experiences in childhood, ego psychology, along with pre-Oedipal object relations theory (see Cocks, 1977; Hughes, 1977,
1983), emphasizes the individual's functioning in response to situations and other human
beings at specific points during a lifetime. Loewenberg (1982, p. 4) uses Brodie's (1981)
study of Richard Nixon as an example of the differences between the earlier and later
models: "Her emphasis on the theme of Nixon the liar from boyhood to maturity, from
parental home to the White House, is unsatisfactory in its neglect of Nixon's many ego
strengths and adaptations in a long political career." History, properly done, sees human
beings acting out of a complex combination of rational and irrational impulses formed by
memory and environment.

The whole trend in psychoanalytic thought toward a more holistic investigation of
"character"—which really began with Freud's ([1916] 1957) ruminations on "Those
Wrecked by Success"—has drawn psychoanalytic theory closer and closer to history in
a mutual concern with the ego—where the internal world of drive, wish, and fantasy
collides and conjoins with the cognitive, rational, and external world of objects and
aims. Reich's (1949) notion of "character armor" constituted another notable step in this
direction through its concern with the phenomenological exterior—"the readily observable and explicitly reported externals of appearance, bearing, manner, conduct, behavior, and personal style" (Loewenberg, 1982, p. 46). Pflanze (1972) used this Reichian
model to good effect in his study of Bismarck.

The psychoanalytic basis for psychohistory has also been criticized for a masculine
bias inherited from Freud and Viennese culture. This bias is congenial with the traditional historical concern with men, an orientation only recently challenged by the twin
twentieth-century forces of social history and feminism. Even though his work helped
free women (and men) from some of the more nonsensical constraints imposed by
Victorian views on sexuality, Freud in some frustration finally asked "Was will das
Weib?" Psychohistory itself has, thus, had to wrestle in particular seriousness with the
issues involved in the historical study of women. Wellman (1978) has argued that the
traditional male bias in psychoanalysis has been exaggerated in most psychohistorical
works because of the traditional concern with the almost exclusively male world of
political leaders and movements.

At the same time, Wellman's arguments do call up the evolution within psychoanalysis
away from libido theory, which, according to Wellman, regarded reproduction (and
hence the achievement of genitality) as the chief function of human beings. This notion
helped put women in their domestic place, fully equipped only for a reproductive role in
society. Wellman contends that humanistic psychology regards a sexually neutral self-
realization as the ultimate aim of the human organism. The trend within psychoanalysis
itself toward ego psychology left behind the strict sexual determinism of early psycho-

analytic theory. Thus, psychohistory draws from a psychoanalytic tradition that is now more generally appropriate for understanding women in history as well as men.

The rise of social history has also contributed to the growing psychohistorical study of women (Smith-Rosenberg, 1975). The natural concern of psychohistorians for matters of family, child rearing, and socialization—as exemplified in the group studies by Demos (1970a, 1970b, 1971, 1982) and Greven (1970, 1978) and the research of Hunt (1970) into the childhood of Louis XIII of France—forges a strong link, according to Smith-Rosenberg (1975), between psychohistory and the historical study of women. Most important, perhaps, psychohistorical works on women are beginning to become a prominent part of the literature, notably with Strouse's (1980) biography of Alice James and a forthcoming biography of Emma Goldman by Wexler (1980).

Prescription in Psychohistory. Another issue in psychohistory centers around the prescriptive tradition inherited from psychoanalysis. Lifton, for example, has come to see himself in the tradition of Freud, the psychoanalyst, rather than of Erikson, the psychohistorian. Prescription, as Lifton (1979, pp. 290–291) himself expresses it, is a concern with "ultimate or immortalizing issues" that manifest themselves most clearly in the human symbolic response to traumatic events such as medieval plagues or the atomic bombing of Hiroshima:

> In the important sequence from Freud to Erikson in great man theorizing, Erikson moved from the instinctual to the more genuinely historical, but in the process might have lost some of Freud's suprapersonal (in our terms, ultimate) theoretical emphasis. Perhaps that loss was inevitable, given Erikson's formidable task of integrating psychoanalytic and historical imagination. But at least some of the difficulty may derive from Erikson's simultaneous attempt to hold to and depart from Freud's basic paradigm as applied to history—holding to instinct while simultaneously substituting identity for it—and in the process perhaps conceptually neglecting that transcendent area of concern Freud sought so valiantly and (from the standpoint of subsequent theorists) frustratingly within the instinctual idiom.

We may discern in Lifton's thought here an interesting mix of urgency and hope. The urgency comes from what we can appropriately call a shared concern of modern civilization: the nuclear destruction of the world—in Freudian terms, the potential victory of Thanatos over Eros (Freud, [1930] 1961). Lifton's hope, on the other hand, springs from his medical background—the ancient impulse to cure—and from the modern social and natural scientific faith in progress. Freud's own turn from medical practice toward philosophy late in life resulted as much from his dispositional rejection of these implicit traditions in medicine and science as from his desire to round out his *Weltanschauung.*

Erikson's psychohistory also displays some strong marks of the prescriptive tradition in psychoanalysis. Erikson seeks to prescribe a cure for the ills of civilization, and the cure revolves around his beloved concept of identity. This desire is apparent in the almost demonic portrait he draws of Martin Luther's father and in his embracing of Mohandas

Gandhi's perceived struggle against "pseudospeciation" (Erikson, 1969). As Erikson (1958) notes with penetrating insight, he himself has constantly searched for his own identity after a childhood disrupted by national tensions. It is no wonder, therefore, that in his work Erikson seeks an amelioration among nations of what Freud called "the narcissism of small differences." Erikson's ideals, however, impart a certain vagueness to his concept of identity and substitute a measure of moral exhortation for hardheaded, critical, and objective analysis (Fitzpatrick, 1977; Kovel, 1974).

This prescriptive tradition is crucially related to the dynamics of psychohistory as an emergent subdiscipline of history. Indeed, the major topic of debate in psychohistory as it moved during the 1970s toward an autonomous articulation of its theory, method, and practice has been whether psychohistory is a scientific rather than a historical discipline. According to DeMause (1974), the chief advocate of psychohistory as a predictive science, the history of childhood reveals progressive stages of development from ancient times to the present. This progress has laid the foundation for the elimination of human conflict through enlightened parenting. There is nothing wrong with DeMause's ethical intent, but here good wishes get in the way of good history. The reductionism contained in this prescriptive historiography has led DeMause to see war and military organizations purely in terms of the infant's experience of the maternal heartbeat. It also brought about his inaccurate prediction that the early relationship between Jimmy Carter and his mother would lead the United States into war in 1979. Conflicting evidence or interpretations are dismissed.

Such uncritical fiddling with the realms of objective and subjective analysis, as well as the exuberant but careless mixing of scientific and historical method, distorts history. Distortion is an omnipresent danger in the application of models to history: Generalizations come to command the exercise, producing caricatures and stereotypes. Whatever use the historian makes of social scientific theories and models, he must respect the reality of change and development in human history; the complexities of history break the bounds of any single theory or model. Although useful work has been done by "culturalists" such as Kardiner (1949) in an anthropological search for "basic personalities" within human groups, the historian, like the psychoanalyst, should tend to look after the unique. One need only recall the limitations of the "national character" studies that were in vogue during the 1940s and early 1950s.

Freud himself built psychoanalysis on the basis of a concern for human disability, a preoccupation that wove together the gloomy strands that came to darken his final philosophical musings. The psychoanalytic movement in general, taking a cue from its founder's own post-World War I turn to a greater appreciation for the functioning of the ego, pursued a course more consistent with the basic medical urge to cure. Under the leadership of neo-Freudians such as Erich Fromm, Karen Horney, and Harry Stack Sullivan, among others, the movement came to expect the healthy human psyche to be able to adjust to, and become productive within, society at large.

Our concern, however, is with the value of various psychoanalytic models for the historical enterprise. Just as Freud's final setting of his philosophical house in order drew his thought away from history by reducing it to the repetition of a prehistorical primal event, the neo-Freudian and medical tendency toward prescription displays the limitations of moral and medical insistence as an adequate approach to historical understanding. To return to Lifton, whose chief source of psychoanalytic inspiration is the work of Otto Rank, we find an emphasis on the sledgehammer events of history that allegedly produce dramatic expressions of the human desire for symbolic—or, as in Lifton's (1968) view of Mao, "revolutionary"—immortality. For Lifton it is the *pathos* of the situation that produces inspirational human action and hence historical meaning. Freud, by contrast (and here we are following Rieff's 1979 analysis of Freud's philosophy), emphasized the *ethos* of man's existence, the (ultimately) macrohistorical predisposition that submerges subsequent actions in a sea of past conditions.

It is a thesis of this chapter that Freud's basic orientation to the past is congenial to the historian's task. The value of psychoanalysis to the historian is its careful detailing of the continuous balance of tension within the individual, who is constantly dealing with the personal realities of physical and mental life. Every historical event, every social structure, interacts with a complex sense of existence and identity, which, though malleable to a degree, is already established on an individual basis. What the historian sees (or should see) is the product of the interaction between the self, as significantly formed by early experiences, and the later events of life and processes of rational choice and action. The careful historian wants to know about the dynamics of the past as it affects the present. Event and structure are crucial, but less so than the *continuous lived experience* of human beings as individuals and in groups. There is, after all, very much more past in the human condition than present.

The virtues of history are found in the careful detailing of its subject matter by means of the unparalleled insight won by perspective, its sober rigor striving to provide a comprehensive and coherent view of a particular period, event, or phenomenon. History is supposed to provide an understanding of the past for its own sake. The problem is that the present century—and the prescriptive tradition in psychoanalysis and psychohistory reflects this—presses for solutions to multiplying and accelerating problems. Given this prescriptive tendency, it is vital that balance and thoughtful eclecticism obtain in the new avenues explored by historians. This caveat means, first of all, that psychohistory be regarded as one tool among many that can be grasped by the historian and not as any sort of fully autonomous science, as DeMause would have it. An insistence, however, on breadth and balance in the historian's approach to his work must also include the recognition that the historian will and should have a philosophical point of view. The crucial point for us is that psychoanalysis and psychohistory have an inherent tendency toward prescription, which—in combination with, or in place of, a more general philosophical or moral commitment—can partially or completely distort the historian's findings.

This critique does not mean to imply that there is no value in the work of those such as Fromm, Reich, and Lifton. It means only that the historian, and especially the psychohistorian, must employ a broader view. It is the virtue of the historicist tradition, for example, that it demands an eye, an ear, and a mind for the unique in time, place, and tradition: the historian opening himself up to the myriad voices in which history speaks.

Problems of Evidence. The availability and suitability of evidence is another especially significant issue for psychohistorians. Evidence from the childhoods of most figures in history, especially for those far in the past, is often unavailable, sketchy, or unreliable. A historian wishing to understand the actions of an adult by questing for the childhood experiences informing them must combine close analysis of the subject's own words, observations by contemporaries, and any discernible patterns of behavior with psychoanalytic theory to extrapolate the nature of early influences. In the process the psychohistorian must take care that the hypothesized quality of small bits of evidence does not become simply a device to compensate for lack of quantity of solid evidence.

A further consequence of what some traditional historians see as the psychohistorian's desperate search for evidence and argument is the problem of circularity. The use of psychoanalytic case studies so common in psychohistorical research has the potential to overwhelm historical material through the scientific virtuosity and clinical confidence of its combination of cause and effect. As one example out of the historical literature on Hitler discussed in extended fashion later in this chapter, we will consider an aspect of the debate over Hitler's sexual constitution. Bromberg (1971, 1974; Bromberg and Small, 1982) and, subsequently, Waite (1977) have argued that Hitler suffered from either monorchism, the congenital lack of a testicle, or cryptorchism, an undescended testicle, and that the symptomatology of monorchid and cryptorchid boys recorded in psychoanalytic case studies matches up with Hitler's behavior throughout his life. Binion (1973, p. 253) rejects this hypothesis by challenging the evidence for Hitler's missing a testicle and by asserting that Bromberg's thesis is circular: "For Bromberg, the alleged aftereffects evidence the supposed formative influences, which then explain the alleged aftereffects, with a circularity that rolls right by the bulk of the records."

Reductionism. The danger of circular reasoning in the reconstruction of the past is a variety of an even larger issue, that of reductionism. A shiny new theory can be intoxicating as it slashes through the thickets of history, revealing the true ground beneath. Such a threat to careful historical research is not unique to psychohistory, but the use of psychoanalytic theory can contribute to the real danger of methodological slash-and-burn. In psychohistory reductionism has taken two forms. The first, more traditional and more common, involves the reduction of a subject's motives (or an era's events or a group's actions) to a single root cause, such as the Oedipus complex. This was the marked tendency of the secret wartime report prepared on Hitler for the Office of Strategic Services by psychoanalyst Walter Langer (1972). The second, and more recent, form of reductionism in psychohistory is exemplified by Binion's (1973, 1976) study of Hitler. Binion's approach, associated with the DeMause school of psychohistorical thought, represents not reductionism *within* the psychohistorical model, as manifest in Langer, but the reduction *of* history *to* psychohistory. For Binion the key to Hitler's adult behavior is not an Oedipus complex but an interlocking complex of psychohistorical states, ranging from Klara Hitler's "maternal trauma" through Adolf's "gas trauma" to Germany's collective "November trauma," which in the end was the cause of Auschwitz and Stalingrad. This latter reductionistic tendency of contemporary psycho-history, while based on valuable research into the history of childhood (DeMause, 1974) and illuminated by Binion's intellectual fireworks, is the greater threat to balanced historical study of the individual and society in history.

In a review of Langer's study of Hitler, Orlow (1974) has wisely and concisely pointed out the dangers of reductionism. First of all, Orlow calls attention to the "ahistorical" bias of Freudian psychoanalysis, which holds that the phenomena of mental life eluci-dated by Freud apply equally to all times and places. Orlow (p. 135) then notes that this generalizing tendency in psychoanalysis is also manifest in Langer's tendency to charac-terize the German masses as "feminine-masochistic" and to ignore the "time-and-class-specific aspects of [Hitler]." Finally, Orlow (p. 137), citing Binion (1973), notes that psychoanalysts and psychohistorians regard "societal abstractions as extensions of personal relations." They believe that they can see behind their subjects' words and deeds what unconsciously was "really meant."

Subjectivity in Psychohistory. History is, as Dilthey (1962) put it, a "human science," in which the subjective—or, as Freud put it, affective—link between historian and subject is as indispensable as it is unavoidable. The role of subjectivity, especially in the psychohistorical study of political figures, constitutes an important aspect of any discus-sion of the weaknesses and strengths of psychohistory. This discussion divides neatly into three sections. The first includes those works of psychological analysis scarred by the author's conscious or unconscious antagonism for his subject. Fortunately, such works are rare, and they are usually written not by historians but by political or personal enemies—an infamous example being Bullitt's (Freud and Bullitt, 1967) attack on Woodrow Wilson.

The second mode of subjectivity is that of identification in both the general and specific sense. Hughes (1964) has argued that the historian must have some sort of emotional tie to a historical subject if he is to acquire the degree of interest, commit-ment, and empathy required to understand the past. This is particularly the case with historical biography, the historical encounter most like that of psychoanalyst and patient. In noting this similarity, Klauber (1968, p. 85) has recalled the work of the great historian Collingwood (1946): "It remains a great advance in philosophical insight to perceive that an act of intuition by identification with the thoughts and feelings of another human being is a creative act which deserves to be distinguished from an act of creative intuition which does not depend upon identification." But we must also assume that between a historian and his subject there most likely exists and grows a web of specific points of psychological contact, a network of shared concerns that opens up one life, or portions of a life, more fully to one historian than to another. The more intense and genuine these concerns, all other things being equal, the greater the insight that most likely will be manifest in the final product. Erikson's psychohistorical work is a good example of what Strozier (1977) calls "disciplined subjectivity." As a psychoanalyst, Erikson (1958) has emphasized the need for the historian to respond to the emotions the historical subject matter awakens in him and rightly sees history and psychoanalysis as kindred disciplines—both seeking multiple explanations for specific events and striving for a coherent understanding of the past.

The third area of historical subjectivity emerges from an often criticized tendency within psychoanalysis toward debunking. In the atmosphere of frantic disillusionment following World War I, Strachey (1918)—with his sketches in *Eminent Victorians*— began the tradition of stripping away the friendly masques produced by the phalanx of official biographies of the Victorian era. This was a necessary corrective, but— especially with the "discovery" of psychoanalysis in the 1920s—it soon led to the substitution of chic diagnosis for factual analysis (Mack, 1971). This tradition, when embraced by historians, flourished responsibly with the historian's traditional emphasis on the careful and comprehensive search for documentation and interpretive balance. The cataclysms of the new century also spurred responsible and concerned interest in the personal dynamics of political leaders who held the lives of millions of people in their hands and in their heads. A healthy skepticism, even cynicism, grew up over the allegedly rational process of politics and leadership—in fact, a liberal dream already frayed and tattered by the violent and demagogic turn of the new century.

Critics of psychohistory, however, have often found the genre guilty of debunking to the point of distortion. Coles (1973) has denounced Clinch's (1973) group portrait of the Kennedy brothers as nothing more than a heavy-handed hatchet job on some prominent achievers by an envious little scholar. Coles prefers the grace of a Freud on Leonardo da Vinci—so much so that Mazlish (1973), who wrote the introduction to the Clinch book, has accused Coles of reserving the role of critic of the high, mighty, and talented to those blessed by the "gift of grace." Clinch's analysis is, in fact, marred by the too often one-dimensional application of psychopathological labels, but Mazlish's response has merit. It is easy to idealize, even etherealize, political leaders, especially charismatic ones, and Coles's defense of the Kennedys has about it the injured sensibility of a Boston liberal Brahmin. Wills (1982), no enemy of liberalism and no friend of psychohistory, is the most recent to lay bare some of the less flattering dimensions of the keepers of the American Camelot. Apart from the difficulties, regularly cited by critics, of forging psychohistorical links between leader and led, analyzing American presidents in the face of national veneration is in general no easy task: easier with Nixon (Mazlish, 1970, 1972; Mazon, 1978; Brodie, 1981) and Johnson (Kearns, 1976), harder with Jefferson (Brodie, 1971, 1974) and Jackson (Rogin, 1976). Lincoln (Strozier, 1982) and Wilson (George and George, 1956) fall somewhere in between, since admiration for them is often mixed with puzzled sympathy.

The virtue of these attempts, whatever their individual faults or merits, lies in the corrective they bring to the image of a president as national leader beyond flesh and blood. American presidents—like the ironsided Bismarck, whose vulnerabilities and defenses have been skillfully revealed by Pflanze (1972; see also Sempell, 1974)—were, are, and always will be human beings with emotions. Although presidents are not the only proper and popular subjects for such study (see Brodie, 1959; Rogow, 1963; Glad,

1966; Mazlish, 1976), given their tremendous power, it seems not only desirable but prudent that we understand their characters. This is the chief justification, even with the genre's limits on perspective and evidence, for the fast psychobiographical sketches of sitting presidents, such as those on Nixon (Mazlish, 1970, 1972) and Carter (DeMause and Ebel, 1977; Mazlish and Diamond, 1980), and for Barber's (1972) continuing attempt to describe and define the "presidential character."

Psychoanalysis and Group Phenomena. How can the psychoanalytic model, with its focus on the individual, help to explain the group phenomena that compose much of the historian's concern? Building on Freud's ([1921] 1955) own attempt, the psychohistorical answers to this question include DeMause's (1981, p. 181) bold conviction that the "science" of psychohistory can, through the empathic analysis of "group fantasy," plumb the "psychology of the largest group." Most other psychohistorians have been much more restrained in their approach to this problem. Mazlish (1968) has pointed out that the psychological characteristics of groups are dynamic, not static, and that regional, ethnic, social, and cultural differences must not be ignored, as, for example, they tended to be in the national character studies of the 1940s and 1950s. Mazlish's (1975) own subsequent study of the lives of James and John Stuart Mill attempts to attack this problem from another direction. Mazlish sees the relationship between Mill *père et fils* as revealing of the social and economic changes of the nineteenth century, which within the family brought Oedipal conflict to the fore—a human dynamic that caught the genial attention of Freud in *fin de siècle* Vienna. Such an approach, similar to Erikson's notion of the "great man" as embodiment of the chief concerns of his era, is a valid way of bridging the gap between the psychoanalyst's essential concern with the individual and the historian's natural interest in the group. The group can also be approached directly, however, as in Loewenberg's (1971) deft motivational analysis of the youthful supporters of national socialism. Combining social history and psychoanalytic insights into the lives of infants and children disrupted by separation and undernourishment, Loewenberg connects the childhood experiences of the members of the generational "cohort" of 1902–1915 in Germany before, during, and immediately after World War I to their later enthusiasm for Hitler and the Nazis.

Yet within the ranks of psychohistorians themselves grave doubts about the success of efforts to bridge the gap "between a psychology of repressed instinctual strivings and a complex and multidimensional historical reality" (Wurgraft, 1975, p. 491) have continued to be expressed. Historian Fred Weinstein and sociologist Gerald Platt have together been at the forefront of a campaign to adapt and change psychoanalytic concepts to explain collective phenomena. In their first collaborative venture (Weinstein and Platt, 1969), they attempted to explain social change by adopting a Freudian instinctual model as modified by ego psychologist Heinz Hartmann and by sociologist Talcott Parsons. Since then, however, Weinstein and Platt (1973) have turned to an ego psychological model, emphasizing the ego's functioning within the social and cultural context at all stages of life. This new model, they (1972, 1975) argue, allows for fruitful new insight into history not offered by more traditional psychoanalytic concerns. The emphasis on the structural, however, has led Weinstein (1980) to produce an analysis of the German response to nazism in which the individual portraits are unsatisfyingly flat and abstract.

Psychohistorians must strive toward a greater understanding of the individual psyche (especially of the leader), political culture, and social collectivities. It is a most difficult task, and at present the primary contribution of psychohistory to history and to political psychology has been an elucidation of the unconscious motives of various individual figures of the past. At the other end of the human polity, it has offered some limited insight into cultural and social concerns through the study of the family and childhood. But the meeting ground of individual leader and group following in politics has remained shrouded, most likely because intervening structural, social, economic, and political factors play a major role in the construction of mass constituencies for individual leaders.

REFERENCES

Barber, J. *The Presidential Character: Predicting Performance in the White House.* (2nd ed.) Englewood Cliffs, N.J.: Prentice-Hall, 1972.

Barzun, J. "The Muse and Her Doctors." *American Historical Review*, 1972, *77*, 36–64.

Besançon, A. "Psychoanalysis: Auxiliary Science or Historical Method?" *Journal of Contemporary History*, 1968, *3*, 149–162.

Binion, R. "Hitler's Concept of *Lebensraum*: The Psychological Basis." *History of Childhood Quarterly*, 1973, *2*, 187–258.

————. *Hitler Among the Germans.* New York: Elsevier, 1976.

Brodie, F. *Thaddeus Stevens: Scourge of the South.* New York: Norton, 1959.

————. "Jefferson Biographers and the Psychology of Canonization." *Journal of Interdisciplinary History*, 1971, *2*, 155–171.

————. *Thomas Jefferson: An Intimate History.* New York: Norton, 1974.

————. *Richard Nixon: The Shaping of His Character.* New York: Norton, 1981.

Bromberg, N. "Hitler's Character and Its Development: Further Observations." *American Imago*, 1971, *28*, 289–303.

————. "Hitler's Childhood." *International Review of Psycho-Analysis*, 1974, *1*, 227–244.

Bromberg, N., and Small, V. *Hitler's Psychopathology.* New York: International Universities Press, 1982.

Clinch, N. *The Kennedy Neurosis: A Psychological Portrait of an American Dynasty.* New York: Grossett & Dunlap, 1973.

Cocks, G. "A. A. Milne: Sources of His Creativity." *American Imago*, 1977, *34*, 313–326.

————. *Psychotherapy in the Third Reich: The Göring Institute.* New York: Oxford University Press, 1985.

Coles, R. "Shrinking History." *New York Review of Books*, Feb. 22, 1973, pp. 15–21; March 8, 1973, pp. 25–29.

Collingwood, R. *The Idea of History.* Oxford, England: Clarendon Press, 1946.

Crews, R. "Analysis Terminable." *Commentary*, 1980, *70* (1), 25–34.

Crosby, F. "Evaluating Psychohistorical Explanations." *Psychohistory Review*, 1979, *7* (4), 6–16.

Crosby, F., and Crosby, T. "Psychobiography and Psychohistory." In S. Long (ed.), *The Handbook of Political Behavior.* New York: Plenum, 1981.

Decker, H. *Freud in Germany: Revolution and Reaction in Science 1893–1907.* Psychological Issues Monograph 41. New York: International Universities Press, 1977.

DeMause, L. "The Evolution of Childhood." *History of Childhood Quarterly*, 1974, *1*, 503–575.

_____. "What Is Psychohistory?" *Journal of Psychohistory*, 1981, *9*, 179–184.

DeMause, L., and Ebel, H. (eds.). *Jimmy Carter and American Fantasy.* New York: Psychohistory Press, 1977.

Demos, J. *A Little Commonwealth: Family Life in Plymouth Colony.* New York: Oxford University Press, 1970a.

_____. "Underlying Themes in the Witchcraft of Seventeenth-Century New England." *American Historical Review*, 1970b, *75*, 1311–1326.

_____. "Developmental Perspectives on the History of Childhood." *Journal of Interdisciplinary History*, 1971, *2*, 315–328.

_____. *Entertaining Satan: Witchcraft and the Culture of Early New England.* New York: Oxford University Press, 1982.

Dilthey, W. *Pattern and Meaning in History: Thoughts on History and Society.* (H. Rickman, ed.) New York: Harper & Row, 1962.

Erikson, E. *Young Man Luther: A Study in Psychoanalysis and History.* New York: Norton, 1958.

_____. *Gandhi's Truth: On the Origins of Militant Nonviolence.* New York: Norton, 1969.

Fitzpatrick, J. "Some Problematic Features of Erik H. Erikson's Psychohistory." *Psychohistory Review*, 1977, *5* (3), 16–27.

Freud, S. *Totem and Taboo.* In J. Strachey (ed.), *The Complete Psychological Works of Sigmund Freud.* Vol. 13. London: Hogarth Press, 1955. (Originally published 1913.)

_____. *Some Character-Types Met with in Psycho-Analytic Work.* Chap. 2: "Those Wrecked by Success." In J. Strachey (ed.), *The Complete Psychological Works of Sigmund Freud.* Vol. 14. London: Hogarth Press, 1957. (Originally published 1916.)

_____. *Group Psychology and the Analysis of the Ego.* In J. Strachey (ed.), *The Complete Psychological Works of Sigmund Freud.* Vol. 18. London: Hogarth Press, 1955. (Originally published 1921.)

_____. *Civilization and Its Discontents.* In J. Strachey (ed.), *The Complete Psychological Works of Sigmund Freud.* Vol. 21. London: Hogarth Press, 1961. (Originally published 1930.)

Freud, S., and Bullitt, W. *Thomas Woodrow Wilson: A Psychological Study.* Boston: Houghton Mifflin, 1967.

Friedländer, S. *History and Psychoanalysis: An Inquiry into the Possibilities and Limits of Psychohistory.* (S. Suleiman, trans.) New York: Holmes & Meier, 1978.

George, A., and George, J. *Woodrow Wilson and Colonel House: A Personality Study.* Don Mills, Ontario: Longman Canada, 1956.

Glad, B. *Charles Evans Hughes and the Illusions of Innocence.* Urbana: University of Illinois Press, 1966.

Greenstein, F. *Personality and Politics: Problems of Evidence, Inference, and Conceptualization.* Chicago: Markham, 1969.

Greven, P. *Four Generations: Population, Land and Family in Colonial Andover, Massachusetts.* Ithaca, N.Y.: Cornell University Press, 1970.

_____. *The Protestant Temperament: Patterns of Child Rearing, Religious Experience and Self in Early America.* New York: Knopf, 1978.

Hughes, H. "History and Psychoanalysis: The Explanation of Motive." In *History as Art and as Science.* New York: Harper & Row, 1964.

Hughes, J. "Toward the Psychological Drama of High Politics: The Case of Bismarck." *Central European History*, 1977, *10*, 271–285.

_____. *Emotion and High Politics: Personal Relations at the Summit in Late Nineteenth-Century Britain and Germany.* Berkeley: University of California Press, 1983.

Hunt, D. *Parents and Children in History: The Psychology of Family Life in Early Modern France.* New York: Basic Books, 1970.

Kardiner, A. *The Psychological Frontiers of Society.* New York: Columbia University Press, 1949.

Kearns, D. *Lyndon Johnson and the American Dream.* New York: Harper & Row, 1976.

Klauber, J. "On the Dual Use of Historical and Subjective Method in Psychoanalysis." *International Journal of Psycho-Analysis*, 1968, *49*, 80-88.

Kovel, J. "Erik Erikson's Psychohistory." *Social Policy*, 1974, *4* (5), 60–66.

Langer, W(alter). *The Mind of Adolf Hitler: The Secret Wartime Report.* New York: Basic Books, 1972.

Langer, W(illiam). "The Next Assignment." *American Historical Review*, 1958, *63*, 283–304.

Lifton, R. *Revolutionary Immortality: Mao Tse-tung and the Chinese Cultural Revolution.* New York: Random House, 1968.

_____. "Psychohistory." *Partisan Review*, 1970, *37*, 11–32.

_____. *The Broken Connection: On Death and the Continuity of Life.* New York: Simon & Schuster, 1979.

Loewenberg, P. "The Psychohistorical Origins of the Nazi Youth Cohort." *American Historical Review*, 1971, *76*, 1457–1502.

_____. "Psychoanalytic Models of History: Freud and After." Paper presented at conference on "History and Psychology: Recent Studies in the Family, Biography and Theory," Stanford University, May 1982.

_____. *Decoding the Past: The Psychohistorical Approach.* New York: Knopf, 1983.

Mack, J. "Psychoanalysis and Historical Biography." *Journal of the American Psychoanalytic Association*, 1971, *10*, 143–179.

Mazlish, B. "Group Psychology and Problems of Contemporary History." *Journal of Contemporary History*, 1968, *3*, 163–177.

_____. "Toward a Psychohistorical Inquiry: The 'Real' Richard Nixon." *Journal of Interdisciplinary History*, 1970, *1*, 49–105.

_____. *In Search of Nixon: A Psychohistorical Portrait.* New York: Basic Books, 1972.

_____. Letter to the Editor. *New York Review of Books*, May 3, 1973, p. 36.

_____. *James and John Stuart Mill: Father and Son in the Nineteenth Century.* New York: Basic Books, 1975.

_____. *Kissinger: The European Mind in American Policy.* New York: Basic Books, 1976.

Mazlish, B., and Diamond, E. *Jimmy Carter: A Character Portrait.* New York: Simon & Schuster, 1980.

Mazon, M. "Young Richard Nixon: A Study in Political Precocity." *The Historian*, 1978, *41*, 21–40.

Meyerhoff, H. "On Psychoanalysis as History." *Psychoanalysis and the Psychoanalytic Review*, 1962, *49*, 3–20.

Orlow, D. "The Significance of Time and Place in Psychohistory." *Journal of Interdisciplinary History*, 1974, *5*, 131–138.

Pflanze, O. "Toward a Psychoanalytic Interpretation of Bismarck." *American Historical Review*, 1972, *77*, 419–444.

Raack, R. "When Plans Fail: Small Group Behavior and Decision-Making in the Conspiracy of 1808 in Germany." *Journal of Conflict Resolution*, 1970, *14*, 3–19.

Reich, W. *Character Analysis.* (2nd ed.) (T. Wolfe, trans.) New York: Orgone Institute Press, 1949.

Rieff, P. *Freud: The Mind of the Moralist.* (3rd ed.) Chicago: University of Chicago Press, 1979.

Rogin, M. *Fathers and Children: Andrew Jackson and the Subjugation of the American Indian.* New York: Random House, 1976.

Rogow, A. *James Forrestal: A Study of Personality, Politics and Policy.* New York: Macmillan, 1963.

Rolle, A. "The Historic Past of the Unconscious." In H. Lasswell, D. Lerner, and H. Speier (eds.), *Propaganda and Communication in World History.* Vol. 3. Honolulu: University of Hawaii Press, 1980.

Sempell, C. "Bismarck's Childhood: A Psychohistorical Study." *History of Childhood Quarterly*, 1974, *2*, 107–124.

Smith-Rosenberg, C. "The New Woman and the Psycho-Historian: A Modest Proposal." *Group for the Use of Psychology in History Newsletter*, 1975, *4* (3), 4–11.

Stannard, D. *Shrinking History: On Freud and the Failure of Psychohistory.* New York: Oxford University Press, 1980.

Strachey, L. *Eminent Victorians.* New York: Putnam, 1918.

Strouse, J. *Alice James: A Biography.* Boston: Houghton Mifflin, 1980.

Strozier, C. "Disciplined Subjectivity and the Psychohistorian: A Critical Look at the Work of Erik H. Erikson." *Psychohistory Review*, 1977, *5* (3), 28–31.

———. *Lincoln's Quest for Union: Public and Private Meanings.* New York: Basic Books, 1982.

Waite, R. *The Psychopathic God: Adolf Hitler.* New York: Basic Books, 1977.

Weinstein, F. *The Dynamics of Nazism: Leadership, Ideology and the Holocaust.* Orlando, Fla.: Academic Press, 1980.

Weinstein, F., and Platt, G. *The Wish to Be Free: Society, Psyche, and Value Change.* Berkeley: University of California Press, 1969.

———. "History and Theory: The Question of Psychoanalysis." *Journal of Interdisciplinary History*, 1972, *2*, 419–434.

———. *Psychoanalytic Sociology: An Essay on the Interpretation of Historical Data and the Phenomena of Collective Behavior.* Baltimore: Johns Hopkins University Press, 1973.

———. "The Coming Crisis in Psychohistory." *Journal of Modern History*, 1975, *47*, 202–228.

Wellman, J. "Some Thoughts on the Psychohistorical Study of Women." *Psychohistory Review*, 1978, *7* (2), 20–24.

Wexler, A. "The Early Life of Emma Goldman." *Psychohistory Review*, 1980, *7* (4), 7–21.

Wills, G. *The Kennedy Imprisonment: A Meditation on Power.* Boston: Little, Brown, 1982.

Wurgraft, L. Review of Weinstein and Platt (1973). *Journal of Interdisciplinary History*, 1975, *5*, 491–496.

Yankelovich, D., and Barrett, W. *Ego and Instinct: The Psychoanalytic View of Human Nature— Revised.* New York: Random House, 1970.

CHAPTER FOUR

POLITICAL PSYCHOLOGY OF DESTRUCTIVE OBEDIENCE AND GENOCIDE

Even while standing in the remains of gas chambers and crematoria at Oświęcim, Poland, most people cannot envision the extent of the genocidal horrors that occurred there fewer than fifty years ago. Endless rows of stark barracks at Birkenau testify to the magnitude of Nazi evil, as does a nearby pond still discolored by the ashes of several hundred thousand victims.

But Nazism cannot be explained as a reversion to an uncivilized or barbarian state, and its enormity is not merely a function of the number of corpses produced. In many ways, twentieth century Germany epitomized modernity; the nation stood at the pinnacle of world achievement in scholarship, technology, and industry. Moreover, science and culture permeated Nazi efforts to bring about a "final solution" to the "Jewish problem." Crude anti-Semitism existed alongside intricate philosophical theory, often within the same mind. Sadistic medical experiments abounded. Meanwhile, a camp orchestra of inmates played classical music for the pleasure of Commandant Höss and his guests.

The killing operations themselves were not technologically complex feats, but modern man's bureaucratic efficiency facilitated the location and transport of victims. Thus, what happened at Auschwitz, at other concentration camps and at the hands of Einsatzgruppen in the East cannot be dismissed simply as savage behavior. We must wonder whether the twelve years between Hitler's accession to power and his suicide in April 1945 were an aberration from a generally benign trend in human civilization, or whether these years reveal something fundamental about the human potential for evil. Put more simply, could a similar catastrophe happen again? Where, and under what conditions?

For several decades, philosophers and theologians have debated the ultimate meaning of the Holocaust (Roth and Berenbaum, 1989). In addition, all branches of the social sciences have applied their disciplinary methodologies to the study of Nazism, discerning lessons about anti-Semitism, fascism, war, the human psyche and civilization itself. Social and political psychologists have been at the forefront of this effort.

During and immediately following the Second World War, psychological studies began to appear offering many hypotheses on anti-Semitism and Nazism. Numerous works drew on psychoanalysis (Ackerman and Jahoda, 1950; Adorno, Frenkel-Brunswik, Levinson, and Sanford, 1950; Bettelheim and Janowitz, 1950; Fromm, 1941) but other approaches were represented as well (Arendt, 1951; Rose, 1948; Simmel, 1948). Despite historian Geoffrey Barraclough's (1981) suggestion that it is "time to ask whether . . . [Nazism] is really worth all the attention sociologists, political scientists, historians, and psychiatrists have given it," social scientific interest in the phenomenon shows few signs of abatement.

So many studies of the psychological aspects of anti-Semitism, prejudice, Nazism, fascism, and genocide have appeared that it would be impossible to explore, or even list, all of them here (Allport, 1954; Dietrich, 1988; Glock and Stark, 1966; Kressel, 1981; Tumin, 1961; Weil, 1985). Many empirical studies have examined more recent, less destructive manifestations of Jew-hatred, frequently in the United States; attempts to extrapolate from these investigations to the Nazi context must proceed with extreme caution.

Psychological approaches to Nazism have attempted to: (1) identify a fascism-prone personality type (Adorno, et al., 1950; Altemeyer, 1981; Eysenck, 1954; Lewis, 1990; Ray, 1972; Rokeach, 1960; Samelson, 1986), (2) determine the psychodynamics behind Hitler, his lieutenants, and other genocidal dictators (Binion, 1976; Borofsky and Brand, 1980; Cocks, 1986; Waite, 1977), (3) delve into the unconscious of the German public (Binion, 1976; Fromm, 1941; Loewenberg, 1971; Terman, 1984), and (4) understand the role of situational pressures and obedience in producing compliance with Nazi orders (Arendt, 1977; Milgram, 1973; Sabini and Silver, 1980).

The readings in this chapter focus on this last approach. We explore how social forces can lead to destructive obedience and, hence, to immoral acts. While we pay particular attention to Nazi genocide, several other instances of dictatorial control and destructive obedience are considered.

Writing about Adolf Eichmann, a top official involved in the implementation of Hitler's "final solution," Hannah Arendt (1977) discusses the way an average-Joe-on-the-street can become a mass murderer. She writes that,

Except for an extra-ordinary diligence in looking out for his personal advancement, he had no motives at all. . . . He *merely*, to put it colloquially, *never realized what he was doing*. . . . It was sheer thoughtlessness—something by no means identical with stupidity—that predisposed him to become one of the greatest criminals of that period. (p. 287)

This "banality of evil" thesis calls for social psychological elaboration. If, for example, the principle holds for Eichmann, a mastermind, how much the more so might it apply to the case of lower-level perpetrators such as concentration camp guards? And, if Nazi killers were not particularly hateful or pathological, then the processes that led them to genocidal behavior might be normal processes—relevant, as well, to far less heinous crimes. The readings in this chapter explore these issues.

Stanley Milgram's famous experiments on obedience to authority (1963, 1973) provide one source of insight into relevant social psychological processes. These experiments, described in selection 14 by Sabini and Silver, support the conclusion that many Nazis obeyed orders simply because "obedience is as basic an element in the structure of social life as one can point to" (p. 1). For Milgram, the consequences of the human tendency to obey are immense; he cites C. P. Snow's conclusion that "When you think of the long and gloomy history of man, you will find more hideous crimes have been committed in the name of obedience than have ever been committed in the name of rebellion" (Milgram, 1973, p. 129). The conclusion is debatable, depending at least in part on how you classify crimes associated with Stalin, Mao, Pol Pot, Robespierre, and others. Nonetheless, the Milgram-Arendt interpretation of Nazi evil is provocative and must be reconciled with our thinking about the Holocaust.

Any attempt to explain Nazism can sound like an effort to justify it. The problem emerges whether one agrees with Milgram's approach, a psychoanalytic model, or other social psychological interpretations. Although condemnation of Nazi acts remains intellectually possible and morally necessary, difficult philosophical questions can arise about the issue of blame. B. F. Skinner's (1971) extreme position is that, because of the absence of free will, no moral condemnation is justifiable in any situation. Although some individuals resisted Nazi pressures to comply, their behavior can be viewed as potentially subject to explanation, either environmental or genetic. Insofar as people do not choose their genes or environments, we cannot readily assign praise or blame to them. Resolution of this ethical and intellectual dilemma lies beyond the scope of this book, but political psychologists who study the Holocaust must keep it in mind.

Another important issue concerns analogies between the Nazi destruction of European Jewry and other events in the past and present. Social scientists, typically, are less apt than historians to view the Holocaust as a unique, incomparable event. Lifton and Markusen (1990), for example, perceive meaningful comparisons between Nazi doctors and nuclear weapons professionals as participants in genocidal systems—although they note differences as well. Generally, social scientists are more likely than historians to search for processes common to other instances of bigotry, genocide, warfare, and dictatorship. When these comparisons detract from the centrality of anti-Semitism in Hitler's ideology and when they lead us to ignore critical details about the Nazi years, they may be inappropriate. However, if Milgram and others are correct about the generality of the social psychological processes that underlie Nazism, then we would expect similar processes to play a role in other crimes of obedience. This is the position taken by Kelman and Hamilton (1990). How tightly one should control use of the Holocaust analogy remains a controversial issue, often reflecting contemporary political disagreements as much as differences in historical interpretation (Dawidowicz, 1981; 1990).

This chapter includes four selections on obedience, control, and the psychology of the Holocaust. Two deal exclusively with Nazi genocide, while a third explores the broader category of "sanctioned massacres." The last selection addresses obedience and control in a very different context: the Communist Chinese thought reform movement. By considering Nazi genocide and Chinese thought reform, in the same chapter, I do not wish to imply moral equivalence between these situations. However, similar psychological mechanisms may have been at work.

John Sabini and Maury Silver, in the first selection (14), consider the relevance of social influence research to the explanation of Nazi perpetrators. Sabini and Silver summarize classic studies by Stanley Milgram, Philip Zimbardo, and Solomon Asch. Often, when social psychologists try to explain the Holocaust, they show inadequate respect for the differences among historical periods and national situations. One strong point of Sabini and Silver's essay is that it avoids simplistic generalizations from experimental studies. Instead, they base conclusions on an examination of the congruence between social psychological evidence and the historical record. Their use of survivor testimony in this context is noteworthy.

Robert Jay Lifton's prolific writings have influenced many areas of political psychology. His selection (15) in this chapter comes from his in-depth analysis, *The Nazi Doctors: Medical Killing and the Psychology of Genocide*. Lifton's theory of "doubling" provides a plausible explanation of how doctors ostensibly devoted to healing could participate in mass murder on a daily basis. Lifton sees the physicians' role as central in Nazi genocide and, also, derives a general psychological model of genocide from his analysis. His controversial approach has been criticized for exaggerating the significance of medical killing in Nazi genocide, minimizing the differences among various instances of mass murder, and relying too heavily on the doubling mechanism (Goldhagen, 1986).

Like Lifton, social psychologists Herbert C. Kelman and V. Lee Hamilton see parallels between the psychological mechanisms underlying killings in Nazi Germany and those in Vietnam. In the brief selection (16) from their recent book, *Crimes of Obedience: Toward a Social Psychology of Authority and Responsibility*, Kelman and Hamilton define a controversial category of sanctioned massacres in which they group the Nazis' destruction of European Jewry, the massacres of American Indians, U.S. activities in Vietnam, great purges in the Soviet Union, the genocide in Cambodia, and many other mass killings. Such a grouping is politically charged. Kelman and Hamilton note that sanctioned massacres vary on several dimensions, but they choose to focus on their similarities. They present a model based on Kelman's earlier work that identifies three processes that are linked to genocide: authorization, routinization, and dehumanization. For the authors, the key psychological forces are not "characterological dispositions to engage in murderous violence or profound hostility against the target." Rather, they argue that,

> The question that really calls for psychological analysis is why so many people are willing to formulate, participate in, and condone policies that call for the mass killings of defenseless civilians.

For the authors, democracies such as the United States are among the major perpetrators of crimes of obedience. The reader may dispute this conclusion, but, nonetheless, Kelman and Hamilton's discussion of social processes involved in genocide merits consideration.

In the final selection (17) in the chapter, John King Fairbank, the eminent historian of China, describes dictatorial control after the Communist revolution in China. The excerpt from Fairbank's *United States and China* summarizes the psychological processes used by the Communists to cause large-scale intellectual and emotional reconditioning of their population. Fairbank considers this personality change in its religious, political, and cultural context. The portrait he paints of this dark period in Chinese history shows how structured situations can be used to bring about extreme changes in political behavior and attitudes. This work and others (Lifton, 1961; Schein, Schneier, and Barker, 1961) delineate the processes by which people can be induced under extreme conditions to abandon their prior values.

The four readings in this chapter suggest that individual moral systems frequently provide weak resistance to situational pressures. Historical and political forces create powerful contexts that coax, cajole, disarm, or threaten individuals until they comply. Under some conditions, the power of the situation may suffice to produce collaboration rather than mere compliance.

Of course, as all the perspectives in the chapter indicate, exceptions always exist. Some people do resist evil, and therein, perhaps, lies some cause for hope.

REFERENCES

Ackerman, N. W., and Jahoda, M. (1950). *Anti-Semitism and Emotional Disorder: A Psychoanalytic Interpretation*. New York: Harper.

Adorno, T. W., Frenkel-Brunswik, E., Levinson, D., and Sanford, R. N. (1950). *The Authoritarian Personality*. New York: Harper & Row.

Allport, G. W. (1954). *The Nature of Prejudice*. Reading, MA: Addison-Wesley.

Altemeyer, B. (1981). *Right-Wing Authoritarianism*. Winnepeg, Canada: University of Manitoba Press.

Arendt, H. (1951). *The Origins of Totalitarianism*. New York: Harcourt, Brace.

———. (1977). *Eichmann in Jerusalem*. New York: Penguin.

Barraclough, G. (1981, 18). Goodbye, Hitler. *The New York Review of Books*, pp. 14–16.

Bettelheim, B., and Janowitz, M. (1950). *Dynamics of Prejudice*. New York: Harper.

Binion, R. (1976). *Hitler Among the Germans*. New York: Elsevier.

Borofsky, G. L., and Brand, D. J. (1980). Personality organization and psychological functioning of the Nuremberg war criminals: The Rorschach data. In J. E. Dimsdale (Ed.), *Survivors, Victims, and Perpetrators*. New York: Hemisphere.

Cocks, G. (1986). Contributions of psychohistory to understanding politics. In M. G. Hermann (Ed.), *Political Psychology* (pp. 139–166). San Francisco: Jossey-Bass.

Dawidowicz, L. S. (1981). *The Holocaust and the Historians*. Cambridge, MA: Harvard University Press.

_____. (1990, 6). How they teach the Holocaust. *Commentary*, pp. 25–32.

Dietrich, D. (1988). National renewal, anti-Semitism, and political continuity: A psychological assessment. *Political Psychology*, *9*(3), 385–411.

Eysenck, H. J. (1954). *The Psychology of Politics*. London: Routledge & Kegan Paul.

Fromm, E. (1941). *Escape from Freedom*. New York: Holt, Rinehart & Winston.

Glock, C. Y., and Stark, R. (1966). *Christian Beliefs and Anti-Semitism*. New York: Harper & Row.

Goldhagen, D. J. (1986). Healers as killers. *Commentary*, 82 (December), 77–80.

Kelman, H. C., and Hamilton, V. L. (1990). *Crimes of Obedience: Toward a Social Psychology of Authority and Responsibility*. New Haven, CT: Yale University Press.

Kressel, N. J. (1981). Hating the Jews: A new view from social psychology. *Judaism*, *30*, 269–275.

Lewis, T. T. (1990). Authoritarian attitudes and personalities: A psychohistorical perspective. *Psychohistory Review*, *18*(2), 141–167.

Lifton, R. J. (1961). *Thought Reform and the Psychology of Totalism*. New York: W. W. Norton.

Lifton, R. J. and Markusen, E. (1990). *The Genocidal Mentality: Nazi Holocaust and Nuclear Threat*. New York: Basic Books.

Loewenberg, P. (1971). The psychohistorical origins of the Nazi youth cohort. *American Historical Review*, 76, 1457–1502.

Milgram, S. (1963). Behavioral study of obedience. *Journal of Abnormal and Social Psychology*, 67, 371–378.

_____. (1973). *Obedience to Authority*. New York: Harper & Row.

Ray, J. J. (1972). Is anti-Semitism a cognitive simplification: Some observations on Australian neo-Nazis. *Jewish Journal of Sociology*, *14*(2), 207–213.

Rokeach, M. (1960). *The Open and Closed Mind*. New York: Basic Books.

Rose, A. (1948). Anti-Semitism's root in city hatred. *Commentary*, pp. 374–378.

Roth, J. K., and Berenbaum, M. (Eds.). (1989). *Holocaust: Religious and Philosophical Implications*. New York: Paragon House.

Sabini, J., & Silver, M. (1980). Destroying the innocent with a clear conscience. In J. E. Dimsdale (Ed.), *Survivors, Victims, and Perpetrators* (pp. 329–358). New York: Hemisphere.

Samelson, F. (1986). Authoritarianism from Berlin to Berkeley: On social psychology and history. *Journal of Social Issues*, *42*, 191–208.

Schein, E. H., Schneier, I., and Barker, C. H. (1961). *Coercive Persuasion*. New York: W. W. Norton.

Simmel, E. (Ed.). (1948). *Anti-Semitism: A Social Disease.* New York: International Universities Press.

Skinner, B. F. (1971). *Beyond Freedom and Dignity.* New York: Alfred Knopf.

Terman, D. (1984). Anti-Semitism: A study in group vulnerability and the vicissitudes of group ideals. *Psychohistory Review, 12*(4), 18–24.

Tumin, M. (1961). *An Inventory and Appraisal on American Anti-Semitism.* New York: Freedom Books.

Waite, R.G.L. (1977). *The Psychopathic God: Adolf Hitler.* New York: Basic Books.

Weil, F. D. (1985). The variable effects of education on liberal attitudes: A comparative-historical analysis of anti-Semitism using public opinion survey data. *American Sociological Review, 50*(4), 458–474.

14

Destroying the Innocent with a Clear Conscience: A Sociopsychology of the Holocaust

JOHN P. SABINI and MAURY SILVER

In Paris on November 7, 1938, Herschl Grynszpan, a 17-year-old Polish Jew, shot and killed Ernst von Rath, third secretary of the German Embassy. In Germany the response was *Kristallnacht*.

During the days of *Kristallnacht*, synagogues were razed, shop windows shattered, thousands of Jewish businesses destroyed, and tens of thousands of Jews attacked, tortured, and humiliated. Nearly 100 Jews were killed. As an outpouring of hatred, vicious anti-Semitism, and unrestrained sadism, *Kristallnacht* appears to display the essence of the Holocaust. To develop an analysis centering on *Kristallnacht*, we would explore such traditional social-psychological issues as the psychology of the mob (cf. Milgram and Toch, 1969), techniques of propaganda (cf. McGuire, 1969), and the character structure of the anti-Semite and fascist (cf. Adorno, Frenkel-Brunswik, Levinson, and Sanford, 1950).

But *Kristallnacht* cannot be our focus. *Kristallnacht*, a pogrom, an instrument of terror, is typical of the long-standing tradition of European anti-Semitism, not the new Nazi order, not the systematic extermination of European Jewry. Mob violence is a primitive, ineffective technique of extermination. It *is* an effective method of terrorizing a population, keeping people in their place, perhaps even of forcing some to abandon their religious or political convictions, but these were never Hitler's aims with regard to the Jews; he meant to destroy them.

Consider the numbers. The German state annihilated approximately six million Jews. At the rate of 100 per day this would have required nearly 200 years. Mob violence rests on the wrong psychological basis, on violent emotion. People can be manipulated into fury, but fury cannot be maintained for 200 years. Emotions, and their biological basis, have a natural time course; lust, even blood lust, is eventually sated. Further, emotions are notoriously fickle, can be turned. A lynch mob is unreliable, it can sometimes be moved to sympathy—say by a child's suffering. To eradicate a "race" it is essential to kill the children.

Thorough, comprehensive, exhaustive murder required the replacement of the mob with a bureaucracy, the replacement of shared rage with obedience to authority. The requisite bureaucracy would be effective whether manned by extreme or tepid anti-Semites, considerably broadening the pool of potential recruits; it would govern the actions of its members not by arousing passions but by organizing routines; it would only make distinctions it was designed to make, not those its members might be moved to make, say, between children and adults, scholar and thief, innocent and guilty; it would be responsive to the will of the ultimate authority through a hierarchy of responsibility—whatever that will might be. It was this bureaucratization of evil, the institutionalization of murder that marked the Third Reich; our focus then will be on the social psychology of individual action within the context of hierarchical institutions. Hence with Eichmann the bureaucrat, not *Kristallnacht*, is where an answer to the question "How could it have happened?" will be sought.

As Arendt (1965) tells it, Eichmann was a disappointment. Those who expected some passionate, deep-seated evil in the character of an organizer of the German death machine were frustrated, not because Eichmann revealed some nobility of character incompatible with a passion to destroy, but because the utter shallowness of the man was inconsistent with any deep principle. It is not the angry rioter we must understand but Eichmann, the colorless bureaucrat, replicated two million times in those who assembled the trains, dispatched the supplies, manufactured the poison gas, filed the paper work, sent out the death notices, guarded the prisoners, pointed left and right, supervised the loading-unloading of the vans, disposed of the ashes, and performed the countless other tasks that also constituted the Holocaust. An excerpt from the Auschwitz diary of SS Professor Dr. Hans Hermann Kremer illustrates the particular quality of murder as bureaucratized in the Third Reich, its place in the life of its operatives, how distant this murder is from passionate impulse, the distance between the rioter and the functionary.

September 6, 1942. Today, Sunday, excellent lunch: tomato soup, half a hen with potatoes and red cabbage (20g. fat), sweets and marvelous vanilla ice . . . in the evening at 8.00 hours outside for a Sonderaktion.*

---

* "The most spectacular of the mass atrocities were called *Sonderaktionen* (special actions). One of these, which was practiced particularly in Auschwitz, was the burning of live prisoners, especially children, in pits measuring 20 by 40 to 50 meters, on piles of gasoline-soaked wood" (Alexander, 1949, reported in Cohen, 1953).

September 9, 1942. This morning I got the most pleasant news from my lawyer, Prof. Dr. Hallermann in Münster, that I got divorced from my wife on the first of this month (Note: I see colors again, a black curtain is drawn back from my life!). Later on, present as doctor at a corporal punishment of eight prisoners and an execution by shooting with small-calibre rifles. Got soap flakes and two pieces of soap. . . . In the evening present at a Sonderaktion, fourth time.*

How could a Sonderaktion and soap flakes possibly be mentioned in the same breath? How could someone participate in mass murder without showing some emotion—distress, anger, or perhaps glee? Our account, then, attempts to explain not mass murder but mass murder of this special sort. Brutality, torture, rage, and even sadism in its restricted sexual sense were not missing from the Holocaust, but they were not its special features. They were neither necessary nor sufficient: what was needed was a machine not a beast. What is novel about the psychology of the Holocaust is not murder but the bloodlessness of the murderer. What needs explanation is not so much how the sadist could murder but how murder could come to occupy the same level of importance as soap flakes.

OBEDIENCE TO AUTHORITY

Eichmann has offered an account of this kind of murder; he has explained that he (and by extension the two million others) were merely doing their jobs (cf. Hilberg, 1961). This was a bizarre attempt to *justify* genocide, but could it be part of a correct *explanation*? Is it possible for someone not a sadist or a psychopath to kill innocent individuals just because ordered to do so? Stanley Milgram (1974), in a brilliant series of social psychological experiments, addressed this question.

The logic of his study was simple. An experimenter ordered subjects to deliver increasingly painful punishment to another person within the context of what the experimenter claimed was an important study of the relation between punishment and learning. Milgram was interested in knowing at what point people would refuse to inflict further punishment on a fellow human being.

In Milgram's experiment the individual is faced with a dramatic choice, one apparently involving extreme pain and perhaps injury to another human being. The subjects are recruited to participate in an experiment on memory. When each arrives at the laboratory, the experimenter tells him and another subject, a kindly, pleasant, avuncular, middle-aged gentleman (actually a confederate) that the study concerns the effects of punishment on learning. After a rigged drawing the lucky subject wins the role of teacher and the confederate becomes the "learner." The teacher and learner are taken to an

* From *Human Behavior in the Concentration Camp* by Elie A. Cohen, Copyright © 1953 by Grossett & Dunlap, Inc. Reprinted by permission of Grossett & Dunlap, Inc.

adjacent room, and the learner is strapped into a chair, electrodes attached to his arms, supposedly to prevent excessive movement; the effect was to make it appear impossible to escape. While strapped in the chair the learner diffidently mentions that he has a heart condition. The experimenter replies that while the shocks may be painful, they cause no permanent tissue damage. The teacher is instructed to read to the learner a list of word pairs, to test him on the list, and to administer punishment, an electric shock, whenever the learner errs. The teacher is given a sample shock of 45 volts (the only real shock ever administered). The experimenter instructs the teacher to increase the intensity of the shock one step on the shock generator for each error. The generator has 30 switches labeled from 15 to 450 volts, 10 times the sample shock. Beneath these voltage readings are verbal labels ranging from "SLIGHT SHOCK" to "DANGER: SEVERE SHOCK" and finally "XX."

The experiment starts routinely. By the fifth shock level, however, the confederate grunts in annoyance, and by the eighth shock level he shouts that the shocks are becoming painful. By the tenth level (150 volts) he cries out "Experimenter, get me out of here! I won't be in the experiment any more! I refuse to go on!" This response makes plain the intensity of the pain, and underscores the learner's *right* to be released regardless of the intensity of the pain. By 270 volts the learner's response becomes an agonized scream, and at 300 volts the learner refuses to supply any further answers. From 300 volts to 330 volts he shrieks in pain at each shock and gives no answer (the teacher is told to treat the failure to answer as an erroneous answer and to continue to shock). From 330 volts on the learner is not heard from, and the teacher has no way to know whether the learner is still conscious or, for that matter, alive (the teacher also knew that the experimenter could not tell about the condition of the victim from his position in the same room as the teacher).

Typically the teacher attempts to break off the experiment many times during the session. When he tries to do so, the experimenter instructs him to continue. If he refuses, the experimenter insists, finally telling him, "You must continue; you have no other choice." If the subject still refuses, the experimenter ends the experiment. The question of interest is the point at which the subject will terminate the experiment.

The situation is extremely realistic and tension-provoking. An observer (Milgram, 1963) has related:

> I observed a mature and initially poised businessman enter the laboratory smiling and confident. Within 20 minutes he was reduced to a twitching, stuttering wreck, who was rapidly approaching a point of nervous collapse. He constantly pulled on his earlobe, and twisted his hands. At one point he pushed his fist into his forehead and muttered: "Oh God, let's stop it." And yet he continued to respond to every word of the experimenter, and obeyed to the end. (p. 377)

We would expect that at most a small minority of subjects would continue to shock beyond the point at which the victim screamed in pain and demanded to be released. We certainly would expect that very, very few people would continue to the point of 450 volts. Indeed Milgram asked a sample of undergraduates, a sample of psychiatrists, and a sample of adults of various occupations to predict whether they would obey the orders of the experimenter. Each of these 110 people claimed that he or she would disobey at some point. Milgram, aware of the fact that people would be unwilling to admit that they themselves would obey such an unreasonable and unconscionable order, asked another sample of middle-class adults to predict how far *other people* would go in such a procedure. The average prediction was that perhaps one person in a thousand would continue to the end. This prediction was very far from the mark. In fact 65 percent (26 out of 40) of the subjects obeyed to the end.

Of course Milgram's subjects were not like Eichmann. Typically they protested, complained, and frequently showed signs of tension while carrying out their task. Arendt's report of Eichmann's prison interviews in Jerusalem shows no corresponding difficulty in carrying out his orders—the Final Solution. But this difference must not obscure the central point: subjects in the experiment *did* continue to shock even though the person they were shocking demanded to be released and withdrew his consent, even though the person they were shocking had ceased responding and might have been unconscious or even dead. Subjects in the experiment were induced to act in ways that we simply would not expect ordinary citizens of no obvious deficit of conscience to act.

In two other variants of the Milgram experiment there was a reduction in the subject's protests and emotional displays and an increase in obedience. In one variation the subject is not himself ordered to pull the switch delivering the shock but rather he performs a different, also essential task, while another person (in reality a confederate) pulls the switch. In this case roughly 90 percent (37 out of 40) of the subjects continued to perform the subsidiary task through 450 volts. The vast majority of the millions implicated in the Holocaust were involved in analogous subsidiary but essential functions. Further, they performed them distant from the actual gassing, burnings, and shootings. Distance from the victim, Milgram found, also has a profound effect on the level of obedience and on the stress experienced in obeying—from 20 percent obedience and great stress in a condition in which the subject has to physically press the victim's hand to the shock plate to virtually complete obedience and little stress in a condition in which the subject's information about the victim's suffering is dependent almost entirely on the verbal designations on the shock machine.

The central problem remains: How could the subjects in the Milgram experiments bring themselves to continue shocking the victim? This problem is exacerbated, not relieved, by the fact that some experienced great tension. If they were that upset by what they were doing, why didn't they stop?

Subjects in the Milgram experiment sometimes turned to the experimenter and asked who was responsible for their shocking the learner. The experimenter replied that *he* accepted full responsibility and subjects seemed to accept this and thus continued shocking. Yet how *could* the experimenter take upon himself their responsibility? Responsibility is not property that can be borrowed, shared, loaned, or repossessed. Responsibility is related to the *proper* allocation of moral praise and blame; assessing a person's responsibility involves considerations of what the person intended to do, what he realized or should have realized, what the individual could or could not have done, and so forth, as well as considerations relating to the gravity of the rule transgressed, the priority of competing claims, and the like. How could the experimenter's offer to assume responsibility alter any of these considerations; hence how could his offer alter whether the subjects were or were not responsible?

We do not doubt that the subjects' feeling of responsibility did affect how they acted; however, pointing to this feeling does not in itself explain the behavior. Consider the following simple, perhaps trivial, but hopefully illuminating example. Imagine that a person bends down and loosens his shoe because he feels that there is a rock in it, and furthermore he in fact discovers a rock. In this case his feeling about the rock fully explains his loosening his shoe. Imagine now a case in which, when he bends down he finds no rock. Although in this case it is also true that he bent down to untie his shoe because he felt that there was a rock in it, his behavior is still not fully explained—the now problematic question of why he felt that there was a rock in his shoe when there was not is left hanging. When we explain someone's behavior by pointing out that he felt that "X" was the case, we use a shorthand that takes for granted that the source of the person's *feeling* that X is the case is the *fact* that X is the case. When the feelings and facts do not coincide, saying that a person did what he did because of the way he felt gives a promissory note that one will explain why the person felt what he felt even though it was not the case. When this promissory note is not delivered on, then the "explanation" is at best misleading.

As for the behavior of Milgram's subjects, while it is correct to point out that they continued to obey because they *felt* that they were not responsible even though they were responsible, we now are obligated to explain how they could feel not responsible when they in fact were,* especially since as people attempting to predict behavior in the experiment, or as jurists considering the crimes of members of the SS, we see quite clearly

---

* The support that the rock-in-the-shoe example lends to our claims about feelings of responsibility and the facts of responsibility rests on the assumption that the statements that "John has a rock in his shoe" and "John is responsible for Bill's death" both are statements about *objective* facts not subjective reactions. Of course statements about rocks and statements about responsibility are different in many ways, but one of these ways is *not* that the former is objective and the latter subjective. We mean by this claim that commonsense actors share and assume that they share criteria they can call upon to tell whether a given person is or is not responsible for his or her actions. (Of course they also have and know they have a shared notion of rocks in shoes—that is why it is also objective.) We are not claiming that there are not difficult cases or even ambiguous cases for the proper application of the notion of responsibility, and we hasten to affirm that claims of responsibility are rather more difficult to apply than claims about rocks in shoes. In addition, we do not claim (nor deny) that the concept of responsibility is cross-culturally universal or invariant. We do hold, however, that *within a culture* it is sensible to talk of responsibility because there are shared criteria for when it is correct to say of a person that he or she is responsible. Our argument, although contrary to the subjectivist, individualistic biases of American psychology, is rooted in both the interpretive sociology of Berger and Luckmann (1967) and the analytic philosophy of Wittgenstein (1958) and Austin (1961). We cannot further develop this argument here but refer the reader to Kovesi's (1967) illuminating discussion on this issue.

that they were responsible. Responsibility is not something like personal property that one can divest oneself of, or that even an experimenter or a Führer can give or take away. How then could these subjects be guilty of this misinterpretation? Understanding how responsibility works in a bureaucracy provides a clue. Within an organization a section head, for example, is responsible for planning a job, assigning responsibilities among the workers, and even relieving some workers of responsibilities. A subordinate is only responsible for carrying out the plan. If the subordinate executes the plan according to specifications, then it is not his or her fault if the larger project fails because the plan was misconceived. The boss was responsible for the plan; the subordinate was responsible for only part of the execution. We could say that here responsibility has been partitioned, taken over, and shared. However, if the organization were indicted, it would be queer indeed for the subordinates to offer to the judge, as Eichmann did (and Milgram's subjects might have had it come to that), the excuse that they were not responsible, that their boss had relieved them of responsibility, and further, they had not constructed the plan but had merely carried it out. To offer such an excuse would be to ludicrously confuse the issues of technical and moral (or legal) responsibility.

The question of *technical* responsibility, the question of who is accountable for which part of a larger plan, arises within an institution and is decided by that institution. Questions of *moral* responsibility *cannot* be confined within institutions and resist resolutions by institutional superiors. Obedient subjects in the Milgram experiment who felt reassured by the experimenter's acceptance of responsibility apparently succumbed to a confusion between these two sorts of responsibility. The obedient Eichmann, at least in some of his moods, refused to the death to concede that such a distinction between technical and moral responsibility *can* be drawn.

So long as our institutions are legitimate and act within the limits of our shared morality, we are, as moral actors, free to ignore the broader question of moral responsibility as a matter of convenience. Ordinarily, convinced of the benevolence of the organizations of which we are a part, we do not trouble ourselves with questions of moral responsibility for the routine doing of our job. Eichmann and Milgram's subjects lost the right to be unconcerned with the moral implications of their actions just when the German state and the experimenter's demands became immoral. Milgram's obedient subjects and Hitler's murderers ought to have seen that these institutions were no longer legitimate, could no longer claim their loyalty, and could no longer settle for them the question of moral responsibility. Milgram's subjects, insofar as they accepted the experimenter's explicit or implicit claim to accept responsibility, failed to see what is, from a distance, so obvious.

MORALITY AND THE LEGITIMACY OF THE AUTHORITY

One might suppose that the failure of Eichmann and the millions like him to perceive the patent immorality of the German state bureaucracy must be different from the failure of

Milgram's subjects to see what had become of the experiment. After all, the magnitude of the failure in the Eichmann case is so much greater, the responsibility so much greater, that it would seem that we need different principles to explain it. We want to assume that the German bureaucrats acted out of a deep anti-Semitism, or perhaps financial self-interest, or perhaps they just sought to avoid the Russian front. We want to see the German failure as motivated in a way that the moral failure of Milgram's subjects seems not to be. Further variants of the Milgram experiment address the question of whether we need to assume such deep and particular motivation.

In one version the experiment is repeated not for the benefit of pure science, under the auspices of august Yale University, but rather for a firm of private industrial consultants located in a somewhat run-down commercial building in an office which barely managed to appear respectable. Yet in this setting, 19 out of 40 subjects obeyed fully. Although this is fewer than the 26 out of 40 at Yale, it is not significantly so. The rather shabby setting in an institution of vague if not questionable aims was not only sufficient to induce subjects to start the experiment but to keep them going to the end.

A second variant further explores the issue of legitimacy. Subjects in the original condition sometimes reported that the reason they continued was that the experiment was fair—the learner had volunteered to be in the experiment. But as an explanation this implies that the subject would not have obeyed if the experiment had not been fair, at least in this restricted sense. This possible explanation was examined in a condition in which the learner, in the presence of the subject and experimenter, agrees to participate only if the experimenter would agree to stop the experiment if and when he, the learner, wanted it stopped. The experimenter agreed. As in the other conditions the learner demands that the experiment be stopped at 150 volts. Sixteen out of 40 subjects continued to the end, even though this was in clear violation of the prior agreement. If anything ought to have undermined the legitimacy of the enterprise, this violation ought to have done so. It did not. These experiments do not explain *why* institutions keep such a strong presumption of legitimacy, why it is so difficult for people to extract themselves on moral grounds, but it does illustrate that people can treat corrupt institutions as legitimate in cases in which it would not seem possible to do so, even though they have *no* ulterior motive. For people to perceive the Nazi government as legitimate even while it was slaughtering millions, it would seem that it was not necessary to personally profit by, for example, taking over confiscated Jewish businesses.

Participating in a "legitimate" enterprise allowed subjects and bureaucrats to ignore the immoral implications of their actions in two ways. First, the issue of moral responsibility for the goals of the organization just does not come up in legitimate institutions; to do their jobs, people do not have to think about such matters. Second, even if subjects or bureaucrats *had* addressed the question of moral responsibility, bureaucratic structure would have helped them answer the question incorrectly; the relation between an individual's action and the rules and commands of an organization obscures personal responsibility.

RESPONSIBILITY AND INTENT

Typically there is a close relation between responsibility and intent—we are responsible for what we intend to do, what we are *trying* to do. If we accidentally cause something that was not our intent, then we have lessened or no responsibility. For example, if we accidentally step on someone's toy poodle, we may be guilty of clumsiness but not cruelty to animals, since we do not intend to hurt the beast. Lack of intent is a quite common ingredient of justifications and excuses in everyday life. An act we do not intend is usually a mistake, an error, an inadvertent consequence, and for these reasons our responsibility for them is usually diminished. In fact the link between responsibility and intent is even tighter: if we were asked what we are doing at a given moment, we would be likely to reply by mentioning the goal of our action, what we are intending. We would not be likely to point out the constituents or consequences aside from our goal or goals. For example, going to the store to get a loaf of bread is also: putting on our coat, going down stairs, walking down the street, wearing down our shoes, passing our friend's house, and, also, contributing to the profits of the grocery store owner, providing employment for the clerks, using up the earth's scarce resources, and so forth. However, of all of these, "going for a loaf of bread" (our goal) is the only one we are likely to see ourselves as "really" doing. The typical Milgram subject was only trying to be a good subject, help the experiment, and, perhaps, contribute to science; one imagines the German bureaucrat, similarly, as trying only to do his job well, follow the rules, perhaps support his family. In both cases the evil they did was not intended; it was perhaps easy to "feel" that the evil was not their doing, to feel that it had an accidental quality. Moreover, in both cases not only was destroying others not something they were trying to do, but, as in the case of the poodle who was accidentally stepped on, it was something they *would never* try to do. Carrying out the evil may even have been something they despised doing while they did it. For all these reasons, it was easy for Milgram's subjects, and at least some bureaucrats, to feel so innocent, so lacking in responsibility for the evil they performed. But feelings aside, they were responsible—not because their protestations of innocent intent were necessarily insincere but because in *these* cases the question of intent is irrelevant to the question of responsibility. No matter how much the evil that was a part, say, of dispatching the trains, when those trains went from Warsaw to Auschwitz, *felt* accidental it was not. Eichmann knew what his actions caused. Eichmann may well have been personally indifferent as to whether the Jews were annihilated, sent to Madagascar, or allowed to fulfill the Zionist dream, and in that sense he did not intend the Holocaust, but he was still responsible because people are responsible for all that they *cause* so long as they can or should see that they cause it. We may *feel* responsible only for what we intend; we *are* responsible for all that we do, and we know it.

Because our *feelings* of responsibility are grounded in our intentions, and bureaucracies arrange that everyone need only intend to follow the rules, the result is that bureaucracies have a genius for organizing evil. The bureaucrat knows what the rules of the bureaucracy dictate that he ought to do; if he should find some action contrary to his inclinations, he can still do it with a clear conscience, since he knows the action is contrary to his inclinations, can be divorced from his intentions. Even if he actually does want to bring about the very thing the bureaucracy tells him to do, and he suspects that it is wrong, he can still correctly maintain that even though he wanted to do it, he would have refrained in light of its questionable moral status were it not for the fact that he was ordered to do it. Of course this is germane to the question of *intent* but irrelevant to the issue of *responsibility*. Insofar as these concepts are muddled, morality is lost from the bureaucracy as a whole; each and every one is allowed to *feel* free of responsibility except, perhaps, the person who put it all together.

An important difference between Eichmann and Milgram's subjects is that Eichmann, unlike the obedient subjects who gave every evidence of detesting their role and resisting it, did not obey orders passively but actively strove to carry them out efficiently, intelligently, creatively, and most important, visibly—after all, his advancement depended on it. And trying to advance was what Eichmann, at least as Arendt tells it, saw himself as doing. Orders from above provided the ready excuse for him to kill millions as his particular pathway to self-advancement. This was why Eichmann was able to complain to his Jewish interrogator of the injustice of his being passed over in his difficult struggle to improve his position. The covering excuse of superior orders allows the individual to pursue personal goals (wealth, status, power, etc.) as well as more altruistic goals (providing for his family).

Doing one's duty is an important virtue, something that might justify actions one would not ordinarily do. A professor might fail a student, for example, keeping him or her out of medical school (inflicting real pain, something ordinarily proscribed), out of a duty to grade fairly, yet we find the teacher virtuous not a sadist. But just as a lack of evil intent does not necessarily absolve one of the responsibility, neither does a virtuous intent. If in pursuit of the virtue of punctuality, we were to jostle an elderly cripple to the ground or refuse to yield the right of way to an ambulance, then we could not offer as an excuse that punctuality was a virtue. Nor can we excuse Eichmann his genocide because he so well exemplified the virtue of adherence to duty.

How could Eichmann find that the dictates of his job had a moral claim that could compete with the injunction not to commit genocide? The bizarre moral climate of Nazi Germany, with its constant propaganda about the "international Jewish conspiracy" directed against the German Volk and Western civilization, was undoubtedly one powerful determinant that led Eichmann to be able to see killing, even of the innocent, as the call of duty and thus as a justification for genocide. Oddly enough, killing even *felt* like duty, like virtue. When the orders of "legitimate" authority are themselves immoral, then the ordinary connections among the proper course of action, moral principles, temptation, and desire contribute to the *subversion* of our perception of right and wrong. To see why, let us return to the details of the Milgram experiment.

Why do we expect subjects not to continue in the Milgram experiment; why did the people Milgram asked predict that people would stop? The simple answer is that we expect people to see that it was right to stop, that their conscience would not let them go on. Let us examine more closely the way we think about conscience and its relation to action.

We ordinarily conceive of action, at least potentially evil action, as having its source in desire. The commonsense view of the drama of morality is that it involves the conflict of desire with duty. We think of the child tempted to play with a forbidden toy or the adult tempted by self-interest to cheat on his or her taxes and these desires opposed by the dictates of conscience. Conscience finds its place in opposition to desire, egoism, internal drives. It is in contrast to desires and wants. Morality, the content of conscience, is perceived by the individual, in Berger and Luckmann's (1967) terms, as an "objective" phenomenon, that is, something beyond the individual's wants, interests, moods, and control. We speak of people knowing what is right and wrong, understanding the moral implications of something, perceiving the moral worth of something. So in the classic conception of moral drama there is a struggle between the drives one has and the duty one knows.

But in the Milgram experiment the source of the subject's wrongdoing is *not* his desire; he correctly perceives himself as *not* wanting to do wrong, *not* wanting to hurt the victim. The demands of the experimenter, *like the moral principles that ought to oppose them* are external, objective, beyond the subject's control or will. Indeed the experiment is constructed to make them external even to the *experimenter*: if the subject attempts to withdraw from the experiment, the experimenter tells the subject, "The experiment requires that you continue" not "I want you to continue." Further, the relation of the experimenter's commands to the purported purpose of the experiment reinforces the view that it is the experiment and the institution of science that requires this awful act, not the experimenter's will. The subject obeys, not because he wants to please the experimenter, but because he sees himself as being required by the experiment to continue. The subject is not tempted to shock the victim; if he is tempted at all, it is to stop. If the individual's conscience were to come into play to oppose his temptation, it would only have the effect of suppressing his inclination to *stop* and encourage his duty to participate. Indeed, even defiant subjects did not attack the experimenter for his immorality but, rather, often apologized for ruining the experiment.

And just as the law in civilized countries assumes that the voice of conscience tells everybody "Thou shalt not kill," even though man's natural desires and inclinations may at times be murderous, so the law of Hitler's land demanded that the voice of conscience tell everybody: "Thou shalt kill," although the organizers of the massacres knew full well that murder is against the normal desires and inclinations of most people. Evil in the Third Reich had lost the quality by which most people recognize it—the quality of temptation. Many Germans and many Nazis, probably an overwhelming majority of them, must have been tempted *not* to murder, *not* to rob, *not* to let their neighbors go off to their doom (for that the Jews were transported to their doom they knew, of course, even though many of them may not have known the gruesome details), and *not* to become accomplices in all these crimes by benefiting from them. But, God knows, they had learned how to resist temptation. (Arendt, 1965, p. 150)

Moreover, Eichmann did not decide one day that committing genocide was his calling. Rather he found himself arranging its logistics as the culmination of his career as a specialist on Jewish affairs. The German people did not decide that their first order priority was the eradication of the Jews and for that reason elected Hitler; the genocide they committed was the outcome, perhaps inevitable, of their political choices. The German bureaucrat, say a dispatcher for the railroad, did not decide to work on the railroad in order to move the Jews to their death; he found himself doing that among his other duties. In all these cases a person's evil is not the consequence of a focal decision to do that evil but rather is a result of a prior commitment. Milgram's obedient teachers did not decide to give the learner a possibly lethal shock; they too reached that point through a process of escalating commitments.

Subjects enter the experiment recognizing some commitment to cooperate with the experimenter; after all, they have agreed to participate, taken his money, and probably to some degree endorse the aims of the advancement of science. When the learner makes his first error, subjects are asked to shock him. The shock level is 15 volts. A 15-volt shock is entirely harmless, imperceptible. There is no moral issue here. Of course the next shock is more powerful, but only slightly so. Indeed every shock is only slightly more powerful than the last. The quality of the subject's action changes from something entirely blameless to something unconscionable, but by degrees. Where exactly should the subject stop? At what point is the divide between these two kinds of actions crossed? How is the subject to know? It is easy to see that there must be a line; it is not so easy to see where that line ought to be. Further, if the subject decides that giving the next shock is not permissible, then, since it is (in every case) only slightly more intense than the last one, what was the justification for administering the last shock he just gave? To deny the propriety of the step he is about to take *is* to undercut the propriety of the step he just took, and this undercuts the subject's own moral position. The subject is trapped by his gradual commitment to the experiment.

Of course in retrospect the inevitable drama of the 450-volt level is built into the structure of the experiment from the first shock. Had subjects perceived this, they might have refused to participate or set some level in advance where they would stop, but apparently they did not. Hitler's program of extermination similarly advanced by degrees. There was an 8-year progression from the first economic measures against the Jews to the construction of the extermination camps. Here too, however, the inevitability of the last step should be clear in the first; Hitler had made his plans perfectly clear in *Mein Kampf* in the 1920s. But still, in both the escalation in the experiment and the escalation of measures against the Jews there was an element of contingency. The learner might not, after all, make enough errors to call for the 450 volts, or the experimenter might call it off; respectable Germans believed that Hitler's "excessive" anti-Semitism was just a political ploy, that he would become more restrained once he assumed the burdens of power, that even if he wanted to he could not really carry out his program of annihilation. Thus it was possible for people to vote for the Nazi party, financially contribute to it, or join the government bureaucracy without intending the

Final Solution, but by a process of gradual commitment become responsible for the horror in its fullness.

Hitler's own sensitivity to the problem of the necessity for gradual action was demonstrated in a 1937 speech. When the most violent anti-Semites of the Nazi party were pressing him to move more forcefully against the Jews, he replied:

> the final aim of our whole policy is quite clear for all of us. Always I am concerned only that I do not take any step from which I will perhaps have to retreat, and not to take any step that will harm us. I tell you that I always go to the outermost limits of risk, but never beyond. For this you need to have a nose more or less to smell out: "What can I still do?" Also in a struggle against an enemy. I do not summon an enemy with force to fight, I don't say: "Fight!" because I want to fight. Instead I say, "I will destroy you!" and now, Wisdom, help me to maneuver you into the corner that you cannot fight back, and then you get the blow right in the heart. (Kotze & Krausnick, cited in Dawidowicz, 1975, pp. 124–125)

BRUTALITY AND EMOTIONAL RESPONSE

There is a powerful objection to our analogy between the behavior of Milgram's subjects and that of the German bureaucrat. The parallel seems especially strained when we focus not on train dispatchers, file clerks, and logistics experts, but on the SS members in the camps themselves. All accounts of actual concentration camp life portray repeated examples of wanton brutality on the part of the SS. In the Milgram experiment, on the other hand, many subjects showed extreme stress while carrying out the experimenter's orders. They held the shock levers down for very brief periods to deliver as little shock as possible within the confines of the experimenter's orders. They tried to resist the experimenter who prodded them into continuing. But the SS guards were even more brutal than the extermination plan required. Perhaps this shows that the commands of authority were simply an excuse, were not the essence of the psychology of the Holocaust. But even if the commands of authority happened to coincide with what the SS wanted to do anyway, still the excuse was an important ingredient in action. As we argued above, there is a gap between wanting to do something and doing it, and by seeming to remove responsibility for action, the commands of authority help close the gap. Second, we should not accept automatically that the egregious brutality of the concentration camps followed from the *inherent* brutality the guards brought to the camp without considering other possibilities.

To focus this discussion we will attempt to set the issue of brutality sharply. We begin with the position that Kogon (1950) develops in his discussion of the camps. By his account the people who made up the SS were the most shiftless, rootless elements of German society. Further, the training the guards received actively selected against any show of sympathy for the prisoners. The result of this process was that the guards were uniformly sadistic individuals, and, by implication, the brutality of the prison camps was a result of having people of this sort, with the tacit approval of the camp authorities.

This view traces the brutality of the camp to individual depravity. An opposing view supported by Cohen (1953), for example, is that the nature of the task of working as a camp guard was sufficient to produce that brutality even if the guards were not initially sadists. These are not exclusive possibilities with regard to the concrete, historical events of the Holocaust; it is likely that each contributed. But for the sake of this analysis, we shall focus on evidence to support the latter view, evidence that circumstances such as the concentration camps can produce such effects, and any evidence at all that the people engaged in running the concentration camps were not necessarily from the start psycho-pathological sadists.

We begin by reviewing a detail of the Milgram experiment. As we have pointed out, although a majority of subjects obeyed the commands of the experimenter, many of them exhibited signs of emotional stress; they were uncomfortable about the pain they were causing. Even if they did not see the moral imperative that they stop, they suffered from no defect of empathy; their emotions if not their intellect and action were in the right place. Further, this emotional reaction could be controlled by moving the teacher either further away or closer to the victim. Moving the victim has no effect on the moral issue of the experiment nor does it enhance the information the subject has about the victim (except, of course, to let him know that the victim has not passed out or been killed, which from the moral point of view should *increase* not decrease obedience). Rather this manipulation seems to work by enhancing the subject's direct emotional response to the victim. Closeness, in Arendt's terms, enhances the temptation to disobey.

Is there any evidence that even an SS member may be bothered by destructive emotional reactions and that the apparatus of extermination took them into account? Consider first the *Einsatzgruppen*, which were the mobile killing squads that Eichmann sent into the East following the German army to perform the on-the-spot slaughter of Jews, Gypsies, homosexuals, and so forth. These units functioned by rounding up the Jews in an area, transporting them to a desolate spot, digging a deep ditch, and then marching the victims to the edge of the ditch where they were shot in the neck, fell into the ditch, and then covered over (dead or alive) with dirt. Although this procedure resembles a firing squad, it is in fact different. A firing squad is inefficient; a concession is made to the scruples of the squad members by having several people shoot at once at the victim. This fact, along with the single blank bullet, obscures the question of who exactly killed the victim. The scale of the job of exterminating the Jews excluded the possibility of such sops to emotionality, hence each squad member shot at only a single target. Steiner (1967) writes about this procedure that:

The new system, on the contrary, personalized the act. Each executioner had "his" victim. . . . Moreover, this personalization of the act was accompanied by a physical proximity, since the executioner stood less than a yard away from his victim. Of course, he did not see him from the front, but it was discovered that necks, like faces, also individualize people. This accumulation of necks—suppliant, proud, fearful, broad, frail, hairy, or tanned—

rapidly became intolerable to the executioners, who could not help feeling a certain sense of guilt. Like blind faces, these necks came to haunt their dreams. (p. 73)

In recognition of the emotional cost to the executioners, they were expected to work for only an hour at a time at this physically not very taxing task. Alcohol was also liberally provided to dull the senses (Musmanno, 1961). According to Steiner's (1967) account, this psychological difficulty played a role in the evolution of the concentration camp system.

The solution to this problem, this psychological limitation of even the best trained and best selected SS men, the most rabid anti-Semites, was the eventual construction of fixed gas chambers. A further giant step in the solution of this problem was taken when it was decided that Jews themselves could be employed to do the loading and unloading of the chambers, thus removing the executioners from the gruesome human facts of their work. This solution posed a problem common to bureaucratic organizations—the problem of manpower turnover. Obviously, performing this task involved a certain amount of training. Further, there were certain subsidiary tasks that needed to be done and also required training (e.g., removing the gold from the mouths of the victims; collecting, sorting, and transporting the personal goods the victims brought with them; maintaining the camp constructed for the SS staff, etc.). To supply this labor a certain number of Jews would have to be kept in the camp for a considerable period of time rather than simply being processed through the death machinery. Thus the concentration camps became places where people lived, for a time, as well as died.

This step in the evolution of the Holocaust could exacerbate the psychological problem in that these victims became, or could become, relatively long-term residents of the camp in day-to-day contact with the guards who must eventually kill them. If it is difficult to shoot or shock a total stranger, how much more difficult it must be to do so to someone one has been in contact with over a period of time. It was not possible to increase the physical distance between victim and executioner to lessen the problem, but it was possible to do something else perhaps psychologically more potent. How could the concentration camp guards be shielded from the facts of their treatment of these human beings they were now forced to see, smell, hear, and on occasion even touch?

Part of the answer is that for the Nazis these were not, after all, fully human beings; they were a subhuman species. Nazi propaganda, developing on centuries of anti-Semitic rhetoric, elaborated the theme that Jews were less than human. But even so, most normal individuals find it difficult to mistreat a household pet. How many of us would be comfortable torturing or killing a chimpanzee? Our emotions, if not our morality, inhibit our brutalizing subhumans as well as humans. Another part of the propaganda was that these captives were dangerous to the Nazi war effort. While stories of the danger may have been compelling to the commandos in the field, such a point of view pales when the potential enemies are in captivity. Ideological notions of the depravity of these groups remain abstract, compared to the physical sight, smell, and expressions of the victims themselves. The captives must somehow not only be labeled as inferior but also must be made to appear that way. This problem was not insolvable.

Goffman (1959, 1963, 1971), in his careful analyses of total institutions, stigma, and self-presentation calls our attention to the ways that the individual must actively present a "worthy self," and to the fact that the presentation of a worthy self exerts a direct and powerful demand for treatment of a kind. To reduce this demand, to nullify it, to subvert its operation, it is useful, if not necessary, to destroy the individual's capacity to present him- or herself as a human being (i.e., as a self-conscious, reflective agent aware of his or her own humanity, dignity, moral worth, and capable of the expressivity typical of the species). While the capacity for such performance and such expression may be innate in a psychological sense, it is still dependent on circumstances. A constant theme of both the literature on the German concentration camps and Solzhenitsyn's accounts of the Russian camps is the perpetual degradation of the inmates.

Starvation, along with reducing the economic burden of the slaves to the slave masters, destroys the body's capacity to produce the range of expressions we take as a sign of affective life. Constant hunger, like constant pain, removes the individual from the social world, fixates attention on the internal state, and hence dehumanizes. Further, the extremes of hunger drive the individual to resort to scavenging through garbage, turning informant, fighting with fellow inmates for a scrap of food (and in the process impeding the development of associations among prisoners necessary to organized resistance). Starvation and constant hunger are extremely effective tools of degradation. Des Pres (1977) points out that some of the prisoners recognized the potential dehumanization in the camps and actively sought to resist it by maintaining standards of cleanliness, sharing packages from home, and preventing suicides.

Perhaps the most potent technique of degradation is to make the individual filthy, to make him stink. As Des Pres and Goffman have emphasized, in modern Western culture the requirement that one remain clean (both of contamination by mud, dirt, and other environmental sources of pollution and, perhaps more importantly, of one's own excrement) is a first and central demand on every child who would be a member of the society. But to do this requires not only a psychological and biological capacity but also social circumstances that make it possible. Baths, showers, and toilets are resources without which it is impossible to maintain the appearance of being a self-conscious, worthy member of the social order. To withdraw these or forbid their use makes it inevitable that the individual will be unable to sustain the immediate, compelling appearance of a worthy self, and makes it easier for another to ignore the moral fact that such a spoiled appearance has no bearing on the question of value or worth.

We cannot claim that all the camp officials recognized the desirable consequences of keeping the prisoners perpetually degraded and planned the camps with that in mind, but at least one official noticed the utility of bestiality after the fact. In an interview with Franz Stangl, Treblinka's commandant, the issue of why the guards degraded the prisoners became explicit:

"Why," I asked Stangl, *"if they were going to kill them any way, what was the point of all the humiliation, why the cruelty?"*

"To condition those who actually had to carry out the policies," he said. "To make it possible for them to do what they did." (Sereny, cited in Des Pres, 1977, p. 67)

Would people who were not already sadists, who did not derive pleasure from torture, wantonly brutalize prisoners even if it is true that under the *command* of authority they might torture them? First, in the Milgram experiments there was some indication that the subjects became angry at the learner. As the experiment progressed they became angry at him for, as they saw it, making the mistakes that caused them to be subjected to such stress. Surely this is an extraordinarily immature response, but we are dealing here with matters of emotion and it is no surprise when emotional responses are immature. But still, none of the subjects went out of his way to further harm the victim, even if they were somewhat angry. On the other hand, the experiment lasted only about an hour, and we do not know how the subjects would have responded were the stress more enduring.

Another source of more direct evidence on this point comes from a study by Zimbardo (1971). Zimbardo's plan was to conduct a 2-week simulation of prison experience to examine the reactions of normal subjects who would play the parts of guards and prisoners. The subjects were all college-age males who happened to be in the area of the experiment (Stanford, California) during the summer, and who answered an ad soliciting paid volunteers. Potential subjects were screened by psychologists using various personality tests; any who were deemed abnormal were excluded.

Zimbardo attempted to capture in the details of his prison the degradation present in American prisons; therefore prisoners were, among other things, forced to give up their personal effects and to wear stocking caps over their heads to obscure their hair styles, a rough and ready equivalent of the shaved heads characteristic of the military and German camps. These male prisoners were given gowns to wear (resembling traditional hospital attire) that looked like, and forced prisoners to walk as if, they were wearing dresses. This costume was designed to make the prisoners appear ludicrous to the guards and themselves since the prisoners, to protect their modesty, had to walk and sit as though they were women wearing dresses. It symbolized, in a very minor way, the emasculation of male prisoners in the camps or prisons.

Guards were also costumed for their part. They were given uniforms, billy clubs, and silver sunglasses to prevent eye contact between themselves and their prisoners. They were instructed to refer to the prisoners by number only, further stripping away the prisoner's identity.

A long list of prison regulations forbade unauthorized talking, required the prisoners to address the guards not by name but with the title "Mr. Correction Officer," forbade the prisoners the use of the bathroom without permission, and required a humiliating stripping and delousing as a first step in prison life.

Although the study was designed to last for two weeks, Zimbardo was forced to cancel it after six days due to the level of brutality the guards had reached and the signs of severe psychological distress on the part of several prisoners. The behavior on the part of the guards could be characterized as an escalation of brutality or, put the other way around, a moral drift. The prisoners reacted in an apathetic, despairing way. Both groups seemed little to take account of the fact that it was "only" an experiment, that they were not really prisoners or guards.

The second day of the experiment was marked by a prisoner rebellion, in reaction to which some familiar features of the concentration camp were imposed spontaneously. For example, the prisoners were subjected to endless roll calls, taking up the better part of the night. Accounts of concentration camp life almost invariably point to the egregiously long assemblies as a feature of daily experience. The prisoners in the experiment were forced to chant songs with content that degraded themselves. This too is a nearly constant theme in the concentration camp literature. Zimbardo's guards took upon themselves the authority to order on-the-spot punishment, confinement to solitary chambers, and to place informants in the cells. Prisoners were assigned senseless tasks or were ordered to perform tasks in the most degrading possible way (e.g., cleaning out toilets with their bare hands). Bathroom privileges were withdrawn, and prisoners were forced to use a bucket in their cells; guards, on occasion, would refuse permission to empty it, another torture endemic to concentration camps. Food was occasionally denied, and, conversely, a prisoner who refused to eat was force fed. These results strongly suggest that perfectly normal people will, in certain circumstances, treat others in a brutal, inhumane way, even though they know that their victims are ordinary people much like themselves, even though they know, literally in this case, that there but for chance would they be.

It is important to distinguish this result from Milgram's. Milgram's subjects were explicitly ordered to shock the victim; subjects showed little inclination to go beyond the necessary infliction of pain. Indeed in one condition of the experiment, Milgram told subjects to pick whatever levels of shock they thought best. Although the experimenter tacitly sanctioned any level at all, just by being there and not stopping the subject when he picked a level, only two of forty subjects went beyond 150 volts, with the majority staying below 60 volts. In the Zimbardo experiment, again with the tacit approval of the authority (the psychologist running the experiment), subjects innovated their own forms of degradation and punishment. A central difference seems to be that Zimbardo set out to degrade the victims, while Milgram did nothing to degrade the learner. A further difference is that Zimbardo's guards acted not alone but in the presence and as part of a group of other guards. We want to know, then, how the presence of peers under the at least passive aegis of an authority might affect one's behavior in this morally significant case.

Milgram (1964) conducted a variant of his experiment to investigate this matter. The subject met not one but three confederates. As in all conditions, one of the confederates was assigned by a fake lottery to the role of learner, the other two and the subject were to be teachers. The experimenter did not tell them what shock level to use but rather told them to decide the proper level among themselves. They were told that they were to give the *lowest* level that any of them wanted, thus the subject had an effective veto on the confederates. As the experiment progressed the two confederates hit upon the idea of increasing the level of shock one 15-volt step with each error; the subject then is faced with the clear option of at least passively going along with the plan or using his veto power to lower the voltage. One further detail is important: the subject himself was assigned the task of actually pulling the lever. In this condition about 18 percent of the subjects continued to shock to the end, 45 percent refused to go above 150 volts, and the remaining subjects broke off somewhere between. If one examines more closely the distribution of shocks that subjects deliver and compares them to the shock levels that subjects choose when neither instructed by authority nor prodded by confederates, one finds that the subject's responses in this condition are a compromise between what the subjects would have done were they left to pick their own level and the responses proposed by the two confederates. The plans of their peers are not as effective as are the orders of authority (only seven as opposed to twenty-six got to the end), but in this case, with the tacit approval of the authority, subjects' actions are swayed in the direction of their peers.

How are we to interpret this result? The significance we give it is that the subjects, as shown in the condition in which they are tested alone, have some rough conception of how much shock is appropriate. Of course this is not a crystal clear matter. As we argued before, it is a matter of degree; they are not *committed* to some level beyond which they will not go. They encounter in the experiment two other people much like themselves who have, however, a different conception of how to balance the competing claims of the learner and the experiment. The opinions of these other subjects seem to influence their own; their conception of the point beyond which they will not go moves up. Why? If the other subjects had a gun on them we would understand why their behavior at least would be affected by the other people's opinion; but the confederates have no gun. As we have suggested elsewhere (Sabini and Silver, 1978) the classic studies by Sherif (1935) are relevant here.

MORAL JUDGMENT AND PEER INFLUENCE

Sherif conducted an experiment in which a subject was asked to fix his attention on a point source of light in a dark room. If you do this you will notice that the light will seem to move, an optical illusion called the autokinetic effect. Sherif then asked the subject how far the light moved. The subject has no frame of reference within which to answer this question, but he tries. If the subject is tested over a series of 50 or 100 trials, his answers tend to accumulate about a central value, they do not evenly distribute themselves along the continuum of plausible answers. If you now take three subjects, each of whom has taken part in this procedure and each of whom has reached some mean, some stable idea as to how far the light is moving, and ask them again in each other's presence to say out loud how far the light has moved, you find that the individuals' judgments tend to converge. Subjects do not experience this procedure as a stressful one in which others are trying to impose their views on them. Rather, since each believes that there is a right answer (if you tell them it's an illusion as Alexander, Zucker, and Brody [1970] did, no convergence occurs), and each knows that he does not know that answer (they can see that they have very little guidance in guessing), and each knows that no one else is sure either (they can see that the other people are in the same position), they give weight to others' opinions in forming their own judgment about this ambiguous matter.

If we take this as a model for the Milgram study, then we might say that when a subject confronted with an ambiguous moral judgment finds two other people who differ about that judgment, he takes into account their views in forming his own opinion. Were the other two subjects in the Sherif experiment known by the third subject to be blind, then we would not expect such convergence; were the two confederates in the Milgram experiment known in advance by the subject to be sadists, we would not expect moral convergence. If this line of thought is correct, then the fact that another sees a behavior as correct and morally tolerable can, in ambiguous situations, lead a person who might a priori find that behavior wrong to find it acceptable.

We can also view these results from the perspective of the subject's presentation of his character before the experimenter, the victim, the two confederates, and of course himself. The subject's response as a compromise between the judgments of the confederate and the very mild shock that if he were on his own he would choose displays his sensitivity to the learner while showing that he respects the opinion of his fellow teachers. He is in this way sensitive to and responsive to all points of view on the matter. He is not only an effective functionary but a "humane" one.

Before we can apply our analysis of the Sherif experiment to either the Zimbardo findings or the concentration camps, we have two limitations to consider: (1) the influence in the Sherif experiment is mutual—a rough compromise occurred. If compromise is what happened in the case of the guards we have been considering, then we must conclude that they were, on the average, sadists, since the mean level of viciousness was so high; and (2) the Sherif experiment takes place in circumstances of ambiguity—no one would call the behavior of concentration camp guards morally ambiguous.

To deal with the first objection, that the Sherif results indicate convergence to a mean, whereas the phenomenon we are trying to explain involves progressively more extreme behavior, we must examine the Sherif experiment more closely. The opinions of the subjects enter into the process of convergence only because the subjects offer their guesses publicly—they externalize their private views. They do it precisely because they are asked to do so by the experimenter; they stand in no danger of being asked, "Who asked you?" In the Zimbardo experiment, on the other hand, presumably no one asked each of the guards for his opinion about the limits of acceptable compulsion to be used to control the prisoners. As a consequence there developed in the Zimbardo experiment several kinds of guards rather than a group with a shared consensus.

The guards could be characterized as falling into one of three groupings. There were the tough but fair guards whose orders were always within the prescribed rules of prison operation. Then there were several guards who were the good guys according to the prisoners, who felt genuinely sorry for the prisoners, who did little favors for them and never punished them. And finally, about a third of the guards were extremely hostile, arbitrary, inventive in their forms of degradation and humiliation, and appeared to thoroughly enjoy the power they wielded when they put on the guard uniform and stepped out into the yard, big stick in hand. (Zimbardo, 1971, p. 14)

But the "good guards' " good heartedness had no apparent effect on the behavior of the more sadistic group; Zimbardo (1971) writes: "In fact, they allowed it to go on, never once interfering with an order by one of the cruel guards. It might even be said that it was the good guards who helped maintain the prison, although the bad guards set the tone" (p. 16). The failure of the "good guards" to act cannot, of course, account for the *inclination* on the part of the others to be brutal, but it does have to do with the absence of group norms, both in the sense of shared understandings about right and wrong and enforceable regulations. Matza (1968) pointed out a similar drift into brutality in some youth gangs he extensively interviewed. He claimed that individual gang members reported that they privately disavowed the delinquent behavior the gang engaged in but that each was afraid to say this out loud for fear of ridicule. In this sort of setting behavior can deteriorate to the level of the least restrained members of the group, not because the other members fully endorse that behavior, but because they are unwilling or unable to make their view known. Private views of morality cannot become anchors for the behavior of others unless those views are expressed; there is even the question of whether these views can remain anchors for the individual who holds them unless they are expressed. The Zimbardo experiment lasted a mere 6 days; could his "good guards" have remained attached to at least their passive unwillingness to take part in the brutality had the experiment continued? Over an extended period of time it might be very difficult for people to hold indefinitely to a moral position they see flaunted by others. Of course they might remain less brutal than the worst guards, but as the worst guards became worse their "temperate" behavior could become quite brutal indeed.

We propose then that in cases in which individuals see others doing what they would not do but do not voice their objections, moral drift occurs. The failure to publicly establish the wrongness of a particular action gives it an implicit legitimacy; even those who would be disposed to find it wrong have difficulty sustaining that view when others, presumably as competent at moral matters as they, give evidence by their actions of finding it acceptable.

Once brutality becomes standard procedure within an institution, it takes on an added legitimacy. As Berger and Luckmann (1967) argue, institutions by their very existence are taken by people, at least prima facie, to be legitimate. This legitimacy is conferred and reinforced by the process of socialization into the institution. Consider the problem a newcomer to an institution has in dealing with practices within it that he or she may find distasteful.

A newcomer is typically in the position of someone who does not know his or her way around and knows it. It is natural to seek information from others to learn how things are done here. The fact that everyone else seems to accept (or at least no one opposes) what would appear at first glance to be brutality suggests prima facie that in the judgment of these people the behavior is acceptable, and this suggests that the behavior is acceptable. Tillion's (1975) account of the "socialization" of a new *Aufseherin*, a female guard at Ravensbruck, suggests this process at work:

> The beginners usually appeared frightened upon first contact with the camp, and it took some time to attain the level of cruelty and debauchery of their seniors. Some of us made a rather grim little game of measuring the time it took for a new Aufseherin to win her stripes. One little Aufseherin, twenty years old, who was at first so ignorant of proper camp "manners" that she said "excuse me" when walking in front of a prisoner, needed exactly four days to adopt the requisite manner, although it was totally new for her. (This little one no doubt had some special gifts in the "arts" we are dealing with here.) As for the others, a week or two, a month at the most, was an average orientation period. (p. 69)

Tillion claims that the *Aufseherinnen*, unlike the male SS guards, were not selected for their brutality. This puts her in accord with Kogon (1950) in the claim that the male SS was a selected band of sadists. But the similar brutality of the female guards suggests, at the same time, the superfluousness of this selection; it suggests that the conditions of the camp were sufficient to socialize guards into the brutality in a relatively brief period without prior selection.

There is still a gap for us to close. The Sherif illustration deals with cases of ambiguity; no one would call the behavior in the camps ambiguous. Can social influences lead people to view clearcut moral matters in such a perverse way if they do not have a prior desire to see them that way? Some evidence from a series of experiments conducted by Asch (1952) may bring us closer to an answer.

Asch recognized that the Sherif demonstration had to do with an entirely ambiguous matter; he expected that if people were given sufficiently clear cases to judge they would not be subject to such influences. To investigate this he constructed an experiment in which people were asked simply to judge which of three lines was equal in length to a fourth. When people made these judgments alone they erred in only a very few cases. Asch asked other subjects to make the same judgments in the presence of a group. The group contained six confederates who were instructed to give a patently wrong answer on some of the trials. Subjects in this condition, then, were asked to make a judgment about a perfectly clear matter in the presence of other people who, presumably, were judging the same relation. How did subjects react?

All (or nearly all) subjects reacted with signs of tension and confusion. Roughly one-third of the judgments subjects made were in error. Nearly 80 percent of the subjects gave the obviously wrong answer on at least one trial. The perception that a few other people make an absurd judgment of a clear, unambiguous physical matter was, then, a very troubling experience, sufficient to cause doubt and in some cases conformity. This procedure lasted only an hour or so. How would subjects have stood up had the procedure lasted for even the four days of Tillion's "little one"? Notice too that here the subject is asked to judge a physical relation, something our nervous system is presumably wired to perceive directly. While we would agree with Durkheim (1933/1893) that moral matters are objective and external, they are clearly not directly tied to the wiring of the nervous system as is the judgment of line length. As Durkheim saw, for moral norms to have the force they have of inhibiting, limiting, and regulating individual action, they must be elements external to the individual, properties not of one's internal subjectivity but of the social world one inhabits. This position confers on moral norms a certain fragility; they are fragile in that others have access to them, they are not our private property. Others' statements about them and, perhaps more importantly, the statements about them implicit in others' behavior must then have weight with regard to our own view. The assumption of mutuality leads to the most basic and primitive form of social influence: influence that arises from taking into account each other's views of our shared social world.

The guards influenced the level of each others' brutality in a further way. In replicating the Asch work Tuddenham and MacBride (1959) asked subjects about their conformity. They were surprised to find that some subjects who had given erroneous judgments reported that they themselves were quite independent of group influence. On further prodding they revealed that, as they understood the situation, the first "subject" who gave a wrong answer was honestly confused about the right answer, but the other "subjects" (in reality confederates) who gave that answer were not themselves confused, they were just following the leader like sheep. These naive subjects then went on to say that while the "followers" conformed on *every* trial they themselves gave the wrong answer on only *some* trials. As they saw it, by comparison they were independent. The "independent" behavior of subjects here is similar to the "humane" behavior of the subjects in the Milgram conformity variant.

Consider this account about a "good guard." Karst (1942) is writing about the night of January 23, 1939 in Dachau. A prisoner had escaped and the remaining 12,000 prisoners were forced to stand for 25 hours in the assembly square with the temperature at 16 below zero C. Two 20-minute breaks were allowed. Many of the already starved and exhausted prisoners collapsed. As was the rule at the German camps, other prisoners were not allowed to go to their aid. Karst was standing next to an old man who fell over dead. He writes:

> The S.S. man moved on, but five minutes later he returned. "Take the body into the hospital," he gave us the order. We were glad that we could move. I bent down to get hold of the body, but I was so stiff that I had absolutely no strength. I could not straighten up and was afraid I would collapse. That would be the end of me: refusal to obey a command. Would the S.S. man draw his revolver? He looked at me, noticed my terror stricken eyes. "Take your time," he said. "Get a cover," he added. I owe to him my life. (Karst, 1942)

For acts of this sort the guard gained the reputation of a "good guard." This act of simple humanity showed him not to be ignorant or insensitive to humane impulses. We recognize the compassion in his action and assess his character accordingly. But still this was Dachau, a slave labor camp. The institution of Dachau itself rivals all constructions of humanity as an embodiment of evil, and this guard was part of it. We see, the author saw, and the guard saw himself as a kind person, but this perception is grounded in the fact that he was personally less brutal than some other guards while working thousands of people to their death. Actions that bespeak an inner self which is pure, a heart of gold, have a direct and compelling impact on our judgment of the character of an individual. In circumstances in which the individual's social world is to some degree humane, we are led to proper conclusions of his or her moral worth; but when those conditions are the hell of the concentration camp, the judgment that a particular guard is a good, humane person measures only our capacity to appreciate irony.

CONCLUSION

The thrust of this chapter has been to bring the phenomena of the camps closer to home, to see how this horror, this inhumanity could have been the product not only of deranged individuals but of normal people placed in deranged and degrading circumstances. We have attempted to draw links between what we know the artisans of the Holocaust did and what ordinary, American people have done in laboratory settings. We have tried to show how this behavior that we cannot understand is more comprehensible if we analyze it in terms of the influences of authority and peer support on people's moral judgments.

There is, however, a danger in this. The task of making something understandable *is* to make us see how it could have happened by showing how it is akin to something we can already grasp. There is a common tendency to slide from understanding to excusing. We are accustomed to thinking that once we have understood how someone came to do something, we are then compelled to forgive. In this case we cannot allow understanding to lead to excuse or forgiveness. As scientists examining the phenomenon, we are committed to trying to discover its similarities with things that we know, how it follows from fundamental facts of human nature; only when this is done do we have an adequate grasp of the phenomenon. We, at the same time, must take the position that no matter how well we understand, no matter how clearly we see the behavior as an expression of something basic to human nature, we cannot alter our moral judgment of these actions or the actors who performed them.

There is a precedent for this paradox. Greek tragedy is absorbed with the attempt to make evil understandable, to relate it to common flaws in human nature. Our appreciation of how hard it is to do right when fate and circumstances conspire to trick us cannot obscure the fact that the measure of human nature is our capacity to do what is right and resist what is wrong.

REFERENCES

Adorno, T., Frenkel-Brunswik, E., Levinson, D., & Sanford, N. *The authoritarian personality.* New York: Harper, 1950.

Alexander, C. N., Jr., Zucker, L. G., & Brody, C. L. Experimental expectations and autokinetic experiences: Consistency theories and judgmental convergence. *Sociometry*, 1970, *33*, 108–122.

Alexander, L. The molding of personality under dictatorship. *Journal of Criminal Law and Criminology of Northwestern University*, May–June 1949, *40*.

Arendt, H. *Eichmann in Jerusalem* (2nd ed.). New York: Viking Press, 1965.

Asch, S. *Social psychology* (Chap. 16). Englewood Cliffs, N.J.: Prentice Hall, 1952.

Austin, J. L. *Philosophical papers.* Oxford: Oxford University Press, 1970.

Berger, P., & Luckmann, T. *The social construction of reality.* Garden City: Anchor Books, 1967.

Cohen, E. *Human behavior in the concentration camp.* New York: Grossett & Dunlap, 1953.

Dawidowicz, L. *The war against the Jews.* New York: Bantam, 1975.

Des Pres, T. *The survivor: An anatomy of life in the death camps.* New York: Pocket Books, 1977.

Durkheim, E. *The division of labor.* (First published 1893). New York: Macmillan, 1933.

Goffman, E. *The presentation of self in everyday life.* New York: Doubleday, 1959.

_____. *Stigma.* Englewood Cliffs, N.J.: Prentice-Hall, 1963.

_____. *Relations in public.* New York: Harper & Row, 1971.

Hilberg, R. *The destruction of the European Jews.* Chicago: Quadrangle Books, 1961.

Karst, G. *The beasts of the earth.* New York: Unger, 1942.

Kogon, E. *The theory and practice of hell: The concentration camps and the system behind them.* London: Secker & Warburg, 1950.

Kovesi, J. *Moral notions.* London: Routledge & Kegan Paul, 1967.

Matza, D. The nature of delinquent commitment. In E. Rubington & M. Winberg (Eds.), *Deviance: The interactionist perspective.* London: Macmillan, 1968.

McGuire, W. J. The nature of attitudes and attitude change. In G. Lindzey & E. Aronson (Eds.), *Handbook of social psychology* (2nd ed.), Vol. 3. Reading, Mass.: Addison-Wesley, 1969, 136–314.

Milgram, S. Behavioral study of obedience. *Journal of Abnormal and Social Psychology*, 1963, *67*, 371–378.

_____. Group pressure and action against a person. *Journal of Abnormal and Social Psychology*, 1964, *69*, 137–143.

_____. Some conditions of obedience and disobedience to authority. *Human Relations*, 1965, *18*, 57–76.

_____. *Obedience to authority.* New York: Harper & Row, 1974.

Milgram, S., & Toch, H. Collective behavior: Crowds and social movements. In G. Lindzey & E. Aronson (Eds.), *Handbook of social psychology* (2nd ed.), Vol. 4. Reading, Mass.: Addison-Wesley, 1969, 507–610.

Musmanno, M. *The Eichmann kommandos.* Philadelphia: Macrae Smith, 1961.

Sabini, J., & Silver, M. Moral reproach and moral action. *Journal for the Theory of Social Behaviour*, 1978, *8*, 103–123.

Sherif, M. A study of some social factors in perception. *Archives of Psychology*, 1935, *27*, 1–60.

Steiner, J. *Treblinka*. New York: Simon & Schuster, 1967.

Tillion, G. *Ravensbruck*. Garden City: Anchor Books, 1975.

Tuddenham, R., & Mac Bride, P. The yielding experiment from the point of view of the subject. *Journal of Personality*, 1959, *27*, 258–271.

Wittgenstein, L. *The blue and brown books*. Oxford: Oxford University Press, 1958.

Zimbardo, P. The Stanford prison experiment: A simulation study of the psychology of imprisonment. Script of slideshow, 1971.

15

The Nazi Doctors

ROBERT JAY LIFTON

Not only will you break through the paralysing difficulties of the time—you will break through time itself . . . and dare to be barbaric, twice barbaric indeed.

THOMAS MANN

Any of us could be the man who encounters his double.

FRIEDRICH DURRENMAT

The key to understanding how Nazi doctors came to do the work of Auschwitz is the psychological principle I call "doubling": the division of the self into two functioning wholes, so that a part-self acts as an entire self. An Auschwitz doctor could, through doubling, not only kill and contribute to killing but organize silently, on behalf of that evil project, an entire self-structure (or self-process) encompassing virtually all aspects of his behavior.

Doubling, then, was the psychological vehicle for the Nazi doctor's Faustian bargain with the diabolical environment in exchange for his contribution to the killing; he was offered various psychological and material benefits on behalf of privileged adaptation. Beyond Auschwitz was the larger Faustian temptation offered to German doctors in general: that of becoming the theorists and implementers of a cosmic scheme of racial cure by means of victimization and mass murder.

One is always ethically responsible for Faustian bargains—a responsibility in no way abrogated by the fact that much doubling takes place outside of awareness. In exploring doubling, I engage in psychological probing on behalf of illuminating evil. For the individual Nazi doctor in Auschwitz, doubling was likely to mean a choice for evil.

Generally speaking, doubling involves five characteristics. There is, first, a dialectic between two selves in terms of autonomy and connection. The individual Nazi doctor needed his Auschwitz self to function psychologically in an environment so antithetical to his previous ethical standards. At the same time, he needed his prior self in order to continue to see himself as humane physician, husband, father. The Auschwitz self had to be both autonomous and connected to the prior self that gave rise to it. Second, doubling follows a holistic principle. The Auschwitz self "succeeded" because it was inclusive and could connect with the entire Auschwitz environment: it rendered coherent, and gave form to, various themes and mechanisms, which I shall discuss shortly. Third, doubling has a life-death dimension: the Auschwitz self was perceived by the perpetrator as a form of psychological survival in a death-dominated environment; in other words, we have the paradox of a "killing self" being created on behalf of what one perceives as one's own healing or survival. Fourth, a major function of doubling, as in Auschwitz, is likely to be the avoidance of guilt: the second self tends to be the one performing the "dirty work." And, finally, doubling involves both an unconscious dimension—taking place, as stated, largely outside of awareness—and a significant change in moral consciousness. These five characteristics frame and pervade all else that goes on psychologically in doubling.

For instance, the holistic principle differentiates doubling from the traditional psychoanalytic concept of "splitting." This latter term has had several meanings but tends to suggest a sequestering off of a portion of the self so that the "split off" element ceases to respond to the environment (as in what I have been calling "psychic numbing") or else is in some way at odds with the remainder of the self. Splitting in this sense resembles what Pierre Janet, Freud's nineteenth-century contemporary, originally called "dissociation," and Freud himself tended to equate the two terms. But in regard to sustained forms of adaptation, there has been confusion about how to explain the autonomy of that separated "piece" of the self—confusion over (as one thoughtful commentator has put it) "What splits in splitting?"[1]*

"Splitting" or "dissociation" can thus denote something about Nazi doctors' suppression of feeling, or psychic numbing, in relation to their participation in murder.† But to chart their involvement in a continuous routine of killing, over a year or two or more, one

---

* This writer seemed to react against the idea of a separated-off piece of the self when he ended the article by asking, "Why should we invent a special intrapsychic act of splitting to account for those phenomena as if some internal chopper were at work to produce them?"[2] Janet meant by "dissociation" the hysteric's tendency to "sacrifice" or "abandon" certain psychological functions, so that these become "dissociated" from the rest of the mind and give rise to "automatisms" or segmented-off symptom complexes.[3] Freud spoke, in his early work with Josef Breuer, of "splitting of consciousness," "splitting of the mind," and "splitting of personality" as important mechanisms in hysteria.[4] Edward Glover referred to the psychic components of splitting or dissociation as "ego nuclei."[5] And, beginning with the work of Melanie Klein, splitting has been associated with polarization of "all good" and "all bad" imagery within the self, a process that can be consistent with normal development but, where exaggerated, can become associated with severe personality disorders now spoken of as "borderline states."[6]

† Henry V. Dicks invokes this concept in his study of Nazi killers.[7]

needs an explanatory principle that draws upon the entire, functioning self. (The same principle applies in sustained psychiatric disturbance, and my stress on doubling is consistent with the increasing contemporary focus upon the holistic function of the self.)[8]

Doubling is part of the universal potential for what William James called the "divided self": that is, for opposing tendencies in the self. James quoted the nineteenth-century French writer Alphonse Daudet's despairing cry *"Homo duplex, homo duplex!"* in noting his "horrible duality"—as, in the face of his brother Henri's death, Daudet's "first self wept" while his "second self" sat back and somewhat mockingly staged the scene for an imagined theatrical performance.[9] To James and Daudet, the potential for doubling is part of being human, and the process is likely to take place in extremity, in relation to death.

But that "opposing self" can become dangerously unrestrained, as it did in the Nazi doctors. And when it becomes so, as Otto Rank discovered in his extensive studies of the "double" in literature and folklore, that opposing self can become the usurper from within and replace the original self until it "speaks" for the entire person.[10] Rank's work also suggests that the potential for an opposing self, in effect the potential for evil, is *necessary* to the human psyche: the loss of one's shadow or soul or "double" means death.

In general psychological terms, the adaptive potential for doubling is integral to the human psyche and can, at times, be life saving: for a soldier in combat, for instance; or for a victim of brutality such as an Auschwitz inmate, who must also undergo a form of doubling in order to survive. Clearly, the "opposing self" can be life enhancing. But under certain conditions it can embrace evil with an extreme lack of restraint.

The Nazi doctor's situation resembles that of one of Rank's examples (taken from a 1913 German film, *The Student of Prague*): a student fencing champion accepts an evil magician's offer of great wealth and the chance for marriage with his beloved in return for anything the old magician wishes to take from the room; what he takes is the student's mirror image, a frequent representation of the double. That double eventually becomes a killer by making use of the student's fencing skills in a duel with his beloved's suitor, despite the fact that the student (his original self) has promised the woman's father that he will not engage in such a duel. This variation on the Faust legend parallels the Nazi doctor's "bargain" with Auschwitz and the regime: to do the killing, he offered an opposing self (the evolving Auschwitz self)—a self that, in violating his own prior moral standards, met with no effective resistance and in fact made use of his original skills (in this case, medical-scientific).[11]*

Rank stressed the death symbolism of the double as "symptomatic of the disintegration of the modern personality type." That disintegration leads to a need for "self-perpetuation in one's own image"[13]—what I would call a literalized form of immortality—as compared with "the perpetuation of the self in work reflecting one's personality" or a creative-symbolic form of immortality. Rank saw the Narcissus legend as depicting both the danger of the literalized mode and the necessity of the shift to the

---

* Rank's viewing of *The Student of Prague*, during a revival in the mid-1920s, was the original stimulus for a lifelong preoccupation with the theme of the double. Rank noted that the screenplay's author, Hanns Heinz Ewers, had drawn heavily on E.T.A. Hoffmann's "Story of the Lost Reflection."[12]

creative mode (as embodied by the "artist-hero").* But the Nazi movement encouraged its would-be artist-hero, the physician, to remain, like Narcissus, in thralldom to his own image. Here Mengele comes immediately to mind, his extreme narcissism in the service of his quest for omnipotence, and his exemplification to the point of caricature of the general situation of Nazi doctors in Auschwitz. [15]

The way in which doubling allowed Nazi doctors to avoid guilt was not by the elimination of conscience but by what can be called the *transfer of conscience*. The requirements of conscience were transferred to the Auschwitz self, which placed it within its own criteria for good (duty, loyalty to group, "improving" Auschwitz conditions, etc.), thereby freeing the original self from responsibility for actions there. Rank spoke similarly of guilt "which forces the hero no longer to accept the responsibility for certain actions of his ego, but to place it upon another ego, a double, who is either personified by the devil himself or is created by making a diabolical pact":[16] that is, the Faustian bargain of Nazi doctors mentioned earlier. Rank spoke of a "powerful consciousness of guilt" as initiating the transfer;[17] but for most Nazi doctors, the doubling maneuver seemed to fend off that sense of guilt prior to its developing, or to its reaching conscious dimensions.

There is an inevitable connection between death and guilt. Rank equates the opposing self with a "form of evil which represents the perishable and mortal part of the personality."[18] The double is evil in that it represents one's own death. The Auschwitz self of the Nazi doctor similarly assumed the death issue for him but at the same time used its evil project as a way of staving off awareness of his own "perishable and mortal part." It does the "dirty work" for the entire self by rendering that work "proper" and in that way protects the entire self from awareness of its own guilt and its own death.

In doubling, one part of the self "disavows" another part. What is repudiated is not reality itself—the individual Nazi doctor was aware of what he was doing via the Auschwitz self—but the meaning of that reality. The Nazi doctor knew that he selected, but did not interpret selections as murder. One level of disavowal, then, was the Auschwitz self's altering of the meaning of murder; and on another, the repudiation by the original self of *anything* done by the Auschwitz self. From the moment of its formation, the Auschwitz self so violated the Nazi doctor's previous self-concept as to require more or less permanent disavowal. Indeed, disavowal was the life blood of the Auschwitz self. †

---

* In his earlier work, Rank followed Freud in connecting the legend with the concept of "narcissism," of libido directed toward one's own self. But Rank gave the impression that he did so uneasily, always stressing the issue of death and immortality as lurking beneath the narcissism. In his later adaptation, he boldly embraced the death theme as the earlier and more fundamental one in the Narcissus legend and spoke somewhat disdainfully of "some modern psychologists [who] claimed to have found a symbolization of their self-love principle" in it.[14] By then he had broken with Freud and established his own intellectual position.
† Michael Franz Basch speaks of an interference with the "union of affect with percept without, however, blocking the percept from consciousness."[19] In that sense, disavowal resembles psychic numbing, as it alters the *valencing* or emotional charge of the symbolizing process.

DOUBLING, SPLITTING, AND EVIL

Doubling is an active psychological process, a means of *adaptation to extremity*. That is why I use the verb form, as opposed to the more usual noun form, "the double." The adaptation requires a dissolving of "psychic glue"[20] as an alternative to a radical break-down of the self. In Auschwitz, the pattern was established under the duress of the individual doctor's transition period. At that time the Nazi doctor experienced his own death anxiety as well as such death equivalents as fear of disintegration, separation, and stasis. He needed a functional Auschwitz self to still his anxiety. And that Auschwitz self had to assume hegemony on an everyday basis, reducing expressions of the prior self to odd moments and to contacts with family and friends outside the camp. Nor did most Nazi doctors resist that usurpation as long as they remained in the camp. Rather they welcomed it as the only means of psychological function. If an environment is sufficiently extreme, and one chooses to remain in it, one may be able to do so *only* by means of doubling.

Yet doubling does not include the radical dissociation and sustained separateness characteristic of multiple or "dual personality." In the latter condition, the two selves are more profoundly distinct and autonomous, and tend either not to know about each other or else to see each other as alien. The pattern for dual or multiple personality, moreover, is thought to begin early in childhood, and to solidify and maintain itself more or less indefinitely. Yet in the development of multiple personality, there are likely to be such influences as intense psychic or physical trauma, an atmosphere of extreme ambivalence, and severe conflict and confusion over identifications[21]—all of which can also be instrumental in doubling. Also relevant to both conditions is Janet's principle that "once baptized"—that is, named or confirmed by someone in authority—a particular self is likely to become more clear and definite. [22] Though never as stable as a self in multiple personality, the Auschwitz self nonetheless underwent a similar baptism when the Nazi doctor conducted his first selections.

A recent writer has employed the metaphor of a tree to delineate the depth of "splitting" in schizophrenia and multiple personality—a metaphor that could be expanded to include doubling. In schizophrenia, the rent in the self is "like the crumbling and breaking of a tree that has deteriorated generally, at least in some important course of the trunk, down toward or to the roots." In multiple personality, that rent is specific and limited, "as in an essentially sound tree that does not split very far down."[23] Doubling takes place still higher on a tree whose roots, trunk, and larger branches have previously experienced no impairment; of the two branches artificially separated, one grows fetid bark and leaves in a way that enables the other to maintain ordinary growth, and the two intertwine sufficiently to merge again should external conditions favor that merging.

Was the doubling of Nazi doctors an antisocial "character disorder"? Not in the classical sense, in that the process tended to be more a form of adaptation than a lifelong pattern. But doubling can include elements considered characteristic of "sociopathic" character impairment: these include a disorder of feeling (swings between numbing and rage), pathological avoidance of a sense of guilt, and resort to violence to overcome "masked depression" (related to repressed guilt and numbing) and maintain a sense of vitality.[24] Similarly, in both situations, destructive or even murderous behavior may cover over feared disintegration of the self.

The disorder in the type of doubling I have described is more focused and temporary and occurs as part of a larger institutional structure which encourages or even demands it. In that sense, Nazi doctors' behavior resembles that of certain terrorists—and members of the Mafia, of "death squads" organized by dictators, or even of delinquent gangs. In all these situations, profound ideological, family, ethnic, and sometimes age-specific ties help shape criminal behavior. Doubling may well be an important psychological mechanism for individuals living within any criminal subculture: the Mafia or "death squad" chief who coldly orders (or himself carries out) the murder of a rival while remaining a loving husband, father, and churchgoer. The doubling is adaptive to the extreme conditions created by the subculture, but additional influences, some of which can begin early in life, always contribute to the process.* That, too, was the case with the Nazi doctors.

In sum, doubling is the psychological means by which one invokes the evil potential of the self. That evil is neither inherent in the self nor foreign to it. To live out the doubling and call forth the evil is a moral choice for which one is responsible, whatever the level of consciousness involved.† By means of doubling, Nazi doctors made a Faustian choice for evil: in the process of doubling, in fact, lies an overall key to human evil.

VARIETIES OF DOUBLING

While individual Nazi doctors in Auschwitz doubled in different ways, all of them doubled. Ernst B., for instance, limited his doubling; in avoiding selections, he was resisting a full-blown Auschwitz self. Yet his conscious desire to adapt to Auschwitz was an accession to at least a certain amount of doubling: it was he, after all, who said that "one could react like a normal human being in Auschwitz only for the first few hours"; after that, "you were caught and had to go along," which meant that you had to double. His own doubling was evident in his sympathy for Mengele and, at least to some extent, for the most extreme expressions of the Nazi ethos (the image of the Nazis as a "world blessing" and of Jews as the world's "fundamental evil"). And despite the limit to his doubling, he retains aspects of his Auschwitz self to this day in his way of judging Auschwitz behavior.

---

* Robert W. Rieber uses the term "pseudopsychopathy" for what he describes as "selective joint criminal behavior" within the kinds of subculture mentioned here.[25]

† James S. Grotstein speaks of the development of "a separate being living within one that has been preconsciously split off and has an independent existence with independent motivation, separate agenda, etc.," and from which can emanate "evil, sadism, and destructiveness" or even "demoniacal possession." He calls this aspect of the self a "mind parasite" (after Colin Wilson) and attributes its development to those elements of the self that have been artificially suppressed and disavowed early in life.[26]

In contrast, Mengele's embrace of the Auschwitz self gave the impression of a quick adaptive affinity, causing one to wonder whether he required any doubling at all. But doubling was indeed required in a man who befriended children to an unusual degree and then drove some of them personally to the gas chamber; or by a man so "collegial" in his relationship to prisoner doctors and so ruthlessly flamboyant in his conduct of selections. Whatever his affinity for Auschwitz, a man who could be pictured under ordinary conditions as "a slightly sadistic German professor" had to form a new self to become an energetic killer. The point about Mengele's doubling was that his prior self could be readily absorbed into the Auschwitz self; and his continuing allegiance to the Nazi ideology and project probably enabled his Auschwitz self, more than in the case of other Nazi doctors, to remain active over the years after the Second World War.

Wirths's doubling was neither limited (like Dr. B.'s) nor harmonious (like Mengele's): it was both strong and conflicted. We see Auschwitz's chief doctor as a "divided self" because both selves retained their power. Yet his doubling was the most successful of all from the standpoint of the Auschwitz institution and the Nazi project. Even his suicide was a mark of that success: while the Nazi defeat enabled him to equate his Auschwitz self more clearly with evil, he nonetheless retained responsibility to that Auschwitz self sufficiently to remain inwardly divided and unable to imagine any possibility of resolution and renewal—either legally, morally, or psychologically.

Within the Auschwitz structure, significant doubling included future goals and even a sense of hope. Styles of doubling varied because each Nazi doctor created his Auschwitz self out of his prior self, with its particular history, and with his own psychological mechanisms. But in all Nazi doctors, prior self and Auschwitz self were connected by the overall Nazi ethos and the general authority of the regime. Doubling was a shared theme among them.

DOUBLING AND INSTITUTIONS

Indeed, Auschwitz as an *institution*—as an atrocity-producing situation—ran on doubling. An atrocity-producing situation is one so structured externally (in this case, institutionally) that the average person entering it (in this case, as part of the German authority) will commit or become associated with atrocities. Always important to an atrocity-producing situation is its capacity to motivate individuals psychologically toward engaging in atrocity.[27]

In an institution as powerful as Auschwitz, the external environment could set the tone for much of an individual doctor's "internal environment." The demand for doubling was part of the environmental message immediately perceived by Nazi doctors, the implicit command to bring forth a self that could adapt to killing without one's feeling oneself a murderer. Doubling became not just an individual enterprise but a shared psychological process, the group norm, part of the Auschwitz "weather." And that group process was intensified by the general awareness that, whatever went on in other camps, Auschwitz was the great technical center of the Final Solution. One had to double in order that one's life and work there not be interfered with either by the corpses one helped to produce or by those "living dead" (the *Muselmänner*) all around one.

Inevitably, the Auschwitz pressure toward doubling extended to prisoner doctors, the most flagrant examples of whom were those who came to work closely with the Nazis— Dering, Zenkteller, Adam T., and Samuel. Even those prisoner doctors who held strongly to their healing ethos, and underwent minimal doubling, inadvertently contributed to Nazi doctors' doubling simply by working with them, as they had to, and thereby in some degree confirmed a Nazi doctor's Auschwitz self.

Doubling undoubtedly occurred extensively in nonmedical Auschwitz personnel as well. Rudolf Höss told how noncommissioned officers regularly involved in selections "pour[ed] out their hearts" to him about the difficulty of their work (their prior self speaking)—but went on doing that work (their Auschwitz self directing behavior). Höss described the Auschwitz choices: "either to become cruel, to become heartless and no longer to respect human life [that is, to develop a highly functional Auschwitz self] or to be weak and to get to the point of a nervous breakdown [that is, to hold onto one's prior self, which in Auschwitz was nonfunctional]."[28] But in the Nazi doctor, the doubling was particularly stark in that a prior healing self gave rise to a killing self that should have been, but functionally was not, in direct opposition to it. And as in any atrocity-producing situation, Nazi doctors found themselves in a psychological climate where they were virtually certain to choose evil: they were propelled, that is, toward murder.

DOUBLING—NAZI AND MEDICAL

Beyond Auschwitz, there was much in the Nazi movement that promoted doubling. The overall Nazi project, replete with cruelty, required constant doubling in the service of carrying out that cruelty. The doubling could take the form of a gradual process of "slippery slope" compromises: the slow emergence of a functional "Nazi self" via a series of destructive actions, at first agreed to grudgingly, followed by a sequence of assigned tasks each more incriminating, if not more murderous, than the previous ones.

Doubling could also be more dramatic, infused with transcendence, the sense (described by a French fascist who joined the SS) of being someone entering a religious order "who must now divest himself of his past," and of being "reborn into a new European race."[29] That new Nazi self could take on a sense of mystical fusion with the German *Volk*, with "destiny," and with immortalizing powers. Always there was the combination noted earlier of idealism and terror, imagery of destruction and renewal, so that "gods . . . appear as both destroyers and culture-heroes, just as the Führer could appear as front comrade and master builder."[30] Himmler, especially in his speeches to his SS leaders within their "oath-bound community,"[31] called for the kind of doubling necessary to engage in what he considered to be heroic cruelty, especially in the killing of Jews.

The degree of doubling was not necessarily equivalent to Nazi Party membership; thus, Hochhuth could claim that "the great divide was between Nazis [meaning those with well-developed Nazi selves] and decent people, not between Party members and other Germans."[32] But probably never has a political movement demanded doubling with the intensity and scale of the Nazis.

Doctors as a group may be more susceptible to doubling than others. For example, a former Nazi doctor claimed that the anatomist's insensitivity toward skeletons and corpses accounted for his friend Hirt's grotesque "anthropological" collection of Jewish skulls. . . . While hardly a satisfactory explanation, this doctor was referring to a genuine pattern not just of numbing but of medical doubling. That doubling usually begins with the student's encounter with the corpse he or she must dissect, often enough on the first day of medical school. One feels it necessary to develop a "medical self," which enables one not only to be relatively inured to death but to function reasonably efficiently in relation to the many-sided demands of the work. The ideal doctor, to be sure, remains warm and humane by keeping that doubling to a minimum. But few doctors meet that ideal standard. Since studies have suggested that a psychological motivation for entering the medical profession can be the overcoming of an unusually great fear of death, it is possible that this fear in doctors propels them in the direction of doubling when encountering deadly environments. Doctors drawn to the Nazi movement in general, and to SS or concentration-camp medicine in particular, were likely to be those with the greatest previous medical doubling. But even doctors without outstanding Nazi sympathies could well have had a certain experience with doubling and a proclivity for its further manifestations.

Certainly the tendency toward doubling was particularly strong among *Nazi* doctors. Given the heroic vision held out to them—as cultivators of the genes and as physicians to the *Volk*, and as militarized healers combining the life-death power of shaman and general—any cruelty they might perpetrate was all too readily drowned in hubris. And their medical hubris was furthered by their role in the sterilization and "euthanasia" projects within a vision of curing the ills of the Nordic race and the German people.

Doctors who ended up undergoing the extreme doubling necessitated by the "euthanasia" killing centers and the death camps were probably unusually susceptible to doubling. There was, of course, an element of chance in where one was sent, but doctors assigned either to the killing centers or to the death camps tended to be strongly committed to Nazi ideology. They may well have also had greater schizoid tendencies, or been particularly prone to numbing and omnipotence-sadism, all of which also enhance doubling. Since, even under extreme conditions, people have a way of finding and staying in situations they connect with psychologically, we can suspect a certain degree of self-selection there too. In these ways, previous psychological characteristics of a doctor's self had considerable significance—but a significance in respect to tendency or susceptibility, and no more. Considerable doubling occurred in people of the most varied psychological characteristics.

We thus find ourselves returning to the recognition that most of what Nazi doctors did would be within the potential capability—at least under certain conditions—of most doctors and of most people. But once embarked on doubling in Auschwitz, a Nazi doctor did indeed separate himself from other physicians and from other human beings. Doubling was the mechanism by which a doctor, in his actions, moved from the ordinary to the demonic . . .

DOUBLING AS GERMAN?

Is there something especially German in doubling? Germany, after all, is the land of the *Doppelgänger*, the double as formalized in literature and humor. Otto Rank, while tracing the theme back to Greek mythology and drama, stresses its special prominence in German literary and philosophical romanticism, and refers to the "inner split personality, characteristic of the romantic type."[33] That characterization, not only in literature but in political and social thought, is consistent with such images as the "torn condition" (*Zerrissenheit*), or "cleavage," and the "passages and galleries" of the German soul.[34] Nietzsche asserted that duality in a personal way by depicting himself as both "the antichrist" and "the crucified"; and similar principles of "duality-in-unity" can be traced to earlier German writers and poets such as Hölderlin, Heine, and Kleist.[35]

Indeed, Goethe's treatment of the Faust legend is a story of German doubling:

> *Two souls, alas, reside within my breast*
> *And each withdraws from and repels its brother.[36]*

And the original Faust, that doctor of magic, bears more than a passing resemblance to his Nazi countrymen in Auschwitz. In Goethe's hands, Faust is inwardly divided into a prior self responsible to worldly commitments, including those of love, and a second self characterized by hubris in its quest for the supernatural power of "the higher ancestral places."* In a still earlier version of the legend, Faust acknowledges the hegemony of his evil self by telling a would-be spiritual rescuer, "I have gone further than you think and have pledged myself to the devil with my own blood, to be his in eternity, body and

---

* The passage concerning the "two souls" continues:

> *One with tenacious organs holds in love*
> *And clinging lust the world within its embraces.*
> *The other strongly sweeps this dust above*
> *Into the higher ancestral places.*

soul."[38] Here his attitude resembles the Auschwitz self's fidelity to evil. And Thomas Mann's specific application of the Faust legend to the Nazi historical experience captures, through a musician protagonist, the diabolical quest of the Auschwitz self for unlimited "creative power": the promise of absolute breakthrough, of conquering time and therefore death; if the new self will "dare to be barbaric, twice barbaric indeed."[39]*

Within German psychological and cultural experience, the theme of doubling is powerful and persistent. Moreover, German vulnerability to doubling was undoubtedly intensified by the historical dislocations and fragmentations of cultural symbols following the First World War. Who can deny the Germanic "feel" of so much of the doubling process, as best described by a brilliant product of German culture, Otto Rank?

Yet the first great poet to take up the Faust theme was not Goethe but the English playwright Christopher Marlowe. And there has been a series of celebrated English and American expressions of the general theme of the double, running through Edgar Allan Poe's "William Wilson," Robert Louis Stevenson's *The Strange Case of Dr. Jekyll and Mr. Hyde*, Oscar Wilde's *Picture of Dorian Gray*, and the comic strip *Superman*. Indeed, the theme penetrates the work of writers of all nationalities: for instance, Guy de Maupassant's *Le Horla* and Dostoevski's novel *The Double*.[41]

Clearly, the Nazis took hold of a universal phenomenon, if one given special emphasis by their own culture and history. But they could not have brought about widespread doubling without the existence of certain additional psychological patterns that dominated Auschwitz behavior. These internalized expressions of the environment of the death camp came to characterize the Auschwitz self, and have significance beyond that place and time.

DOUBLING: THE BROADER DANGER

Although doubling can be understood as a pervasive process present in some degree in most if not all lives, we have mainly been talking about a destructive version of it: *victimizer's doubling*. The Germans of the Nazi era came to epitomize this process not because they were inherently more evil than other people, but because they succeeded in

---

The historian of German literature Ronald Gray finds patterns of "polarity and synthesis" in various spheres of German culture: Luther's concept of a God who "works by contraries," the Hegelian principle of thesis and antithesis, and the Marxist dialectic emerging from Hegel. In all of these, there is the "fusion of opposites," the rending of the individual as well as the collective self, and the passionate quest for unity.[37] One could almost say that the German apocalyptic tradition—the Wagnerian "twilight of the gods" and the general theme of the death-haunted collective end—may be the "torn condition" extended into the realm of larger human connectedness and disconnectedness.

* Mann also captures the continuity in doubling by speaking of the "implicit Satanism" in German psychology, and by having the devil make clear to the Faust figure that "we lay upon you nothing new . . . [but] only ingeniously strengthen and exaggerate all that you already are."[40]

making use of this form of doubling for tapping the general human moral and psychological potential for mobilizing evil on a vast scale and channeling it into systematic killing.

While victimizer's doubling can occur in virtually any group, perhaps professionals of various kinds—physicians, psychologists, physicists, biologists, clergy, generals, statesmen, writers, artists—have a special capacity for doubling. In them a prior, humane self can be joined by a "professional self" willing to ally itself with a destructive project, with harming or even killing others.

Consider the situation of the American psychiatrist doing his military service during the Vietnam War. In working with Vietnam veterans, I was surprised by their special animosity toward "chaplains and shrinks." It turned out that many of these veterans had experienced a mixture of revulsion and psychological conflict (the two were difficult to distinguish in the midst of Vietnam combat) and were taken to either a chaplain or a psychiatrist (or the assistant of either), depending upon the orientation of the soldier himself or of his immediate superior. The chaplain or the psychiatrist would attempt to help the GI become strong enough to overcome his difficulties and remain in combat, which in Vietnam meant participating in or witnessing daily atrocities in an atrocity-producing situation. In that way, the chaplain or psychiatrist, quite inadvertently, undermined what the soldier would later come to view as his last remnant of decency in that situation. The professional involved could do that only because he had undergone a form of doubling which gave rise to a "military self" serving the military unit and its combat project. One reason the chaplain or psychiatrist was so susceptible to that doubling was his misplaced confidence in his profession and his professional self: his assumption that, as a member of a healing profession, whatever he did healed. In this case, the military self could come to subsume the professional self. Thus, psychiatrists returning from Vietnam to their American clinical and teaching situations experienced psychological struggles no less severe than those of other Vietnam veterans.[42]

Consider also the physicist who is for the most part a humane person devoted to family life and strongly opposed to violence of any kind. He may undergo a form of doubling from which emerges what we can call his "nuclear-weapons self." He may actively involve himself in making the weapons, argue that they are necessary for national security and to combat Soviet weapons, and even become an advocate of their use under certain circumstances as a theorist of limited nuclear war. It is precisely his humane commitment to democracy and family life (his prior self) that enables him to claim similar humanity for his nuclear-weapons self despite its contribution to devices that could slaughter millions of people. He can do what he does because his doubling is part of a functional psychological equilibrium.[43]

In light of the recent record of professionals engaged in mass killing, can this be the century of doubling? Or, given the ever greater potential for professionalization of genocide, will that distinction belong to the twenty-first century? Or, may one ask a little more softly, can we interrupt the process—first, by naming it?

NOTES

1. Paul W. Pruyser, "What Splits in Splitting?," *Bulletin of the Menninger Clinic* 39 (1975): 1–46.
2. Ibid., p. 46. See also Jeffrey Lustman, "On Splitting," in Kurt Eissler et al., eds., *The Psychoanalytic Study of the Child*, vol. 19 (1977), pp. 19–54; Charles Rycroft, *A Critical Dictionary of Psychoanalysis* (New York: Basic Books, 1968), pp. 156–57.
3. See Pierre Janet, *The Major Symptoms of Hysteria* (New York: Macmillan, 1907) and *Psychological Healing* (New York: Macmillan, 1923). See also Leston Havens, *Approaches to the Mind* (Boston: Little, Brown, 1973), pp. 34–62; and Henri F. Ellenberger, *The Discovery of the Unconscious* (New York: Basic Books, 1970), pp. 364–417.
4. Sigmund Freud and Josef Breuer, *Studies on Hysteria*, in *Standard Edition of the Works of Sigmund Freud*, James Strachey, ed. (London: Hogarth Press, 1955 [1893–95], vol. II, pp. 3–305.
5. Edward Glover, *On the Early Development of Mind: Selected Papers on Psychoanalysis* (New York: International Universities Press, 1956 [1943]), vol. I., pp. 307–23.
6. Melanie Klein, "Notes on Some Schizoid Mechanisms," *International Journal of Psychoanalysis* 27 (1946):99–110; and Otto F. Kernberg, "The Syndrome," in *Borderline Conditions and Pathological Narcissism* (New York: Jason Aronson, 1973), pp. 3–47.
7. Henry V. Dicks, *Licensed Mass Murder: A Socio-Psychological Study of Some SS Killers* (New York: Basic Books, 1972).
8. See, for example, Erik H. Erikson, *Identity: Youth and Crisis* (New York: W. W. Norton, 1968); Heinz Kohut, *The Restoration of the Self* (New York: International Universities Press, 1977); Henry Guntrip, *Psychoanalytic Theory, Therapy and the Self* (New York: Basic Books, 1971); and Robert Jay Lifton, *The Broken Connection: On Death and the Continuity of Life* (New York: Basic Books, 1983 [1979]).
9. William James, *The Varieties of Religious Experience: A Study in Human Nature* (New York: Collier, 1961 [1902]), p. 144.
10. Rank's two major studies of this phenomenon are *The Double: A Psychoanalytic Study* (Chapel Hill: University of North Carolina Press, 1971 [1925]); and "The Double as Immortal Self," in *Beyond Psychology* (New York: Dover, 1958 [1941]), pp. 62–101.
11. Rank, *Double* [10], pp. 3–9; Rank, *Beyond Psychology* [10], pp. 67–69. On "Der Student von Prag," see Siegfried Kracauer, *From Caligari to Hitler: A Psychological History of the German Film* (Princeton: Princeton University Press, 1947), pp. 28–30.
12. E.T.A. Hoffmann, "Story of the Lost Reflection," in J. M. Cohen, ed., *Eight Tales of Hoffmann* (London, 1952).
13. Rank, *Beyond Psychology* [10], p. 98.
14. Ibid.
15. On Rank's "artist-hero," see Rank, *Beyond Psychology* [10], pp. 97–101.
16. Rank, *Double* [10], p. 76.
17. Ibid.
18. Rank, *Beyond Psychology* [10], p. 82.
19. Michael Franz Basch, "The Perception of Reality and the Disavowal of Meaning," *Annual of Psychoanalysis*, 11 (New York: International Universities Press, 1982): 147.

20. Ralph D. Allison, "When the Psychic Glue Dissolves," *HYPNOS-NYTT* (December 1977).
21. The first two influences are described in George B. Greaves, "Multiple Personality: 165 Years After Mary Reynolds," *Journal of Nervous and Mental Disease* 168 (1977): 577–96. Freud emphasized the third in *The Ego and the Id*, in the *Standard Edition of the Works of Sigmund Freud*, James Strachey, ed. (London: Hogarth Press, 1955 [1923]), vol. XIX, pp. 30–31.
22. Ellenberger, *Unconscious* [3], pp. 394–400.
23. Margaretta K. Bowers et al., "Theory of Multiple Personality," *International Journal of Clinical and Experimental Hypnosis* 19 (1971):60.
24. See Lifton, *Broken Connection* [8], pp. 407–9; and Charles H. King, "The Ego and the Integration of Violence in Homicidal Youth," *American Journal of Orthopsychiatry* 45 (1975):142.
25. Robert W. Rieber, "The Psychopathy of Everyday Life" (unpublished manuscript).
26. James S. Grotstein, "The Soul in Torment: An Older and Newer View of Psychopathology," *Bulletin of the National Council of Catholic Psychologists* 25 (1979):36–52.
27. See Robert Jay Lifton, *Home From the War: Vietnam Veterans, Neither Victims Nor Executioners* (New York: Basic Books, 1984 [1973]).
28. Rudolf Höss, quoted in Karl Buchheim, "Command and Compliance," in Helmut Krausnick et al., *Anatomy of the SS State* (New York: Walker, 1968 [1965]), p. 374.
29. Christian de La Mazière, *The Captive Dreamer* (New York: Saturday Review Press, 1974), pp. 14, 34.
30. John H. Hanson, "Nazi Aesthetics," *The Psychohistory Review* 9 (1981):276.
31. Sociologist Werner Picht, quoted in Heinz Höhne, *The Order of the Death's Head: The Story of Hitler's S.S.* (New York: Coward-McCann, 1970 [1966]), pp. 460–61.
32. Rolf Hochhuth, *A German Love Story* (Boston: Little, Brown, 1980 [1978]), p. 220.
33. Rank, *Beyond Psychology* [10], p. 68.
34. Koppel S. Pinson, *Modern Germany: Its History and Civilization* (2nd ed.; New York: Macmillan, 1966), pp. 1–3 (last phrase is from Nietzsche's *Beyond Good and Evil*).
35. Ronald Gray, *The German Tradition in Literature, 1871–1945* (Cambridge: Cambridge University Press, 1965), pp. 3, 79.
36. *Faust*, quoted in Pinson, *Germany* [34], p. 3.
37. Gray, *Tradition* [35], pp. 1–3.
38. Walter Kaufmann, *Goethe's Faust* (New York: Doubleday, 1961), p. 17.
39. Thomas Mann, *Doctor Faustus: The Life of the German Composer Adrian Leverkühn as Told by a Friend* (New York: Alfred A. Knopf, 1948 [1947]), p. 243.
40. Ibid., pp. 249, 308.
41. Rank, *Double* [10]; see also Robert Rogers, *A Psychoanalytic Study of the Double in Literature* (Detroit: Wayne State University Press, 1970).
42. Lifton, *Home* [27], chap. 6.
43. Steven Kull, "Nuclear Nonsense," *Foreign Policy* 20 (spring 1985):28–52.

16

Sanctioned Massacres

HERBERT C. KELMAN and V. LEE HAMILTON

The slaughter at My Lai is an instance of a class of violent acts that can be described as sanctioned massacres (Kelman, 1973): acts of indiscriminate, ruthless, and often systematic mass violence, carried out by military or paramilitary personnel while engaged in officially sanctioned campaigns, the victims of which are defenseless and unresisting civilians, including old men, women, and children. Sanctioned massacres have occurred throughout history. Within American history, My Lai had its precursors in the Philippine war around the turn of the century (Schirmer, 1971) and in the massacres of American Indians. Elsewhere in the world, one recalls the Nazis' "final solution" for European Jews, the massacres and deportations of Armenians by Turks, the liquidation of the kulaks and the great purges in the Soviet Union, and more recently the massacres in Indonesia and Bangladesh, in Biafra and Burundi, in South Africa and Mozambique, in Cambodia and Afghanistan, in Syria and Lebanon. Sanctioned massacres may vary on a number of dimensions. For present purposes, however, we want to focus on features they share. Two of these are the *context* and the *target* of the violence.

Sanctioned massacres tend to occur in the context of an overall policy that is explicitly or implicitly genocidal: designed to destroy all or part of a category of people defined in ethnic, national, racial, religious, or other terms. Such a policy may be deliberately aimed at the systematic extermination of a population group as an end in itself, as was the case with the Holocaust during World War II. In the Nazis' "final solution" for European Jewry, a policy aimed at exterminating millions of people was consciously articulated and executed (see Levinson, 1973), and the extermination was accomplished on a mass-production basis through the literal establishment of a well-organized, efficient death industry. Alternatively, such a policy may be aimed at an objective other than

232

extermination—such as the pacification of the rural population of South Vietnam, as was the case in U.S. policy for Indochina—but may include the deliberate decimation of large segments of a population as an acceptable means to that end.

We agree with Bedau's (1974) conclusion from his carefully reasoned argument that the charge of U.S. genocide in Vietnam has not been definitively proven, since such a charge requires evidence of a specific genocidal *intent*. Although the evidence suggests that the United States committed war crimes and crimes against humanity in Indochina (see Sheehan, 1971; Browning and Forman, 1972), it does not show that extermination was the conscious purpose of U.S. policy. The evidence reviewed by Bedau, however, suggests that the United States did commit genocidal acts in Vietnam as a means to other ends. Central to U.S. strategy in South Vietnam were such actions as unrestricted air and artillery bombardments of peasant hamlets, search-and-destroy missions by ground troops, crop destruction programs, and mass deportation of rural populations. These actions (and similar ones in Laos and Cambodia) were clearly and deliberately aimed at civilians and resulted in the death, injury, and/or uprooting of large numbers of that population and in the destruction of their countryside, their source of livelihood, and their social structure. These consequences were anticipated by policymakers and indeed were intended as part of their pacification effort; the actions were designed to clear the countryside and deprive guerrillas of their base of operations, even if this meant destroying the civilian population. Massacres of the kind that occurred at My Lai were not deliberately planned, but they took place in an atmosphere in which the rural Vietnamese population was viewed as expendable and actions that resulted in the killing of large numbers of that population as strategic necessities.

A second feature of sanctioned massacres is that their targets have not themselves threatened or engaged in hostile actions toward the perpetrators of the violence. The victims of this class of violence are often defenseless civilians, including old men, women, and children. By all accounts, at least after the first moments at My Lai, the victims there fit this description, although in guerrilla warfare there always remains some ambiguity about the distinction between armed soldiers and unarmed civilians. As has often been noted, U.S. troops in Vietnam had to face the possibility that a woman or even a child might be concealing a hand grenade under clothing.

There are, of course, historical and situational reasons particular groups become victims of sanctioned massacres, but these do not include their own immediate harmfulness or violence toward the attackers. Rather, their selection as targets for massacre at a particular time can ultimately be traced to their relationship to the pursuit of larger policies. Their elimination may be seen as a useful tool or their continued existence as an irritating obstacle in the execution of policy.

The genocidal or near-genocidal context of this class of violence and the fact that it is directed at a target that—at least from an observer's perspective—did not provoke the violence through its own actions has some definite implications for the psychological environment within which sanctioned massacres occur. It is an environment almost totally devoid of the conditions that usually provide at least some degree of moral justification for violence. Neither the reason for the violence nor its purpose is of the kind that is normally considered justifiable. Although people may disagree about the precise point at which they would draw the line between justifiable and unjustifiable violence, most would agree that violence in self-defense or in response to oppression and other forms of strong provocation is at least within the realm of moral discourse. In contrast, the violence of sanctioned massacres falls outside that realm.

In searching for a psychological explanation for mass violence under these conditions, one's first inclination is to look for forces that might impel people toward such murderous acts. Can we identify, in massacre situations, psychological forces so powerful that they outweigh the moral restraints that would normally inhibit unjustifiable violence?

The most obvious approach—searching for psychological dispositions within those who perpetrate these acts—does not yield a satisfactory explanation of the phenomenon, although it may tell us something about the types of individuals most readily recruited for participation. For example, any explanation involving the attackers' strong sadistic impulses is inadequate. There is no evidence that the majority of those who participate in such killings are sadistically inclined. Indeed, speaking of the participants in the Nazi slaughters, Arendt (1964) points out that they "were not sadists or killers by nature; on the contrary, a systematic effort was made to weed out all those who derived physical pleasure from what they did" (p. 105). To be sure, some of the commanders and guards of concentration camps could clearly be described as sadists, but what has to be explained is the existence of concentration camps in which these individuals could give play to their sadistic fantasies. These opportunities were provided with the participation of large numbers of individuals to whom the label of sadist could not be applied.

A more sophisticated type of dispositional approach seeks to identify certain charac-terological themes that are dominant within a given culture. An early example of such an approach is Fromm's (1941) analysis of the appeals of Nazism in terms of the prevalence of sadomasochistic strivings, particularly among the German lower middle class. It would be important to explore whether similar kinds of characterological dispositions can be identified in the very wide range of cultural contexts in which sanctioned massacres have occurred. However general such dispositions turn out to be, it seems most likely that they represent states of readiness to participate in sanctioned massacres when the opportunity arises rather than major motivating forces in their own right. Similarly, high levels of frustration within a population are probably facilitators rather than instigators of sanctioned massacres, since there does not seem to be a clear relationship between the societal level of frustration and the occurrence of such violence. Such a view would be consistent with recent thinking about the relationship between frustration and aggression (see, for example, Bandura, 1973).

Could participation in sanctioned massacres be traced to an inordinately intense hatred toward those against whom the violence is directed? The evidence does not seem to support such an interpretation. Indications are that many of the active participants in the extermination of European Jews, such as Adolf Eichmann (Arendt, 1964), did not feel any passionate hatred of Jews. There is certainly no reason to believe that those who planned and executed American policy in Vietnam felt a profound hatred of the Vietnamese population, although deeply rooted racist attitudes may conceivably have played a role.

To be sure, hatred and rage *play a part* in sanctioned massacres. Typically, there is a long history of profound hatred against the groups targeted for violence—the Jews in Christian Europe, the Chinese in Southeast Asia, the Ibos in northern Nigeria—which helps establish them as suitable victims. Hostility also plays an important part at the point at which the killings are actually perpetrated, even if the official planning and the bureaucratic preparations that ultimately lead up to this point are carried out in a passionless and businesslike atmosphere. For example, Lifton's (1973) descriptions of My Lai, based on eyewitness reports, suggest that the killings were accompanied by generalized rage and by expressions of anger and revenge toward the victims. Hostility toward the target, however, does not seem to be the *instigator* of these violent actions. The expressions of anger in the situation itself can more properly be viewed as outcomes rather than causes of the violence. They serve to provide the perpetrators with an explanation and rationalization for their violent actions and appropriate labels for their emotional state. They also help reinforce, maintain, and intensify the violence, but the anger is not the primary source of the violence. Hostility toward the target, historically rooted or situationally induced, contributes heavily toward the violence, but it does so largely by dehumanizing the victims rather than by motivating violence against them in the first place.

In sum, the occurrence of sanctioned massacres cannot be adequately explained by the existence of psychological forces—whether these be characterological dispositions to engage in murderous violence or profound hostility against the target—so powerful that they must find expression in violent acts unhampered by moral restraints. Instead, the major instigators for this class of violence derive from the policy process. The question that really calls for psychological analysis is why so many people are willing to formulate, participate in, and condone policies that call for the mass killings of defenseless civilians. Thus it is more instructive to look not at the motives for violence but at the conditions under which the usual moral inhibitions against violence become weakened. Three social processes that tend to create such conditions can be identified: authorization, routinization, and dehumanization. Through authorization, the situation becomes so defined that the individual is absolved of the responsibility to make personal moral choices. Through routinization, the action becomes so organized that there is no opportunity for raising moral questions. Through dehumanization, the actors' attitudes toward the target and toward themselves become so structured that it is neither necessary nor possible for them to view the relationship in moral terms.

AUTHORIZATION

Sanctioned massacres by definition occur in the context of an authority situation, a situation in which, at least for many of the participants, the moral principles that generally govern human relationships do not apply. Thus, when acts of violence are explicitly ordered, implicitly encouraged, tacitly approved, or at least permitted by legitimate authorities, people's readiness to commit or condone them is enhanced. That such acts are authorized seems to carry automatic justification for them. Behaviorally, authorization obviates the necessity of making judgments or choices. Not only do normal moral principles become inoperative, but—particularly when the actions are explicitly ordered—a different kind of morality, linked to the duty to obey superior orders, tends to take over.

In an authority situation, individuals characteristically feel obligated to obey the orders of the authorities, whether or not these correspond with their personal preferences. They see themselves as having no choice as long as they accept the legitimacy of the orders and of the authorities who give them. Individuals differ considerably in the degree to which—and the conditions under which—they are prepared to challenge the legitimacy of an order on the grounds that the order itself is illegal, or that those giving it have overstepped their authority, or that it stems from a policy that violates fundamental societal values. Regardless of such individual differences, however, the basic structure of a situation of legitimate authority requires subordinates to respond in terms of their role obligations rather than their personal preferences; they can openly disobey only by challenging the legitimacy of the authority. Often people obey without question even though the behavior they engage in may entail great personal sacrifice or great harm to others.

An important corollary of the basic structure of the authority situation is that actors often do not see themselves as personally responsible for the consequences of their actions. Again, there are individual differences, depending on actors' capacity and readiness to evaluate the legitimacy of orders received. Insofar as they see themselves as having had no choice in their actions, however, they do not feel personally responsible for them. They were not personal agents, but merely extensions of the authority. Thus, when their actions cause harm to others, they can feel relatively free of guilt. A similar mechanism operates when a person engages in antisocial behavior that was not ordered by the authorities but was tacitly encouraged and approved by them—even if only by making it clear that such behavior will not be punished. In this situation, behavior that was formerly illegitimate is legitimized by the authorities' acquiescence.

In the My Lai massacre, it is likely that the structure of the authority situation contributed to the massive violence in both ways—that is, by conveying the message that acts of violence against Vietnamese villagers were *required*, as well as the message that such acts, even if not ordered, were *permitted* by the authorities in charge. The actions at My Lai represented, at least in some respects, responses to explicit or implicit orders. Lieutenant Calley indicated, by orders and by example, that he wanted large numbers of villagers killed. Whether Calley himself had been ordered by his superiors to "waste" the whole area, as he claimed, remains a matter of controversy. Even if we assume, however, that he was not explicitly ordered to wipe out the village, he had reason to believe that such actions were expected by his superior officers. Indeed, the very nature of the war conveyed this expectation. The principal measure of military success was the "body count"—the number of enemy soldiers killed—and any Vietnamese killed by the U.S. military was commonly defined as a "Viet Cong." Thus, it was not totally bizarre for Calley to believe that what he was doing at My Lai was to increase his body count, as any good officer was expected to do.

Even to the extent that the actions at My Lai occurred spontaneously, without reference to superior orders, those committing them had reason to assume that such actions might be tacitly approved of by the military authorities. Not only had they failed to punish such acts in most cases, but the very strategies and tactics that the authorities consistently devised were based on the proposition that the civilian population of South Vietnam—whether "hostile" or "friendly"—was expendable. Such policies as search-and-destroy missions, the establishment of free-shooting zones, the use of antipersonnel weapons, the bombing of entire villages if they were suspected of harboring guerrillas, the forced migration of masses of the rural population, and the defoliation of vast forest areas helped legitimize acts of massive violence of the kind occurring at My Lai.

Some of the actions at My Lai suggest an orientation to authority based on unquestioning obedience to superior orders, no matter how destructive the actions these orders call for. Such obedience is specifically fostered in the course of military training and reinforced by the structure of the military authority situation. It also reflects, however, an ideological orientation that may be more widespread in the general population, as some of the data presented in this volume will demonstrate.

ROUTINIZATION

Authorization processes create a situation in which people become involved in an action without considering its implications and without really making a decision. Once they have taken the initial step, they are in a new psychological and social situation in which the pressures to continue are powerful. As Lewin (1947) has pointed out, many forces that might originally have kept people out of a situation reverse direction once they have made a commitment (once they have gone through the "gate region") and now serve to keep them in the situation. For example, concern about the criminal nature of an action, which might originally have inhibited a person from becoming involved, may now lead to deeper involvement in efforts to justify the action and to avoid negative consequences.

Despite these forces, however, given the nature of the actions involved in sanctioned massacres, one might still expect moral scruples to intervene; but the likelihood of moral resistance is greatly reduced by transforming the action into routine, mechanical, highly programmed operations. Routinization fulfills two functions. First, it reduces the necessity of making decisions, thus minimizing the occasions in which moral questions may arise. Second, it makes it easier to avoid the implications of the action, since the actor focuses on the details of the job rather than on its meaning. The latter effect is more readily achieved among those who participate in sanctioned massacres from a distance—from their desks or even from the cockpits of their bombers.

Routinization operates both at the level of the individual actor and at the organizational level. Individual job performance is broken down into a series of discrete steps, most of them carried out in automatic, regularized fashion. It becomes easy to forget the nature of the product that emerges from this process. When Lieutenant Calley said of My Lai that it was "no great deal," he probably implied that it was all in a day's work. Organizationally, the task is divided among different offices, each of which has responsibility for a small portion of it. This arrangement diffuses responsibility and limits the amount and scope of decision making that is necessary. There is no expectation that the moral implications will be considered at any of these points, nor is there any opportunity to do so. The organizational processes also help further legitimize the actions of each participant. By proceeding in routine fashion—processing papers, exchanging memos, diligently carrying out their assigned tasks—the different units mutually reinforce each other in the view that what is going on must be perfectly normal, correct, and legitimate. The shared illusion that they are engaged in a legitimate enterprise helps the participants assimilate their activities to other purposes, such as the efficiency of their performance, the productivity of their unit, or the cohesiveness of their group (see Janis, 1972).

Normalization of atrocities is more difficult to the extent that there are constant reminders of the true meaning of the enterprise. Bureaucratic inventiveness in the use of language helps to cover up such meaning. For example, the SS had a set of *Sprachregelungen*, or "language rules," to govern descriptions of their extermination program. As Arendt (1964) points out, the term *language rule* in itself was "a code name; it meant what in ordinary language would be called a lie" (p. 85). The code names for killing and liquidation were "final solution," "evacuation," and "special treatment." The war in Indochina produced its own set of euphemisms, such as "protective reaction," "pacification," and "forced-draft urbanization and modernization." The use of euphemisms allows participants in sanctioned massacres to differentiate their actions from ordinary killing and destruction and thus to avoid confronting their true meaning.

DEHUMANIZATION

Authorization processes override standard moral considerations; routinization processes reduce the likelihood that such considerations will arise. Still, the inhibitions against murdering one's fellow human beings are generally so strong that the victims must also be stripped of their human status if they are to be subjected to systematic killing. Insofar as they are dehumanized, the usual principles of morality no longer apply to them.

Sanctioned massacres become possible to the extent that the victims are deprived in the perpetrators' eyes of the two qualities essential to being perceived as fully human and included in the moral compact that governs human relationships: *identity*—standing as independent, distinctive individuals, capable of making choices and entitled to live their own lives—and *community*—fellow membership in an interconnected network of individuals who care for each other and respect each other's individuality and rights (Kelman, 1973; see also Bakan, 1966, for a related distinction between "agency" and "communion"). Thus, when a group of people is defined entirely in terms of a category to which they belong, and when this category is excluded from the human family, moral restraints against killing them are more readily overcome.

Dehumanization of the enemy is a common phenomenon in any war situation. Sanctioned massacres, however, presuppose a more extreme degree of dehumanization, insofar as the killing is not in direct response to the target's threats or provocations. It is not what they have done that marks such victims for death but who they are—the category to which they happen to belong. They are the victims of policies that regard their systematic destruction as a desirable end or an acceptable means. Such extreme dehumanization becomes possible when the target group can readily be identified as a separate category of people who have historically been stigmatized and excluded by the victimizers; often the victims belong to a distinct racial, religious, ethnic, or political group regarded as inferior or sinister. The traditions, the habits, the images, and the vocabularies for dehumanizing such groups are already well established and can be drawn upon when the groups are selected for massacre. Labels help deprive the victims of identity and community, as in the epithet "gooks" that was commonly used to refer to Vietnamese and other Indochinese peoples.

The dynamics of the massacre process itself further increase the participants' tendency to dehumanize their victims. Those who participate as part of the bureaucratic apparatus increasingly come to see their victims as bodies to be counted and entered into their reports, as faceless figures that will determine their productivity rates and promotions. Those who participate in the massacre directly—in the field, as it were—are reinforced in their perception of the victims as less than human by observing their very victimization. The only way they can justify what is being done to these people—both by others and by themselves—and the only way they can extract some degree of meaning out of the absurd events in which they find themselves participating (see Lifton, 1971, 1973) is by coming to believe that the victims are subhuman and deserve to be rooted out. And thus the process of dehumanization feeds on itself.

REFERENCES

Arendt, H. (1964). *Eichmann in Jerusalem: A report on the banality of evil.* New York: Viking Press.

Bakan, D. (1966). *The duality of human existence.* Chicago: Rand McNally.

Bandura, A. (1973). Social learning theory of aggression. In J. F. Knutson (Ed.), *Control of aggression: Implications from basic research.* Chicago: Aldine-Atherton.

Bedau, H. A. (1974). Genocide in Vietnam. In V. Held, S. Morgenbesser, & T. Nagel (Eds.), *Philosophy, morality, and international affairs* (pp. 5–46). New York: Oxford University Press.

Browning, F., & Forman, D. (Eds.). (1972). *The wasted nations: Report of the International Commission of Enquiry into United States Crimes in Indochina, June 20–25, 1971*. New York: Harper & Row.

Fromm, E. (1941). *Escape from freedom*. New York: Rinehart.

Janis, I. L. (1972). *Victims of groupthink: A psychological study of foreign-policy decisions and fiascoes*. Boston: Houghton Mifflin.

Kelman, H. C. (1973). Violence without moral restraint: Reflections on the dehumanization of victims and victimizers. *Journal of Social Issues*, 29 (4), 25–61.

Levinson, S. (1973). Responsibility for crimes of war. *Philosophy and Public Affairs*, 2, 244–273.

Lewin, K. (1947). Group decision and social change. In T. M. Newcomb & E. L. Hartley (Eds.), *Readings in social psychology*. New York: Holt.

Lifton, R. J. (1971). Existential evil. In N. Sanford, C. Comstock, & Associates, *Sanctions for evil: Sources of social destructiveness*. San Francisco: Jossey-Bass.

———. (1973). *Home from the war—Vietnam veterans: Neither victims nor executioners*. New York: Simon & Schuster.

Schirmer, D. B. (1971, April 24). My Lai was not the first time. *New Republic*, pp. 18–21.

Sheehan, N. (1971, March 28). Should we have war crime trials? *The New York Times Book Review*, pp. 1–3, 30–34.

17

Thought Reform in China

JOHN KING FAIRBANK

THOUGHT REFORM

The Communist achievement in organization, among a people so recently famous for their lack of it, depended upon the inspiring, coercing, or manipulating of individual personalities. Building upon methods used in Yenan to Leninize the party (as well as to convert Japanese war prisoners), Liu Shao-ch'i and other organizers developed empirical procedures to deal with every type of enemy or supporter. When American prisoners of war in Korea "confessed" to germ warfare and collaborated with their Chinese captors, they were responding to techniques developed through use with Chinese of all sorts, including party members. As a result of these methods capitalists and rich peasants smilingly gave their property to the state, professors scathingly denounced their Western bourgeois education, secondary school students devotedly gave their lives to party work.

These diverse phenomena represented the real Communist effort at revolution, to change Chinese thinking and behavior. Though very diverse, thought reform generally had certain common features: control of the environment, both of the person physically and of the information available to him (this was now true of the whole country); the stimuli both of idealism and of terror, intermixed; and a grim psychological experience, undergone with guidance through successive phases and intensified by the manipulation of one's sense of guilt and shame. The Chinese slang term "brainwashing" imparted perhaps too much mystery to a process faintly visible elsewhere in religious crusades of the past, only now more thoroughly organized. Modern psychologists can explain how privation, prolonged insecurity, and tension, combined with extended fatigue and repetitive indoctrination, can shatter the individual's sense of inner identity and create pressures from which the only escape for many is submission to authority and acceptance at least temporarily of new attitudes and concepts. This coercing of the human mind, quite different in degree from the mild voluntary form of American advertising methods, is still only partially understood and exploited. Spread over the world it would create the ultimate crisis of individualism. Perhaps it is not surprising that in China, where the practical art of human relations has been more fully developed than anywhere else, these psychological methods should be so advanced.

For the Chinese student class, from whom the CCP had to get its cadres, this intellectual-emotional reconditioning was carried out in the big revolutionary colleges set up through the reorganization and expansion of the educational system. Thousands of trainees went through indoctrination courses of several months' duration. A center of this type containing 4000 students might be subdivided into classes of one or two hundred and then into study groups of six to ten persons. A psychiatrist who analyzed the process, Robert Lifton, divided a typical six-month thought reform into three stages—first, group identification, a period of togetherness and considerable freedom and enthusiasm. During this stage major Marxist-Leninist-Maoist concepts were studied and discussed mainly in small groups. A free exchange of views, with a high esprit de corps, led the trainee to expose himself and engage wholeheartedly in a "thought mobilization."

The second phase was one of induced emotional conflict within each individual. The daily schedule continued to be physically exhausting. The milieu, carefully controlled, now seemed to close in. The individual submitted his first summary of his own life and thought. As criticism and self-criticism intensified, the dangers of being rejected became apparent. The evils within the old individual were now attacked, not merely the old society in the abstract, and the student strove to dig up his failings and correct them. Group pressures were focused by experienced leaders so that each individual became heavily involved emotionally, under assault. He might struggle with himself and be "struggled with" by his group-mates over an excess of subjectivism or objectivism, of opportunism or dogmatism, bureaucratism or individual heroism, and so forth. The individual who attempted to hold back and resist the process took a psychological beating. Each participant was completely alone, isolated within himself like all his fellows. Under this pressure, similar to that used against prisoners, the individual soon felt guilt (he had sinned and should be punished) and also a sense of shame (he had lost face and self-esteem), which created intense humiliation. In attacking himself, he was thus prepared for confession and self-condemnation, feeling as though he were mentally ill and needed a cure.

The third phase was that of submission and rebirth. When his final thought summary or confession was accepted by the group and the authorities, the individual was likely to feel exhilarated, cleansed, a new person. This months-long process was on a larger scale a sort of induced religious conversion, like those of our own revival meetings, but with added elements of pressure and psychotherapy. The individual had been manipulated, the wellsprings of his own nature had put him under pressure, and the relief from this self-induced tension was associated with the external authority of the party, on whom he should henceforth be dependent. For the party's aim was not only to control disciplined activists but also to improve their performance by changing their idea of themselves, their goals and values. They renounced family and father and accepted the party and the revolution in their place.

This process was most successful with malleable young minds. In the case of older intellectuals, particularly returned students from the West, criticism, self-criticism, and confession could only be an overlay of their formative experience. Many statements by Peking professors were pro forma. They denounced the corrupting influence of the bourgeois West and their former subjection to it, possibly with some sense of guilt at having been seduced or alienated from their native culture. But the net effect of their self-criticism was less to change these individuals than to align them properly in the public eye as supporters of the new order. Thus the one class who might represent a Western non-Communist influence neutralized themselves and presented no model for youth.

COMMUNISM AND CONFUCIANISM

Few who have lived in China will assume that a revolution, however irresistible, can quickly remake the immovable Middle Kingdom. Our schematic account of thought reform should not imply that it could easily remake the Chinese personality. However, the strategy was long term, to maintain a controlled environment of lip service if not love for the regime until the new socialist generation could take over.

Out of the Chinese inheritance, moreover, authoritarian traditions could be invoked for modern purposes. Thus Confucianism in one of its aspects has a certain resonance with Marxism—not an identity, only a partial overlap. This point of resonance was in the unity of theory and practice. The Bolshevik emphasis on putting theory into revolutionary practice contended that theory was no good in itself but must be applied in activity, as part of an effort not only to understand the world but to change it. Marxism as a "science of history" when put into practice must become an ethic, a personal philosophy animating one's entire thought and conduct. Self-criticism was a necessary part of discipline for this purpose. It was also a Communist doctrine that Marxist-Leninist theory should be applied according to the content of each national background, blending Communist ideas with the local tradition. As Mao said, "We must unify appropriately the general truth of Marxism with the concrete practice of the Chinese revolution."

Communist self-criticism was reminiscent of the Confucian doctrine of self-cultivation in the form associated particularly with the sixteenth-century philosopher Wang Yang-ming (1472–1529). Wang attacked the dualism of knowledge and action. In Wang's view, as David Nivison puts it, "To know is to know how and to know that one ought." The completely sincere man must express his moral perceptions in equally moral conduct. Wang and others therefore urged self-cultivation as a process by which the true philosopher can bring his thought and conduct into consonance, so that knowledge is realized in action and action contributes to knowledge. This idea was echoed in Sun Yat-sen's "Knowledge is difficult, action is easy" and later by Chiang Kai-shek.

While Confucian self-cultivation was not a group affair, it stressed the moral improv-ability of human nature, the ancient Chinese belief that through proper ethical instruction and exhortation, man can be made into a more social being. Individual self-cultivation and group self-criticism have something in common. Thought reform at Yenan made use of traditional Chinese terminology and invoked Confucian sanctions. The good Commu-nist, according to Liu Shao-ch'i, must discipline himself through self-cultivation, through "watching himself when alone," so as to become flexibly and resourcefully obedient to the party's leadership. Through greater consciousness of the historical influences playing upon him, it was argued, he might indeed achieve a certain feeling of freedom within the confines of the historical process. Thus where Confucianism instilled loyalty to family, father, and emperor, Maoism now diverted it to the people, the party, and the leader. The classics were quoted for this purpose.

CRITICISM, LITERARY AND POLITICAL

In thought reform, the Chinese literary world was obliged to follow Mao Tse-tung's dictum on literature and art of 1942, that they are political tools in the class struggle and thoroughly subordinate to politics. The full force of meetings, denunciations, and special publications was assembled to attack Hu Shih as the symbol of "decadent American bourgeois pragmatism." One campaign was against his interpretation of the famous eighteenth-century novel *The Dream of the Red Chamber* as an autobiographical work. Communists preferred to see in it the inner collapse of China's feudal society, thus salvaging this fascinating book from China's heritage as belonging to "the people," like other selected heroes, poets, and cultural inheritances. The campaign simultaneously discredited Western-type literary criticism based on historical research, as part of the attack upon Chinese liberalism and its foreign allies.

But the Communist party's creative writers still tended occasionally to be critics, the same as in the Soviet Union. Some who had gained fame attacking the evils of the old order now criticized imperfections in the new, particularly the Central Committee's claim through its literary commissar, Chou Yang, to be the final arbiter of artistic excellence. A rebellious disciple of Lu Hsün named Hu Feng was pilloried for this in a nationwide campaign. Eventually his denunciators, like Ting Ling, were also denounced and purged by Chou Yang (who was himself to be purged in 1966).

Just as thought reform and other campaigns winnowed the population, separating out potential enemies and recruits, so the great corpus of China's historical inheritance had to be reappraised in Marxist-Leninist terms and integrated into the new state-and-culture. "Applying the universal principles of Marxism-Leninism to the concrete real-ities of China" was a never-ending process. Most of China's glorious past, for example, had to be put by definition within the Marxian period of "feudalism." Precisely when "capitalism" had begun in China was disputed; but since 1840, it was argued, foreign "capitalist imperialism," allied with domestic "feudal reaction," had checked and distorted China's "normal" capitalist development. Such formulas, imposed upon academic learning for political purposes, raised some new questions and absorbed scholarly attention.

CHAPTER FIVE

PUBLIC OPINION, THE MASS MEDIA, AND DEMOCRACY

This chapter examines public opinion in democratic countries. At least since the days of John Locke and Jean-Jacques Rousseau, scholars have considered the sources, content, and impact of public sentiments. During the past half-century, the refinement of polling techniques has greatly enhanced our ability to explore these issues scientifically. Simultaneously, new communication and broadcast technology has transformed the way the public acquires and expresses its attitudes. Social scientists have approached public opinion and political communication from various academic disciplines; empirical and theoretical analyses are abundant. Sociology and communication departments often house these research programs, but public opinion and political communication are central concerns of political psychologists as well.

Perhaps the most critical questions today remain those that preoccupied the earliest students of political sentiments in democracies. How *does* the public think and act? How *should* the public think and act? What are the limits of the public's capabilities? Where do public sentiments originate? What impact do the mass media have on public opinion and policy? How does the public participate in democratic politics?

Although few political scientists express much confidence in the wisdom and virtue of mass opinion, some versions of democratic ideology hold the common person's attitudes in high regard. *The Federalist Papers* notwithstanding, many people equate democracy with rule by *vox populi*. Hence, Al Smith's much-quoted remark that "all the ills of democracy can be cured by more democracy."

Bob Grant, a bombastic radio talk show host in New York City, is one who shows his faith in this position by scowling his social panacea across the radio waves every

246

evening: "Your influence counts—use it!" Three widely held assumptions underlie Grant's injunction to his listeners: 1) the public possesses or can form meaningful opinions on a wide range of issues, 2) the public has the power—current or potential, direct or indirect—to influence policy, and 3) better policies will result if the public uses its influence than if it refrains from intervening. For those who wish to challenge these assumptions, public opinion research provides ample ammunition.

Walter Lippmann (1922, 1925), an early and tremendously influential student of public opinion, waxed cynical about the public's potential to influence policy for the better. In *The Phantom Public*, Lippmann calls attention to:

> the inherent absurdity of making virtue and wisdom dependent on 51 percent of any collection of men. . . . The practical realization that the claim was absurd has resulted in a whole code of civil rights to protect minorities and in all sorts of elaborate methods of subsidizing the arts and sciences . . . so they might be independent of the operation of majority rule. (p. 58)

Moreover, Lippmann claims that:

> when public opinion attempts to govern directly it is either a failure or a tyranny. It is not able to master the problem intellectually, nor to deal with it except by wholesale impact. The theory of democracy has not recognized this truth because it has identified the functioning of government with the will of the people. This is a fiction. The intricate business of framing laws and of administering them through several hundred thousand public officials is in no sense the act of the voters nor a translation of their will. (pp. 70–71)

Lippmann wrote *The Phantom Public* and his earlier classic, *Public Opinion*, without the advantages of modern survey research. As we shall see in the readings, some of his conclusions are quite consistent with subsequent scientific findings.

In contrast to Lippmann, however, pollster Daniel Yankelovich (1991) speaks with optimism about an expanded role for the public. Yankelovich recognizes the limitations of the public identified in several decades of survey research, but sees a greater danger in relegating public debate to cadres of experts. He calls for the media and political leaders to define the country's choices on vital issues more clearly so that the public *can* exercise effective judgment. Moreover, he believes that we need to draw a distinction between top-of-the-head opinions and more considered judgments. When the latter are involved, public opinion, according to Yankelovich, can play a crucial role in determining policy.

The normative debate concerning the proper role for public opinion in a democracy continues, and many positions have been expressed. Often, this debate has provided the motivation behind empirical research programs.

The large body of research and scholarship on public opinion has been reviewed in several texts (Erikson, Luttbegg, and Tedin, 1988; Hennessy, 1985; Oskamp, 1991).

Much of this research concerns the role the public plays, can play, or should play in a democracy. For example, public opinion researchers explore:

- how people conceptualize political matters and how they organize their political thinking (Campbell, Converse, Miller, and Stokes, 1960; Converse, 1964; Judd and Milburn, 1980; Nie, Verba, and Petrocik, 1979);
- the foundations of mass political tolerance (Bobo and Licari, 1989; McClosky and Brill, 1983; Mueller, 1988);
- the correspondence between mass and elite political opinions (Converse, 1964; Kressel, 1987; Neuman, 1986);
- demographic and trend analysis of public opinion on economic, social, and political issues (Erikson, Luttbegg, and Tedin, 1988; Oskamp, 1991; Smith, 1990);
- the effects of dramatic events on public opinion (Adams and Heyl, 1981; Riley and Pettigrew, 1976);
- the impact of public opinion on the political process (Cohen, 1973; Key, 1961; Sudman, 1982);
- the impact of the mass media on public opinion (Iyengar and Lenart, 1989; Katz, 1987; Kraus and Davis, 1976);
- the application of survey and mass communication research to the design of campaign strategy (Diamond and Bates, 1988; Gopoian and Brown, 1989; Nimmo, 1970; Sabato, 1981).

Many political psychologists focus on links between public opinion and other psychological concerns. Early research attempted to identify motivational and unconscious foundations of public opinion (Adorno, Frenkel-Brunswik, Levinson, and Sanford, 1950; Smith, Bruner, and White, 1956). For example, many political opinions correlated with authoritarianism, as measured by the F-scale and related instruments (Kirscht and Dillehay, 1967). Social psychological variables such as machiavellianism, dogmatism, locus of control, and self-esteem have been studied in connection to public opinion.

Recently, political psychologists have focused on cognitive foundations of public opinion. Cognitive style, cognitive complexity, cognitive sophistication, schematic processing, and many other cognitive approaches have been employed widely during the past few years (Barner-Barry, 1990; Conover and Feldman, 1984; Neuman, 1986).

This chapter includes four selections. The first three readings—Neuman (18), McClosky and Zaller (19), and Verba and Nie (20)—provide thoughtful analyses of the public's role in maintaining democracy in the United States. Finally, Iyengar, Peters, and Kinder (21) offer empirical evidence for a cognitive model of the impact of television news.

In the few years since W. Russell Neuman's *The Paradox of Mass Politics* first appeared, his book has had much influence on public opinion research. Combining methodological expertise with a creative, integrative approach to theory, Neuman discusses many matters that concern political psychologists, including political cognition and political socialization. The portion of Neuman's work in this anthology (18) presents his analysis of the paradox of mass politics, which he defines as "the gap between the expectation of an informed citizenry put forward by democratic theory and the discomforting reality revealed by systematic survey interviewing." Neuman's resolution of this paradox is facilitated by his segmentation of the American public, based upon political sophistication categories.

Herbert McClosky's contributions to political psychology span many decades (McClosky, 1958; 1967; 1983); in this excerpt from *The American Ethos* (19), he teams up with John Zaller. In the empirical body of their book, McClosky and Zaller determine that Americans still hold many general values—equality, freedom, individualism, private property—endorsed by the founding fathers. However, Americans interpret these values and their application in very different ways than the founding fathers had intended.

The reprinted selection is the concluding chapter of *The American Ethos*. In this chapter, McClosky and Zaller argue that most Americans currently support democracy more heartily than they support capitalism. Based on empirical and theoretical analyses, the authors offer some informed speculation about the future of American democracy and capitalism.

The next reading is an excerpt from Sidney Verba and Norman Nie's *Participation in America: Political Democracy and Social Equality.* Verba and Nie consider a broad spectrum of political participation including voting, campaign activity, communal activity, and "particularized contacting" of elected officials. They conclude that "participation is unequally distributed throughout the society because the qualities that lead some to choose to participate—motivation, skills, resources—are not equally distributed." Social status and the civic attitudes that accompany it are important determinants of participation. Verba and Nie's 1972 study has stood the test of time fairly well (Wolfinger and Rosenstone, 1980). However, it is worth remembering their contention that the most important questions are normative.

> How much participation ought there to be? Who should participate? How should political leaders respond to the voice of the people? And in general how adequate is American democracy, and how might it be improved? (p. 1)

Research cannot resolve these issues, but it can provide us with a more accurate empirical foundation for discussion.

In the final piece (21), Shanto Iyengar, Mark D. Peters, and Donald R. Kinder report on two experiments that examine the consequences of viewing televised network news. Their study provides a clear example of how experimentation can enhance our understanding of political communication—if it is supplemented by field research. In addition, Iyengar, Peters, and Kinder offer a useful integration of media research and cognitive psychology.

REFERENCES

Adams, W. C. and Heyl, P. (1981). From Cairo to Kabul with the networks, 1972–1980. In W. C. Adams (Ed.), *Television Coverage of the Middle East* (pp. 1–39). Norwood, NJ: Ablex.

Adorno, T. W., Frenkel-Brunswik, E., Levinson, D., and Sanford, R. N. (1950). *The Authoritarian Personality*. New York: Harper & Row.

Barner-Barry, C. (1990). Political psychology in the 1980s and the cognitive perspective. In S. Long (Ed.), *Annual Review of Political Science* (Vol. 3, pp. 198–220). Norwood, NJ: Ablex.

Bobo, L. and Licari, F. C. (1989). Education and political tolerance. *Public Opinion Quarterly, 53*, 285–308.

Campbell, A., Converse, P. E., Miller, W. E., and Stokes, D. E. (1960). *The American Voter*. New York: Wiley.

Cohen, B. C. (1973). *The Public's Impact on Foreign Policy*. Boston: Little, Brown.

Conover, P. J. and Feldman, S. (1984). How people organize the political world: A schematic model. *American Journal of Political Science, 28*(Feb.), 95–126.

Converse, P. E. (1964). The nature of belief systems in mass publics. In D. E. Apter (Ed.), *Ideology and Discontent* (pp. 206–261). New York: Free Press.

Diamond, E. and Bates, S. (1988). *The Spot: The Rise of Political Advertising on Television* (Revised ed.). Cambridge, MA: MIT Press.

Erikson, R. S., Luttbegg, N. R., and Tedin, K. L. (1988). *American Public Opinion: Its Origins, Content, and Impact* (Third ed.). New York: Macmillan.

Gopoian, J. D. and Brown, S. R. (1989). Public opinion and campaign strategy. In S. Long (Ed.), *Political Behavior Annual* (Vol. 2, pp. 103–124). Boulder, CO: Westview Press.

Hennessy, B. (1985). *Public Opinion*. Monterey, CA: Brooks/Cole.

Iyengar, S. and Lenart, S. (1989). Beyond "minimal consequences": A survey of media political effects. In S. Long (Ed.), *Political Behavior Annual* (Vol. 2, pp. 21–38). Boulder, CO: Westview Press.

Judd, C. M. and Milburn, M. A. (1980). The structure of attitude systems in the general public: Comparisons of a structural equation model. *American Sociological Review, 45*, 870–890.

Katz, E. (1987). Communications research since Lazarsfeld. *Public Opinion Quarterly, 51*, s25–s45.

Key, V. O. (1961). *Public Opinion and American Democracy*. New York: Alfred A. Knopf.

Kirscht, J. P. and Dillehay, R. C. (1967). *Dimensions of Authoritarianism: A Review of Research and Theory*. Lexington, KY: University of Kentucky Press.

Kraus, S. and Davis, D. (1976). *The Effects of Mass Communication on Political Behavior*. University Park, PA: Pennsylvania State University Press.

Kressel, N. J. (1987). Ideological correspondence between Senators and their constituents. *Psychological Reports, 60*(3, pt. 2), 1131–1137.

Lippmann, W. (1922). *Public Opinion*. New York: Macmillan Free Press.

———. (1925). *The Phantom Public*. New York: Harcourt, Brace and Company.

McClosky, H. (1958). Conservatism and personality. *American Political Science Review, 52*, 27–45.

———. (1967). Personality and attitude correlates of foreign policy orientation. In J. N. Rosenau (Ed.), *Domestic Sources of Foreign Policy* (pp. 51–109). New York: Free Press.

McClosky, H. and Brill, A. (1983). *Dimensions of Tolerance: What Americans Believe About Civil Liberties.* New York: Russell Sage.

Mueller, J. (1988). Trends in political tolerance. *Public Opinion Quarterly*, *52*, 1–25.

Neuman, W. R. (1986). *The Paradox of Mass Politics.* Cambridge, MA: Harvard University Press.

Nie, N. H., Verba, S., and Petrocik, J. R. (1979). *The Changing American Voter.* Cambridge, MA: Harvard University Press.

Nimmo, D. (1970). *The Political Persuaders.* Englewood Cliffs, NJ: Prentice-Hall.

Oskamp, S. (1991). *Attitudes and Opinions* (2nd ed.). Englewood Cliffs, NJ: Prentice Hall.

Riley, R. and Pettigrew, T. F. (1976). Dramatic events and attitude change. *Journal of Personality and Social Psychology*, *34*, 1004–1115.

Sabato, L. J. (1981). *The Rise of Political Consultants: New Ways of Winning Elections.* New York: Basic Books.

Smith, M. B., Bruner, J. S., and White, R. W. (1956). *Opinions and Personality.* New York: Wiley.

Smith, T. W. (1990). Liberal and conservative trends in the United States. *Public Opinion Quarterly*, *54*(4), 479–507.

Sudman, S. (1982). The president and the polls. *Public Opinion Quarterly*, *46*, 301–310.

Verba, S. and Nie, N. H. (1972). *Participation in America: Political Democracy and Social Equality.* New York: Harper & Row.

Wolfinger, R. E. and Rosenstone, S. J. (1980). *Who Votes?* New Haven, CT: Yale University Press.

Yankelovich, D. (1991). *Coming to Public Judgment: Making Democracy Work in a Complex World.* Syracuse, NY: Syracuse University Press.

18

The Paradox of Mass Politics:
Knowledge and Opinion in the
American Electorate

W. RUSSELL NEUMAN

Until public opinion polling and scientific sampling techniques were invented in the 1920s and 1930s, the voice of the people was the voice of those who chose to speak out—those who voted, wrote letters to editors, went to public meetings, wrote to legislators, or hired professional lobbyists to represent their interests in the corridors of power. Of course, most everyone had a vague sense of public opinion at large from occasional contacts with friends and associates. But since individuals tend to associate with people like themselves, such informal measures were (and continue to be) misleading. The pioneers of survey research were thus shocked, when they systematically assessed the political knowledge of the electorate, to find such low levels of interest and information.

The paradox of mass politics is the gap between the expectation of an informed citizenry put forward by democratic theory and the discomforting reality revealed by systematic survey interviewing. The paradox raises serious questions. How different are the views of those few who actively attempt to influence political decisions on a day-to-day basis from the views of the many who simply monitor the news media half-attentively and occasionally make it to the polls to vote? Do the masses and elites process political information in distinctly different ways? To the extent that there are differences, how do they affect the workings of the democratic process?

These questions are not new. Walter Lippmann (*Public Opinion*, 1922) puzzled over how the public could be expected to understand the complexities of international diplomacy and military strategy during the First World War well enough to offer meaningful guidance to their elected officials. Similarly, Joseph Schumpeter (*Capitalism, Socialism, and Democracy*, 1942) concluded that on most political and economic issues the level of reasoning of the average citizen is primitive, even infantile. The well-educated are no exception. He cited the example of a lawyer who has been professionally trained to evaluate evidence carefully and critically as it is introduced in the courtroom. This same lawyer, when later in the day it comes time to read a political story in the newspaper, reacts instinctively and primitively to the facts and arguments at hand. Simon (*Administrative Behavior*, 1945) and Downs (*An Economic Theory of Democracy*, 1957) further developed the theory of how people make decisions when they have less than full information and limited time and energy to seek it out.

This book [*The Paradox of Mass Politics*] takes a fresh look at these issues, paying particular attention to electoral politics. The starting point is the paradox itself. Major election surveys from the period 1948 to 1980 provide the evidence on the character of the average citizen's political interest and knowledge, cognitive style, political opinions, and awareness of central public issues. Although it is difficult to calibrate the minimum necessary threshold of public knowledge, by most benchmarks the level of public awareness is disturbingly low. Yet all studies of decision-making in Washington indicate that an articulate voice of attentive public opinion is being heard. Where is this voice coming from?

Four theories have attempted to resolve this paradox. The first theory, which emerged from the early voting studies, emphasized that public opinion is *stratified*. Although the average citizen may not be terribly well-informed on an issue, there are opinion leaders within the community who are articulate, active, and indeed well-informed. Through a complex, multilevel communications process, the issues are discussed and evaluated, and ultimately public views are voiced, usually by means of the opinion-leader stratum.

The second theory, also based on the early voting studies, emphasized the *pluralism* of public opinion. Each citizen need not be an expert on each issue. There exist issue publics, or groups of concerned citizens who have a special awareness about and expertise in matters which affect them directly. Veterans track veterans' affairs; businessmen track business regulations. The resolution to the paradox is pluralism.

The third theory, which emerged in the 1970s, concluded that the portrait of the unsophisticated citizen is an artifact of the 1950s, which were an unusually quiescent period in American politics. As a result of the polarized politics of the 1960s, characterized by student and urban unrest and the ideological candidacies of Barry Goldwater and, later, George McGovern, a *changed American voter* emerged. In response to the more intense political environment, the average citizen proved to be more politically concerned, more aware of the issues, and more attuned to ideological disputes.

The fourth and final theory, also from the 1970s, dealt with the technical issues involved in the measurement of ideology, issue voting, and opinion consistency over time. This *methodological critique* asserted simply that the portrait of an unsophisticated citizenry is false, the unfortunate result of errors in measurement.

Although each response is plausible and offers a potentially attractive resolution to the paradox of mass politics, each turns out to be fundamentally flawed. The notion of a two-step flow of information back and forth between opinion leaders and the mass public is incomplete and misleading. The pluralism of opinions and interests that exists among citizens does not in fact correspond to a pluralism of political expertise. Nor has the American voter changed, for patterns of knowledge, interest, and awareness established in the 1950s have proven over time to be remarkably consistent. And the basic findings about low citizen interest and sophistication have persisted, despite methodological adjustments and refinements.

The key to the paradox, it turns out, lies in a reformulation of the first theory, the theory of opinion stratification. Most studies of political stratification have inferred this phenomenon from measures of education, participation, or the expression of opinions. In doing so, they risk a tautology. The central issue is the correlation between political knowledge and either opinion or behavior. To analyze that correlation, one must have an independent measure of political knowledge and sophistication, so as not to entangle the argument hopelessly. Such a measure of political sophistication would assess the individual's interest in political life, knowledge of political institutions, groups, and issues, and conceptual sophistication. This index of political sophistication is here recalculated for each of a series of nine voting studies covering the period 1948–1980.

The theory of political stratification, as well as common sense, would suggest that the more sophisticated members of the citizenry have more numerous, stable, and structured opinions and a more clear-cut ideological position. Surprisingly, the findings derived from the voting studies do not support these hypotheses. The relationship between sophistication and these variables tends to be small or nonexistent. This is a puzzling finding, which represents, in a sense, another paradox within the main paradox. As for the relationship of sophistication to voting and other forms of political participation, the expected strong linkage again turns out to be incomplete and nonlinear. It is not that political sophistication is unrelated to political opinion and behavior. Rather, the linkage is subtle and complex. The theory of political stratification requires a major reformulation.

A central issue concerns the origins of sophistication, or how it is that some citizens become relatively well-informed and involved while others are oblivious to the entire political process. Analysis of the demographic roots of sophistication reveals a spiral process of the acquisition of political knowledge. This is a gradual process in which interest breeds knowledge which, in turn, breeds further interest and knowledge over time. Related issues concern political learning from the mass media and the linkage between sophistication and political alienation and authoritarianism.

Despite the accumulated results of over thirty years of election surveys, there is a nagging sense that the paradox remains unresolved. The system apparently works quite well despite a generally low level of public interest in and knowledge about the political world. A full resolution to the paradox requires a demonstration that the system does indeed work well, which would lead the book into quite a different direction. But the formulation that, under the circumstances, the system works as well as it does focuses attention on how the system works.

There are three elements to an evolving theory of the impact of sophistication on opinion and behavior. The first focuses on the distribution of political sophistication in the mass electorate. It identifies three distinct styles of political involvement, a theory of three publics. The original notion of stratification developed in the voting studies posited a substantial stratum of opinion leaders, generally the better-educated members of the electorate, and implied a gently sloping distribution from the least to the most sophisticated. Actually, there is a large and undifferentiated middle mass, including the great majority of those who have advanced to a college education or beyond. This large central group, perhaps 75 percent of the population, accounts for a number of the surprisingly weak correlations between knowledge and opinion or behavior. At the top of the sophistication distribution is a distinct but very small group of political activists. Their level of knowledge and cognitive style is much like that of professional politicians, journalists, and political analysts. But their numbers are so small, perhaps a few percent of the population, that they hardly influence the results of a representative national survey. They are articulate and active, however, and their views and concerns make up much of what is heard as "public opinion," just as they did before survey sampling was invented. At the bottom of the sophistication continuum is a third distinct group of apoliticals who seldom pay attention to or participate in public affairs. They constitute about a fifth of the population. The key to both the paradox of mass politics and the theory of three publics is a recognition that the bulk of the population is neither political nor apolitical; it lies in between. Most people can be mobilized to political action, they half-attentively monitor the flow of political news, but they run for the most part on a psychological automatic pilot.

The second and third elements of the theory of political sophistication concern the distinctions between issues and nonissues and between attitudes and nonattitudes. Public opinion has been characterized as a sleeping giant. Most of the time it is passive and unresponsive. But when aroused, it has effects on the polity that are significant and immediate. Government officials and representatives deal with literally hundreds of distinct issues in any given week. And they have some sophisticated knowledge of each issue. They may well have taken a position on many, perhaps most of them. They are also aware that tiny but alert and vocal groups of individuals are concerned about each of these issues. But in the public at large there is awareness or concern about only a few of these issues, perhaps a half-dozen or so that receive prominent attention in the media. The key to the democratic process is the fluidity of the public agenda, the possibility that at any minute what was once the concern of a tiny group of activists may suddenly crystallize the attention of the mass electorate and become a matter about which they do indeed have real opinions and real knowledge. The evolving theory, then, emphasizes public opinion as process, the setting of the public agenda, the process by which nonissues become issues, and, at the individual level, the process by which nonopinions become opinions. Therein lies the key to the paradox.

Each of these conclusions and interpretations is subject to challenge. The line between the active elite and the mass public is not clear-cut. New efforts at the assessment of mass political knowledge may reveal that the pluralism of knowledge and interest extends much farther into the mass electorate than the evidence has so far revealed. These concerns, no doubt, will continue to attract the attention of political scientists.

. . . .

TOWARD A THEORY OF POLITICAL SOPHISTICATION

Politics is more difficult than physics.

—ALBERT EINSTEIN

As is often the case in research of this sort, the accumulated findings on the nature of political sophistication in the mass citizenry have raised as many questions as they have answered. The paradox of mass politics persists. What at first glance seemed to be a self-evident positive correlation between sophistication and the expression, stability, and structuring of political opinions evaporates under closer scrutiny. Those who are more sophisticated are more likely to vote and to participate in political life beyond voting, but the relationships reflect intriguingly nonlinear patterns. The phenomenon of proxy voting seems to be more prevalent in the middle ranges of sophistication rather than, as might have been expected, among the bottom strata. Clearly the public is highly stratified in its interest in and knowledge about politics. But the character of that stratification and the relationship between sophistication and other central factors of political belief and behavior are subtle and complex.

The strategy so far has been to evaluate each set of relevant variables in search of clues to resolve the paradox. The clues have accumulated, but they have not yet fallen together into a coherent whole. A full-scale theory of political sophistication and its role in mass politics may still lie beyond our grasp.[1] But the findings do converge and provide the outline of such a theory. It is based on three central themes: the shape of the stratification curve which reveals three distinct publics, the distinction between issues and nonissues, and the distinction between attitudes and nonattitudes.

The Theory of Three Publics

The debate over whether the mass public is or is not sophisticated presents an awkward dichotomy. It is always possible to derive a seemingly straightforward test of political knowledge on which the majority of the population will fail utterly. It is equally easy to identify a critical issue or a political actor about which the electorate has accumulated a fair amount of information, thus appearing to be reasonably well informed. Such polemic loops represent a seductive distraction. The key step forward is to recognize that the shape of the sophistication distribution is more significant than its mean value.

The generalized sophistication curve is derived from the converging pattern of many previously described distributions. Although political sophistication is defined and measured as a continuous variable, the curve has two inflection points which generate the theory of three publics (Figure 1). There is no clear and unmistakable dividing line between these publics, but their different patterns of behavior suggest that the distinctions are politically important.

The bulk of the population, perhaps 75 percent, share a homogeneous pattern of opinion and behavior. They are marginally attentive to politics and mildly cynical about the behavior of politicians, but they accept the duty to vote, and they do so with fair regularity. This is the great middle stratum.

Another stratum of the public, about 20 percent, is markedly different. They are a self-consistent and unabashedly apolitical lot. They do not share the common norms which stress the importance of keeping informed about politics or of voting, and their

Figure 1. Theory of Three Publics

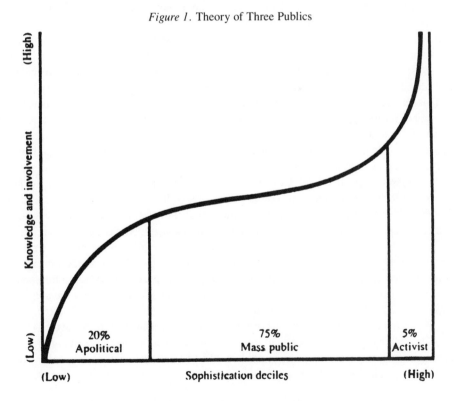

behavior dramatically reflects this posture. For example, the information on voting behavior and perceived duty to vote . . . reflects this sharp falling off in the bottom two deciles. Also, those in the bottom stratum are refreshingly candid about not having any political opinions. . . . Furthermore, content analyses of the natural language used to describe political objects reveal a number of instances of an apolitical stratum of roughly 20 percent of the population. . . .

A much smaller stratum, perhaps less than 5 percent of the population, contains the political activists. Members of this highest stratum of political sophistication exhibit uniquely high levels of political involvement. . . .

Previous research on the stratification of mass political involvement has derived similar figures (Berelson et al., 1954; Dahl, 1963).

The shape of the sophistication distribution has important political consequences. For one thing, the two ends of the curve are self-consistent. The apolitical and activist strata are both characterized by self-reinforcing values and behavior. For the large middle mass, however, the generalized norms of civic duty are at odds with their habitual political behavior. In all likelihood, falling short of the general cultural norms of political attentiveness bothers most citizens very little and contributes only in the minutest way to their accumulated guilt and neuroses. But this normative tension explains the dynamics of the opinion-giving situation which serves as the basis for survey research interviews. The proxy voting and knowledge gap phenomena, for example, characterize the coping strategies of the mass citizenry. Since so much of the statistical analysis of survey and behavioral data is based on the assumption of normal distributions and linear relationships, an empirical approach to political stratification which does not take into account the unique character of these three groups can generate misleading conclusions.

This theory is analogous to the concept of political literacy. The apoliticals can be thought of as fundamentally illiterate, so they are naturally immune to repeated attempts to politicize and mobilize them. They lie below a critical threshold which puts them outside the flow of meaningful political communications. The middle mass can then be characterized as having modest literacy. They keep track of the most important issues with modest effort, but they lack the background information and rich vocabulary necessary for the quick and convenient processing of large amounts of political information. They can communicate political ideas, but they are hunt-and-peck typists. In contrast, the activists are avid readers and lucid speakers. Since virtually all of the professional politicians, journalists, and political analysts fall into the highest stratum, they may well share an ingrained incapacity to understand that the vocabulary of politics is interpreted in somewhat different ways by the middle mass, and in stumbling across this phenomenon from time to time, they may mistake the middle mass for the apolitical stratum at the bottom of the continuum.

One reason that large proportions of the electorate are relatively inattentive has to do with the fact that processing political information has costs. This is a central finding and is fundamental to the theory of three publics. Most citizens rationally minimize the time and effort required to monitor the political environment by a variety of strategies. They monitor fundamental issues, such as war, peace, and economic health, but having determined that a crisis is not at hand, they turn their attention to more immediate and directly rewarding pursuits:

> Rational citizens in an uncertain world are under great pressure to cut down the quantity of scarce resources they use to obtain political information . . . In any society marked by an extensive division of labor in the presence of uncertainty, the cost of information is bound to be different for different men. Hence the amount of data it is rational for one man to acquire can be much greater or smaller than the amount that is rational for another man to acquire. This conclusion is valid even when the returns from information are identical for all. (Downs, 1957, pp. 220, 236)

The information-processing strategies of the average citizen parallel the findings on decisionmaking in administrative organizations (Simon, 1947; Popkin et al., 1972). Unfortunately, the information costs perspective has not yet been integrated into the traditions of behavior and survey research. Thus far, the methodological disputes about issue voting have apparently overwhelmed the efforts of those who would redirect the inquiry.

Applying the notion of information cost explicitly to mass political behavior, however, puts traditional concerns in a new light. Proxy voting, for example, is generally identified as an unfortunate phenomenon. The notion of apolitical wives dependent on their husbands' advice, or of union members blindly following the voting instructions of their shop stewards, seems anathema to the basic ideals of civic duty. But from the information cost perspective, this behavior is rational and functional. When in doubt, ask someone who knows. It is unnecessary to recompile and reevaluate all the available political data when a trusted friend or colleague has already completed the task.

In a similar vein, when it appeared that General Eisenhower's avuncular personal characteristics substituted for the evaluation of his policy positions in the minds of the mass electorate, researchers were greatly concerned (Campbell et al., 1960). But in the absence of strongly differentiated policy positions, reliance on cues of personal competence and leadership ability is an entirely reasonable and rational strategy in voting. The reasonableness of proxy voting is confirmed by the fact that the middle level of political interest and knowledge, not the lowest one, is the level that exhibits the highest likelihood of proxy voting. Again, the critical swing voters and the protest voters are prominently represented in the middle and upper levels rather than at the lowest level of the sophistication continuum.

The picture of uninformed voters in the election booth staring vainly at their shoes in search of cues to help in their vote decision is in all likelihood not a hyperbole. No doubt in each election year, literally millions of crib sheets are taken into voting booths to help voters keep the names of the candidates straight. Such scenarios emphasize the information costs in mass political behavior, but they also reinforce a false dichotomy between uninformed proxy voters and well-informed, issue-oriented, rational voters. Proxy voting and reliance on nonissue cues to the competence of political candidates are all an important part of day-to-day political behavior throughout the full range of the sophistication continuum, from the least to the most informed.

The theory of three publics presumes a bottom stratum of apoliticals whose self-consistent world view leads them to ignore political stimuli and to avoid participating in political life. The middle and upper levels of sophistication are the groups that make the biggest difference in day-to-day political conflict. But within the theory of mass society, the concepts of mobilization and extremist politics draw attention to this bottom stratum (Kornhauser, 1959).

The term *know-nothings*, drawn originally from the American movement of the 1850s, has a straightforward meaning and has been incorporated into the survey research tradition: "All persons do not offer equal targets for information campaigns. Surveys consistently find that a certain proportion of the population is not familiar with any particular event. Offhand, it might be thought that information concerning that event was not distributed broadly enough to each of them, but . . . there is something about the uninformed which makes them harder to reach no matter what the level or nature of the information. . . . There exists a hard core of chronic 'know-nothings.' " (Hyman and Sheatsley, 1947, p. 413).

Marx had a similar concept of a bottom stratum "lumpenproletariat," which he felt was easily propagandized, manipulated, and mobilized to work against the interest of the working classes. He was explicit about the social character of this bottom stratum: "Vagabonds, discharged soldiers, discharged jailbirds, escaped galley slaves, swindlers, mountebanks, lazzaroni, pickpockets, tricksters, gamblers, procurers, brothel keepers, porters, literati, organ grinders, rag pickers, knife grinders, tinkers, beggars—in short, the whole indefinite, disintegrated mass, thrown hither and thither" (Marx, 1852, p. 75).

This notion of a gullible and mobilizable antidemocratic force lies at the core of mass society theory. Because the members of this apathetic stratum lack political experience, so the theory goes, at times of crisis they may turn out in large numbers to support a demagogue. Such are the critical weaknesses of extreme political stratification. Both established conservative authorities and revolutionaries like Marx eye this group suspiciously.

For the most part the findings run contrary to the mass society scenario. They are not definitive, however, because the theory posits the existence of a demagogic, charismatic, and antidemocratic leader, most prominently symbolized by Adolf Hitler. In the absence of a time of crisis and a demagogic appeal, therefore, the theory remains untested. The milder forms of demagogy represented by Senator Joseph McCarthy and Governor George Wallace give some perspective on the issue. In general, the protest voting associated with the support of McCarthy and Wallace came chiefly from the middle level of the sophistication continuum rather than the bottom stratum (Rogin, 1967; Converse et al., 1969). Under different historical conditions the results might have been different. But given the relatively mild political climate of the last three decades in the United

States, the know-nothing stratum remained largely out of earshot and unavailable for political appeals of all varieties. Perhaps even more than the rest of the public, discharged jailbirds and brothel keepers are preoccupied by the day-to-day concerns of personal economic survival and have little time for political life.

The general concerns of the mass society theory nevertheless persist. The notion that active participation in the cross-cutting cleavages of political life leads to self-restraint and political maturity is wishfully naive. Student activists of the extreme left in the 1960s and their conservative counterparts of the fundamentalist religious right, as well as other single-issue constituencies, contain many of the brightest, most articulate, and most politically aware members of their cohorts. The mass society theory has been looking for trouble at the wrong end of the sophistication continuum.

The notion of a knowledge gap emphasizes the disjuncture between the relatively high levels of voting participation and the relatively low levels of political information and knowledge. There is a further gap between voting and more active forms of political behavior. Although substantial majorities of the eligible population make their way to the polls each presidential election year, less than one in twenty manage to participate beyond voting.

If voters were rationally calculating the efficient use of their political efforts, they would spend more time in smaller political groups where their efforts are more likely to make a difference than contributing an infinitesimal fraction to the aggregate vote (Olson, 1965). The notion of information costs and rationally instrumental participation is correct as far as it goes. But political participation involves more than instrumental behavior.

The overlapping motivations for voting were highlighted in the 1964 presidential election (Lang and Lang, 1968). Media reports of early election returns potentially influence the behavior of those who have not yet made it to the polls, and in 1964, when the final results from the East confirmed a landslide for Lyndon Johnson while the polls were still open in the West because of time zone differences, large numbers of Californians voted late in the day in spite of, or possibly because of, having heard the news. Potential voters became more eager to vote, rather than discouraged, as a result of having heard about the returns from the East. Thus, voting is substantially a psychological expression of political partisanship by which individuals "go on record" as continuing to support their long-standing party affiliation. Voting is an expressive act and civic obligation independent of party affiliation:

Many, perhaps most, Americans grew up with the idea that voting for president is a sacred duty. Their positive attitude toward the responsibilities of citizenship develop long before they have specific perception of who the officeholders are and the functions they perform or of the parties and what each stands for. A person's sense of obligation to cast a ballot as an expression of his civic-mindedness prevails even when the vote appears to have no purpose, as in an uncontested election or one which offers the voters a choice between Tweedledee and

Tweedledum. Consequently the proportions among various population groups who vote in a presidential election reflect the prevalence of this general attitude. It is not very much affected by either the closeness of the race or the specific issues at stake. (Lang and Lang, 1968, p. 140)

The ritualistic nature of voting and public political participation parallels other collective ritual acts in primitive societies and in religion (Himmelstrand, 1960; Edelman, 1964; Milbrath, 1965). But the majority of voting studies and, by definition, all of the research on issue voting emphasize the voting act as a rational calculus. The instrumental and expressive components of the voting act are not clear-cut alternatives. The two overlap in the minds of most voters. On the instrumental side, it is unlikely that a citizen's vote will tip the scale and provide victory for one candidate over another. But a surprising number of elections in the United States are relatively close races, with candidates only a few percentage points apart, and like the sweepstakes participant who faces odds of a million to one, the individual voter is psychologically inclined to expect the unexpected. The blurred lines between voting as an instrumental and an expressive act help to put in perspective the disjuncture between voting and more active forms of political participation. Voting is culturally defined as an important, symbolic, civic duty; active participation in campaigns and contact with political authorities are not.

The question of the competence of the average citizen has served as a fulcrum of tension between the widely held egalitarian-democratic ideals and the persistent results of survey research on mass political behavior. Although the aggregate level of political sophistication in the United States is not necessarily below the critical threshold for a viable political system, it is less than one might prefer. The empirical analysis of political sophistication, however, should not be defined as the study of political pathology. If individuals opt not to vote or to pay much attention to the flow of political information, that may well be a rational and quite reasonable decision to marshal scarce resources and energies for other, more directly rewarding pursuits. The stratification of political attentiveness and involvement is a natural and inevitable factor of mass political life.

But because of the tension between the empirical reality and democratic norms and the tradition of survey research not to embarrass respondents, research on these issues has been awkwardly indirect and inferential. A coordinated and convergent effort at measuring political sophistication and knowledge might help to integrate democratic theory and empirical research. In time, agreed-upon measures of sophistication, like measures of party identification, could become fundamental variables in the empirical study of American politics. The measure of political sophistication used here turns out to be almost as stable over time as party identification, with self-correlations of .70 over a four-year period, compared to .80 for party identification. The roots of political sophistication are as deep in the socialization process, and its impacts on attitudes and behavior are as strong, as those of party affiliation.

Sophistication has important direct effects. It is strongly linked, for example, with both voting behavior and participation beyond voting. But a unique character of cognitive phenomena such as sophistication is their propensity toward interactive effects. That is, sophistication influences the nature of the relationships between other variables. This is critically important to the development of future research designs. Thus, if sophistication is defined as openness to political communications, it is not necessarily in itself a causal agent. For example, it will not cause protest behavior. But in those circumstances where there are political stimuli to mobilize protest among a particular political group, the most sophisticated strata of that group will be the first to perceive and respond to those stimuli. In this example, sophistication is the intervening, catalytic variable which increases the likelihood that one variable, the mobilization stimuli, will influence another variable, political behavior.

At the upper end of the sophistication continuum, congressmen, journalists, or private philanthropists might, in response to a relatively small story in the newspaper, be so sensitive to the political issue involved as to devote their primary energy in the following months to an attempt to get a bill passed or to raise public consciousness about a particular episode or issue. They represent the elite. They are intellectually, professionally, and financially able to respond. At the low end of the sophistication continuum, there are individuals with limited horizons and political vocabularies who, although they are aware of the importance of strong political stimuli, such as an impending war or economic depression, do not define these world events as amenable to political influence. They simply do not respond to political stimuli in political terms. The great bulk of the citizenry fall in between these two extremes. They frequently ignore large numbers of political stimuli. They frequently interpret political stimuli in nonpolitical terms. But on occasion they respond to a political appeal by contributing time or money. More frequently, perhaps, they make a mental note that a particular event or issue ought to be taken into account the next time a major election rolls around.

Neither conservatives nor liberals are, in general, more sophisticated than the other, although both liberals and conservatives have strong intuitively based, if divergent, perceptions to the contrary. The fact of the matter is that increasing sophistication does not lead to either conservatism or liberalism. Political ideologues of both the left and the right often appear to be anything but sophisticated because of their overreliance on simplistic catchphrases. At the same time, there are others among the citizenry who can outline the case for a conservative or liberal policy with the subtlety, thoroughness, and persuasiveness of a well-trained lawyer.

As is familiar from the legal profession, when one digs deeper into a particular case or policy issue, one can find factual examples, legal norms, and philosophical principles that might be used to support either side. Most policy debates entail trade-offs between important values, such as equity and efficiency. When liberals and conservatives differ, it is usually because their priorities among those values are different, not because the facts and principles of the matter are so obvious as to lead the sophisticated mind to an inevitable conclusion.

Issues and Nonissues

Imprecise language about what constitutes a political issue has been a principal contributor to controversy over the nature of mass politics. Examples are legion. The McCarthy era of the early 1950s in American politics was characterized by a generalized public concern, perhaps even paranoia, over the presence of Communist sympathizers or party members in positions of authority. Senator McCarthy did not invent the issue of communism, but he discovered its spectacular ability to thrust him onto the front pages of the nation's newspapers and to lead him to be described as the most influential individual in Washington next to the President, indeed to have the era named after him. The cold war dominated the international scene, the war in Korea brought it to the attention of the mass electorate in the most vivid and visceral terms, and the headlines daily echoed the charges and countercharges swirling about the senator from Wisconsin.

These were strong political stimuli indeed. But when in 1954 members of the public were asked about their fears and hopes for the future of their own lives and their country, less than 2 percent mentioned the issue of communism (Stouffer, 1955). The lesson is clear. Communism per se is not an issue. It is intimately intertwined with issues of both domestic and foreign policy. It is a political symbol of emotional weight, but it is not in itself an issue. The irony of data of this sort derives from the attempt to condense the jumble of assumptions, symbols, concerns, and strategic trade-offs that attend the historical fact of international communism into a single survey question.

Likewise, such recent historical concerns as civil rights, Vietnam, and even Watergate involved complexities and subtleties not easily captured by survey items. Lyndon Johnson, for example, was able to pull a survey from his pocket and point with pride to the clear "fact" that the majority of American citizens supported "our boys fighting in Vietnam." At the same time, other surveys revealed that an overwhelming majority of the electorate felt it was a mistake to have become involved in Vietnam in the first place.

One fundamental lesson which can be drawn from the distinction between issues and nonissues is a recognition of the procrustean character of the issue-voting model. As legend has it, Procrustes was a highwayman from ancient Attica who would stretch or abbreviate his victims when they did not conform to the length of his iron bed. One need not pause to examine the psychological roots of Procrustes' fixation on precision and order. But the vividness of the legend brings special power to the adjective procrustean.

The issue-voting model requires researchers to impute rationality to a subset of voters based on the apparent correlations between the issue preferences of the voters and the positions of the candidates. Issue perceptions and party identification are causally intertwined, and some individuals may "rationalize" a vote decision by bringing their own and their chosen candidate's perceived positions into alignment after the fact. Furthermore, although voters and candidates may thus agree on some issues, such issues may be neither salient nor relevant to the vote decision. To review a series of political issues one at a time exaggerates the importance of issue voting by continually reapportioning the same observed variance.

The issue-voting model does unfortunate violence to the realities of mass political behavior. Trying to estimate the rationality and in turn the sophistication of public choice from fragmentary correlations between candidate and voter on policy issues is both unpromising and misleading. If the underlying concern of democratic theory is with the average voter's understanding of fundamental policy issues, then knowledge and understanding of issues should be measured directly.

Research on the role of issues in voting behavior is proceeding apace but is moving away from the original model of issue voting which calculates and adds together the distances between voters' opinions and the perceived positions of the candidates. The new work emphasizes political cognition, the distinction between issues and nonissues, the importance of symbolic politics, and the difficulty of rationally calculating which candidate might best serve a voter's self-interest (Fiorina, 1981; Conover and Feldman, 1984a-b; Anderson, 1985; Brady, 1985; Kinder and Sears, 1985; Miller, 1985; Sniderman et al., 1985).

Ironically, it is often in the interest of politicians to be as vague as possible when speaking out on public issues. In a two-party system both parties tend to maximize their vote appeal by adopting centrist positions. But there are systematic constraints on this practice, for if all parties adopted precisely centrist positions on all possible policy matters, the electorate would become increasingly frustrated and withdrawn. At the same time, if one party ventured toward an extremist position, it might well lose more than it gained in vote appeal. The gap between the need to appear articulate and the dangers of being too specific is often filled by artful ambiguity. Political strategists gain the most if their language can give the impression of a resonance with the opinions of voters while avoiding actually taking a position. Political rationality, in short, "leads political parties in a two-party system to becloud their policies in a fog of ambiguity" (Downs, 1957, p. 136).

A recent study disclosed that a striking feature of candidates' rhetoric is its extreme vagueness: "The typical campaign speech says virtually nothing specific about policy alternatives; discussions of the issue are hidden away in little-publicized statements and position papers. Even the most extended discussions leave many questions unanswered; in short, policy stands are infrequent, inconspicuous and unspecific" (Page, 1978, p. 153). On thirty-three issue areas during the 1968 presidential campaign, Humphrey made a policy proposal in the average-issue area in 6 percent of his speeches, and Nixon did so in 4 percent. And many of the "issue positions" were one-line allusions to positions taken elsewhere. Even these rare references to an issue seldom involved an unambiguous policy. In a major speech on economic policy, for example, Nixon, after criticizing the evils of inflation and lambasting the Democrats for causing it, concluded that he favored a "responsible fiscal policy." Given the backdrop of criticizing Democratic overspending, Nixon might be assumed to have meant budget cuts, but he never actually said so (Page, 1978).

In view of the fact that candidates pound the podium, list numerous issues as being important, and routinely promise to take appropriate action without explaining in detail what they have in mind, the voters' strategy of semiattentiveness makes perfect sense. Paying more attention does not mean that they will actually learn more about the candidates' positions, understand better the political controversies of the day, or use the machinery of electoral politics more effectively.

One of the central findings about the nature of political pluralism is the scarcity of issues on the public agenda at any point in time. Most individuals can handle no more than seven factors simultaneously in the process of decisionmaking (Miller, 1956). Given the diversity of individuals involved and the complexity of social and political institutions, such a limitation theoretically need not apply in the aggregate. But in order for an issue to have a meaningful impact in the electoral arena, though it need not attract the attention of a majority of voters, some meaningful plurality is required.

The 1980 election is typical. Respondents were asked, "As you know, the government faces many serious problems in this country and in other parts of the world. What do you personally feel are the most important problems the government in Washington should try to take care of?" They were encouraged to give up to three answers to that question, and their responses were indeed diverse, including over 300 distinct issues. But the number of issues receiving prominent attention was small. Inflation was the prominent concern, reflecting 19 percent of total issues mentioned, the Iranian hostage crisis and unemployment were tied for second place at 11 percent, and national defense was noted in 6 percent of the responses. Two other issues, the energy crisis and foreign affairs, garnered 3 percent of the responses, and the remaining issues did not exceed 2 percent. Most of the other issues mentioned were of potential political significance, including such obvious questions as the Middle East, civil protection, mass transportation, immigration policy, and taxes. But they did not aggregate to significant political prominence.

The magic number seven may not be far off the mark for the aggregate public agenda. It is literally true that massive events like Watergate, Vietnam, and the Iranian hostage crisis, by grabbing the headlines and filling the front pages, push other ongoing political issues to the back pages of the paper, to the end of the television newscasts, and to the deeper recesses of public consciousness.

The distribution of public issues is similar to the distribution of political sophistication in the mass electorate (Figure 2). Though the shape of the curves differs a bit, the dynamic of the movement of issues up and down the curve is perhaps as significant to understanding the process of mass politics as the fundamental character of the sophistication curve. Whatever the universe of potential political issues is, the number receiving prominent attention is infinitesimal. It is not the shape of the curve but the movement of issues within it that keeps the political system as a whole alert and responsive.

Attitudes and Nonattitudes

There are three schools of thought on the use of survey research data. The first school, those scholars, pollsters, and marketing researchers who use survey research heavily, routinely gloss over the weaknesses of the methodology. The second school, those

Figure 2. Evolution of Public Issues

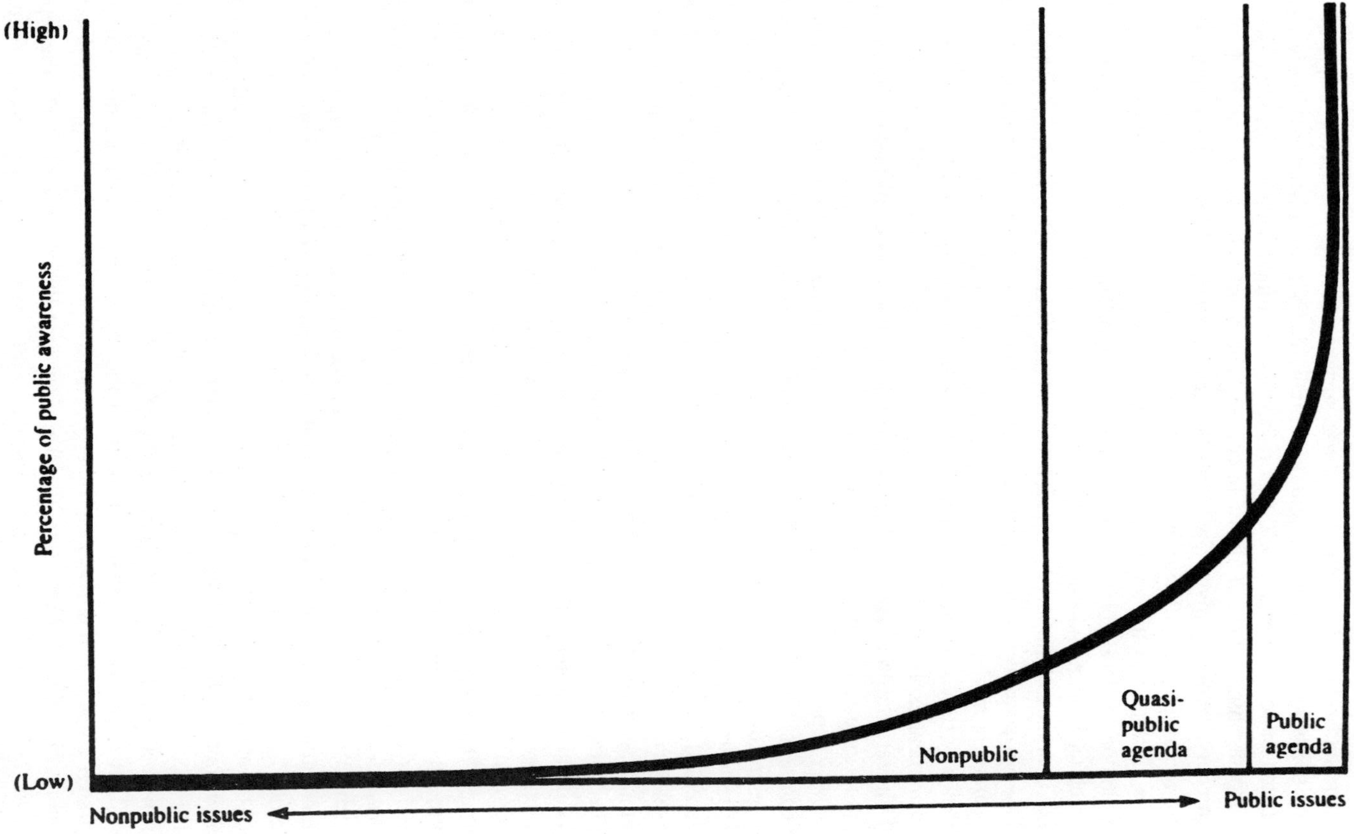

Percentage of public awareness

(High)

(Low)

Public
agenda

Quasi-
public
agenda

Nonpublic

Public issues

Nonpublic issues

scholars and researchers who do not use survey research, are deeply skeptical of its ability to assess the beliefs and opinions of individuals in a realistic way. These scholars are much more comfortable with the richer research methodologies of the case study, participant observation, or depth interview. The third school is comprised of those researchers, including myself, who use survey research but feel uneasy about it. This group represents a small cluster of researchers who, in addition to sharing a sense of unease, feel that, with appropriate refinements and necessary qualifications in the presentation of data, survey research has an important role to play in social science research (Schuman and Presser, 1981).

The character of the survey research method deeply colors the conclusions drawn from it. This is especially true for public attitudes and political life. Researchers should build a measurement model at the same time they attempt to build a model of social processes. In that way they can incorporate their understanding of the limitations and biases of measurement explicitly into their theorizing about the real world (Blalock, 1982).

It appears that the emperor has no attitudes. That wonderful fable of the emperor strutting in his underwear at the front of the parade offers a poignant lesson. It is an especially popular tale among children who understand instantly the basic psychology of pretending to know or see something in response to social expectations. In the fable, a pair of greedy and conniving tailors manipulate the emperor, his court, and the public, and then shrewdly leave the kingdom before the truth is out. In the case of public opinion research, the perpetrators are neither shrewd nor conniving. They are more like the Lockele drummers of the Congo who refused to believe that Europeans did not also communicate by drums.

The parallel with the underdressed emperor is nevertheless a limited one. Most citizens do have carefully developed opinions on some issues and partial or vague opinions on most issues. Cautious survey research, after offering respondents every opportunity to volunteer that they do not have an opinion on a particular issue, finds routinely that 80 percent of the respondents insist on offering one. Furthermore, these opinion distributions are stable in the aggregate over time and correlate in modest degree with the traditional demographic and behavioral variables. This is not a conspiracy; it is a paradox.

Perhaps these phenomena could best be termed quasi-attitudes. The measured public opinion on an issue is a mixture of carefully thought out, stable opinions, half-hearted opinions, misunderstandings, and purely random responses. In the case study of attitudes toward federal involvement in power and housing, respondents were divided into a clear dichotomy of stable versus random opinions and, by inference, an equally clear division between attitudes and nonattitudes (Converse, 1970). The item dealt with an unusually abstract and philosophical issue of government involvement in private enterprise. Thus, the estimate that 80 percent of the responses were either no-opinions or random is atypical and not necessarily characteristic of other issues. Other more salient and concrete political objects, such as the incumbent President or the enduring reputations of the major political parties, stimulate more structured and persisting opinions from the electorate, with only 20 percent expressing no opinion or offering random responses. Measured public opinion on most other issues falls somewhere between these two extremes, with from 20 to 80 percent basing their response on quasi-attitudes, a mixture of guesswork, various linguistic cues in the question wording, and the context of the item in the questionnaire. They are not strictly random. The same question wording and questionnaire context may well generate the same response if the question is later repeated. But because of the ambiguities of the language and the loose linkage between the question and the basic political beliefs held by the respondents, the question response is relatively labile.

The problem of quasi-attitudes is that they are not easily identified. Nonattitudes, quasi-attitudes, and true attitudes blur into one another. Even in response to sustained encouragement from the interviewer, most respondents cannot themselves distinguish their more deeply rooted opinions from those less clearly tied to basic political beliefs. Opinion stability over time does not help much in separating true from quasi-attitudes because there are a variety of nonpolitical as well as political sources of attitude consistency over time.[2]

Survey research ought to rely as often as possible on procedures that identify the opinion pattern for the population as a whole, as well as for smaller subpublics for whom, as best can be determined, the question at hand is politically salient and meaningfully linked to persisting political beliefs and values. Such procedures, in effect, take pluralism seriously.

Paradox Redux

This book has come full circle to the paradox of mass politics, namely, how the political system works as well as it does given the low level of political awareness and knowledge in the mass electorate. Since a paradox is by definition the simultaneous existence of two logically incompatible phenomena, the options for resolving the paradox are to discount the first phenomenon, discount the second, or demonstrate that they are not in fact incompatible. Skeptics might conclude that the average citizen is neither thoughtful nor informed, that such behaviors are incompatible with democratic theory, and that the system does not work very well. Optimists would disagree, observing that mass democracy requires a modestly attentive and knowledgeable public, the system in fact works quite well, and the data used to demonstrate low levels of public sophistication are erroneous, resulting from poorly designed research methods.

In fact, however, both of the propositions are correct: the mass public is for the most part uninterested and unsophisticated, and in consideration of that fact, the system does indeed work remarkably well. The political elites of this country perceive and act within the constraints of an attentive public will. Even for those many obscure and narrowly defined issues which are clearly not in the public eye, the elected and administrative elites have the shared sense that such issues could move into the public eye quite quickly, and they behave accordingly. There is a very small, attentive top stratum of the mass public which is paying close attention, writing letters, and making its presence felt in Washington along with the professional lobbying establishment. The paradox is resolved because the two phenomena are not incompatible.

The key finding is that the mass public is stratified along a sophistication continuum. On most issues, the great majority of citizens are inattentive and uninformed. But, as with many social phenomena of this sort, there is a natural and effective division of labor. The division is not properly described as pluralism, because that term would imply that all citizens have developed a sophisticated opinion in specialized areas and are aligned with a demographic or organized interest group which connects them to the centers of power.

A more appropriate model is that of three publics. The bottom stratum includes the roughly 20 percent of the population who do not monitor the political realm at all and are unlikely to be mobilized to political action by even the most extreme political crisis or case of economic self-interest. At the top of the continuum is a group of active and attentive individuals, who represent approximately 5 percent of the population. For many political matters the effective size of this group could be much smaller, measuring a fraction of 1 percent of the population as a whole. The great majority of the population lie between these two extremes and monitor the political process half-attentively, but they can be alerted if fellow citizens sound the political alarm. Over the past thirty years such issues as Vietnam, Watergate, civil rights, women's rights, and a multitude of more narrowly defined issues have risen to public attention and then receded from it. The dynamism of the political agenda, the fluid movement of issues from obscurity to prominence, is a critical factor in resolving the paradox of mass politics (Neuman and Fryling, 1985).

This paradox involves the tension between the workings of the polity in aggregate, which seems to give evidence of a certain energy, intelligence, and alertness to political issues, and of the individual citizen, who does not:

> In real life, no one acts on the theory that he can have a public opinion on every public question . . . The purpose, then, is not to burden every citizen with expert opinions on all questions, but to push that burden away from him towards the responsible administrator . . . The private citizen, beset by partisan appeals for the loan of his Public Opinion, will soon see, perhaps, that these appeals are not an appeal to his intelligence . . . As his civic education takes account of the complexity of his environment, he will concern himself about the equity and the sanity of procedure, and even this he will in most cases expect his elected representative to watch for him . . . Only by insisting that problems shall not come up to him until they have passed through a procedure, can the busy citizen of a modern state hope to deal with them in a form that is intelligible. (Lippmann, 1922, pp. 250–252)

Lippmann's language emphasizes the notion of formal procedure. Actually, the complex process of setting the public agenda and the rise and decline of public issues involves a number of informal elements as well. The citizen depends on personal friends and colleagues as well as formally designated representatives for cues of what is important enough politically to require attention. The principal difference between Lippmann's perspective on the paradox and the one put forward here is the emphasis in this analysis on the shape of the stratification curve. Lippmann described a single entity, the public, and contrasted it with the corresponding role of public official. But the evidence reviewed here points to the potentially pivotal role of an informally defined activist elite within the mass public.

Ironically, because of the standard sampling procedures of survey research, there are only hints and fragments of evidence about this activist elite. Both the apolitical and the mass publics are large enough to provide ample proportions in a survey data to make their character evident. A special survey design that oversamples the activist group will be necessary to follow up the evidentiary fragments with systematic inquiry. The conflict between seeing the essence of politics in the activities of the elite stratum and seeing it in the slower tidal movements of the full electorate needs to be reformulated. The essence of politics lies in the subtle interactions between the elite stratum and the mass public.

Schumpeter, two decades after Lippmann, came to a similar conclusion in confronting the paradox. He contrasted a naive model of mass democracy with a revised model emphasizing the *modus procedendi* of elite-mass interaction: "Most students of politics have by now come to accept the criticisms leveled at the classical doctrine of democracy . . . centered in the proposition that 'the people' hold a definite and rational opinion about every individual question" (Schumpeter, 1942, p. 269). Schumpeter describes how the workings of the system in aggregate overcome the limitations of the individual citizen.

If Lippmann and Schumpeter are still read and cited today—and they certainly seem to be—how is it that their message is so little heard? Survey research is not the culprit. It provides a very limited picture of the political process; but so do the other methodological approaches, including depth interviews with political activists. The culprit is perhaps the premium paid to specialized single-method research. One scholar becomes a specialist in the study of political parties or bureaucracies using case studies and institutional analysis. Another becomes a public opinion analyst and survey researcher. The two need not define their areas of interest as overlapping, and frequently they do not. In some measure the insights of Lippmann and Schumpeter find little resonance in modern research because such ideas run against the grain of the dominant methodologies.

The character of American political stratification also explains differences between American and other political cultures. One of the most frequent lessons of comparative politics is the fragile character of democratic institutions. The rare longevity of democratic institutions distinguishes the American case (Verba and Nie, 1972; Verba et al., 1978). The level of voluntary political stratification in the American system is as high as or higher than other developed political systems. In many marginally democratic or nondemocratic political systems, individual citizens shrug off corruption or unresponsiveness in their government, explaining either that it is not their concern or that they can do little. It is the persistent character of the American political culture to assume that, when a crisis arises, the citizenry will mobilize and respond. This is a political culture of naiveté. The widely shared naiveté shapes the character of the American political system, elites and middle strata alike.

There is another irony that emerges from the stratification of American politics. The average citizens feel that they need not study a political issue in depth in order to have a meaningful opinion on it. People find it quite natural to be asked about matters of foreign affairs and budgetary policy and to have their opinions listened to and taken seriously. Such norms are reflected in the American jury system. There is a fundamental belief that, if the populace are given the opportunity to review the facts of a case in a fair and open setting, their aggregate judgment is equal to, and in many cases preferable to, the unconstrained opinion of even the most brilliant jurists the legal system can provide.

Senator Roman Hruska was widely ridiculed when in 1970 he defended the mediocrity of Nixon's new nominee to the Supreme Court by commenting, "There are a lot of mediocre judges and people and lawyers. They are entitled to a little representation, aren't they? We can't have all Brandeises, Frankfurters, and Cardozos." The ridicule in this case was well deserved. But those many citizens who insist that they would rather be governed by the first two thousand names in the telephone book than by the faculty of Harvard University do not speak from a lack of political wisdom. In fact, they put the issue in a new light. There is a dynamic balance between the special talents of the political elite and the political system which generates the elite. It remains important to balance the specialized knowledge of the elite and the generalized common sense of the mass polity.

There is an American tradition of the man from Missouri who has to be shown. This self-made individual of rural origins and modest education is unimpressed by the sophistry and abstractions of aloof political debate. His attention focuses on the bottom line. Similarly, the unsophisticated citizen enters the voting booth, goes through the straightforward mental calculations of deciding whether the country is in an economic recession or at war, and, if it is not, votes for the incumbent. This style of political thought is not a bad yardstick in comparison with the vagaries of most campaign rhetoric. These considerations need not be the only ones to enter the voter's mind. Discussions with friends and a casual monitoring of an open political communication system will from time to time bring other concerns to the attention of the typical voter. Personal, nonpolitical concerns may also enter this voter's mind. But if an issue of fundamental political significance comes to the fore, the average voter in particular and the electorate in general are likely to recognize it as such.

NOTES

1. The methodologists and philosophers of science have put forward explicit definitions of what is and is not a "theory" (Hemple, 1952; Nagel, 1961; Kaplan, 1964). The theory derived here does not offer rigorously derived, lawlike hypotheses and corollaries. It rather poses a set of

issues and a corresponding set of operationalized core variables which allow for empirical testing. The theory draws from the original paradox a concern with the basic elements of democratic theory, in particular, the meaningful participation of the mass public in modern politics. It pays special attention to the political cognition of the individual citizen. Thus, while other voting research has emphasized demographic variables or the role of political parties, the emphasis of this research is on sophistication as the core variable.

2. Perhaps the best available approach to this problem, though expensive and time consuming, is the use of multi-item indices. The apparent correlation between any two opinion indices will appear to be reassuringly strong, in the range of .20 to as high as .50. But the mathematics of most linear correlation coefficients relies heavily on the top strata of respondents whose responses are consistently distant from the mean. For the purposes of these coefficients, the 20 to 80 percent of the population who either register no opinion or lie close to the population mean are, in statistical terms, almost irrelevant.

REFERENCES

Anderson, K. (1985). *Causal Schemas in Political Thinking*. Paper presented at Midwest Political Science Association. Chicago, IL.

Berelson, B., Lazarsfeld, P., and McPhee, W. (1954). *Voting: A Study of Opinion Formation in a Presidential Campaign*. Chicago: University of Chicago Press.

Blalock, H. (1982). *Conceptualization and Measurement in the Social Sciences*. Beverly Hills, CA: Sage.

Brady, H. E. (1985). *Chances, Utilities, and Voting in Presidential Primaries*. Occasional Paper No. 85-5. Cambridge, MA: Center for American Political Studies, Harvard University.

Campbell, A., Converse, P. E., Miller, W. E., and Stokes, D. E. (1960). *The American Voter*. New York: Wiley.

Conover, P. J. and Feldman, S. (1984a). How people organize the political world: A schematic model. *American Journal of Political Science*, 28(Feb.), 95–126.

———. (1984b). *Where Do They Stand? Inference Processes and Political Perception*. Paper for Annual Meeting of American Political Science Association, Washington, D.C.

Converse, P. E., Miller, W. E., Rusk, J. G., and Wolfe, A. C. (1969). Continuity and change in American politics: Parties and issues in the 1968 election. *American Political Science Review*, 63, 1083–1105.

Converse, P. E. (1970). Attitudes and non-attitudes: The continuation of a dialogue. In E. Tufte (Ed.), *The Quantitative Analysis of Social Problems* (pp. 168–189). Reading, MA: Addison-Wesley.

Dahl, R. (1963). *Modern Political Analysis*. Englewood Cliffs, NJ: Prentice Hall.

Downs, A. (1957). *An Economic Theory of Democracy*. New York: Harper and Row.

Edelman, M. (1964). *Symbolic Uses of Politics*. Urbana, IL: University of Illinois Press.

Fiorina, M. (1981). *Retrospective Voting in American National Elections*. New Haven, CT: Yale University Press.

Hemple, C. (1952). Fundamentals of concept formation in empirical science. *International Encyclopedia of United Science*, 2, 7.

Himmelstrand, U. (1960). *Social Pressures, Attitudes, and Democratic Processes.* Stockholm: Almquist and Wiksell.

Hyman, H. H. and Sheatsley, P. B. (1947). Some reasons why information campaigns fail. *Public Opinion Quarterly, 11*(3), 412–423.

Kaplan, A. (1964). *The Conduct of Inquiry.* San Francisco: Chandler.

Kinder, D. R. and Sears, D. O. (1985). Public opinion and political action. In G. Lindzey and E. Aronson (Eds.), *The Handbook of Social Psychology* (vol. 2, pp. 659–741). New York: Random House.

Kornhauser, W. (1959). *The Politics of Mass Society.* New York: Free Press.

Lang, K. and Lang, G. (1968). *Politics and Television.* Chicago: Quadrangle Books.

Lippmann, W. (1922). *Public Opinion.* New York: Macmillan Free Press.

Marx, K. (1963). *The 18th Brumaire of Louis Bonaparte.* New York: International Publishers.

Milbrath, L. (1965). *Political Participation.* Chicago: Rand McNally.

Miller, G. A. (1956). The magical number seven, plus or minus two: Some limits on our capacity for processing information. *Psychological Review, 63,* 81–97.

Miller, A. (1985). *Information Processing and Political Candidates.* Paper for Midwest Political Science Association. Chicago.

Nagel, E. (1961). *The Structure of Science: Problems in the Logic of Scientific Explanation.* New York: Harcourt Brace and World.

Neuman, W. R. and Fryling, A. C. (1985). Patterns of political cognition: An exploration of the public mind. In S. Kraus and R. Perloff (Eds.), *Mass Media and Political Thought.* Beverly Hills, CA: Sage.

Olson, M. (1965). *The Logic of Collective Action: Public Goods and the Theory of Goods.* Cambridge, MA: Harvard University Press.

Page, B. (1978). *Choices and Echoes in Presidential Elections.* Chicago: University of Chicago Press.

Popkin, S. J., Gorman, J. W., Phillips, G., and Smith, J. A. (1972). Comment: What have you done for me lately? Toward an investment theory of voting. *American Political Science Review, 70,* 779–805.

Rogin, M. P. (1967). *The Intellectuals and McCarthy: The Radical Specter.* Cambridge, MA: MIT Press.

Schuman, H. and Presser, S. (1981). *Questions and Answers in Attitude Surveys: Experiments on Question Form, Wording, and Context.* New York: Academic Press.

Schumpeter, J. A. (1942). *Capitalism, Socialism, and Democracy* (Third ed.). New York: Harper and Row.

Simon, H. A. (1976). *Administrative Behavior.* New York: Free Press.

Sniderman, P. M., Hagen, M. G., Tetlock, P. E., and Brady, H. E. (1985). *Reasoning Chains: A Causal Model of Policy Reasoning in Mass Publics.* Working Paper No. 75. Berkeley, CA: Survey Research Center, University of California.

Stouffer, S. A. (1955). *Communism, Conformity, and Civil Liberties.* New York: Doubleday.

Verba, S. and Nie, N. H. (1972). *Participation in America.* New York: Harper and Row.

Verba, S., Nie, N., and Kim, J. (1978). *Participation and Political Equality.* New York: Cambridge University Press.

19

The American Ethos:
Public Attitudes Toward Capitalism
and Democracy

HERBERT MCCLOSKY and JOHN ZALLER

In the course of this book [*The American Ethos*] we have seen that the ideals to which the nation's Founders appealed—values such as freedom, equality, individualism, and private property—are, for the most part, still prized by Americans and their opinion leaders. Yet, despite this continuity, dramatic changes have occurred in the norms through which these general values have been translated into everyday practice. Suffrage, for example, once largely limited to white males who owned property, has been extended to include all adults, of both genders and of every race and religion; the right to speak, publish, and worship freely has been greatly expanded and strengthened; and the notion of equality has been extended to encompass women, blacks, and other dispossessed minorities as well as the poor.

Changes in the norms of capitalism have been equally dramatic: Americans have increasingly favored a form of capitalism in which the economy is subject to government regulation. Numerous laws now cover such matters as industrial and banking practice, labor relations, the hiring of minorities, the safety of manufactured products, protection against environmental damage, minimum wages and pension programs, and in some cases even the prices a business enterprise may charge for its products or services. The laissez-faire economy of the nineteenth century, in short, has given way to a more regulated economy in which business and government share responsibility for many key economic decisions.

These and related changes have transformed the federal government from an institution primarily concerned with domestic order and national security into a complex network of agencies that seeks to regulate the economy, protect the rights of the citizenry, and provide assistance to those unable to care for themselves. These changes in the practices of capitalism and democracy, however, have not developed in a steady stream. Rather, the nation has seemed, at least in this century, to swing from periods in which the values of capitalism are emphasized to other periods in which democratic values are stressed. The 1920s and 1950s, for example, were decades in which business values were dominant and matters of social and political equality excited relatively little public interest. During the decade of the 1930s, by contrast, unrestrained capitalism was on the defensive as Franklin D. Roosevelt and the New Deal pressed for greater popular control of the economy and a more equal distribution of the nation's wealth. Capitalism was again on the defensive in the 1960s and early 1970s, as public concern for such democratic values as the right of dissent, due process, and racial and sexual equality assumed a dominant position in the nation's politics. The early 1980s seemed to herald another swing toward capitalism, with the conservative administration of Ronald Reagan claiming to have received a popular mandate to revive individual initiative, reduce government regulation of the economy, reinforce the "work ethic," and promote business productivity by cutting taxes.[1]

These swings in the national mood reflect a strain that lies at the heart of the American ethos. While most Americans favor a competitive, private economy in which the most enterprising and industrious individuals receive the greatest income, they also want a democratic society in which everyone can earn a decent living and has an equal chance to realize his or her full human potential. Since these two sets of values often conflict with each other in practice, the mood of the country may shift from one era to another as the values of one tradition or the other predominate. In one period the nation may be shocked by society's failure to fulfill the democratic promise of American life for the poor, the unemployed, and other disadvantaged groups, and may accelerate its efforts to rectify this failure; in the next period, however, many people may complain that the nation has gone too far in pursuing these goals and may advocate a shift back toward a more conservative, laissez-faire, and procapitalist course.

There appears, however, to be a marked asymmetry in these swings: movements in the procapitalist direction have increasingly turned out to be little more than holding actions, efforts that have only temporarily halted a long-term trend toward government efforts to assist the needy, broader individual liberties, and greater popular control over the economy. Thus the gains made by the Coolidge, Hoover, and Eisenhower administrations on behalf of free enterprise capitalism in the 1920s and 1950s were largely undone by the liberal Democratic administrations that followed. National swings in the prodemocratic direction, by contrast, have tended to produce enduring changes in American life. Thus the Nixon and Ford administrations, despite their conservatism, showed little inclination to return to the policies of racial segregation or overt sexual discrimination that had prevailed in earlier decades. Nor, on balance, did they slow the movement toward social and economic equality implicit in the welfare state. And even though the Reagan administration succeeded in reversing certain policies relating to civil rights and the welfare state, it is doubtful that these reversals can be made permanent. By Reagan's third year in office, there were signs that the push to trim welfare spending and cut back federal regulation of the economy had run its course and that the pendulum had begun to swing back. The administration, for example, was unable to win congressional approval for further cutbacks in domestic spending, and was even being forced to accept the partial restoration of funds in some welfare programs.

The long-term result of this asymmetry is that norms relating to such democratic values as freedom of expression, due process of law, and equality of rights and opportunities are now more firmly entrenched and substantially broader in scope than they were in the nineteenth century, while the norms relating to the values of capitalism are more qualified and circumscribed. This is not to say that capitalist values have lost their standing in American public opinion; we have seen that this is clearly not the case. But in almost every sphere of economic enterprise, the regulation of business has grown far more extensive than it was in the past.

What this suggests is that the democratic tradition is more securely rooted in the nation's political culture than is the capitalist tradition. As further evidence for this claim, we might cite long-term changes in the arguments by which each tradition attempts to justify itself to the public. For example, the industrial tycoons of an earlier era claimed a virtually unlimited right to do whatever they wished with *their* property, *their* factories, *their* capital—and even *their* employees. As entrepreneurs, they declared their right to pursue profit in whatever manner they wished, and to force weaker competitors into submission. The public's needs or wishes were scarcely considered. The capitalists of that day felt no need to appeal to values outside the capitalist tradition itself; private enterprise and the associated values of property, competition, initiative, and hard work were their own justification. Today, however, businessmen express markedly different attitudes. Although they still claim to possess certain entrepreneurial rights, they no longer thunder about them as they once did. Indeed, the public defense of capitalism, for example, boasts that the system aims above all to serve the interests of the people. Businessmen condemn government regulation less because it interferes with their inalienable right to use their property as they wish, than because it allegedly leads to higher prices and wasteful inefficiencies that (they contend) the public ultimately pays for. In opposing high taxes on business profits, they no longer rest their argument solely on the claim that such taxes are unjust, but contend that low taxes will foster individual initiative and promote capital formation, thus leading to greater prosperity for all.

Some of these arguments, to be sure, are not new. The emphasis now given them, however, is far greater than in the past and testifies to the inability of modern capitalists to present themselves in the heroic postures so often assumed by their predecessors. Their reliance on democratic rhetoric reflects a realistic appreciation of the kinds of appeals that are most likely to succeed in the political arena. The proponents of democracy, on the other hand, rarely if ever appeal to values outside the democratic tradition itself. They assume that freedom, equality, and popular sovereignty are, in America at least, recognized as values that require no higher justification.

As a further indication of the stronger and more secure standing of the democratic tradition, one might compare the range of public debate over issues relating to capitalism with the range of debate over issues relating to democracy. With respect to capitalism, one can, of course, readily find respected public figures who advocate a return to laissez-faire. Elsewhere among the elites one encounters numerous people who, though accepting capitalism as an economic system, are highly critical of many of its features and want to modify them. Here and there among the elites, one can even find strong liberals and socialists who favor the public ownership of large industries, a greater role for workers in managing factories, and a major redistribution of wealth. Thus economic debate in the United States, though mainly occurring within relatively limited boundaries, ranges from support for laissez-faire to support for welfare capitalism or even a mixed economy with marked socialist features.

The range of elite debates over democracy is distinctly narrower. Except for a handful of political extremists, one finds few if any opinion leaders who openly oppose such values as freedom or equality or who advocate any form of authoritarian rule. No political parties of any standing in the United States advocate a one-party system, the abolition of elections, a government-controlled press, or the prohibition of dissent. Conservatives and liberals differ over the degree to which democratic values ought to be extended, but neither camp challenges the definitive features of democracy itself.

Data from our public opinion surveys offer further evidence on the relative standing of the two traditions. Table 1 shows that our opinion leaders—the principal repositories of the ethos—score higher than the general public in their support for democratic values, but not for capitalist values. Approximately 74 percent of the opinion leaders in our Opinions and Values study registered high scores on the scale of democratic values, compared with only 33 percent of the general population. On the capitalism scale, however, the scores of the opinion leaders were no higher than those of the general public. The same pattern of elite-mass differences turns up in our Civil Liberties study.

Is it possible, however, that the summaries of elite opinion reported in Table 1 conceal important differences among various elite subgroups? Table 2 enables us to evaluate this question by disaggregating our Civil Liberties elite samples into seven subgroups. Inspection of the data makes it plain that although elite subgroups vary considerably in their attitudes toward capitalism and democracy, certain uniformities exist. All seven elite subgroups score substantially ahead of the general public in support for both democratic values and the values of the welfare state. By contrast, differences between elite and mass support for capitalism are small and inconsequential. The same tendencies show up among the five elite subgroups in the OVS study. Among a broad range of politically active and influential Americans, then, the values of democracy and the welfare state enjoy greater support (at least by comparison with the attitudes of the mass public) than do capitalist values. Insofar as elites influence the course of the nation's

Table 1. Support for Capitalism, Democracy, and the Welfare State Among Elites and the General Public[a]

	Democracy	*Capitalism*	*Welfare state*
General public[b] (N = 938)	33	32	34
Opinion leaders[b] (N = 845)	74	30	69
General public[c] (N = 1,019)	33	30	37
Community influentials[c] (N = 856)	65	34	53

[a] Cell entries are percentage of each sample scoring high on each scale.
[b] Opinions and Values of Americans survey, 1975–77.
[c] Civil Liberties study, 1978–79.

development, they are likely to guide it toward a fuller realization of democratic values and—very likely—a more fully developed welfare state.

Other evidence suggesting the stronger relative standing of democratic values is reported in Table 3, where we see that young people are substantially more likely than their elders to register strong support for both democracy and the welfare state. They are also much less likely than their elders to support capitalism in its laissez-faire form. If the attitudes expressed by young people persist as they advance in age, the gradual replacement of older population cohorts by younger ones will in the future produce higher overall levels of support for democracy and the welfare state, and diminished support for laissez-faire capitalism.

But will the attitudes of the young in fact persist as they advance in age? This question, though vital for assessing future trends in support for capitalism and democracy, is difficult to answer. The crux of the problem is that one cannot be certain whether the differences in attitudes among age groups represent generational differences or life-cycle differences. In other words, do the differences between young and old represent differences in the prevailing values at the time they came to political maturity (and which they presumably carry forward into succeeding years), or do they represent changes that develop as individuals advance in age? Today's generation of older Americans, for example, attained political maturity during an era in which democratic values were less widely accepted than they are now, when the welfare state activities of the federal government were minimal or just beginning, and when private enterprise was still largely unfettered by regulatory laws. Today's generation of young adults, by contrast, attained political maturity in the aftermath of the civil rights and civil liberties activism of the 1960s, in a period in which laissez-faire capitalism had been superseded by the mixed economy of the modern welfare state. If (in keeping with the generational explanation) we assume that both young and old have been most deeply influenced by the

Table 2. Support for Capitalism, Democracy, and the Welfare State Among Elite Subgroups[a]

	General public (N = 1,019)	Lawyers and judges (N = 255)	Clergy (N = 61)	College professors and administrators (N = 65)	Editors and reporters (N = 58)	Elementary teachers and administrators (N = 107)	Officers of private organizations (N = 49)	Public officials (N = 47)	Total community influentials (N = 856)
Democracy	33	85	51	83	84	54	63	47	65
Capitalism	30	34	34	23	31	24	41	32	34
Welfare capitalism	37	50	60	62	52	50	54	53	53

SOURCE: Civil Liberties study, 1978–79.

[a] Cell entries are percentage of each subgroup scoring high on each scale.

Table 3. Effect of Age on Attitudes Toward Capitalism, Democracy, and the Welfare State[a]

	Ages 18–30 (N = 217)	Ages 31–45 (N = 284)	Ages 46–65 (N = 278)	Ages 66+ (N = 153)
Democracy	57	38	21	11
Capitalism	16	30	39	43
Welfare state	47	32	32	26

SOURCE: Opinions and Values of Americans survey, 1975–77.

[a] Cell entries are percentage of each age group scoring high on each scale.

values prevalent in their formative years, and subsequently reinforced by their age cohorts, the attitudes of the young would be bound to differ from those of their elders in ways consistent with the findings in Table 3. However, the findings reported in Table 3 are also consistent with a life-cycle explanation, which would argue that people become less liberal and less democratic as they grow older.

The two explanations, then, are not mutually exclusive: both are plausible and can be defended, and both appear to be at work. From the available evidence, we have reason to believe that the attitudes learned by the younger generation toward democracy, capitalism, and the welfare state will in some measure be carried forward into the next decades—even if they are somewhat attenuated by life-cycle changes. Studies of public attitudes toward freedom of speech and racial equality, as we noted in earlier chapters, have documented a dramatic rise in popular support for these values over the past two decades. These studies, moreover, have attributed a substantial part of this rise to generational replacement—that is, to the dying out of an older, less well educated, less tolerant generation and its replacement by younger, better educated, and more tolerant generations.[2]

Unfortunately, no comparable studies of age-related differences have been conducted on attitudes toward capitalism or the welfare state. It seems highly unlikely, however, that Americans will in the foreseeable future favor a return to laissez-faire capitalism or countenance the dismantling of the welfare state. Our data on elite opinions offer little evidence that political leaders would be sympathetic to a sustained conservative shift of this kind. Moreover, to judge from our findings, most Americans have become thoroughly accustomed to, and dependent on, the services of the welfare state—including unemployment insurance, government controls of pollution, consumer protection services, old age and health insurance, federal savings insurance, and dozens of other such regulations and services. Since elderly citizens benefit greatly from many of these programs, there will be little incentive for Americans to turn against "welfare capitalism" as they advance in age.

In sum, our data provide reasons to expect that, ceteris paribus, the process of generational replacement will lead to higher levels of popular support for democratic values, as well as continued and possibly greater support for some form of the welfare state.

The popularity of democratic values in the nation's political culture, which we have now documented in a variety of ways, takes on particular significance in light of the potential conflicts between the values of capitalism and democracy. That is, the high standing of democratic values suggests that any conflicts that arise are likely to be resolved in ways that are more favorable to democracy than to capitalism. But what are the chances that serious conflicts *will* arise between capitalism and democracy in the future? And if such conflicts do develop, what kinds of modifications in American institutions are likely to result?

In regard to the first question, the intensity of conflict between the two traditions in the past has depended mainly on the performance of capitalist institutions. When capitalism has been associated with a relatively broad distribution of economic opportunities and a fair measure of social equality—as it was in the early nineteenth century—conflict between the two traditions, while by no means absent, has not been severe. At times, however, capitalism has produced—or has seemed to produce—dramatic inequalities between the rich and the poor, attempts by the business classes to dominate the government, and a narrow range of opportunities for debtors, workers, small farmers, and the unpropertied classes generally. Under such circumstances, democratic values have been invoked in order to justify reforms of the free enterprise system.

If the American private enterprise system performs fitfully in the future, exacerbating rather than reducing the serious social and economic inequalities that still exist, further efforts are likely to be made to modify capitalism, even at the expense of violating some of its most cherished values. And even if capitalism performs fairly well, providing a comfortable standard of living for most people but failing to provide adequately for the disadvantaged, pressure for economic reform would, in our view, still exist. In keeping with the growing strength of the egalitarian elements of the ethos, Americans are increasingly reluctant to ignore completely the needs of the poor, or to dismiss some members of society as simply not worth worrying about . . . 78 percent of the public affirm that "all people are equally worthy and deserve equal treatment," while only 7 percent say that the poor "don't have much to contribute to society."

We are not suggesting, of course, that the favored economic classes are about to become crusaders for economic justice and a redistribution of wealth. That is an unlikely prospect. Our belief, rather, rests on what we have discovered about the attitudes of opinion leaders. With the exception of conservative elites, virtually every elite subgroup we have been able to study exhibits a strong commitment to the values of democracy and the welfare state but tempers its support for the values of capitalism by deep-seated skepticism about what private enterprise can accomplish when left unregulated by government.[3] Many members of the opinion elite, moreover, regard the existence of a sizable underclass of impoverished citizens as a standing indictment of the economic system that has produced them. When, as a result of normal swings in the nation's mood and voting tendencies, some of these liberally inclined elites come to power, they will attempt to mobilize public support for a renewed assault on the poverty and cultural deprivation that the private enterprise system has been unable to eliminate on its own. In view of the widespread support for egalitarian values that we have been able to document in this study, there is reason to believe that such appeals for economic reform will meet with a fair degree of success.

Having argued that the future of capitalism depends on its effectiveness in producing and equitably distributing the goods and services Americans expect, we should nevertheless add that it is difficult to know exactly how well capitalism must perform in order to forestall major efforts at economic reform. Judgments about "how good is good enough" are obviously subjective—and liberals and conservatives, laissez-faire capitalists and socialists, will reach different conclusions when making those judgments. Objective indicators of the performance of capitalism—indexes of inflation, unemployment, levels of productivity, income distribution, and the nation's standard of living— are bound to affect judgments about the necessity for economic reform. But in the end, the decision about how well capitalism must perform in order to forestall significant changes will be a political judgment, with all the uncertainty that such assessments entail.

If the performance of the capitalist economy appears to falter, and if efforts are therefore made to reform it, what kinds of changes are likely to result? One probability is that even if capitalism falters badly, Americans will be reluctant to press for the abolition or wholesale transformation of the economic system. As we have seen, most Americans continue to support the basic values of the capitalist economy and strongly reject recommendations for change along socialist lines, such as wage leveling or public ownership of the means of production. A second point, easy to overlook, is that given the nation's political traditions, the impulse to economic reform might initially result in pressures for "more capitalism" rather than less. As the Reagan administration has demonstrated, one approach to a faltering economy is to prescribe a return to laissez-faire. For some, this prescription is an appealing one: it preserves the basic features of capitalism, diminishes the size of government, promises to lower taxes, and reduces government intervention in economic affairs.

If, however, the free enterprise system fails to deliver on the promises made by its proponents, new efforts to modify it seem inevitable. These efforts are likely to take the form of renewed pressure for some version of welfare capitalism—a system in which the basic institutions of private enterprise are retained, but in which government plays a major role in regulating the economy and redirecting resources to individuals, groups, and even business enterprises in need of help. We say this because our data make it plain that Americans favor most of the specific programs associated with welfare capitalism. Study after study has shown that while Americans continue to express distaste for big government, they nonetheless repeatedly call upon government to alleviate the problems that arise when capitalism is left to operate on its own. This attitude, as we have seen, is especially prevalent among liberal and democratic elites. These opinion leaders, though for the most part committed to fundamental capitalist values, believe that government has a moral responsibility to correct whatever inequities and abuses arise from the workings of the private enterprise system.

Popular expectations that government will intervene to correct social and economic injustice and to ensure at least minimum standards of personal well-being have continued to rise among the American public for the past half-century. Over time, they are bound to rise even further in response to the play of democratic forces and the competition among elites for public favor. As the size of the attentive, educated, and democratically oriented public expands and becomes increasingly articulate in its demands, a freely elected government cannot help but respond. Notwithstanding the efforts of conservative administrations to scale back the welfare state and to reinstate laissez-faire, pressure from both elites and the general population for the reestablishment or expansion of government services to which several generations have become habituated is likely to prove irresistible. Our argument, then, can be summarized as follows: conflicts between capitalism and democracy remain a recurrent feature of American life; when these conflicts surface, they are likely to be resolved in ways predominantly favorable to the democratic tradition; and some type of welfare capitalism is the institutional form this resolution is likely to take.

NOTES

1. For discussions of whether it is reasonable to interpret the 1980 election as a "mandate" for conservative policies, see Stanley Kelley, Jr., *Interpreting Elections* (Princeton, N.J.: Princeton University Press, 1983); Warren Miller and J. Merrill Shanks, "Policy Directions and Presidential Leadership: Alternative Interpretations of the 1980 Presidential Election," *British Journal of Political Science*, 12 (1982), pp. 299–356.
2. See James A. Davis, "Communism, Cohorts, Conformity, and Categories: American Tolerance in 1954 and 1972–73," *American Journal of Sociology*, 81 (November 1975), pp. 491–513; D. Garth Taylor, Paul Sheatsley, and Andrew Greeley, "Attitudes toward Racial Integration," *Scientific American* (June 1978), pp. 42–50.
3. Obviously, one could locate vocational or ideological subgroups (for example, bankers, conservative activists) who would exhibit extraordinarily high levels of support for capitalist values. We believe, however, that the twelve occupational subgroups in the OVS and Civil Liberties studies are broadly representative of American elite opinion.

20

Participation and Equality: Who Gets What and How?

SIDNEY VERBA and NORMAN H. NIE

The theme of this book [*Participation in America*] has been political participation in America: What is it? Who does it? What difference does it make? We have tried to answer these questions in the framework of some general considerations about processes associated with participation. This in turn leads to a consideration of some fundamental issues and dilemmas of democracy.

The extent of democracy in a nation is often measured by the availability of political rights: the right to vote, to hold office, to speak up and challenge incumbent leadership, to associate freely with one's fellow citizens in political activity. The history of democratic government can be traced in terms of the extension of these rights so that they are equally available to all citizens.

Such rights can and have been justified as ends in themselves—one of the components of the good polity and society is the equality of access to political rights. But political rights are also justified in terms of their consequences: A society in which there is equal political access may be a better society because of the results of that access. Political rights give the citizenry control over the government and lead to better public policy, policy more closely attuned to the needs and desires of the citizenry. Though most theorists of democracy have conceded many weaknesses in public control over governmental policy—the public is ill-informed, short-sighted, changeable, disorganized—most agree that public policy arising from free participation of citizens and contention among them is, in the long run, to be preferred to more despotic policy.

Thus opportunities to participate are valued because they are expected to lead to more responsive and accountable government. In addition, they are expected to have a close relationship to another democratic value—equality. To give the masses of a society political rights is to give them an important resource—power over governmental activities. And if that resource is equally available to all citizens, it can be used to further social equality. Lower-status citizens are numerous. This, coupled with equal political access, should allow those deprived socially and economically to induce the government to carry out policies that will reduce that deprivation. But does it work that way?

One of the simplest but most important findings in our book [*Participation in America*] is that participation does indeed make some difference. If we accept as a measure of responsiveness the extent to which community leaders adopt the same agenda for community action as that of the citizenry, our data support the conclusion that where citizens are participant, leaders are responsive. That participation makes a difference is hardly surprising—most theorists of democracy have assumed it. Yet it has not often been demonstrated that there is indeed a relationship between citizen activities and leader responsiveness.

But the relationship between participation and leadership responsiveness is not that simple. The source of the complexity of this relationship lies, we believe, in the nature of participation and in what it means to make participation equally available to all. Equal rights to participate are just that: *rights*, not obligations. Some may take advantage of these rights, others may not. The result is that participation is unequally distributed throughout the society because the qualities that lead some to choose to participate—motivation, skills, resources—are not equally distributed.

Given unequal distribution of participation, it could still be that those who have the greatest need for governmental services would participate the most. Their greater need would be motivation enough for higher activity levels. Under some circumstances this happens—though more than just objective levels of need are required.[1] As our data . . . indicated, there is a slight tendency—when all else is held constant (such as social status and race)—for those with serious personal welfare problems to participate more. The point is that all else is not constant in the actual political world. The slight tendency for those with severe personal needs to participate more is overwhelmed by the fact that such individuals come from lower social and economic groups. In fact, they participate far less than those citizens who do not have such severe problems.

STATUS AND PARTICIPATION

A major force leading to participation, as our study shows, is associated with social status and the civic attitudes that accompany it. This skews the participant population in the direction of the more affluent, the better educated, those with higher-status occupations. Furthermore, most of the other forces that modify the workings of the standard socioeconomic model tend—in the United States—to accelerate its effects. Affiliation with voluntary associations increases the disparity in participation between the social levels. So does affiliation with a political party (except in relation to voting). Further-more, with the exception of group consicousness among blacks, the political beliefs among the mass public that we have found to be related to participation all tend to increase the participation disparity between the social levels. The conservative political beliefs among upper-status Republicans seem to be the most potent political ideology in America, in the sense that they seem to have an independent effect as motivations to participate. In sum, the standard socioeconomic model of the process of politicization works in America, resulting in an overrepresentation of upper-status groups in the participant population. The additional forces we study increase that overrepresentation.

The fact that the processes of politicization work as they do in the United States has consequences in terms of how governmental leaders respond to citizens. Participation is a potent force; leaders respond to it. But they respond more to the participants than to those who do not participate. Thus, if participants come disproportionately from the upper strata, they are the ones to whom leaders will respond. The "linking" role of participation is crucial here. As shown . . . community leaders and activists have similar social backgrounds: leaders, like activists, tend to come from upper-status groups. But it is not simply this similarity in social background that leads to greater concurrence. What counts is that upper-status citizens participate more. In short, the process of politiciza-tion and its consequences in the United States looks something like the following:

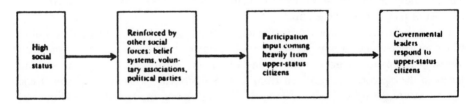

The results of this process are illustrated in Figure 1, which summarizes the participa-tion "payoff" received by the different status groups at various levels of participation. In that figure we divide our sample into five groups based on their overall participation rates. Each of these groups is in turn divided into three socioeconomic levels. Last, we indicate the concurrence scores received by each of the fifteen groups. The height of the various bars indicates the concurrence score for each group (the score is circled in the bars). The width of the bars indicates the proportion of each group in the population as a whole (a figure given as a percentage at the top of each bar).

We can consider our concurrence measure to be an indicator of how much an individual or group gets from the government. The fact that concurrence measures how frequently leaders agree with a citizen on priorities makes this interpretation of the measure quite reasonable. Figure 1 can then be interpreted in an interesting way. The higher a bar, the more the average member of that particular group receives from the government; the wider the bar, the larger that particular group is as a proportion of the population. And, indeed, the area of the bar can be thought of analogously to the "net" effects we discussed

Figure 1. Participation and Concurrence for Three Socioeconomic Groups:
Individual-Level Data

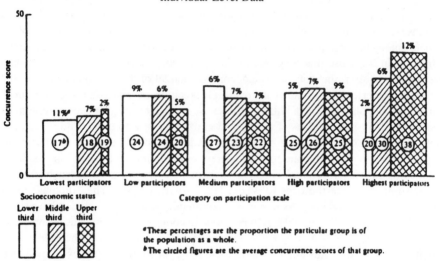

earlier—how much benefit an average member of a group receives multiplied by the number of members of the group.

Consider the concurrence scores (the height of the bars) received by members of the three socioeconomic groups at various points on the participation scale. Among the lowest participants, there is little if any difference across the three socioeconomic levels in the concurrence received from leaders. Only two points on the concurrence scale separate the upper- and lower-status citizens among the lowest participants. But consider the contrast among the highest participants at the other end of the graph. At the high participation level, a big difference exists in the concurrence scores of the citizens from the several socioeconomic levels; indeed, among high participators, upper-status citizens receive almost twice as much concurrence as lower-status ones (38 v. 20 points on the concurrence scale). In fact, we find that lower-status citizens in the highest participation category receive *less* concurrence than do less active lower-status citizens.

A consideration of the proportions of the population who fall into the various groups (the width of the bars) rounds out the picture. It also helps explain why highly active lower-status citizens, despite their activity, do so poorly when it comes to leader concurrence. Consider the category of highest participators. The upper-status citizens are more likely to be in that category than in any other; indeed, they form more than half of the highest participator category. Citizens from the lower socioeconomic group are less likely to be in that category than in any other; they form only about 10 percent of the set of highest participators. Thus, not only do upper-status citizens receive much higher concurrence when they participate, but there are many more of them who actively participate and receive that high score. The overall effect, roughly indicated by the height and width of the bars, reflects this larger "output" that they receive.

Furthermore, the small number of citizens of lower social status who are found among the highest participators explains why they receive relatively little responsiveness despite their high activity rate. . . . [W]e showed that those who are active are likely to differ from the citizenry as a whole. They are less likely to be faced with severe personal welfare problems, less likely to perceive such problems as the major issue in the community, and less likely to think that the government should intervene to deal with such problems. This deviation from the population as a whole is . . . due to the generally higher social status of these activists.

But those lower-status citizens found in the highest participation category differ sharply from the rest of the activists. Our data indicate that they are much more likely to face severe welfare problems than are the other activists. In fact, of all fifteen groups contained in Figure 1—three status groups on each of five participation levels—the lower-status activists report such problems most frequently.[2] The problem is that there simply are not enough of them among the activists. If we look at the category of highest participants we see that upper-status citizens outnumber lower-status ones by six to one. The result is that as individuals, the upper- and lower-status citizens in that highest participant category may be equally active. But the larger number of upper-status citizens—more likely to be opposed to welfare, less likely to be in need of it—drown out the voices of the lower-status ones.

Thus, Figure 1 illustrates, as graphically as any data presented in this book, that participation helps those who are already better off. In general, lower-status citizens participate less than do upper-status ones. And even when some of them become active, their preferences are not communicated to leaders as adequately as are those of the upper-status activists, because they are such a small minority of the activist population.

These data are relevant to a puzzle to which we have alluded at various points in our book [*Participation in America*]: How can our data on the conservative bent of the American participant population square with the obvious signs of radicalization in the United States? Our data on the attitudes toward the Vietnam war found among different activist groups—in particular the differences between the demonstrators and the group of letter writers—suggested that we were dealing with two different phenomena: a small group of highly noticeable activists and a larger group active in less dramatic ways. The former were more dovish, the latter more hawkish.

Figure 1 is, we believe, a strong illustration of this phenomenon. We find a group of very active lower-status citizens, and a group that differs strikingly from all other groups in the salience to themselves of welfare problems. They are likely to be a highly assertive group. But though quite visible, they remain a small group—only 2 percent of the population, and they are counterpoised against the almost glacial pressure of a much larger number of conservative activists. The latter group may not speak as dramatically, but as our data on the relative concurrence received by the upper- and lower-status activists make clear, they speak very effectively.[3]

The close relationship among social status, participation, and responsiveness is our major conclusion about American politics. This stress on the importance of social status conflicts with some common notions. Observers have often commented on the lack of a class basis for American politics. On the institutional level, political parties in the United States are not organized on a class basis; America is famous for the absence of an effective socialist party. There is less class-based voting in the United States than in most of the other English-speaking democracies,[4] and American political parties are less likely than parties elsewhere to recruit activists from particular class groups.[5] Furthermore, the absence of class-based parties is paralleled by the situation *vis-à-vis* public belief systems. Citizens in the United States are not known for the strength of their political ideologies. Especially noteworthy is the absence of class-based ideology as a guide to political behavior.[6]

Yet class relates strongly to participation rates. Indeed—and we think these data are quite surprising—social status has a closer relationship to political participation in the United States than in all but one of nine other countries for which it was possible to obtain data based on measurements similar enough to allow comparison. The data are in Table 1. The relationship is roughly as strong in India as in the United States; but in the other eight nations the status-participation relationship is weaker than in the United States.[7] As all our analysis has shown, this strong relationship between social status and participation has a significant impact on governmental performance.

Why should class, in its relationship to American politics, appear at once so weak and so strong? The answer may be that it is just the absence of an explicit class basis of politics in an institutional or an ideational sense that explains the close relationship in the behavioral sense. If there were more class-based ideologies, more class-based organizations, more explicit class-based appeal by political parties, the participation disparity between upper- and lower-status citizens would very likely be less. Group consciousness among blacks illustrates how a group-based belief system can reduce the participation

Table 1. Correlation of Social Status and Participation in Ten Countries*

Civic culture data		Cross-national program data	
U.S.	.43	India	.38
U.K.	.30	U.S.	.37
Italy	.28	Nigeria	.31
Mexico	.24	Netherlands	.18
Germany	.18	Austria	.10
		Japan	.07

* We present two separate sets of correlation because the data come from two different studies. In each column the measures are comparable, but not across the columns, because different measures are used. This explains the two different figures for the U.S.

disparity. But that, of course, works only for blacks. More generally, the absence of institutions and ideas associated with social status makes, paradoxically, such status a more potent force in American politics.

In this sense, our data may reflect the contemporary results of the historical development of American politics: the absence of a socialist movement, the development of an economically rather than politically oriented trade union movement, the development of a dominant ideology in which class had no place. Such an interpretation, of course, goes beyond our data. But it does suggest some intriguing questions that can be asked about the patterns of participation in other nations whose historical developments differ from those in America—a task of comparative analysis to which we intend to turn.[8]

THE MODES OF PARTICIPATION

Along with stressing social status, we have emphasized the multiplicity of ways citizens can participate. The different modes of activity are engaged in by different sets of citizens, citizens who differ in their orientations to politics. More important, the different modes influence leaders in different ways: The electoral modes of activity (particularly voting) influence leaders by the application of diffuse pressure rather than the communication of specific information about the preferences of the activists. The nonelectoral modes of activity influence through communication of information. The differences among the alternative modes of participation closely relate to a long-standing debate on how citizens can best influence the government. For some analysts, the most important control by citizens over leaders is via elections, in which citizens periodically choose leaders. Effective social policy is maximized if citizens limit their participation to that mode, for citizens cannot effectively rule on more detailed matters. Other scholars have stressed the importance of citizen participation in the between-election period, participation more directly focused on the specific needs and interests of the citizens. Governmental policy that most effectively satisfies citizen needs would come in response to the activities of citizens and groups participating *vis-à-vis* their more narrow interests. Out of the clash of such interests effective social policy emerges.

Our data indicate that both means of citizen control—the pressure of the electoral process and the information of nonelectoral activity—are important ways of achieving governmental responsiveness. Indeed, the combination of the two, where the diffuse pressure of high voting rates combines with high rates of more information-rich activity, leads to greatest leader responsiveness. But the electoral modes differ from the nonelectoral, at least in communities where there is less consensus among citizens as to what the government ought to do. In that kind of community, the more communication of preferences through nonelectoral activity, the lower the overall level of responsiveness of community leaders. And, though we must use caution in extrapolating from our analysis of communities to national politics, one can assume that national politics is more likely to resemble that in the less consensual communities—diversity being much greater across the nation than in any particular community. This suggests that in general, nonelectoral politics in the United States (the activity by which specific groups and individuals try to influence governmental policy) is more likely to skew governmental policy in favor of the particular participant groups and away from a more general "public interest"—if we can interpret that term to refer to the modal preferences of the public.[9]

Such a conclusion is not intended to denigrate the nonelectoral modes of politics. They do have the important ability to communicate fairly precise preferences, but for that reason they benefit only those who use them.

Participation, looked at generally, does not necessarily help one social group rather than another. The general model of the sources and consequences of participation that we have presented could work in a number of ways. It could work so that lower-status citizens were more effective politically and used that political effectiveness to improve their social and economic circumstances. Or it could work, as it appears to do in the United States, to benefit upper-status citizens more. It depends on what organizations, parties, and belief systems exist, and how these all affect participation rates. Participation remains a powerful social force for increasing or decreasing inequality. It depends on who takes advantage of it.

The 1960s, at the end of which our study was conducted, was (it has become a cliché to point out) a time of turmoil and political frustration. A good deal of the frustration focused on the inadequacy of participatory mechanisms in America. Some of our data may explain this. For one thing, the inequality of use of participatory means may be a reason for the search for alternative techniques by citizens who do not find the government as responsive as they would like. Second, the fact that much protest activity comes from an intense but small proportion of the population—a small proportion that is, in turn, counterbalanced by a larger body of steady activists from the other end of the political and social scales—may help explain why so much protest activity flares up, catches the public's attention, and then dies down, leaving behind little substantive change in policy.

Last, consider some changes over time traced by our data. The number of citizens with those characteristics that would lead them to participate in politics—for instance, the number with higher levels of education—has been steadily expanding. Further, the number of citizens actually participating in politics seems to have grown at a rate even faster than that which the expansion in education would predict. But at the same time, political activity takes place more and more in circumstances that are not congenial to effective participation. More and more the setting for participation has become the large city or the suburb, not the well-defined smaller community that fosters political activity. More and more the subject matter of participation has become national or metropolitan issues rather than local issues which citizens can more effectively control.

Thus the actual and potential participant population has grown just when effective participation becomes more difficult. Citizens may be participating more, but enjoying it less.

NOTES

1. Studies of reasons why men revolt have shown that objective deprivation is but one component of a set of forces that lead deprived groups to political violence. See Harry Eckstein, "On the Etiology of Internal Wars," *History and Theory*, vol. 4 (1964). pp. 133–163.
2. On a series of closed questions about problems facing the respondent as well as a similar open question, the small group of lower-status activists constantly expressed a higher level of need.
3. One caution should be mentioned. The data in Figure 1 come from our sample of sixty-four communities, since it is only in such places that we have the data to measure concurrence between leaders and citizens. They do not, therefore, include data from the urban cores. Perhaps the poor are more active and effective there. Without our concurrence measures in large cities we cannot compare the effectiveness of the poorer strata in the urban core with their effectiveness elsewhere. But we can compare their participation. And there is some tendency for the socioeconomic model to work more strongly outside of the urban core, but only a slight tendency. In the sixty-four communities on which our analysis in Figure 1 is based, socioeconomic status correlates at .39 with participation. In the larger cities, it correlates at .33. These data suggest that what we say about our sixty-four communities could be said about larger places, though the disparity between the upper- and lower-status groups on the amount and effectiveness of participation might be somewhat less severe in the latter places.

   Another caution is in order. Our data refer to leader-citizen concurrence within the framework of the local community. Would the same general pattern hold if we considered the match between citizens and national policy makers? Our data provide no answer, though we suspect the pattern would not be *that* different. However, the pattern would obviously depend on what kind of administration were in power. The concurrence scores for the lower-status activists would be much higher under an administration interested in more radical economic policies.
4. See Robert Alford, *Party and Society* (Chicago: Rand McNally, 1963).
5. See Rokkan and Campbell, "Norway and the United States."
6. See, for example, Louis Hartz, *The Liberal Tradition in America* (New York: Harcourt, 1955), Chap. 1.
7. The data in the left column of Table 1 are discussed in Nie, Powell, and Prewitt, "Social Structure and Political Participation"; those in the right column in Verba, Nie, and Kim, *The Modes of Democratic Participation: A Cross-National Comparison*. Data such as those in Table 1 cry out for further analysis along the lines suggested in this book. Such remain on the agenda for the future.
8. In this connection it is interesting to consider some data from Yugoslavia—the latest nation to join our cross-national studies of participation. (These data became available only after the completion of this manuscript.) Our argument that the strong relationship between social status and participation in the United States depends, at least in part, on the fact that social

status differences receive little explicit recognition in terms of political ideology or political institutions leads to an interesting and somewhat counter-intuitive hypothesis about Yugoslavia. In Yugoslavia, for a quite different set of reasons, social status differences receive little explicit recognition in political institutions or ideology. If our argument is correct, one should find a close relationship between status and participation in Yugoslavia as well. And we do find a correlation of .35 between socioeconomic status (based on a measure of income plus education) and political participation. Thus, Yugoslavia has about the same correlation as the United States and India, the two nations where we had previously found the relationship to be strongest.

   The data on Yugoslavia are quite preliminary and require closer analysis. But the point is intriguing.

9. This conclusion is, we believe, quite consistent with the powerful argument made by Lowi about interest group politics in America. See Theodore Lowi, *The End of Liberalism.*

21

Experimental Demonstrations of the "Not-So-Minimal" Consequences of Television News Programs

SHANTO IYENGAR, MARK D. PETERS, and
DONALD R. KINDER

[The press] is like the beam of a searchlight that moves restlessly about, bringing one episode and then another out of the darkness into vision.

W. LIPPMANN (1922)

Four decades ago, spurred by the cancer of fascism abroad and the wide reach of radio at home, American social scientists inaugurated the study of what was expected to be the sinister workings of propaganda in a free society. What they found surprised them. Instead of a people easily led astray, they discovered a people that seemed quite immune to political persuasion. The "minimal effects" reported by Hovland and Lazarsfeld did much to dispel naive apprehensions of a gullible public (Lazarsfeld, Berelson, and Gaudet 1944; Hovland, Lumsdaine, and Sheffield 1949). Moreover, later research on persuasion drove home the point repeatedly: propaganda reinforces the public's preferences; seldom does it alter them (e.g., Katz and Feldman 1962; Patterson and McClure 1976; Sears and Chaffee 1979).[1]

Although politically reassuring, the steady stream of minimal effects eventually proved dispiriting to behavioral scientists. Research eventually turned elsewhere, away from persuasion, to the equally sinister possibility, noted first by Lippmann (1922), that media might determine what the public takes to be important. In contemporary parlance, this is known as agenda setting. Cohen put it this way:

> the mass media may not be successful much of the time in telling people what to think, but the media are stunningly successful in telling their audience what to think about. (1963, p. 16)

Do journalists in fact exert this kind of influence? Are they "stunningly successful" in instructing us what to think about? So far the evidence is mixed. In a pioneering study that others quickly copied, McCombs and Shaw (1972) found that the political problems voters thought most important were indeed those given greatest attention in their media. This apparently successful demonstration, based on a cross-sectional comparison between the media's priorities and the aggregated priorities of uncommitted voters in one community, set off a torrent of research. The cumulative result has been considerable confusion. Opinion divides over whether media effects have been demonstrated at all; over the relative power of television versus newspapers in setting the public's agenda; and over the causal direction of the relation between the public's judgments and the media's priorities. (For reviews that vary in their enthusiasm, see Becker, McCombs, and McCleod 1975; Erbring, Goldenberg, and Miller 1980.) A telling indication of this confusion is that the most sophisticated cross-sectional study of agenda setting could do no more than uncover modest and mysteriously context-dependent effects (Erbring, Goldenberg, and Miller 1980). In short, "stunningly successful" overstates the evidence considerably.

But the problem may rest with the evidence, not the hypothesis. Along with Erbring and his colleagues, we believe that much of the confusion is the result of the disjuncture between cross-sectional comparisons favored by most agenda setting researchers, on the one hand, and the agenda setting hypothesis, which implies a dynamic process, on the other. If problems appear and disappear—if they follow Downs's (1972) "issue-attention cycle"—then to look for agenda setting effects cross-sectionally invites confusion. If they are to be detected, agenda setting effects must be investigated over time.

Though few in number, dynamic tests of agenda setting do fare better than their cross-sectional counterparts. Funkhouser (1973), for example, found substantial concurrence between the amount and timing of attention paid to various problems in the national press between 1960 and 1970 and the importance accorded problems by the American public. These results were fortified by MacKuen's more sophisticated and more genuinely dynamic analysis (MacKuen and Coombs 1981). MacKuen discovered that over the past two decades fluctuations in public concern for problems like civil rights, Vietnam, crime, and inflation closely reflected changes over time in the attention paid to them by the national media.

For essentially the same reasons that motivate dynamic analysis, we have undertaken a pair of experimental investigations of media agenda setting. Experiments, like dynamic analysis, are well equipped to monitor processes like agenda setting, which take place over time. Experiments also possess important advantages. Most notably, they enable authoritative conclusions about cause (Cook and Campbell 1978). In our experiments in particular, we systematically manipulated the attention that network news programs devoted to various national problems. We did this by unobtrusively inserting into news broadcasts stories provided by the Vanderbilt Television News Archive. Participants in our experiments were led to believe that they were simply watching the evening news. In fact, some participants viewed news programs dotted with stories about energy shortages; other participants saw nothing about energy at all. (Details about the procedure are given below in the Methods section.) By experimentally manipulating the media's agenda, we can decisively test Lippmann's assertion that the problems that media decide are important become so in the minds of the public.

Our experimental approach also permits us to examine a different though equally consequential version of agenda setting. By attending to some problems and ignoring others, media may also alter the standards by which people evaluate government. We call this "priming." Consider, for example, that early in a presidential primary season, the national press becomes fascinated by a dramatic international crisis, at the expense of covering worsening economic problems at home. One consequence may be that the public will worry more about the foreign crisis and less about economic woes: classical agenda setting. But in addition, the public's evaluation of the president may now be dominated by his apparent success in the handling of the crisis; his management (or mismanagement) of the economy may now count for rather little. Our point here is simply that fluctuations in the importance of evaluational standards may well depend on fluctuations in the attention each receives in the press.

Another advantage of experimentation is the opportunity it offers to examine individual-level processes that might account for agenda setting. Here we explore two. According to the first, more news coverage of a problem leads to the acquisition and retention of more information about the problem, which in turn leads to the judgment of the problem as more important. According to the second, news coverage of a problem provokes the viewer to consider the claims being advanced; depending on the character of these ruminations, agenda setting will be more or less powerful.

In sum, we will: (1) provide authoritative experimental evidence on the degree to which the priorities of the evening newscasts affect the public's agenda; (2) examine whether network news' priorities also affect the importance the public attaches to various standards in its presidential evaluations; and (3) further exploit the virtues of experimentation by exploring individual cognitive processes that might underlie agenda setting.

METHOD

Overview

Residents of the New Haven, Connecticut area participated in one of two experiments, each of which spanned six consecutive days. The first experiment was designed to assess the feasibility of our approach and took place in November 1980, shortly after the presidential election. Experiment 2, a more elaborate and expanded replication of Experiment 1, took place in late February 1981.

In both experiments, participants came to two converted Yale University offices to take part in a study of television newscasts. On the first day, participants completed a questionnaire that covered a wide range of political topics, including the importance of various national problems. Over the next four days participants viewed what were represented to be videotape recordings of the preceding evening's network newscast. Unknown to the participants, portions of the newscasts had been altered to provide sustained coverage of a certain national problem. On the final day of the experiment (24 hours after the last broadcast), participants completed a second questionnaire that again included the measures of problem importance.

Experiment 1 focused on alleged weaknesses in U.S. defense capability and employed two conditions. One group of participants (N = 13) saw several stories about inadequacies in American defense preparedness (four stories totalling eighteen minutes over four days). Participants in the control group saw newscasts with no defense-related stories (N = 15). In Experiment 2, we expanded the test of agenda setting and examined three problems, requiring three conditions. In one group (N = 15), participants viewed newscasts emphasizing (as in Experiment 1) inadequacies in U.S. defense preparedness (five stories, seventeen minutes). The second group (N = 14) saw newscasts emphasizing pollution of the environment (five stories, fifteen minutes). The third group (N = 15) saw newscasts with steady coverage of inflation (eight stories, twenty-one minutes). Each condition in Experiment 2 was characterized not only by a concentration of stories on the appropriate target problem, but also by deliberate omission of stories dealing with the two other problems under examination.

Participants

Participants in both experiments responded by telephone to classified advertisements promising payment ($20) in return for taking part in research on television. As hoped, this procedure produced a heterogeneous pool of participants, roughly representative of the New Haven population. Participants ranged in age from nineteen to sixty-three, averaging twenty-six in Experiment 1 and thirty-five in Experiment 2. They were drawn primarily from blue collar and clerical occupations. Approximately 30 percent were temporarily out of work or unemployed. Blacks made up 25 percent and women, 54 percent of the participants in Experiment 1 and 10 percent and 61 percent, respectively, in Experiment 2.

Participants were first scheduled for one of several daily sessions. Each of these sessions, with between five and ten individuals, was then randomly assigned to one of the two conditions in Experiment 1, or one of the three conditions in Experiment 2.[2] Random assignment was successful. Participants in the defense condition in Experiment 1 did not differ at all in their demographic characteristics, in their political orientations, or in their political involvement from their counterparts in the control condition, according to day 1 assessments. The sole exception to this pattern—the control group had a significantly larger proportion of black participants (38 vs. 15 percent, $p < .05$)—is innocuous, since race is unrelated to the dependent variables. And in Experiment 2, across many demographic and attitudinal pretreatment comparisons, only two statistically significant differences emerged: participants in the defense condition reported watching television news somewhat more often ($p < .05$), and participants in the pollution condition were somewhat less Democratic ($p < .03$). To correct for this, party identification has been included as a control variable, where appropriate, in the analyses reported below.

Manipulating the Networks' Agenda

On the evening before each day's session, the evening national newscast of either ABC or NBC was recorded. For each of the conditions being prepared, this broadcast was then copied, but with condition-inappropriate stories deleted and condition-appropriate stories inserted. Inserted stories were actual news stories previously broadcast by ABC or NBC that were acquired from the Vanderbilt Television News Archive. In practice, the actual newscast was left substantially intact except for the insertion of a news story from the VTNA pool, with a condition-irrelevant story normally deleted in compensation. All insertions and deletions were made in the middle portion of the newscast and were spread evenly across experimental days. In Experiment 1 the first newscast was left unaltered in order to allay any suspicions on the part of the participants, and for the next three days a single news story describing inadequacies in U.S. military preparedness was inserted into the broadcasts. Similar procedures were followed in Experiment 2, except that we added material to all four newscasts. The stories comprising the treatments in both experiments are listed and described in the Appendix.[3]

Avoiding Experimental Artifacts

In both experiments we undertook precautions to guard against "demand characteristics" (Orne 1962)—cues in the experimental setting that communicate to participants what is expected of them. In the first place, we initially presented to participants a diverting but wholly plausible account of our purpose: namely, to understand better how the public evaluates news programs. Participants were told that it was necessary for them to watch the news at Yale to ensure that everyone watched the same newscast under uniform conditions. Second, editing was performed with sophisticated video equipment that permitted the cutting, adding, and rearranging of news stories without interrupting the newscast's coherence. Third, though key questionnaire items were repeated from pretest to posttest, they were embedded within a host of questions dealing with political affairs, thus reducing their prominence. The success of these precautions is suggested by postexperimental discussions. Not a single participant expressed any skepticism about either experiment's real purpose.

We also tried to minimize the participants' sense that they were being tested. We never implied that they should pay special attention to the broadcasts. Indeed, we deliberately arranged a setting that was casual and informal and encouraged participants to watch the news just as they did at home. They viewed the broadcasts in small groups, occasionally chatted with their neighbors, and seemed to pay only sporadic attention to each day's broadcast. Although we cannot be certain, our experimental setting appeared to recreate the natural context quite faithfully.

RESULTS

Setting the Public Agenda

We measured problem importance with four questions that appeared in both the pretreatment and posttreatment questionnaires. For each of eight national problems, participants rated the problem's importance, the need for more government action, their personal concern, and the extent to which they discussed each with friends. Because responses were strongly intercorrelated across the four items, we formed simple additive indices for each problem. In principle, each ranges from four (low importance) to twenty (high importance).[4]

The agenda setting hypothesis demands that viewers adjust their beliefs about the importance of problems in response to the amount of coverage problems receive in the media. In our experiments, the hypothesis was tested by computing adjusted (or residualized) change scores for the importance indices and then making comparisons across conditions. Adjusted change scores measure the extent to which pretest responses underpredict or overpredict (using OLS regression) posttest responses (Kessler 1978). Participants whose posttest scores exceeded that predicted by their pretest scores received positive scores on the adjusted change measure; those whose posttest scores fell short of that predicted received negative scores.

Table 1 presents the adjusted change scores for each of the eight problems inquired about in Experiment 1. In keeping with the agenda-setting hypothesis, for defense preparedness *but for no other problem*, the experimental treatment exerted a statistically significant effect ($p < .05$). Participants whose news programs were dotted with stories alleging the vulnerability of U.S. defense capability grew more concerned about defense over the experiment's six days. The effect is significant substantively as well as statistically. On the first day of the experiment, viewers in the experimental group ranked defense sixth out of eight problems, behind inflation, pollution, unemployment, energy, and civil rights. After exposure to the newscasts, however, defense ranked second, trailing only inflation. (Among viewers in the control group, meanwhile, the relative position of defense remained stable.)

Experiment 2 contributes further support to classical agenda setting. As in Experiment 1, participants were randomly assigned to a condition—this time to one of three

Table 1. Adjusted Change Scores for Problem Importance: Experiment 1

	Condition	
Problem	Defense	Control
Defense*	.90	−.79
Inflation	−.49	.23
Energy	−.40	.22
Drug addiction	−.19	−.48
Corruption	−.67	.05
Pollution	−.58	.60
Unemployment	.28	.54
Civil rights	−.27	−.27

* $p < .05$, one-tailed t-test.

conditions, corresponding to an emphasis upon defense preparedness, pollution, or inflation. Changes in the importance of defense, pollution, and inflation are shown in Table 2. There the classical agenda setting hypothesis is supported in two of three comparisons. Participants exposed to a steady stream of news about defense or about pollution came to believe that defense or pollution were more consequential problems. In each case, the shifts surpassed statistical significance. No agenda setting effects were found for inflation, however. With the special clarity of hindsight, we attribute this single failure to the very great importance participants assigned to inflation before the experiment. Where twenty represents the maximum score, participants began Experiment 2 with an average importance score for inflation of 18.5!

As in Experiment 1, the impact of the media agenda could also be discerned in changes in the rank ordering of problems. Among participants in the defense condition, defense moved from sixth to fourth, whereas pollution rose from fifth to second among viewers in that treatment group. Within the pooled control groups, in the meantime, the importance ranks of the two problems did not budge.

Taken together, the evidence from the two experiments strongly supports the classical agenda setting hypothesis. With a single and, we think, forgivable exception, viewers exposed to news devoted to a particular problem become more convinced of its importance. Network news programs seem to possess a powerful capacity to shape the public's agenda.

Priming and Presidential Evaluations

Next we take up the question of whether the media's agenda also alters the standards people use in evaluating their president. This requires measures of ratings of presidential performance in the designated problem areas—national defense in Experiment 1, defense, pollution, and inflation in Experiment 2—as well as measures of overall appraisal of the president. For the first, participants rated Carter's performance from "very good"

Table 2. Adjusted Change Scores for Problem Importance: Experiment 2

Problem	Condition		
	Pollution	Inflation	Defense
Pollution	1.53**	−.71	−.23
Inflation	−.11	.11	−.06
Defense	−.44	−.34	.76*

*p < .05.
**p < .01.

to "very poor" on each of eight problems including "maintaining a strong military," "protecting the environment from pollution," and "managing the economy." We measured overall evaluation of President Carter in three ways: a single five-point rating of Carter's "*overall performance* as president"; an additive index based on three separate ratings of Carter's *competence*; and an additive index based on three separate ratings of Carter's *integrity*.[5]

In both Experiments 1 and 2, within each condition, we then correlated judgments of President Carter's performance on a particular problem with rating of his overall performance, his competence, and his integrity. (In fact these are partial correlations. Given the powerful effects of partisanship on political evaluations of the kind under examination here, we thought it prudent to partial out the effects of party identification. Party identification was measured in both experiments by the standard seven-point measure, collapsed for the purpose of analysis into three categories.)

At the outset, we expected these partial correlations to conform to two predictions. First, when evaluating the president, participants will weigh evidence partly as a function of the agenda set by their news programs. Participants exposed to stories that question U.S. defense capability will take Carter's performance on defense into greater account in evaluating Carter overall than will participants whose attention is directed elsewhere; that is, the partial correlations should vary according to the broadcasts' preoccupations, in keeping with the priming hypothesis. Second, the priming effect will follow a semantic gradient. Specifically, priming is expected to be most pronounced in judgments of Carter's overall performance as president, somewhat less apparent in judgments of his competence, a personal trait relevant to performance; and to be least discernible in judgments of his integrity, a personal trait irrelevant to performance.

Experiment 1 treated our two predictions unevenly. As Table 3 indicates, the first prediction is corroborated in two of three comparisons. Steady coverage of defense did strengthen the relationship between judgments of Carter's defense performance and evaluations of his overall job performance, and between judgments of Carter's defense performance and integrity, as predicted. However, the relationship reverses on judgments of Carter's competence. And as for our second prediction, Experiment 1 provides only the faintest encouragement.

Table 3. Correlations between Overall Evaluations of Carter and Judgments of Carter's Performance on Defense as a Function of News Coverage: Experiment 1

	Coverage emphasizes defense	Coverage neglects defense
Carter's overall performance	.59	.38
Carter's competence	.03	.58
Carter's integrity	.31	.11

(Table entries are first-order Pearson partial correlations, with party identification held constant.)

More encouraging is the evidence provided by Experiment 2. As Table 4 indicates, our first prediction is upheld in eight of nine comparisons, usually handsomely, and as predicted, the effects are most striking for evaluations of Carter's overall performance, intermediate (and somewhat irregular) for judgments of his competence, and fade away altogether for judgments of his integrity.

In sum, Experiments 1 and 2 furnish considerable, if imperfect, evidence for priming. The media's agenda does seem to alter the standards people use in evaluating the president. Although the patterns are not as regular as we would like, priming also appears to follow the anticipated pattern. A president's overall reputation, and, to a lesser extent, his apparent competence, both depend on the presentations of network news programs.

Mediation of Agenda Setting

Having established the consequences of the media's priorities, we turn finally to an investigation of their mediation. One strong possibility is information recall. More news coverage of a problem leads to the acquisition and retention of more information. More information, in turn, leads individuals to conclude that the problem is important.

Participants in both experiments were asked to describe "what the news story was about" and "how the story was presented" for each story they could recall something about. We coded both the number of stories as well as the volume of information participants were able to recall. We then correlated recall with participants' posttest beliefs about the importance of the target problem, controlling for their pretest beliefs.

In Experiment 1 the partial correlation using the number of defense stories recalled was $-.13$ (ns); in the case of volume of defense information recalled it was even tinier $(-.03)$. The recall hypothesis also failed in Experiment 2. Here, for reasons of parsimony, we pooled the importance and recall data across the three conditions. The appropriate partial correlation between the number of news stories recalled and posttest importance, controlling for pretest importance was, $-.20$ (ns). Recall of information seems a most unlikely mediator of agenda setting.

The failure of the recall hypothesis led us to consider a second possibility, that agenda setting might be mediated by covert evaluations triggered by the news stories. This hunch is consistent with a growing body of experimental research in which people are invited to record their thoughts as a persuasive message is presented. These thoughts are later classified as unfavorable, favorable, or as neutral to the persuasive message. It turns out that attitude change is predicted powerfully by the intensity and direction of such covert evaluations: the greater the number of unfavorable reactions, the lower the level of attitude change and vice versa. (For a detailed review of these experiments see Petty, Ostrom, and Brock 1981.)

This result extends with little effort to agenda setting. Viewers less able or willing to counterargue with a news presentation should be more vulnerable to agenda setting. To test this hypothesis, participants in Experiment 2 were asked to list "any thoughts, reactions, or feelings" about each news story they recalled. These responses were then scored for the number of counterarguments, with an average inter-coder correlation across the three treatment problems of .86. Consistent with the covert evaluation hypothesis, such counterarguing was inversely related to increases in problem importance. The partial correlation between the number of counterarguments (concerning news stories about the treatment problem) and posttest importance, controlling for initial importance, was $-.49$ ($p < .05$) in the defense treatment group; $-.35$ (ns) in the inflation treatment group; and $-.56$ ($p < .05$) in the pollution treatment group. Pooled across conditions, the partial correlation was $-.40$ ($p < .05$).[6]

And who are the counterarguers? They are the politically involved: those who claimed

Table 4. Correlations between Overall Evaluations of Carter and Judgments of Carter's Performance on Specific Problems as a Function of News Coverage: Experiment 2

	Coverage emphasizes defense	Coverage neglects defense
Carter's overall performance	.88	.53
Carter's competence	.79	.58
Carter's integrity	.13	$-.17$

	Coverage emphasizes pollution	Coverage neglects pollution
Carter's overall performance	.63	.42
Carter's competence	.47	.56
Carter's integrity	.33	.15

	Coverage emphasizes inflation	Coverage neglects inflation
Carter's overall performance	.63	.39
Carter's competence	.71	.38
Carter's integrity	.07	.08

(Table entries are first-order Pearson partial correlations, with party identification held constant.)

to follow public affairs closely, who reported a higher level of political activity, and who possessed more political knowledge. Of these three factors, political knowledge appeared to be the most consequential. In a regression analysis, pooling across the experimental groups, counterarguing was strongly predicted only by political knowledge (Beta = .43, $p < .05$).[7]

To summarize, agenda setting is strengthened to the degree audience members fail to counterargue. Agenda setting appears to be mediated, not by the information viewers recall, but by the covert evaluations triggered by the news presentations. Those with little political information to begin with are most vulnerable to agenda setting. The well informed resist agenda setting through effective counterarguing, a maneuver not so available to the less informed.[8]

CONCLUSION

Fifty years and much inconclusive empirical fussing later, our experiments decisively sustain Lippmann's suspicion that media provide compelling descriptions of a public world that people cannot directly experience. We have shown that by ignoring some problems and attending to others, television news programs profoundly affect which problems viewers take seriously. This is so especially among the politically naive, who seem unable to challenge the pictures and narrations that appear on their television sets. We have also discovered another pathway of media influence: priming. Problems prominently positioned in television broadcasts loom large in evaluations of presidential performance.[9]

How long do these experimental effects persist? We cannot say with certainty. Our results are generally consistent with MacKuen's time-series analysis of agenda setting, which finds news media to exert persisting effects on the judgments the public makes regarding the country's most important problems (MacKuen and Coombs 1981). We also know that our experimental effects survive at substantial levels for at least twenty-four hours, since posttests in both experiments were administered a full day after the final broadcast. This is a crucial interval. The dissemination of television news is of course periodic, typically following cycles of twenty-four hours or less. The regularity and frequency of broadcasts mean that classical agenda setting and priming are, for most people, continuous processes. When news presentations develop priorities, even if rather subtle ones as in our experiments, viewers' beliefs are affected—and affected again as new priorities arise.

Political Implications

We do not mean our results to be taken as an indication of political mischief at the networks. In deciding what to cover, editors and journalists are influenced most by organizational routines, internal power struggles, and commercial imperatives (Epstein 1973; Hirsch 1975). This leaves little room for political motives.

Unintentional though they are, the political consequences of the media's priorities seem enormous. Policy makers may never notice, may choose to ignore, or may postpone indefinitely consideration of problems that have little standing among the public. In a parallel way, candidates for political office not taken seriously by news organizations quickly discover that neither are they taken seriously by anybody else. And the ramifications of priming, finally, are most unlikely to be politically evenhanded. Some presidents, at some moments, will be advantaged; others will be undone.

Psychological Foundations

On the psychological side, the classical agenda setting effect may be a particular manifestation of a general inclination in human inference—an inclination to overvalue "salient" evidence. Extensive experimental research indicates that under diverse settings, the judgments people make are swayed inordinately by evidence that is incidentally salient. Conspicuous evidence is generally accorded importance exceeding its inferential value; logically consequential but perceptually innocuous evidence is accorded less (for reviews of this research, see Taylor and Fiske 1978; Nisbett and Ross 1980).

The analogy with agenda setting is very close. As in experimental investigations of salience, television newscasts direct viewers to consider some features of public life and to ignore others. As in research on salience, viewers' recall of information seems to have little to do with shifts in their beliefs (Fiske, Kenny, and Taylor 1982). Although this analogy provides reassurance that classic agenda setting is not psychologically peculiar, it also suggests an account of agenda setting that is unsettling in its particulars. Taylor and Fiske (1978) characterize the process underlying salience effects as "automatic." Perceptually prominent information captures attention; greater attention, in turn, leads automatically to greater influence.

Judgments are not always reached so casually, however; according to their retrospective accounts, our participants occasionally quarreled with the newscasts and occasionally actively agreed with them. Counterarguing was especially common among the politically informed. Expertise seems to provide viewers with an internal means for competing with the networks. Agenda setting may reflect a mix of processes therefore: automatic imprinting among the politically naive; critical deliberation among the politically expert.

Alterations in the standards by which presidents are evaluated, our second major finding, may also reflect an automatic process, but of a different kind. Several recent psychological experiments have shown that the criteria by which complex stimuli are judged can be profoundly altered by their prior (and seemingly incidental) activation. (For an excellent summary, see Higgins and King 1981.) As do these results, our findings support Collins and Loftus's (1975) "spreading-activation" hypothesis. According to Collins and Loftus, when a concept is activated—as by extended media coverage—other linked concepts are made automatically accessible. Hence when partic- ipants were asked to evaluate President Carter after a week's worth of stories exposing weaknesses in American defense capability, defense performance as a general category was automatically accessible and therefore relatively powerful in determining ratings of President Carter.

Methodological Pluralism

Over twenty years ago, Carl Hovland urged that the study of communication be based on field *and* experimental research (Hovland 1959; also see Converse 1970). We agree. Of course, experimentation has problems of its own, which our studies do not fully escape. That our participants represent no identifiable population, that our research setting departs in innumerable small ways from the natural communication environment, that the news programs we created might distort what would actually be seen on network newscasts—each raises questions about the external validity of our results. Do our findings generalize to other settings, treatments, and populations—and to the American public's consumption of evening news particularly? We think they do. We took care to avoid a standard pitfall of experimentation—the so-called college sophomore problem— by encouraging diversity in experimental participants. We undertook extra precautions to recreate the natural communication environment: participants watched the broadcasts in small groups in an informal and relaxed setting. And we were careful not to tamper with standard network practice in constituting our experimental presentations.

Limitations of experimentation—worries about external validity especially— correspond of course to strengths in survey-based communication research. This com- plementarity argues for methodological pluralism. We hope our results contribute to a revitalization of Hovland's dialogue between experimental and survey-based inquiries into political communication.

NOTES

1. Our abbreviated history of this vast literature is necessarily incomplete, conspicuously so at two points. In the first place, "minimal consequences" has critics of its own, Robinson (1976) being the most vocal. Robinson argues that network news and public affairs programming are largely responsible for the sharp increases in Americans' political cynicism over the past fifteen years. In the second place, we do not mean to suggest that researchers should abandon tests of persuasion. "Minimal consequences" is an apt phrase to describe effects of short- term media presentations, but over the longer haul, media effects produced by repetitious presentations may prove to be substantial.
2. Initially, each condition in both experiments was to be represented by three independent groups of viewers so that condition, session, and time of day would be independent. This arrange- ment prevailed in Experiment 2 but not in Experiment 1, where early attrition forced us to combine the defense sessions, thus confounding condition and time of day. Fortunately, this

adjustment does not threaten the integrity of the experimental design, as comparisons reported in text show.

3. Had participants viewed the actual newscasts each evening and compared them to the version presented on the subsequent day, they might well have discovered our alterations. This possibility was circumvented by instructing participants not to view the national network newscasts at home during the week of the study.

4. The wording of these items is given below:

> Please indicate how important you consider these problems to be.
> Should the federal government do more to develop solutions to these problems, even if it means raising taxes?
> How much do you yourself care about these problems?
> These days how much do you talk about these problems?

> Index reliability was assessed with Cronbach's Alpha. In Experiment 1, the obtained values for the defense importance indices were .77 and .79. In Experiment 2, the alpha values ranged from .69 to .89.

5. On the importance of and distinction between competence and integrity, consult Kinder, Abelson, and Peters 1981. The specific trait terms were smart, weak, knowledgeable (competence), and immoral, power-hungry, dishonest (integrity). The terms were presented as follows: How well do the following terms describe former President Carter: extremely well, quite well, not too well, or not well at all? The average intercorrelation among the competence traits was .43 in Experiment 1 and .62 in Experiment 2. For the integrity traits the correlations were .60 and .30.

6. Typical counterarguments were: in the defense condition a viewer reacted to a story depicting Soviet superiority over the U.S. in the realm of chemical warfare by saying, "The story was very one sided and made me feel even more strongly that the military is overfunded." In the pollution condition, a viewer reacted to a story on the evils of toxic waste: "Overdone—reporter admitted to no evidence to link this with lung disease." Counterarguments with respect to inflation news were comparatively rare. Most came in the form of remarks critical of President Reagan's proposed cuts in social programs.

7. And who are the politically knowledgeable? Presumably they are people who over some interval in their past paid special and abiding attention to media presentations bearing on their perhaps idiosyncratic interests, and hence developed a particular point of view—a point of view that current media presentations have difficulty budging.

8. These results work against the claim that the classical agenda setting and priming effects are special products of artificially high levels of attention induced by our experimental setting. In the first place, as we argued earlier, attention did not seem to be artificially high. Second, the information recall results imply the greater the attention, the *less* (marginally) beliefs are changed. Third, the counterarguing results imply, similarly, that the more "alert" viewers are, the *more* able they are to defend themselves against the media's priorities. All this suggests that our experimental setting, if anything, *underestimates* the influence of network news.

9. In a pair of experiments conducted since the two reported here, we found additional strong support both for classical agenda setting and for priming. The new experiments demonstrated also that priming depends not only on making certain evidence prominent but also on its relevance; priming was augmented when news presentations portrayed the president as responsible for a problem (Iyengar, Kinder, and Peters 1982).

REFERENCES

Becker, L. B., McCombs, M. C., and McCleod, J. 1975. The development of political cognitions. In *Political communication: issues and strategies for research.* ed. S. H. Chaffee, Beverly Hills: Sage.

Cohen, B. 1963. *The press and foreign policy.* Princeton: Princeton University Press.

Collins, A. M., and Loftus, E. F. 1975. A spreading-activation theory of semantic processing. *Psychological Review* 82:407–28.

Converse, P. E. 1970. Attitudes and non-attitudes: continuation of a dialogue. In *The quantitative analysis of social problems.* ed. E. R. Tufte, Reading, Mass.: Addison-Wesley.

Cook, T. D., and Campbell, D. T. 1978. *Quasi-experimentation.* Chicago: Rand McNally.

Downs, A. 1972. Up and down with ecology—the "issue attention cycle." *Public Interest* 28:38–50.

Epstein, E. J. 1973. *News from nowhere.* New York: Random House.

Erbring, L., Goldenberg, E. N., and Miller, A. H. 1980. Front-page news and real-world cues: a new look at agenda setting by the media. *American Journal of Political Science* 24:16–49.

Fiske, S. T., Kenny, D. A., and Taylor, S. E. 1982. Structural models for the mediation of salience effects on attribution. *Journal of Experimental Social Psychology* 18:105–27.

Funkhouser, G. R. 1973. The issues of the sixties: an exploratory study of the dynamics of public opinion. *Public Opinion Quarterly* 37:62–75.

Higgins, E. T., and King, G. 1981. Category accessibility and information-processing: consequences of individual and contextual variability. In *Personality, cognition, and social interaction*, ed. N. Cantor and J. Kihlstrom. Hillsdale: Lawrence Erlbaum.

Hirsch, P. M. 1975. Occupational, organizational and institutional models in mass media research. In *Strategies for communication research.* ed. P. Hirsch et al., Beverly Hills: Sage.

Hovland, C. I. 1959. Reconciling conflicting results derived from experimental and survey studies of attitude change. *American Psychologist* 14:8–17.

Hovland, C. I., Lumsdaine, A., and Sheffield, F. 1949. *Experiments on mass communication.* Princeton: Princeton University Press.

Iyengar, S., Kinder, D. R., and Peters, M. D. 1982. The evening news and presidential evaluations. Unpublished manuscript.

Katz, E., and Feldman, J. 1962. The debates in the light of research: a survey of surveys. In *The great debates.* ed. S. Krauss, Bloomington: Indiana University Press.

Kessler, R. 1978. The use of change scores as criteria in longitudinal research. *Quality and Quantity* 11:43–66.

Kinder, D. R., Abelson, R. P., and Peters, M. D. 1981. Appraising presidential candidates: personality and affect in the 1980 campaign. Paper delivered at the Annual Meeting of the American Political Science Association, New York City, September.

Lazarsfeld, P., Berelson, B., and Gaudet, H. 1944. *The people's choice.* New York: Columbia University Press.

Lippmann, W. 1922. *Public opinion.* New York: Harcourt, Brace.

MacKuen, M. J., and Coombs, S. L. 1981. *More than news: media power in public affairs.* Beverly Hills: Sage.

McCombs, M. C., and Shaw, D. 1972. The agenda setting function of the mass media. *Public Opinion Quarterly* 36:176–87.

Nisbett, R. E., and Ross L. 1980. *Human inference: strategies and short-comings of social judgment.* Englewood Cliffs, N.J.: Prentice-Hall.

Orne, M. T. 1962. On the social psychology of the psychology experiment. *American Psychologist* 17:776–83.

Patterson, T. E., and McClure, R. D. 1976. *The unseeing eye: the myth of television power in national elections.* New York: G. P. Putnam.

Petty, R. E., Ostrom, T. M., and Brock, T. C. 1981. *Cognitive responses in persuasion.* Hillsdale: Lawrence Erlbaum.

Robinson, M. J. 1976. Public affairs television and the growth of political malaise. *American Political Science Review* 70:409–32.

Sears, D. O., and Chaffee, S. H. 1979. Uses and effects of the 1976 debates: an overview of empirical studies. In *The great debates, 1976: Ford vs. Carter.* ed. S. Krauss, Bloomington: Indiana University Press.

Taylor, S. E., and Fiske, S. T. 1978. Salience, attention and attribution: top of the head phenomena. In *Advances in experimental social psychology, Vol. II.* ed. L. Berkowitz, New York: Academic Press.

APPENDIX

Day	Network	Length (min)	Content
			Experiment 1
1	ABC	1.40*	Increases in defense spending to be proposed by the incoming Reagan Administration.
2	ABC	4.40	Special assignment report on the declining role of the U.S. as the "arsenal of democracy." Story notes the declining level of weapons production since the early seventies and points out the consequences on U.S. ability to respond militarily.
3	NBC	4.40	Special segment report on U.S. military options in the event of Soviet aggression in the Persian Gulf region. Story highlights Soviet superiority in conventional forces and tanks and suggests that a U.S. "rapid deployment force," if used, would be overwhelmed.
4	ABC	1.10*	Air crash in Egypt during joint U.S.-Egyptian military exercises.
		4.30	Special assignment report on the low level of education among incoming military recruits. Describes resulting difficulty in the use of advanced equipment and shows remedial education programs in place.
			Experiment 2
Defense 1	ABC	4.40	Declining role of the U.S. as the "arsenal of democracy" (see above).

APPENDIX (*continued*)

Day	Network	Length (min)	Content
2	NBC	4.00	Special report on the readiness of the National Guard. Notes dilapidated equipment being used and lack of training among members.
3	NBC	3.00*	Growing U.S. involvement in El Salvador; draws parallel with Vietnam.
4	ABC	2.00	Deteriorating U.S.-USSR relations over El Salvador.
4	ABC	4.00	Special report on U.S. capability to withstand a chemical attack. Story highlights the disparity in the production of nerve gases between the U.S. and USSR and notes the vulnerability of U.S. forces to chemical weapons.
Pollution			
1	ABC	2.20	Congressional hearings on toxic waste in Memphis.
		2.10	Report on asbestos pollution in the soil and resulting dangers to health for residents of the area.
2	ABC	2.40	Toxic dumping in a Massachusetts community and the high rate of leukemia among the town's children.
3	NBC	2.10*	Underground coal fire in Pennsylvania; carbon monoxide fumes entering residents' homes.
4	ABC	5.10	Special features on the growing dangers from toxic waste disposal sites across the nation. Sites shown in Michigan, Missouri, Louisiana, and California.
Inflation			
1	ABC	2.30*	Reagan's approach to inflation to concentrate on government spending reductions. Results of a public opinion poll concerning cuts in government spending reported.
		2.20*	Taxpayers in Michigan protest the high level of taxes.
2	ABC	2.20*	Reagan's plans to deal with inflation discussed.
		4.10	Special report on supply-side economics as a means of controlling inflation; view of various economists presented.
3	NBC	3.00*	Latest cost of living statistics announced in Washington and reaction from the Administration and Congress.
		1.20*	Reaganomics discussed at a House committee hearing.
4	ABC	3.00	Special report on economic problems in the U.S. and the prospects for improvement under the Reagan Administration.
		2.30*	Democrats attack the proposed cuts in social services and programs.

* Story appeared live in original newscast.

CHAPTER SIX

THE PSYCHOLOGY OF
INTERNATIONAL CONFLICT

The Constitution of UNESCO states, in part, that,

> since wars begin in the minds of men, it is in the minds of men that the defences of peace must
> be constructed; . . . [and] that a peace based exclusively upon the political and economic
> arrangements of governments would not be a peace which could secure the unanimous,
> lasting, and sincere support of the peoples of the world. . . . (Cited in Hajnal [1983, p. 403])

Adopted in London on November 16, 1945, this constitution focuses attention on the psychological origins of international conflict. The document further suggests that ignorance, misunderstanding, misperception, and mistrust lie at the roots of problems that arise among nations. Although the UNESCO constitution does not use explicitly the language of psychopathology, many writers and politicians have described war as a manifestation of collective mental illness. Thus, some portion of the educated public, at least since the global wars of this century, has grasped intuitively the relevance of psychology to international politics. If "the minds of men" is where wars begin, then perhaps those scholars who study human behavior, feelings, and thought processes have something important to contribute.

In the years during and immediately following World War II, some psychologists and psychiatrists began to examine international affairs. Most sought to apply lessons of individual psychology more or less directly to the interpretation of warfare and conflict. Studies appeared that drew heavily on psychoanalysis, learning theory, and other branches of psychology; what they typically lacked was a firm grounding in political science.

Herbert Kelman (1965) recounts the history of these efforts and identifies a fundamental flaw in many early psychological approaches to the study of international politics. He explains that

> some psychological writers starting from individual behavior have tended to overemphasize the role of aggression . . . based on the assumption that the behavior of states consists, after all, of the behavior of individuals. This assumption, however, ignores the fact that the behavior of nations is the aggregation of a variety of behaviors on the part of many individuals, representing different roles, different interests, different degrees of influence on final decisions, and contributing in very different ways to the complex social processes that eventuate in a final outcome such as war. . . . There are certainly things to be learned from the psychology of aggression that are relevant to international relations, but they cannot be applied automatically; only by starting from an analysis of international relations at their own level can one identify the points at which such application becomes relevant. (pp. 5–6)

Kelman's important (1965) book, *International Behavior: A Social-Psychological Analysis*, helped to crystallize the orientation to international affairs that dominates contemporary political psychology. This approach draws heavily on social psychology and attempts to articulate the points at which psychology is relevant to international political processes. The social psychological emphasis shows up in frequent efforts to elucidate the interaction between the individual, on one hand, and the group, nation, or social system on the other.

Kelman sees social psychological approaches to international relations as both "broader and narrower than the study of international politics" (p. 30). Some questions—for example, concerning cross-national exchanges or children's dreams about international conflict (Bilu, 1989)—may legitimately interest political psychologists, without having clear or immediate application to international politics. At the same time, many critical questions in international politics lie beyond the purview of social psychology, for example, some matters of political economy.

Kelman's discussion of the scope of social psychological approaches to international politics remains useful. According to Kelman, some research efforts fall into the category of how individuals relate themselves to their country, other countries, people from other countries, the international system in general, war, peace, and related issues. Studies in this category focus on: 1) attitudes toward international affairs, 2) national and international loyalties, 3) stereotypes and images of other countries, and 4) cross-national contacts.

A second research category concerns more directly the behavior of nations and their decision-makers. Studies in this category focus on: 1) the role played by public opinion in the foreign policy process, 2) the part of individual leaders in the formation and execution of foreign policy, and 3) negotiation and interaction processes in conflict and conflict resolution. Social psychologists also can contribute to the formulation of policy recommendations and the development of theory and methodology in international relations.

During the past few decades, social and political psychologists have conducted much research on these issues. Many mainstream foreign policy analysts remain unconvinced about the usefulness of political psychology to the study of international conflict, but a growing cadre of scholars have been deriving policy recommendations from this body of knowledge (Cohen, 1973; Janis, 1982, 1985; Jervis, 1976; Jervis, Lebow, and Stein, 1985; Kelman, 1987).

Typically, two general approaches have characterized the study of international politics. One focuses on the structure of the international system and how this structure influences rational preferences and strategy; economics often provides models, metaphors, and insights for analysts using this approach. States are seen as motivated by rational pursuit of their material interests. The other orientation highlights foreign policy decision-making and the impact of domestic political realities on outcomes in international politics. Political psychology typically figures most prominently in this second approach, although it is not irrelevant to the first (Telhami, 1990). Most political psychologists acknowledge the importance of structural explanations of international politics, but view them as insufficient. As Ole Holsti writes,

> They may broadly describe the menu of choices before policy makers, but they cannot give us much guidance on which meals will be selected, by whom, and why. . . . They cannot identify completely the nature and sources of interests and preferences because these are unlikely to derive solely from the structure of the system. Ideology, beliefs about international relations and opponents, and domestic considerations are often at least as important. Consequently, structural models are also unable to specify adequately how interests and preferences change. Structural theories tend to focus on power and its distribution, but these variables can explain outcomes in international affairs only in the most general way. (Holsti, 1989, p. 496).

Political psychologists attempt to construct models of conflict, conflict management, and decision-making that permit closer and more specific understanding of international affairs than that provided by the structuralists.

Most often, during the 1970s and 1980s, political psychologists focused their efforts on the nuclear threat and U.S.-Soviet relations (Barner-Barry, 1990; Blight, 1986; White, 1984). At present, political psychologists are just beginning to revise and reinterpret theories in light of the dramatic changes in East-West relations that occurred in the late 1980s. It remains to be seen how well concepts developed during the Cold War will withstand the changes, although one might predict a shift in attention to regional crises across the globe as the threat of nuclear war and superpower conflict recedes.

Political psychologists have already devoted significant efforts to understanding the Arab-Israeli dispute (Gilboa, 1987; Kelman, 1987; Kelman and Cohen, 1986; Kressel, 1987a, 1987b; Vallone, Ross, and Lepper, 1985) and, to a lesser extent, regional conflicts in Northern Ireland (Dutter, 1988), Latin America (Etheredge, 1985), and Iraq (Post, 1991; White, 1991). Research also has addressed psychological aspects of modernization and North-South relations (Inkeles, 1983; Pye, 1979).

More specifically, a partial list of topics explored by political psychologists includes:

- the impact of small group processes upon decision-makers (Janis, 1982),
- patterns and sources of misperception among decision-makers and the general public (Jervis, 1976; White, 1984),
- the integrative complexity of thought processes and belief systems of international leaders (Tetlock, 1983a, 1983b),
- nationalism, ideologies, and world politics (Kosterman and Feshbach, 1989; Rubinstein and Smith, 1988),
- the impact of leaders' personalities on their international preferences, for example, regarding the use of force (Etheredge, 1978),
- assessment of the personalities of international leaders at a distance (Winter, Hermann, Weintraub, and Walker, 1991; Winter and Stewart, 1977),
- the processes by which governments learn and fail to learn from past errors (Etheredge, 1985),
- the effects of stress on the management of international crises (Janis, 1985; Janis and Mann, 1977),
- trends in mass and elite public opinion on international issues (Wittkopf, 1990),
- the impact of public attitudes on foreign policy formation (Cohen, 1973),
- mass media coverage of international affairs (Cohen, 1963; Epstein, 1973),
- the use of third-party mediation and workshops in conflict resolution (Cohen, Kelman, Miller, and Smith, 1977; Kelman and Cohen, 1986).

Several of these topics have been discussed in other sections of this reader.

This chapter includes six selections. Philip E. Tetlock (22) and Stanley Hoffmann (23) consider broad, overarching issues in the psychology of international conflict; they each suggest agendas for subsequent research and policy advising. Although the international situation has changed dramatically since Tetlock and Hoffmann wrote their essays, we can still benefit from their intelligent guidelines for the integration of political and psychological analysis. In the next selection, Irving L. Janis (24) explains how he developed the groupthink concept to explain recurrent barriers to effective decision-making in high-level policy groups. Janice Gross Stein, in reading 25, discusses current status of the "misperception" approach to international relations. The final two selections by myself (26) and Bernard C. Cohen (27) consider public opinion, the mass media, and international politics.

Philip E. Tetlock's article (22) provides an excellent introduction to the political psychology of international affairs. Tetlock, a prolific researcher on the thought processes and belief systems of foreign policy decision-makers, considers the ways in which psychologists (as psychologists) can become involved in foreign policy debates. He summarizes many studies and focuses attention on the practical implications of research. Tetlock believes that psychological expertise in three areas is most relevant: 1) social judgment and decision-making processes, 2) negotiation and social influence processes, and 3) "assessment-at-a-distance" methodologies that examine personality and other psychological dimensions of international leaders. He shows specifically how these forms of expertise might lead to the formulation of sound foreign policy advice, while also noting some limitations of the approach.

The next piece (23) is Stanley Hoffmann's presidential address to the International Society of Political Psychology. Hoffmann is a renowned expert on French politics and international relations. In his address, he discussed a split between *traditionalists* and *radicals*—a division based on views concerning the nuclear age and Soviet-American confrontation. (Both of Hoffmann's groups seem to the left of the American political center.) He explains where the two groups diverge in their thinking and, then, attempts to forge a common agenda for political psychologists interested in international affairs. Interested readers may wish to consult several responses to Hoffmann's essay (Holt, 1986; Montville, 1986; Stein, 1986).

Few researchers have contributed more to social and political psychology than Irving L. Janis. His early works on attitude change, persuasion, stress, health psychology, counseling, and other topics have helped to shape many research domains. However, none of Janis's writings have been more influential than his studies of decision-making, crisis management, and groupthink (Janis, 1982, 1985, 1989; Janis and Mann, 1977). Every year, new studies appear that examine groupthink in a wide variety of contexts (Hart, 1991). The brief selection (24) by Janis in this volume tells how he initially developed the groupthink hypothesis and explains its relevance to several important decisions, including the Bay of Pigs. Interested readers should consult Lloyd Etheredge's (1985) study of American policy in Latin America for an argument against Janis's use of groupthink to explain the Bay of Pigs decision. Janis (1989) includes a rejoinder to Etheredge.

Janice Gross Stein's article evaluates the strengths and limitations of Robert Jervis's "misperception" approach. Jervis and his colleagues (including Stein) have written several influential works about misperception in international politics (Jervis, 1976; Jervis, Lebow, and Stein, 1985). They consider, among other things, how the belief systems of decision-makers color judgments and assessments. Jervis provides an insightful analysis of the ways leaders draw lessons from history. He concludes his classic book *Perception and Misperception in International Politics* with prescriptions to policy makers on how to avoid common misperceptions. Stein's article (25) argues that systematic consideration of political and strategic factors must supplement psychological studies of misperception.

The next two selections examine how the public and the mass media deal with international affairs. My article (26) looks at media coverage of the Arab-Israeli conflict, focusing especially on charges of bias frequently made by pro-Arab and pro-Israeli partisans. These charges frequently confuse conceptual, empirical, and normative judgments, sometimes intentionally to gain political capital and sometimes because of various cognitive processes. The article offers a psychopolitical analysis of bias accusations and concludes with advice for journalists and researchers.

Bernard C. Cohen, the author of the final selection, has written major studies of public opinion and media coverage of foreign affairs (Cohen, 1963, 1973). The brief excerpt in this volume is drawn from *The Public's Impact on Foreign Policy*. Prior to Cohen's work, we had a reasonable understanding of the characteristics and distribution of foreign policy attitudes and some comprehension of how these attitudes were formed and transmitted. However, we possessed very sketchy information about how public opinion entered the policy process. By interviewing foreign policy officials and integrating a good deal of pre-existing research literature, Cohen painted a credible portrait of the linkage process. In this selection, he summarizes the many ways public opinion can reach policy makers and offers suggestions for increasing their responsiveness to the public.

REFERENCES

Barner-Barry, C. (1990). Political psychology in the 1980s and the cognitive perspective. In S. Long (ed.), *Annual Review of Political Science* (vol. 3, pp. 198–220). Norwood, NJ: Ablex.

Bilu, Y. (1989). The other as a nightmare: The Arab-Israeli conflict as reflected in children's dreams in Israel and the West Bank. *Political Psychology*, *10*(3), 365–390.

Blight, J. G. (1986). How might psychology contribute to reducing the risk of nuclear war? *Political Psychology*, 7, 617–660.

Cohen, B. (1963). *The Press and Foreign Policy*. Princeton, NJ: Princeton University Press.

———. (1973). *The Public's Impact on Foreign Policy*. Boston: Little, Brown.

Cohen, S. P., Kelman, H. C., Miller, F. D., and Smith, B. L. (1977). Evolving intergroup techniques for conflict resolution: An Israeli-Palestinian pilot workshop. *Journal of Social Issues, 33*, 165–189.

Dutter, L. E. (1988). Changing elite perceptions of the Northern Irish conflict, 1973–1983. *Political Psychology, 9*, 129–154.

Epstein, E. J. (1973). *News From Nowhere*. New York: Random House.

Etheredge, L. S. (1978). *A World of Men: The Private Sources of American Foreign Policy*. Cambridge, MA: MIT Press.

———. (1985). *Can Governments Learn?: American Foreign Policy and Central American Revolutions*. New York: Pergamon.

Gilboa, E. (1987). *American Public Opinion Toward Israel and the Arab-Israeli Conflict*. Lexington, MA: Lexington Books.

Hajnal, P. J. (1983). *Guide to UNESCO*. New York: Oceana Publications.

Hart, P. 't (1991). Irving L. Janis's "Victims of Groupthink." *Political Psychology, 12*(2), 247–278.

Holsti, O. (1989). The political psychology of international politics: More than a luxury. *Political Psychology, 10*(3), 495–500.

Holt, R. R. (1986). Bridging the rift in political psychology: An open letter to Stanley Hoffmann. *Political Psychology, 7*(2), 235–244.

Inkeles, A. (1983). *Exploring Individual Modernity*. New York: Columbia University Press.

Janis, I. L. (1982). *Victims of Groupthink: Psychological Studies of Policy Decisions and Fiascoes* (Second ed.). Boston: Houghton Mifflin.

_____. (1985). International crisis management in the nuclear age. *Applied Social Psychology Annual, 6*, 63–86.

_____. (1989). *Crucial Decisions: Leadership in Policymaking and Crisis Management.* New York: Free Press.

Janis, I. L. and Mann, L. (1977). *Decision Making: A Psychological Analysis of Conflict, Choice and Commitment.* New York: The Free Press.

Jervis, R. (1976). *Perception and Misperception in International Politics.* Princeton, NJ: Princeton University Press.

Jervis, R., Lebow, R. N., and Stein, J. (1985). *Psychology and Deterrence.* Baltimore, MD: Johns Hopkins University Press.

Kelman, H. C. (ed.). (1965). *International Behavior: A Social-Psychological Analysis.* New York: Holt, Rinehart & Winston.

_____. (1987). The political psychology of the Israeli-Palestinian conflict: How can we overcome the barriers to a negotiated solution. *Political Psychology, 8*, 347–363.

Kelman, H. C. and Cohen, S. P. (1986). Resolution of international conflict: An interactional approach. In S. Worchel and W. G. Austin (eds.), *Psychology of Intergroup Relations* (pp. 323–342). Chicago: Nelson-Hall.

Kosterman, R. and Feshbach, S. (1989). Toward a measure of patriotic and nationalistic attitudes. *Political Psychology, 10*(2), 257–274.

Kressel, N. J. (1987a). Biased judgments of media bias: A case study of the Arab-Israeli dispute. *Political Psychology, 8*, 211–227.

_____. (1987b). Elite editorial favorability and American public opinion: A case study of the Arab-Israeli conflict. *Psychological Reports, 61*(1), 303–313.

Montville, J. V. (1986). A commentary on Stanley Hoffmann's presidential address. *Political Psychology, 7*(2), 219–222.

Post, J. M. (1991). Saddam Hussein of Iraq: A political psychology profile. *Political Psychology, 12*(2), 279–290.

Pye, L. W. (1979). Political modernization: Gaps between theory and reality. *The Annals of the American Academy of Political and Social Science, 442*, 28–39.

Rubinstein, A. Z. and Smith, D. E. (1988). Anti-Americanism in the third world. *The Annals of the American Academy of Political and Social Science, 497*, 35–45.

Stein, H. F. (1986). On professional allegiance in the study of political psychology. *Political Psychology, 7*(2), 245–253.

Telhami, S. (1990). *Power and Leadership in International Bargaining: The Path to the Camp David Accords.* New York: Columbia Unversity Press.

Tetlock, P. E. (1983a). Cognitive style and political ideology. *Journal of Personality and Social Psychology, 45*(1), 118–126.

_____. (1983b). Policy-makers' images of international conflict. *Journal of Social Issues, 39*(1), 67–86.

Vallone, R. P., Ross, L. and Lepper, M. R. (1985). The hostile media phenomenon: Biased perception and perceptions of media bias in coverage of the Beirut massacre. *Journal of Personality and Social Psychology, 49*, 577–585.

White, R. (1984). *Fearful Warriors: A Psychological Study of U.S.-Soviet Relations.* New York: Free Press.

_____. (1991). Empathizing with Saddam Hussein. *Political Psychology, 12*(2), 291–308.

Winter, D. G., Hermann, M. G., Weintraub, W. and Walker, S. G. (1991). The personalities of Bush and Gorbachev measured at a distance: Procedures, portraits and policy. *Political Psychology, 12*(2), 215–246.

Winter, D. G. and Stewart, A. (1977). Content analysis technique for assessing political leaders. In M. G. Hermann (ed.), *A Psychological Examination of Political Leaders* (pp. 27–61). New York: Free Press.

Wittkopf, E. R. (1990). *Faces of Internationalism: Public Opinion and American Foreign Policy.* Durham, NC: Duke University Press.

22

Psychological Advice on Foreign Policy: What Do We Have to Contribute?

PHILIP E. TETLOCK

The future of civilization, perhaps even that of the human race, hinges on our ability to avoid nuclear war. This point has been made so repeatedly and, on occasion, so eloquently that it needs no amplification here (cf. Dyson, 1984; Katz, 1982; Sagan, 1983; Schell, 1980). The consensus, however, begins and ends on that point. Wide disagreement exists on the best means for avoiding nuclear war. In the United States, for example, there exists a broad range of opinion. At one end of the continuum, there are the nuclear use theorists, who believe that the only truly secure forms of deterrence are those that convince one's adversaries that one possesses the capability and resolve to "prevail" at any level of nuclear conflict (Gray, 1982). At the other end of the continuum, there are the proponents of partial or even total unilateral disarmament, for whom the use of nuclear weapons as instruments of foreign policy is morally abhorrent. Toward the middle of the continuum, one finds proponents of the mutual-assured-destruction school of thought: The key to preserving peace lies in ensuring that neither side ever acquires the power to launch a first strike that would eliminate the ability of the other to retaliate (Bundy, Kennan, McNamara, and Smith, 1982; McNamara, 1983).

It is misleading to represent these different policy positions on a single continuum—as if preference for more or less nuclear weaponry were the only issue at stake. Advocates of the competing positions differ on a complicated, and difficult to disentangle, mixture of factual and moral issues: What types of risks is the Soviet Union prepared to take to achieve its geopolitical objectives? What are these objectives? What types of risks should the United States be prepared to take to achieve its geopolitical objectives? What

320

should these objectives be? What are the likely short- and long-term consequences of pursuing new policy initiatives—be they nuclear weapons systems, arms control agreements, or military, political, or economic interventions in zones of contested influence? Not surprisingly, given the variety of important issues at stake and the lack of precision in definitions of key terms on both sides (What, for example, does prevailing in a nuclear war really mean? What exactly is "minimal deterrence" or a "vital interest"?), debates between schools of thought tend to be acrimonious, with each side simply reiterating its own position and disparaging the arguments of the other side either as being naive (a label applied to advocates of more "liberal" conflict spiral positions) or as representing a Neanderthal mentality (a label applied to advocates of more "conservative" deterrence positions). As I have noted elsewhere (Tetlock, 1983a), such debates are doomed to be unproductive: The loose intellectual ground rules under which the debates are conducted guarantee a conceptual impasse. Advocates of each side possess a seemingly unlimited capacity to interpret evidence in terms that are at least consistent with their own initial assumptions concerning the nature of the international predicament confronting humanity.

In this article, I explore contributions that psychologists can make toward improving the quality of foreign policy debates in general and debates on problems of American–Soviet relations in particular. It is useful to begin by explicitly stating the conception of foreign policy that guides my analysis. The fundamental goal of any foreign policy is to develop and maintain relationships with other states that promote the security and welfare of one's own state. If policymakers are to be successful in achieving this goal, they must perform a variety of cognitively and emotionally demanding tasks. They must clearly define their own state's interests and values, make difficult judgments concerning the relative importance of these interests and values, and carefully weigh the costs and benefits of alternative strategies of pursuing them. Knowing one's own objectives, moreover, is not enough; one must also understand the perceptions and concerns of the other side and how the other side is likely to react to policy initiatives of one's own state. Policymakers need to be aware of situations in which conflicts of interest are likely to emerge and of the best ways to achieve mutually acceptable accommodations of such conflicts without abandoning what policymakers deem to be vital national interests.

I distinguish three interrelated ways in which psychologists (qua psychologists) can become involved in foreign policy debates. First, psychologists can become involved in their capacities as experts on social judgment and decision-making processes. Here the focus is on how psychological variables—be they rooted in personality, cognitive, or small-group processes—can bias or distort the processing of policy-relevant information. The goal is to identify and minimize these potential sources of error and bias. Second, psychologists can contribute as experts on negotiation and social-influence processes. Here the focus shifts from the decision-making process to the actual dynamics of interstate bargaining and negotiation. The goal is to explore the psychological assumptions that policymakers rely on in choosing influence strategies and to assess the degree to which these assumptions are in accord with existing research evidence. Third, psychologists can contribute as experts on "assessment-at-a-distance" methodologies that permit the operationalization of psychological constructs from archival or historical records. Here the focus shifts from bargaining and negotiation processes in general to a concern with determining the power of psychological variables to predict the behavior of particular individuals (or collectivities) under specified circumstances. Such data can presumably then be fed directly into policy calculations.

I will examine examples of each of these forms of involvement in foreign policy. My purpose in doing so is neither to defend nor to condemn past efforts, although my remarks may on some occasions sound supportive and on others more critical. My objective is to acquaint a broad readership with the diverse ways in which psychological research findings may be helpful to policymakers who are charged with the extraordinarily complex task of managing relations with other states.

PROCEDURAL ADVOCACY

Procedural advocacy refers to efforts that aim at improving the quality of the foreign policy-making process (advising policymakers on *how* they should think) but that stop short of recommending that policymakers adopt particular arguments or proposals (advising policymakers on *what* they should think). Procedural advocacy can take a variety of forms (Axelrod, 1976; Fischhoff, Lichtenstein, Slovic, Derby, and Keeny, 1981; George, 1980; Janis, 1982; Janis and Mann, 1977; Jervis, 1976; Tetlock, 1983a). It is possible, however, to identify three guiding assumptions underlying all forms of procedural advocacy: (a) an implicit or explicit normative model that specifies what high-quality or rational decision making looks like; (b) an empirically grounded analysis that specifies how psychological variables can lead to serious deviations from these normative models; and (c) the view that it is possible, through individual or organizational interventions, to reduce these psychological sources of error and bias.

Normative Models of High-Quality Decision Making

Substantial consensus exists on what constitutes high-quality or rational decision-making procedures (cf. Fischhoff et al., 1981; George, 1980; Janis and Mann, 1977). Decision makers need to consider a broad range of policy options, carefully appraise the potential consequences of these options, assess the relevance of these consequences to their basic values, squarely recognize conflicts that emerge among basic values, and display a willingness to revise their opinions in response to new evidence. Although no one claims that adherence to these rules guarantees a satisfactory outcome in any given situation, or that deviation from these rules automatically results in failure, most analysts of decision making agree that adherence to these rules does at least increase the probability of satisfactory outcomes, especially in complex, ambiguous, and changing environments.

Deviations From Normative Models

Substantial consensus also exists that actual decision making often falls far short of the demanding requirements of normative models. This evidence—which comes from such diverse methodological sources as laboratory experiments and simulations, personality assessment, content analyses of archival documents, and historical case studies—points to a number of ways in which psychological variables can produce sharp departures from rational-actor standards (for reviews, see George, 1980; Janis, 1982; Jervis, 1976; Tetlock, 1983b; Tetlock and McGuire, 1986). Evidence has accumulated that supports the following conclusions.

1. Personality needs and themes that bear no logical connection to foreign policy issues are systematically related to foreign policy preferences (Etheredge, 1978; Hermann, 1976; McClosky, 1967; Tetlock, 1981; Walker, 1983; Winter and Stewart, 1976). For instance, persons who score high on measures of dominance and power motivation are more likely to endorse hard-line postures toward other nations than are low scorers on these measures. Foreign policy attitudes often seem to be extensions of broader psychological or interpersonal dispositions.

2. Cognitive biases and errors that have been documented in laboratory work also emerge in foreign policy settings (Axelrod, 1976; George, 1980; Jervis, 1976; Lebow, 1981; Tetlock and McGuire, 1986). Although it is hard to estimate the pervasiveness of these biases and errors with precision, a growing body of work in political science provides numerous—and rather compelling—examples of the intrusion of cognitive shortcomings into high-level national security deliberations. Policymakers have been found to rely heavily on theory-driven as opposed to data-driven processing of incoming evidence, to employ superficial and simplistic forms of analogical reasoning in drawing lessons from history, to be slow in recognizing political or situational constraints on the behavior of adversaries, to deny or avoid value tradeoffs inherent in many international relations problems, and to be excessively confident in the correctness of their judgments and predictions. To compound the problem, many of these errors or biases appear to be exacerbated in high-stress crisis situations, which frequently promote rigid, conceptually simple functioning (Hermann, 1972; Janis and Mann, 1977; Staw, Sandilands and Dutton, 1981; Suedfeld and Tetlock, 1977).

3. Small-group dynamics—pressures toward conformity and ingroup cohesiveness—can restrict the range of policy options that decision-making groups consider, inhibit the expression of deviant viewpoints, and discourage thoughtful, self-critical analysis of popular viewpoints (George, 1980; Janis, 1982; Tetlock, 1979). In brief, interpersonal patterns of behavior that are activated in small groups often may amplify rather than correct biases that are rooted in individual cognitive and motivational processes.

This list is illustrative, certainly not exhaustive. It nonetheless captures the pessimistic tone of recent work on decision making in general and on foreign policy in particular. Decision makers are commonly depicted as cognitive misers (Fiske and Taylor, 1984) who rely on simple and fallible heuristics that permit them to make up their minds quickly and with confidence in the correctness of their decisions. Unfortunately, our understanding of judgmental shortcomings has advanced much more rapidly than our understanding of the extent to which these shortcomings can be overcome. Much of what has been written on improving the foreign-policy-making process is highly speculative.

Reduction of Psychological Sources of Error

What practical steps might be taken to minimize potential psychological impediments to high-quality decision making? Proposed solutions tend to reflect the theoretical orientation of the proposer. For example, a concern for the impact of personality variables on the decision-making process leads one to consider the feasibility of screening mechanisms designed to prevent certain types of individuals from achieving high office (Clark, 1971). A concern for cognitive limits on rationality leads one to consider decision aids that sensitize individual policymakers to the fallibility of their own judgment and that increase their awareness of and control over their own cognitive processes (Fischhoff et al., 1981). A concern for interpersonal and small-group constraints on rationality leads one to consider broader organizational reforms designed to increase incentives for complex and open-minded policy analysis (George, 1980; Janis, 1982).

When applied to foreign policy contexts, some proposed remedies are impractical. The idea of personality screening of high-level policymakers quickly comes into conflict with important political values and norms (e.g., in democracies, the right of elected officials to assume office and appoint the individuals who will control key governmental bureaucracies). Screening systems are also unlikely to be able to maintain even the pretense of ideological neutrality.

Other proposed remedies are more practical and deserve careful scrutiny. For instance, Axelrod (1976) has proposed using the cognitive mapping technique to assist policymakers in "externalizing" their implicit and explicit beliefs about causal relationships (what leads to what?) in foreign policy problems. Axelrod's procedure may have a variety of beneficial consequences. It may facilitate detection of dubious hidden premises in arguments, serious gaps in knowledge, and errors of fact or logic embedded in key arguments. Systematically comparing the cognitive maps of different policymakers may also facilitate detection of exact points of disagreement and possible methods for resolving them.

A related technique, formal decision analysis, could play a similar role. Decision analysts would encourage those who make foreign policy (as they have encouraged many other types of policymakers) to decompose complex problems into constituent parts. Many psychological shortcuts in decision making would be blocked off as policymakers systematically tried to list (a) the variety of possible courses of action open to them; (b) the variety of possible consequences of each option and the likelihood of each consequence occurring; and (c) their evaluations of each consequence on a common utility metric (Raiffa, 1968). Decision analysis might be particularly useful in clarifying sources of disagreement among policymakers (e.g., factual versus value disagreements) as well as in assessing "bottom-line" differences in the expected utility that different policymakers attach to options (Hammond and Adelman, 1976).

Both cognitive mapping and formal decision analysis focus on fine-tuning the judgmental processes of individual decision makers. Alexander George (1980) and Irving Janis (1982) have offered procedural prescriptions that nicely complement these individual-level interventions. They have been concerned with fostering small-group and organizational norms that guarantee the representation of diverse points of view and evidence in the foreign-policy-making system. For instance, George's multiple advocacy approach "accepts the fact that conflicts over policy and advocacy in one form or another are inevitable in a complex organization" (George, 1980, p. 193). The challenge is to make good use of such conflicts by creating and maintaining an institutional framework for structured, balanced debate among policy advocates drawn from different parts of the organization. Practically, multiple advocacy could go hand in hand with cognitive mapping and decision analysis. Multiple advocacy greatly expands the range of informational inputs into the cognitive systems of individual policymakers; cognitive mapping and decision analysis provide powerful tools for systematically representing and communicating in succinct form different perspectives on key issues. The two approaches jointly may well lead to a higher quality and more complex decision-making process than is commonly observed—one in which a broad range of options are considered, the pros and cons of competing proposals are thoroughly aired, and difficult tradeoffs and ambiguities are candidly acknowledged rather than suppressed (cf. Tetlock, 1983c).

Reactions to proposals for procedural reform. To many psychologists, these procedural reforms may seem uncontroversial, even obvious. Many policymakers may, however, have the opposite reaction. The problems for which solutions are being proposed are not widely recognized or understood to be problems. The language of psychological analysis has yet to be absorbed into the language of the foreign-policy-making community in the same way that concepts of economic theory or deterrence theory have been absorbed. As a result, implementation of even modest procedural reform is likely to run into considerable, even steely, resistance. Psychologists bearing such advice should be prepared for often unenthusiastic receptions from the policy-making community. During the Kennedy administration, Dean Acheson bluntly told Richard Neustadt (a political scientist who suggested that the president should typically be exposed to many viewpoints prior to making decisions): "I know your theory. You think the President should be warned. You're wrong. The President should be given confidence" (in Steinbruner, 1974, p. 332).

Advocates of procedural reform need to be sensitive to the hidden costs of adopting their recommendations (see George, 1980). Policymakers are extremely busy people who cannot afford to spend much time or energy on most decisions. Advice that requires time- and energy-consuming analysis and debate is practical for only the most important issues. Policymakers also want to keep bureaucratic and political infighting within their

administrations to a tolerable minimum. Advice that requires highlighting serious disagreements (thereby magnifying their symbolic importance) may exacerbate intra-
governmental conflict. For political and personal reasons, policymakers may often be
reluctant to acknowledge the painful value tradeoffs that are implicit in many decisions.
Advice that requires confronting these tradeoffs is therefore not likely to be popular.
Finally, procedural advice may sometimes be too effective in sensitizing decision makers
to the complexity of policy problems. It may lead decision makers to vacillate, to appear
inconsistent to friends and foes alike, and to fail to act quickly in situations that call for
prompt action. In many cases, it may indeed be better to rely on simple, easy-to-execute
choice heuristics with clear-cut policy implications than to temporize in the hope of
identifying a best or utility-maximizing solution (Jervis, 1982; Kleinmuntz and Kleinmuntz, 1981).

In brief, there are no magical procedural solutions that guarantee a wise and judicious
foreign policy. In any given case, one must balance the benefits that are likely to accrue
from vigilant, complex analysis against the personal and political costs of undertaking
such analysis. Policymakers must decide how to decide (Einhorn and Hogarth, 1981;
Payne, 1982). Psychologists who advocate procedural reform in foreign-policy-making
systems need to make a strong case that (a) the problems that the reforms are designed to
cure do actually exist; and (b) the "costs" of implementing the reforms are substantially
outweighed by the effectiveness of the reforms in reducing serious blunders and miscalculations.

GENERATING POLICY-RELEVANT KNOWLEDGE

Procedural advocates draw on psychological research on social judgment and decision
making in designing proposals for improving the policy-making process. Procedural
advocates generally stay neutral, however, on such politically sensitive questions as,
What types of evidence and values should policymakers take into account in arriving at
specific decisions? and How exactly should policymakers weight these considerations in
arriving at final judgments? Procedural advocates can maintain neutrality on these issues
because they focus on abstract threats to the rationality of the policy-making process—
threats that, in principle, could affect the rationality of decision making in any domain of
life. The question inevitably arises: In what ways can psychological knowledge be
utilized to inform the *content* of foreign policy decisions?

I propose here that psychological theory and research can be harnessed not only to
improve the policy-making process but also to improve the quality and soundness of the
assumptions that policymakers rely on in deciding how to deal with specific states in the
international system. Foreign-policy-makers can be thought of as intuitive influence
theorists who spend much of their working lives attempting to influence, and being
influenced by, the policy initiatives of other states. The influence tactics that policymakers adopt are profoundly colored by psychological and political assumptions they

hold concerning (a) the most effective strategies for eliciting desired responses from other states and (b) the nature of other states and the probable responses of these states under various hypothetical contingencies. Errors or gaps in these guiding assumptions can lead to the adoption of influence tactics that prompt unexpected (and frequently very unwelcome) international responses (cf. George, 1980; George and Smoke, 1974; Jervis, 1976, 1982; Lebow, 1981).

In the next section, I consider some examples of ways in which behavioral science research can enrich the assumptions that have been used to guide and justify American policy toward the Soviet Union. I argue that the dominant matrix of guiding assumptions—loosely known as deterrence theory—represents a very limited and constrained way of thinking about the superpower relationship. A more comprehensive theory of international influence processes is needed—a differentiated theory (George, 1980; Pruitt, 1981) that takes into account the full range of influence tactics that are open to policymakers (competitive and coordinative) and that offer at least general guidelines concerning the conditions under which different tactics (or mixtures of tactics) are likely to be effective in protecting or advancing important objectives.[1] In the succeeding section, I take up the problems that arise in applying general theories of influence processes to particular problems. Policymakers are typically not interested in the "truth content" of general psychological propositions; they want to know what policy will achieve desired results in a specific situation. The question here becomes, Can psychological concepts and research methods be used to bridge the inevitably large gap between the abstractions of theory and the concrete demands of praxis?

Toward a Comprehensive Theory of International Influence

Foreign policy is in its most fundamental sense the exercise of social influence. But that statement by itself is not very informative. Foreign-policy-makers face an enormous variety of influence tasks. To take a specific example, American policymakers in the post–World War II era have had a number of stated influence objectives in their dealings with the Soviet Union. Among other goals, they have sought to prevent the Soviet Union from launching a thermonuclear attack on the United States and its allies, to prevent the Soviet Union and its allies from using conventional forces to invade American allies, to prevent the Soviet Union from using low-level violence and political or economic instrumentalities to encroach on Western spheres of influence, and—as a long-term goal—to encourage gradual change in the nature of the Soviet Union itself.

Deterrence theory. One or another variant of deterrence theory has provided the conceptual underpinnings of American policy toward the Soviet Union (Brodie, 1946, 1959; Brown, 1979; Kaufmann, 1954; Weinberger, 1981; Woolsey, 1984). Although major doctrinal and policy disagreements exist, deterrence theorists tend to share the following assumptions: (a) The Soviet Union is an expansionist power willing to incur moderate—perhaps even substantial—risks to challenge American national security interests,

(b) the Soviet Union can be deterred from "aggressive" action by threats of punishment (or threats of denial of gain) that lead the Soviet leadership to conclude that the expected utility of aggression is substantially lower than that of accepting the status quo, (c) generating this conclusion in the Soviet leadership requires a threat that, if enacted, is sufficiently large to make the consequences of aggression truly less attractive than those of accepting the status quo, and (d) generating this conclusion also requires that the Soviet leadership believe that the American leadership possesses both the resolve and capability to enact the threat—factors that jointly influence the *credibility* of the threat.

Deterrence theory has been tremendously influential in the policy-making community. It provides policymakers with a coherent, reasonably simple, and readily communicated rationale for making key national security decisions. From a social-psychological point of view, however, deterrence theory possesses serious limitations that circumscribe its usefulness as a general framework for foreign policy analysis (cf. George, 1980; George and Smoke, 1974; Lebow, 1981, 1983).

First, the theory presumes a definition of the problem that is at least debatable. Soviet foreign policy conduct is posited to spring from expansionist motives activated by vulnerable commitments, not from defensive or security concerns, as conflict spiral theorists maintain (Deutsch, 1983; Etzioni, 1962; Osgood, 1962; White, 1984). The theory also presumes an unchanging, unitary rational-actor model of the leadership of the adversary (cf. Allison, 1971)—what may well be the international analogue of the fundamental attribution error in person perception (Ross, 1977). Many historical observers have suggested that national governments typically consist of shifting political and bureaucratic coalitions that seek or oppose confrontation with other states for their own independent reasons (e.g., Jervis, Lebow and Stein, 1985). An adequate theory of international influence would take into account the diverse ways in which the internal political dynamics of states can prompt them to challenge the status quo (Lebow, 1981) and the steps that defender states might take to minimize the "perceived need" to challenge the status quo.

A second, serious limitation is the theory's one-sided focus on threats as instruments of social influence. Policymakers have traditionally employed a much broader range of tactics in their efforts to shape the conduct of other states, including not only competitive tactics (such as threats, faits accomplis, and ultimatums) but also coordinative tactics (such as proposing compromises, symbolic tension-reducing initiatives, and cooperation with third-party mediators) and mixed competitive–coordinative tactics (cf. Craig and George, 1983; Pruitt, 1981).

A third flaw, which flows directly from the previous two, is the insensitivity of many deterrence theorists to the potential negative side effects of a pure-threat policy (cf. Brehm, 1966; Deutsch, 1973; Kelman and Bloom, 1973; Lebow, 1981; White, 1984). Threats may activate interrelated psychological and political processes that actually increase the likelihood of aggression and war. Threats may do so by inducing psychological reactance (motivating the threatened party to assert its freedom to perform the forbidden act), by increasing the threatened party's concern for saving face in the eyes of domestic political and international audiences (it does not want to acquire a reputation for weakness), and by leading the threatened party to conclude that it is impossible to arrive at a stable modus vivendi with the source of the threat. Threats may also exacerbate the insecurity of the other side, thus triggering a conflict spiral of mutually escalating hostility and an arms race that culminates in a war that no one wants (Holsti, 1972; Kelman and Bloom, 1973; Lebow, 1981). Deterrence theory, however, largely ignores these issues; like many other theories, it is insensitive to its own boundary conditions.

Fourth, and most crucial from a policy-making perspective, deterrence theory offers surprisingly little guidance in solving the multitude of specific problems that arise in devising actual threats to influence other states. With a few noteworthy exceptions (e.g., Schelling, 1960, 1966), the theory fails to address key questions such as the following:

1. How should one calibrate threats to specific situations? What are the costs—beyond possible losses in credibility—of relying on severe threats? How should one design threats to avoid provoking undesired responses from adversaries? On this latter point, for example, the research literature suggests that presenting threats as warnings (Snyder and Diesing, 1977) or as promises (Rubin and Lewicki, 1973) enhances their effectiveness. The literature also suggests that threats that appear "legitimate" in the eyes of an adversary (cf. Kelley, 1965) are more likely to induce compliance. Why do these relationships exist? Such findings certainly cannot be deduced from, and are difficult to assimilate into, a traditional deterrence framework.

2. In what ways should threats be combined and synchronized with coordinative policy initiatives such as concessions or other tension-reducing moves? Both laboratory research and archival research indicate that under a rather broad range of circumstances, a fair-but-firm reciprocity strategy works better than either a pure-threat or pure-appeasement posture—"works better" in the sense of triggering more mutually advantageous patterns of interaction (Axelrod, 1984; Druckman, 1983; Esser and Komorita, 1975; George, Hall, and Simon, 1971; George and Smoke, 1974; Leng and Wheeler, 1979; Lindskold, 1978; Oskamp, 1971; Pruitt, 1981; Snyder and Diesing, 1977). Concessions in conjunction with firmness on the key issues (what Pruitt has called flexible–rigidity) frequently facilitate solutions to conflicts of interest that both parties prefer to continued or escalated competition. What explains the superiority of mixed influence strategies of this sort? Do properly timed concessions serve important face-saving functions that make it psychologically and politically easier for the other side to back down (George and Smoke, 1974; Kelman, 1982; Pruitt, 1981; Schlenker, 1980; Snyder and Diesing, 1977)? And what qualifications need to be attached to the above claims? Again, deterrence theory offers little help in answering these questions.

3. Finally, if deterrent threats are most effective when carefully calibrated and phrased and when integrated into an overall reciprocity strategy, how does one ensure that potential adversaries correctly interpret these threats? Too-subtle signals can be easily lost in the noise of surrounding dramatic events (Jervis et al., 1985). How does one ensure that potential adversaries heed all the facets of one's multifaceted influence

strategy? And how does one ensure that, if heeded, the different components of one's strategy do not cancel each other out—that one's concessions do not negate the impression of firmness and that one's threats do not negate the impression of fairness? In brief, how does the beleaguered decision maker come up with a mixed strategy that achieves the desired effects of deterrence but moderates the ill effects?[2]

Is there a viable alternative? Granting that deterrence theory possesses fundamental shortcomings, what can be offered in its place? Unfortunately, no full-grown alternative exists. The foregoing remarks do, however, illustrate that the general shape of an alternative has begun to emerge from the work of social psychologists and political scientists on bargaining and negotiation processes. The research literature points to the need for a much more complex theory of influence processes than traditional deterrence analyses provide—a theory that points to the need for different mixes of influence tactics in different historical–political situations. But, that said, it must be conceded that the research literature, too, has serious limitations. Available evidence is far from totally consistent (Druckman, 1983; Pruitt, 1981). Moreover, even if it were totally consistent, translating theoretical abstractions and empirical trends into specific policy proposals is no easy task. It is one thing to claim that a reciprocity strategy usually "works better" than rival strategies; it is another thing to claim that a reciprocity strategy is most appropriate in a particular political context. In Verba's (1967) words, "generalizations fade when we look at particular cases" (p. 116). It is necessary to take into account the many circumstances unique to the case at hand, each circumstance a potential boundary condition for the "law" one wishes to apply. Caution is obviously in order, for the history of psychology abounds with examples of the main effects of today becoming the first- and second-order interaction effects of tomorrow (cf. Cronbach, 1975; Gergen, 1978).

Even if one could be reasonably confident that the general principle applied to a specific case, one would still confront the profound problem of implementing the reciprocity strategy. What exactly does it mean to say that the United States should pursue a reciprocity strategy in its dealings with the Soviet Union? Reciprocity can be operationalized in a seemingly infinite variety of ways. Does reciprocity mean adopting some variant of Osgood's (1962) Graduated and Reciprocal Initiatives in Tension Reduction (GRIT) proposal, in which the United States attempts to initiate a de-escalation process through a series of carefully planned unilateral concessions? And what exactly should these concessions be—halting development of the MX missile, cessation of deployment of intermediate-range nuclear missiles in Western Europe, announcement of a "no first use" policy, or, perhaps, all of the above (cf. Deutsch, 1983; White, 1984)? How do we know that in operationalizing the reciprocity strategy in a particular way, we have struck the right balance between conciliatoriness and resistance to exploitation? Presumably, some kind of corrective feedback mechanism needs to be built into the policy formula. How does one decide whether a given Soviet response is sufficiently conciliatory or refractory to warrant a response in kind?

In my opinion, psychologists are wise to avoid staking their professional credibility on particular policy proposals. Taking positions on such detailed issues requires extrapolating far beyond existing psychological knowledge and taking stands on highly ambiguous political and moral issues (e.g., What are the geopolitical intentions of the Soviet leadership? How great a risk of appearing too open to exploitation or too threatening should one take?).

Crisis prevention and management. Psychological theory and research does not lead directly to policy prescriptions; policy prescriptions rest on complex amalgams of psychological, political, and moral assumptions. Psychological theory and research do, however, highlight issues that prudent policymakers should take into account if those policymakers do indeed wish to avoid war in international confrontations. Alexander George's path-breaking research on crisis prevention and management is the best illustration of work in this vein. In discussing the practice of deterrence and compellence in international politics, George (1980) did not presume to tell policymakers whether they should use threats of force in specific situations. On the basis of his own inductive-historical research, he did, however, identify several generic problems that policymakers need to solve if they are to be successful in tailoring a strategy of deterrence or compellence to specific situations. For instance, he identified six classes of considerations that need to be addressed by policymakers who contemplate the use of coercive tactics to shape the behavior of other states:

1. What are the risks of presenting an explicit or implicit ultimatum that specifies a deadline for compliance? Can the risks be controlled?
2. How does one deal with the conflict between the need to pressure the opponent into compliance (for example, cease invading a particular nation) and the requirement of effective crisis management of slowing the pace of events to give the opponent time to evaluate the situation?
3. How should one calculate the timing of the threat to make certain it will be regarded as credible?
4. How should one calculate the timing of negotiations with the opponent?
5. How does one formulate a "carrot-and-stick" policy that makes compliance the most attractive option to the adversary? How threatening should the consequences of noncompliance be? How appealing should the consequences of compliance be?
6. How can rewards and threats be designed so that they do not interfere with each other?

Influence theorists such as George make a vital contribution by highlighting the complexity of the issues that must be confronted and the variety of "things that can go wrong" in making major foreign policy decisions. The products of such analyses are similar in important respects to "fault trees" that engineers use to assess the various ways in which complex physical systems can fail (cf. Fischhoff, Slovic, and Lichtenstein, 1978). Influence fault trees may eventually come to play an important troubleshooting role in the foreign policy field by sensitizing decision makers to gaps or omissions in their cognitive representations of policy problems.

At this point, however, it is important to recall the cognitive, emotional, and small-group processes that may make it difficult to cope with complex tradeoffs in choosing influence tactics. My discussion of error and bias in the decision-making process revealed a variety of psychological pressures to simplify policy problems. The discussion of influence processes complements this earlier discussion by pointing to specific ways in which psychological pressures to simplify issues can lead to serious miscalculations. Achieving a well-balanced mix of foreign policy influence tactics requires the ability and willingness to see events from different points of view (including that of one's opponent), to recognize tensions between important objectives, and to develop guidelines for resolving tensions between these objectives (cf. Lebow, 1983).[3]

Situational Diagnosis

Developing a theory of interstate influence that acknowledges the limitations of pure deterrence approaches is a step in the right direction. Policymakers should be sensitized to the wide range of influence tactics open to them and to the variety of contextual factors that can shape a target's responses to these tactics. Useful as such theory may be as a framework for organizing one's thinking about problems of foreign policy in general, it does not satisfy the needs of policymakers for guidance in coping with concrete real-world problems. How does one go about bridging or at least closing the conceptual void between general theoretical analyses of influence processes and policy debates over the best strategies for dealing with specific states at specific times?

Theoretical analyses of social influence yield, at best, conditional generalizations for selecting influence strategies. Under one set of conditions, policymakers should empha-size one type of strategy; under another set of circumstances, they should emphasize another type of strategy. But such advice begs the question of how one determines whether the preconditions for adopting a given strategy are actually met in a given situation. What conceptual model, for instance, best fits current American–Soviet relations: some form of deterrence or conflict spiral model? Is the Soviet Union an expan-sionist power prepared to take large risks to achieve highly ambitious goals (cf. R. Osgood, 1981; Wildavsky, 1983)? Or is the Soviet Union best thought of as a conservative status quo power preoccupied with minimizing internal or external threats to its own security (cf. White, 1984)? Or is the Soviet foreign policy guided by some complex mixture of defensive and opportunistic offensive motives? The answers one provides to these questions have important implications for the relative importance one attaches to deterrence versus reassurance in designing a foreign policy strategy toward the Soviet Union.

To what extent can behavioral science research methods help to clarify such important psychological "unknowns" in foreign policy debates? Is it possible to develop empirical techniques that permit one to assess the comparative validity of the psychological premises that underlie competing policy proposals? Cautious optimism appears to be warranted. A rich variety of assessment-at-a-distance methodologies have been developed in the last 15 years that permit investigators to operationalize psychological constructs such as images of the enemy, motivational themes, and cognitive style from archival data sources such as interviews and speeches (for reviews, see Hermann, 1976; Tetlock, 1983b). Applications of these techniques to specific foreign policy settings raise the (perhaps naive) promise of reformulating, in much more tractable, empirical terms, the often polemical exchanges between advocates of competing policy positions. For example, conflicting motivational attributions for Soviet conduct may to a considerable extent be reducible to different methods of interpreting the action–reaction dynamics of American–Soviet relations (e.g., How do the Soviets respond to seemingly conciliatory or threatening American policy initiatives?) and to different methods of reading expressed Soviet perceptions and goals in official publications (e.g., How much weight should one attach to the statements of different sources in different time periods?).[4]

American–Soviet interactions. One promising application of systematic research methods (especially content analysis) has been to the study of American–Soviet interactions. The general goal of work in this area has been to explore interdependencies between the rhetoric and policy initiatives of the two superpowers. Available evidence is encouraging to advocates of some form of reciprocity strategy in American dealings with the Soviet Union. The evidence quite consistently indicates that conciliatory behavior tends to elicit accommodative responses and that belligerent behavior tends to elicit refractory responses. For example, this was the general finding of Gamson and Modigliani (1970) in their study of American–Soviet relations between 1945 and 1963. Compatible results emerged from Jensen's (1984) analyses of negotiating tactics in strategic arms control talks between 1969 and 1979 (concessions tend to elicit concessions), Leng's (1984) analyses of links between American threats of force in crises and Soviet reactions (threats of force trigger responses in kind; carrot-and-stick policies with less specific threats trigger more accommodative Soviet responses), and Tetlock's (1985; Tetlock and McGuire, 1985) time-series analyses of links between the foreign policy rhetoric and actions of the superpowers between 1945 and 1983 (less integratively complex rhetoric by one side elicits less integratively complex rhetoric from the other side; less complex rhetoric by a given side is also associated with an increased likelihood of that side undertaking major military–political interventions in other countries and a decreased likelihood of arriving at mutually acceptable agreements or treaties with the other superpower).

These results suggest that some form of reciprocity dynamic characterizes American–Soviet relations. But the results are far from conclusive. Skeptics can challenge, for example, the act-classification rules used by past (predominantly liberal) investigators. The skeptics might argue that tactical retreats or concessions extracted as a result of Western resolve or strength should not be classified as conciliatory. Soviet foreign policy goals, in this view, do not change; only the tactics vary. Such objections raise difficult conceptual and methodological issues that need clarification. What rules should guide act classification? In what ways do the act-classification rules of deterrence and conflict spiral observers differ? What, if anything, would hardline deterrence theorists accept as evidence of conciliatory Soviet behavior? Research on American–Soviet interaction has not yet confronted these questions, but sophisticated theoretical and methodological tools do exist for exploring possible answers (e.g., the act-frequency model of Buss and Craik, 1983). At a minimum, work on these questions would raise the quality of the debate on influence strategy in American–Soviet relations. Observers of such debates would be in a much better position to specify exact points of disagreement between models and to assess the degree to which advocates of competing models have advanced falsifiable versions of their positions.

Soviet leadership. Behavioral science research methods can also be applied to the study of trends over time and to individual differences in the Soviet leadership (cf. Bialer, 1981; Breslauer, 1984; Dallin, 1981; Hermann, 1980; Herrmann, 1985; Hough, 1981; Stewart, Warhola, and Blough, 1983). The materials that such studies have to work with are necessarily sparse (e.g., limited biographical information, public statements); nonetheless, these studies can be suggestive of interesting transformations and perhaps cleavages in elite Soviet opinion. Public commitments to particular perceptions or values may not represent the true perceptions and values of the speaker. But such statements do represent consequential political acts that commit the speaker to particular positions in the eyes of important domestic and international audiences (cf. Graber, 1976). As such, these statements may provide valuable clues to future directions in Soviet policy and likely Soviet reactions to various types of Western initiatives.

For example, we still know disconcertingly little about intergenerational differences in Soviet policy preferences—a topic that assumes great importance as the cohort of leaders who acquired high positions in the late Stalin era rapidly relinquishes power to the Gorbachev generation. To what extent do significant intergenerational differences in attitudes exist toward détente, economic reform, arms control, political liberalization, and a host of more specific domestic and international issues? To what extent do significant intergenerational differences exist in style or sophistication of thought (cf. Bialer, 1980; Hough, 1981)? Are the foreign policy objectives of the younger generation likely to be more or less ambitious than those of its predecessors? In a major crisis, would the new generation of leaders be more or less prone to raise the stakes and pursue a highly competitive influence strategy in dealings with the United States? Why might such intergenerational effects exist (e.g., the need of a new leadership to establish its legitimacy via external triumphs, the need to place higher priority on solving domestic economic and social problems than on foreign policy, the dimming memory of World War II, different political socialization experiences)?

If we know little about intergenerational differences in outlook, we know even less about individual differences within generations. The new political leaders of the Soviet Union—Gorbachev, Shevardnadze, Chebrikov, Ryzhkov and so forth—are the subject of much speculation, but little of it is systematic. Application of research techniques such as content analysis (qualitative or quantitative) and expert ratings of personality and political style based on biographical data would help to clarify what is and is not known of Soviet leaders (cf. Hermann, 1980; Stewart et al., 1983; Tetlock, 1986). Knowledge generated from these techniques should not, moreover, be regarded as a mere foreign policy frill. Ultimately, American leadership choices of policy tactics for influencing the Soviet Union rest on implicit or explicit psychopolitical assessments of the Soviet leadership.

CONCLUSIONS

No neat, nonarbitrary line divides psychological issues from political and moral issues. Making policy decisions requires taking stands on subtle mixtures of factual issues (some of which rest on psychological judgments, others on political ones) and moral issues (which require setting priorities among objectives and standards of acceptable risk). I have argued here that psychologists can make important contributions to foreign policy debates in their capacities as psychologists—that existing theory and research findings can shed considerable light on the psychology of the policy-making process and on the validity of the psychological assumptions that guide policy decisions. But complete value neutrality is an illusion. Psychologists who bring existing knowledge to the attention of the policy-making community are committing a political act with potential political consequences. The general objective—improving the quality of foreign policy decisions—is uncontroversial, even platitudinous; nonetheless, much room for argument exists over what constitutes improvement and over what forms of psychological involvement are likely to promote improvement.

The proposals advanced in this article, like all efforts at social problem solving, are predicated on a complex blend of psychological, political, and moral assumptions (Lynn, 1978). I have tentatively assumed, for example, that improving the quality of the policy-making process and the soundness of the knowledge that decision makers rely on to create policy will reduce the likelihood of serious miscalculations that unnecessarily magnify or exacerbate international conflict. Skeptics might well note, however, the enormous difficulties that arise in thoroughly defending this proposition. How exactly does one determine whether the decision-making process is of "high quality"? How exactly does one go about operationalizing procedural reforms such as multiple advocacy that are designed to ensure high-quality decision making? Who decides, for example, how wide a range of viewpoints should be represented in a policy-making system? By what criteria should that decision be made? (How unreasonable must a position be to be dismissed summarily?) At what point do the costs of procedural reforms outweigh their likely benefits? How exactly does one assess the soundness of the psychological and political assumptions underlying foreign policy decisions? How does one assess the degree to which psychological advice has achieved its stated objective of reducing the likelihood of "serious miscalculations that unnecessarily magnify or exacerbate international conflict"? What constitutes an unnecessary magnification of conflict? Does not the answer depend, at least in part, on what one deems to be vital national interests? Is any national interest important enough to justify an increased likelihood of war—in particular, nuclear war? Is the problem fundamentally a moral–political one (policymakers hold the "wrong" values and are too tolerant of the risks of war), a psychopolitical one (policymakers hold faulty or simplistic assumptions about the international environment and how best to cope with it), or a systemic–technological one (given the anarchic nature of the international system and the momentum of technological development of weapons systems, policymakers are doing the best they can in an "irrational" situation). Perhaps the truth is best represented by some combination of these alternatives.

It is appropriate to close with such a list of questions, some of which just may not be answerable, others of which may possess only partial or vague answers. Our understanding of how psychological knowledge can be applied to the solution of real-world dilemmas of foreign policy remains incomplete. It is unrealistic, moreover, to expect productive research psychologists to drop what they are doing and rush to apply their skills to these issues. Interest in foreign policy issues appears to be cyclical in the psychological research community, waxing and waning with the level of tension in the international environment. Such intermittent interest is not adequate to sustain the types of cumulative theoretical and research efforts necessary to develop and apply policy-relevant knowledge to problems of international relations.

What is needed is much more encouragement of interdisciplinary training and research projects that bring together scholars with complementary forms of expertise. The field requires the active participation of basic psychological researchers (individuals whose work currently bears on foreign policy concerns only at an abstract level, such as a concern with decision making or social influence processes), experts in political science and international relations (whose work has yielded insights into how psychological variables shape foreign policy outcomes in interaction with variables at other levels of analysis), and "area" experts (whose work focuses on the cultural, political, and economic systems of the nation states that are the objects of foreign policy). Perhaps most important, if such collaborative interdisciplinary work is to have an impact on the actual conduct of foreign policy, a new type of specialist is needed. A number of writers (Lynn, 1978; Masters, 1984) have noted the serious problems that arise in forging links between behavioral science research findings and social policy and have argued for the emergence of a new professional role: the policy liaison specialist, whose task is to assist policymakers in translating the theoretical and empirical work of academic writers into specific proposals. As I have shown, the work of such specialists will not be easy. Formidable conceptual and methodological obstacles exist simply to extrapolating solutions to particular problems from general theory or aggregate data. The more we come to understand these difficulties, the more we come to understand the limited, but nonetheless real, relevance of the psychological literature and the forms that responsible advocacy on foreign policy issues can take.

NOTES

1. Although I focus on psychological assumptions of deterrence theory in general, detailed investigation is needed of the social influence assumptions underlying other policy formulations, including the Nixon–Kissinger détente strategy (George, 1980) and countervailing doctrines of nuclear deterrence (Jervis, 1984).
2. Achieving a well-balanced mix of influence tactics is difficult in a world of conventionally armed states. Jervis (1984) made a powerful case that, if anything, the tensions between conflict and cooperation become even more acute in a nuclear world of mutual assured destruction. He argued that the tradeoffs created by the nuclear revolution are so stressful (e.g., the perceived need to use nuclear weapons for deterrence and the prospect of total destruction) that people have sought to escape from them in a variety of ways (e.g., seeking a perfect ballistic missile defense system, advocating total nuclear disarmament, supporting general freezes on current weapons systems and technologies, and developing doctrines espousing limited nuclear war that "conventionalize" nuclear weapons). Jervis suggested, however, that all proposed escapes are illusory and that no fully satisfactory resolution of the tensions may be possible.
3. Even assuming that one knows what would constitute a well-balanced foreign policy, one still faces the extraordinarily difficult task of rallying and maintaining domestic political support for such a policy (George, 1980). This problem raises a whole new set of complex social-psychological issues beyond the scope of this article.
4. Conflicting attributions of Soviet intentions are not, of course, entirely reducible to clashing interpretations of foreign policy behavior and rhetoric. Debates also focus on the proper inferences to be drawn from Soviet conventional and nuclear force configurations. These debates, although often highly technical in nature, can be usefully viewed from a psychological perspective. Major asymmetries exist in the American and Soviet arsenals—asymmetries that can be traced to the different histories, geographies, and technological capabilities of the two powers. These asymmetries, in turn, create enormous obstacles to the negotiation of mutually acceptable understandings in arms control. As Steinbruner (1985) noted, there are powerful psychological and political pressures on both sides to emphasize asymmetries that work to one's disadvantage and to downplay asymmetries that work to one's advantage.

REFERENCES

Allison, G. T. (1971). *Essence of decision.* Boston: Little, Brown.
Axelrod, R. (1976). *Structure of decision.* Princeton, NJ: Princeton University Press.
———. (1984). *The evolution of cooperation.* New York: Basic Books.
Bialer, S. (1980). *Stalin's successors: Leadership, stability, and change in the Soviet Union.* New York: Columbia University Press.
———. (1981). *The domestic context of Soviet foreign policy.* Philadelphia: Lippincott.
Brehm, J. (1966). *A theory of psychological reactance.* New York: Academic Press.
Breslauer, G. W. (1984). Is there a generation gap in the Soviet party establishment? Demand articulation by RSFSR provincial party first secretaries. *Soviet Studies, 36,* 1–25.

Brodie, B. (1946). *The absolute weapon*. New York: Harcourt Brace.

———. (1959). *Strategy in the missile age*. Princeton, NJ: Princeton University Press.

Brown, H. (1979). *Department of Defense annual report, F.Y. 1982*. Washington, DC: U.S. Government Printing Office.

Bundy, M., Kennan, G., McNamara, R. and Smith, G. (1982). Nuclear weapons and the Atlantic alliance. *Foreign Affairs, 60*, 753–768.

Buss, D. M., and Craik, K. H. (1983). The act frequency approach to personality. *Psychological Review, 90*, 105–126.

Clark, K. B. (1971). The pathos of power. *American Psychologist, 26*, 1047–1057.

Craig, G. A., and George, A. L. (1983). *Force and statecraft: Diplomatic problems of our time*. New York: Oxford University Press.

Cronbach, L. J. (1975). Beyond the two disciplines in scientific psychology. *American Psychologist, 30*, 116–127.

Dallin, A. (1981). The domestic sources of Soviet foreign policy. In S. Bialer (Ed.), *The domestic context of Soviet foreign policy* (pp. 335–408). Philadelphia: Lippincott.

Deutsch, M. (1973). *The resolution of conflict*. New Haven, CT: Yale University Press.

———. (1983). The prevention of World War III: A psychological perspective. *Political Psychology, 4*, 3–32.

Druckman, D. (1983). Social psychology and international negotiations: Processes and influences. In R. F. Kidd & M. J. Saks (Eds.), *Advances in applied social psychology* (Vol. 2, pp. 51–81). Hillsdale, NJ: Erlbaum.

Dyson, F. (1984). *Weapons and hope*. New York: Harper & Row.

Einhorn, H., & Hogarth, R. M. (1981). Behavioral decision theory. *Annual Review of Psychology, 32*, 53–88.

Esser, J. K. and Komorita, S. (1975). Reciprocity and concession-making in bargaining. *Journal of Personality and Social Psychology, 31*, 864–872.

Etheredge, L. S. (1978). *A world of men*. Cambridge, MA: MIT Press.

Etzioni, A. (1962). *The hard way to peace*. New York: Crowell-Colber.

Fischhoff, B., Lichtenstein, S., Slovic, P., Derby, S., and Keeny, R. L. (1981). *Acceptable risk*. New York: Cambridge University Press.

Fischhoff, B., Slovic, P., and Lichtenstein, S. (1978). Fault trees: Sensitivity of estimated failure estimates to problem representation. *Journal of Experimental Psychology: Human Perception and Performance, 2*, 330–344.

Fiske, S. T. and Taylor, S. (1984). *Social cognition*. Reading, MA: Addison-Wesley.

Gamson, W. and Modigliani, A. (1970). *Untangling the cold war*. Boston: Little, Brown.

George, A. L. (1980). *Presidential decision-making in foreign policy: The effective use of information and advice*. Boulder, CO: Westview Press.

———. (1983). *Managing U.S.–Soviet rivalry: Problems of crisis prevention*. Boulder, CO: Westview Press.

George, A. L., Hall, D. and Simon, W. (1971). *The limits of coercive diplomacy*. Boston: Little, Brown.

George, A. L., and Smoke, R. (1974). *Deterrence in American foreign policy: Theory and practice*. New York: Columbia University Press.

Gergen, K. J. (1978). Experimentation in social psychology: A reappraisal. *European Journal of Social Psychology, 8*, 507–527.

Graber, D. (1976). *Verbal behavior and politics.* Urbana: University of Illinois Press.

Gray, C. S. (1982). Dangerous to your health: The debate over nuclear strategy and war. *Orbis, 26,* 327–349.

Hammond, K. R., and Adelman, L. (1976). Science, values, and human judgment. *Science, 194,* 389–396.

Hermann, C. (1972). *International crises: Insights from behavioral research.* New York: Free Press.

Hermann, M. G. (1976). *The psychological examination of political leaders.* New York: Free Press.

———. (1980). Assessing the personalities of Soviet politburo members. *Personality and Social Psychology Bulletin, 6,* 332–352.

Herrmann, R. K. (1985). Analyzing Soviet images of the United States. *Journal of Conflict Resolution, 29,* 665–697.

Holsti, O. R. (1972). *Crisis, escalation, war.* Montreal, Canada: McGill-Queens University Press.

Hough, J. (1981). *Soviet leadership in transition.* Washington, DC: The Brookings Institution.

Janis, I. L. (1982). *Victims of groupthink.* Boston: Houghton Mifflin.

Janis, I. L. and Mann, L. (1977). *Decision making.* New York: Free Press.

Jensen, L. (1984). Negotiating strategic arms control. *Journal of Conflict Resolution, 28,* 535–559.

Jervis, R. (1976). *Perception and misperception in international politics.* Princeton, NJ: Princeton University Press.

———. (1982, June). *Perception and misperception: An updating of the analysis.* Paper presented at the fourth annual meeting of the International Society of Political Psychology, Washington, DC.

———. (1984). *The illogic of American nuclear strategy.* Ithaca, NY: Cornell University Press.

Jervis, R., Lebow, R. N., and Stein, J. (1985). *Psychology and deterrence.* Baltimore, MD: Johns Hopkins University Press.

Katz, A. M. (1982). *Life after nuclear war: The economic and social impacts of nuclear attacks on the United States.* Cambridge, MA: Ballinger.

Kaufmann, W. (1954). *Military policy and national security.* Princeton, NJ: Princeton University Press.

Kelley, H. H. (1965). Experimental studies of threats in negotiations. *Journal of Conflict Resolution, 9,* 77–105.

Kelman, H. C. (1982). Creating the conditions for Israeli–Palestinian negotiations. *Journal of Conflict Resolution, 26,* 39–75.

Kelman, H., and Bloom, A. (1973). Assumptive frameworks in international politics. In J. Knutson (Ed.), *Handbook of political psychology* (pp. 261–295). San Francisco, CA: Jossey-Bass.

Kleinmuntz, D. N., and Kleinmuntz, B. (1981). Systems simulation decision strategies in simulated environments. *Behavioral Science, 26,* 294–304.

Lebow, R. N. (1981). *Between peace and war.* Baltimore, MD: Johns Hopkins University Press.

———. (1983). The deterrence deadlock: Is there a way out? *Political Psychology, 4,* 333–354.

Leng, R. J. (1984). Reagan and the Russians: Crisis bargaining, beliefs and the historical record. *American Political Science Review, 78,* 338–355.

Leng, R. J., and Wheeler, H. (1979). Influence strategies, success, and war. *Journal of Conflict Resolution, 23*, 655–684.

Lindskold, S. (1978). Trust development, the GRIT proposal, and the effects of conciliatory acts on conflict and cooperation. *Psychological Bulletin, 85*, 382–402.

Lynn, L. E. (1978). *Knowledge and policy: The uncertain connection.* Washington, DC: National Research Council.

Masters, J. (1984). Psychology, research, and social policy. *American Psychologist, 39*, 851–862.

McClosky, H. (1967). Personality correlates of foreign policy orientation. In J. Rosenau (Ed.), *Domestic sources of foreign policy* (pp. 51–109). New York: Free Press.

McNamara, R. (1983). The military role of nuclear weapons. *Foreign Affairs, 62*, 68–70.

Osgood, C. (1962). *An alternative to war or surrender.* Urbana: University of Illinois Press.

Osgood, R. (1981). *Containment, Soviet behavior, and grand strategy*: Berkeley, CA: Institute of International Studies.

Oskamp, S. (1971). Effects of programmed strategies on cooperation in the prisoner's dilemma game. *Journal of Conflict Resolution, 15*, 225–259.

Payne, J. (1982). Contingent decision behavior. *Psychological Bulletin, 92*, 382–402.

Pruitt, D. (1981). *Negotiation behavior.* New York: Academic Press.

Raiffa, H. (1968). *Decision analysis.* Reading, MA: Addison-Wesley.

Ross, L. (1977). The intuitive psychologist and his shortcomings: Distortion in the attribution process. In L. Berkowitz (Ed.), *Advances in experimental social psychology* (Vol. 10, pp. 173–220). New York: Academic Press.

Rubin, J., and Brown, B. (1975). *The social psychology of bargaining and negotiation.* New York: Academic Press.

Rubin, J., and Lewicki, R. J. (1973). A three-factor experimental analysis of promises and threats. *Journal of Applied Social Psychology, 3*, 240–257.

Sagan, C. (1983). Nuclear war and climatic catastrophe. *Foreign Affairs, 62*, 257–292.

Schell, J. (1980). *The fate of the earth.* New York: Knopf.

Schelling, T. C. (1960). *The strategy of conflict.* Cambridge, MA: Harvard University Press.

———. (1966). *Arms and influence.* New Haven, CT: Yale University Press.

Schlenker, B. R. (1980). *Impression management: The self-concept, social identity and interpersonal relations.* Monterey, CA: Brooks/Cole.

Snyder, G., and Diesing, P. (1977). *Conflict among nations.* Princeton, NJ: Princeton University Press.

Staw, B. M., Sandilands, L. E., & Dutton, J. E. (1981). Threat–rigidity effects in organizational behavior: A multilevel analysis. *Administrative Science Quarterly, 26*, 501–524.

Steinbruner, J. (1974). *A cybernetic theory of decision.* Princeton, NJ: Princeton University Press.

———. (1985, August). U.S. and Soviet security perspectives. *Bulletin of the Atomic Scientist, 22*, 89–93.

Stewart, P., Warhola, J. W., and Blough, R. (1983). Issue salience and foreign policy role specialization in the Soviet politburo of the 1970's. *American Journal of Political Science, 26*, 1–22.

Suedfeld, P., and Tetlock, P. E. (1977). Integrative complexity of communications in international crises. *Journal of Conflict Resolution, 21*, 169–184.

Tetlock, P. E. (1979). Identifying victims of groupthink from public statements of decision-makers. *Journal of Personality and Social Psychology, 37*, 1314–1324.

_____. (1981). Personality and isolationism: Content analysis of senatorial speeches. *Journal of Personality and Social Psychology, 41*, 737–743.

_____. (1983a). Policy-makers' images of international conflict. *Journal of Social Issues, 39*, 66–86.

_____. (1983b). Psychological research on foreign policy: A methodological overview. In L. Wheeler (Ed.), *Review of personality and social psychology* (Vol. 4, pp. 45–78). Beverly Hills, CA: Sage.

_____. (1983c). Accountability and complexity of thought. *Journal of Personality and Social Psychology, 45*, 74–83.

_____. (1985). Integrative complexity of American and Soviet foreign policy statements: A time-series analysis. *Journal of Personality and Social Psychology, 49*, 1565–1585.

_____. (1986). *Assessing the cognitive and rhetorical styles of Soviet leaders.* Paper delivered at the annual meeting of the American Psychological Association, August 1986, Washington, DC.

Tetlock, P. E., and McGuire, C. (1985). Integrative complexity as a predictor of Soviet foreign policy behavior. *International Journal of Group Tensions, 14*, 113–128.

_____. (1986). Cognitive perspectives on foreign policy. In S. Long (Ed.), *Political behavior annual* (Vol. 1, pp. 255–273). Boulder, CO: Westview. (Reprinted in R. White [Ed.], *Psychology and the prevention of nuclear war.* New York: New York University Press).

Verba, S. (1967). Some dilemmas in comparative research. *World Politics, 20*, 111–127.

Walker, S. (1983). The motivational foundations of political belief systems: A reanalysis of the operational code construct. *International Studies Quarterly, 27*, 179–201.

Weinberger, C. (1981). *Testimony before U.S. Senate Committee on Foreign Relations Hearings on Strategic Weapons Proposals* (Part 1, 97th Congress, 1st session). Washington, DC: U.S. Government Printing Office.

White, R. (1984). *Fearful warriors: A psychological study of U.S.–Soviet relations.* New York: Free Press.

Wildavsky, A. (1983). *Beyond containment: Alternative American policies toward the Soviet Union.* San Francisco, CA: Institute for Contemporary Studies.

Winter, D., and Stewart, A. (1976). Content analysis as a technique for assessing political leaders. In M. Hermann (Ed.), *The psychological examination of political leaders* (pp. 27–61). New York: Free Press.

Woolsey, R. J. (1984). *Nuclear arms: Ethics, strategy, and politics.* San Francisco, CA: Institute for Contemporary Studies.

23

On the Political Psychology of Peace and War: A Critique and an Agenda[1]

STANLEY HOFFMANN

INTRODUCTION

What brings us together here is the conviction that politics—the task of defining the goals of a community, of choosing and pursuing the means to reach them, and of selecting the leaders—cannot be understood except by reference to the intentions of the actors, and to the perceptions that shape their acts. The term political psychology is a pleonasm: not all psychology is about politics, thank goodness, but politics is wholly psychological. Even those of my colleagues who study the political behavior through quantitative techniques or formal theory operate from assumptions (far too often implicit only) about the motives and goals of human behavior.

My subject is one particular branch of politics: The study of international relations—and, within that branch, the study of strategic and diplomatic behavior. It is a fascinating and frustrating subject, for two reasons at least. First, there seems to be something implacably constant about the logic of behavior of sovereign actors in the international state of nature. The differences in size, complexity, economic and social structure, relations between the public and the private, which exist between, say, the Greek *polis* and a contemporary nation-state are enormous (and make nostalgic laments about past communal life quite irrelevant). But the student of present-day world politics who turns to Thucydides finds in his masterpiece, certainly not relief, but enlightenment and shock. The empires and nations of today seem to be playing the same ballet: the music may be different; the choreography hasn't changed. Second, our fate depends on the future of interstate relations. In the nuclear age, some states have the capacity to put an end to the show, and to much of civilization, for the first time in history.

The fact that the show has been playing for so long, through so many upheavals and holocausts from which mankind as a whole has always recovered, and above all the fact that the world remains organized in separate communities whose internal needs and passions are the dominant concerns of most citizens, explain why, so often, they fail to worry enough about the implications and perils of the game of states, about the threats to peace and the risk of war. This is why they tend to leave these worries to experts, or to leaders elected or selected on quite other grounds than wisdom or skill in foreign affairs. On the other hand, the awareness of danger that cannot fail to come either with expertise or from reflections about the drift of the world explains why, in many countries, a large portion of the educated public, especially among intellectuals and professionals, and a smaller fraction of the citizenry have been sounding the alarm.

It is about that part of the alarmed public which consists of students of world politics that I want to talk about: Not about that segment of the public that either reacts with blind faith in the leadership's policy, or with a ritualistic ethnocentric self-righteousness that justifies Erik Erikson's remarks about pseudospeciation. Nor about that unfortunately large body of experts that consists of policy scientists who serve, write for, or rationalize the decisions of, the nations' leaders, because they share the goals and outlook of these leaders, see themselves as mere technicians, or—as in so many countries—are simply not allowed to question the leaders' assumptions. These two populations are part of our problem. But there is another part: a deep split among those of us who are professionally concerned with world politics, and disturbed or anguished by politics-as-usual.

In a recent issue of *Political Psychology* Richard Smoke (Smoke, 1984) described two "universes of discourse" for the same topic—survival in the nuclear age and the era of Soviet-American confrontation. He was talking about the anti-nuclear movement on one side, the "mainstream national security analysts" on the other. I am referring to the same division, but even among those of us who are not in charge or advisers of official policy. Smoke labeled these two viewpoints the deterrence model and the abolitionist model, thus focusing on nuclear weapons. The focus is right, although perhaps too narrow. The labels are more questionable, for in the camp of what Smoke calls the deterrence model there are many critics of deterrence, aware of its past failures and multiple ambiguities, and in the other camp there are people who believe that nuclear weapons cannot be wiped out.

The split exists. It is not about values: The concern for survival, the anxiety about black-and-white thinking, cognitive closure, and deadly miscalculations are the same in both groups. Nor is it necessarily about what each camp expects if politics continues as usual—those who appear shortsighted to the other group are often far from reassured about the outcome of the current contests of states. It is, above all, a split about *what is possible,* which is tied to a different reading of reality. In order to simplify, I will use my own labels. I am aware of their limitations, but I wanted them to be as neutral as possible. I will refer to *traditionalists* and *radicals.* The two groups agree on the obvious: the existence of international anarchy, of a state of nature in which the actors pursue their separate goals without a common superior and without any broad consensus of values. In such a state, the resort to force is an ever-present possibility, and the actors spend much of their time preparing for, or against, this use, calculating the forces of potential or actual rivals; the common norms or procedures are weak and permanently imperiled. Thus, both groups begin with what Rousseau deplored: the absence of a "general unity of mankind," the division of mankind into separate units.

This is all, I think, that the two groups agree on. The traditionalists' reading of reality is often denounced, by the radicals, as complacent, or as a denial of reality, or even as resulting from an identification with those who cause the present dangers. I will not deny that some of the less sophisticated champions of what, in my branch of political science, is called the realist school of international affairs, often sound as if they believed that what is is fine, and that this state of affairs could be well managed as long as the actors are rational and pursue moderate goals.

But many traditionalists, even among those who accept the label of realism, have no illusions about rationality or the "rational actor" model of decision-making. They know that the very fragmentation of mankind breeds both the emotional distortions that students of prejudices, ideologies, national images, and national styles describe, and the cognitive distortions which the parochialism of perceptions, the uncertainty about the motives of other players or about the costs and benefits of alternative courses, the policy-makers' own need for consistency, the organizational pressures for continuity or loyalty, and the weight of past commitments or current domestic constraints inevitably entail. They know that the many contests among states, the states' desire to dominate or determination not to be dominated, inject into their concerns considerations, both about image and about power, that twist their definition of needs, their selection of ends, their choice of means, in strange ways. They know that deterrence has often failed in the past, and that such fiascoes also are of the essence in a world of fragmented units and perceptions in conflict; for what is defensive to one power is offensive to the other, and each actor constantly has to choose between a move that could fail to deter because the rival will interpret it as a provocation, and a policy that could fail to deter because the rival will interpret it as a sign of weakness and appeasement. And yet states, yesterday and today, still aim at deterring each other, not because, by necessity, any evidence of inferiority, any deficiency of power *must* lead to blackmail or attack—as several writers have pointed out, there are many factors of self-deterrence at work (Lebow, 1984)—but because there is always a *risk* that weakness might tempt a rival or foe. To be prepared for the worst in a situation in which Gresham's law operates, is a basic, unavoidable, rule of thumb.

The traditionalists' approach to reality is thus neither uncritical nor Panglossian. Indeed, it could be called doubly tragic: because—like their Founding Father, Thucydides—they are fully aware of the errors and horrors the actors unceasingly commit, *and* because they do not believe that the essence of world politics is susceptible to drastic and early change, barring disasters. In their eyes, easy, quick transcendence, a sudden mutation, is not at all possible. They do not, usually, rule out the emergence of identities wider than the current nation-states; but they note that, in the past, the widening of identity has been both slow and violent, and that, today, the creation of a nation-state out of far narrower identities is still unfinished business in much of the world; today, in the states, there are more demands for narrower than for wider identities. Traditionalists do not deny that states might learn new modes of cooperation to cope with common needs and fears, and gradually tame violence in their relations; they are aware of the forces and processes that operate across borders, reduce the autonomy of the states, and sometimes create actors other than the states. But they are not convinced that transnational agents, be they multinational corporations or religious movements, always contribute to peace, or that transnational forces are more integrative than disruptive. They remain skeptical about the states' willingness to give up fully either sovereignty, however leaky, or arms, however suicidal, and they remain aware of the enormous potential for interstate violence that lies in the countless powder kegs of domestic strife.

Above all, they look at international politics as a field with rules of its own, derived from the very nature of the international milieu. Any reasoning by analogy, for instance, from the domestic politics of well-integrated nations, is thus seen by them as a mistake (they are, on the whole, very dubious about deriving "lessons" for state behavior from labor mediation). They realize that violence, which it is the function of the state to curb within its borders, is both a result and a perpetuator of international anarchy; but they also realize that neither one of the two techniques that have produced wider identities— but never an end to war—in history: conquest, and voluntary association, is likely to eliminate anarchy and violence in the near future. Consequently, what is on their agenda is, on the one hand, a better, deeper, broader understanding of the theoretical logic of interstate relations, of the different political, sociological, and psychological factors that affect it in practice, of the specialized grammars of diplomacy, war, trade, etc . . . ; on the other hand, a (modest, by necessity) agenda of reforms, aimed at introducing as much moderation, as many opportunities for cooperation and the pooling of sovereignties, as much taming of the beast, as the structure and the logic allow.

When the traditionalists look at the world, they see nuclear weapons, of course. Their failure to march for abolition results neither from love of the bomb (what a silly idea!), nor from a conviction that nuclear deterrence will always be successful, nor from a denial of the peril. It comes from their conviction that the very nature of international reality rules it out. When they look at the world, they see the contest between Washington and Moscow, of course; and they do not, usually, agree among themselves either about Soviet intentions, behavior and achievements, or about American actions and effects, or about the best way of dealing with the contest. But they believe that it too cannot be transcended, both because it is of the very essence of international politics that the two biggest actors must be rivals, that the growth of the power of one must cause fear in the other, that each one shall see the other as malignant, itself as benign; and also because *these* two actors have (objectively, as *Pravda* would say) widely conflicting interests and worldviews.

It seems to me (I am traditionalist, in case you didn't know it) that the radicals' approach differs from what precedes in three ways. I will try—knowing that many, perhaps most of you are not traditionalists—to be as fair as possible, but it is clearly a traditionalist's view of the radicals that I will offer, along with an explanation of why my group takes issue with their approach. Let me make one thing perfectly clear, as someone used to say: Not all the radicals are psychologists, social psychologists, psychoanalysts or psychiatrists. Some of these are to be found wandering or toiling among the traditionalists, and there are a number of political scientists and jurists among the radicals. What I will say about them may be more true of some than of others, but I am concerned here with ideal-types rather than with a complete coverage of all the nuances.

First, the radicals' impulse is *therapeutic*, whereas the traditionalists' is *analytic*. Insofar as the latter are concerned with "cures," interested in suggesting norms for behavior that would make the international "state of war" less lethal, they derive these prescriptions from their sense of the limits of the possible: they insist that the steps to be taken remain, so to speak, within the boundaries of the stage on which the ballet is performed. The radicals—even when they agree with the description of the stage offered by the traditionalists—begin with a critique and rejection of the whole show. One side takes the show as a given, even as they deplore its flaws and wish for revisions. The other side is so sensitive to cacophony, so worried about the potential for disaster, that it denounces not only the players, but also those who seem—to them—largely satisfied with analysis and resigned to the fundamental status quo.

This is why I talked about a different reading of reality. One group, looking at the show, concludes that it is utopian to wish it away, or to suggest cures whose adoption cannot be imagined unless it were already fundamentally different from what it is now and has been for ages. The other group, looking at the new weapons on the stage, and remembering the show's past breakdowns, argues that the only way of preventing the fire next time is to move to a totally new stage, and to change the play and the actors.

As I said already, not all the traditionalists promise world peace, nor do all the radicals believe in the mathematical certainty of nuclear war and winter. But they are convinced that the very impossibility of a mutation *before* disaster limits the scope and indeed the types of measures that can realistically be taken to avoid it. Radical impatience with what is (wrongly) often interpreted as a professional commitment of traditional analysts to the perpetuation of the current state of their field—as a failure on their part, as well as on the part of statesmen, to be shaken, like Ionesco's characters, by the sudden irruption of rhinoceroses in our midst—is matched by traditionalist annoyance at what is often perceived as mere rhetoric of indignation, denunciation, and exorcism, fist shaking at unwelcome facts, and unfair name calling addressed to actors who, caught in a game they did not invent, do, at best, what they can to keep it from blowing up and, more usually, at least what they have been selected for.

This brings us to a second difference. The radicals, who tend (often correctly) to perceive the policy scientists' stance as a *trahison des clercs*, write and behave as if they were above the fray, seeing through the rationalizations statesmen endlessly provide, and the stereotypes in which citizens cloak their fears, frustrations, and aggressions. At the same time, they can't help but belong to different communities: While calling for a global identity, they remain, say, Americans or British, or Indian, or Israeli. Their recommendations are usually addressed to, or hurled at, their own governments or (in the case of many intellectuals from less powerful countries who deal with the global cold war) at the superpowers. The underlying assumption, once again, is that the seriousness of the peril should push their own national government, or, in the latter case, the great powers' leaders, into adopting the drastic measures needed for salvation.

The traditionalists, even when, in their own work, they try scrupulously to transcend national prejudices and to seek scientific truth, believe that it is unrealistic to expect *statesmen* to stand above the fray: By definition, the statesmen are there to worry not only about planetary survival, but—first of all—about national survival and safety. To be sure, they ought to be able to see how certain policies, aimed at enhancing security, actually increase insecurity all around. But there are sharp limits to how far they can go in their mutual empathy or in their acts (unlike intellectuals in their advice), as long as the states' antagonisms persist, as long as uncertainty about each other's intentions prevails, and as long as there is reason to fear that one side's wise restraint, or unilateral moves toward "sanity," will be met, not by the rival's similar restraint or moves, but either by swift or skillful political or military exploitation of the opportunity created for unilateral gain, or by a formidable domestic backlash if national self-restraint appears to result in external losses, humiliations or perceptions of weakness.

There is little point in saying that the state of affairs which imposes such limits is "anachronistic" or "unrational." To traditionalists, the radicals' stance—condemnation from the top of Mount Olympus—can only impede understanding of the limits and possibilities of reform. To be sure, the fragmentation of mankind is a formidable obstacle to the solution of many problems that cannot be handled well in a national framework, and a deadly peril insofar as the use of force, the very distinctive feature of world politics, now entails the risk of nuclear war.

But one can hardly call anachronistic a phenomenon—the assertion of national identity—that, to the bulk of mankind, appears not only as a necessity but also as a positive good, since humanity's fragmentation results from the very aspiration to self-determination. Many people have only recently emerged from foreign mastery, and have reason to fear that the alternative to national self-mastery is not a world government of assured fairness and efficiency, but alien domination.

As for "unrationality," the drama lies in the contrast between the rationality of the whole, which scholars are concerned about—the greatest good of the greatest number, in utilitarian terms—and the rationality or greatest good of the part, which is what statesmen worry about and are responsible for. What the radicals denounce as irrational and irresponsible from the viewpoint of mankind is what Weber called the statesman's ethic of responsibility. What keeps ordinary "competitive conflict processes" (Deutsch, 1983)—the very stuff of society—from becoming "unrational" or destructive, is precisely what the nature of world politics excludes: the restraint of the partners either because of the ties of affection or responsibility that mitigate the conflict, or because of the existence of an outsider—marriage counselor, arbitrator, judge, policeman or legislator—capable of inducing or imposing restraints.

Here we come to a third point of difference. The very absence of such safeguards of rationality, the obvious discrepancy between what each part intends, and what it (and the whole world) ends with, the crudeness of some of the psychological mechanisms at work in international affairs—as one can see from the statements of leaders, or from the media, or from inflamed publics—have led many radicals, especially among those whose training or profession is in psychoanalysis or mental health, to treat the age-old contests of states in terms, not of the psychology of politics, but of individual psychology and pathology.

There are two manifestations of this. One is the tendency to look at nations or states as individuals writ large, stuck at an early stage of development (similarly, John Mack (1985) in a recent paper talks of political ideologies as carrying "forward the dichotomized structures of childhood"). One of my predecessors writes about "the correspondence between development of the individual self and that of the group or nation," and concludes "that intergroup or international conflict contains the basic elements of the conflict each individual experiences psychologically" (Volkan, 1985). Robert Holt, from the viewpoint of cognitive psychology, finds "the largest part of the American public" immature, in a "phase of development below the Conscientious" (Holt, 1984). The second related aspect is the tendency to look at the notions statesmen or publics have of "the enemy," not only as residues of childhood or adolescent phases of development, but as images that express "disavowed aspects of the self" (Stein, 1985), reveal truths about our own fears and hatreds, and amount to masks we put on the "enemy," because of our own psychological needs.

Here is where the clash between traditionalists and radicals is strongest. Traditionalists do not accept a view of group life derived from the study of individual development or family relations, or a view of modern society derived from the simplistic Freudian model of regressed followers identifying with a leader. They don't see in ideologies just irrational constructs, but often rationally selected maps allowing individuals to cope with reality. They don't see national identification as pathological, as an appeal to the people's baser instincts, more aggressive impulses or unsophisticated mental defenses; it is, as Jean-Jacques Rousseau so well understood, the competition of sovereign states that frequently pushes people from "sane" patriotism to "insane" nationalism (Rousseau's way of preventing the former from veering into the latter was, to say the least, impractical: to remain poor in isolation). Nor do they see anything "primitive" in the nation's concern for survival: It is a moral and structural requirement.

Traditionalists also believe that the "intra-psychic" approach distorts reality. Enemies are not mere projections of negative identities; they are often quite real. To be sure, the Nazis' view of the Jews fits the metaphor of the mask put on the enemy for one's own needs. But were, in return, those Jews who understood what enemies they had in the Nazis, doing the same? Is the Soviet domination of Eastern Europe, is the Soviet regime's treatment of dissidents, was the Gulag merely a convenient projection of our intra-psychic battles? Clichés such as the one about how our enemy "understands only force" may tell us a great deal about ourselves; but sometimes they contain half-truths about him, and not just revelations about us. Our fears flow not only from our private fantasies but also from concrete realities and from the fantasies which the international state of nature generates.

In other words, the psychology of politics which traditionalists deem adequate is not derived from theories of psychic development and health; it is derived from the logic of the international milieu, which breeds the kind of vocabulary found in the historians and theorists of the state of nature: fear and power, pride and honor, survival and security, self-interest and reputation, distrust and misunderstanding, commitment and credibility. It is also derived from the social psychology of small or large groups, which resorts to the standard psychological vocabulary that describes mental mechanisms or maneuvers and cognitive processes: denial, projection, guilt, repression, closure, rigidity, etc. . . . But using this vocabulary does not imply that a group whose style of politics is paranoid is therefore composed of people who, as private individuals, are paranoid. Nor does it relieve us of the duty to look at the objective reasons and functions of these mental moves, and of the duty to make explicit our assumptions about what constitutes a "healthy," wise, or proper social process.

Altogether, traditionalists find the mental health approach to world affairs unhelpful. Decisions about war and peace are usually taken by small groups of people; the temptation of analyzing their behavior either, literally, in terms of their personalities, or, metaphysically, in terms borrowed from the study of human development, rather than in those of group dynamics or principles of international politics is understandable. But it is misleading. What is pathological in couples, or in a well-ordered community, is, alas, frequent, indeed normal, among states, or in a troubled state. What is malignant or crazy is usually not the actors or the social process in which they are engaged: it is the possible results.

The grammar of motives which the mental health approach brands as primitive or immature is actually rational *for the actors*. Traditionalists fear that this particular approach leads to the substitution of labels for explanations, to bad analysis and fanciful prescriptions. Bad analysis: the tendency to see in group coherence a regressive response to a threat, whereas it often is a rational response to the "existential" threats entailed by the very nature of the international milieu. Or the tendency to see in the effacement or minimization of individual differences in a group a release of unconscious instincts, rather than a phenomenon that can be perfectly adaptive—in response to stress or threats—or result from governmental manipulation or originate in the code of conduct inculcated by the educational system, etc. . . . The habit of comparing the state, or modern society, with the Church or the army, and to analyze human relations in these institutions in ways that stress the libidinal more than the cognitive and superego factors, or equate libidinal bonds and the desire for a leader. The view that enemies are above all products of mental drives, rather than inevitable concomitants of social strife at every level. Or the view that the contest with the rival fulfills internal needs, which may be true, but requires careful examination of the nature of these needs (psychological? bureaucratic? economic?), obscures the objective reasons of the contest, and risks confusing cause and function.

Indeed, such analysis is particularly misleading in dealing with the present scene. The radicals are so (justifiably) concerned with the nuclear peril that the traditional ways in which statesmen and publics behave seem to vindicate the pathological approach. But this, in turn, incites radicals to overlook the fundamental ambiguity of contemporary world politics. On the one hand, there is a nuclear revolution—the capacity for total destruction. On the other hand, many states, without nuclear weapons, find that the use of force remains rational (in terms of a rationality of means) and beneficial at home or abroad—ask the Vietnamese, or the Egyptians after October 1973, or Mrs. Thatcher after the Falklands, or Ronald Reagan after Grenada.

The superpowers themselves, whose contest has not been abolished by the nuclear revolution (it is the stakes, the costs of failure that have, of course, been transformed), find that much of their rivalry can be conducted in traditional ways—including limited uses of force—below the level of nuclear alarm. They also find that nuclear weapons, while— perhaps—unusable rationally, can usefully strengthen the very process that has been so faulty in the prenuclear ages: deterrence (this is one of the reasons for nuclear proliferation). The pathological approach interprets deterrence as expressing the deterrer's belief that his country is good, the enemy's is bad. This is often the case, but it need not be; it can also reflect the conviction that one's country has interests that are not mere figments of the imagination, and need to be protected both because of the material costs of losing them, and because of the values embedded in them. As for war planning, it is not a case of "psychological denial of unwelcome reality" (Montville, 1985), but a—perhaps futile, perhaps dangerous—necessity in a world where deterrence may once more fail.

The prescriptions that result from the radicals' psychological approach also run into traditionalist objections. Even if one accepts the metaphors of collective disease or pathology, one must understand that the "cure" can only be provided by politics. All too often, the radicals' cures consist of perfectly sensible recommendations for lowering tensions, but fail to tell us how to get them carried out—they only tell us how much better the world would be, if only "such rules could be established" (Deutsch, 1983).

Sometimes, they express generous aspirations—for common or mutual security— without much awareness of the obstacles which conflicting interests, fears about allies or clients, and the nature of the weapons themselves, continue to erect. Sometimes, they too neglect the ambiguity of life in a nuclear world: The much lamented redundancy of weapons, a calamity if nuclear deterrence fails, can also be a cushion against failure. Finally, many of the remedies offered are based on an admirable liberal model of personality and politics: the ideal of the mature, well-adjusted, open-minded person (produced by liberal education and healthy family relations) transposed on the political level, and thus accompanied by the triumph of democracy in the community, by the elimination of militarism and the spread of functional cooperation abroad.

But three obstacles remain unconquered: first, a major part of the world rejects this ideal and keeps itself closed to it (many of the radicals seem to deny it, or to ignore it, or to believe it doesn't matter). Second, the record shows that real democracies, in their behavior toward non-democratic or less "advanced" societies, do not conform to the happy model (think of the U.S. in Central America). Third, the task of reform, both of the publics and of the statesmen, through consciousness raising and education is hopelessly huge, incapable of being pursued equally in all the important states, and—indeed—too slow if one accepts the idea of a mortal nuclear peril.

These, then, are the dimensions of a split that should not be minimized or denied.

A COMMON AGENDA

Dialogues of the deaf risk becoming battles of the equally self-righteous. The exasperation of each group with the other has already contributed to the divisions and confusions of the peace movement in this country. What is at stake in this quarrel is more than a "narcissism of small differences," or a rivalry of scientific imperialisms: This is precisely why I have spent so much time on it. But there is a danger: forgetting what the two groups have in common, and what separates them from all those who consider the structure and logic of world politics not only hard to transcend, but reasonably safe, or desirable. On two conditions, the groups I have described could cooperate fruitfully and extensively. What I shall do now is to outline, sketchily, an agenda for cooperation.

The first of the two conditions is that those traditionalists who, in their work, have stressed what one could call "hard" factors, such as power and interests (and who therefore tend to be more impressed by the monotonous recurrence of the same steps on the stage, because they concentrate on the logic of behavior of competing units), show themselves more willing to move into the jungle of perceptions, images, and distortions that provide both for the many variations on the constant themes, and for the multiple quirks of a "logic" that forces the actors to engage in apparently rational calculations yet rarely saves them from huge errors and disastrous surprises. Second, the radicals should accept the validity of some of the criticisms I have presented—and especially the idea that one must enter into that very logic (however much one disapproves its effects), and understand both its rules and the hold it has on statesmen and on citizens. Indeed, one must accept, in Raymond Aron's terms, the notion that "institutional tensions show in individual tensions, but we cannot diagnose and define the former by studying the latter" (UNESCO, 1957), and even the notion that what would be considered pathological in an individual is often perfectly normal in society and politics. Let us turn to the common agenda.

There is nothing original about it. Some of it has already been undertaken, both by political scientists interested in what actually goes on in the minds of decision-makers, and by social psychologists concerned either with small groups that make political decisions or with the collective beliefs, attitudes and behavior of political communities—scholars such as Alex George, Robert Jervis, Ned Lebow, Irving Janis, Herbert Kelman. It is an agenda both for research and for prescriptions, and it is based on three major assumptions.

The first is the need for a more sophisticated model of political community. There is an almost infinite number of ways in which leaders and followers relate to each other, and in which what Montesquieu called *corps intermédiaires*—organized groups—complicate the picture. The rather crude model Freud derived from Le Bon may approximate reality in some cases of extreme anomie and distress, but it accounts neither—as Philip Rieff has pointed out—for the modern bureaucratized polity, nor for the ego functions often served by the state, nor for the way in which the state can often strengthen rather than undermine the citizens' superegos, nor for the criss-crossing of loyalties whenever groups are allowed to form and to promote their interests freely. How much the leaders can twist and shape the minds of the followers depends on the regime, the laws, the mores, and the moments. Even societies in distress do not all behave in the same way; the outcome depends on national patterns of ideas and behavior, and also on what kind of "heroic leadership" is available for guidance—or for surrender: an FDR or a Hitler, a Mao or a de Gaulle.

Next, despite the inevitably competitive character of international politics, despite the failure of the liberal and social-democratic dream of a harmonious coexistence of nation-states under law and through trade, conflict, the stuff of social life, need not be as violent and destructive as it often is when it breaks out in a structure of anarchy, where autonomous actors are able to resort to force. This suggests both a warning and a goal. On the one hand, we cannot ask *now* that statesmen and publics behave *as if* that structure had been discarded, *as if* a global society comparable to a well-functioning polity had already been established; nor should we think that such a society will necessarily be built on the model of the state as we know it. "World government," should it ever come, would be very different, more differentiated, diffuse and decentralized, than the governments of nations.

On the other hand, we ought to study the possibility of acts and policies that, from within the present anarchic system, nevertheless depart from "politics as usual," and move toward a different kind of international system. It would still be fragmented and conflictual, no doubt, but with far stricter limits on the use of force, and far greater opportunities for cooperative arrangements in all the realms (security included) where unilateral action is insufficient or actually self-defeating.[2] I have in mind a system in which the priority which so many states, old or new, want to give to their internal economic and social development would be rewarded, and quests for aggrandizement or diversion through violent conflict beyond one's borders would be firmly and collectively resisted.

Finally, when it comes to the central issues of today, even though the Soviet-American conflict has extraordinarily deep roots and is unlikely to melt away, even though what McGeorge Bundy has called existential deterrence is a fact of life, which no amount of denunciation will wipe out, we must see to it that the cold war between Washington and Moscow continues to stay cold. This is unlikely, unless areas of cooperation are found and the nuclear arms race is controlled. Moreover, we must never forget that deterrence is not a Procrustean (albeit hard) bed. Its stability is constantly challenged by technology, its ability to prevent war thanks to the nuclear revolution is constantly put in doubt by the attempts both superpowers make to find ways of actually using nuclear weapons should deterrence fail, its credibility is shaken by the theological disputes about what kinds of capabilities deter most, and about what kinds of threats deterrence can effectively protect one from (nuclear threats only? Against oneself only or also against allies?).

What sort of research on peace and war in the past (distant and present) do these assumptions suggest? I will make five recommendations.

In the first place, insofar as one of the causes of war in the modern world—since the French Revolution—is the bursting of the reservoir of *collective emotions and passions*, we need to do more work to find out to what extent and when such feelings and images constitute mere restraints on the freedom of action of governments; to what extent and when they actually push statesmen in directions states might otherwise not have taken; to what extent and when certain beliefs and attitudes (I am thinking of those of so many people in the U.S.A. toward Communism and toward the peoples of Central America) give a green light, if not a *carte blanche*, to the government; and to what extent and when they are little more than a stagnant, often stinking pool that can be stirred up either by the media or by interest groups or by political parties or by the governments for their own purposes.

There are vast amounts of data, for all the wars, and major crises leading to wars, of the last 150 years. My own research, both about the 1930s and about contemporary world politics, suggests that the public at large, and sometimes the decision-makers themselves, are often extraordinarily susceptible to sudden crystallizations of fears, prejudices, and interpretations produced by small but influential groups whose members come together from many circles: politics, business, the media, the intelligentsia, etc. And these crystallizations then guide, or misguide, both the public and the government, because they seem to offer a convincing explanation of a bewildering world and a convenient road map.

Also, this research shows that the more the public is torn between conflicting fears, the more it tries to ignore and deny the lesser fear, in order to conjure the bigger one, and thus achieve a fragile, fallacious cognitive and emotional consistency. Indeed, insofar as collective images and prejudices are concerned, or episodes in which large amounts of people display those symptoms of regression, of scapegoating, or of massive denial of reality that can be catastrophic in their effects, we need more understanding—from social psychologists—of the mental mechanisms at work. (Do we really know how individuals who are dispersed, who live in different places and groups, produce a sort of collective mind, mood, and pattern of conduct that may be quite independent of, and often contrary to, their character and behavior as individuals?)

We also need, from other social scientists, to find out more about the economic and social factors, the cultural traditions, the historical marks, that explain when and why such phenomena occur, and why certain ideological choices appear to those who make them answers, not only to the needs of their personality, but to their experience in society. Again, Europe in the 1930s, but also the Arab-Israeli conflict, or the first cold war, provide endless material.

Second, the work that has already been undertaken about the behavior of small *groups of decision-makers* faced with issues of war and peace needs to be expanded. Thanks to the research of several of the authors I have named, we begin to have a sort of repertory of the mental and organizational mistakes most commonly found—information processed according to misleading postulates, overvaluation of past successes, excessive investments in established policies, exaggeration of the costs of alternatives, inability to empathize with foreign decision-making groups or to understand their concerns, a stake in beliefs that justify the existence or importance of one's agency, etc.

But the many case studies we now have, most of which focus on disasters, often reach contradictory conclusions. For instance, we find many cases in which "groupthink" (Janis, 1982)—a form of concurrence and closure under stress in which loyalty to the leader or to the organization plays a major role (but so does the desire for effectiveness)—seemed to be an important factor of failure. However, we also find cases in which fiasco resulted from the divisions of the decision-making groups, from the outside pressures that weighed on them, from their inability to control or discipline "deviants" or dissidents (Lebow, 1981).

Clearly, we need to know more about the circumstances in which it is unanimity that is dangerous, and those in which it is discord; and we have to be more precise and discriminating in our concept of decision-making "groups": The structures, degrees of intensity and openness vary considerably. We have to be more systematic about the effects of failure; sometimes, they force statesmen into a corrective relaxation of the tensions that had produced the crisis (Lebow discusses Fashoda and the Cuban missile crisis); sometimes, however, they have exactly the opposite result: a determination to be tougher the next time. Indeed, the gradual erosion of restraints through repeated crises that, while "managed," leave one or even both sides feeling cheated is one of the major causes of ultimate disasters.

We should not neglect the importance of the "map of the world"—derived from past experiences, education, expectations, images of the collective self and of others—that is often common to decision-makers of very different backgrounds and personalities (and hence helps provide "groupthink"), as in America's Vietnam drama—or even to actors otherwise divided over tactical and bureaucratic issues (as in the Reagan Administration, or in the German leadership in July 1914). Moreover, we need to go beyond the small circle of decision-makers, and look at the way in which their decisions are either institutionalized and turned into policies which bureaucratic momentum preserves long beyond any justification, or else are subtly undermined or neutralized by bureaucratic independence or resistance. Here, organizational strategies, group dynamics, and the impact of personality come together.

Third, some shoddy books have given "psycho-history" a bad reputation. However, insofar as decisions on peace and war are made by leaders who experience and interpret the logic of world politics in different ways, we need more studies in the *psychology of leadership*—as long as they do not conform too slavishly to the Lasswellian psycho-pathological approach. At least they should understand that even in cases of displacement of private frustrations on public objects, what matters is what the leader does with what may be pathological in him—and especially with his aggression—as well as the ways in which, in his public performance, his character fits, filters, and is reshaped by, the demands of the role—how it is, so to speak, harnessed, constrained or on the contrary let loose by the nature of the country's institutional system. In particular, how do all these factors interact in foreign policy crises?

What is also needed, of course, is an understanding of the many variables that intervene between character and policy decisions on war and peace. Many wars have occurred because the leaders were far too ordinary or mediocre (1914), others because one dangerously charismatic leader managed to provoke a conflagration (1939). Average leaders caught in the logic of their role, or subjected to too many pressures, can make fatal mistakes (the appeasers); partly psychopathic leaders can be extremely cautious abroad (Stalin), or use their talents, for a while, in brilliantly instrumental ways (Hitler, 1933–1939).

Fourth, after this rather grim series of invitations to look at wreckage, let us turn to the historical record in more encouraging directions. We need to examine more systematically, not only the way in which crises have been managed or mismanaged in the past, but on the one hand the whole art of *crisis avoidance and prevention:* why and how some tensions never burst into crises, some conflicts were defused or remained moderate despite (or perhaps, because of) expectations of trouble and without leaving deep scars on the international system. To what extent were such successes due to military deterrence, to what extent were other factors—calculations of interests, or moral restraints— decisive? On the other hand, we also need to study all the cases of successful *conflict resolution* in order to evaluate both the contributions—positive and negative—made by negotiated or imposed settlements, and the role played by other factors, psychological and political.

Fifth, what can we learn from the record of past and contemporary cooperation? We need to study what Karl Deutsch and his associates once called "*security communities*" (Deutsch, 1957), the oases of peace and cooperation in the desert of conflict and competition: What has made such zones possible, under what conditions have they lasted, what has it taken for former enemies to overcome their hostility and become associates (has it always been the combination of exhaustion and emergence of a greater threat that lies behind Franco-German reconciliation?).

In a comparable vein, the research launched, in recent years, by teams of political scientists and political economists, about what Robert Keohane and Joseph Nye have called *international regimes* (1977)—clusters of norms and procedures that allow states to bargain and cooperate for the joint pursuit of interests and needs which hostile or separate action could not serve—the conditions in which such regimes can be established, surmount crises, or collapse, and the reasons why some last and others don't, is of considerable importance to political psychology. For we find here leaders and (often transnational) groups at work, often—for once!—in highly creative ways. We also find, in some cases, the expectations, calculations and demands of larger groups—farmers, bankers, businessmen, fishermen, sailors and aviators—focusing on the benefits (or costs) of such regimes. Thus, they provide a learning experience in new forms and frameworks of political behavior.

All of these suggestions aim at using the tools, theories, and insights of a variety of disciplines in order to dredge the huge pond that lies in between the very simple, stark landscape described by the theory of interstate behavior—the logic of strategic-diplomatic conduct—and the jungle of past and present international and national events. This logic, as I have stated above, tells us that conflicting units in search of "rational" policies will make mistakes because of misperceptions, miscalculations, and the mischief of uncertainty. It does not tell us how each unit will, at any moment, interpret what is "rational" for it, nor what those distortions and gropings in the dark will be.

Is there anything the two groups of political psychologists could also do in order to ensure that the steps of the actors will, in the future, be more enlightened, keep the world safe from destruction, and move toward the kind of world society with minimal interstate violence I have alluded to?

We all can, of course—as intellectuals and as citizens—push for the causes that we hold essential and warn, protest, petition, and pressure against those we deem evil. Since we are undoubtedly divided, politically as well as methodologically, there might seem little point in offering a program for action: It could add one more split to the Society! But I have been talking about those students of world affairs who *are* alarmed by current trends; and I think it is possible for an association of scholars and professionals to engage, in their daily work, in activities—writings, lectures, all the forms of public education—that could help preserve peace, go beyond that fragile and ominous accumulation of deadly weapons called deterrent which, as the American Catholic bishops have said, is only conditionally acceptable as a lesser evil, and inch us toward a safer world. Let me suggest, again, five directions.

One is a matter of action and research. At a time of growing ethnocentrism and parochialism in this country, when the public and much of the political class oscillates between the conviction that we know what is good for others and the desire to be left alone by them, it is essential for us to broaden our membership abroad and to multiply *scientific contacts and cooperative projects* with colleagues from other countries.

We need, of course, candor: Too often, for instance, meetings of American independent scholars or professionals with Soviet not so independent counterparts turn either into ritual, generalized proclamations of common interests and denunciations of obstacles to peace and friendship, or into traps or encounters between masochists and sadists—when only moves or mistakes of Western governments are described as dangerous, and no mention is found of the massive contribution Moscow has often made to international tensions or Western distrust.

Only candor, indeed, will make such exchanges useful: for they will, then, provide Soviet experts who are, I repeat, not purely private citizens, with valuable insights into our ways of working at common problems. And we need these contacts in order to understand, and then to spread our understanding of, the images, prejudices, perceptions, hopes and fears of representatives of foreign cultures. Whenever we can foster a project that would entail the cooperation of people from nations in conflict, Americans and Russians, Israelis and Palestinians, South Africans and Africans from the frontline states, we have a chance, however small, of being useful.

My second and third suggestions are also for research and action. They take us back to this country. My second suggestion concerns our contest with Moscow. Despite all the tons of literature already produced (I have contributed to it myself) there is no adequate and convincing study of the sum of obstacles: mental as well as institutional, economic and political, etc., that reduce the ability of any American Administration to go as far in the direction of unilateral restraint, or tacit understandings for arms control, as the nature of the Soviet-American contest and the need to preserve essential American interests abroad would actually permit, to settle on and stick to a narrower definition of these interests (or to a more sensible interpretation of the "Soviet threat"), and to pursue toward Moscow the mix of competition and cooperation that seems prudent and desirable. Recent studies on the failure of detente in the 1970s are a useful beginning, but no more; here, one needs the concerted efforts of political scientists, social psychologists, economists, sociologists, and historians of *mentalités* capable of helping us understand the formation of American beliefs and attitudes toward the use of force, or toward radical social revolutions.

We ought to pursue in particular the task that has been brilliantly undertaken by a number of scholars—political scientists such as Seweryn Bialer, Marshal Shulman, Robert Legvold, Alexander Dallin, and psychologists such as Ralph White—about *American perceptions and misperceptions of the Soviet Union*, in order to understand the origins of these beliefs and attitudes, to evaluate the extent to which they are rational reactions to Soviet conduct, and to ascertain the degree to which they are distortions, expressions of American prejudices and insecurities.

It would be important to report on and to combat our misperceptions, while remembering that comparable work about Soviet misperceptions of America is unlikely to be undertaken in the USSR. Indeed, it would be important for the American public and decision-makers to know more about those Soviet views, in order for us, as a nation, to avoid feeding and reinforcing the Soviets' own anxieties and their own tendencies to black-and-white thinking.

Of course, a better understanding of mutual feelings is not likely to eliminate conflict: Many of the respective perceptions are based on fact, or spring from strongly held values. But few things are more striking, in the Soviet-American relationship, than the failure of each side to evaluate and to take into account the psychological effect of its moves, or statements, on the other. What I suggest here might help our statesmen at least become more aware both of the impact of their own behavior, and of some of the reasons for the Soviets'.

My third item is about *nuclear weapons*, again. Changes in technology and the tense Soviet-American rivalry in recent years are rapidly making the prospects for significant arms control more hopeless. We need to do what the Bishops did—acquire, if we don't have it already, the technical and military expertise necessary in order to make informed suggestions about and generate public pressure for the kinds of measures—unilateral acts, tacit deals, and explicit agreements—that would make the inevitably nuclear world more livable. They ought altogether to shore up crisis stability (i.e., ensure that in a crisis neither side could believe it has an advantage in striking first, or would be decisively worse off if struck first), reduce the number of conflict situations in which a bad turn of events might incite a party to initiate the use of nuclear weapons in the hope that escalation will be prevented or controllable, keep the nuclear arsenals verifiable, and gradually and drastically reduce them, starting with the elimination of the most destabilizing systems.

While many of my radical, or abolitionist, colleagues will find such measures insufficient or flawed, I recommend the comprehensive list of dos and don'ts recently compiled by my Harvard colleagues in *Hawks, Doves and Owls*. Their "agenda for avoiding nuclear war," insofar as it stresses the most likely peril—war coming out of miscalculations, of mismanaged crises, of "loss of control and nonrational factors" (1985)—fits exactly my concern, whatever minor disagreements I may have on certain points.

Fourth, an item for creative reflection: What kinds of *international or regional regimes* are conceivable *in the realm of security*—a domain in which past mechanisms of restraint (such as the balance of power) are either not relevant to or not sufficiently effective for our needs, and never fully amounted to what we now call regimes? Under what political conditions could they be set up? What favorable balance of advantages and restrictions would be likely to attract states, especially states in conflict, to such innovations? How far could one go in separating the establishment of mutual controls and limitations on arms, from the solution of underlying disputes? How much expansion and development of international institutions and safeguards would be required? Needless to say, such research would have to be done area by area (preferably, again, with the participation of experts from each area): Measures such as demilitarized or denuclearized zones that make sense in one part of the world make much less sense in others.

Finally, another item—for reflection above all, but also, ultimately, for action: What are the qualities citizens of free countries should want in those of their *leaders* who will have to deal with international conflicts in a nuclear world? George Ball's lament about resistance to complexity suggests one major missing element in American leadership. The public's desire for both strength and peace sets the outer limits within which American leaders can move. But inside those limits, there are many possibilities; and recent experiences have mainly shown us what ought to be avoided. Heroism and crookedness are equally dangerous, albeit for different reasons; so is ignorance of the outside world, which risks breeding delusions about the righteousness of our course and a simplistic projection of our past achievements. Mere managerial skills, or the gift for public relations and spectacle, are clearly not enough.

In the United States and elsewhere, our schools of public service train for expertise and for administrative cleverness. What they should be more concerned with is character and insight—a sense of the needs of people, more than mastery of the techniques of public policy; a grasp of the traditions, ambitions and dreams of foreign leaders; a mix of responsibility, imagination, and honesty; a balance between the ability to compromise and a steadfast defense of essential principles.

What can be done, in complex mobile and acquisitive societies where the notion and lure of a career prevail over old values of service, to identify, nurture, encourage and reward those who have the necessary qualities? We have tended to let established patterns of selection produce whatever they can, however faulty these structures and procedures may have become. They certainly have, in the United States, where we all are, as a result, too often left at the mercy of money, blind ambition, or chance. Neither for the solution of our domestic problems, nor for the sake of peace, can we afford to be so indifferent, or so resigned, to what ultimately determines our fate.

NOTES

1. Presidential address, International Society of Political Psychology, Washington, June 20, 1985.
2. See Hoffmann (1978 and 1981), *Primacy or World Order* and *Duties Beyond Borders*.

REFERENCES

Allison, G., Carnesale, A., and Nye, J. (1985). *Hawks, Doves and Owls.* Norton, New York. p. 210.

Deutsch, M. (1957). *Political Community and the North Atlantic Area.* Princeton University Press, Princeton.

_____. (1983). The prevention of World War III: A psychological perspective. *Polit. Psychol.* 4(1): 6, 26.

Hoffmann, S. (1978). *Primacy or World Order.* McGraw-Hill, New York.

_____. (1981). *Duties Beyond Borders.* Syracuse University Press, Syracuse.

Holt, R. (1984). Can psychology meet Einstein's challenge? *Polit. Psychol.* 5(2): 222.

International Organization (Spring 1982), Krasner, S. (ed.).

Janis, I. L. (1982). *Victims of Groupthink.* Houghton Mifflin, Boston.

Keohane, R., and Nye, J. (1977). *Power and Interdependence.* Little, Brown, Boston.

Lebow, R. N. (1981). *Between Peace and War.* Johns Hopkins University Press, Baltimore.

_____. (1984). Windows of opportunity: Do states jump through them? *Int. Sec.* 9(1): 147–186.

Mack, J. (1985). Toward a collective psychopathology of the nuclear arms competition. *Polit. Psychol.* 6(2): 307.

Montville, J. V. (1985). Introduction. *Polit. Psychol.* 6(2): 211.

Smoke, R. (1984). The 'peace' of deterrence and the 'peace' of the antinuclear war movement. *Polit. Psychol.* 5(4): 741–748.

Stein, H. F. (1985). Psychological complementarity in Soviet-American relations. *Polit. Psychol.* 6(2): 257.

UNESCO (1957). In *The Nature of Conflict.* p. 178.

Volkan, V. (1985). The need to have enemies and allies: A developmental approach. *Polit. Psychol.* 6(2): 221.

24

Groupthink

IRVING L. JANIS

The idea of "groupthink" occurred to me while reading Arthur M. Schlesinger's chapters on the Bay of Pigs in *A Thousand Days*. At first I was puzzled: How could bright men like John F. Kennedy and his advisers be taken in by such a stupid, patchwork plan as the one presented to them by the C.I.A. representatives? I began wondering if some psychological contagion of complacency might have interfered with their mental alertness.

I kept thinking about this notion until one day I found myself talking about it in a seminar I was conducting at Yale on the psychology of small groups. I suggested that the poor decision-making performance of those high officials might be akin to the lapses in judgment of ordinary citizens who become more concerned with retaining the approval of the fellow members of their work group than with coming up with good solutions to the tasks at hand.

When I re-read Schlesinger's account I was struck by many further observations that fit into exactly the pattern of concurrence-seeking that has impressed me in my research on other face-to-face groups when a "we" feeling of solidarity is running high. I concluded that a group process was subtly at work in Kennedy's team which prevented the members from debating the real issues posed by the C.I.A.'s plan and from carefully appraising its serious risks.

By now I was sufficiently fascinated by what I called the "groupthink" hypothesis to start looking into similar historic fiascoes. I selected for intensive analysis three that were made during the administrations of three other American presidents: Franklin D. Roosevelt (failure to be prepared for Pearl Harbor), Harry S. Truman (the invasion of North Korea) and Lyndon B. Johnson (escalation of the Vietnam war). Each decision was a group product, issuing from a series of meetings held by a small and cohesive group of government officials and advisers. In each case I found the same kind of detrimental group process that was at work in the Bay of Pigs decision.

In my earlier research with ordinary citizens I had been impressed by the effects—both unfavorable and favorable—of the social pressures that develop in cohesive groups: in infantry platoons, air crews, therapy groups, seminars and self-study or encounter groups. Members tend to evolve informal objectives to preserve friendly intra-group relations, and this becomes part of the hidden agenda at their meetings. When conducting research on groups of heavy smokers, for example, at a clinic established to help people stop smoking, I noticed a seemingly irrational tendency for the members to exert pressure on each other to increase their smoking as the time for the final meeting approached. This appeared to be a collusive effort to display mutual dependence and resistance to the termination of the sessions.

Sometimes, even long before the final separation, pressures toward uniformity subverted the fundamental purpose. At the second meeting of one group of smokers, consisting of twelve middle-class American men and women, two of the most dominant members took the position that heavy smoking was an almost incurable addiction. Most of the others soon agreed that nobody could be expected to cut down drastically. One man took issue with this consensus, arguing that he had stopped smoking since joining the group and that everyone else could do the same. His declaration was followed by an angry discussion. Most of the others ganged up against the man who was deviating from the consensus.

At the next meeting the deviant announced that he had made an important decision. "When I joined," he said, "I agreed to follow the two main rules required by the clinic—to make a conscientious effort to stop smoking, and to attend every meeting. But I have learned that you can only follow one of the rules, not both. I will continue to attend every meeting but I have gone back to smoking two packs a day and I won't make any effort to stop again until after the last meeting." Whereupon the other members applauded, welcoming him back to the fold.

No one mentioned that the whole point of the meetings was to help each person to cut down as rapidly as possible. As a psychological consultant to the group, I tried to call this to the members' attention and so did my collaborator, Dr. Michael Kahn. But the members ignored our comments and reiterated their consensus that heavy smoking was an addiction from which no one would be cured except by cutting down gradually over a long period of time.

This episode—an extreme form of groupthink—was only one manifestation of a general pattern that the group displayed. At every meeting the members were amiable, reasserted their warm feelings of solidarity and sought concurrence on every important topic, with no reappearance of the unpleasant bickering that would spoil the cozy atmosphere. This tendency could be maintained, however, only at the expense of ignoring realistic challenges—like those posed by the psychologists.

* * *

The term "groupthink" is of the same order as the words in the "newspeak" vocabulary that George Orwell uses in *1984*—a vocabulary with terms such as "doublethink" and "crimethink." By putting "groupthink" with those Orwellian words, I realize that it takes on an invidious connotation. This is intentional: groupthink refers to a deterioration of mental efficiency, reality testing and moral judgment that results from in-group pressures.

When I investigated the Bay of Pigs invasion and other fiascoes, I found that there were at least six major defects in decision-making which contributed to failures to solve problems adequately.

First, the group's discussions were limited to a few alternatives (often only two) without a survey of the full range of alternatives. Second, the members failed to re-examine their initial decision from the standpoint of non-obvious drawbacks that had not been originally considered. Third, they neglected courses of action initially evaluated as unsatisfactory; they almost never discussed whether they had overlooked any non-obvious gains.

Fourth, members made little or no attempt to obtain information from experts who could supply sound estimates of losses and gains to be expected from alternative courses. Fifth, selective bias was shown in the way the members reacted to information and judgments from experts, the media and outside critics; they were only interested in facts and opinions that supported their preferred policy. Finally, they spent little time deliberating how the policy might be hindered by bureaucratic inertia, sabotaged by political opponents or derailed by the accidents that happen to the best of well-laid plans. Consequently, they failed to work out contingency plans to cope with foreseeable setbacks that could endanger their success.

I was surprised by the extent to which the groups involved in these fiascoes adhered to group norms and pressures toward uniformity, even when their policy was working badly and had unintended consequences that disturbed the conscience of the members. Members consider loyalty to the group the highest form of morality. That loyalty requires each member to avoid raising controversial issues, questioning weak arguments or calling a halt to soft-headed thinking.

Paradoxically, soft-headed groups are likely to be extremely hard-hearted toward out-groups and enemies. In dealing with a rival nation, policymakers constituting an amiable group find it relatively easy to authorize dehumanizing solutions such as large-scale bombings. An affable group of government officials is unlikely to pursue the difficult issues that arise when alternatives to a harsh military solution come up for discussion. Nor are they inclined to raise ethical issues that imply that this "fine group of ours, with its humanitarianism and its high-minded principles, could adopt a course that is inhumane and immoral."

The greater the threat to the self-esteem of the members of a cohesive group, the greater will be their inclination to resort to concurrence-seeking at the expense of critical thinking. Symptoms of groupthink will therefore be found most often when a decision poses a moral dilemma, especially if the most advantageous course requires the policymakers to violate their own standards of humanitarian behavior. Each member is likely to become more dependent than ever on the in-group for maintaining his self-image as a decent human being and will therefore be more strongly motivated to maintain group unity by striving for concurrence.

Although it is risky to make huge inferential leaps from theory to practice, we should not be inhibited from drawing tentative inferences from these fiascoes. Perhaps the worst mistakes can be prevented if we take steps to avoid the circumstances in which group-think is most likely to flourish. But all the prescriptive hypotheses that follow must be validated by systematic research before they can be applied with any confidence.

The leader of a policy-forming group should, for example, assign the role of critical evaluator to each member, encouraging the group to give high priority to airing objections and doubts. He should also be impartial at the outset, instead of stating his own preferences and expectations. He should limit his briefings to unbiased statements about the scope of the problem and the limitations of available resources.

The organization should routinely establish several independent planning and evaluation groups to work on the same policy question, each carrying out its deliberations under a different leader.

One or more qualified colleagues within the organization who are not core members of the policy-making group should be invited to each meeting and encouraged to challenge the views of the core members.

At every meeting, at least one member should be assigned the role of devil's advocate, to function like a good lawyer in challenging the testimony of those who advocate the majority position.

Whenever the policy issue involves relations with a rival nation, a sizable block of time should be spent surveying all warning signals from the rivals and constructing alternative scenarios.

After reaching a preliminary consensus the policy-making group should hold a "second chance" meeting at which all the members are expected to express their residual doubts and to rethink the entire issue. They might take as their model a statement made by Alfred P. Sloan, a former chairman of General Motors, at a meeting of policymakers:

"Gentlemen, I take it we are all in complete agreement on the decision here. Then I propose we postpone further discussion until our next meeting to give ourselves time to develop disagreement and perhaps gain some understanding of what the decision is all about."

It might not be a bad idea for the second-chance meeting to take place in a relaxed atmosphere far from the executive suite, perhaps over drinks. According to a report by Herodotus dating from about 450 B.C., whenever the ancient Persians made a decision following sober deliberations, they would always reconsider the matter under the influence of wine. Tacitus claimed that during Roman times the Germans also had a custom of arriving at each decision twice—once sober, once drunk.

Some institutionalized form of allowing second thoughts to be freely expressed might be remarkably effective for breaking down a false sense of unanimity and related illusions, without endangering anyone's reputation or liver.

PEARL HARBOR: GENIALITY AND SECURITY

On the night of Dec. 6, 1941—just 12 hours before the Japanese struck—Admiral Husband E. Kimmel (Commander in Chief of the Pacific Fleet) attended a dinner party given by his old crony, Rear Admiral H. Fairfax Leary, and his wife. Other members of the in-group of naval commanders and their wives were also present. Seated next to Admiral Kimmel was Fanny Halsey, wife of Admiral Halsey, who had left Hawaii to take his task force to the Far East. Mrs. Halsey said that she was certain the Japanese were going to attack. "She was a brilliant woman," according to Captain Joel Bunkley, who described the party, "but everybody thought she was crazy."

Admiral Leary, at a naval inquiry in 1944, summarized the complacency at that dinner party and at the daily conferences held by Admiral Kimmel during the preceding weeks. When asked whether any thought had been given to the possibility of a surprise attack by the Japanese, he said, "We all felt that the contingency was remote . . . and the feeling strongly existed that the Fleet would have adequate warning of any chance of an air attack." The same attitude was epitomized in testimony given by Captain J. B. Earle, chief of staff, Fourteenth Naval District. "Somehow or other," he said, "we always felt that 'it couldn't happen here.' "

From the consistent testimony given by Admiral Kimmel's advisers, they all acted on the basis of an "unwarranted feeling of immunity from attack," though they had been given a series of impressive warnings that they should be prepared for war with Japan.

Most illuminating of the norm-setting behavior that contributed to the complacency of Kimmel's in-group is a brief exchange between Admiral Kimmel and Lieutenant Commander Layton. Perturbed by the loss of radio contact with the Japanese aircraft carriers, Admiral Kimmel asked Layton on Dec. 1, 1941, to check with the Far East Command for additional information. The next day, discussing the lost carriers again with Layton, he remarked jokingly: "What, you don't know where the carriers are? Do you mean to say that they could be rounding Diamond Head [at Honolulu] and you wouldn't know it?" Layton said he hoped they would be sighted well before that.

This exchange implies an "atmosphere of geniality and security." Having relegated the Japanese threat to the category of laughing matters, the admiral was making it clear that he would be inclined to laugh derisively at anyone who thought otherwise. "I did not at any time suggest," Layton later acknowledged at a Congressional hearing, "that the Japanese carriers were under radio silence approaching Oahu. I wish I had."

But the admiral's foolish little joke may have induced Layton to remain silent about any vague, lingering doubts he may have had. Either man would risk the scornful laughter of the other—whether expressed to his face or behind his back—if he were to express second thoughts such as, "Seriously, though, shouldn't we do something about the slight possibility that those carriers might *really* be headed this way?" Because this ominous inference was never drawn, not a single reconnaissance plane was sent out to the north of the Hawaiian Islands, allowing the Japanese to win the incredible gamble they were taking in trying to send their aircraft carriers within bombing distance of Pearl Harbor without being detected.

That joking exchange was merely the visible part of a huge iceberg of solid faith in Pearl Harbor's invulnerability. If a few warm advocates of preparedness had been within the Navy group, steamed up by the accumulating warning signals, they might have been able to melt it. But they would certainly have had a cold reception. To urge a full alert would have required presenting unwelcome arguments that countered the myth of Pearl Harbor's impregnability. Anyone who was tempted to do so knew that he would be deviating from the group norm: the others were likely to consider him "crazy," just as the in-group regarded Mrs. Halsey at the dinner party on the eve of the disaster when she announced her deviant opinion that the Japanese would attack.

ESCALATION IN VIETNAM: HOW COULD IT HAPPEN?

A highly revealing episode occurred soon after Robert McNamara told a Senate committee some impressive facts about the ineffectiveness of the bombings. President Johnson made a number of bitter comments about McNamara's statement. "That military genius, McNamara, has gone dovish on me," he complained to one Senator. To someone in his White House staff he spoke even more heatedly, accusing McNamara of playing into the hands of the enemy. He drew the analogy of "a man trying to sell his house while one of his sons went to the prospective buyer to point out that there were leaks in the basement."

This strongly suggests that Johnson regarded his in-group of policy advisers as a family and its leading dissident member as an irresponsible son who was sabotaging the family's interest. Underlying this revealing imagery are two implicit assumptions that epitomize groupthink: We are a good group, so any deceitful acts that we perpetrate are fully justified. Anyone who is unwilling to distort the truth to help us is disloyal.

This is only one of the many examples of how groupthink was manifested in Johnson's inner circle.

A PERFECT FIASCO: THE BAY OF PIGS

Why did President Kennedy's main advisers, whom he had selected as core members of his team, fail to pursue the issues sufficiently to discover the shaky ground on which the faulty assumptions of the Cuban invasion plan rested? Why didn't they pose a barrage of penetrating and embarrassing questions to the representatives of the C.I.A. and the Joint Chiefs of Staff? Why were they taken in by the incomplete and inconsistent answers they were given in response to the relatively few critical questions they raised?

Schlesinger says that "for all the utter irrationality with which retrospect endowed the project, it had a certain queer logic at the time as it emerged from the bowels of government." Why? What was the source of the "queer logic" with which the plan was endowed? If the available accounts describe the deliberations accurately, many typical symptoms of groupthink can be discerned among the members of the Kennedy team: an illusion of invulnerability, a collective effort to rationalize their decision, an unquestioned belief in the group's inherent morality, a stereotyped view of enemy leaders as too evil to warrant genuine attempts to negotiate, and the emergence of self-appointed mind-guards.

Robert Kennedy, for example, who had been constantly informed about the Cuban invasion plan, asked Schlesinger privately why he was opposed. The President's brother listened coldly and then said: "You may be right or you may be wrong, but the President has made his mind up. Don't push it any further. Now is the time for everyone to help him all they can."

Here is a symptom of groupthink, displayed by a highly intelligent man whose ethical code committed him to freedom of dissent.

Robert Kennedy was functioning in a self-appointed role that I call being a "mind-guard." Just as a bodyguard protects the President and other high officials from physical harm, a mind-guard protects them from thoughts that might damage their confidence in the soundness of the policies which they are about to launch.

25

Building Politics into Psychology: The Misperception of Threat

JANICE GROSS STEIN

INTRODUCTION

Psychological research has contributed immeasurably to the analysis of the misperception of threat in international relations. Particularly in the last decade, political psychologists have drawn on theories of attribution, estimation, and judgment to document the distorting impact of cognitive biases on the perception of threat across a wide range of international contexts and cases. More recently, they have traced motivated error and the consequent misperception of threat to leaders' fears, needs, and interests. Often, however, the psychological analysis has been strikingly apolitical. This essay concludes that analysis of the psychological processes of misperception is not enough and argues that politics must be built back into the analysis of the misperception of threat.

We look first at the impact of cognitive and motivated error on the misperception of threat. We consider the impact of schematas, heuristics, and biases which culminate in unconscious cognitive error and then examine the consequences of need, fear, and interests which result in unacknowledged motivated error. The deliberate and self-conscious manipulation of threat by political leaders is excluded from this analysis. When leaders deliberately minimize or exaggerate the threat an adversary poses, they do not unconsciously misperceive but deliberately distort.

We then consider cognitive and motivated error as mediating variables and examine the political and strategic factors which may either make these errors more likely or compound their impact. In part because political and strategic variables are often omitted, the essay concludes that explanations of the misperception of threat are deficient in three important ways.

Current theories do not consider systematically the critical interaction among cognitive heuristics and biases and their cumulative impact on the misperception of threat in international relations. Nor do they integrate affective and cognitive processes in their explanation of distorted threat perception. Finally, they do not consider systematically the impact of political and strategic factors which condition the likelihood and intensity of misperception. Unless politics are explicitly built into psychological explanations of threat perception in international relations, political psychologists will continue to work with inadequate theory and will limit their capacity to speak to the policy community.

THE PROCESSES OF MISPERCEPTION

In international relations, threats are broadly of two kinds. When leaders use strategies like deterrence, for example, they signal their commitment and resolve in part by issuing threats to a would-be challenger. This kind of threat, by its nature, is conditional. One leader threatens another with harmful consequences that are under the control of the threatener if the target does not comply with the request. What is relevant to the success of the strategy is not the threat itself but its perception; there is often a considerable gap between the intentions of the leader who issues the threat and its perception by another.

Leaders perceive not only those threats that are communicated by another party but also those that inhere in the environment. We term these "situational threats" (McClelland, 1975: 19). Accuracy in the perception of situational threats is even more problematic for policymakers to achieve and for scholars to establish. People may read their environment very differently: one may perceive a situation as threatening while another will consider the same set of conditions to be benign. Even analysts, who are less immediately involved than policymakers and often have the advantage of hindsight, can disagree subsequently among themselves about the substance and the scope of the threat leaders confronted.

In order to assess the scope of misperception, a standard of accurate perception is required. Even with the advantage of hindsight, assessment of accuracy is often not obvious. Although threats that are issued by one party to another are often communicated explicitly and their content is known, leaders and analysts can still debate the intentions that underlie the threat. Assessment of the perception of situational threats is still more troublesome; the dangers inherent in a situation are rarely unambiguous. Senior American officials, intelligence analysts, and political leaders varied widely, for example, in their estimate of the threat inherent in the political crisis in Iran in the autumn of 1979.

Where good documentary evidence is available and the intentions of those who issue the threat are well-established, we can compare leaders' perceptions of threat to the intentions of those who threatened and to their capabilities and make a judgment of accuracy (Levy, 1983: 73–80). Where such evidence is not available or, as frequently happens, is open to multiple interpretation, assessment of the accuracy of threat perception is far more difficult. Under these circumstances, we treat threat perception as a process rather than as an outcome and consider deviations from generally accepted norms of inference and judgment (Jervis, 1986a). Again, since standards of rationality vary and leaders rarely approximate these norms, evaluating processes of perception can also create controversy (Jervis, 1976: 117–142; Stein and Tanter, 1980: 3–20). Nevertheless, because the perception of threat is in its essence a psychological process, the explanation and evaluation of misperception as a process is useful.

Four sets of factors can contribute to the underestimation or overestimation of threat. We look first at the explanations provided by cognitive psychologists who examine the impact of central cognitive constructs and biased processes of thinking on threat perception. Second, we examine the impact of leaders' needs, fears, and interests on their perception of threat; here the crucial explanatory variable is the motivated errors leaders make. Third, attributes of the international strategic environment may contribute to the process of misperception; the workings of the international "security dilemma," for example, where the security of one requires the insecurity of another, encourages the overestimation of threat. Fourth, we look at the additional impact of the political and institutional context on leaders' definitions of their interests and on their processes of threat perception. Strategic threat is perceived in a political context which shapes leaders' expectations, their needs, and their interests. Very little systematic work has been done on the impact of critical political processes which can define the parameters of threat perception.

Before beginning the analysis of the misperception of threat, some important caveats are in order. First, any explanation of misperception must be tentative until it is validated through the systematic analysis of cases where the perception of threat was relatively accurate. Some of the important contributory factors to misperception may be present as well when leaders perceive threats with minimal distortion. In looking primarily at cases of distorted threat perception, we can identify the necessary conditions of misperception but we cannot establish their importance.

Second, we seek to explain two kinds of misperception, the *underestimation* and the *overestimation* of threat. As will become apparent, the same explanatory variables can result at times in one kind of distortion and at times in another. Stalin's expectations about Hitler, for example, were a major factor in his underestimation of the threat of a German attack whereas Anthony Eden's beliefs about President Gamul Ab'dul Nasir of Egypt contributed to his overestimation of threat. Similarly, leaders' needs can at times induce them to minimize or exaggerate threat. President Carter, operating in a harsh domestic political climate created in part by the Soviet invasion of Afghanistan, responded unwittingly with an exaggerated estimate of the Soviet threat. Israel's political leaders, on the other hand, faced an imminent election in the autumn of 1973; although they did not do so consciously, it was very much in their interest to minimize the threat posed by Egyptian army maneuvers that October. In assessing the contribution of explanatory variables to processes of misperception, it is important to try to specify, insofar as possible, when and how each is likely to lead to the minimization or the maximization of threat.

Third, we look at each of the explanatory factors in sequence. Each of these variables—cognitive predispositions and biases, motivated error, the strategic environment, and domestic political processes and politics—can independently confound threat perception. These factors, however, are often not independent of one another but interdependent. Political and strategic factors can interact with cognitive processes and motivated error to multiply the obstacles to accurate threat perception. Domestic and international pressures can encourage leaders unconsciously to minimize or exaggerate their estimates of threat to achieve their political purposes. In explaining the processes of misperception, the interaction of these variables may be more important than the independent impact of any single factor.

Cognitive Sources of the Misperception of Threat

Belief Systems. Cognitive psychologists have examined the distorting impact of cognitive "schemata" and "scripts" as well as a series of heuristics and biases which color threat perception. The most important is the overwhelming impact of leaders' expectations and beliefs on their perceptions. Individuals who think, reason, and learn impose structure on a complex world by the concepts they develop of themselves and others. Any acquisition of knowledge involves categorization and the use of "schematas" that relate new information to prior knowledge (Abelson, 1973; Anderson, 1982; Edelman, 1977; Kelley, 1972; Lau and Sears, 1986; Reder and Anderson, 1980; Thorndyke and Hayes-Roth, 1979; and Schank and Abelson, 1977). These belief systems or "schemata" are essential; without them, no individual could organize or interpret the enormous amount of information potentially relevant to any problem. Yet these belief systems constrain and condition how and what leaders perceive.

In October 1973, Israel's leaders believed that Egypt would not attack until the Egyptian air force could strike at Israel in depth and at Israel's airfields in particular, and second, that Syria would attack only in conjunction with Egypt (Stein, 1985: 64). Using this as the organizing concept to interpret a great deal of evidence of Egyptian military activity, intelligence analysts discounted the possibility of preparation for an attack and interpreted the activity in the field as annual military maneuvers. Their low estimate of the likelihood of attack was reinforced by their confidence in Israel's military superiority; beliefs reinforced one another. The "theory" of analysts in military intelligence drove the interpretation of the evidence and led to a serious underestimation of threat. In this case, the errors of intelligence analysts are best explained by deeply rooted cognitive bias rather than by motivated error; unlike their political colleagues who were facing reelection, no obvious benefit accrued from a tranquil strategic environment.

Anthony Eden's estimation of the threat posed by Egypt's nationalization of the Suez Canal in 1956 illustrates the impact of cognitive predispositions on the overestimation of threat. The prime minister's formative experience was Britain's appeasement of Mussolini and Hitler in the 1930s, appeasement that resulted in war. Frequently, leaders tend to learn only superficially from history; their beliefs are shaped by recent events, by events that they or their country experienced directly, by events that happened when they were first coming to political awareness, and by events that had major consequences (Jervis, 1976: 177–204, 217–221, 262–270; Lebow, 1985a). Eden's experience preceding the second world war met at least three of these criteria. Fifteen years later, when confronted with the Egyptian nationalization of the canal, Eden could only see President Nasir as yet another dictator. He did not consider the critical differences between Nasir in Egypt in 1956, and Mussolini in 1935 and Hitler in Germany in 1938. Rather, he saw what he expected to see and what he expected to see was a threat of massive proportions.

Lack of Empathy in Contrasting Cognitive Contexts. Closely related to the overwhelming impact of beliefs is the effect of the lack of empathy on the misperception of threat. Empathy refers to the capacity to understand others' perception of their world, their conception of their role in that world, and their definition of their interests. Leaders are frequently unable to empathize, in part because of a difference in cognitive contexts. When sender and recipient use quite different contexts to frame, communicate, or interpret signals, the opportunities for miscalculation and misjudgment multiply. As Jervis (1985) argues, it is very difficult for one set of leaders to imagine how another sees them. This is so in part because the relevant evidence is often difficult to obtain but, even more important, because leaders' beliefs about themselves are frequently so powerful that it is hard to conceive that others hold a different view (Fiske and Taylor, 1984; Lebow and Stein, 1987). Consequently, leaders are often deficient in their capacity to empathize. Awareness of how and why an adversary feels threatened, for example, is an important component of empathy but political leaders often display no sensitivity to their adversary's sense of vulnerability while they dwell heavily on their own perception of threat.

This inability to empathize intrudes at both ends of the signalling process to confound the perception of threat. The leaders who issue the threat are frequently insufficiently sensitive to the way their adversary sees them and, consequently, overconfident that they can design and communicate clearly the appropriate threat. The target interprets the threat from a different cognitive context and deduces meaning that is unintended. International history is rich with examples of this kind of misperception.

Ernest May describes the failure of the attempts by the United States to coerce Spain over Cuba in 1898 (1961: 161). When President McKinley threatened "other and further action" in the "near future" in his annual message to Congress, Spanish leaders simply did not perceive the threat. The translation of the message circulated to members of the Spanish cabinet had extensive marginal notation but the threat was not highlighted. On the contrary, since the statement praised the offer of autonomy to the rebels, the Foreign Minister considered the message "very satisfactory."

The threat was not poorly executed. Indeed, the message seemed clear enough to

American leaders, but it was not perceived by Spanish leaders who approached Cuba from a wholly different political perspective. Because of this difference in cognitive context, Spanish leaders not only underestimated but missed entirely the threat issued by the United States. The United States, of course, had no way of knowing that Spanish leaders had not "heard" their threat.

Lebow documents a similar case of underestimation of threat by India's leaders in 1961 (1981: 216–222). Chinese soldiers surrounded and cut off several Indian outposts that had been set up in contested areas of Ladakh. After they demonstrated their capability to isolate Indian soldiers, the Chinese pulled their forces back, thinking that the threat was unmistakable but hoping that India would withdraw quietly because violence had been avoided. China's leaders seriously misjudged how Indian leaders were likely to interpret their action.

The Indian estimate of the Chinese action was dramatically different. They interpreted the withdrawal as a lack of resolve and as testimony to Chinese military inferiority; consequently they determined to occupy as much of the disputed territory as they could. India's leaders underestimated the Chinese threat in part because of the difference in cognitive contexts of the two sets of leaders. Nehru, Menon, and their advisers believed that Peking was reluctant to attack India because it feared defeat. In fact, in large part because China was persuaded of its military superiority, its leaders believed that a show of force followed by military restraint on their part might encourage compromise by India. Prime Minister Nehru was also persuaded that China would not attack because it wanted to avoid being labeled the aggressor by the nonaligned states. This second assessment was particularly important in framing the context in which India's leaders evaluated Chinese actions. In large part because of the limits to empathy and the differences in cognitive contexts, the Chinese threat was so badly misinterpreted that it provoked rather than deterred further military action by India.

Similarly, the profound ideological differences between the United States and the Soviet Union have repeatedly impaired their capacity to empathize and exaggerated their perception of threat. Because leaders of both superpowers are deficient in their capacity to empathize, to understand how the other sees them, they are each prone to misinterpret benign actions as threatening. When, for example, the United States offered to extend aid to the Soviet Union to assist in the reconstruction of its economy after the war, Soviet leaders suspected that the United States was seeking a market to absorb the expected surplus of peacetime production (Gaddis, 1972: 174–98). Ideological, political, and cultural differences reinforce this tendency to read the other's signals and actions as threatening and offensive.

Evidence from a variety of cases suggests that ideological, political, or cultural differences in cognitive contexts can easily constrain the capacity to empathize and result in serious error in threat perception (Lebow and Stein, 1987). Whether threats are overestimated or minimized will be very much a function of the specifics of the differences, but the general proposition holds. Because adversaries often do not relate to one another in terms of a common frame of reference and do not empathize with each other, threats are easily misinterpreted.

The Heuristics of "Availability" and "Representativeness." In addition to these deeply rooted and fundamental impediments to threat perception, cognitive psychologists have identified a number of specific heuristics which can impair processes of perception and attribution. People are "cognitive misers": Because of well-defined cognitive limits, their processing of information is selective (Anderson, 1982; Fiske and Taylor, 1984). Heuristics refer to shortcuts in the processes of information retrieval which leaders use to gain access to information stored within their organizing schemas and belief systems. Two of the most pervasive are "availability" and "representativeness." Leaders tend to interpret threats in terms of what is easily available in their cognitive repertoire (Tversky and Kahneman, 1973). Often what is most available to policymakers are their own intentions, plans, and experiences and, consequently, they tend to perceive the actions of others in their light.

The estimates of the German air threat generated by the British Air Ministry in the period preceding World War II illustrate the impact of availability on the misperception of threat (Jervis, 1985: 23). British officials argued that the best criteria for judging Germany's rate of expansion were those which governed the rate at which the Royal Air Force could establish new units. Similarly, because the RAF emphasized strategic bombardment, they inferred that Germany planned to attack their cities. In both cases, British officials overestimated German capability in the air and the threat this posed.

Through almost exactly the same process of reasoning, Israel's military intelligence underestimated the likelihood of an Egyptian attack in 1973. Because Israel relied so heavily on its air force as its primary offensive instrument, military and political leaders were receptive to an intelligence evaluation that stressed the deterrent effectiveness of Israel's air force; an Egyptian attack, therefore, was considered unlikely before 1975, the earliest date by which Egypt could acquire and absorb the required aerial capability (Stein, 1985: 64). The availability of Israel's strategic planning led intelligence analysts to estimate Egyptian intention to attack in light of these plans. The result was a serious underestimation of threat. In both these cases, leaders misperceived threat in part because the most available referent was a self-image rather than an image of the other. This bias toward self-image as an available referent to evaluate others is likely to be greater when differences in cognitive contexts are greater; the one is likely to reinforce the other, with serious consequences for the perception of threat.

The bias of "representativeness" can also influence the perception of threat (Jervis, 1986b). Generally, people tend to exaggerate the similarity between one event and a class of events because they pay inadequate attention to base rate statistics, or the probability that the event is part of a general class independent of any specific information about the particular event (Ajzen, 1977; Bar-Hillel, 1977). We have already noted Anthony Eden's classification of President Gamul Ab'dul Nasir as yet another dictator.

Although Mussolinis and Hitlers are exceedingly rare in the history of international politics, Eden quickly assumed that Nasir was representative of this class of leaders. In this case, it is very likely that both availability and representativeness worked together to compound the misperception of threat.

The "Egocentric" Bias. The "egocentric" bias refers to the predilection of people to see themselves as the central point of reference when they explain the actions of others (Ross and Sicoly, 1979; Fiske and Taylor, 1984; and Jervis, 1976: 343–355). When people exaggerate the causal significance of their own actions and discount the importance of other factors, they overestimate the linkages between themselves and the behavior of others. They tend, in consequence, to exaggerate threat for two closely related reasons: first, because they overestimate the extent to which another's behavior is targeted at them and, second, because they exaggerate the degree to which the behavior of others is the result of their prior actions.

Lebow *et al.* (1988) document the impact of the egocentric bias in their analysis of President Carter's perception of the Soviet threat after Afghanistan. Both dimensions of the bias worked to inflate Carter's estimate of the scope of the Soviet threat. He had come to office with a relatively benign perception of the Soviet Union and had made the improvement of America's relationship with the Soviet Union a cornerstone of his foreign policy. After the invasion, however, Carter rejected the hypothesis that the Soviet Union had engaged in defensive action of a beleaguered ally and saw the United States and the western world as the target of the Soviet invasion. Carter's perception is consistent with people's tendency to exaggerate the extent to which they are the target of another's action. This tendency prompts leaders to interpret the behavior of others as threats to which they must respond.

Second, and even more striking, Carter interpreted the Soviet invasion as a failure of American deterrence, even though in preceding years the United States had made no effort to deter Soviet action in Afghanistan. It is difficult to explain the self-inflicted estimate of failure and the escalated perception of Soviet threat without reference to the second dimension of the egocentric bias. Because American leaders exaggerated the extent to which Soviet behavior was the result of their own prior actions, even dovish members of the administration could conclude that the principal incentive for the Soviet Union had been the near certainty that the Soviet Union could "move with impunity." In reaching this conclusion, American policymakers discounted other explanations of Soviet action and placed themselves at the center of Soviet calculations. The interactive effect of these two dimensions of the egocentric bias was a dramatically heightened perception of Soviet threat and the corollary requirement of a firm American response.

Overconfidence. A closely related bias of overconfidence further complicates the signalling and the perception of threat. People generally tend to be too confident of their capacity to make complex judgments and perform complicated mental operations (Fischhoff *et al.*, 1977). This bias can have dangerous consequences insofar as leaders tend to overestimate their ability to design and communicate appropriate threats and to assess the intentions of their adversary (Jervis, 1982).

In his analysis of American strategy in Vietnam, Theis (1980) demonstrates repeated misperception by leaders in Hanoi of threats carefully designed and calibrated in Washington. American policymakers were confident, for example, that their adversary would be sensitive to fine differences in the deployment of American forces in the south. Leaders in North Vietnam, however, gave these kinds of factors no weight in their assessment of American intentions because they were unaware of their significance.

Leaders in the target state can also be overconfident in their perception of threat and insensitive to alternative explanations of action. During the Cuban missile crisis, there was widespread agreement that the Soviet Union had placed missiles in Cuba as part of a broadly based offensive strategy. No serious attention was given to the alternative hypothesis that the Soviet Union was motivated in large part by new information that the United States knew of its strategic vulnerability. In November of 1961, the deputy secretary of defense, Roswell Gilpatric, publicly spoke of American strategic superiority and the weakness of the Soviet ICBM system. Soviet leaders thereby learned of the enhanced American intelligence capability to assess Soviet forces. Even more to the point, they knew that the United States knew of their strategic weakness. Yet, the following year, Kennedy and almost all his advisers dismissed the proposition that the Soviet Union was motivated even in part by weakness. As subsequent evidence and argument would show, theirs was an overconfident and exaggerated perception of the Soviet threat (Lebow, 1983, 1987). In this case, it is likely that the egocentric bias interacted with the propensity of overconfidence to shape the American perception of threat. In a skewed analysis, the United States saw itself as the primary determinant of Soviet action and, with little hesitation or doubt, expressed confidence in their assessment and excluded any other interpretation of their adversary's intentions.

The "Proportionality" Bias. Political psychologists have paid particular attention to the assumptions people tend to make about the appropriate relationship between means and ends. Generally, leaders expect their adversary to expend efforts proportionate to the ends they seek. Consequently, they make inferences about the intentions of others from the costs and consequences of the actions they initiate (Komorita, 1973; Jervis, 1985: 15; Lebow et al., 1988). When a state incurs high costs, others assume that important objectives were at stake for the leadership. Even if leaders consider the costs of an adversary's action to be low, but judge the immediate stakes to be lower still, they will perceive threat from this lack of proportion. As Jervis (1985: 15) argues, the "how" is more important than the "what": leaders are likely to perceive a threat if an adversary demonstrates a high propensity to take risks or ignores accepted procedure. When an opponent infringes upon an accepted norm of behavior, leaders infer that their adversary is no longer bound by conventional restraints and is, therefore, a serious threat (Cohen, 1979: 165, 177). Because they estimate the costs of "breaking the rules" as high, they consider the threat proportionately serious.

This bias toward proportionality inflates the perception of threat. Related in part to the bias toward overconfidence, it ignores the difficulty that people are often poor judges of the costs and consequences of an action they choose and that leaders may also differ in their concepts of cost. American officials judged the political and military costs of the Soviet invasion of Afghanistan to be extremely high—the disruption of detente, the loss of the SALT II treaty—and consequently reasoned that Soviet objectives were commensurate with these costs. As Lebow *et al.* (1988) argue, only an extreme interpretation of Soviet intentions could justify the consequences the Soviet leadership incurred. Ironically, the costs were as high as they were in part because the punishment inflicted by American leaders was a function of their heightened perception of threat. American officials ignored this circularity in their reasoning. Moreover, it is striking that despite their recent experience in Vietnam, no senior American leader advanced the proposition that Soviet leaders had misjudged the consequences of their intervention.

The "Fundamental Attribution Error." Psychologists who study cognitive processes of attribution examine how people characteristically construct explanations. In their research they have identified a fundamental error, people's tendency to exaggerate the importance of dispositional over situational factors when they explain undesirable behavior of others and the corresponding tendency to emphasize situational rather than dispositional factors when they are explaining their own behavior (Jones and Nisbett, 1971; Kelley and Michela, 1980; Nisbett and Ross, 1980; Ross, 1977).

This error in attribution contributes significantly to the overestimation of threat. Like the egocentric bias, it transforms effect into intent. Soviet officials tend, for example, to attribute the high level of American defense spending to the dispositional factor of the contradictions of capitalism and its inherent opposition to the Soviet Union. Their own defense spending, they insist, is situationally determined; it is a reaction to American militarism (Milburn *et al.*, 1982). The dramatic increase in the perception of the Soviet threat by officials in the Carter administration also illustrates the impact of this fundamental error. In explaining the Soviet intervention, American officials gave almost no weight to the situational factors which might have constrained the Soviet leadership, despite repeated efforts by Soviet officials to convey to Washington the scope of their dilemma (Garthoff, 1985: 903, 905, 907). Rather they looked almost exclusively to dispositional factors and estimated threatening intentions from Soviet action; misplaced causation contributed significantly to the misperception of threat. In this case, moreover, the fundamental attribution error worked together with the egocentric and proportionality biases to compound the perception of Soviet threat.

Attribution of Greater Coherence and Centralization. Leaders frequently tend to attribute greater coherence to their adversary than the evidence warrants (Jervis, 1976: 319–329; Levy, 1983). Leaders overestimate the control their adversaries have over their machinery of government and attribute intent to all their actions. This frequently misplaced attribution of centralized decisionmaking is consistent with the attempt to assimilate discrepant information to existing images and beliefs.

This process often works to inflate the perception of threat. It is most apparent in the interpretation of defense spending by an adversary. Many analysts in the United States, for example, assess Soviet defense spending as the product of a centrally coordinated and coherent plan even though they are aware of the bureaucratic pulling and hauling which characterizes their own processes of defense allocation. In 1962, for example, senior American officials gave no thought to the possibility that interservice rivalry may have been a factor in encouraging Khrushchev to risk the placement of missiles in Cuba even though they themselves had just gone through intense bureaucratic struggles with the air force and navy over force missions and numbers of weapons (Ball, 1980). Soviet leaders similarly speak of the central role of the military-industrial complex in the United States in driving up levels of defense spending (MccGwire, 1987).

The cognitive biases that we have identified contributed in important ways to the misperception of threat by political leaders. Because they were pervasive and distorting, they frequently had harmful effects upon strategy. Moreover, in many of these cases biases interacted with one another to aggravate misperception. Although the case evidence suggests that cognitive errors occur in clusters, existing psychological theory tends to treat these biases singly. Exploring the covariation among biases remains an important theoretical and research challenge both when biases compete with one another and when they reinforce each other to compound misperception.

The near ubiquity of cognitive biases and heuristics is an even more serious problem. Because they are generally characteristic of processes of attribution, estimation, and judgment, they do not appear to be related in any special way either to specific kinds of needs and interests or to types of political and strategic situations. We return to these difficulties and their implications for theory and policy after we examine the motivated misperception of threat.

MOTIVATED MISPERCEPTION OF THREAT

Explanations of motivated misperception locate error within the broader context of psychological fears and needs rather than expectations. They ask fundamental political as well as psychological questions: What needs are met by misperception? whose interests are served? Motivated biases result from unacknowledged, subconscious needs and fears and from emotional stress which is generated by leaders' political and strategic interests as they see them. Because motivated errors can be situated within a broader political and strategic context, they may be easier to identify and classify.

Motivated errors provoke some of the same pathologies identified by cognitive psychologists. Although they flow from fears, needs, and interests, they become manifest in some of the same biases of inconsistency management, absence of empathy, egocentricity, overconfidence, proportionality, and pathologies of attribution. Indeed, the principal difference between the two psychological explanations is not so much in the biases they identify but rather in the source of the errors (Lebow, 1981: 111–112). Psychologists who emphasize motivation give attention to the impact of fears and needs while cognitive psychologists look to processes of information management in an uncertain and complex environment. When motivated error culminates in pathologies of interpretation and judgment indistinguishable from cognitive biases, it too contributes to both the overestimation and the minimization of threat.

International history is rich with examples of motivated underestimation of threat. Janis and Mann (1977: 57–58, 107–33), in their analysis of decisionmaking, identify a pattern of "defensive avoidance," characterized by efforts to avoid, dismiss, and deny warnings that increase anxiety and fear. Although policymakers continue to think about the problem, they ward off anxiety by practicing selective attention and other forms of distorted information processing. When actually confronted with disturbing information, leaders will alter its implications through a process of wishful thinking. At the core of this repertoire of techniques of inconsistency management is the need to control and reduce fear (Janis, 1967; and Lazarus, 1966). When the perception of threat simultaneously evokes fear and a feeling of helplessness, defensive avoidance and distortion become more acute.

Defensive avoidance contributed significantly to the underestimation by British officials of the likelihood that Argentina was seriously contemplating a military challenge in the Falklands. British leaders could find no satisfactory policy option to deal with the growing threat of Argentinian military action. In part because they were reluctant to use military force, yet anxious to protect the islanders, they faced an intense and apparently irreconcilable conflict of values. Under these circumstances, as expected, they ignored repeated indications that Argentinian leaders were preparing to use force, discounted the scope of the Argentinian threat, and took refuge in defensive avoidance (Lebow, 1985b: 180–202).

Similar dynamics were at work in the American underestimation of the threat in Iran. Gary Sick, a member of the National Security Council with responsibility for Iran during the Carter Administration, writes: "At least equally important for the relative lack of attention paid to Iran during this critical period was the underlying realization that there were no attractive options available to Washington" (1985: 77). Sick argues that the spectre of Vietnam loomed large and neither the president nor his principal advisers were "philosophically prepared" to consider military intervention in a civil war in the third world. Moreover, many of his principal advisers in the State Department were strongly opposed to the Shah's repressive policies. Consequently, Sick concludes:

> since there were very few realistic policy options available, and since any substantial change
> in policy involved actions that were certain to be politically distasteful or worse, people were
> inclined to keep their thoughts to themselves. The combined effect was to stifle communica-

tion . . . and to encourage procrastination in the hope that the situation would resolve itself somehow. (1985: 78)

Even when leaders are not frightened and hopeless, their needs can motivate error. A careful reading of studies of intelligence failures suggests a process of motivated underestimation (Betts, 1982; Handel, 1976). In the autumn of 1973, for example, Israel's leaders were preparing for a general election and, in their campaign rhetoric, members of the governing coalition emphasized the calm along the borders and the improved strategic situation. In this kind of political climate, political leaders may have unconsciously discounted the growing evidence of Egyptian and Syrian military preparations and conjointly inflated evidence that deterrence was secure.

This tendency to wishful thinking and motivated denial of threatening information was reinforced by the satisfaction of Israel's leaders with the status quo. The policy implications which flowed from their analysis were attractive: no mobilization of civilian reserves unless Israel's leadership was absolutely convinced that Egypt was irrevocably committed to attack. Such a restrictive requirement for certainty reduced the attractiveness of any significant strategic response at the same time as leaders were motivated to dismiss evidence of threat (Stein, 1985). The result, predictably, was strategic and tactical surprise when Egyptian and Syrian forces attacked.

In his analysis of British intelligence during the '30s, Wark (1985) finds a similar process at work. Intelligence analyses of German military strength did not shape policy, but policy shaped intelligence estimates. Under Neville Chamberlain, estimates of German capabilities increased, making a military confrontation with Germany less attractive. In 1939, when the scope of Hitler's ambitions became unmistakably apparent, estimates of relative German capabilities declined as British leaders prepared for war. Vested interest in a particular policy can best explain both the overestimation and the underestimation of the military threat posed by Hitler's Germany.

Psychologists who study cognitive and motivated error make a singular contribution to the explanation of the misperception of threat. At least in the first instance, they can explain both the remarkable degree of insensitivity adversaries display to each other's signals and exaggerated perceptions of threat. Analysis of cognitive biases alone, however, cannot establish the likely direction of misperception or its probable occurrence; the direction of motivated errors is far easier to specify. Preliminary research indicates, moreover, that motivational biases are not random occurrences but rather responses to underlying political and/or strategic conditions (Lebow and Stein, 1987). It is to these political and strategic conditions that we now turn.

The Strategic Roots of the Misperception of Threat

Analysts traditionally have looked to the strategic environment as an important source of the distortion of threat. In particular, scholars have examined the impact of the "security dilemma" on the exaggeration of threat and the especially dangerous consequences which flow from the distorted perception which is more likely in this kind of strategic environment (Butterfield, 1951; Herz, 1950; Jervis, 1976, 1978; and Snyder, 1985). The distinguishing characteristic of a security dilemma is that behavior perceived by adversaries as threatening and aggressive is initiated as a defensive response to an inhospitable strategic environment. What one set of leaders sees as defensive another sees as offensive. A "perceptual security dilemma" may develop, however, when strategic and psychological factors interact and strategic assessments are exaggerated or distorted by perceptual biases; in effect, leaders overrate the advantages of the offensive, the magnitude of unfavorable power shifts, and the hostility of their adversaries (Snyder, 1985).

In 1914, for example, leaders did confront elements of a security dilemma (Snyder, 1984; Van Evera, 1984). As French fortifications improved, German security required the vulnerability of Russian forces in Poland; without this vulnerability, both Russia and France could mobilize to full strength and then attack jointly. Russian security, however, excluded precisely such a weakness: Russia could not tolerate a decisive German advantage in a short war and so planned a 40 percent increase in standing forces by 1917. In this strategic situation, defensive preparation by Russia was an offensive threat to Germany and, conversely, a defensive strategy by Germany suggested immediate military action against Russia. Although offense was operationally more difficult than defense, Russia's slow mobilization created the incentive to develop offensive strategies to solve defensive problems. When offense and defense became virtually indistinguishable, threat perception escalated dramatically.

Although the strategic environment was inhospitable and dangerous, Germany's leaders exaggerated the threat and, as Snyder (1985: 170) argues persuasively, reasoned inside out. They overestimated the hostility of their adversaries and, consequently, assumed the inevitability of a two-front war. The attractiveness of a preventive war-fighting strategy then became overwhelming; indeed, the general staff gave no serious consideration after 1890 to the possibility of a defensive strategy. German military planners overestimated the threat posed by their adversaries in ways that psychological theories expect and then argued that an offensive capability was the least unsatisfactory option. Once they did so, Germany's neighbors confronted a real security dilemma. Insofar as they could not distinguish between offense and defense, their perception of the German threat escalated.

In 1914, the strategic environment conditioned and facilitated the overestimation of threat. The inhospitability of the strategic environment was compounded by the motivated errors of the German military whose strong commitment to an offensive military strategy is otherwise inexplicable. As Janis and Mann (1977) would predict, these motivated errors occurred when the German military felt itself up against a very difficult strategic situation with no obvious solution. Predictably again, the result was catastrophe.

A school of German historians disputes this interpretation of German misperception of the Russian and French threat as motivated error. Rather, it argues that the structural contradictions of German society were powerful inducements to the deliberate exaggeration of threat (Fischer, 1975). Important industrial and economic groups benefited directly, they suggest, from the heightened perception of danger and the defense spending that followed. The political leadership alleviated the social tensions and sharp class conflict in Germany at the time, at least in part, by their emphasis on the growing external threat (Gordon, 1974). If this interpretation is correct, then Germany's overestimation of threat was not the result of misperception by its leadership but rather a deliberate manipulation of threat in response to alarming political as well as strategic factors. Evidence of the thinking of the German military over a long period of time, however, suggests a sustained preoccupation with a two-front war. This preoccupation was independent of changes in domestic political and social tension.

Closely related to the impact of the international security dilemma on the distortion of threat are unfavorable changes in the relative balance of power (Cohen, 1979; Knorr, 1976). When the trends in the balance of military capabilities alter in favor of an adversary or leaders perceive an unfavorable shift, the ensuing sense of vulnerability and fear promote an exaggerated estimate of threat. In the autumn of 1986, for example, some senior military officers in Israel estimated that Syria was preparing for imminent attack. Their perception of threat was in part a function of Syrian military activity in southern Lebanon but more broadly a response to their estimates of unfavorable trends in the balance of military capabilities.

Vulnerability ensues not only from changes in relative capabilities but also from geostrategic conditions. Shallowness of space, unsettled borders, the absence of strategic depth, repeated or protracted warfare, can all promote a collective sense of vulnerability and an exaggerated perception of threat (Knorr, 1976; Cohen, 1979). Analysts of Israel's foreign policy have suggested, for example, that its acute perception of threat can only be understood in the context of its strategic vulnerability and its repeated experience of attack and war (Brecher, 1972; Yaniv, 1987).

Leaders can exercise considerable care in the interpretation of changes in the relative strategic balance, mindful of the motivation to exaggerate threat under these kinds of conditions. They can be especially vigilant if they are aware that a "security dilemma" is at work, distorting and multiplying the perception of threat. In this kind of strategic environment, policies must be carefully designed to reduce spirals of mutual fear and reinforcing threat (Jervis, 1976: 58–113). Especially in this kind of environment, threat-based strategies like deterrence may not only be inappropriate but also provocative and dangerous (Lebow and Stein, 1987).

The Political Roots of the Misperception of Threat

Leaders operate not only in the international system but in their domestic political environment as well. Very often, leaders' perception of threat is conditioned by their domestic political needs and interests and by the institutional nexus of policy. Graham Allison (1971) argues that "where you stand determines where you sit," that position in the institutional hierarchy determines predisposition and preference. Threat perception can similarly be seen as partly a function of institutionalized rivalry (Freedman, 1977; Prados, 1982). Snyder (1984) finds, for example, that the German military had a far more exaggerated perception of the threat posed by Germany's neighbors than did the civilian leadership. It is no coincidence that this acute perception of threat was accompanied by a strong commitment to an expensive offensive strategy; perception and interest coincided.

In a well-known process, civilian and military officials responsible for defense often unwittingly exaggerate threat to increase the size of budgetary allocations. In his analysis of policymaking on Vietnam, Betts (1977) finds that operational military analysts seeking to justify missions tended to overestimate threat while autonomous intelligence analysts were considerably less alarmed. More recently, a comparison of the analyses of the Soviet threat by the Central Intelligence Agency and the Pentagon finds distinct institutional differences (Gordon, 1986). Consistently, the CIA has been less pessimistic in its analysis of the Soviet military threat than has the Pentagon: it has disputed assertions by the Pentagon that the Soviet SS-19 missile has the accuracy to be an effective first-strike weapon; it has concluded that the United States previously exaggerated the yield of the Soviet underground tests of nuclear weapons and questioned allegations that the Soviet Union has violated the 1974 Threshold Test Ban Treaty; it has provided a more cautious reading of the pace of Soviet research on antimissile systems; and it has disputed Pentagon estimates of Soviet military spending and concluded that Soviet defense spending has been constant for years.

Analysts attribute this difference to two closely related political processes. First, unlike the Defense Intelligence Agency, whose intelligence reports are commissioned by the Pentagon even though they circulate through the government, the CIA provides intelligence to a variety of Government agencies and increasingly to Congress. Its analysts are therefore inherently less vulnerable to political pressure and less likely to shape their analysis unconsciously to conform to the expectations and preferences of a particular consumer. Second, Pentagon analysts may unwittingly exaggerate Soviet military capabilities in order to secure support for the budgetary requests submitted to Congress. This consistent difference in the pattern of threat perception appears to be related systematically to institutional interests.

The impact of the institutional context of leaders' perceptions is not simple and unidirectional. Leaders can also influence the form and content of information that flows through the hierarchy. Merely by making their expectations or preferences known, policymakers can encourage their subordinates to report or emphasize information supportive of those expectations and preferences. Perspectives confirmed and reconfirmed over time become more and more resistant to discrepant information. In this way, selective attention, denial, or any motivated error that results from the efforts of policymakers to cope with alarming information can be institutionalized. Again, the result is significant distortion in threat perception.

A RESEARCH AGENDA

The arguments and the evidence we have just reviewed are troubling. The arguments are troubling because the theory on which they are based is still primitive and inchoate; we have no integrated theory of misperception. The evidence is troubling because it suggests that the obstacles to accurate threat perception are so many and so pervasive. Indeed it seems unlikely that leaders could avoid committing all the most important cognitive errors or that the political and strategic conditions which motivate misperception can be controlled. Indeed, it might be more appropriate to ask not how, when, and why threats are misperceived, but, rather, how and when threats are accurately perceived.

A short but accurate answer is that we do not know. We do not know enough about the conditions that promote effective signalling and reasonably accurate perception of threat. This indeed is the critical question, both analytically and from a policy perspective. Policy and theory are closely related to one another and the imperatives of both suggest several broad lines of research.

First, we need to know when and how threat is accurately perceived, in what kinds of political and strategic environments. The first priority is to identify cases in history where leaders have perceived the threat that was issued with some degree of accuracy. It would be especially useful to identify cases where leaders were divided in their evaluation of threat (Barnhart, 1987). It would then be possible to hold the strategic, political, and institutional influences constant and to explore the impact of different cognitive and motivational processes on threat perception. With the benefit of hindsight, we could ask "what did leaders do right," "how did they do it," and "how did they differ systematically from those who were wrong?" How did Churchill and Chamberlain differ, for example, in their processes of threat assessment? Some analysts have speculated that Churchill was right for the wrong reasons, that he did not differ significantly from Chamberlain in the cognitive processes that he used to evaluate the threat from Germany, but that he was lucky enough to begin with the "right" set of organizing beliefs.

This kind of controlled comparison is essential if we are to create a systematic body of knowledge about threat perception. Our analysis of cases of misperception at best permits us to identify both the immediate and the structural factors that are associated with distortion. It may well be, however, that some of these same factors are also present when perception is far more accurate. If this is so, then these factors may be necessary but unimportant components of a more general explanation of misperception. On the other hand, they may prove critical.

We also need to know a great deal more about the interaction of important psychological processes when leaders misperceive threat. Here, the difficulty lies principally with psychological theories rather than with the available historical evidence. The theoretical challenge is twofold. First, cognitive psychologists have yet to develop a set of theoretically related propositions to explain distorted attribution, estimation, and judgment. The impact of heuristics and biases is well-established but we do not know when they occur or how they interact. Second, psychologists have not yet integrated the cognitive and affective dimensions in a theoretically coherent explanation. We look briefly at each of these challenges and their implications for the analysis of the perception of threat.

Cognitive psychology analyzes the organizing schemas and belief systems which are fundamental to cognition but does not specify the relationship of schemas to beliefs nor the processes of formation and change in the crucial elements in the cognitive repertoire (Jervis, 1986c: 327–328). Processes of cognitive change are clearly important to changes in threat perception over time.

Cognitive psychologists also identify a set of discrete heuristics and biases whose relationship to one another and to substantive and situational factors remains as yet unexplicated. The limited evidence that we have reviewed indicates that at times these biases appear in patterned clusters rather than independently of one another and suggests a number of propositions for further investigation.

Our evidence suggests, for example, that the bias toward self-image as an available referent to evaluate others is likely to be greater when differences in cognitive contexts are great and the propensity to empathy is low; the latter seemed to reinforce the former. We noted as well that the attribution of greater coherence and centralization to an adversary was consistent with the attempt to assimilate discrepant information to existing beliefs; it reinforced processes of inconsistency management. Analysis of Carter's perception of the Soviet threat also indicates that the bias toward proportionality interacted with a tendency to overconfidence, egocentricity, and fundamental errors of attribution to inflate his perception of threat. Finally, the underestimation of the likelihood of an Egypt attack by Israel's leaders in 1973 can be explained by a "theory-driven" process of judgment, by the heuristic of availability, and by the reinforcing impact of the bias toward self-image. In these two cases, heuristics and biases reinforced one another and were easily interpreted. When biases contradict each other, however, existing theory does not specify their relative importance, the likelihood that one will supercede the other, nor the conditions under which each is likely to occur.

This first cut at the evidence suggests the necessity to encourage psychologists and political analysts to identify clusters of biases which are theoretically coherent and integrated and to examine the interactive effects of contradictory heuristics and biases. We need as well to reread contemporary international history to isolate patterned misperception empirically. When did biases occur together and what kind of impact did they have on the misperception of threat? What kinds of errors are characteristic of different kinds of biases? Are leaders insensitive to their adversary's values and interests, for example, because of an inability to empathize, because of the bias toward egocentricity, and/or because of the tendency to discount unpleasant information? An analysis of the interaction of the most important errors in theory and practice is a critical prerequisite of a better explanation of misperception.

Cognitive explanations have also paid inadequate attention to the context in which people make their estimates and choices. Psychologists debate whether biases identified in the laboratory are replicated outside (Cronbach, 1975; Ebbeson and Koncini, 1980; Jungermann, 1983). Some suggest that distortion is magnified in the laboratory while others suspect that experimental procedures often result in an underestimation of the magnitude of inferential biases (Nisbett and Ross, 1980: 250–254). Jervis (1986c: 324) suggests, for example, that cognitive processing may vary with the importance of the issue to the decision maker, that performance may improve on problems that are central rather than trivial, but Nisbett and Ross dispute the proposition that important judgments will be made through better quality cognitive processes (1980: 220–22). If Jervis's proposition is sustained in a political and strategic context, the underestimation or overexaggeration of threat may be less when the intrinsic interests at stake are central to political leaders.

Psychological theories must also attempt to integrate cognitive and affective dimensions in their explanations of attribution, estimation, and judgment. Cognitive and motivated error are often treated dichotomously, in part because they are derived from different theoretical assumptions and organizing principles. One tradition within psychology treats cognition and affect as separate systems that operate largely independently of one another (Zajonc, 1980; Zajonc *et al.*, 1982). This separation is contested, however, by two broad traditions within psychology which examine the relationship between cognition and affect.

The first asks how thought processes shape what people feel and treats cognition as the antecedent variable. Experimental studies have examined how arousal, cognitive complexity, cognitive organization, and the fitting of new information to affect-laden schema shape affective reactions to new stimuli (Mandler, 1975; Strongman, 1978; Linville, 1982a,b; Tesser, 1978; Fiske, 1981, 1982). Research has also demonstrated that attributions about the results of past outcomes and thoughts about one's alternative outcomes both contribute to emotion (Weiner, 1980; Kahneman and Tversky, 1982).

Psychologists have also examined how feelings shape the way people think. Studies suggest several sources of motivational influence on attribution: the need for self-esteem (Miller, 1976; Sicoly and Ross, 1977); the need for social approval (Arkin *et al.*, 1980; Bradley, 1978; Tetlock, 1980); the need to believe in a "just world" (Lerner and Miller, 1978); and the need for effective control (Miller *et al.*, 1978: 599). Other research suggests that intense emotion affects information processing and interrupts both attention and memory (Nielson and Sarason, 1981; Brown and Kulik, 1977). Fear and anxiety in particular interrupt cognitive processes and can culminate in distorted processes of defensive avoidance and hypervigilance (Janis and Mann, 1977; Fiske and Taylor, 1984: 332–333). A careful review of the most important evidence, however, suggests that the data are also open to nonmotivational, information-processing explanations (Tetlock and Levi, 1982).

The relationship between affect and cognition is complex and difficult to specify and test (Fiske and Taylor, 1984: 338–339; Lau and Sears, 1986: 359; Tetlock and Levi,

1982). Experimental studies have not yet succeeded in disentangling the impact of one on the other. The failure to specify the relationship between cognition and affect is troubling both when the two sets of theoretical expectations diverge and when they converge (Lazarus, 1982).

When cognitive and motivational explanations differ in their theoretical predictions, interpretation of the evidence permits some assessment of their relative importance even in the absence of good theory. In one of the few cases where they do diverge, the evidence suggests that Carter's decision in 1979 to attempt to deter the Soviet Union in the Persian Gulf conforms more closely to the expectations of a motivational model than to a cognitive explanation (Lebow et al., 1988; Lebow, 1981: 149–228). Even then, the absence of adequate theoretical specification of the relationship between cognitive and motivated error is troubling, since evidence of both kinds of errors is present.

The lack of an integrated explanation is far more serious when the evidence is incomplete. To return to an earlier proposition, insofar as the "importance" of an issue and affect are not entirely independent of one another, motivational explanations would challenge the proposition that performance outside the laboratory may improve on problems that are central rather than trivial. They would predict rather that the greater affect associated with "important" interests would decrease performance and make the misperception of threat more likely.

A second kind of controversy stems not from divergent expectations but rather from an inability to separate the cognitive and affective components of a central theoretical concept. In Germany in 1914, in India in 1962, and in Israel in 1973, cognitive and motivational explanations converge; the political needs of leaders reinforced the impact of cognitive biases and heuristics (Lebow, 1981: 119–147, 216–223; Stein, 1985; Lebow and Stein, 1987). Because the expectations converge, the evidence cannot discriminate between the two explanations nor establish the relative impact of cognition and affect.

If political psychologists are to improve the precision and power of explanations of the misperception of threat, we must look more carefully at the interaction among cognitive heuristics and biases. We must also address the relative importance of affect and cognition on the distorted processes of attribution, estimation, and judgment that contribute to the misperception of threat. These are not easy tasks, both because the theory is only beginning to develop and because behavioral evidence often does not permit distinction between the two perspectives.

Consideration of psychological processes alone will not be sufficient. The evidence suggests that the misperception of threat can often be understood as unconsciously motivated responses to leaders' needs, fears, or interests that are in turn shaped in part by their political, institutional, and strategic environments. Political psychologists must attempt as well as identify the political and strategic conditions which promote or diminish the occurrence of the important cognitive and motivational biases.

EPILOGUE: THEORY AND POLICY

In the analysis of international conflict, we seek not only to build better theory but also to speak usefully to the policy community. This will be difficult to do if the misperception of threat is largely the result of fundamental cognitive biases. Insofar as these errors are both characteristic and unrelated to specific situations, policy recommendations to minimize the impact of cognitive bias are likely to be trivial or banal. The theory that we now have does not permit us to say a great deal that is useful to policymakers.

It is true that leaders would correct their errors if they were aware that their perceptions of threat were biased. Consequently, there is some value in sensitizing leaders to the pervasiveness of the most important kinds of errors. They can be urged to have greater empathy, to reconstruct the fundamental political beliefs of their adversary. They can be pressed to consider basic differences in cultural and ideological beliefs. They can be warned to guard against overconfidence and overgeneralization. The advice to leaders to be aware of these biases and to try to compensate for them may be correct, and leaders may even try to do so, but they are not likely to be terribly successful, given the pervasiveness and deeply rooted nature of these kinds of cognitive errors. We cannot avoid the obvious conclusion: Insofar as the misperception of threat is largely a function of fundamental cognitive biases, leaders can do little but resort to threat less frequently, with greater caution, and with greater awareness of the high risk of misperception by the target.

The evidence that we have reviewed is not, however, entirely discouraging. On the contrary, it suggests that motivated error may occur with some frequency. In reading history, it is difficult at times to separate motivated and cognitive errors empirically because some of the processes can be similar and neither leaves direct behavioral traces. By searching for the political and strategic conditions which evoke fear and need, however, we can try to situate distorted threat perception within its broader political context and identify patterns of motivated biases. Our evidence suggests, for example, that domestic political crises and security dilemmas create a heightened sense of vulnerability. This sense of weakness increases the likelihood of motivated error and, in turn, of distorted threat perception.

This kind of proposition must be the subject of further research across cases of both distorted and accurate perception of threat. If a relationship between strategic and political conditions and motivated error is substantiated, it would have implications not only for theory but for policy. In deciding whether or not to use threat, leaders could be advised to pay special attention to the political and strategic environment of their adversaries and to their sense of vulnerability. A great deal of historical evidence suggests that when leaders feel themselves vulnerable, threats may provoke rather than deter (Jervis, 1976; Lebow, 1981; Lebow and Stein, 1987; Stein, 1987). Insofar as the political and strategic preconditions of vulnerability can be identified, leaders can be given at least a rough rule of thumb to distinguish those conditions which are especially likely to motivate misperception.

In the final analysis, however, there is no "technical fix" to the fundamental problems associated with the transmission and perception of threat. The use of threat is natural and ubiquitous, but problematic. It is problematic because of the deeply rooted cognitive and motivated errors which confound its transmission and perception. Tinkering with modes of signalling, channels of communication, or the format of the message is likely to have an impact only at the margin. Attempts to control bureaucratic rivalries or manipulate domestic political environments are not likely to fare much better.

Far more important are the basic political and strategic factors which condition both the formulation and the impact of threat in an adversarial relationship. Threats, after all, are used to try to manage political and strategic problems. Psychological research can illuminate the fundamental obstacles to accurate perception of threat but we must put politics back into the psychology of misperception. It is imperative that political psychologists specify the international and domestic conditions which make cognitive and motivated error more likely and thereby exacerbate the misperception of threat with all its attendant costs and consequences.

REFERENCES

Abelson, R. (1973). The structure of belief systems. In Schank, R., and Colby, K. (eds.), *Computer Models of Thought and Language*, W. H. Freeman, San Francisco, pp. 287–339.

Ajzen, I. (1977). Intuitive theories of events and the effects of base rate data on prediction. *J. Personal. Social Psychol.* 35: 303–314.

Allison, G. (1971). *Essence of Decision: Explaining the Cuban Missile Crisis.* Little, Brown, Boston.

Anderson, J. R. (1982). *The Architecture of Cognition.* Harvard University Press, Cambridge.

Arkin, R. M., Appelman, A. J., and Burger, J. M. (1980). Social anxiety, self-presentation, and the self-serving bias in causal attribution. *J. Personal. Social Psychol.* 38: 23–55.

Ball, D. (1980). *Politics and Force Levels: The Strategic Missile Program of the Kennedy Administration.* University of California Press, Berkeley and Los Angeles.

Bar-Hillel, M. (1977). *The Base-Rate Fallacy in Probability Judgments*, Decision Research, Eugene, Oregon.

Barnhart, M. A. (1987). *Japan Prepares for Total War: The Search for Economic Security, 1919–1941*, Cornell University Press, Ithaca.

Betts, R. (1977). *Soldiers, Statesmen, and Cold War Crises*, Harvard University Press, Cambridge.

———. (1982). *Surprise Attack*, Brookings Institution, Washington, D.C.

Bradley, G. W. (1978). Self-serving biases in the attribution process: A reexamination of the fact or fiction question. *J. Personal. Social Psychol.* 36: 56–71.

Brecher, M. (1972). *The Foreign Policy System of Israel: Setting, Images, Process.* Oxford University Press, London.

Brown, R., and Kulik, J. (1977). Flashbulb memories. *Cognition* 5: 73–99.

Butterfield, H. (1951). *History and Human Relations*, Collins, London.

Cohen, R. (1979). *Threat Perception in International Crisis.* The University of Wisconsin Press, Madison.

Cronbach, L. (1975). Beyond the two scientific disciplines of scientific psychology. *Am. Psychologist* 30: 116–127.

Ebbeson, E. B. and Koncini, V. J. (1980). On the external validity of decision making research: What do we know about decisions in the real world? In Wallsten, T. S. (ed.), *Cognitive Processes in Choice and Decision Behavior*, Lawrence Erlbaum, Hillsdale, N.J., pp. 21–45.

Edelman, M. (1977). *Words That Succeed and Politics That Fail.* Academic Press, New York.

Fischer, F. (1975). *War of Illusions: German Policies from 1911 to 1914*, trans. M. Jackson, Norton, New York.

Fischhoff, B. Slovic, P. and Lichtenstein, S. (1977). Knowing with certainty: The appropriateness of extreme confidence. *J. Exp. Psychol. Hum. Percept. Perform.* 3: 522–564.

Fiske, S. T. (1981). Social cognition and affect. In Harvey, J. (ed.), *Cognition, Social Behavior and the Environment*, Lawrence Erlbaum, Hillsdale, N.J., pp. 227–264.

———. (1982). Schema-triggered affect: Applications to social perception. In Clark, M. S., and Fiske, S. T. (eds.), *Affect and Cognition: The 17th Annual Carnegie Symposium on Cognition*, Lawrence Erlbaum, Hillsdale, N.J., pp. 55–78.

Fiske, S. T. and Taylor, S. E. (1984). *Social Cognition.* Addison-Wesley, Reading, Mass.

Freedman, L. (1977). *U.S. Intelligence and the Soviet Strategic Threat*, Macmillan, London.

Gaddis, J. L. (1972). *The United States and the Origins of the Cold War, 1941–1947*, Columbia University Press, New York.

Garthoff, R. L. (1985). *Detente and Confrontation: American-Soviet Relations from Nixon to Reagan*, Brookings Institution, Washington, D.C.

Gordon, M. R. (1974). Domestic conflict and the origins of the first world war: The British and the German cases. *J. Mod. Hist.* 46: 191–226.

———. (1986). C.I.A., evaluating Soviet threat, often is not so grim as Pentagon. *The New York Times*, 16 July.

Handel, M. (1976). Perception, deception, and surprise: The case of the Yom Kippur War. *Jerusalem Peace Papers*, 19, Leonard Davis Institute of International Relations, Jerusalem.

Herz, J. (1950). Idealist internationalism and the security dilemma. *World Politics* 2: 158–180.

Janis, I. (1967). Effects of fear arousal on attitude change: Recent developments in theory and experimental research. In Berkowitz, L. (ed.), *Advances in Experimental Social Psychology*, *Vol. 3*, Academic Press, New York.

Janis, I., and Mann, L. (1977). *Decision Making: A Psychological Analysis of Conflict, Choice, and Commitment*, Free Press, New York.

Jervis, R. (1976). *Perception and Misperception in International Politics*, Princeton University Press, Princeton.

———. (1978). Cooperation under the security dilemma. *World Politics* 30: 167–214.

———. (1982). Deterrence and perception. *International Security* 7: 3–32.

———. (1985). Perceiving and coping with threat. In Jervis, R., Lebow, R. N., and Stein, J. G. *Psychology and Deterrence*, The Johns Hopkins University Press, Baltimore, pp. 13–33.

———. (1986a). *War and Misperception*, Paper presented to a conference on the origins and prevention of major wars. Durham, N.H.

———. (1986b). Representativeness in foreign policy judgments. *Polit. Psychol.* 7: 483–506.

———. (1986c). Cognition and political behavior. In Lau, R. R., and Sears, D. O. (eds.), *Political Cognition*, Lawrence Erlbaum, Hillsdale, N.J., pp. 319–336.

Jones, E. E. and Nisbett, R. E. (1971). The actor and observer: Divergent perceptions of the causes of behavior. In Jones, E. E., Kanouse, D. E., Kelley, H. H., Nisbett, R. E., Valins, S., and Weiner, B. (eds.), *Attribution: Perceiving the Causes of Behavior*, General Learning Press, Morristown, N.J., pp. 79–94.

Jungermann, H. (1983). The two camps on rationality. In Scholz, R. W. (ed.), *Decision Making under Uncertainty*, Elsevier, Amsterdam, pp. 63–86.

Kahneman, D. and Tversky, A. (1982). The simulation heuristic. In Kahneman, D., Slovic, P., and Tversky, A. (eds.), *Judgment under Uncertainty: Heuristics and Biases*, Cambridge University Press, New York, pp. 201–208.

Kelley, H. (1972). *Causal Schemata and the Attribution Process*, General Learning Press, Morristown, N.J.

Kelley, H. and Michela, J. (1980). Attribution theory and research. *Annu. Rev. Psychol.* 31: 457–501.

Knorr, K. (1976). Threat perception. In Knorr, K. (ed.), *Historical Dimensions of the National Security Problem*, University Press of Kansas, Lawrence, Kansas, pp. 78–119.

Komorita, S. S. (1973). Concession-making and conflict resolution. *J. Conflict Res.* 17: 745–762.

Lau, R. R. and Sears, D. O. (1986). Social cognition and political cognition: The past, present, and the future. In Lau, R., and Sears, D. O. (eds.), *Political Cognition*, Lawrence Erlbaum, Hillsdale, N.J., pp. 347–366.

Lazarus, R. (1966). *Psychological Stress and the Coping Process*, McGraw-Hill, New York.

———. (1982). Thoughts on the relations between emotion and cognition. *Am. Psychologist* 37: 1019–1024.

Lebow, R. N. (1981). *Between Peace and War: The Nature of International Crisis*, The Johns Hopkins University Press, Baltimore.

———. (1983). The Cuban missile crisis: Reading the lessons correctly. *Political Science Quarterly* 98: 431–458.

———. (1985a). Generational learning and conflict management. *Int. J.* 40: 555–585.

———. (1985b). Miscalculation in the South Atlantic: The origins of the Falklands War. In Jervis, R., Lebow, R. N., and Stein, J. G. *Psychology and Deterrence*, The Johns Hopkins University Press, Baltimore, pp. 89–124.

———. (1987). Deterrence failures revisited. *Int. Sec.* 12: 197–213.

Lebow, R. N. and Stein, J. G. (1987). Beyond deterrence: Building better theory. *J. Social Issues* 43: 155–169.

Lebow, R. N., Stein, J. G., and Cohen, D. S. (1988). Afghanistan as inkblot: Assessing cognitive and motivational explanations of foreign policy. Under review.

Lerner, M. J. and Miller, D. J. (1978). Just world research and the attribution process: Looking back and ahead. *Psychological Bull.* 81: 1030–1051.

Levy, J. S. (1983). Misperception and the causes of war: Theoretical linkages and analytical problems. *World Polit.* 36: 76–99.

Linville, P. W. (1982a). Affective consequences of complexity regarding the self and others. In Clark, M. S. and Fiske, S. T. (eds.), *Affect and Cognition: The 17th Annual Carnegie Symposium on Cognition*, Lawrence Erlbaum, Hillsdale, N.J., pp. 79–110.

———. (1982b). The complexity-extremity effect and age-based stereotyping. *J. Personal. Social Psychol.* 42: 193–211.

Mandler, G. (1975). *Mind and Emotion*, Wiley, New York.

May, E. (1961). *Imperial Democracy*, Harcourt, Brace, New York.

MccGwire, M. (1987). *Military Objectives in Soviet Foreign Policy*, Brookings Institution, Washington, D.C.

McClelland, C. (1975). Crisis and threat in the international setting: Some relational concepts. Threat Recognition and Analysis Project Technical Report 28, University of Southern California. International Relations Research Institute, Los Angeles.

Milburn, T. W., Stewart, P. D., and Herrmann, R. K. (1982). Perceiving the other's intentions, USA and USSR. In Kegley, C., and McGowan, P. (eds.), *Foreign Policy, U.S.A., USSR*, Sage International Yearbook of Foreign Policy Studies, Sage Publications, Beverly Hills.

Miller, D. T. (1976). Ego-involvement and attributions for success and failure. *J. Personal. Social Psychol.* 34: 901–906.

Miller, D. T., Norman, S. A., and Wright, E. (1978). Distortion in person perception as a consequence of need for effective control. *J. Personal. Social Psychol.* 36: 593–607.

Nielson, S. L., and Sarason, S. G. (1981). Emotion, personality, and selective attention. *J. Personal. Social Psychol.* 41: 945–960.

Nisbett, R. E. and Ross, L. (1980). *Human Inference: Strategies and Shortcomings of Social Judgment*, Prentice-Hall, Englewood Cliffs, N.J.

Prados, J. (1982). *The Soviet Estimate: U.S. Intelligence Analysis and Russian Military Strength*, Dial Press, New York.

Reder, L. M. and Anderson, J. R. (1980). A partial resolution of the paradox of inference: The role of integrating knowledge. *Cognitive Psychol.* 12: 447–472.

Ross, L. (1977). The intuitive psychologist and his shortcomings: Distortions in the attribution process. In Berkowitz, L. (ed.), *Advan. Exp. Social Psychol.* Vol. X, Academic Press, New York, pp. 174–214.

Ross, M. and Sicoly, F. (1979). Egocentric bias in availability and attribution. *J. Personal. Social Psychol.* 37: 322–326.

Schank, R. and Abelson, R. (1977). *Scripts, Plans, Goals, and Understanding: An Inquiry into Human Knowledge Structures*, Lawrence Erlbaum, Hillsdale, N.J.

Sick, G. (1985). *All Fall Down*, Penguin, New York.

Sicoly, F. and Ross, M. (1977). Facilitation of ego-biased attributions by means of self-serving observer feedback. *J. Personal. Social Psychol.* 35: 734–741.

Snyder, J. (1984). Civil-military relations and the cult of the offensive, 1914 and 1984. *International Security* 9: 58–107.

———. (1985). Perceptions of the security dilemma in 1914. In Jervis, R., Lebow, R. N., and Stein, J. G. *Psychology and Deterrence*, The Johns Hopkins University Press, Baltimore, pp. 153–179.

Stein, J. G. (1985). Calculation, miscalculation, and deterrence II: The view from Jerusalem. In Jervis, R., Lebow, R. N., and Stein, J. G. *Psychology and Deterrence*. The Johns Hopkins University Press, Baltimore, pp. 60–88.

———. (1987). Extended deterrence in the Middle East: American strategy reconsidered. *World Polit.* 39: 326–352.

Stein, J. G. and Tanter, R. (1980). *Rational Decision Making: Israel's Security Choices, 1967*, Ohio State University Press, Columbus, Ohio.

Strongman, K. T. (1978). *The Psychology of Emotion*, Wiley, New York.

Tesser, A. (1978). Self-generated attitude change. In Berkowitz, L. (ed.), *Advances in Experimental Social Psychology*, Vol. 11, Academic Press, New York, pp. 289–338.

Tetlock, P. E. (1980). Explaining teacher explanations for pupil performance: An examination of the self-presentation interpretation. *Social Psychological Quart.* 43: 283–290.

Tetlock, P. E. and Levi, A. (1982). Attribution bias: On the inconclusiveness of the cognition-motivation debate. *J. Exp. Social Psychol.* 18: 68–88.

Theis, W. (1980). *When Governments Collide*, University of California Press, Berkeley.

Thorndyke, P. W. and Hayes-Roth, B. (1979). The use of schemata in the acquisition and transfer of knowledge. *Cognitive Psychol.* 11: 82–105.

Tversky, A. and Kahneman, D. (1973). Availability: A heuristic for judging frequency and probability. *Cognitive Psychol.* 5: 207–232.

Van Evera, S. (1984). The cult of the offensive and the origins of the First World War, *Int. Sec.* 9: 58–107.

Wark, W. (1985). *The Ultimate Enemy: British Intelligence and Nazi Germany, 1933–1939*, Cornell University Press, Ithaca.

Weiner, B. (1980). A cognitive (attribution-) emotion action model of motivated behavior: An analysis of judgment of help-giving. *J. Personal. Social Psychol.* 39: 186–200.

———. (1982). The emotional consequences of causal attributions. In Clark, M. S., and Fiske, S. T. (eds.), *Affect and Cognition: The 17th Annual Carnegie Symposium on Cognition*, Lawrence Erlbaum, Hillsdale, N.J., pp. 185–210.

Yaniv, A. (1987). *Deterrence without the Bomb: The Politics of Israeli Strategy*, D. C. Heath, Lexington, Mass.

Zajonc, R. B. (1980). Feeling and thinking. Preferences need no inferences. *Am. Psychologist* 35: 151–175.

Zajonc, R. B., Pietromonoco, P., and Bargh, J. (1982). Independence and interaction of affect and cognition. In Clark, M. S., and Fiske, S. T. (eds.), *Affect and Cognition: The 17th Annual Carnegie Symposium on Cognition*, Lawrence Erlbaum, Hillsdale, N.J., pp. 211–228.

26

Biased Judgments of Media Bias: A Case Study of the Arab-Israeli Dispute

NEIL J. KRESSEL

Since the birth of the Jewish state in 1948, hundreds of commentaries have appeared on American media coverage of the Arab-Israeli dispute. Each time the conflict flares anew, more articles turn up in both academic journals and popular publications. Not surprisingly, most critiques are driven by a desire to demonstrate bias—either against Israel or against the Arab states.

On one hand, a barrage of articles accuse the American press of engaging in "adversary journalism" against Israel and, in some instances, of turning the Jewish state into the "scapegoat of the world media" (e.g., Isaac, 1980; Feith, 1980; Alexander, 1982; Peretz, 1982b; Podhoretz, 1982; Chafets, 1984). On the other hand, an even larger number of articles charge the American media with inequitable pro-Israel and anti-Arab biases (e.g., Baha el-Din, 1971; Suleiman, 1961, 1974; Asi, 1981a, b; Said, 1981).

To some extent, this apparent contradiction can be explained by noting the dates of the accusations. Israel supporters seldom objected to coverage prior to the (1973) Yom Kippur War; their discontent peaked during the aftermath of the (1982) Lebanon War (Peretz, 1982b; Podhoretz, 1982; ADL, 1982; Chafets, 1984). Arab supporters, however, expressed particular dissatisfaction with coverage of the (1967) Six Day War (Adams, 1971; Suleiman, 1970, 1974; Baha el-Din, 1971; Asi, 1981a). Although pro-Arab writers, for the most part, continue to view the media as anti-Arab, they have grown somewhat more satisfied with coverage during the past decade (Ibrahim, 1974; Shaheen, 1980; Asi, 1981b). Still, the dates of the accusations offer only partial guidance since coverage of the same events, on many occasions, has drawn denuncia-tions from both sides.

Conflicting accusations have led many fairminded readers to throw up their hands in despair, concluding that little of value can be distilled from the voluminous writings on this topic and that our knowledge of Middle East media coverage lies in disarray. Others optimistically have interpreted conflicting bias charges as evidence of media equity, balance, and impartiality. In other words, if both Arabs and Israelis consider the Western media biased against them, then, the media *ipso facto* must produce reasonably unprej-udiced coverage.

This paper presents a brief overview of articles charging the American mass media with unfair bias in coverage of the Arab-Israeli conflict. Kressel (1983) offered a more detailed review of journalistic and empirical studies on media coverage of the conflict; Asi (1981a) also reviewed numerous empirical articles on this topic. The present study differs from prior efforts insofar as it focuses upon the perspectives of partisan critics. The paper's goals are (1) to review and categorize accusations of bias, (2) to distinguish between the normative, conceptual, and empirical issues involved in judgments of bias, and (3) to suggest an overall vantage point from which we may most usefully view the debate over media bias.

PRO-ARAB CRITICISM OF THE AMERICAN MASS MEDIA

Since pro-Arab perspectives on American media coverage have been changing over the past decade, it is not a straightforward matter to identify the elements of a mainstream pro-Arab critique. Moreover, different Arab supporters have highlighted different is-sues. Nontheless, most accusations of anti-Arab media bias have included some combi-nation of the following points.

1. The American mass media consistently present unbalanced coverage; this bias shows up as *a disproportionate number of unfavorable references to Arab states, their leaders, and their actions. Similarly, bias is evident in a disproportionate number of favorable references to Israel.* Although present in news articles, the imbalance is most blatantly apparent in editorials, features, and cartoons. Although some pro-Arab writers have acknowledged a move toward balance in press coverage during the past few years, none have argued that the American press is no longer biased against Arabs (Suleiman, 1965, 1970, 1974, 1975; Farmer, 1968; Terry, 1971, 1974, 1975; Asi, 1981a, b; and many others).

2. The American media paint *a blatantly distorted and untrue picture of the Arab-Israeli conflict.* Frequent citations of false images in the media include (1) Jewish settlement made the desert bloom but Palestinian Arabs left the land untended, (2) Zionism is a basically liberal philosophy, (3) Israel is the underdog in the Middle East, (4) Palestinians are terrorists, (5) Jews did not force Palestinian Arabs to leave their

homes in 1948 but instead urged them to stay, (6) the Arab-Israeli conflict, at bottom, stems from Arab anti-Judaism (Suleiman, 1965, 1974; Said, 1981; Shaheen, 1981).

3. The media present *too much coverage of Israel and too little of the Arabs*; this leads to greater familiarity and, hence, partiality toward Israel (Padelford, 1979; Asi, 1981a; Weisman, 1981a, b; and many others).[1]

4. Conspiracy, editorial bans, and other barriers have made it *impossible or extremely difficult for pro-Arab views to appear in print in the United States* (Raspberry, 1973; Suleiman, 1965; Ward, 1969; Baha el-Din, 1971; Adams, 1971). Some Arab commentators object to the prominence of Jews in media professions, claiming that this destroys the chances for fair coverage. Also, pro-Arab writers frequently complain that their views are denied fair consideration; instead, pro-Arab opinions are delegitimized by labeling them as anti-Jewish.

5. *Cultural insensitivity, stereotyping, and racist imagery* predominate in American media coverage of the conflict (Suleiman, 1970; Baha el-Din, 1971; Shaheen, 1979, 1980; Cooley, 1981; Said, 1981).

6. The American mass media use *double standards* when judging actions of Israel and the Arab states. For example, critics have argued that Palestinian attacks against Israelis generally are labeled "terrorist" while Israeli bombings of Arab villages are called "retaliatory" (Suleiman, 1965, 1970; Cooley, 1981; Said, 1981; Weisman, 1981a).

PRO-ISRAEL CRITICISM OF THE AMERICAN MASS MEDIA

By nearly all accounts, the Jewish state had little about which to object in mass media coverage of the conflict prior to 1973.[2] After the Yom Kippur War, however, many pro-Israel authors perceived an erosion of support for Israel. During the late seventies and early eighties, pro-Israel critiques of the media grew in frequency and severity. Unlike pro-Arab writings which often had appeared in academic form, pro-Israel commentaries mostly involved impressionistic accounts focusing upon coverage of specific events. Still, a mainstream pro-Israel critique of the mass media might include some combination of the following elements:

1. Since the Yom Kippur War, the American mass media have moved away from their formerly objective treatment of the conflict. In recent years, the media have made *disproportionately unfavorable references to Israel and disproportionately favorable references to Arabs*. This new imbalance shows up in the orientation of news and feature stories, the positions of editorials, the imagery of cartoons, and other ways.

2. In their efforts to present more "evenhanded" coverage, many journalists have distorted the truth and painted a *badly flawed and inaccurate picture of the Arab-Israeli dispute*. According to pro-Israel writers, the distorted image has several common components: (1) overplaying Arab moderation, e.g., saying Sadat attacked Israel in 1973

in order to lay the groundwork for peace; (2) portraying Arab institutions in terms more palatable to American readers, e.g., calling the Saudi political system a "desert democracy"; (3) whitewashing the PLO and downplaying its terrorism; (4) portraying Israel as more militaristic and less committed to peace than the Arabs; (5) devoting disproportionate attention to Israel's activities on the West Bank; (6) getting many facts wrong in coverage of the Lebanon War (Rubin, 1975/1976; Isaac, 1980; Feith, 1980; Hadar, 1980; Blitzer, 1980; Barlas, 1981; ADL, 1982; Peretz, 1982b; Podhoretz, 1982; Baum, 1982; Sidorsky, 1982).

  3. *Political barriers of various sorts bar American journalists from presenting objective reports* about the conflict. The most severe objection of this sort holds that Western reporters operate under fear of terrorist reprisals (Chafets, 1982; Wall, 1982; Peretz, 1982a; Timmerman, 1983). Other critics have charged that reporters, in order to maintain access to Arab countries, must write stories acceptable to their hosts.

  4. *The mass media, to some degree, have started to display anti-Jewish tendencies.* This prejudice shows up in several ways: (1) invidious stereotypes about Jewish control of the media and government; (2) vulgar anti-Jewish imagery, particularly in political cartoons; (3) declaration of Jewish group interests as illegitimate; (4) collusion of anti-Israel partisans with traditional anti-Jewish activists (Podhoretz, 1982; Volkmann, 1982; and others).

  5. *The mass media, especially television, emphasize the vivid and the concrete; these emphases have resulted in unfavorable coverage of Israel in recent years*—particularly in the Lebanon War. The bias stems from broadcast media's inability to deal adequately with historical, background, and long-term forces; for example, the attacking army in any war, however just, seems evil through the lens of TV cameras particularly suited for capturing rubble and dead bodies. Thus, viewers of television coverage of the war in Lebanon did not learn the truth about the invasion (Roeh, 1981; Miller, 1982; Peretz, 1982b; ADL, 1982).

  6. The mass media employ *double standards* in deciding what to cover and how to judge Israel and the Arabs. Numerous pro-Israel writers (e.g., Alexander, 1982; Podhoretz, 1982) have cited coverage of the massacres at Sabra and Shattila as evidence of double standards. They have asked why equally voluminous and condemnatory coverage was not given to similar massacres in the past committed entirely by Arabs. Moreover, they have argued that Israel's indirect involvement received stronger condemnation than the direct involvement of the actual Christian murderers. Podhoretz (1982) sees employment of double standards as pervasive and regards their use as one defining characteristic of media anti-Semitism.

BIASED RESEARCH ON MEDIA BIAS

The critiques of media coverage offered by pro-Arab writers and pro-Israel writers contain some structural similarities. Both groups cite: (1) unbalanced and disproportionately unfavorable coverage, (2) distorted and untrue media portrayals of the conflict, (3) prejudice and stereotyping, (4) employment of double standards, and (5) various unfair political and organizational barriers to an objective coverage. In addition, pro-Arab commentators have highlighted quantitative underrepresentation in media coverage. Pro-Israel writers have discussed limitations inherent in the media themselves—such as broadcast media's weakness at handling contextual background.

One simple truth goes a long way toward explaining the curious literature on media bias. Differing perceptions about media coverage are linked *inextricably* to disagreements over facts and interpretations concerning the conflict itself. Although certain relatively minor issues may be agreed upon regardless of political orientation, it is impossible to conceive of a situation in which Arab partisans, Israel partisans, and the unaligned would agree on judgments of bias.

Since each side would readily offer its own scholars to resolve disagreement, there is no sense in leaving the question to the experts. This limitation applies equally to middle-of-the-road or neutral experts; there is no reason to believe they have a monopoly on political truth.

THE PROBLEM WITH "SCIENTIFIC" STUDIES

In much research on Middle East media coverage, "scientific" approaches have obscured the centrality of normative and political issues. After reviewing several studies of media bias on matters not related to the Arab-Israeli conflict, content analysis methodologist Klaus Krippendorff (1980) concluded that most such studies "suffer from the lack of defensible criteria" for determining bias. This problem clearly underlies most quantitative, content analytic studies of media coverage of the Arab-Israeli conflict. Typically, studies addressing the bias question have rested upon one or the other of two fallacious assumptions:

1. Fair coverage of the Arab-Israeli conflict would tell the version of the story accepted by oneself.

2. Fair coverage of the Arab-Israeli conflict would say half nice things about the Arabs and half nice things about the Israelis.

Neither assumption is compelling. In the first instance, the problem is obvious. In the second case, one need only imagine problems in using the principle to cover, say, Stalin; should the mass media have reported 50 percent favorable items about the Soviet leader and 50 percent about his victims? Should half the *New York Times* editorials have supported Stalin and half opposed him? Or should they have remained neutral?

In numerous content analytic studies of media coverage of the Arab-Israeli conflict, these difficulties have been ignored (Suleiman, 1965, 1971, 1974, 1975; Terry, 1971, 1974, 1975; Padelford, 1979; Asi, 1981a; and others). Most frequently, pro-Arab researchers have conducted the studies. They usually have started by citing the range of Arab charges against the American mass media—conspiracy, double standards, lies, racism, etc. Then, without explaining the critical difference between these accusations and the accusation of unbalanced (or unfavorable) coverage, the studies claim to have resolved the bias question scientifically.

Researchers in this area seldom have been explicit about their definitions of bias but, usually, the operational definition is based on one or more of the following criteria:

1. Widespread negative imagery about Arab states, leaders, and customs,

2. A disproportionate number of negative utterances about Arab states, leaders, and customs,

3. A disproportionate number of positive utterances about Israel,

4. Overwhelming editorial support for Israel's case in the Arab-Israeli conflict.

Samples of mass media coverage are then subjected to formal content analysis. In concluding sections, studies finding *unfavorable* coverage claim to have demonstrated *unfair media bias* and the need for the media to mend their ways. Quite clearly, no such conclusions can follow from these studies. Content analytic studies explore what messages the media send; they cannot assess the validity or fairness of these messages.

Studies of textbook coverage of the Middle East have suffered from the same problem (e.g., Al-Qazzaz, 1975; Griswold, 1975; Perry, 1975; Kenny, 1975). One study (Abu-Laban, 1975) even claimed that "content analyses of school textbooks . . . indicate that at both the formal and informal levels, pressure has been exerted to influence (sic) a predominantly one-sided approach to the Arab-Israeli conflict." How content analysis made this magical leap of inference was not explained.

THE PROPER ROLE FOR EMPIRICAL STUDIES

Although content analytic studies do not get us very far in discussions of media bias, they do add significantly to our empirical knowledge about media coverage of the conflict. For instance, studies have investigated (1) changes in media favorability and attentiveness toward the Arab-Israeli conflict, (2) differences between broadcast and print media, (3) differences among various newspapers and among the networks, (4) changes in favorability and attentiveness to various sub-issues of the conflict, (5) changes in favorability and attentiveness to various leaders and countries in the conflict, (6) journalists' criteria for coverage of events in the conflict, (7) coverage of the Arab-Israeli conflict in comparison to coverage of other international conflicts, (8) political orientations of media professionals, (9) case studies of how dramatic events have been covered, (10) the relationship between media coverage and public opinion, and a host of other topics. To the extent that these studies have focused upon empirical issues (e.g., favorability) and avoided the confusion of scientific measurement with normative judgment (e.g., of unfairness), they have been able to expand our empirical knowledge about media coverage of the conflict.

Kressel (1983) reviewed quantitative studies of media coverage of the Arab-Israeli conflict in detail. According to that literature review, several empirical generalizations emerge about coverage:

1. The mass media send a picture of the conflict heavily dominated by dramatic events.

2. During the 1970s, the Middle East emerged as the most frequently covered foreign policy story in the American mass media.

3. As a rule, favorability of the American mass media has paralleled the favorability of the United States government policy—whatever it has been at various times.

4. From the birth of Israel until very recently, the American mass media favored Israel in coverage of the conflict. Israel's relative advantage, however, was diluted by the bulk of coverage which was overwhelmingly nonpartisan or middle-of-the-road.

5. From 1972 through the end of 1982, at least, media support for Israel declined steadily. Over this same period, there was a dramatic rise in media support for Palestinians.

6. During war years, coverage was most favorable to Israel in 1967 and 1948, less favorable in 1956 and 1973, and least favorable in 1982.

7. Regarding editorials in five major newspapers between 1972 and the end of 1982, the *Wall Street Journal* was most favorable to Israel, the *New York Times* came next, followed by the *Washington Post* and the *Los Angeles Times*. The *Christian Science Monitor* was least favorable, by far. During the previous decade, the order was similar, except that the *New York Times* came first, followed by the *Wall Street Journal*.

Other empirical conclusions of this sort have been drawn from well-designed quantitative studies of media favorability. An error occurs when authors and critics attempt to derive normative conclusions from these studies.

UNTRUTHS, DOUBLE STANDARDS, SLANTS, AND JOURNALISTIC NORMS

The question arises whether all investigations of bias regarding the Arab-Israeli conflict are flawed inherently. To answer this question, we must consider separately various types of media criticism.

For editorials, features, news analyses, and cartoons, the problems of observer values and perspectives are most obvious. Charges of bias in these categories nearly always indicate mere disagreement. Two types of commentaries are useful here: (1) identification of exertions of partisan influence upon editors and (2) identification of racist imagery and invidious stereotyping. Beyond this, debate about bias in editorial positions might focus more fruitfully upon the issues of the conflict themselves.

When critics consider news coverage, however, they validly may identify violations of generally accepted journalistic standards in news reporting. For example, it is possible to document straightforward errors of fact. During the Lebanon War in 1982, reporters regularly cited inflated casualty figures from PLO sources without proper attribution (ADL, 1982; Peretz, 1982; Cody and Ramati, 1982; Muravchik, 1983). While this sort of critique provides a useful check on media tendencies to violate their own standards, it is limited, by its nature, to documentation of short-term errors and cannot lead to a clearcut assessment of overall media bias. (See, for example, the interpretation by Morris, 1982.) Whether one judges errors of fact to be incidental or fundamental depends upon one's overall orientation to the conflict.

In general, agreement between observers becomes more difficult as the unit of media under consideration becomes larger; it is relatively easy to agree retrospectively about particular errors of fact, say, in a single broadcast. It is much more difficult, however, to agree about overall coverage of an event or series of events. On the Lebanon War, for example, it probably can be said that journalists sometimes broke with generally accepted standards in ways that were unfair to Israel; similarly, the media often broke with professional standards during the Six Day War in ways that were unfair to Arabs. One's opinion on *overall* coverage of either event, however, still depends upon political partisanship and values.

On the other hand, critics might investigate the styles and language of news coverage. For example, when disagreements exist, do partisan tones creep into the reporting of the position of either side? For example, when both sides express their positions, is one side typically said to have "suggested new directions for progress in peace talks" while the other is said to have "declared its stance"? Empirical research has shown that partisan language in news coverage of the Middle East occurs infrequently and is diluted by a great deal of neutral coverage. Still, Kressel (1983), using Terry's (1974) data, has found some evidence for correlation between a newspaper's editorial stance and its subtle slants in news coverage.

Another accusation holds that the media's choice of events for coverage reflects unfair bias. For example, concentration on controversial Saudi domestic practices (e.g., "Death of a Princess" telecast) angers many Arab supporters. Similarly, concentration on the Israeli military and Israeli treatment of Arabs on the West Bank strikes many Israeli partisans as unfair. Since the media's greatest power probably lies in its ability to set agendas (McCombs and Shaw, 1972), these concerns are understandable. However, choice of events for coverage always depends upon news judgments of reporters and editors; these judgments, in turn, inescapably derive to some degree from values and political perspectives.

In addition, editors legitimately make judgments about what their readers would find interesting. One such criterion was pointed out by Raab (1982) in an attempt to explain anti-Israel double standards in judgments of newsworthiness. He cited the media's "theory of discontinuity; otherwise known as man-bites-dog." In other words, since the media perceive Israel as a basically democratic and just society, its misdeeds are newsworthy; for the Arabs, the opposite is true. This criterion, itself, reflects Raab's political orientation but it does point out additional difficulty in discerning bias. Thus, in the final analysis, selection of events for coverage must rest upon political orientations and values as much as on journalistic norms.

Both sides frequently have charged that the media use double standards in judging the conduct of Israel and the Arab nations; this issue cannot be addressed scientifically. For example, pro-Israel commentators have claimed that Israel's indirect role in the massacre at Sabra and Shattila was scrutinized by the media with a fine-toothed comb while many similar massacres in Syria and Lebanon, more or less, have been ignored. Also, Israelis have argued that the mass media treated them more harshly than the Lebanese Christian perpetrators of the massacre were treated. Arab supporters might reasonably retort that the analogy to other massacres is invalid, that the facts are different, or that Israel's injustices against the Palestinians, at bottom, were more extreme. Alternatively, Arab supporters could concede the point in the particular instance and, then, hurl counter-charges of anti-Arab double standards in other cases. To say the least, debate would be unlikely to proceed fruitfully.

Similar problems weaken charges that the media fail to provide proper context for individual events. To be sure, some media provide *more* contextual and background information than other media; television and radio generally provide the least. However, the decision about *which version of context* to present remains dependent, by definition, upon political perspective and values. For example, pro-Israel commentators desired more historical background to explain why Israel invaded Lebanon in 1982; they claim Israel was portrayed as an invading power without any justification. Yet, regarding the 1973 Yom Kippur War, few Israel supporters would have desired a lengthy description of the justification for the Arab attack—certainly not by a reporter at all sympathetic to the Arabs.

Some writers have pointed out, sensibly, that television prefers nonanalytic, vivid scenes (Roeh, 1981); others have charged that war coverage almost never captures the political context of events (Miller, 1982). Television's emphasis on simple, exciting, and vivid scenes worked against Israel in the Lebanon War; it probably led to more positive coverage during the 1967 war.

ORGANIZATIONAL AND POLITICAL BARRIERS TO FAIR COVERAGE

To some extent, journalistic investigations and organizational studies of media behavior can shed light on barriers to free debate on the Arab-Israeli conflict in the United States—particularly by uncovering exertions of illegitimate influence. If accurate, investigations of terrorist constraints on news coming out of the Middle East constitute a meaningful addition to discussions of media coverage (Peretz, 1982a). In the final

POLITICAL PSYCHOLOGY

analysis, though, such journalistic and scholarly investigations can identify some of the forces that produce media coverage but they cannot answer basic questions about media bias. Too many additional factors influence the production of the news.

MORAL RELATIVISM

Some values are commonly held by Arab supporters and Israel supporters. Thus, there is a basis for some agreement. We may expect many people, regardless of their political orientation, to object to extreme racism or, in some instances, outright lying. Clear demonstrations of errors in fact, prejudice, and invidious stereotyping, on occasion, can convince even partisans from the other side.

For most questions concerning bias, however, we are left with epistemological and moral relativism; our judgments about media coverage depend upon our values and political orientations. Where these come from, of course, is a central preoccupation of sociologists of knowledge (Berger and Luckmann, 1966).

SOCIAL PSYCHOLOGICAL PERSPECTIVES ON THE BIAS DEBATE

The evaluation of media coverage and the judgment of media bias—at least in part—involve processes of social perception and cognition. A substantial and time-honored body of research highlights the extent to which preconceived theories and opinions can color partisans' evaluations of evidence (Allport, 1954; Nisbett and Ross, 1980). For example, Lord *et al.* (1979) asked advocates and opponents of the death penalty to examine an identical pair of studies that provided mixed results on the effectiveness of capital punishment as a deterrent. Partisans of each position saw the studies as supportive of their own outlook; they readily accepted confirmatory aspects of the studies and discounted conflicting aspects. The general principle that emerges from Lord *et al.* (1979) and other research is that partisans tend to find support in evidence that non-partisan observers deem inconclusive or impartial; this process is called biased assimilation.

At first blush, partisans' evaluations of media coverage of the Arab-Israeli conflict seem inconsistent with this tendency. However, the contradiction exists only at a superficial level; further examination shows that the "hostile media" phenomenon, in fact, is a consequence of the general confirmatory bias in cognition. Vallone *et al.* (1985) explain that,

Partisans who have consistently processed facts and arguments in light of their preconceptions and prejudices (accepting information at face value, or subjecting it to harsh scrutiny, as a function of its congruence with these preconceptions and prejudices) are bound to believe that the preponderance of reliable, pertinent evidence favors their viewpoint. Accordingly, to the extent that the small sample of evidence or argument featured in a media presentation seems unrepresentative of this larger "population" of information, perceivers will charge bias in the presentation and will be likely to infer hostility and bias on the part of those presenting it.

Social judgment theory (Sherif and Hovland, 1961; Kiesler *et al.,* 1969) provides a related perspective on partisans' accusations of media bias. According to this theory, when people are "involved" in an issue, their own stands provide a powerful internal reference point for subsequent judgments. If a position is expressed that falls relatively far from their own outlook, they will completely reject the discrepant position. If a person is heavily involved in the issue, he/she will have a very wide latitude of rejection. As a consequence of rejecting highly discrepant positions, the person's own sense of correctness will solidify. This will occur regardless of the "objective validity" of the discrepant positions. Anything short of partisan media support will fall within the latitude of rejection, and hence be perceived as bias. Uninvolved parties will have much smaller latitudes of rejection and, hence, be much less likely to perceive bias.

According to these social psychological perspectives, partisans may agree about the actual content of the media presentations and still disagree about their fairness. Another social psychological approach suggests that partisans may perceive and remember very different stimuli in mass media coverage. Hastorf and Cantril's classic (1954) study of partisan perceptions of illegitimate violence in an intercollegiate football game illustrates the phenomenon. After viewing a film of the contest, Dartmouth and Princeton supporters each perceived the other side as having engaged in continuous, illegitimate atrocities and their own side as having retaliated occasionally. This suggests that pro-Arab partisans and pro-Israel partisans might in fact perceive different stimuli when they examine the same sample of media coverage.

Vallone *et al.* (1985) conducted a recent experiment to investigate the social psychological underpinnings of partisan judgments of bias in media coverage of the 1982 massacre of Palestinians at Sabra and Shattila. The researchers asked partisan Stanford University students to evaluate segments of television news coverage of the tragedy. The study concluded the following:

1. Partisans on both sides evaluated media coverage as biased against their own side.

2. Partisans *perceived* the coverage differently, remembering different aspects of the media presentations.

3. Arab and Israel supporters both evaluated "middle-of-the-road" and "gray" accounts of events as unfair and biased.

4. The more knowledgeable and more emotionally involved the partisan, the more likely he/she was to charge bias.

Thus, empirical evidence from Vallone *et al.*'s (1985) study supports the three social psychological processes outlined above: the confirmatory bias in evaluating evidence, the tendency for deeply involved partisans to have a wide latitude of rejection, and the tendency for partisans to perceive (and misperceive) stimuli in accordance with their overall perspective. While these explanations suggest that charges of bias may evolve out of predictable cognitive, perceptual, and psychological processes, it should be emphasized that they cannot resolve questions concerning the objective validity of the accusations.

THE POLITICS OF BIAS ACCUSATIONS

Perhaps, it is most realistic to understand arguments about media bias in a political context. If one can influence the press, one controls a powerful weapon. Whatever the media's real power, partisans on each side believe that media influence both public opinion and government policy in the United States. Historians may argue about the veracity of Israeli and Arab perspectives on the conflict. The outcome of the conflict itself, however, will no doubt be influenced more by which side can marshal the resources necessary to get its views across. In large part, this depends upon whether Arab supporters or Israel supporters convince relatively uninvolved parties of the truth and morality of their positions. Since this task requires a facade of objectivity, the whole endeavor involves an essentially mythic pretense that one's own orientation derives from "objective" facts. To the extent that media coverage fails to support one's arguments, the accuracy of that coverage must be questioned. In addition, charges of media bias may constitute an attempt to encourage preferential treatment by the media.

For partisans (in their own eyes—if not in the eyes of some political scientists), media criticism plays a significant political role; to my mind, this role is not necessarily immoral. If people are willing to back up their values and politics with guns, I see no reason why they should not use words. Admittedly, though, this judgment rests upon personal values.

SUMMARY

We may draw several conclusions about charges of unfair media coverage of the Arab-Israeli conflict:

1. The media should not be easy prey to accusations of bias. Moreover, they ought not rely upon "evenhandedness," "balanced content," or "middle-of-the-road politics" as guidelines for coverage of the conflict.

2. "Scientific," content analytic studies of media bias have obscured the centrality of values and political orientations in judgments of unfair coverage. When done properly, however, content analyses can enhance significantly our empirical knowledge about media treatment of the Arab-Israeli conflict.

3. While the media do have an obligation to adhere to certain journalistic norms and

standards, it is difficult—if not impossible—to invoke these norms without making normative and conceptual judgments.

4. Since pro-Arab, pro-Israel, and middle-of-the-road analysts share certain values and political orientations, it is possible (but rare) to obtain agreement on some matters. In general, agreement is most likely when the amount of media coverage considered is small and when violations of norms are blatant, e.g., overt racist stereotyping.

5. Demonstrations of illegitimate exertions of influence and other barriers to fair coverage are useful. Most often, however, these demonstrations concern relatively isolated instances and seldom can establish the significance of such factors in the overall determination of media favorability.

6. Structural constraints predispose the mass media towards certain types of coverage. For example, television is drawn towards vivid imagery and away from presentation of historical background. Sometimes, limitations in media capabilities produce coverage favorable to Israel and sometimes they produce coverage favorable to the Arabs.

7. Judgments of media bias rest upon three social psychological processes: a general, cognitive confirmatory bias in judging evidence, a tendency for deeply involved partisans to have a wide latitude of rejection, and a tendency for partisans to perceive (and misperceive) media stimuli in accordance with their overall views.

8. Media criticism may also be understood as a partisan, political tool.

NOTES

1. Some social psychological research supports this notion that mere familiarity and exposure can lead to increased liking; see, for example, Zajonc (1968).
2. Immediately following the Six Day War, some pro-Israel writers began to complain about very unfavorable coverage in some "leftist" publications but, for the most part, these objections did not concern mainstream media (e.g., Forster and Epstein, 1974).

REFERENCES

Abu-Laban, S. M. (1975). Stereotypes of Middle East Peoples. In Abu-Laban, B., and Zeadey, F. T. (eds.), *Arabs in America: Myths and Realities*, The Medina University Press International, Wilmette, Ill.

Adams, M. (1971). European media and the Arabs. In Jabara, A. and Terry, J. (eds.), *The Arab World from Nationalism to Revolution*, The Medina University Press International, Wilmette, Ill.

Alexander, E. (1982). Israel: Scapegoat of the world media. *Congress Monthly, 49*, May, 4–5.

Allport, G. W. (1954). *The Nature of Prejudice*, Addison-Wesley, Reading, Mass.

Anti-Defamation League. (1982). *Television Network Coverage of the War in Lebanon*, Unpublished study prepared by Garth-Furth International, New York.

Asi, M. O. (1981a). *Arabs, Israelis and U.S. Television Networks: A Content Analysis of How ABC, CBS and NBC Reported the News between 1970–1979*, Unpublished Ph.D. dissertation, Ohio University, Athens, Ohio.

———. (1981b). Arabs, Israelis and TV news: A time-series content analysis. In Adams, W. (ed.), *Television Coverage of the Middle East*, Ablex, Norwood, N.J.

Baha el-Din, A. (1971). World media and the Arabs: an Arab perspective. In Jabara, A., and Terry, J. (eds.), *The Arab World from Nationalism to Revolution*, The Medina University Press International, Wilmette, Ill.

Barlas, S. (1981). Bending the news at the Washington Post. *Moment*, May, 30–36.

Baum, P. (1982). Congress charges bias in ABC's "Fortress Israel" program. *Congress Monthly* 49 (May, 3).

Berger, P. L., and Luckmann, T. (1966). *The Social Construction of Reality*, Doubleday, Garden City, N.Y.

Blitzer, W. (1980). The media's Mideast. *The New Republic*, April 26, 14–17.

Chafets, Z. (1982). Once again the West uses a double standard to malign Israel's good name. *The Boston Globe*, October 13.

———. (1984). *Double Vision: How the Press Distorts America's View of the Middle East*, Morrow, N.Y.

Cody, E., and Ramati, P. (1982). Covering the Invasion of Lebanon, *Washington J. Rev.* September 18–21.

Cooley, J. K. (1981). The news from the Mideast: A working approach. *The Middle East J.* 35: 465–480.

Farmer, L. (1968). All we know is what we read in the papers. *Middle East Newsletter*, February, 1–5.

Feith, D. J. (1980). Israel, the Post, and the shaft. *Middle East Review*, 7(4): 8(1): 62–66.

Forster, A., and Epstein, B. (1974). *The New Anti-Semitism*, McGraw-Hill, New York.

Griswold, W. J. (1975). *The Image of the Middle East in Secondary School Textbooks*, Middle East Studies Association, New York.

Hadar, L. T. (1980). Behind the New York Times Middle East coverage. *Middle East Rev.* 7(4), 8(1): 56–61.

Hastorf, A., and Cantril, H. (1954). They saw a game: A case study. *J. Abnorm. Social Psychol.* 49: 129.

Ibrahim, S. (1974). American domestic forces and the October war. *J. Palestine Studies* 4: 55–81.

Isaac, R. J. (1980). Time against Israel. *The New Republic*, October 18, 18–23.

Kenny, L. M. (1975). The Middle East in Canadian social science textbooks. In Abu-Laban, B., and Zeadey, F. T. (eds.), *Arabs in America: Myths and Realities*, The Medina University Press International, Wilmette, Ill.

Kiesler, C. A., Collins, B. E., and Miller, N. (1969). *Attitude Change*, Wiley, New York.

Kressel, N. J. (1983). *American Public Opinion and Mass Media Coverage of the Arab-Israeli Conflict, 1948–1982*, Unpublished Ph.D. dissertation, Harvard University, Cambridge, Mass.

———. (1984). *The Relationship between Aggregate Mass Media Coverage and American Public Opinion: A Case Study*, Paper presented at the 39th annual conference of the American Association for Public Opinion Research, Lake Delavan, Wisconsin, May.

Krippendorff, K. (1980). *Content Analysis: An Introduction to Its Methodology*, Sage, Beverly Hills, Calif.

Lord, C. G., Ross, L., and Lepper, M. R. (1979). Biased assimilation and attitude polarization: The effects of prior theories on subsequently considered evidence. *J. Personal. Social Psychol.* 37: 2098–2109.

McCombs, M. E., and Shaw, D. L. (1972). The agenda-setting function of the mass media. *Public Opin. Quart.* 36: 176–187.

Miller, M. C. (1982). How TV covers wars. *The New Republic* 187: 27, 26–33.

Morris, R. (1982). Beirut—and the press—under siege. *Columbia Journalism Rev.* November/December, 33.

Muravchik, J. (1983). Misreporting Lebanon. *Policy Rev.* 23: 11–16.

Nisbett, R., and Ross, L. (1980). *Human Inference: Strategies and Shortcomings of Social Judgment*, Prentice-Hall, Englewood Clifs, N.J.

Padelford, E. A. (1979). *The Regional American Press: An Analysis of Its Reporting and Commentary on the Arab-Israeli Situation*, Unpublished Ph.D. dissertation, American University, Washington, D.C.

Peretz, M. (1982a). A journalistic cover-up. *The New Republic.* 186(10): 9–10.

_____. (1982b). Lebanon eyewitness. *The New Republic.* 187: 5, 15–23.

Perry, G. (1975). Treatment of the Middle East in American high school textbooks. *J. Palestine Studies* 4: 46–58.

Podhoretz, N. (1982). J'accuse. *Commentary* 74: 3, 21–31.

Qazzaz, A. (1975). Images of the Arab in American social science textbooks. In Abu-Laban, B., and Zeadey, F. T. (eds.), *Arabs in America: Myths and Realities*, The Medina University Press International, Wilmette, Ill.

Raab, E. (1982). Is the Jewish community split? *Commentary*, 74(5): 21–25.

Raspberry, W. (1973). (Column). *The Washington Post*, December 31, p. 49.

Roeh, I. (1981). Israel in Lebanon: Language and images of storytelling. In Adams, W. (ed.), *Television Coverage of the Middle East*, Ablex, Norwood, N.J.

Rosenfeld, S. (1982). Dateline Washington: anti-Semitism and U.S. foreign policy 47: 172–183.

Rubin, B. (1976). The media and the Middle East. *Middle East Rev.* 28–32.

Said, E. W. (1981). *Covering Islam: How the Media and the Experts Determine How We See the Rest of the World*, Pantheon, New York.

Shaheen, J. (1979). The television Arab: Hollywood's nigger. *Middle East Int.* 97: April 13, 10.

_____. (1980). The Arab stereotype on television. *The Link*, 13: 2, 24.

_____. (1981). Images of Saudis and Palestinians: a review of major documentaries. In Adams, W. (ed.), *Television Coverage of the Middle East*, Ablex, Norwood, N.J.

Sherif, M., and Hovland, C. I. (1961). *Social Judgment*, Yale, New Haven, Conn.

Sidorsky, D. (1982). Balance and responsibility in the media. *Midstream* 28: 6, 17–29.

Suleiman, M. W. (1965). An evaluation of Middle East news coverage of seven American news magazines, July–December 1956. *Middle East Forum* 41: 9–30.

_____. (1968). Mass media and the June conflict. *Arab World* 16: 10–11, 59–65.

_____. (1970). American mass media and the June conflict. In Abu-Lughod, I. (ed.), *The Arab-Israeli Confrontation of June 1967: An Arab Perspective*. Northwestern University Press, Evanston, Ill.

_____. (1974). National stereotypes as weapons in the Arab-Israeli conflict. *J. Palestine Studies* 3: 114–117.

_____. (1975). Perceptions of the Middle East in American magazines. In Abu-Laban, B., and

Zeadey, F. T. (eds.), *Arabs in America: Myths and Realities*, The Medina University Press International, Wilmette, Ill.

Terry, J. (1971). A content analysis of American newspapers. In Jabara, A., and Terry, J. (eds.), *The Arab World from Nationalism to Revolution*, The Medina University Press International, Wilmette, Ill.

_____. (1974). 1973 U.S. press coverage of the Middle East. *J. Palestine Studies* 4: 121–123.

_____. (1975). The Western press and the October war: A content analysis. In Aruri, N. H. (ed.), *Middle East Crucible*, The Medina University Press International, Wilmette, Ill.

Timmerman, K. (1983). How the PLO terrorized journalists in Beirut. *Commentary* 75(1): 48–49.

Vallone, R. P., Ross, L., and Lepper, M. R. (1985). The hostile media phenomenon: biased perception and perceptions of media bias in coverage of the Beirut massacre. *J. Personal. Social Psychol.* 49: 577–585.

Volkmann, E. (1982). *A Legacy of Hate*, Franklin Watts, New York.

Wall, H. (1982). *Censorship by Terror*, press release, B'nai Brith Anti-Defamation League, New York, February.

Ward, W. (1969). The semantics of anti-Semitism. *The Middle East Newsletter.* 3(4): 2–3.

Weisman, J. (1981a). Blind spot in the Middle East: Why you don't see more Palestinians on TV. *TV Guide.* 29: 43.

_____. (1981b). Blind spot in the Middle East: the problems of access and image. *TV Guide.* 29: 44.

Zajonc, R. B. (1968). Attitudinal effects of mere exposure. *J. Personal. Social Psychol. Monogr. Suppl.* 9(2): part 2.

27

The Public's Impact on Foreign Policy

BERNARD C. COHEN

THE MANY SHAPES OF PUBLIC OPINION

Public opinion presents itself to foreign policy officials in a multitude of shapes. At its simplest, it may be one or two long-established and "reliable" voices: a given newspaper, perhaps, and a few people with business connections in a given part of the world. For others, it may be a formless and perhaps unexpected surge, like a tidal wave: "We get exposed to the public from all possible angles and sources, when something stirs them up—a Nasser, an Ayub. Then you hear from your mother, from your Congressman, from the whole pack." If in the process of examining the variety of public contacts I impose a certain order on them, I would enjoin the reader never to forget the often confused quality of the original. In the very confusion of voices arises the need for officials to pick and choose those whose timbre they like—to "order" them ultimately according to their *own* preferences, as they seek to define and implement what they believe to be the public or national interest.

It is not only my mode of organizing and presenting the forms of public opinion that is a synthetic act. The larger construct itself, the over-all structure of opinion shapes and sources, is a creation which—I think it is fair to say—no single foreign affairs official ever experiences. As the sum-total (or a reasonable approximation thereto) of the varied perceptions and exposures of a broad sample of foreign policy makers, the construct may be regarded as an attempt to specify the foreign policy "opinion elite" in practical terms. [1] But, to repeat the burden of the paragraph above, it is important to remember that what we call the opinion elite is only a summation, an abstraction. In reality this opinion elite has no unitary character or even existence. Few of its component parts interact in any way; rather, they participate in discrete and discontinuous realms. In short, in its public opinion aspects, the foreign policy process is riddled with pluralism.[2] And the initiative in what to listen to, or what to hear, or even whom to call on remains most of the time, as we shall see, with the official.

For discussion purposes, the first and major distinction to be made with regard to public opinion is between those sources—people and groups—which are known or are identifiable to officials and those sources which are impersonal and faceless. The crucial difference here is whether the sources carry recognizable personal or political identification marks, with all that these imply for psychic or political leverage, and not whether the relationships are face-to-face. For example, I include in the first group the press, even where officials may never see the reporters or editorial writers involved; and I include in the second group the face-to-face meetings with strangers that officials have whenever they go on the lecture circuit.

The "Identifiable" sources may be combined into three major groupings: "Intimates," "Specialists," and "Institutions." The category of "Intimates" includes figures not ordinarily understood to be significant bearers of opinion—(1) members of one's family, primary or extended; (2) close friends; (3) colleagues within the State Department who are not involved in one's own policy problems. "Specialists" have in common a knowledge, experience, or skill in policy areas that not only sets them apart from all other opinion sources but qualifies them to be treated as "equals" by officials. Among them will be found (4) notables, or "important people," many of whom have in fact served in the Department in the past; (5) experts, men of skill or other resource in particular policy areas, many of whom are currently qualified to serve in the Department; (6) advisory boards, composed both of notables and experts who are currently serving the Department in advisory capacities. "Institutions" comprise the groups, organizations, and enterprises that are so commonly thought to be the significant bearers of public opinion that they are often treated as unofficial branches of government—(7) interest groups and (8) the press. This category also includes an official branch of government, (9) the Congress, for reasons that will be made clear in the discussion below.

The "Faceless" or "Impersonal" sources are fewer in number, but much larger in the number of people whose opinions they encompass. The sources include: (10) the mail that comes to the government on foreign policy questions, most of it ending up in the State Department; (11) audiences which officials see from time to time over the top of a lectern; (12) demonstrative behavior of one sort or another; and (13) public opinion polls.

This listing does not exhaust the sources of public opinion on foreign policy, nor is it the only way these sources can be combined; but it does include the sources of opinion most in evidence in the Department and most salient in the minds of Department officials.[3]

THE EMERGING PICTURE

This broad canvass of public opinion as perceived by State Department officials is only one step in the exploration of the public's impact on foreign policy; we have to go on, now, to questions of appraisal, evaluation, effects—to consider how external opinion is assimilated into the internal governmental processes of foreign policy formulation. But before we do, we should take note of the picture that is beginning to emerge: the ingredients of public opinion as they are experienced in the State Department are substantially and significantly different from the standard ingredients, or aggregations, as they are defined by political scientists and other outside observers.

We conventionally portray opinion as manifesting itself chiefly in the form of public opinion polls, organized interest-group activity, newspaper editorials, and, less often, letters to public officials and to newspapers; and sometimes we even let one or two of these forms carry the whole burden. These forms or categories of external opinion are of course the most clearly visible from the outside, and they also encompass the largest number of articulated viewpoints. But it is not much of an exaggeration to say that these categories, designed to enlarge our vision of nongovernmental participation in policy processes, have become blinders; they have come to delimit artificially the areas in which we look for the content of public opinion and thus for its consequences. From the perspective of the foreign policy official in Washington, the opinion landscape takes on rather different contours. The polls and editorials move into the background, along with most of the mail. Organized interests and particular groups are somewhat more common, although in narrow areas of specialization and with varying entrées to the front. In the foreground stand the Congress and the "working press" and all the other individual "contacts," formal and informal, that we have seen make up the private and professional worlds of the foreign policy official. The implications for both the theory and practice of representation and of responsive government are extensive, and I shall consider them later. Simply to point the way, however, I would draw attention here to the findings of Warren Miller and Donald Stokes and others, to the effect that Congressmen themselves (despite what foreign policy officials think) may not in fact come very close to understanding, reflecting, or acting upon the foreign policy attitudes of their constituents.[4]

INCREASING THE POLITICAL VALUE OF OPINION

The core of the problem of improving responsiveness lies in *enlarging the utility* of outside opinion for foreign policy officials. More specifically, increasing the value of outside opinion as a preferential input into the decision making process means improving its competitive standing vis-à-vis the many other considerations of bureaucratic, national, and international politics that go into the formulation of foreign policy. But if we wish to magnify its utility, to increase its value, we have to start with a realistic understanding of its present utility, its present value. Why, in brief, is external opinion important to foreign policy officials at all? Why do they respond to it as much (or as little) as they do, and in the ways—substantially instrumental and manipulative—that they do?

The answer to this question is surprisingly obvious, though it is not easy to formulate it in a simple sentence. It lies in the ordinary procedures of bureaucratic life, in the peculiar mixture of politics and administration that defines the opportunities that are open to an official to get something accomplished. The impulses of electoral ambition do not apply here; but that does not mean that men are without ambition here.[5] On the contrary, the force that moves the typical official is a *personal* ambition to *do* something that seems important to him and to do it well. To repeat a point I made earlier in this book, the official is not a "mindless bureaucrat" but a knowledgeable person with some convictions about the value and appropriateness of particular courses of action.[6] To accomplish his purposes, to prevail in a setting in which other officials may have equally strong convictions of a different stripe, he needs that elusive, undefinable variable, "support." In practice, "support" means two different things. First, it means the explicit agreement of individuals and groups, inside and outside the government, who are regarded as knowledgeable and "important" on the question by the various contend- ers—"important" in the sense that their views are disproportionately persuasive. Any- one who has ever participated, however remotely, in a decision making process of a substantially consensual variety will recognize the special weight accorded to the positions of a few people, a personal power that is based on such things as substantive knowledge and past experience with respect to the issue, reputation for fairness and for sound judgment, expressive capacity, as well as formal institutional authority. When these people align themselves with a particular proposal, apparent majorities coalesce, decisions acquire legitimacy, and officials can proceed in the expectation that others will take subsequent actions necessary to carry them out. Second, support means the absence of explicit disagreement of other individuals and groups, inside and outside the govern- ment, who are also regarded as knowledgeable and important by the contenders. When those who might be expected, by virtue of their known interests and their past behavior, to take a position against a proposal *fail* to do so, their silence is taken for consent, or at least as a tacit statement that they will not obstruct the execution of the decision.[7] "Support," then, is a variable mixture of the active agreement and cooperation of some people and the passive acquiescence of others; and where the mix is very different from this, where apparent majorities do not coalesce, where officials have no confidence that decisions will be met by affirmative "follow-up" action, they talk of "lack of support."

There is, of course, a very large subjective component in this process, since votes are rarely taken. Hence my use of the phrase "apparent majorities." Officials are obliged to make the best guesses they can concerning the alignment of relevant "others" and the resulting legitimacy and viability of proposed courses of action. Some things, to be sure, can be undertaken at almost any level in the absence of great attention to or conviction about majorities; experience *is* a reasonably good guide with respect to those matters which are, by virtue of the lack of sustained interest anywhere else, effectively within the discretionary power of officials. And at the higher levels some things can be done without lining up support in advance, because the persuasiveness of the President or the Secretary of State can be mobilized, in the event of untoward difficulty, to help sustain the decision. But for nonroutine problems at almost all levels and especially at the working level, rather more of consequence hangs on the capacity of officials to make correct guesses about the "alignment of forces," to use the Soviet expression. Officials, as I noted earlier, are motivated by the desire to see something develop, to make it happen with an economy of effort, to appear knowledgeable and competent and effective and not stupid or foolish. To the extent that external opinions—widely defined—seem to them to be a part of an existing alignment of forces, or to look as if they might be useful or harmful in constructing or reconstructing a different political alignment, officials have an interest in being responsive to them, in one manner or another.

How well do present practices in the assessment of opinion serve these purposes to which opinion is put? And what might be done differently to enlarge its usefulness to officials and thus their incentive to be responsive? To take the evaluative question first: on the face of it, one is tempted to say that officials are reasonably satisfied with what they "know" about outside opinion, and they make little effort to improve on that knowledge. Scattered, almost accidental, exposures to such opinion, and intuitions about its larger structure and significance, give them more information than they can in fact use, granted the primacy of other considerations in the formulation of foreign policy decisions. But to say that is simply to restate the problem, and in the process to suggest a quite different answer: external opinion has such a subordinate place in decision making, and needs for it are so easily and impressionistically met, precisely *because* so much of it is so useless so much of the time—because it is not readily convertible into political currency, because it has no major "clout," because it makes, or seems to make, little difference in any political alignment. At the risk of overstating the matter by treating opinion collectively, it does not address itself very precisely to the problems that are up for decision, it does not speak out knowledgeably and persuasively at points in time when matters are still fluid, and it brings to bear few sanctions or penalties of a political, bureaucratic or personal kind when it is ignored. Small wonder, then, that officials can comfortably disband their efforts to find out what people may be thinking, rely on their casual contacts and their intuitions and on convenient surrogates in the press and in the Congress, and be manipulative and instrumental in their approach to particular groups and to the public in general.

Is there any way to modify this situation? What might be done differently? There is quite clearly little point in urging officials to mend their ways, to pay more attention to external opinion. That merely encourages a patronizing attitude on their part and prompts them to construct more elaborate ways to try to shape that opinion into supportive postures—varieties of responsiveness that are sufficiently well developed as things are now. And there is little point in devising more elaborate mechanisms, in or out of government, for uncovering more and more information about the state of public opinion of the kind that is currently available; that merely makes the pile of useless information even higher. What we are looking for, rather, are ways to increase the political weight of those elements in public opinion that have some potentiality of participating in a policy (as distinct from simply a public) debate. This means, above all else, encouraging a deeper commitment to such participation on the part of those foreign policy "attentives" who have or who can acquire political resources—knowledge and information, experience and sound judgment, leadership, access to the media of mass communication, access to legislative power. In terms of the kinds of public sources I referred to earlier in this book, this means most particularly "notables," academic and other subject-matter specialists, either singly as individuals or in formal or informal advisory groups, and even interest groups, including those collectively referred to as the "peace movement."[8] It means a more assiduous cultivation of foreign policy problems, at an early stage in their development, by the media of communication, so that these participants would have better information resources at earlier phases in the policy making process. It means a more active exercise by members of Congress of their constitutional powers and political interests in foreign affairs—also at the formative stages of foreign policy. This is especially important because the Congress starts off with more than ordinary capabilities as a form of public opinion. It means, further, that some thought be given to the problem of how to improve the focus or the clarity of external opinions of a more general kind, so that their political relevance is better understood by foreign policy officials. One way that this might be accomplished, for example, would be through survey research teams whose mission would be to explore the cognitive and affective dimensions of opinion on diverse policy alternatives, rather than merely the distribution of opinion on the officially favored policy or some variants of it. The so-called "Stanford Poll" which performed this function with respect to Vietnam War alternatives in the spring of 1966 is a good example of the possibilities here, though they need not be limited to national samples.[9] A Congress that is concerned about the responsiveness of the Executive branch to public preferences in the foreign policy field may well reconsider its opposition to the use of public funds for opinion polling of this kind, under conditions of direction or control that keep it independent of Executive branch interests and perspectives.[10]

No foreign policy establishment, of course, could possibly incorporate all such public views, once these have been clarified and communicated more effectively.[11] But neither can it possibly incorporate all the views on any subject that are expressed *within* the establishment. To give something to everybody is, in the end, to give them nothing. What matters, rather, is that a wide range of relevant views and preferences both inside and outside the government get a reliable chance to be heard and to be seriously assessed before important commitments are made. This is what we mean by responsiveness—not simply that one's views get accepted in the final choices. One can devise mechanical ways to ensure a *chance* for private citizens as well as for government officials to be heard on issues of foreign policy; but if those views are to be seriously assessed, they must have substance and weight—they must be intellectually and practically persuasive in order to be politically meaningful, even if not, in the end, acceptable. It is in the cultivation of such skills and resources on the part of people outside of government that we might hope to find a key to greater responsiveness within it, on the part of foreign policy officials.

NOTES

1. See Gabriel A. Almond, *The American People and Foreign Policy*, 2d ed., New York: Praeger, 1960; and James N. Rosenau, *Public Opinion and Foreign Policy*, New York: Random House, 1961, for a specification of the opinion elite in categoric or definitional terms.
2. See Robert A. Dahl, *Who Governs?* New Haven: Yale University Press, 1961. James N. Rosenau seems to be arguing the contrary in *National Leadership and Foreign Policy*, Princeton: Princeton University Press, 1963, when he says, "Apparently national opinion-makers do interact frequently, and apparently they are getting to know one another" (p. 331). But his "national opinion leaders" comprise only a small portion of the opinion elite as I describe it in these pages.
3. On an earlier occasion, after studying the process of policy formation on a single foreign policy issue, I ventured some hypotheses about the nature of external opinion as it was differentially experienced at the Executive and Congressional levels. See Bernard C. Cohen, *The Political Process and Foreign Policy*, Princeton: Princeton University Press, 1957, pp. 94–109. The present study obviously does not permit direct testing of any of these hypotheses; indeed, by treating the Congress here as an opinion *source* and not as a *target* (as in the earlier study) I have made direct comparison impossible. Despite these formal inadequacies, this current exploration of the opinion environment of the State Department is not irrelevant to those earlier concerns, since I am still talking about the way foreign policy makers perceive their opinion environment.
4. See Warren E. Miller and Donald E. Stokes, "Constituency Influence in Congress," *American Political Science Review*, Vol. 57, No. 1, March 1963, pp. 45–56; the summary of roll-call voting studies in Cleo H. Cherryholmes and Michael J. Shapiro, *Representatives and Roll Calls*, Indianapolis: Bobbs-Merrill, 1969, Chapter 7; and Cohen, *The Press and Foreign Policy*, pp. 238–241.
5. See Joseph Schlesinger, *Ambition and Politics*, Chicago: Rand McNally, 1966. For a different view of the role of ambition, see Kenneth Prewitt, "Political Ambition, Volunteerism, and Electoral Accountability," pp. 5–17.
6. Roger Hilsman's *To Move a Nation*, Garden City: Doubleday, 1967, speaks eloquently to this point.
7. See Hoopes, *The Limits of Intervention*, p. 98.
8. This position is not unlike that reached by Gabriel A. Almond nearly twenty-five years ago, in *The American People and Foreign Policy*, 1st ed., New York: Harcourt, Brace, 1950. It may seem retrogressive in a period when pluralism and "the power elite" are under serious attack. It is worth pointing out, however, that any regime, and especially a revolutionary one, would face comparable problems in the location of authority and responsibility for foreign policy making and that, *if* it were also to be held to some standard of continuing

responsiveness to external opinion, the structural problem would persist even though its ideological content and the direction of policy had changed.

9. For a fuller analysis of the Stanford data following the initial release, see Sidney Verba *et al.*, "Public Opinion and the War in Vietnam," *American Political Science Review*, Vol. 61, No. 2, June 1967, pp. 317–333. For an analysis of press reactions to the Stanford Poll, see Nelson W. Polsby, "Political Science and the Press: Notes on Coverage of a Public Opinion Survey on the Vietnam War," *The Western Political Quarterly*, Vol. 22, No. 1, March 1969, pp. 47–60.

10. See the recommendation of the National Policy Panel of the United Nations Association of the United States of America for "a federally-financed, but independently operated polling operation." *Beyond Vietnam: Public Opinion and Foreign Policy*, New York: UNA-USA, February 1970, p. 8.

11. See Frederick B. Hoyt's discussion of the contradictory demands made on the State Department by American groups in China in the period between the two World Wars, and of the Department's inability to meet them all: "Americans in China and the Formation of American Policy, 1925–1937," unpubl. Ph.D. dissertation, Department of History, University of Wisconsin—Madison, 1971.

ABOUT THE EDITOR

Neil J. Kressel is Chairperson of the Department of Psychology at William Paterson College of New Jersey. He also has taught at Harvard University, New York University, and Stevens Institute of Technology.